CARDINAL RED
THE HISTORY OF WOKING F.C.

by Roger Sherlock and Robert Cumming

This book is dedicated to Sue, wife of co-author Roger Sherlock, who tragically passed away on the 16th June 1995

Published by:

SPORTS PROMOTIONS

First published in Great Britain by
CNR SPORTS PROMOTIONS

CNR SPORTS PROMOTIONS
32 Swale Road
Cove
Farnborough
Hampshire
GU14 9NJ

British Library Cataloguing in Publication Data
A catalogue record for this book is available from the British Library

Printed in Great Britain by
The Basingstoke Press (75) Ltd

Cover Design: Matthew Sherlock
Latest Photography: Tony Charters

ISBN 0-9525023 0 5

CNR SPORTS PROMOTIONS

CONTENTS

ACKNOWLEDGEMENTS

(FROM THE AUTHORS AND THE PUBLISHER)

There are many people we have to thank for helping us to gather information for this book. To name everyone is virtually impossible, our apologies are made now for any omissions. So here in no particular order are thanks to:

Michael Andrews, Bill Beminster, Janet Croucher, Bryon Croucher, Peter Cowle, Mike Deavin, Paul Elmer, Geoff Ellis, Brian Flippard, Ron Hicks, Mary Hitchcock, Geoff Hamm, Clarrie Jarman, Fred Keefe, Phil Ledger, Peter Love, Charlie Mortimore, John Mortimore, Alan Petchey, Reg Stratton, Les Sherlock, Neil Sherlock, Matt Sherlock, Ian Tuckey, John Gloster, Tom Patterson, Newspaper Library Colindale, Woking Football Club, Woking Library, Woking News and Mail, Surrey Advertiser, The Press Association, Steve Allan, Tony Charters and Derek Rowlands of The Basingstoke Press (75) Limited.

Chris Richardson (CNR Sports Promotions) the publisher, for his enthusiasm and commitment to the book over several years. Ann Richardson for her DTP skills and the welcome help of Sheila Herbert and Ann Harrap.

Lastly, without the consideration and understanding of our own families, this book could not have been written. Thank you Woking Football Club and everyone who supports the club for your patience and good humour over that last few years whilst waiting for this labour of love to come to fruition.

Sadly Roger Sherlock's wife Sue, tragically passed away this year and very recently, Bob Reeves of an earlier era in the book, died suddenly aged 77 years old.

It is impossible to account for every happening and circumstance in the family life of a football club like Woking - nevertheless we hope this history gives a good recognition of those that have stood by the club for over a century.

FOREWORD

By Sir Bobby Charlton C.B.E.

One of the most pleasurable aspects of being well known in football circles is my involvement in different activities associated with the vast spectrum of the football scene.

This is one such occasion for me. It is indeed a great honour to be asked to write the foreword to this book on the history of Woking Football Club.

I have always admired the tenacity shown by individuals in researching the detail for such a publication. The hours spent in tracing and verifying the most obscure fact is true dedication.

Football does not revolve just around the top clubs, such as Manchester United and Arsenal, it's also about the thousands of dedicated administrators, supporters and players, who week in and week out give their spare time, to ensure all the small and not so small clubs across the length and breadth of Britain survive and in many cases thrive.

Many of the top British footballers both past and present began their careers on the village green, learning the basic skills at amateur and non-league level.

Brother Jack and I came through the hot-bed of football in the north-east, being taught to keep our feet firmly on the ground.

Despite attaining the pinnacle of football achievement in winning the World Cup Final at Wembley in 1966 we never forgot our football roots.

This is why it is particularly pleasing to see a book dedicated to Woking, who are an ambitious GM Vauxhall Conference club pressing for football league status.

Football fans throughout the country were certainly aware of Woking's FA Cup exploits in 1990-91 when West Bromwich Albion were defeated 4-2 at the Hawthorns. A slim 1-0 defeat at Goodison Park against Everton in the following round ensured national news coverage for the club.

Who can predict what the future holds for Woking Football Club. Wimbledon, who competed against Woking in the Isthmian League only thirty years ago showed that it is possible to achieve Premier League status despite existing on a low budget.

The authors of this book are obviously Woking Football Club fanatics who have put together a magnificent edition for the readers of football history. I shall certainly enjoy browsing through the pages, as I am sure you will.

CARDINAL RED
THE HISTORY OF WOKING F.C.
GOLDLEAF CONSTRUCTION

INTRODUCTION

By Leslie A Gosden MBE
President, Woking Football Club

To be asked to write the introduction for this book is indeed an honour for me. As many of you know I have been associated with Woking Football Club for many years. It therefore seems appropriate, and it is certainly with pleasure, to place on record some items of interest encountered as a supporter of the club these seventy odd years.

I can recall a match at Hobbs Meadow, Kingfield in the early 1920's involving Guildford United, later to become Guildford City Football Club, in the F.A. Cup, when Hodgson of Guildford and Tilley of Woking were sent off. This was a very unusual occurrence.

Les Smith, F. A. Councillor (left), presenting Les Gosden, MBE (right) with a memento for over 50 years service to football at Woking (5th May 1985)

Then came our move to Kingfield Sports Ground and a memorable F.A. Cup match in 1926 with Charlton Athletic, when Johnny Price missed a penalty in a 3-1 defeat.

In those days such stalwart players as George Turner, Vic Pearce, Henry Crane, Arthur Cartlidge, Ernie Payne and Tommy Briggs, to name but a few, spring to mind.

In season 1930-31 the semi-final of the Amateur Cup was reached. I can remember queuing up in the Broadway for a train direct to the Spotted Dog to play Clapton. May scored the only goal which took us to Ilford to play the semi-final against Wycombe Wanderers. Alas we lost 3-0.

I was invited to join the club in 1930 and met such dedicated members as "Dad" Saunders - Secretary/Treasurer, Frank Lewry, Freddie Piggot, Alf Seabrook, Frank Wakeford, Fred Bannister and many others, including my old friend Clarrie Jarman, who at the age of 97 still enjoys watching Woking play at home.

With the help of the foregoing I was elected onto the Committee, became caretaker Chairman in 1940 and Chairman in 1945/46. Elected President in 1960 and retired as Chairman in 1965.

As the Isthmian League was the top amateur organisation of football in the country we were at times struggling to maintain our membership.

The outbreak of war 1939 curtailed the activities of football in general. We were lucky our Kingfield Ground was requisitioned to provide recreational facilities for troops billeted in the area.

With the assistance of military personnel and Clarrie Jarman, who provided the necessary backbone to keep the club playing in the South East Combination League throughout the period of the war.

Towards the end of the war, the Woking Football and Sports Ground Company Limited, decided to wind up the Company and put the land on the market.

With the end of the War in Europe in sight, the Public meeting was held in the Christ Church Hall in May 1945 under the heading 'Revival and Survival of Woking Football Club! The hall was full to capacity.

The meeting was chaired by Ralph Brown, a local dentist, was so successful that we were in a position at the end of the meeting to consider the purchase of the freehold title of Kingfield Sports Ground.

I was proud to have been a member of that team, which included such enthusiastic gentlemen as Bryn Davies, Harry Goddard, Clarrie Jarman, Bob Reeves and Len Ledger, father of Philip Ledger JP our Honorary Secretary-Football.

The revival, together with survival, was supported by the Shareholders in the Woking Sports Ground Company Limited, who donated their shares, and all the members of the Woking Football Supporters Club who, unfortunately, were disbanded in 1975. Not forgetting the help given by the public at large, which enable us to face the future with confidence.

The restoration of competitive Amateur Football had many problems. Whilst we enjoyed many good results, top players were in demand. Nevertheless, our efforts were rewarded by winning the Amateur Cup in 1958. A great occasion for all who worked so hard over many years.

Soon after this the Amateur status disappeared, commercialisation came to the foreground, non-league football as we know it today was born.

The good times certainly outweighed the bad times but I can speak for my associates and say we were always optimistic. In some small way we helped to create the shape and the history of the club.

Thirty-six years after our first Wembley triumph I was fortunate enough to be able to witness our successive F.A. Trophy victories. All the efforts put in by so many to keep the club thriving over all those years was fully justified.

It now only remains to be seen whether or not income will match the outgoings necessary for progress, improved facilities and, above all, a winning side and at the same time remain solvent. For the answer we will need to look into the Crystal Ball and hope, remembering that honest endeavour will always outlive adversity, enabling us to face the future with confidence.

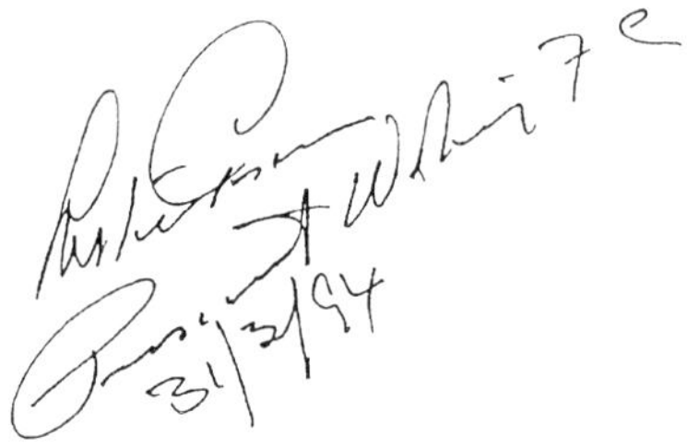

Chapter 1

WOKING FOOTBALL CLUB

A HISTORY

LANDMARKS

A century is a long time. To put this time span in perspective one needs to examine briefly the life styles and pace of the late 1880's compared with that of the early 1990's

Only then is it very apparent that modern times are a quantum leap away from the beginning.

At the birth of Woking Football Club in 1887, the motor car was celebrating its first year. Long distance travel tended to be beyond the common man, although the rail link between Woking and London had been present for some fifty years. Road travel was both uncomfortable and time consuming. It was, therefore, sometimes not unusual for outlying communities to be isolated and existing somewhat in a time warp.

Compare this with the frenzied activity of today, all parts of the globe reachable within 24 hours. Instant access via the telephone. Television in every home beaming pictures from the far reaches of the world. Traffic jams on the M25, crowded tube trains, in fact very little time for personal reflection.

Most of the young men who dashed around enthusiastically after the round ball on the village green in the first season, would more than likely be grandfathers before they saw an aeroplane.

If they could be transported through time to the present day, stopping at various points to see the progress of the club, they would find it hard to believe what they saw.

It is interesting to note that in January 1894 at a complimentary dinner for the members of the team, paid for by the supporters, the Chairman, Dr Eager, proposed a toast "Football, past, present and future", and stated that "he could not predict the future of football in Woking". He would, no doubt, be more than satisfied if he was privy to the club's present position and achievements.

In reviewing the club over a century, it is not possible to record every detail. As with all history, much detail is lost, never recorded, only existing in the life span of the people involved at the time.

Records can show results, scorers, appearances and league tables, but these are only statistics, not the heart of the club.

Landmarks must be sought which explain much more in a short space of time. What transformed the club from a village green kick-about outfit into today's successful non-league concern, recognised as such nationally and in many parts of the world.

Three landmarks have arguably made the most impact in shaping the history of Woking Football Club. Progress, or the precursor of progress, is the common thread linking these three events; a cup game against a top ranking Football Club, the signing of a player, and the appointment of a manager.

Twenty-one years after its formation the club was drifting into obscurity; no money, no prospects, playing in a league which it had outgrown. The club was stagnating. As with many things in life, if there is no progress, no advancement, there is a danger the process will eventually go into reverse.

The 11 January 1908 proved to be a milestone in Woking's short history. It was the kick-start that the club needed. The team that season were well balanced and talented, but it was still an amazing achievement to fight through five qualifying rounds of the F.A. Cup, or English Cup, as it was known then.

The first round draw paired them with Bolton Wanderers, one of the original twelve members of the Football League currently competing in Division 1 and losing cup finalists in 1904. Four members of that cup side played against Woking.

Major giantkilling in those far off days was unheard of, and the result was a predictable 5-0 defeat, but the manner of Woking's play and sportsmanship made a lasting impression on their illustrious opponents and probably, more importantly, the press. Bolton were so impressed, they came to Woking the following season to play a friendly match.

Due to the most favourable national coverage and the financial rewards, the Bolton match was instrumental in shaping the club's future. From being a purely local club, Woking made the national news which undoubtedly influenced the gentlemen of the Isthmian League into electing them as a playing member from 1911.

The Isthmian League was the Premier Amateur Combination at that time in which Woking competed with distinction for the next eighty-one years.

The financial remuneration from the Bolton game, which amounted to £210 cleared all existing monetary anxieties, allowing the club to prepare for the future. A £130 debit balance at the beginning of the season blossomed into a three-figure credit balance at the season's end.

This cash surplus was the buffer Woking required to prepare for Senior Amateur status and provide the infrastructure essential for all potentially successful clubs.

Other events that followed, although significant in terms of the history of the club, would not have existed if the Bolton match had not taken place. The pathway through history would have materialised in another direction.

The Woking Team that played at Bolton in the English Cup.

Standing (left to right) E.T. Engall (Hon Sec), C. Shoesmith, R.S. Stevenson, J.C. Adams, F.S. Lintott, C.S. Salisbury, A. Wells (Assistant Sec), H. Langtree (Committee), T.C. Gloster (Vice President)

Seated J. Kyle, R. Pook, G.H. Hutton, A.H. Bell, Fred Butt

On ground J. Monk, A.V. Pearce

After hostilities ceased in 1945, the club had to be reformed and debts cleared. The generosity of many people, especially the club's Chairman, Mr L Gosden, enabled the freehold of the Woking Sports Ground at Kingfield to be purchased. Although the club now had a permanent home, the first few seasons after the war achieved nothing more than a mid-table position in the League. Then in August 1953, more than forty-five years and two world wars after the Bolton match, the second significant landmark in the club's history occurred.

Charlie Mortimore signed for the club, a former amateur international forward, who had been a regular in Aldershot's Football League side for the four previous seasons. A shy, quiet spoken school teacher, respected by all, who led by example. His belief in total football changed the fortunes of Woking in a few short years. The 50's became a purple decade for Woking Football Club. Two Surrey Senior Cup wins, topping the table briefly in 1955, finishing second in the league in 1956-57 with a century of goals, and providing four players in one game to the England Amateur International XI. Winning the Amateur Cup in 1958 was undoubtedly the jewel in the crown. It was fitting that Charlie Mortimore, (who had transformed Woking into a team recognised for its dedication to playing pure football), lifted the cup at Wembley before 71,000 on the 12 April, his thirtieth birthday.

Charlie Mortimore, England Amateur International. Woking star from 1953 to 1965. Prolific goalscorer.

Those of us who were fortunate enough to be there will never forget the day, the adrenaline surges during the game, and the subsequent balcony parade of the players at the Albion Hotel. Heady days indeed!

Woking was now recognised as a team that always played football as it should be played. This was Charlie Mortimore's legacy. Future Woking teams played this style of football, not always with success, but certainly always pleasing to the eye. Generations of supporters grew accustomed to this approach and demanded nothing less.

The 60's and 70's limped by with some peaks, but mostly troughs. 1978/79 and 1979/80 were good years, but the improvement did not continue. Attendances dropped with loss of revenue. Good players were not attracted to the club, playing standards fell, and the club became seriously in debt. After a number of near misses, the club was relegated from the Premier Division in 1982-83.

Further relegation to Division 2, two seasons later, could have been the death knell of Woking. During this period of decline the club's trustees and committee, made up of men with Woking running through their veins, rescued the club from mediocrity and, perhaps, from folding. Messrs. Gosden, Hills, Ledger and many others give their spare time, and more, and by a mixture of good management, a certain amount of faith and possibly a touch of good luck at times, saved the club from extinction.

What was the catalyst that eventually provided the spark to light the fires again? It came in September 1984, although this date is more significant in retrospect. Geoff Chapple was appointed manager. As with the signing of Charlie Mortimore thirty-one years earlier, there was no immediate shout of 'Eureka'. Progress was initially slow, but a firm base was being fashioned.

Possibly a crystal ball would have foretold the next ten years, but would it have been believed. Fairy tales only happen in story books - or do they?

A former Woking midfield player in the 1970's, noted for his strength and commitment, a proven manager with success at Windsor and Eton, Chapple could not totally turn the tide in his first season. Relegation to Division 2 South may have been a blessing in disguise. Under Chapple's influence and energy the building of a team, on and off the field, capable of winning had begun.

Promotion to Division 1 in 1986-87, promotion to the Premier Division in 1989-90.

Possibly Woking's finest hour came in 1990-91, a place in the all-time list of

Geoff Chapple

giantkillers was achieved with the defeat of second division West Bromwich Albion at the Hawthorns in the F.A. Cup 4-2, and the slender 1-0 loss to first division giants Everton in the next round, made Woking a household name overnight.

The most satisfying season in the history of the club followed in 1991-92 when the coveted Isthmian League Title was won for the first time by a massive eighteen points. Promotion to the Vauxhall Conference followed, and in 1994 a glorious 2-1 victory against Runcorn at Wembley in the F.A. Trophy was achieved.

In ten years Geoff Chapple had masterminded promotion four times, beaten a second division side in the F.A. Cup and frightened the life out of a first division side, reached the County Cup Final four times, winning twice, winning the League Cup, and were the losing finalists in the Loctite Cup. The pinnacle undoubtedly was the winning of the F.A. Trophy, which must rank at least on a par with the Amateur Cup success thirty-six years earlier.

Retaining the Trophy and achieving runners-up spot in the Conference in season 1994-95 was an even greater triumph for Geoff.

He was deservedly awarded a testimonial pre-1995-96 season against West Ham.

Chapter 2

BEGINNINGS

Let us move backwards in time to twenty-one years before the Bolton cup-tie. The pioneers of Woking Football Club were taking the first tentative but enthusiastic steps to promote organised football in the Woking area. Enthusiasm and persistence were the most important factors in establishing a newly formed club, especially in the South, where rugby was the number one winter sport, and the interest of the masses was, to say the least, minimal.

For the citizens of Woking in 1995 it would be difficult to visualise the conditions in the Woking Station District at the birth of `the club in 1887. There was only a handful of shops in Chertsey Road and the High Street, no made-up roads or main drainage, and a population (mostly in the outlying district), of about 8,000. Modern Woking no more than a village rising round a railway station called Woking Common built fifty years before on heathland.

It was ironic that the accelerated urban growth of Woking with increase of population was linked to death. Successive cholera epidemics in London and the churches' refusal to allow burials outside consecrated church grounds, resulted in overcrowded insanitary conditions within the burial grounds. Cremation was not generally accepted at this time.

Legislation was quickly passed to establish a national cemetery. Woking was chosen as a prime site and the newly formed London Necropolis & National Mausoleum Company acquired 2,600 acres in the Woking Parish, but only 400 acres were used to develop the cemetery.

The balance was sold to speculators who could see the potential of the area. Vast profits were to be made from buying and selling land for development.

It was against this background of great change and increasing population that Woking Football Club was formed.

There was no local newspaper, as the "Woking News and Mail" did not publish until 1894, but an item in the "Surrey Advertiser & County Times", (which covered mainly the Guildford area), issued on Saturday 22 October 1887, read as follows:-

> *FOOTBALL An Association Club has been started at Woking. Several matches are already arranged. A general meeting will be held at the Railway Hotel, (Mr Squibbs), on Wednesday next (26 October), to elect officers and arrange other matches".*

This general meeting was recorded in the "West Surrey Times & County Express", issued on Saturday 29 October 1887.

> *"WOKING FOOTBALL CLUB"*

President	*Mr Alfred Wright*
Captain	*Mr A E Mason*
Vice Captain	*Mr Woodruff*
Committee	*Messrs. Trimm, Glover, Hicks, Laker, Gloster and Beattie.*

> *Mr T Eldridge, Chertsey Road, Woking was elected Hon. Secretary and Treasurer to whom all gentlemen wishing to join the club will kindly send their names.*
>
> *The club plays under the Association Rules and is open to accept challenges from clubs in the district. The first match will be played at home to Chertsey on 5 November, kick-off 3 pm.*
>
> *Practice days are Wednesdays and Saturdays in the field adjoining the Railway Hotel.*
>
> *The first official football match completed by Woking Football Club was reported in the "Surrey Advertiser" as follows:-*

"FOOTBALL

Woking Station v Chertsey

The opening match of the season under Association Rules was played on the Wheatsheaf ground on Saturday, (5th November 1887), between the above mentioned clubs in the presence of numerous spectators, the result being a defeat for the visitors by 6 goals to 2. As this is the first attempt of a new club, the result bids well for the future prosperity of the home team."

A more comprehensive report was printed in 12 November 1887 edition of the "West Surrey Times".

"WOKING v CHERTSEY

Played at Woking on Saturday (5 November). This was the first match of the season for the Woking Club and the game resulted in a victory for them by six goals to one.

The visitors kicked off and after a short struggle scored their first and only goal. The good play of Mason, O'Connor, Railton and Beattie was especially noticeable.

Railton secured the first goal for Woking. Eldridge, Tomlinson, O'Connor and Mason also scored, the last named scored twice.

Appended is a list of the teams:

CHERTSEY

Goal: Hook, Backs: Skeats and Harris, Half-backs: Percy and McMunday, Forwards: Woodgate and Blaker (right wing), Payne (Captain) (centre), Parsons, Sizmur and Martin (left wing).

WOKING

Goal: A Keys, Backs: Trimm and Robertson, Half-backs: T Eldridge, O'Connor and E Laker, Forwards: Railton and Tomlinson (right wing), Mason (Captain) (centre), Beattie and Butt (left wing)".

It was not unknown in these early times for newspapers to disagree about the final goal tally. This is not surprising as teams regularly disputed the number of goals scored.

The lack of goal nets and crossbars made the referee's (or umpire as he was then called), task very difficult. Goals could only be awarded if the scoring side claimed a goal.

Nevertheless, although the actual number of goals scored by Chertsey was uncertain, the victory was not in dispute. Unfortunately, this was the first and only win during that inaugural season, but better times were ahead.

Various reports appeared in the Surrey Advertiser and County Times during that first season.

Weybridge Swifts were too strong for Woking in both home and away fixtures. The match at Woking resulted in a victory for Weybridge by 9 goals to nil. This game was played on the 19th November 1887 and was reported as follows:

"Owing to the bad state of the ground good play was impossible. After a one-sided game ended in a victory for the Swifts by 9-0. Mason played well for Woking."

In the return match played on the 28th January 1888, Weybridge Swifts again won comfortably by 10 goals to nil, although in the West Surrey Times the score was reported as 15 to nil.

The report in the Surrey Advertiser was fairly comprehensive:

"Played at Weybridge Green. This being the 1st Season of the Woking club they are far from strong and several players did not turn up. Woking had to play with some men who had never kicked a ball before, only having four reliable men who worked very hard for Woking namely Robertson, Trimm, Tomlinson and Eldridge.

The Woking team was P. More (goalkeeper), Robertson (captain) and Trimm (backs), Laker, Waters, C. Heane (half-backs), Eldridge (centre), Tomlinson, Beattie, Butt, Gale (forwards)".

Of the eight results traced the first game against Chertsey was the only game won. The game against Tillingbourne on 10th March 1888 ended in a 1-1 draw. The other six games were lost.

For the first few seasons the club colours were cardinal and white vertical stripes, with the change to halves not occurring until 1894.

Wheatsheaf Common was the first ground with the players changing in the Wheatsheaf Inn, Chobham Road. Players had to take their own soap and towel and draw water from the Wheatsheaf Well.

It was primitive compared with today's plush dressing rooms but no doubt was just as enjoyable. The income in the first season was about 12 shillings (60p) which just about met the expenses for the dressing room.

Prior to the start of the season 1888-89 the annual meeting was reported in the Surrey Advertiser as follows.

> *15th September 1888:- "The annual meeting of Woking Football Club was held at the Temperance Hall on Wednesday evening when there was a fair attendance of members.*
>
> *Mr. E. C. Boyle presided. Mr. Robertson was re-elected captain and Mr. J. Tomlinson was appointed hon. secretary and treasurer.*
>
> *Mr. E. C. Boyle kindly consented to accept the offer of president. It was stated that the Rev. J. Back of Horsell had granted the use of his meadow for the club's matches during the coming season, of which a number had already been arranged."*

The meadow was on a site at Church Hill Estate, Horsell, now occupied by houses in Horsell Vale. Rev. John Back's claim to fame was by association. His nephew Canon Norman Pares played in the Old Etonians team which won the F.A. Cup by defeating Clapham Rovers in 1879.

He was afterwards the Vicar of Horsell for many years (1897 to 1935). Visitors to St. Mary-the-Virgin Horsell Church can view his memorial to his mother Katherine Pares, a three-light stained glass window, the Adoration of the Shepherds commissioned in 1903.

There was a distinct improvement in the playing record for the second season. Of the 15 games traced five games were won.. Victories were achieved over Tillingbourne, Caxton (Guildford), Weybridge Swifts, Chertsey and Guildford.

As was usual during this early period of Association Football, disputes were common. In the game against Caxton (Guildford), which Woking won 4-3, Caxton disputed one of Woking's goals to such an extent that their report indicated a 3-3 draw. Woking's officials were so incensed over the "bad sportsmanship" of Caxton that they immediately cancelled the return fixture.

Castle School (Guildford) were new opponents who proved too strong in defeating the 'Wokingites' home and away. The famous Farnfield brothers were associated with Castle School. It was the six Farnfield brothers (four of them blues) who destroyed Woking in the F.A. Cup of 1905-06. Whilst playing for New Crusaders the Farnfields scored all 16 goals in Woking's record 16-0 defeat.

Prior to the commencement of the 1889-90 season the general meeting was held in the Temperance Hall. Mr. E.C . Boyle was re-elected president. Mr. H.W. Robertson was appointed secretary. Mr. J.E. O'Connor succeeded Mr. J. Trimm as captain. Mr. O'Connor was described as having originally been one of the starters of Wolverhampton Wanderers and having played for West Bromwich Albion and Aston Villa.
Mr. J. Tomlinson was appointed treasurer.

Many of these early pioneers were respected pillars of the community. Mr. O'Connor was a local schoolmaster who became headmaster of Goldsworth School. J.H. Stedman worked in the family business which gave the name to Brewery Road, Horsell. Robert Mossop became the first clerk to the Woking Urban District Council. The Ridler brothers Bert and Harold joined the cloth and became reverends. Many of the top footballers at this time were university educated and made the church their vocation in life.

The first fixture card was printed for season 1889-90 which commenced on 5th October and ended on the 29th March.

Printing was completed by Mr. Moore at the premises which would be used to print the Woking News and Mail, although this local newspaper did not appear until 1894.

Twenty-two matches were arranged including two 2nd XI games. Snow and bad weather cancelled seven of these fixtures.

Of the first six matches played two were drawn and four were lost. The first fixture of the season was against Addlestone played at Woking on 5th October 1889. The result was a 3-3 draw and Woking's team that day was, Trimm, O'Connor, Railton, Robertson, Boorman, Pritchard, Tomlinson, Seddon, Ryde, Mossop and Laker.

The club's expenses from 1st October 1889 to 1st January 1890 totalled £1.17s.2d and was itemised as follows:

> *Four football bladders 8/- (40p), mending football cases and laces 1/- (5p), stamps, telegrams etc 10/6 (52½p), material for flags 2/6 (12½p), two jerseys not sold 9/8 (48p), four teas for outside players 4/- (20p) and two new posts 1/6 (7½p).*

What a contrast with football finance today.

Wins were achieved against Weybridge Rose, St. Georges College and Hersham with draws against Addlestone, twice, both 3-3, Castle School, and Shere. All the games played were "local", travel was by train, bicycle or cart, although road travel was both time consuming and uncomfortable.

Extracts from Hon. Secretary, H.W. Robertson's pocket book for seasons 1889-90 and 1890-91.

Note that referees were called umpires.

For the first few years Addlestone, Hersham, Weybridge and Guildford would figure prominently in the fixture list.

An interesting comment appeared in the Surrey Advertiser on the 12th October 1889.

> *"The Woking Football Club are an up-and-coming club with two or three good men included in the team. It is however to be regretted that the inhabitants of Woking (and the same may be said of Guildfordians) do not take more interest in and give better support to such sports. What more encourages a team than a little cheering and praise. Outdoor games it must be remembered are not only conducive to health and manliness but they have largely helped to make England what she is today".*

Apathy appeared to be present one hundred years ago, so perhaps times do not change that much.

Association football grew from strength to strength during the years before the turn of the century. New clubs were springing up right across the country. The football league commenced in 1888 but no Southern clubs applied to join. Professionalism in sport was frowned on in the South. The amateur in true Corinthian Spirit was the way forward. League football was synonymous with professionalism and hence the competition was boycotted initially by the amateur south.

Woking at this time appeared oblivious to the in-fighting between amateurism and professionalism and for the next five seasons only friendly matches were played. Various grounds were used including Wheatsheaf Common and the field at the junction of Chobham Road and Woodham Road.

In season 1890-91 three of the first four games were won; the best start yet. Although snow and frost decimated January the playing record was highly satisfactory. Up to the 14th March nine games had been won with one draw and three losses. Fifty-four goals were scored with only twenty two conceded. Of the games traced in the local newspapers victories were achieved against Hersham, Shere, Shalford, Castle School (Guildford), Shalford Swifts and Guildford (probably the 2nd XI).

A further influx of players appeared on the scene including F. Ryde, N.L. Railton, J.C. Railton, Frank Butt, G. Bevis, F. Heane, Sam Sharman, S. Gale, C. McLaren, J. Salisbury, F. Tilley, S.H. Knight and F.P. Quinton.

Two snippets of information appeared in the Surrey Advertiser and County Times.

> *28 February 1891. "The local football team played the Shalford Swifts at Woking on Saturday last. About 2 minutes before the cessation of play an accident occurred to one of the Wokingites. C. Railton who had been playing with his usual dash appears to have fallen and broken his left collar bone. He was unaware of the extent of the injuries at the time and continued to play during the short period remaining. Subsequently, however he was taken home in a cart and medically attended. Woking won 5-0."*

The following snippet indicated the social importance attached to football at that time:

> *28 March 1891. "A fancy dress football match to be played on Saturday next. Anyone wishing to play in the same are invited to kindly send their names (stating what costume they wish to play in) to H.W. Robertson hon. sec. of Woking F.C. who will be pleased to enter their names. Kick-off will be at 3.30 sharp. This finished the season.*
>
> *Following is a list of the fancy dress men:-*

H. Ridler	*(Jester)*
H. Holley	*(Harlequin)*
W.S. White	*(Policeman)*
R. Mossop	*(Buffalo Bill)*
H. Robertson	*(the clown carrots)*
S. Gale	*(Jockey)*
R.E. Robertson	*(Highlander)*
N.L Railton	*(Nigger)*
A. Spoofindyke	*(French soldier)*
Rolfe	*(Country Clown)*
P. More	*(Policeman)*

* * * * * * *

The number of games played in season 1891-92 has not been fully traced. By the 19th March 15 games had been played with nine wins and six losses, 40 goals were scored with 27 against. Of the traceable games, victories were recorded against Chertsey, Addlestone, Weybridge Rovers, Stoke Pioneer, Caxton (Guildford), Ripley and Shalford. Losses were recorded against Hersham, Addlestone, and Guildford.

An interesting fixture was a game against Everton at Everton on 19th December 1891. Evidently this game was arranged to provide the Woking Club with funds. A party from Woking made the journey. Unfortunately the result has not yet been traced.

Matches were cancelled during part of January to mourn for the death of the Duke of Clarence. It was some years later that the Duke of Clarence was reputed to be the infamous Jack the Ripper. This will never now be proved although no doubt the speculation will continue.

Of the team that played against Chertsey, in the first ever match for Woking Football Club, H.W. Robertson, J. O'Connor, E. Laker, H. Beattie and F. Butt were still playing during this season.

There were a couple of items recorded in the Surrey Advertiser. On the 17th March 1892, there was a reference to a football club concert at the Goldsworth Hall and a general meeting was reported in the 6th May edition.

> *"Woking held a general meeting at the Temperance Hotel, Woking Station for the purposes of winding-up the season and receiving the accounts. The latter showed a very satisfactory state of things as the club closes the year with a balance to the good of over 22s (£1.20p). Various matters in connection with the work of the club were discussed and it was decided to enter for the Junior League competition next year.*

Season 1892-93 saw Woking sustain two heavy defeats in the opening four games. A 6-2 defeat at Ripley and a 7-2 beating at Chertsey was followed by four straight victories including a 7-1 success against Weybridge 2nd XI.

Football in January was virtually wiped out as heavy frosts and arctic conditions made pitches unplayable. Only two games were traced in the new year, both at home. Nine Elms and Chertsey defeated Woking 3-2 and 5-0 respectively.

Old favourites Robertson, Laker, Tomlinson and O'Connor were still mentioned in local reports of the games.

* * * * * * *

Now firmly established, Woking F.C. affiliated to the Surrey County Football Association in October 1893. Sam Sharman had become captain and vice-presidents included Mr. C. Harvey Combe, M.P. and Mr. W.H. Corrie, J.P. (Chairman of the Woking Local Board, the predecessor of the Woking Urban District Council). It is a little staggering nowadays to find that Woking opened season 1893-94 with a match against Ripley, which was won 3-0 and that in the two following weeks lost to Chobham (2-5) and Stoke Recreation (1-2).

Seven straight wins during November and December included a 7-0 victory against Chertsey and a 7-4 thriller against Walton 2nd XI.

As the season looked like being the best ever, the supporters gave a complimentary dinner to the players.

This was reported as follows in the Surrey Advertiser issued on the 20th January 1894.

> ***COMPLIMENTARY DINNER TO THE FOOTBALL CLUB 16TH JANUARY***
>
> *"Because the season has been so successful the supporters gave a complimentary dinner to the members of the team in the large dining hall of the Liberal Club. Catering by Mr. Burton of Chertsey Road. The chair was occupied by D. Eager, also present H.W. Gloster (vice-chairman), Wenham, Clamp, Eager jun, H.W. Gloster jun, Tomlinson, Brown, Church, Stokes, Lovitt, Cook, Merryfield, Haskon, Raggett, T. Gloster, J. Stedman, H. Hart, Pary, Atkinson, Allen, Heane, Sharman (capt), Robertson (secretary), Harris, Bevis, Quinton, Duffett, Clinton, Watkins, R. Gloster, E. Gale, Dorset, Pope, Aslett, D. Gloster C.L. Smith, G. Gloster.*

Record justly proud played 18 lost 3. This was the sixth year of the club. Their first season was by no means encouraging as only one match had been won. They had not had the assistance of the outside public as was the case now.

At the present time although they had a small numerical membership they possessed the best record in the county of Surrey".

The chairman then proposed "Football past, present and future". "What would be the future of football he could not predict". Mr Tomlinson responded and said that when he was a member of the team the club occupied a very different position to now. The great deal of advancement was due to Mr. Robertson the Secretary."

It was not unexpected that the next game after the dinner was lost, to Addlestone 2-3, but four consecutive wins brought Woking back into line.

Atkinson and Quinton forged a successful left wing partnership with F. Heane established on the right wing. Bevis played in goal with Robertson and A.W. Kirton being the full backs. Sam Sharman and H.B. Ridler completed the defence/wing halves.

Of the 19 recorded games 14 were won, a truly successful season.

One interesting item in the Surrey Herald dated 24th March 1894, indicated the problems still present at the grass roots level.

In football matters the Chertsey Club is most unfortunate. The Saxons had arranged a match at Chertsey with Woking for last Saturday. They have received several severe defeats during the season and on Saturday they looked like receiving a no less severe one than the others. When they had played some 35 minutes, however and had succeeded in bursting two footballs and allowed their opponents to score four goals, the match had to be stopped as there were no fresh balls forthcoming.. Such an ending to the game would indicate that it was, if not brilliant, at least vigorous.

* * * * * * *

More new names including those of Messrs G. and R. Gloster and A. Wells appeared on the committee in 1894-95. Posters announcing the matches, bore the footnote "Admission 3d, Boys 1d, Ladies free. Play, Wet or Fine."

Robertson had retired from playing with C. Barkshire taking his place at full back. E.H. Ridler had taken over the goalkeeping spot and a new name slotted into Woking's central defence. Bradshaw Galway Popham or simply the Reverend Popham played when the duties of the Church allowed him to do so. In the attack C.J. Bromfield generally played at centre-forward with E. Inwood an international deaf player playing next to him.

Of the 17 games traced, 13 were won, 1 was drawn and 3 lost. Inwood, Quinton, and Bromfield appeared regularly on the score sheet.

Even in those far off days the officials were given some abuse but some did not turn the other cheek as was shown in the Surrey Herald of 27th October 1894.

"Hersham Football Club went to Woking. A pretty rough game took place with the conduct of the spectators pretty disgraceful. One of the two gentlemen who in particular "marked" the linesman may have regretted it by this time. All through the game the official bore patiently all the insults thrown at him. As soon as play had finished there was a slight blacking of eyes and when justice had been done to the principal offender, an inquiry led to the discovery that his "pal" was missing. He had evidently recognised the truth of the old adage that discretion is the better part of valour."

Of the results traced Woking had losses against Ripley, Aldershot and Weybridge Rose. In the return matches revenge was achieved against Ripley and Aldershot to the tune of 6-0 and 6-1 respectively. Cranleigh and Farncombe were both defeated 6-0 with Hermitage Wanderers being thrashed 8-1.

This was the last season that only friendly matches were played as the West Surrey League was joined for season 1895-96.

Pullinger's Bakery - Players used to change there before a game.

Wheatsheaf Hotel - Opposite Wheatsheaf Common, one of the original grounds.

Railway Hotel - original training ground behind the Hotel.

Chapter 3

WEST SURREY LEAGUE AND BEYOND

1895 - 1896

Woking .joined the West Surrey League for the 1895-96 season. Other members of this league were Guildford, Addlestone, Walton, Dorking and Godalming. Not much of a league perhaps, as only ten games were played but the competition was different. Friendlies were only competitive for ninety minutes each game whereas the league games stretched from October to March. A lost game was a setback but could be retrieved throughout the rest of the season.

Woking performed admirably and finally won the league with a one point margin over Guildford achieved in the last game of the season.

Woking were trailing Godalming by 2-1 until Quinton popped up with the equaliser three minutes from the end.

Rev. Popham captain of Woking received the cup from the Mayor of Godalming, Mr. J.C. Collier J.P. This was Woking's first ever trophy.

Woking Football Club, winners of the West Surrey League 1895-96.

Left to right Back Row A. Wells (assistant sec.), C.R. Barkshire, E.B. Eyre, F. Duffett, S. Sharman, Rev. B.G. Popham.
Seated P.K. Allen, F.P. Quinton, E.H. Ridler, H. Knight, H.B. Ridler, H.W. Robertson (hon.sec.)
Seated on Ground W.H. Monk, S.S. Mossop

Three weeks after winning the league, Woking defeated the Rest of the League in the traditional champions challenge match played at Godalming by 3 goals to 1. E.H. Ridler(2) and E.S. Wendover(1) were the Woking goalscorers.

The Ridler brothers, Rev. Popham and Quinton played in all the league games. Twenty-one league goals were scored with Quinton top scoring with 6, Duffett and Inwood scored 3 each.

Friendly matches were still played throughout the season, sixteen results have been traced with Woking winning 13 games, drawing two and losing only one. Three players scored hat-tricks during the season Inwood, E.H. Ridler, and Quinton.

The first league season was arguably the most successful in Woking's short history. The reserve XI were also very successful winning 13, drawing 2 and losing 6, scoring 79 with 42 against.

Games against Weybridge Rose and Charterhouse Violets gave the reserve's season a floral slant.

Due to the success of the first league season a complimentary dinner for the Woking Football Team was discussed and to further this object a meeting was arranged for Tuesday 24th March 1896.

> *"To be held at Messrs Geddes and Austins offices at 7 o'clock when any help which can be given will be gladly received. A committee consisting of Messrs F.C. Peake, Askam, Wenham, Monk, S.C. Knight, Dr Eager, Capt. Swan and Mr. T.L. Smith (secretary pro-*

tem) have been formed to take steps in the matter." WOKING NEWS AND MAIL, FRI 20 MAR 1896.

The dinner to celebrate the season took place at the Onslow Hall, Guildford Road, Woking on 22nd April 1896. Speakers at the dinner were Dr. T.C. Eager, the Rev. W.F.T. Hamilton (first Vicar of Christ Church, Woking), the Rev. B.G. Popham, Messrs. R.N. Stevens, C. Barkshire, A.G. Clinton, H.W. Robertson, J.B.S. Lancaster, W.R. Skeet and Kirbell (hon. secretary of the League).

The menu was Oxtail or Mock Turtle soup; Roast Sirloin or Boiled Beef, Roast or Boiled Mutton, Veal and Ham; Stewed Fruits, Custard, Blancmange, Fruit Tarts and Jellies; Cheese and Salad.

It was also noted in the Woking News of 3rd April 1896 "that Mr. E.F. Inwood (Deaf and Dumb International) member of Woking F.C. has been selected as Captain of the London Deaf and Dumb team who are going to Stretford near Manchester on Saturday to play a Manchester team."

1896 - 1897

Season 1896-97 commenced with a meeting reported in the Woking News and Mail 11th September 1896.

"Woking Football Club meeting held in Christ Church Rooms, Present were Rev. Popham (chairman), Robertson (hon. sec.), A. Wells (assistant hon. sec.), Gunning (treasurer), Messrs R.,D.,G. and T. Gloster.

A conversation arose to the utilising £9 in the bank for a dressing room, but it was considered £50 was needed. Project was abandoned.. The question of a roller for the ground was raised. Woking Urban District Council to be approached for the use of their steam roller."

Guildford proved to be the strongest team in the West Surrey League, defeating Woking both home and away 4-1 and 4-0 respectively. Woking only dropped one other point during the season in a 2-2 draw at home to Addlestone. Walton were heavily defeated twice 6-0 and 5-2 and Godalming were thrashed 6-1.

E.H. Ridler was the top league scorer with 8 goals, newcomer P. Hutton notched 7 goals including a hat-trick against Walton. Quinton scored 5, P.K. Allen and T. Denny scored 4 each.

The backbone of the side was basically unchanged from last season with the Ridler brothers, the Rev. Popham, Quinton, Knight, Allen, Monk, Eyre and Inwood still performing. Denny, Hutton and Kemp made the breakthrough into the first eleven.

Fifteen frendlies were traced with nine being won and three lost. In an 8-3 victory at Ripley, Denny scored 4.

New teams played in friendly games included Borough Polytechnic, Molesey, St. Michaels (Camberley) and Eastleigh.

1897 - 1898

Season 1897-98 was successful with the League being won for the second time in three years. Woking also made their first appearance in the Surrey Senior Cup competition.

It was an achievement therefore to reach the Final. Victories against Kenley 3-0 and Guys Hospital 2-1 paired Woking against Croydon Park in the third round. A 1-1 draw at Croydon was turned into a 4-1 victory in the home replay. The semi-final at Weybridge against Surbiton Hill was watched by 1,750 people. A 0-0 draw ensured a return to Weybridge for a replay which was equally as close, but a goal from A.E. Reid brought Woking a hard-fought 1-0 success.

The final played at Guildford was against the powerful Weybridge side of those days. A 4-0 defeat was certainly no disgrace.

The Rev. Popham was once again captain with E.B. Eyre vice-captain and G.F. Hawkins and A. Heane holding similar positions in the reserves.

Among the committee members were Messrs. Knight, Kemp and Quinton all regular players. The ground was still at Horsell but a new dressing room at Mr. Pullinger's, Chobham road was in use.

Although the third league game at home to Guildford resulted in a heavy 5-1 defeat the other nine games were duly won including a 1-0 victory at Guildford before 2,000 spectators. A goal from P. Dalton won the championship for Woking.

Massive victories were registered against Chertsey 9-2 with Quinton scoring 4 and Slater 3. Walton were defeated 12-0 and 13-0. In the first game hat-tricks were scored by Allen, Quinton and Dalton. Stansfield collected five goals and Dalton another hat-trick in the 13-0 triumph. Two further hat-tricks were scored in the league, Stansfield in a 6-1 defeat of Addlestone and Slater in a 4-0 success at Chertsey.

Stansfield who won a regular place in the team scored 12 goals in 9 league games. Both Slater and Quinton scored 10 league goals each. Slater also scored 12 goals in cup and friendly matches.

Of the 13 friendly matches traced 7 were won and 3 were lost. Eastleigh were defeated 8-1 and Ewell 7-1.

Ridler, Slater and Quinton played in all league and cup games. The last game of a successful season was lost 3-0 to the Rest of the League.

1898 - 1899

Season 1898-99 was a poor season with only three league games won out of twelve. The league was now known as the East and West Surrey League.

First round exits against Townley Park 2-1 in the Surrey Senior Cup and Guildford by 4-1 in the Charity Cup ensured there were no trophies for Woking this season.

League wins were achieved against Dorking twice and Addlestone, but heavy defeats 6-1 against Guildford, 5-0 against Addlestone and 5-2 against Godalming placed Woking in the bottom half of the table. Freddy Butt, who would give sterling service to Woking for a number of seasons played in all the games. H.B. Ridler was still playing but E.H. Ridler only played one friendly. George Hutton who played on for a further ten years alternated between goalkeeper and left wing, being equally proficient at both. Popham played his last game and was replaced by G.F. Hawkins.

Top scorer was Lemon with four in four games. Butt and Slater managed three each.

Of the ten friendly games recorded five were won and four were lost. Fred Butt scored four goals in a 6-0 victory over Basingstoke. Old favourite and former skipper Sammy Sharman played in eight of the league games but generally the old guard was on its way out to be replaced by the new youngsters.

The gate receipts for the season had dropped from £45 to £25, railway fares and players refreshments amounted to £15, an increase of £6 from last season. Subscriptions had dropped from £53 to £27. The debt was approximately £31 which was carried to next season, although £25 had been received plus £3 promised so that only a £3 shortfall would actually be carried over to the next season.

1899 - 1900

Season 1899-1900 was marginally better than the previous season but in terms of threatening for honours it was a non-event.

Rev. H. Marriot was voted in as Chairman, Rev. Popham, treasurer, G. Gloster, secretary and F. Quinton, Captain.

The highlight of the season was only known in hindsight. A young man two months passed his 16th birthday made his debut at the end of the year in a friendly against Brookwood. Evelyn Henry Lintott also scored the winner in a 2-1 victory. Lintott was reputedly the finest footballer ever produced by Woking.

Evelyn was one of five brothers who played for Woking around the turn of the century. Unfortunately his stay with Woking was relatively short. In 1905, he went to Exeter College for teacher training and from then was available only occasionally. Taking up a teaching post at Willesden in 1907 he assisted Q.P.R. as an amateur playing in a new position at left half. Two months later he was England's left half against Ireland and held his place against Wales and Scotland. He also played in five Amateur Internationals.

At the end of that season he signed as a professional and was then transferred to Bradford City , then in the First Division. He gained three more international caps that season but injury kept him out of the game for some time. He moved to Leeds City in 1913-14 but the war ended his career and life as on 1st July 1916 Lieut. E.H. Lintott was killed in the Battle of the Somme.

A poor start to the league season saw Woking thrashed by Addlestone 5-1 and at home to Godalming only produced a 4-4 draw. In the next five league games Woking only scored 4 goals, but as the defence conceded 3 goals only one game was lost. A double victory in the last two league games against Kingston gave Woking a mid-table position. Quinton top-scored with 6 goals in 7 league games and D. Keenan scored 5 in 6 league games.
Dr. Cappe of Brookwood Hospital made his debut for Woking.

Eyre and G.F. Hawkins played in all 12 league games with Fred Butt and C. Fox playing in 10.

In the Surrey Senior Cup, Woking progressed into the 2nd round after a 1-1 draw at Wandsworth. Wandsworth scratched as they couldn't raise a team for the replay. Quinton scored a hat-trick in a hard fought 4-3 victory against Alleyn College (Dulwich). Despite another goal from Quinton, Woking lost 2-1 to Weybridge in the third round.

Fourteen friendly matches were traced with Woking winning nine and drawing two. Keenan scored 9 in six matches, Fred Butt scored 7 goals and Fox and Hutton each scored five.

The new century did not initially bring too much joy to the supporters of the club.

1900 - 1901

Woking finished bottom of the East and West Surrey League in season 1900-01 and were beaten in the first round of the Senior Cup. Only three League games were won, twice against Camberley and a fine 4-2 home win against Kingston.

The team was in the development stage, twenty year old Stacey Lintott played in six league games, his brother 17 year old Evelyn established himself as a goalscorer notching 6 goals in 11 league games. Fred Butt scored freely with 8 in 14 games and George Hutton finally managed to persuade the selectors that the outfield was his best position. H.B. Ridler a strong defender only managed to play in two league games and his strength was no doubt missed.

G.F. Hawkins who was to become the Woking U.D.C. chief engineer only missed one league game.

Fred Butt scored the only league hat-trick of the season in a 4-1 home victory against Camberley and at the end of the season played for the Rest of the League in the Champions challenge match.

Reigate Priory knocked out Woking in the first round of the Senior Cup by 2-1 after drawing 2-2 at the first meeting.

The number of victories in friendly matches was also much lower than usual. Of the 16 games played only 7 victories were recorded. Fred Butt scored 12 goals in 15 games and Hutton hit 9 in 16 games.

Four Woking players were selected by Surrey Wanderers for their Easter tour of Europe including Berlin, Budapest and Vienna. They were F. Kemp, S.H. Knight, G.F. Hawkins and F.P. Quinton. However, their departure left a shortage of players. Woking were forced to borrow Brooks, Woodcock and Bullock from Brookwood Football Club.

1901 - 1902

At the AGM held in September a small deficit was recorded. This was cleared after an instant collection had raised £2 one shilling and sixpence.

The matter of betting on matches was raised. It was emphasised that the club was purely amateur and this activity must be stopped and would be dealt with by the committee led by the President, A.H. Godfrey.

The "Ites" as Woking were then nicknamed, showed improved form in season 1901-02.

Only two league games were lost, both to Guildford by the same score 2-0. Thirty-five goals were scored in 12 league games with Camberley being defeated 6-0 (including an E. Lintott hat-trick) and 5-0. Lintott scored four in a 6-1 victory against Kingston. Lintott, Hutton and Butt again scored the bulk of the league goals with 10, 8 and 8 respectively.

The main difference this season was the defence which only conceded 12 league goals. Parker, Dalton, Hawkins, Knight, F.S. Lintott, Walker and W.H. Monk provided this stability.

In the Senior Cup, Barnes were defeated 4-2, with two goals from E. Lintott. Three more from Lintott ensured Woking defeated Redhill 4-1. A very strong West Norwood side defeated Woking 5-1 in the 4th round.

Nine friendlies were traced with five wins and two draws. Fred Butt scored six, including a hat-trick against Norwood and Evelyn Lintott scored five to take his tally to 21 goals in 23 games.

An interesting crowd of 750 watched the home league game with Guildford.

C.S. Salisbury played his first game in the friendly against West Ham Garfield in December 1901. Twenty years later almost to the day he played his last game. 218 games and 65 goals was a glowing testament to his skill and dedication.

1902 - 1903

Season 1902-03 was fairly successful without actually winning any trophies. Runners-up position in the league was achieved although Redhill won the championship comfortably at the first attempt.

Woking completed six victories, one draw and three losses. Two losses in the first three games put paid to any ideas of winning the championship.

In the home game against Guildford an attendance of 750 saw Woking lose 3-1. Goals from Lintott and Quinton in the penultimate game gave Woking a 2-1 revenge victory which pipped Guildford for the runner-up spot.

The Surrey Senior Cup provided Woking with an 11-0 success at home to Camberley in the first round, Freddy Butt scored five goals, Lintott claimed a hat-trick and Quinton weighed in with a brace.

Two goals from Lintott enabled Woking to thrash Guildford 4-0 in the next round and two from Hutton settled the tie against Ewell 3-2. Townley Park ended hopes of Surrey Senior Cup success with a 3-1 victory in the 4th round. A solitary goal from Lintott was not enough.

Guildford were defeated 3-2 in the 1st round of the Charity Shield but Weybridge just proved too strong by 1-0 in the semi-final played at Guildford.

Fourteen friendlies were traced with nine victories and three draws. Big wins were achieved against Old Exonians, Weybridge and Kettering Ath: 7-0, 7-0 and 9-1 respectively.

E.H. Lintott scored 36 goals in 31 games. This included 5 hat-tricks and a five. Fred Butt scored 18 goals and Hutton 13 goals. Hawkins, skipper Dalton and 6ft 4in Stacey Lintott were the mainstays in defence, with Evelyn Lintott, Fred Butt and Hutton providing the punch in attack. J.B. Monk, who would play a major role in Woking's team for the next eight or so years, played his first league games.

The two energetic secretaries G. Gloster and A. Wells and the selection committee prevented any serious difficulties by utilising all available players; the reserves being available whenever required in "right good sportsmanship manner".

"A new pavilion was erected during the past winter at considerable cost and the Executive have done all in their power to extinguish the debt. They have met with a considerable amount of success in this direction and though not wiping the debt off entirely, there is every hope during the coming season."

1903 - 1904

Season 1903-04 produced a fitting and brilliant climax with the Surrey Charity Shield being won against Townley Park after a titanic struggle. The season started on more ambitious lines than in former years by entering the F.A. Cup and the Amateur Cup for the first time. It was considered that cup-ties would create more interest than friendlies. Unfortunately it did not have the desired effect. The luck of the draw went against Woking. In the F.A. Cup an away draw at Bromley ended in a 5-0 thrashing. Godalming were defeated 3-1 in the first round of the Amateur Cup with goals by Hutton, Kyle and Cottam, but Townley Park put an end to any aspirations Woking had in the competition with a 4-0 beating.

These defeats plus early losses in the league had a depressing effect upon players, supporters and finances. The unsettled state of the team with changes of men and positions gave Woking only two wins in the first ten games.

In the early matches the task of satisfactorily filling the places occupied last season by Quinton, Crossley and Sinclair was difficult and the poor form of defence especially G.F. Hawkins, who was eventually dropped and resigned from the club shortly after, led to the run of unsatisfactory results.

The team at length started to evolve, Evelyn Lintott who succeeded to the captaincy moved back to centre-half with instant success, which installed him in the Surrey Team. J.B. Monk also moved back into the half-back line and with Stacey Lintott as the other half-back, it was reputedly the most accomplished half-back line in Surrey. Freddy Butt was also converted to full back with much success.

Jack Kyle was a new recruit to the forward line and he was to play for many seasons scoring well over 150 goals up to the first world war, which ended his Woking career.

Despite their poor start to the season Woking ended as runners-up to Guildford in the East and West Surrey League with 9 victories from 14 games.

Cuthbert Lintott brother to Evelyn and Stacey, was a natural goalscorer but unfortunately because of business commitments was unable to turn out for Woking regularly. In the ten games he played he scored 12 goals. Four were scored in a 7-2 victory over Walton, but he saved two for Townley Park in the final of the Charity Shield. Two thousand were present at Guildford as the game went into extra time at 2-2. The teams were ordered to play until there was a result. Half-an-hour produced nothing but with 3 minutes of a further 20 minutes of extra play left Cuthbert Lintott headed in the winner. The Charity Shield was won for the first time after 2 hours 20 minutes play.

E. Lintott and G. Hutton played in all 31 games with Fred Butt only missing one game. F.G. Knott claimed the goalkeeping spot with a certain amount of success. R.R. Cottam top scored with 14 goals followed by C.W. Lintott on 12. One sad occasion was the death in November of Ernest Laker a founder member of the club.

1904 - 1905

Season 1904-05 was very successful with the winning of the East and West Surrey League and reaching the final of the Charity Shield for the second year running. Unfortunately Woking reserved one of their poorer performances of the season in losing 3-1 to Croydon.

Thirty-three games were played with 25 victories and only 7 losses. A total of 117 goals were scored and only 46 were let through. Two main causes were attributed to the success of the season. In comparison with the previous season, when chopping and changing the players did not allow the team to settle until after a dozen games, the number of players who did most of the work during the season was twelve.

Captain E.H. Lintott moved up to centre-forward as goals were being missed. Although he did not score all the goals, his influence on the other forwards was inspirational.

F.S. Easton, a Hastings man who came from Brookwood slotted into the back position with considerable success. With Lintott moving into the attack the half-back line of F.S. Lintott, C.E. Hawkins and J.B. Monk performed successfully.

Of the forwards Hutton and Firmin formed an exceptional left-wing, Jack Kyle on the right started poorly but came good as the season progressed.

In the F.A. Cup, two rounds were successfully negotiated with Guildford and Croydon Wanderers both defeated 4-1. For the privilege of watching the game against Guildford, 1,150 paid £27. Southern United proved too strong in the next round by 8 goals to 1.

In the Amateur Cup two rounds were also won both away to Godalming and the Royal Engineers. In the latter game 2,000 watched Cottam(2) and Fred Butt score in a 3-1 victory. Reigate Priory despite being under siege for most of the game defeated Woking 1-0. This was the only game in which Woking did not score a goal.

Revenge was sweet in the Senior Cup with a 2-1 success but Dulwich were too strong by 4-2 in the next round.

Guildford were again defeated 4-1 this time in the Charity Shield. A 2-1 victory at home to Kingston gave Woking the chance to retain the shield but Croydon had other ideas before 2,000 spectators.

Fifty-six goals were scored in 14 league games. The easiest win was 10-1 against Guildford 'A' in which E. Lintott, Hutton and Salisbury scored hat-tricks. The league was won by virtue of a 3-0 victory at home to Guildford before 1,200 spectators. In all games E. Lintott scored 27 goals in 32 games, Hutton 23 in 29 games and Kyle 18 in 29 games. J.B. Monk did not miss a game. The best individual score was Lintott's five goals in a 8-0 victory against Richmond Athletic.

1905 - 1906

Season 1905-06 was disastrous in comparison with the previous two. Before the season commenced it was known that E. Lintott would only be available during college vacation. Easton left the district, Firmin went to Godalming and C.E. Hawkins was poached by Guildford. F.S. Lintott missed half the games due to injuries and Fred Butt and Jack Kyle decided to retire although there was a change of mind later. Of the younger players Vic Pearce made the most impact. J.B. Monk fulfilled his promise with a tremendously consistent season. Of the old guard, Hutton and Salisbury were the shining stars of the forward line. Considering the poorness of the season, Hutton's 17 league goals in 16 games including one four and one hat-trick, was a magnificent effort.

Fifth place out ten teams in the league (now reverted to the West Surrey League) was a below average performance although a 7-0 victory at home to Walton, a 7-1 victory at Chertsey and a 3-3 draw at home to runaway champions Kingston were good performances.

Not one of the Cup and Shield games was won. New Crusaders, who should have been called Farnfield F.C., destroyed Woking in a record 16-0 defeat in the F.A. Cup. Six Farnfield bothers played for New Crusaders and five of them scored all 16 goals.

First round defeats in the Amateur Cup, the Senior Cup and the Charity Shield as well as the F.A. Cup must have been a record for Woking. Of the eleven friendly fixtures played six were won and four were lost.

There was a certain amount of criticism in the local paper. It was suggested that Woking needed "to look after its present players and new ones, so that all the best local talent that is young is not signed on by other clubs. September 1st is too late to wake up". Criticism is not a modern phenomenon it was there in 1906 and probably at an earlier age.

1906 - 1907

Due to the demise of Addlestone Football Club, Woking obtained the services of two exceptional footballers at the start of season 1906-07. A.H. (Daisy) Bell a full-back who would gain international honours in the future and Charlie Adams certainly the best goalkeeper in Surrey. With the ground tenure secured for another season, the club had a very good season under George Hutton's captaincy.

At a general meeting held in the autumn the question of players expenses was raised. The subject was very sensitive as there was still conflict between professional and amateur status. The club ruling was that expenses of any player would only be paid for away matches. This appeared to be too "black and white" so the agreement was to give the committee discretionary powers.

Again in most of Woking's previously successful seasons a settled side was essential. Basically twelve players played in the majority of the games. The half-back line of Vic Pearce, J.B. Monk and F.S. Lintott was very strong. Either F. Butt or R. Stevenson was Bell's full-back partner. The forward line of C. Shoesmith, R. Pook, J. Kyle, G. Hutton and C.S. Salisbury was fairly potent in front of goal.

Evelyn Lintott played in odd games during college vacations. In the league game at Haslemere, Evelyn turned out at centre-forward, scoring six in an 11-1 victory. He went one better in a late-March friendly against Bowes Park scoring 7 in a 9-0 victory.

In a league season of protests three games had to be replayed, but at the end Kingston took league honours with Woking remaining as runners-up. The only points Kingston dropped were in a 2-0 home loss to Woking, with R. Pook and J. Kyle scoring the goals. Woking's only loss was 1-0 to Kingston in the reverse fixture.

As well as the 11-1 success against Haslemere, Farncombe were defeated 9-2 with Pook scoring 3, Chertsey perished 6-1 with Kyle scoring 3. Another six was registered in a 6-0 home victory against Haslemere.

The F.A. Cup was not entered this season and Kingston defeated Woking in the Amateur Cup, albeit at the third attempt. At Woking 1,100 watched a 1-1 draw; in the replay Kingston were leading 1-0 when the game was abandoned in extra time. The second replay at Guildford ended 3-2 in Kingston's favour.

Clapham defeated Woking 1-0 at the semi-final stage of the Senior Cup. Earlier victories had been achieved against Surbiton Hill 4-1 and with more difficulty a single goal from Kyle just beating Old Tiffinians.

Revenge was sweet in the Charity Shield as Kingston were defeated 2-0 in the first round.

Two goals each from Kyle and Pook were enough to defeat Guildford 4-1. The final against Croydon was a repeat of two years previously, but the 3-1 result this time was in Woking's favour. A crowd 4,000 turned up at Guildford to see Woking's victory.

Only one defeat was recorded in friendlies with five victories and three draws.

Pook with 17 goals just pipped Kyle with 16 goals. E. Lintott with the help of a 7 and a 6 totalled 15 goals in 11 games. Hutton weighed in with 12 goals. Cuthbert Lintott only played in two league games but against Farncombe he scored all three goals in a 3-1 success.

Altogether a very successful season which would be surpassed in 1907-08.

1907 - 1908

In season 1907-08 Woking astonished the Amateur football world by their magnificent achievement in fighting their way through the qualifying rounds to the last 64 in the F.A. Cup and playing Bolton Wanderers at Bolton on January 11th 1908. This remarkable feat placed Woking very definitely on the football map and undoubtedly led in 1911, to their election to the Isthmian League, the country's premier Amateur combination.

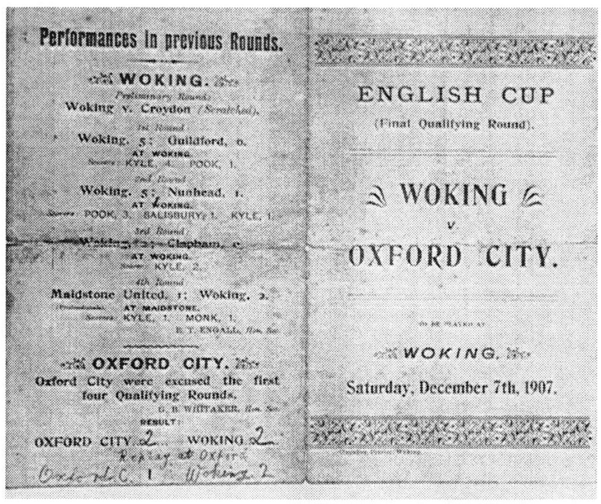
Performances in previous Rounds.

WOKING.

Woking v. Croydon

Woking, 5; Guildford, 0.
AT WOKING
KYLE, 4. POOK, 1.

Woking, 5; Nunhead, 1.
AT WOKING.
POOK, 3. SALISBURY, 1. KYLE, 1.

AT WOKING.
KYLE, 2.

Maidstone United, 1; Woking, 2.
AT MAIDSTONE.
KYLE, 1. MONK, 1.

OXFORD CITY.
Oxford City were excused the first four Qualifying Rounds.
G. B. WHITAKER

RESULT:
OXFORD CITY 2 WOKING 2
Replay at Oxford
Oxford C. 1 Woking 2

ENGLISH CUP
(Final Qualifying Round).

WOKING
v
OXFORD CITY.

WOKING.

Saturday, December 7th, 1907.

English Cup
Woking v Oxford City Programme 1907

The Bolton year was certainly a memorable one in the Club's history as only four games were lost all season. These were an opening day friendly to Clapham (home) 3-2, Bolton in the F.A. Cup 5-0, Kingston (away) in the Amateur Cup 2-1 (after a goal-less draw at Woking) and Nunhead in the Surrey Senior Cup Final at Guildford 2-0.

It was interesting to note that the first West Surrey League fixture was not played until the 14th December. Nevertheless the league was duly won without completing three of the fixtures.

Of the thirteen games played, twelve were won and one away to Guildford was drawn. Cranleigh were defeated 10-0 and 6-0, Farnham perished 7-0 and Chertsey were beaten 6-1. Of the 55 goals scored, Kyle scored 19 and notched 41 in all matches, including two 4's and two hat-tricks. F. Buck scored 13 in 9 league matches. It was not only the forward line that excelled, as the defence only let through four league goals.

Prior to the start of the season, the use of a new ground in Pembroke Road had been secured. This removal to new quarters involved the club in considerable expense as a new pavilion had also been erected.

Eighteen cup-ties were played, only in the Amateur Cup was progress not made. Kingston defeated 10 men Woking 2-1 after a 0-0 draw at Woking. The Charity Shield was successfully defended, although Woking did not play well during the competition. Farnham were only beaten by 2-1 after a 1-1 draw and a rare goal by J.B. Monk was enough to knock out Godalming 1-0. In the final at Guildford, Dorking were defeated by the odd goal in three. Goals by Harrison and Shoesmith before 3,500 spectators retained the Shield.

There were some better performances in the Senior Cup, Leatherhead were despatched 5-0, and 1,600 were present to see a Kyle hat-trick defeat Dulwich 4-2 after a 2-2 draw at Dulwich. A 3-0 revenge win against Kingston paired Woking against Nunhead in the Final. Nunhead proved too strong with a 2-0 victory.

In the F.A. Cup five rounds were safely negotiated. Kyle bagged four in a 5-0 victory over Guildford. A Pook hat-trick helped defeat Nunhead 5-1. Clapham were the next victims as a Kyle brace gave Woking a 2-0 win. Maidstone, a professional side, were defeated 2-1. Oxford provided stiff opposition drawing 2-2 at Woking. Torrential rain flooded the Oxford ground for the replay, but 2,500 people saw Woking win 2-1 on a nearby college ground.

Action photograph from Woking's cup-tie against Bolton Wanderers at Burnden Park on January 11th 1908

The 100 or so Woking supporters who made the round trip of 450 miles to Bolton saw Woking defeated 5-0, but their sportsmanlike

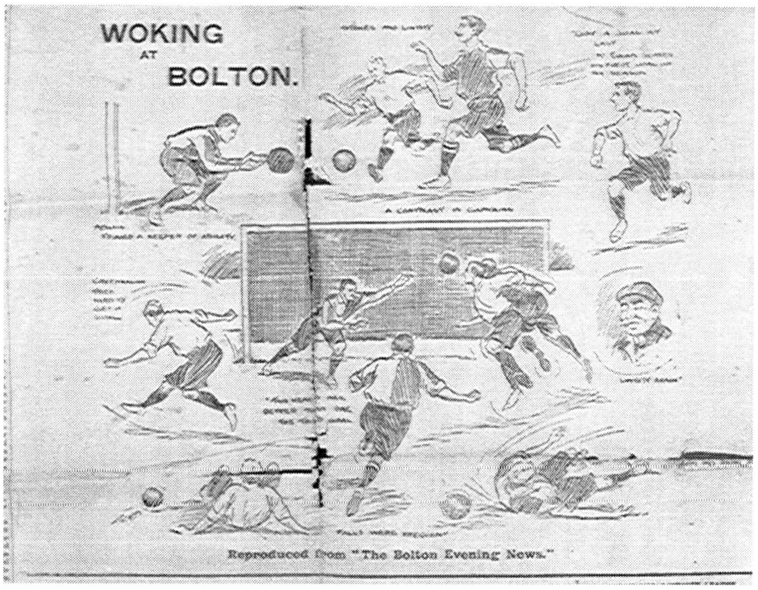

Cartoon reproduced from "The Bolton Evening News" depicting characters from the historic English Cup (F.A. Cup) tie at Bolton on January 11, 1908

approach made an impression with the Bolton team, its supporters and management.

With one or two exceptions, 13 players, thanks to the absence of injuries, carried the club through the season.

Success on the field ensured a financial success. Approximately £210 was received from the Bolton game. With the expense of a new ground the financial gains more than paid for these costs and ensured financial stability for a number of seasons.

The team at Bolton which would retain a prominent place in Woking's history was J.C. Adams, R. Stevenson, A.H. Bell, A.V. Pearce, J.B. Monk, F.S. Lintott, F. Butt, J Kyle, C.S. Salisbury, R. Pook, G. Hutton.

1908 -1909

Season 1908-09 was bound to be an anti-climax after the euphoria of the previous season. The only trophy won was the Lymposs Cup, played at the end of April when Guildford were defeated 2-0.

The highlight of the season was the friendly game against Bolton Wanderers, 1,600 turned up at Pembroke Road to see the visitors win 4-1.

In the West Surrey League, Woking remained unbeaten until the 18th game but only one point in the last three games lost Woking the championship. Nevertheless the league performances were generally good. The introduction of B. Daniels at centre-forward half-way through pepped up the scoring. Daniel's individual tally was 16 goals in 12 games; this included two hat-tricks and a four.

Henry Crane also made his league debut and scored a hat-trick in his second game. Henry became one of the legends of Woking Football Club playing on until 1923; being the most respected player and captain, the Charlie Mortimore of his time.

As often happens, after an excellent season in the Cups, Woking lost at the first attempt in the F.A. Cup, Summerstown being just too strong at 3-2. The 1st Battalion Leicester Regiment beat Woking 2-1 in the first round of the Amateur Cup.

Cranleigh were soundly defeated 4-0 in the Senior Cup, but the Guards Depot (Caterham) were too strong at 2-0 in the 4th round.

The East Lancashire Regiment became the third army team to defeat Woking during the season; this time 2-0 in the Charity Shield.

Basically the defence remained the same although C.W. Day shared the full-back spot with Stevenson. Pearce, F.S. Lintott and Monk played in all games, but it was in the forward line that changes were made.

Pook emigrated, Hutton played in only half the games as he came to the end of a long career. Butt, Kyle and Salisbury played spasmodically.

R. Hill came into the forward line scoring four in eleven league games. C. Shoesmith scored 7 in 21 league games and Kyle managed five goals in his eight league games.

A.H. Bell was the travelling reserve in the England party to play Sweden and he was also selected in the squad of 33 for the Olympic Games.

The season was not unsuccessful as only eleven games were lost in 35 played, but comparisons with 1907-08 were inevitable, so in the context of that season, 1908-09 was not memorable.

1909 - 1910

Two Cup Finals were lost at the end of the 1909-10 season, Dulwich defeated Woking 2-1 in the replayed Senior Cup Final at Redhill after a 0-0 at Norbiton. Windsor and Eton easily beat the Cardinals 3-0 before 2,000 in the Oxford Hospital Cup Final.

Despite this disappointing wind-up the season was superior to 1908-09 with only eight losses in 35 games.

Among the very satisfactory features of the 21 cup ties was the progress in the Amateur Cup. Four qualifying rounds were won; Farncombe, Clapham, Farnham and Old Kingstonians were easily defeated with Jack Kyle scoring in each round. In the first round they were only beaten at Nunhead 5-4 after a great struggle. Kyle hit two goals to maintain his scoring record.

Strangely enough in the second qualifying round of the F.A. Cup, Summerstown defeated Woking for the second year in succession, this time by 5-4, Kyle again scored twice.

There was a series of hard struggles in the Senior Cup involving three Isthmian League teams and also Kingston the Charity Shield winners. West Norwood were defeated at the second attempt 2-0 after a 2-2 draw. Kingston were defeated 3-0 in the next round. The semi-final against Nunhead was as tough as the meeting earlier in the Amateur Cup, but this time Woking were victorious 2-1 after a 0-0 first meeting.

The final against Dulwich ended goal-less and despite a Henry Crane goal in the replay Dulwich finally won 2-1.

Walton who finished bottom of the West Surrey League surprisingly defeated Woking 2-0 in the Charity Shield.

Only eleven of the sixteen league games were completed due to lack of time.

Two matches were lost, one against Old Kingstonians the eventual champions and one against Hersham.

Only one game was lost at home in all competitions and this result was reversed, as Old Kingstonians played an ineligible man in this F.A. Cup tie.

A good deal of the success of the team was due to the fact that the personnel had remained practically constant throughout the season. The work done by Mr. E.T. Engall, the hon. secretary and Mr. A. Wells his assistant, should not be overlooked.

Jack Kyle scored 31 goals in 31 games with R. Hill notching 19 in 30 games. C.S. Salisbury came back well after an indifferent previous season with 9 in 28 games. F.S. Lintott retired before the season started, but H.J. Crane made the position his own. Fred Butt also hung up his boots. Both Lintott and Butt had made a major contribution to the success of Woking Football Club.

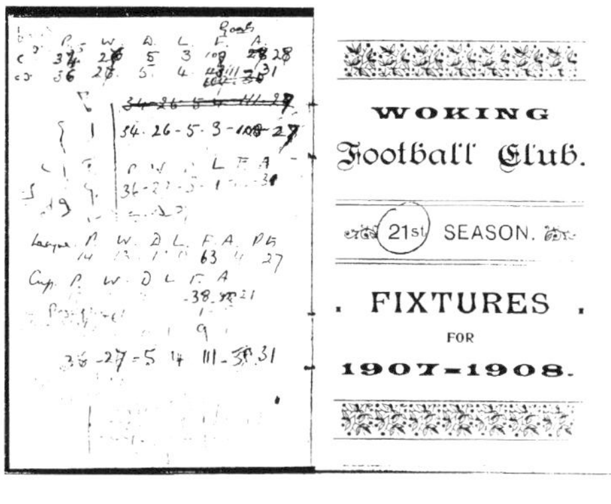

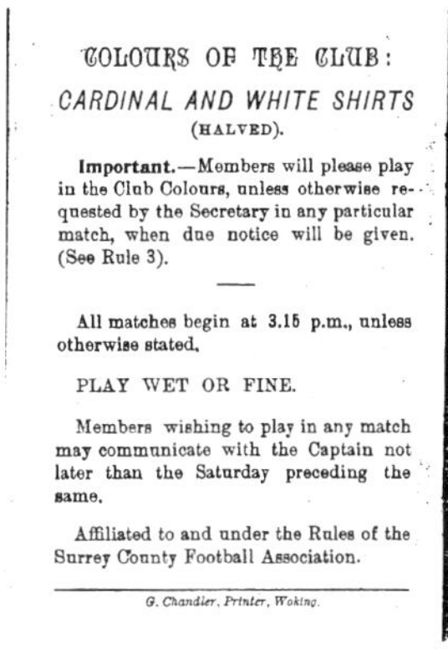

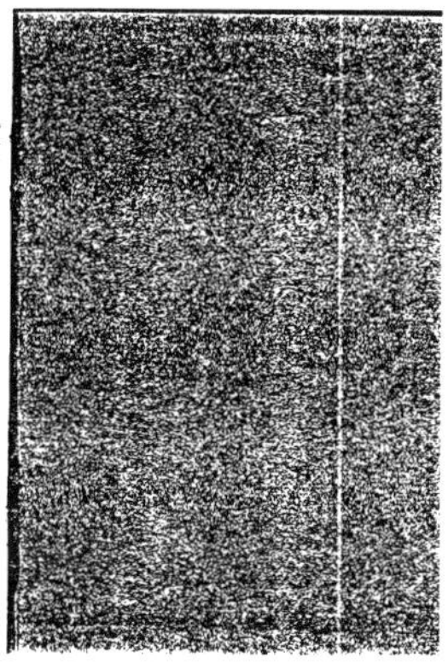

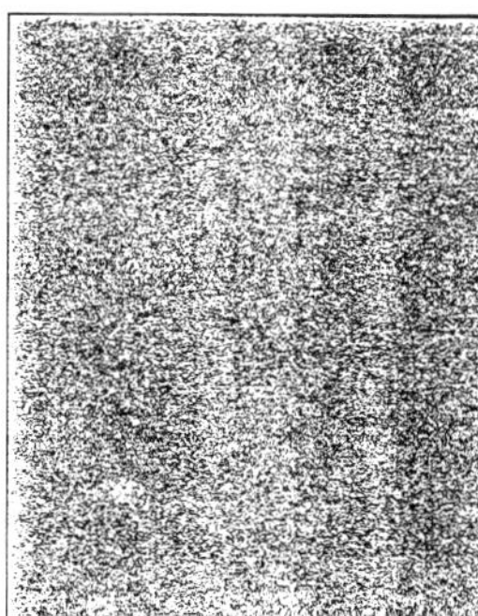

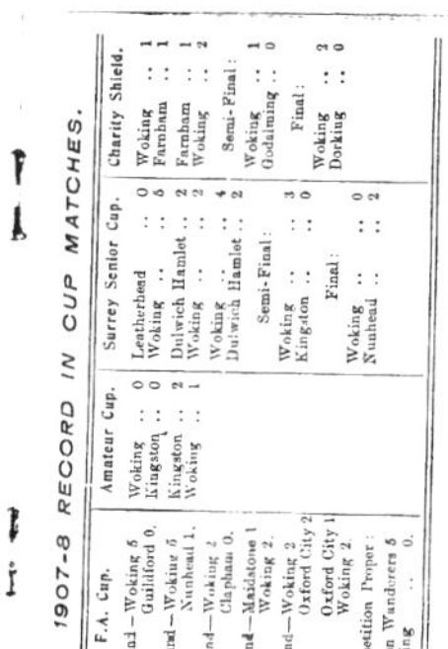

Example of Yearly Fixture Cards both front covers and inside pages. The handwritten calculations for 1907-1908 is the work of R.H. Gibbons, editor of the Woking News and Mail

Further international honours were conferred on Woking's skipper 'Daisy' Bell and half-a-dozen of Woking's regular side were called upon to assist Surrey, namely Bell, Salisbury, Kyle, Monk, Pearce and Shoesmith.

1910 - 1911

Season 1910-11 was the last in the West Surrey League for the first eleven. Unfortunately the championship was not won but third place was a satisfactory effort behind Walton and Guildford. Both of these teams were defeated at home, in fact Walton, the eventual champions were hammered 5-1 with Jack Kyle scoring twice. A month later Walton gained revenge in some style 6-1. Woking's best victory was an 8-1 success against Farncombe in which Jack Kyle scored five. H. Swallow nearly matched Kyle's individual score with four in a 5-0 victory against Godalming. In fact Swallow notched nine goals in one April week. He followed up his four with a midweek hat-trick against Hersham and two goals against Cranleigh on the following saturday.

Old Kingstonians were the bogey side throughout the season. In the league a 2-2 draw at Pembroke Road was followed by a 5-0 loss away and then a 7-2 thrashing ended Woking's interest in the F.A. Cup; a much closer 1-0 defeat before 2,000 people prevented a place in the Charity Shield Final, but the biggest disappointment was the 2-1 loss in extra time of a replayed Surrey Senior Cup Final at Guildford. According to the newspaper report it was a disputed goal that defeated Woking after Henry Crane had equalised from the penalty spot.

Woking had reached the final of the Senior Cup by defeating the Guards Depot by a solitary Kyle goal. Farnham fell 2-0 and Dulwich were defeated in the semi-final 2-1 at Norbiton before 1,600 spectators. The path to the semi-final of the Charity Shield was more difficult, Walton the West Surrey League champions were defeated 2-0. It took three goals to defeat runners-up Guildford. Swallow, Kyle and Crane scored them to finally win the tie 3-0.

A hat-trick by Salisbury enabled Woking to defeat Clevedon 4-3 in the first round of the Amateur Cup, but defeat at Wycombe by the same score in the next round ended Woking's interest for this season.

A.H. 'Daisy' Bell was re-elected captain at the start of the season and he led his troops with his usual dedication. Harry Swallow topped the scoring with 17 goals, Jack Kyle scored 16 and Salisbury scored ten goals. The balance of the side remained good, Charlie Adams missed a number of games in goal but W. Skeet was an able deputy. The defence was not as mean as in previous seasons but Bell, Crane and M. Warner were generally steady. Monk and Crane missed only a few games between them. Up front Jack Kyle was still scoring regularly and he was ably backed up by Swallow and Salisbury. The famous Lintott name was again in the Woking side with Evelyn's younger brother Keith playing four league games.

Next season would be a new venture with Isthmian League giants awaiting.

Woking Melrose team photograph 1910-1911, taken at Pembroke Road. Players that can be identified: Back row, fifth from the left, Harry Gloster. Centre row, fourth from the left, Horace Lutley. Seated on the grass from the left, Compton and goalkeeper, Harry Drawley

Chapter 4

THE ISTHMIAN CHALLENGE BEGINS

1911-1912

A new era began for Woking Football Club as the Isthmian League invited Woking for competition in season 1911-12.

The first game on 9th September resulted in a 1-1 draw at London Caledonians. J. Hartley scored Woking's first goal in the new league.

In retrospect the result looked good, as London Caledonians ended up as champions. The next three games were lost including the first home game against Nunhead. A cracking match that ended 5-4 to Nunhead was witnessed by 1,000 spectators.

Charlie Adams returned in the next match which had the effect of tightening the defence. The first victory was against Oxford by 2-0 with Kyle and A.W. Humphreys scoring the goals.

Two more draws followed, so after nine games Woking's record was not too inspiring with one victory and four draws. The position started to improve just before Christmas with a 2-1 victory at home to Clapton.

In the final eight games four were won and one was drawn. Woking did London Caledonians a favour by defeating runners-up Ilford 2-1, Humphreys and Salisbury were the scorers.

A final 8-0 victory at home to Shepherds Bush with H.E. Crick netting four, pushed Woking into a respectable mid-table position, Humphreys top scored with 10 league goals, and Harry Swallow finished a close second on 9 goals.

Dorking defeated Woking 3-2 in the preliminary round of the F.A. Cup. More success came in the Amateur Cup with an easy 5-0 victory against Pokesdown and a tough extra time 2-1 victory at Redhill; the 2,000 crowd saw Salisbury hit the winner.

The entertaining northern giants from Middlesbro', Eston Utd, proved too strong in the 3rd round, defeating Woking 4-2 in their own backyard.

For the first round of the Surrey Senior Cup, 1,600 crammed into Pembroke Road, but Dulwich scored an easy 4-1 victory, with Arthur Grove obtaining Woking's consolation goal.

Walton and Camberley were defeated in the first two rounds of the Charity Shield 4-2 and 4-1 respectively. The semi-final against Guildford Pinks did not provide a result until the third meeting. After two 1-1 draws, the Pinks finally won 2-1 against an under strength Woking side.

Among the friendlies played was the first meeting between Woking and Ferenevarosi Torna Club of Buda-Pesth, Hungary. Woking just lost 3-2.

For the last game of the season Woking lost 2-1 to the Kings Royal Rifles in aid of the Titanic disaster fund.

The basis of the team changed very little from the previous season with Adams, Bell, Crane, J.B. Monk, M. Warner, Salisbury, Swallow, Johnson, Kyle and Shoesmith playing the majority of the games.

Humphreys who scored 17 goals and S.J. Love were the newcomers who came into the side. Other double figure scorers were Jack Kyle with fourteen and Harry Swallow with twelve.

The first season at a higher level was entirely satisfactory with a mid-table league position being achieved.

1912 - 1913

Season 1912-13 was Woking's cup year, both the Senior Cup (for the first time) and the Charity Shield were won. In the first round of the Senior Cup, Kingston were beaten 2-1 with goals from Bennett and Swallow. The second round tie at Dorking was abandoned in extra time, because of a pitch invasion, with Woking leading 2-1. In the replay which was played at Pembroke Road, Woking won relatively comfortably 3-1.

Old Kingstonians provided the opposition in the semi-final at Summerstown. They had defeated Woking regularly over the years, but the bogey was duly laid with a 3-0 victory, Kyle, Swallow and Lewis scoring the goals.

Close to 5,000 spectators paid £105 to see Woking and Metrogas contest the final at Old Kingstonians. A special train from Woking brought in as many as 1,000 supporters whilst another 500 came by other means. The Old Kent Road also contributed a considerable quota to the attendance. In a good tight contest, Woking just had the edge with goals from Salisbury and Kyle to bring the cup to Woking for the first time. The players with captain Henry Crane to the fore, were met by a great crowd at the Station and the team acknowledged the cheers from the balcony of the Albion Hotel.

L.R. Lewis who was in the Dorset Regiment transferred to Ireland near the seasons end. Three times however for a semi-final and two finals, Lewis was given permission to cross the Irish Sea and assist Woking to win all three games. Lewis in fact scored six times in his ten cup games.

The Charity Shield was won more easily with Old Kingstonians being defeated by two Harry Swallow goals. In the earlier rounds Camberley were defeated 4-0 and Farnham gave Woking their record victory with an unbelievable 17-4 scoreline. H.C. Bennett scored six, Swallow five and Vic Pearce a hat-trick. Kyle planted four into Guildford Pinks' net to record a 7-1 semi-final success.

Woking defeated Cranleigh 2-0 and West Norwood 4-1 before losing to Nunhead 2-1 in the 2nd Qualifying Round of the F.A. Cup.

Dulwich claimed Woking's scalp in the first round of the Amateur Cup with an impressive 5-0 display.

The 1912-13 team which beat Metrogas 2-0 in the Surrey Senior Cup Final at the Old Kingstonians' ground at Norbiton.

Left to right, Standing, A. Grove, E. Norris, J.B. Monk, E. Yarham, S.J. Love, C.S. Salisbury. Seated, L.R. Lewis, J. Kyle, A.H. Bell, H.J. Crane (Capt), H. Swallow, A.V. Pearce.

Woking's league record changed little from the previous season, finishing exactly half-way with the same number of points, nineteen.

A.V. Pearce, played over 230 league and cup games at half-back between 1905 and 1921. The photograph was taken in 1913 with the Surrey Senior Cup and the Surrey Charity Shield.

The first three league games were won including an excellent 3-1 victory at eventual runners-up Leytonstone. Unfortunately the next seven games produced only one win at bottom club West Norwood. In contrast the following five matches produced three wins and two draws. Jack Kyle scored a hat-trick in a 5-1 win at Shepherds Bush, but only two draws in the final five games prevented Woking from finishing in the top half.

Bell, Crane, Kyle, Pearce and Salisbury were still playing and formed the backbone of the team. W.E. Yarham replaced Charlie Adams in goal. J.B. Monk only played a couple of games. Norris, Bennett and Lewis all made their mark during the season.

Harry Swallow top-scored with 22, closely followed by Jack Kyle with 20 goals, Bennett managed 12 and Lewis with 9.

Harry Swallow played all 33 games with Bell only missing one cup game. Crane played in 31, Love missed only three.

There was no doubt that the winning of the premier County Trophy was the highlight of a very satisfactory season.

1913 - 1914

The last season (1913-14) prior to the outbreak of the First World War, was a total disaster. Woking finished rock bottom with three points. Only one game was won and this was against West Norwood who finished second to bottom.

In the first game London Caledonians, who again won the championship just won 1-0. A draw at Clapton was the only point gained until that one elusive victory on 4th April.

Perhaps the side grew old together. Players such as Bell and Kyle would play their last games for Woking, both great servants over the years, but probably past their best.

Only eleven league goals were scored and 61 conceded, both the lowest and the highest in the league.

Kingston knocked Woking out the F.A. Cup at the third attempt. In the second match, Woking were leading 2-1 but the game was abandoned in extra time. The third game also went to extra time but this time Kingston won 2-1.

First time exits were made in the Amateur Cup against 1st Kings Royal Rifles, the Surrey Senior Cup 5-1 at Metrogas and 2-1 against the Royal Sussex Regiment in the Charity Shield. Marlow ended Woking's interest in the Oxford Hospital Cup by 2-1 with 'Daisy' Bell scoring one of his few goals.

Jack Kyle scored six goals which was extremely low for a club top scorer.

Bell, Crane and Arthur Grove played in 19 of the 20 league games. It was unfortunate that the replacement players were not of a suitable high standard essential for success in the Isthmian League.

Fortunately the application for re-election was accepted but Woking had six years to wait for league action as War was declared.

Woking played one friendly in September 1914 against Nunhead which was lost 1-0 and in January 1915 against the 84th Company Royal Engineers which was lost 4-3, but Woking youth was at War.

So the Great War removed five football seasons and also finished football careers that had never started. Woking's greatest player Evelyn Lintott fell in the Battle of the Somme in 1916.

Evelyn Lintott. Lieutenant in the 15th Battalion, West Yorkshire Regiment - the Leeds 'Pals'. Killed in action, July 1916, at the Battle of the Somme.

Nevertheless, there was great optimism and enthusiasm for the start of the 1919-20 football season. The league had expanded to twelve clubs with New Crusaders and Shepherds Bush dropping out and Tufnell Park, Casuals and Civil Service coming in.

1919 - 1920

The first season after the war (1919-20) did not start very productively. A creditable 2-2 draw was achieved at Leytonstone in the first game but the next six league games were all lost.

It was reminiscent of the season prior to the outbreak of the war, when only three points were obtained. As well as the poor league performances, the F.A. Cup, the Amateur Cup and the Surrey Charity Shield were all lost at the first hurdle.

In the F.A. Cup a good performance at Guildford against the Pinks before 3,000 spectators gave Woking a replay. The Pinks had obviously learnt from the first game as they destroyed Woking 11-2, and the lesson was recalled as they cruised to a 6-0 victory in the Charity Shield a month later. RAE Farnborough proved far too strong in the Amateur Cup giving Woking a 5-1 hammering.

Only an abandonment in extra time prevented Woking from losing out before Christmas in the four major cup competitions. Bad light stopped the Surrey Senior Cup tie with Metrogas 3-2 in front. Three days into the new year Metrogas completed the victory with a 4-2 win.

The league position was improved slightly with a double victory over bottom club Casuals either side of Christmas.

With only nine games left Woking looked doomed with only five points from thirteen games. The introduction of the front runners E. Dorkins and G.V. Hunter prompted by H.E. Gowan at half-back and crosses supplied by Salisbury gave Woking a new dimension to their play. Four victories and two draws enabled Woking to climb out of the bottom two. Dorkins scored nine goals in nine games.

A vast crowd of 2,000 saw Woking run the champions Dulwich to a close 2-1 game but a Dorkins goal was not quite enough.

Henry Crane, Vic Pearce and Henry Phillips provided the link with the pre-war team, although Cecil Salisbury had played many games prior to 1913-14. G. Smith, H. Gowler, W. Christie and E. Gooch played in the majority of games.

Dorkins was the top scorer with 9 goals, followed by E. Gooch and G. Cockran with eight apiece.

Goalkeeper Phillips, who had replaced Skeet a victim of the war, only missed one cup game.

Crane, Pearce and George Smith all played 20 league games. C.H. Over, F.E Smith and L.C. Johnson all playing members in 1913-14 played in a few games during the season.

The club had survived the first post-war season but only just.

1920 - 1921

Season 1920-21 was a great disappointment after the promising end to the previous season. Dorkins who had notched a goal-a-game last season did not score for the first three games and then left the club.

Leytonstone again provided Woking with a point in the first game of the season. Richard Thorne-Thorne scored on his debut. He was a class player who eventually played for England amateurs. Unfortunately although he enjoyed a long career, he never played more than a handful of games each season for Woking.

There was a problem scoring goals all season, but four were smashed into the Oxford net to give Woking their first league victory of the season at the end of October. It was January 1st before the Civil Service were defeated 2-1 to register Woking's second win. The third and last win was a 2-1 victory at home to Casuals in mid-February.

The final two league games were home and away to Dulwich. A 4,000 crowd saw Dulwich triumph 2-0 in their home fixture but Woking gained a 2-2 draw at Pembroke Road. Eighteen hundred saw Gooch score Woking's two goals.

A final league position of third from bottom was the same as last season but with four fewer points. Only sixteen goals were scored in 22 league games which was a very poor reward.

In the Cups and Shield only one tie was won. This was against Walton in the F.A. Cup by 4-2. Kingstonian defeated Woking 3-2 in the next round, despite Gowler netting twice.

Guildford Pinks again dented Woking's hopes with a 1-0 scoreline in the Amateur Cup. Redhill won 5-1 in the Senior Cup and a poor result at home to Camberley ended Woking's interest in the Charity Shield.

Crane and Pearce were still battling away only missing one game each. George Griffin came in for Phillips in goal and only missed three games. Forty-five players were used in an attempt to find the winning combination.

The meagre ration of goals were shared around with Gowler, Thorne-Thorne and Gooch claiming four each.

Woking only just survived, for the second season running, having to apply for re-election.

The number of teams for 1921-22 were increased from twelve to fourteen, with Wycombe Wanderers and Wimbledon being the new clubs. Both these clubs would be a tremendous asset to the league over many years.

A permanent sports ground at Kingfield had been obtained. The levelling of the ground had begun. The newly formed limited company "The Woking Football and Sports Ground Ltd" would provide sports facilities on an eleven acre site for Woking Football Club, Woking Cricket Club and Woking Hockey Club. The future was therefore secured. The Company has a capital of £4,000 divided into ordinary shares of £1. There were seven directors, Messrs J. Hutchinson-Driver J.P., R.G. Bullock, T.C. Gloster, A. Hardy, A.F. Jones, B. Pain and Dr. B.B. Thorne-Thorne O.B.E. An agreement was entered into, whereby the option to purchase the Kingfield site at the agreed price of £150 per acre plus an additional sum of £250 being payable to the tenant as compensation for loss of crops.

1921 - 1922

The Kingfield Sports Ground was still being prepared, so for season 1921-22 home games were played at Hobbs Field in Kingfield. Hobbs Dairy Sports Field was close to the current Westfield Football ground in Woking Park.

Only Griffin and Crane from the previous season played regularly in the side. Newcomers H.H. Thayers, H.J. Norcott, A.V. Badcock, J. Stocks, A.P. Coe, J. Shaw, and

T.W. Inseal played major roles during the season.

The league season began with losses at Ilford and Dulwich, who would finish as Champions and Runners-up, and a slim 1-0 victory at home to West Norwood. Nevertheless a nine-match unbeaten league run extended into the new year.

A vast crowd of 3,000 spectators turned out to see Woking draw 1-1 against Ilford. This 18 week undefeated league run ended with a 4-2 loss at London Caledonians, but by later defeating Wimbledon 2-1 before a crowd of 5,000, placed Woking in joint top position with Ilford.

Suddenly the bubble burst, as not one of the final nine games were won and only three points gained. Woking tumbled from joint top to 10th position.

Although the finish was disappointing the general performance of the team far outstripped anything from recent league programmes. The newcomers linked well, with Thayers and Badcock scoring the goals, and Shaw, Norcott, Stocks, along with Crane and Griffin defending superbly. Thorne-Thorne who only played in four games during the season became Woking's third amateur international, joining the elite group of "Daisy" Bell and Evelyn Lintott.

In the F.A. Cup, recently formed professionals of the Southern League, Guildford Utd, defeated Woking 2-1 after extra time in a replay after a 2-2 draw at Guildford. 5,000 watched the replay. Guildford Pinks, now in the Athenian League, ended Woking's Amateur Cup year with a 2-1 victory in the second qualifying round. The first qualifying round at Surrey Senior side Dorking, provided an astonishing game. Dorking went 3-0 up but Woking through a Harry Thayers hat-trick equalised in normal time and scored three more during extra time to win the tie 6-3.

First round exits occurred in the Senior Cup 3-1 at Nunhead and 2-1 at home to Kingstonian in the Charity Shield.

Griffin played in all games with Crane and Thayers missing one game each.

Thayers was the top scorer with eighteen goals, Badcock scored nine goals with Withers and Tilley scoring six each.

George Turner who would play a leading role throughout the 1920's made his debut and in fact scored three goals in six games.

Altogether a promising season with home gates also showing a healthy increase compared with previous seasons.

Woking Football Club 1921 - 1922

Chapter 5

KINGFIELD SPORTS GROUND; HOME AT LAST

1922 - 1923

Woking's new sports ground was formally opened on Whit Monday 1922 with an attractive programme of games and sports. The principal features of the day's events was a cricket match, a lawn tennis tournament, children's sports, a tug-of-war and a concert. The formal opening ceremony was performed by Mr. F.H.A. Booth of Hoe Place.

On the 26th August 1922, the first competitive football match was played in brilliant sunshine before a tremendous crowd of over 3,000. Tufnell Park were the opposition. Woking opened the scoring with Coe finding the net after 70 minutes. Unfortunately to spoil the day the visitors equalised two minutes from the end.

Only one win, Oxford by 4-2, was achieved in the first ten games. The euphoria created by the acquisition of a new ground soon ceased.

Ilford, the previous seasons champions, scored seven goals against Woking in both the home and away games. Woking's problem was in defence; too many goals were conceded. As well as two sevens from Ilford, Dulwich smashed Woking for six and in an amazing game Wycombe defeated Woking 9-4 before 4,000 spectators.

Three consecutive victories against Wimbledon, West Norwood and Dulwich kept Woking out of the bottom two, although the next six games with only two draws kept Woking on the re-election tightrope.

Wins against Casuals 4-1, London Caledonians 2-1 and a very comfortable 2-2 draw at runners-up Nunhead, enabled Woking to finish third from bottom.

Some moderate success came in the cup competitions. The F.A. Cup produced three victories 1-0 against RAMC, 3-1 against Surrey Senior League newboys, RAE (Farnborough), and an excellent 3-0 victory at Kingstonian after a 2-2 draw at Woking. In a tight struggle Woking just lost 1-0 to Guildford Utd in the 2nd qualifying round.

Woking Football Club 1922 - 1923

Left to right Standing (front) 1st Tom Gloster, 3rd A.V. Badcock, 6th G. Griffin, 7th Jock Shaw, 9th "Dad" Saunders. Seated 1st Harry Thayers, 3rd Arthur Grove, 4th Henry Crane,

Three qualifying ties were also won in the Amateur Cup. Guildford Pinks, Farnham United Breweries and Royal Engineers (Aldershot) were all defeated. In the first round it took two replays before Erith & Belvedere finally defeated Woking 6-1.

Livesey Utd in their only London League season, were defeated 6-2 in the Senior Cup before fellow London League side Mitcham Wanderers, surprisingly won 1-0 at Kingfield. The Charity Shield Final was reached with victories at Kingstonian and Wimbledon. Five Thousand, five hundred attended the final at Wimbledon but Woking were totally outclassed by London League side Summerstown 6-1.

The Oxford Hospital Cup Final was held over for a season. Wycombe and Marlow were both beaten in the earlier rounds.

The basic structure of the team remained. Henry Crane was once again the captain. Griffin, Norcott, Stocks, Thayers and Shaw played most of the games. N.J. Harman, L.W. Urpeth, G.F. Turner and T.M.R. Briggs were the newcomers who made the grade.

Thayers was the top scorer for the second year running with 17 goals, Harman scored 12 and Briggs and Withers scored 11 each. Len Ledger, father of the present secretary Phil Ledger, played six games and was stated as being an uncompromising wing half.

1923 - 1924

Season 1923-24 was significant for only one event; the retirement of Henry Crane, captain of Woking. Henry was the last link of the pre-war Woking and the last of the "old school". His name will go down in local soccer history alongside stalwarts like E.H. Lintott, A.H. Bell, J. Kyle, C.S. Salisbury and A.V. Pearce. George Turner took over the captaincy, a post he then held for many seasons.

A few untried players played in the first league game at home to Wycombe, which was lost 6-1. Changes were made, which reaped dividends with a home victory against Leytonstone and a goal-less draw at home to Nunhead.

L.E. Montgomery, ex-Addlestone, who had played against Woking for Tufnell Park in the inaugural match at Kingfield, had replaced Griffin in goal. G. Turner, H. Norcott, J. Shaw and W.C. Elsworth formed the nucleus of the defence. B.V. Griffiths, H. Thayers, N. Harman and A. Gilbert were in the main the strike force. Woking were the lowest scorers in the league with only 31 in 26 games.

By mid-December, Woking were bottom of the league with only one win and three draws from eleven games. Then on the Saturday before Christmas, top of the table Dulwich visited Woking and the inevitable shock occurred, a strike by Gilbert was enough in a rousing 1-0 victory.

Three draws and a 1-0 victory over Oxford with only two goals conceded gave some hope of climbing the league table, but an unbelievable 11-2 loss at Oxford, who finished second to bottom, destroyed the confidence. Only one point was gained in the next five games. Winning two games and drawing one out of the last four pulled Woking out of the re-election positions.

The victory against London Caledonians in the last game was a personal triumph for H.L. Longhurst who scored Woking's four goals in a 4-1 win.

Woking made very little impact in the major cups. Wellington Works knocked Woking out of the F.A. Cup by 6-2. A first round loss in the Amateur Cup against RASC (Aldershot) by 3-1 did not inspire any great confidence. The two Surrey competitions provided some entertainment.

Surrey Senior League Champions, Farnham U.B.'s, were defeated 1-0 in the Senior Cup after a 1-1 draw. A crowd of 5,000 watched a 3-3 thriller at Wimbledon in the next round and despite a Harman hat-trick, Woking just lost 3-4 in the replay.

Summerstown, now in the Athenian League, won 2-1 at Woking in the Charity Shield after Kingstonian had been defeated 2-0 in the first round.

In the held over Oxford Hospital Cup Final, Woking were soundly beaten 5-2 by Oxford, and 4-0 by Oxfordshire Senior Cup holders Cowley in the 1923-24 final.

Harman was the top scorer with 11 goals, Gilbert scored 8 with Thayers seven. Turner missed only one game, with Shaw playing all but two; Norcott played 33 out of 37 and Montgomery turned out in 32 games.

Woking's record against the top three in the league was two wins, two draws and two losses, a good record for a side finishing third from bottom.

1924 - 1925

Season 1924-25 started off very poorly with an 8-1 reverse at Clapton. Five Thousand fans watched the eventual league runners-up destroy the Woking defence. Two 1-0 defeats against London Caledonians who eventually won the league by two points from Clapton and a 3-1 reverse at Nunhead left Woking with no points from four games.

E.A. Thomas made an emphatic debut by scoring all four goals in a 4-2 victory at home to Wycombe. The return of Harry Thayers as strike partner gave the side some much needed punch. A 0-0 draw with Tufnell Park was followed by a 6-1 mauling of Casuals with Thomas again netting four goals. He netted another two in a 5-2 reverse at St. Albans and a hat-trick against Reigate Priory from the Southern Amateur League in a 8-3 Surrey Senior Cup victory gave Thomas a dream start with 13 goals in 5 games.

In the Christmas games a fine 2-0 victory at home to Clapton and a 1-1 draw at Wycombe indicated that Woking's fortunes were on the change.

Unfortunately the next six games were lost. Thomas played his last game in a 4-5 thriller against Leytonstone. Wins against Ilford and Nunhead and a 2-2 draw at Dulwich gave Woking some hope but the final six games were lost. Woking therefore finished rock bottom with 13 points, seven behind second to bottom Oxford.

Woking had a small flurry in the F.A. Cup, Camberley from the Surrey Senior League, were defeated 5-1 with C.V. Maidment scoring two of the goals. Two goals each from Stimson and R. Smith defeated Wellington Works 4-1. A crowd of 3,000 watched Woking defeat Tooting Town of the London League 3-1. Summerstown defeated Woking 2-0 at the second attempt in the second qualifying round. The first game was abandoned at 23 minutes when the referee collapsed and died.

Farnham U.B.'s, champions of the Surrey Senior League in consecutive years, defeated Woking 3-1 in the Amateur Cup after a 2-1 first qualifying round victory against the Royal Engineers.

Woking were again defeated by Farnham U.B.'s, this time 4-2 in the Senior Cup after easy victories against Reigate Priory and Weybridge (Surrey Senior League) in previous rounds, R.G. Stimson scored hat-tricks in both these games.

A 4,000 attendance saw Woking lose 2-1 to Kingstonian at the first attempt in the Charity Shield.

George Turner captain of Woking only missed two games. Montgomery, Maidment, Stimson and Thayers played twenty or more league games. Norcott took part in 26 league and cup games, Shaw played in 21 and Harman played in 19 but had lost his scoring touch. Tommy Briggs played in 8 games from early March but he was powerless to stop the slide.

Reg Stimson scored 18 goals in 29 games, Thomas finished with 16 goals in 14 games. Cyril Maidment scored seven and Harry Thayers six.

For the first time since 1914 Woking had to apply for re-election.

1925 - 1926

Woking made their usual poor start to season 1925-26. The visit to Leytonstone, with a largely experimental defence proved disastrous with an 8-1 defeat. Changes were made which resulted in a 1-0 victory at home to London Caledonians. This was the only win in the next eight games although three were drawn. The tide turned at the end of November when two goals from Ledger helped defeat Wimbledon at Kingfield 4-3.

A debut goal from Johnny Price and one from C. Woodards sent Leytonstone home with a 2-0 defeat. Four wins from the next five games moved Woking into a respectable mid-table position. Twenty goals were scored in these five games and fifteen goals were conceded. Attacking football appeared to be Woking's policy. Dick Fitzgerald's debut game was a 5-4 victory at Wimbledon in which he scored four times. A hat-trick in a 4-3 victory at Clapton gave him seven goals in his first two games for Woking, which must constitute something of a record.

A fast and furious game at Wycombe ended the winning run with a 6-4 defeat. The goal scoring continued in April with a 3-2 home victory against Oxford and two 3-3 home draws against Ilford and St. Albans. The former game was seen by a crowd of 2,000. In the final game against league champions Dulwich, Woking were committed to attack and lost 7-5 despite two goals each from Joe Perryman and L.W. Urpeth.

The final league position of 9th was a major improvement over last seasons bottom spot. Fifty-six goals were scored in 26 games but a very high 73 goals conceded indicated Woking's weakness.

Cup ties did not produce much excitement. In the F.A. Cup Woking were defeated by Wellington Works at the third attempt. A 2-0 lead during extra time in the second match was meaningless as the game was abandoned due to bad light. A very weak Woking side lost 3-1 in the third match. The 2nd Rifle Brigade ended Woking's participation in the Amateur Cup with a resounding 5-1 score.

A Wheatcroft hat-trick helped defeat Casuals 6-1 in the Surrey Senior Cup but despite two goals from Harman, Kingstonian proved superior in the second round with a 4-2 victory before a crowd of 6,000.

Kingstonian again knocked out Woking, this time in the semi-final of the Charity Shield. It was a more decisive 5-1 score line.

New players C. Pope, J. Wheatcroft and J. Elliott joined old favourites Turner, Shaw, Montgomery, Thayers and Maidment. Wheatcroft was the top scorer with 14 goals with Harman scoring nine goals. Fitzgerald scored 9 goals in five games, Woodward scored 7 in seven and Joe Perryman scored 5 goals in eight games.

W.J. Price made his debut scoring twice in three games. There were a few more goals to come from "Johnny" before he turned professional with Fulham. Dick Fitzgerald would also claim many goals in the next few seasons. In three consecutive games, two league and one friendly, Dick scored 4, 3 and 4 times. Rather a prolific start.

Forty-nine players wore the Cardinal and White shirts during the season. This indicated an unsettled side although six players turned out twenty or more times in the league.

Woking Reserve XI. Winners Surrey Intermediate Charity Cup 1925 - 26

Left to right Standing C. Salisbury, J. Perryman, A.C. Carr, S. Sturt, C. Dyason, V. Waller, L. Ledger, A Lush (sec.). Seated H. Peel, R. Heaseman, J. Elliott, H. Gowler (Capt.), W. Pelham, R. Humphreyies, S. Matthews (Trainer).

1926 -1927

Once again the early league results were poor. An opening game defeat at Leytonstone 6-3 was possibly due to some experimental changes that didn't come off. Nevertheless it was a marginal improvement over the three previous seasons openers, which had ended 8-1, 8-1 and 6-1.

Despite the poor start, only two wins in the first eleven games, season 1926-27 was the best since 1912-13 when both the County Cup and the Shield were won.

Perryman, Price, Wheatley and Fitzgerald were a formidable strike force ably backed up by arguably Woking's best ever half-back line of Arthur Cartlidge, Ernie Payne and Tommy

Briggs. Cartlidge would play for England Amateurs and Briggs for Scotland Amateurs.

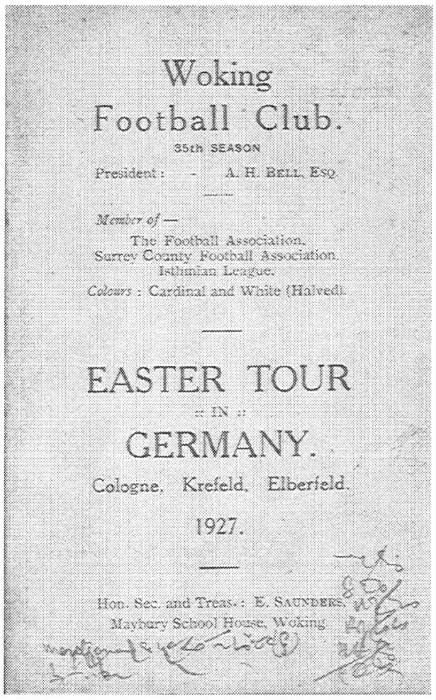

Woking
Football Club.
35th SEASON
President: - A. H. Bell, Esq.

Member of —
The Football Association.
Surrey County Football Association.
Isthmian League.
Colours: Cardinal and White (Halved).

EASTER TOUR
:: IN ::
GERMANY.
Cologne, Krefeld, Elberfeld.
1927.

Hon. Sec. and Treas.: E. Saunders,
Maybury School House, Woking

Easter Tour in Germany 1927.
Itinerary Card. Three games played, two draws, one loss.

In the early months of the season very few league games were played. Progress in both the F.A. Cup and the Amateur Cup competitions restricted the league programme to nine games before the new year. Twenty goals were scored but 25 were conceded. In five away games Woking scored three in four of them but due to their shaky defence only one win was recorded.

Five qualifying rounds of the F.A. Cup were won, all home ties against Surrey Senior side Aldershot Traction (4-1), RAMC (3-2), Guildford Utd (2-0) before a crowd of 5,481, Thorneycroft of the Hampshire League (5-1) and Leytonstone (3-0). Perryman scored in every tie notching seven goals.

Charlton Athletic of Division 3 (South) came to Woking in the F.A. Cup 1st round and finally won 3-1, although Price missed a penalty for Woking at 1-1. The official attendance was given as 5,593 but from the gate receipts of £373 there was no doubt that 8,100 was closer to the actual attendance.

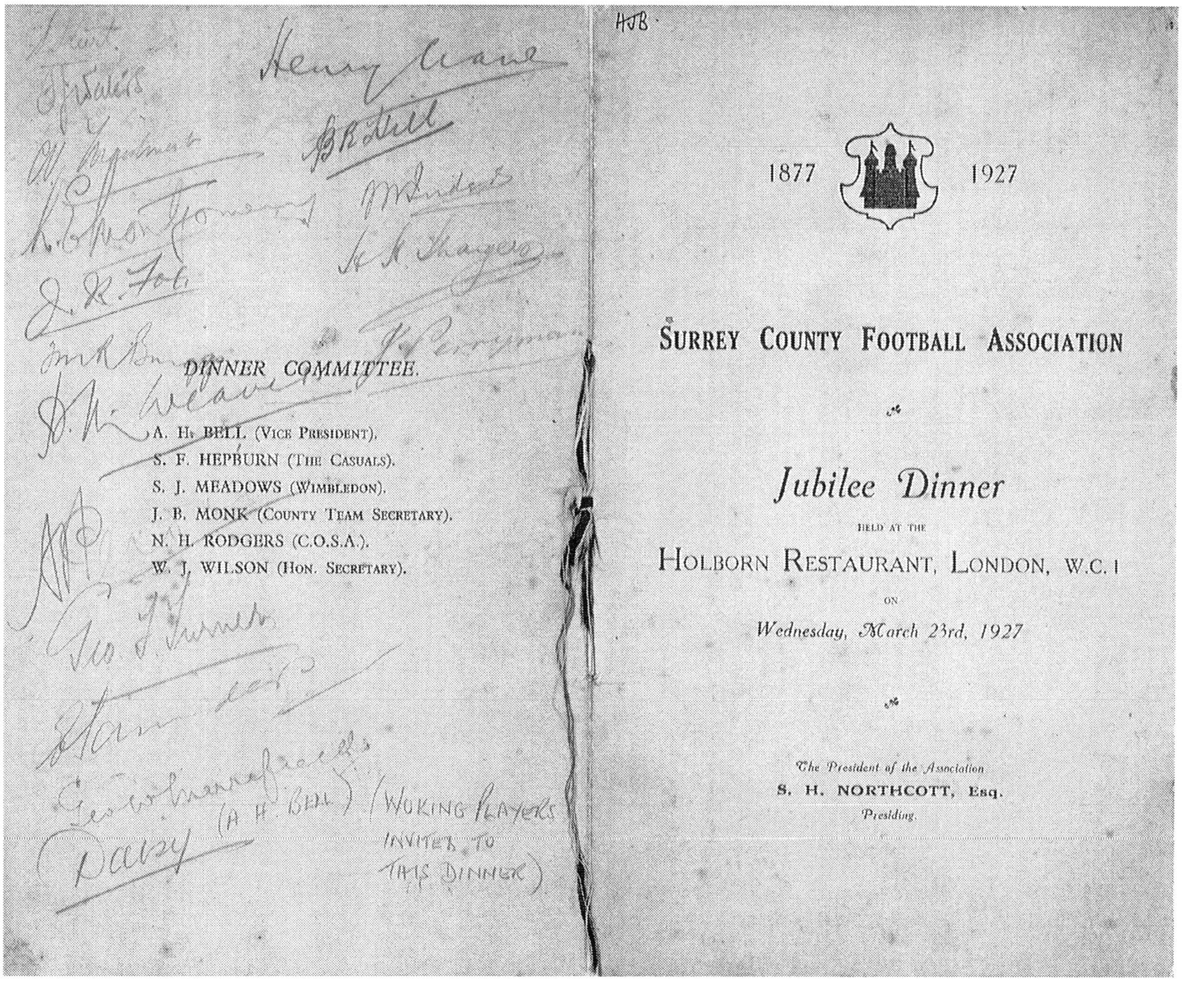

DINNER COMMITTEE.
A. H. Bell (Vice President).
S. F. Hepburn (The Casuals).
S. J. Meadows (Wimbledon).
J. B. Monk (County Team Secretary).
N. H. Rodgers (C.O.S.A.).
W. J. Wilson (Hon. Secretary).

1877 1927

Surrey County Football Association

Jubilee Dinner
held at the
Holborn Restaurant, London, W.C.1
on
Wednesday, March 23rd, 1927

The President of the Association
S. H. Northcott, Esq.
Presiding.

Surrey County F.A. Jubilee Dinner 1927
Woking Players A.H. Bell and J.B. Monk on Dinner Committee.

Four qualifying rounds in the Amateur Cup were comfortably won with Price scoring in each round, including four against Addlestone (5-1) and three against RASC (7-0). A home tie in the first round against the Isthmian League champions to be, St. Albans, was lost 4-1.

The league programme took off in the new year with only one defeat in eight games. In three successive home games Woking scored five. An 8-0 drubbing at Nunhead in March and a 4-2 loss at home to St. Albans slowed Woking's climb up the table but five wins and a draw in the final seven games placed Woking a respectable 5th.

The Surrey Senior Cup was duly won in the last game of the season at Guildford. A crowd of 7,000 saw Athenian side Redhill defeated 3-0. Joe Perryman had scored in every round including an incredible 7 in an 8-3 defeat of Epsom.

Turner, Price and Montgomery played in most of the games being ably backed up by Payne, Perryman, Wheatley, Maidment, Briggs, Cartlidge, Thayers, Pope and Fitzgerald.

Perryman scored 41 in 35 games, Price 36 in 40, Wheatley 17 in 30 and Fitzgerald 11 in 21.

Woking made two overseas visits losing 5-2 to Ajax Sporting Club before 8,000 and playing an Easter tournament in Germany. The Good Friday game against Kölner (Cologne) was lost heavily 6-0 but the final games against Elberfeld and Krefeld were both drawn 3-3. It was interesting to note that players were advised to "take soap, boot polish, a towel and plain white football shirt".

1927 - 1928

For the first time for many years Woking had a winning start to season 1927-28. Ilford who finished one place ahead of Woking were smashed 7-4 at Kingfield with Fitzgerald and Price both claiming hat-tricks.

Cartlidge had left the club and Briggs played only one game so Maidment and Wheatley shared the No.4 spot with Sherlock and Cable competing for the No. 6 shirt. Montgomery, Turner and Payne were still battling in defence with P.J. Clifford staking his claim at full-back. Price, Fitzgerald and Perryman scored the majority of the goals with E. Moore providing the service from the wing.

In the two premier cup competitions Woking defeated Weybridge 6-2 in the preliminary round of the F.A. Cup but newly named Guildford City away proved too strong as, 6,013 watched Woking defeated by 3-0.

The Casuals provided stiff opposition in the Amateur Cup, but after holding Woking to 2-2 at Kingfield they were heavily defeated 5-1 in the replay.

Woking disappointed in the second round losing untypically 1-0 at home to London Caledonians.

Four wins and a draw in the first five games was the best league start for years. Last season's champions St. Albans were beaten 3-0 before a crowd of 3,000 at Kingfield. Wycombe ended the run 3-1. It was this failure to defeat teams below them that probably cost Woking the championship. Middle of the table Leytonstone defeated Woking twice but the loss to bottom club Tufnell Park 2-0 was unbelievable.

Perryman scored two hat-tricks against the Civil Service (6-1) and Dulwich (5-3), Price scored three against Tufnell Park (5-2) and four against the Civil Service (8-2).

St. Albans retained the championship with 35 points. Woking finished four points behind in fourth place, their highest finish in the Isthmian League.

In the Charity Shield, Casuals defeated Woking 4-1 in the first round. A more determined effort was made to hold onto the Surrey Senior Cup. Mitcham Wanderers and Casuals were defeated 2-0 and 3-1 respectively. Price scoring in both encounters. Price, Fitzgerald and Perryman scored the goals which defeated Nunhead 3-1 in the semi-final at Wimbledon. The final at Kingstonian which drew a 4,000 crowd was an anti-climax as Woking performed badly in losing 3-0.

Turner only missed one game with Payne and Montgomery missing two games. Wheatley, Moore, Price and Fitzgerald were also regulars. It was this continuity that helped promote good team play. Price, Fitzgerald and Payne travelled with the Isthmian League squad to Berlin in the close season.

For the second season running most of the goals were scored by Price, 28 in 31 games, Perryman notched 22 in 22 games and Fitzgerald 21 in 30 games.

Price who played for England Amateurs during the season had signed amateur forms for Brentford in the new year, but he would sign pro' forms in the close season and become a firm favourite at Fulham.

During March work was started on a new stand. It was designed by Mr. H.A. Whitburn and would seat approximately 350. The Supporters Club had provided the funds through their own enterprise.

1928 - 1929

Season 1928-29 was unsuccessful. The strength of the last two seasons, namely the high number of goals scored, deserted Woking. Only 39 goals, joint lowest in the league, were scored in 26 league games.

The loss of Price and Fitzgerald was partly responsible for the drought. The latter played one game, on Christmas day against Wimbledon. In a 5-3 victory he scored three goals.

Turner had a new full-back partner in F. Gary, who played in most of the games. Payne had gone. He was replaced at centre-half initially by G.B. Harvey, then by Maidment. Wheatley played a number of games in defence but a new face, Ken Blunden played in 18 league and cup games. H. May took over the No. 8 shirt with some success.

Woking started the season with a 1-0 home victory against the whipping boys, Civil Service. Thirteen games later on Christmas Day, Woking recorded their second win. In January three consecutive victories were recorded at home to Wycombe and Oxford and away to Casuals. Three heavy home defeats followed with Tufnell Park and St. Albans scoring five each and Ilford winning (4-2). Three victories followed against Nunhead, Civil Service and Leytonstone, but defeats by Wycombe (1-7) and Clapton (1-2) prevented Woking climbing up the table.

Woking were exempted until the 4th qualifying round of the F.A. Cup when Tooting Town of the London League were duly despatched 3-1, but Newport away in the first round was too much and the final score 7-0 reflected the difference in the sides.

Barking Town of the Athenian League destroyed Woking 6-1 in the Amateur Cup. Wimbledon went one better defeating Woking 7-1 in the Senior Cup and 5-2 in the Charity Shield. Perryman scored all three goals against Wimbledon.

The semi-final of the Surrey Combination Cup, in which Guildford won comfortably 4-1, was watched by 2,955 who paid £102 for the privilege

Montgomery, Moore, Turner, Perryman and Gary played in the majority of the games. H. May supported Perryman in attack with W.C. Galbally providing the subtle crosses.

Perryman scored 18 goals in 28 games, Moore was next with 7 goals. The rest of the goals were shared among many.

One of Woking's few good games was in defeating Nunhead the eventual champions 2-1 in their own backyard.

Attendances fell dramatically as the side did not perform with any consistency. The position of second to bottom was probably correct.

1929 - 1930

Season 1929-30 started off very poorly. A largely experimental side was heavily defeated 6-1 at Leytonstone. Woking's only victory in the first nine league games was a 4-2 success at home to London Caledonians.

Montgomery and Turner were still playing; Sam Craddock came in at centre-half, Lockwood played at wing-half and G.L. Moseley and Wilf Chitty settled into the forward line. The major find of the season however was a multi-talented striker, Billy Warnes, who would play for England Amateurs during his career.

With all these changes the team did not settle down quickly. On the Saturday before Christmas Nunhead were the visitors. Changes were made; Gary came in to partner Turner at full-back, C. Seddon replaced W. Stevens at half-back, A.W. Bolton and an old favourite Fitzgerald played up front.

The effect was immediate Fitzgerald scored three in a 5-4 victory. Wimbledon were despatched twice over Christmas 4-2 and 6-2. Bolton scored a hat-trick at Wimbledon (4-2) and another two on Boxing Day in the reverse fixture. Seven wins and a draw in eight games moved Woking into a respectable league position. Thirty-three goals were scored in these eight games. Bolton, who only played six games, scored 8 goals and Fitzgerald scored in each of his three games to register 6 goals.

Fortunately when Bolton and Fitzgerald did not play, Moore stepped into the forward slot and Perryman notched six goals in five games, this included four goals against Ilford in a final score of 9-3.

Although the final nine games only produced three wins and three draws, the final league position was a respectable fifth.

Mitcham Wanderers knocked Woking out of the F.A. Cup 2-1 at Kingfield and later in the season repeated this success 1-0 in the Surrey Charity Shield. In the County Cup four goals from stand-in centre-forward F. Gary helped eliminate Whyteleafe 9-3. Nunhead defeated Woking 2-1 in the next round after the first game ended 1-1.

Four qualifying rounds of the Amateur Cup were safely negotiated. Three of them were against Army sides. First round opponents Hampstead Town proved just too strong in a 3-2 defeat.

Moseley, Craddock, Montgomery and Lockwood played in all but a handful of games. Warnes scored 16 goals, Moore 15 goals and Moseley 14 goals were the main scorers. Useful scoring contributions were made by H. May 8, Chitty 6 and as stated earlier by Bolton, Fitzgerald and Perryman.

In September Danny Shea, an England full international forward with West Ham, Blackburn and Fulham, commenced duties as Woking's first professional trainer coach.

A sad occasion at the end of the season was the leaving of George Turner to take up an appointment in Uganda. He served Woking for ten years, eight as captain and played twenty-five times for Surrey. A true clubman in every sense.

Left A.V. Badcock 1920 to 1925, 40 league & cup games
Right Arthur Grove 1910 to 1921, 77 league and cup games

Ken Blunden 1927 to 1937, 102 league and cup games

L.E. Montgomery 1923 to 1932
One of Woking's top goalkeepers playing 280 league and cup games

Jock Shaw 1921 to 1926
Over 150 league & cup appearances

Arthur Cartlidge
Amateur international 1925 to 1927
28 league & cup appearances

Dick Fitzgerald 1925 to 1931
65 league & cup appearances
scoring 51 goals

Cyril Maidment 1922 to 1929
Over 130 league & cup games.

Johnny Price 1925 to 1928
74 league & cup appearances scoring 66 goals. Turned professional with Fulham.

Ernie Payne 1926 to 1928
70 league & cup games.
One third of the legendary half-back line of Cartlidge, Payne and Briggs.

Six-a-side Easter Tournament late 1920's or early 1930's.
Woking winners of the senior section, Stan Sturt is the goalkeeper.
Three seated (left to right) Harry Thayers, Dick Fitzgerald, V. Lee.

The following is a report by MIKE BONDY, on an F.A. Cup match, Woking v Charlton Athletic in 1926:

GROUND RECORD ATTENDANCES: Number 29

KINGFIELD SPORTS GROUND: 8,100

WOKING (0) 1 CHARLTON ATHLETIC (0) 3

Price 64 Rankin 46, Cairns 71, Tricker 73

F.A. Cup, 1st Round Saturday, November 27th, 1926.

Blessed with home ties throughout the qualifying rounds of the 1926/7 F.A. Cup competition, Woking made most of their good fortune and swept aside the opposition without the need of any replays. Victories were achieved against the Aldershot Traction Co. 4-1 (Price 2, Cartlidge, Perryman), R.A.M.C. 3-2 (Price, Perryman, Sewell), Guildford United 2-0 (Perryman 2), Thorneycrofts 5-1 (Perryman 2, Wheatley 2, Price) and Leytonstone 3-0 (Price, Wheatley, Perryman). Woking were now in the competition proper for only the second time in their history, the first being back in 1907/8 when they had gone down 0-5 to First Division Bolton Wanderers at Burnden Park in Round One (the equivalent of the 3rd Round today). In the Isthmian League, the Cardinals had only played 5 games and were bottom, but his told a totally false tale, for with all the various cup games they'd been involved in, the team had in fact reeled off a run of 9 successive wins and were on the crest of a wave. Charlton's form was pretty patchy, they were destined to finish a fairly modest 13th in Division 3 South, but against that had one of the better defence records in the Football League.

Away from home the 'Robins' found life generally hard, goals were difficult to find, and wins infrequent, though leading up to this tie they surprisingly notched 2 consecutive victories on the ground of Northampton 1-0, Norwich City 3-2. Woking had more than a fair chance of causing an upset, stimulating enormous interest in the tie. At the time, the official ground attendance figure of paying spectators was given as below 6,000 (receipts £375-3s-0d), but the evidence suggests that this was actually far removed from the numbers who were inside, and there seems little doubt that the Kingfield ground held over 8,000 people that Saturday afternoon.

Soon after the start, Woking's inside right Wheatley was struck hard in the face by the ball, and had to leave the field for a short spell, with treatment to a nose bleed. A free-kick from the touchline, gave home keeper, Montgomery, the first goalmouth action of the match, and he cleared the ball well with his right fist to avert any danger. Price then tested Preedy with a firm drive, which the Charlton goalie took cleanly to his chest. The game was fast and open, with play switching from first one end of the field, and then to the other. Woking left winger Lee slanted a free-kick across Charlton's area, and outside right Thayers promptly struck the ball well at an angle from some distance. His shot looked to be hurtling in under the crossbar, but Preedy leaped high to flick the ball over the top for a corner. This brought warm applause from the crowd, the best effort of the match so far. Woking's full-backs Turner and Pope were both playing well, their steady and effective work snuffing out much of Charlton's threat.

At half-time honours were even, neither side had scored, and many onlookers fancied the Cardinals chances, with the team kicking into their favourite goal for the 2nd period. Charlton though had other ideas, and within 60 seconds had taken the lead with a simple goal. The visitors winger Horton hared down the left touchline, and after Turner's back heeled clearance had temporarily halted him, he regained possession, then squared the ball into the goalmouth, where Rankin, a yard or so out, had an easy tap-in past Montgomery. This score took the wind out of Woking's sails for a while, but hey were back pressing for an equaliser, and got their reward after 64 minutes. Thayers centre was allowed to pass by Perryman, who, with great awareness stepped aside to the Price fire in a strong well directed shot, a second before an opponents challenge. Preedy got his hand to the ball, but was powerless to prevent it entering the net. Hardly had the excitement died down when Perryman was tripped in the penalty area, but Price pout his spot-kick straight into Preedy's arms. Charlton, relieved by their escape, regained the lead four minutes later when Cairns headed neatly in, following a clever attacking move between Davies and Sherlaw. A free-kick sealed Woking's fate in the 73rd minute, for as Tricker drove a shot in from outside the box, a colleague ducked down, right in front of the unsighted keeper, and the ball flew into the net.

Charlton's cup hopes were dashed 4-1 at Bristol Rovers in the next round, but Woking's season finished with the Surrey Senior Cup, and a healthy 5th spot in the Isthmian League.

WOKING: L.E. Montgomery, G.F. Turner, C. Pope, S. Sherlock, E. Payne, T.M.R. Briggs, H.H. Thayers, E. Wheatley, J. Perryman, W.J. Price.

CHARLTON: Preedy, Middleton, Devine, Paterson, V. Lee, Davies, Armitage, Sherlaw, Tricker, Cairns, Rankin, Horton.

Chapter 6

AMATEUR CUP SEMI-FINAL, THREE CONSECUTIVE CHARITY SHIELD FINALS - ALL LOST, THEN WORLD WAR II

1930 - 1931

Season 1930-31 was centred around the Amateur Cup. The semi-final was reached but unfortunately Wycombe proved to be too strong on the day and were the eventual winners of the Cup.

The league games became of secondary importance and this no doubt contributed to the final position of third from bottom.

Billy Warnes had the honour of playing for England Amateurs, winning his first cap against Ireland in Belfast on 15th November and his second cap in February against Wales in which he scored two goals in a 5-0 victory.

Of the playing personnel Montgomery started his 8th season as first team goalkeeper. H.E. Turner replaced his namesake George Turner as full-back partner to A. Beadle. Seddon, Craddock and Lockwood were the first choice half-backs. Warnes was partnered by May and Mason settled into the centre-forward position once Moseley and Fitzgerald had stopped playing. Generally D. Bateman was the number eleven with R. Watson, H. Greenwood and F. Stockley at various times claiming the number ten shirt. A total of 45 players turned out in league and cup games during the season.

In the F.A. Cup two rounds were won, Whyteleafe Albion of the London League 5-1 and Casuals 4-0, before Kingstonian ended Woking's interest with a 3-1 victory. Five thousand five hundred paid £179 to see the game. Kingstonian also ended Woking's Surrey Senior Cup campaign this time 5-1. They proved to be a bogey side as they won 6-2 and 2-0 in the league.

Egham of the Spartan League defeated Woking 3-2 in the Charity Shield to avenge last seasons 2-1 loss.

Woking F.C. 1930 - 1931 Amateur Cup Semi-Finalists

Left to right Back Row Danny Shea (Trainer), H. Turner, L Montgomery (committee), S. Sturt, G.W. Mason, A. Beadle, H. Greenwood, E. Saunders (committee), A.H. Fell (committee) Seated Middle Row W.H. Warnes. H. May, S. Craddock (Captain), F. Stockley, D. Bateman Seated Front J. Chapman, F.B. Lockwood

Guildford City again won the Surrey Combination Cup, although two replays were required. May's two goals could not prevent a 4-2 defeat.

Sam Craddock 1921- 1931
65 League & Cup appearances

Although the first league game was lost to London Caledonians (3-0) a Warnes hat-trick helped defeat Ilford away 5-4 and a single Watson goal gained revenge at London Caledonians. Three games were lost including a tight 4-3 at Champions-to-be Wimbledon.

By the time the Amateur Cup 1st round commenced in mid-December, Woking had played eleven league games. Four had been won and two were drawn.

Cambridge Town a Spartan League side were defeated 3-1 in the first round, Athenian side Leyton who had won the cup in 1927 and 1928 and were beaten finalist in 1929, were heavily defeated 4-0 by a rampant Woking. Western League side Portland Utd, travelled up from Grove Corner but were edged out 2-1 before 4,500 in the 3rd round. Clapton who three weeks earlier had defeated Woking 8-4 in the league were defeated by a May goal in the 64th minute of this fourth round cup-tie. Semi-final opponents Wycombe, who had already defeated Woking twice in the league, made it three times before 7,300 at Ilford. The 3-0 scoreline emphasised Wycombe's superiority on the day.

The rest of the league programme was an anti-climax although a weakened side defeated league leaders Dulwich 4-1 away.

H. May was the top goalscorer with 19 goals, Mason and Warnes each scored 16 goals.

In an Easter tour of Belgium, Woking lost 2-1 to Klub Kladno (Prague) before 12,000 but the second match ended 4-4 with Sporting Anderlecht.

Johnny Price again played on the Kingfield turf when Fulham came to Woking for a friendly match.

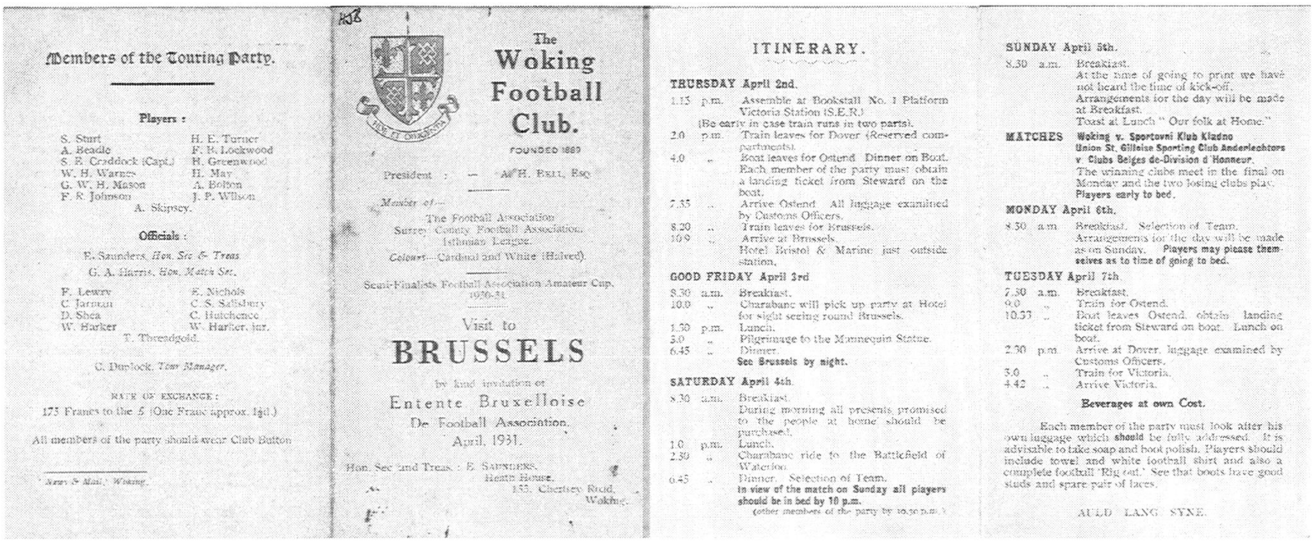

Members of the Touring Party.

Players :

S. Sturt — H. E. Turner
A. Beadle — F. B. Lockwood
S. E. Craddock (Capt.) — H. Greenwood
W. H. Warnes — H. May
G. W. H. Mason — A. Bolton
F. R. Johnson — J. P. Wilson
A. Skipsey.

Officials :

E. Saunders, *Hon. Sec & Treas*
G. A. Harris, *Hon. Match Sec.*

F. Lewry — E. Nichols
C. Jarman — C. S. Salisbury
D. Shea — C. Hutchence
W. Harker — W. Harker, jnr.
T. Threadgold.

C. Durlock, *Tour Manager.*

RATE OF EXCHANGE :
175 Francs to the £ (One Franc approx. 1½d.)

All members of the party should wear Club Button

"News & Mail," Woking.

The Woking Football Club.
FOUNDED 1889

President : — A. H. Bell, Esq.

Member of—
The Football Association
Surrey County Football Association.
Isthmian League.
Colours—Cardinal and White (Halved).

Semi-Finalists Football Association Amateur Cup, 1930-31.

Visit to
BRUSSELS
by kind invitation of
Entente Bruxelloise
De Football Association.
April, 1931.

Hon. Sec and Treas. : E. Saunders,
Heath House,
133, Chertsey Road,
Woking.

ITINERARY.

THURSDAY April 2nd.

1.15 p.m. Assemble at Bookstall No. 1 Platform Victoria Station (S.E.R.)
(Be early in case train runs in two parts).
2.0 p.m. Train leaves for Dover (Reserved compartments).
4.0 „ Boat leaves for Ostend. Dinner on Boat. Each member of the party must obtain a landing ticket from Steward on the boat.
7.35 „ Arrive Ostend. All luggage examined by Customs Officers.
8.20 „ Train leaves for Brussels.
10.9 „ Arrive at Brussels.
Hotel Bristol & Marine just outside station.

GOOD FRIDAY April 3rd

8.30 a.m. Breakfast.
10.0 „ Charabanc will pick up party at Hotel for sight seeing round Brussels.
1.30 p.m. Lunch.
3.0 „ Pilgrimage to the Manneqain Statue.
6.45 „ Dinner.
See Brussels by night.

SATURDAY April 4th.

8.30 a.m. Breakfast.
During morning all presents promised to the people at home should be purchased.
1.0 p.m. Lunch.
2.30 „ Charabanc ride to the Battlefield of Waterloo.
6.45 „ Dinner. Selection of Team.
In view of the match on Sunday all players should be in bed by 10 p.m.
(other members of the party by 10.30 p.m.)

SUNDAY April 5th.

8.30 a.m. Breakfast.
At the time of going to print we have not heard the time of kick-off.
Arrangements for the day will be made at Breakfast.
Toast at Lunch " Our folk at Home."

MATCHES **Woking v. Sportovni Klub Kladno**
Union St. Gilloise Sporting Club Anderlechtors v. Clubs Belges de-Division d'Honneur.
The winning clubs meet in the final on Monday and the two losing clubs play.
Players early to bed.

MONDAY April 6th.

8.30 a.m. Breakfast. Selection of Team.
Arrangements for the day will be made as on Sunday. **Players may please themselves as to time of going to bed.**

TUESDAY April 7th.

7.30 a.m. Breakfast.
9.0 „ Train for Ostend.
10.33 „ Boat leaves Ostend, obtain landing ticket from Steward on boat. Lunch on boat.
2.30 p.m. Arrive at Dover, luggage examined by Customs Officers.
3.0 „ Train for Victoria.
4.42 „ Arrive Victoria.

Beverages at own Cost.

Each member of the party must look after his own luggage which **should** be fully addressed. It is advisable to take soap and boot polish. Players should include towel and white football shirt and also a complete football 'Rig out.' See that boots have good studs and spare pair of laces.

AULD LANG SYNE.

Itinerary for the visit to Brussels, April 1931. Two games were played, one lost and one drawn

1931 - 1932

Season 1931-32 did not achieve anything remarkable, second to bottom in the league and knocked out of the major cups quickly. The only success was in the Charity Shield with the final being contested against Nunhead. A close 2-1 defeat relegated Woking to runners-up position.

turned professional in November with Crystal Palace. Local players Fred Buckmaster and Harry Hooker were given their chance up-front.

A reasonable league start with four wins in eight games deteriorated after Christmas with only two wins in fourteen starts.

Leyland Motors of the Surrey Senior League were easily defeated 5-0 in the F.A. Cup with

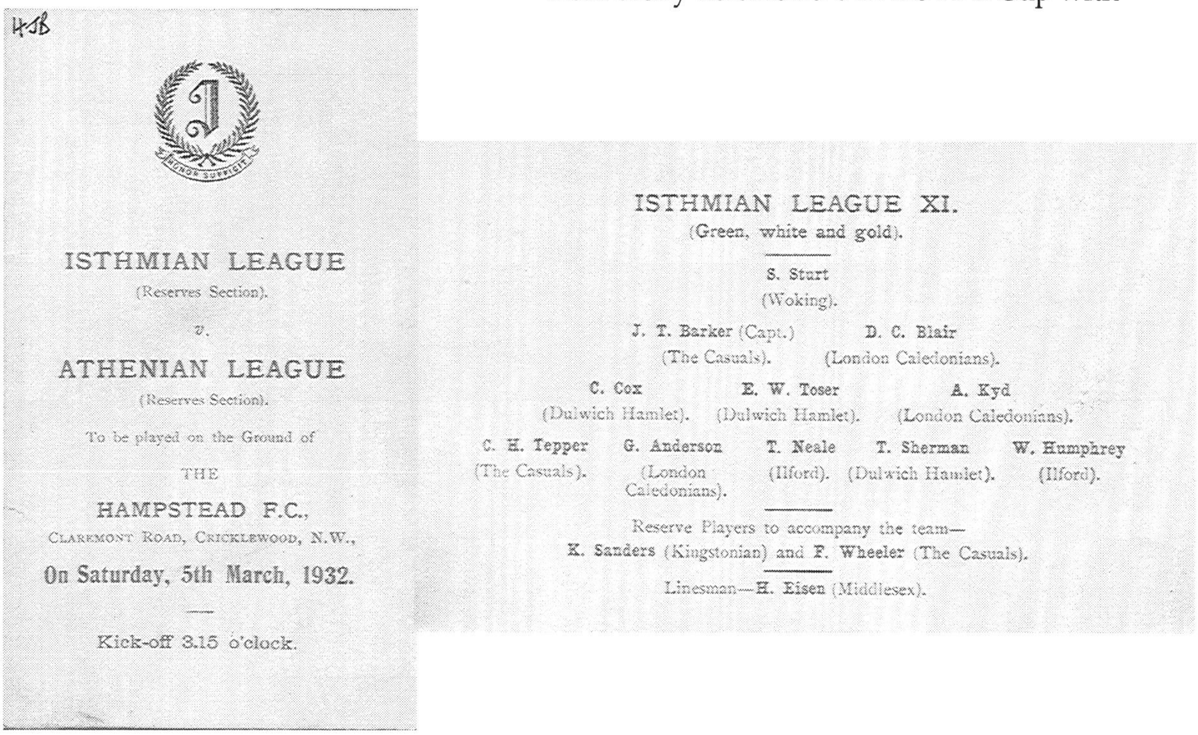

ISTHMIAN LEAGUE
(Reserves Section).
v.
ATHENIAN LEAGUE
(Reserves Section).
To be played on the Ground of
THE
HAMPSTEAD F.C.,
CLAREMONT ROAD, CRICKLEWOOD, N.W.,
On Saturday, 5th March, 1932.
Kick-off 3.15 o'clock.

ISTHMIAN LEAGUE XI.
(Green, white and gold).
S. Sturt (Woking).
J. T. Barker (Capt.) (The Casuals). D. C. Blair (London Caledonians).
C. Cox (Dulwich Hamlet). E. W. Toser (Dulwich Hamlet). A. Kyd (London Caledonians).
C. H. Tepper (The Casuals). G. Anderson (London Caledonians). T. Neale (Ilford). T. Sherman (Dulwich Hamlet). W. Humphrey (Ilford).
Reserve Players to accompany the team—
K. Sanders (Kingstonian) and F. Wheeler (The Casuals).
Linesman—H. Eisen (Middlesex).

Isthmian League, Reserve Section representative game, March 1932.
Stan Sturt was the Surrey goalkeeper.

Only H.E. Turner, Warnes and May of last seasons regulars started in the first game, which was lost by the odd goal in five at St. Albans. Newcomer C.H. Breeze scored on his debut.

Stan Sturt started off in goal although Montgomery, who was playing in his last season, appeared in half the games making his final and 280th appearance in March 1932. Montgomery was one of Woking's greats and ranked high among Woking's goalkeepers.

J. O'Donnell, J. Tompkins and H. Greenwood started off as the half-back line, N. Osgood came in at centre-back and with Tompkins signing on for Fulham, Ken Blunden had an extended run in the team.

Warnes played intermittently, as he was a regular in Arsenal's combination side. May

Breeze scoring twice. Athenian leaguers Sutton were too strong in the next round, defeating Woking 4-1. Maidenhead of the Spartan league overcame Woking 4-0 in the Amateur Cup.

Bateman scored twice against Guildford Pinks to secure a 3-1 win in the Senior Cup but in the second round despite Warnes scoring a goal, Wimbledon won at Kingfield 3-1.

Almost four thousand saw Guildford City retain the Combination Cup 4-1 at Guildford. Replay wins against teams from the Surrey Senior League, Dorking 4-0 after a 3-3 draw and two goals each from Breeze and Warnes defeated Camberley & Yorktown 4-3 after a 2-2 draw in the semi-final of the Charity Shield. In the final at Wimbledon, Nunhead defeated Woking 2-1.

Warnes finished top scorer with 14 goals in 24 games, Breeze scored 12 in 26 games. Other contributions came from Hooker 8 goals, May 7 in 11 games and Buckmaster 7 goals.

This was the first of a number of mediocre seasons leading up to the second world war.

A friendly against Fulham saw the Cottagers field four ex-Cards in Price, Tompkins, Watson and Potts.

1932 - 1933

Season 1932-33 was memorable because of the goalscoring exploits of Ronnie Rooke and the longest run to date in the Amateur Cup comprising seven games.

Tenth place in the league was a major improvement over the previous season, although inconsistency was a major problem. Big victories against St. Albans (6-1), Wycombe (5-1) and Ilford (5-3) were interspersed with three 5-1 defeats.

Once again an experimental team played in the first game with disastrous results. A 5-1 defeat at Oxford was followed by a 2-2 draw at home to Wimbledon and a 5-1 reverse in the return match. Buckmaster scored in the three games.

One of Woking's better performances was a 2-2 draw at Dulwich before 6,000 spectators. Dulwich ended-up as league champions.

Ronnie Rooke, who was destined to play only 25 games for Woking, played his first on the 10th September and his last game on the 11th March. He scored in both and finished with a grand total of 29 goals in 25 matches. This included four against Hampshire League side Basingstoke in the Amateur Cup and hat-tricks against Wycombe and St. Albans. In March he signed as professional for Crystal Palace and remained a prolific goalscorer throughout his career, which finally won him a league championship medal in 1947-48 with Arsenal.

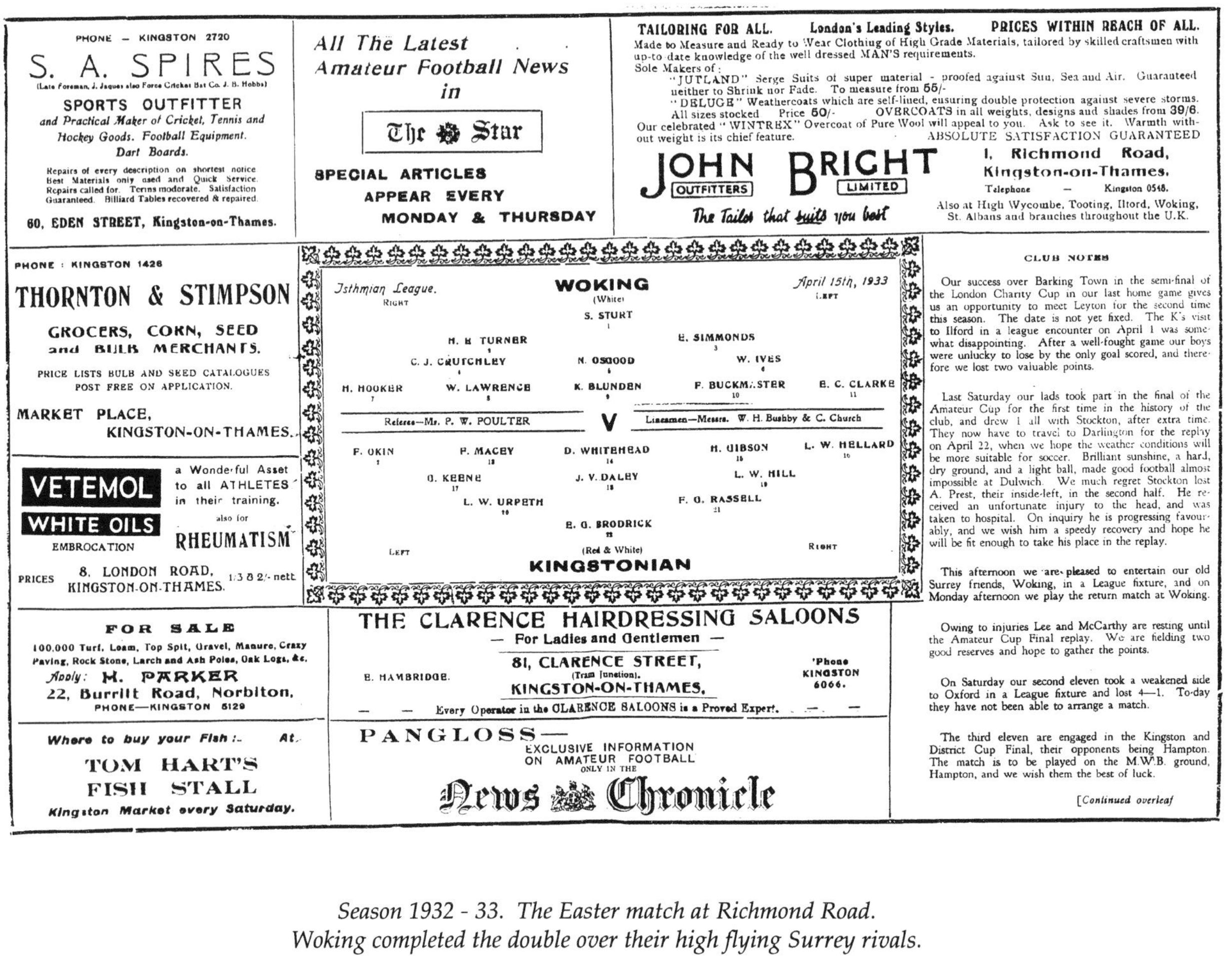

Isthmian League. April 15th, 1933

WOKING (White)

Right				Left
		S. STURT 1		
	H. B. TURNER 2		E. SIMMONDS 3	
	C. J. CRUTCHLEY 4	N. OSGOOD 5	W. IVES 6	
H. HOOKER 7	W. LAWRENCE 8	K. BLUNDEN 9	F. BUCKMASTER 10	E. C. CLARKE 11

Referee—Mr. P. W. POULTER V Linesmen—Messrs. W. H. Bushby & C. Church

Left				Right
F. OKIN 12	P. MACEY 13	D. WHITEHEAD 14	H. GIBSON 15	L. W. HELLARD 16
	G. KEENE 17	J. V. DALEY 18	L. W. HILL 19	
	L. W. URPETH 20		F. G. RASSELL 21	
		E. G. BRODRICK 22		

(Red & White) **KINGSTONIAN**

CLUB NOTES

Our success over Barking Town in the semi-final of the London Charity Cup in our last home game gives us an opportunity to meet Leyton for the second time this season. The date is not yet fixed. The K's visit to Ilford in a league encounter on April 1 was somewhat disappointing. After a well-fought game our boys were unlucky to lose by the only goal scored, and therefore we lost two valuable points.

Last Saturday our lads took part in the final of the Amateur Cup for the first time in the history of the club, and drew 1 all with Stockton, after extra time. They now have to travel to Darlington for the replay on April 22, when we hope the weather conditions will be more suitable for soccer. Brilliant sunshine, a hard, dry ground, and a light ball, made good football almost impossible at Dulwich. We much regret Stockton lost A. Prest, their inside-left, in the second half. He received an unfortunate injury to the head, and was taken to hospital. On inquiry he is progressing favourably, and we wish him a speedy recovery and hope he will be fit enough to take his place in the replay.

This afternoon we are pleased to entertain our old Surrey friends, Woking, in a League fixture, and on Monday afternoon we play the return match at Woking.

Owing to injuries Lee and McCarthy are resting until the Amateur Cup Final replay. We are fielding two good reserves and hope to gather the points.

On Saturday our second eleven took a weakened side to Oxford in a League fixture and lost 4—1. To-day they have not been able to arrange a match.

The third eleven are engaged in the Kingston and District Cup Final, their opponents being Hampton. The match is to be played on the M.W.B. ground, Hampton, and we wish them the best of luck.

[Continued overleaf

Season 1932 - 33. The Easter match at Richmond Road. Woking completed the double over their high flying Surrey rivals.

There were very few changes in the defensive formation Sturt, H.E. Turner, E. Simmonds, Crutchley, Osgood, and Ives played in the majority of the games. Buckmaster, Perrett, Hooker, Blunden and Rooke were involved in the art of scoring goals. During the season Rooke notched 29 goals, Harry Hooker scored 12, with Buckmaster, Perrett and Blunden claiming 9 apiece.

Sturt and Crutchley played in all the games and Ives and Buckmaster missed only two each.

Ken Blunden who took over at centre-forward after Rooke's departure, totalled seven goals in his first four games in the number 9 shirt.

Woking would have finished in the top five but losing the last three games prevented this.

Spartan League Metropolitan Police defeated Woking in the 1st Qualifying Round of the F.A. Cup after a 5-3 defeat of Surrey County Side Walton in the preliminary round, in which Rooke scored twice. Nunhead won 1-0 at Woking in the Senior Cup and Guildford City defeated Woking 2-0 in the Surrey Combination Cup.

Woking fought through four qualifying rounds of the Amateur Cup. Rooke's four finished off Basingstoke 4-2. Three Army sides were then defeated. A first round 3-0 victory over London Caledonians gave Woking a second round tie at Slough. Despite Rooke scoring this twelfth Amateur Cup goal, Slough Spartan League runners-up walloped Woking 6-1.

In the Surrey Charity Shield, Camberley and Redhill were only just defeated but the final against the London League runners-up was something of a massacre with Epsom winning at a canter 5-0.

The season itself was full of interest for the spectators, although no cups were won.

1933 - 1934

Season 1933-34 had very few highlights with the league campaign starting off badly with four straight losses and finishing with six losses and a draw. Woking finished bottom of the league. Eighty-one goals were conceded which was the highest of the fourteen teams.

New players in the first team were full back Johnny Cowle who partnered H.E. Turner. F. Hollingsworth played in the half-back line with Crutchley and Ken Blunden, who came in at centre-half after Christmas. Bill Lawrence finally claimed a spot in the forward line, Buckmaster was partnered by newcomer J. Francis. Corporal L. East played in the early games scoring 9 goals in 13 matches before being posted away.

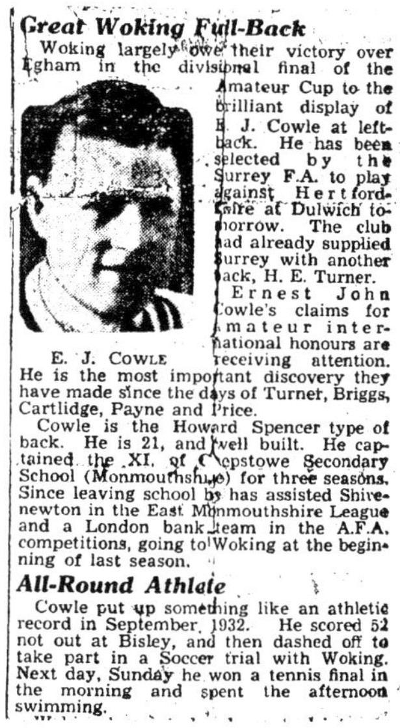

Great Woking Full-Back

Woking largely owe their victory over Egham in the divisional final of the Amateur Cup to the brilliant display of E. J. Cowle at left-back. He has been selected by the Surrey F.A. to play against Hertfordshire at Dulwich to-morrow. The club had already supplied Surrey with another back, H. E. Turner.

E. J. COWLE

Ernest John Cowle's claims for amateur international honours are receiving attention. He is the most important discovery they have made since the days of Turner, Briggs, Cartlidge, Payne and Price.

Cowle is the Howard Spencer type of back. He is 21, and well built. He captained the XI. of Chepstowe Secondary School (Monmouthshire) for three seasons. Since leaving school he has assisted Shirenewton in the East Monmouthshire League and a London bank team in the A.F.A. competitions, going to Woking at the beginning of last season.

All-Round Athlete

Cowle put up something like an athletic record in September, 1932. He scored 52 not out at Bisley, and then dashed off to take part in a Soccer trial with Woking. Next day, Sunday he won a tennis final in the morning and spent the afternoon swimming.

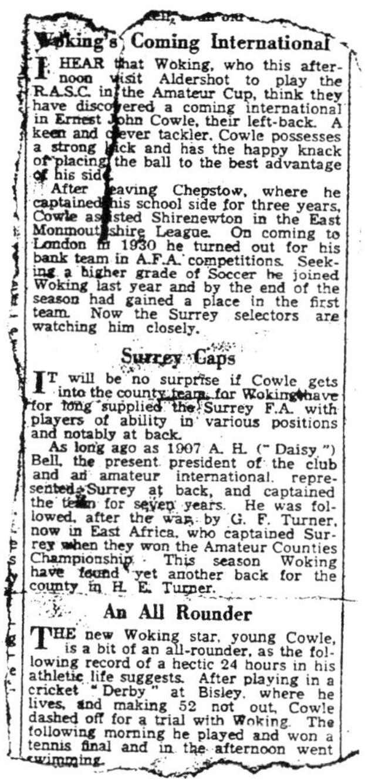

Woking's Coming International

I HEAR that Woking, who this afternoon visit Aldershot to play the R.A.S.C. in the Amateur Cup, think they have discovered a coming international in Ernest John Cowle, their left-back. A keen and clever tackler. Cowle possesses a strong kick and has the happy knack of placing the ball to the best advantage of his side.

After leaving Chepstow, where he captained his school side for three years, Cowle assisted Shirenewton in the East Monmouthshire League. On coming to London in 1930 he turned out for his bank team in A.F.A. competitions. Seeking a higher grade of Soccer he joined Woking last year and by the end of the season had gained a place in the first team. Now the Surrey selectors are watching him closely.

Surrey Caps

IT will be no surprise if Cowle gets into the county team, for Woking have for long supplied the Surrey F.A. with players of ability in various positions and notably at back.

As long ago as 1907 A. H. ("Daisy") Bell, the present president of the club and an amateur international, represented Surrey at back, and captained the team for seven years. He was followed, after the war, by G. F. Turner, now in East Africa, who captained Surrey when they won the Amateur Counties Championship. This season Woking have found yet another back for the county in H. E. Turner.

An All Rounder

THE new Woking star, young Cowle, is a bit of an all-rounder, as the following record of a hectic 24 hours in his athletic life suggests. After playing in a cricket "Derby" at Bisley, where he lives, and making 52 not out, Cowle dashed off for a trial with Woking. The following morning he played and won a tennis final and in the afternoon went swimming.

Two newspaper cuttings from November 1933, praisingthe footballing virtues of Johnny Cowle, Woking's left-back, who despite losing the war years from his career, still played 107 league and cup games.

The success of the season was centre-forward S.H. Faggetter who scored in his first five games. He scored 15 in 13 games including hat-tricks against Clapton 5-1 and St. Albans 5-4 and four against Tooting in the Charity Shield 6-2.

Other high individual scorers were East who scored three against Tufnell Park 4-2, Ken Blunden a hat-trick in a 4-4 thriller at Wimbledon, and Lawrence's four in a 5-0 victory in the Charity Shield over P.O. Engineers of the London League.

The defence conceded at least one goal in all league games and eleven times four goals were let though.

Peter West replaced Sturt in goal after Christmas in an attempt to prevent goals, Blunden, Griffiths and Faggetter came into the team but the flow of goals against continued.

Of interest to cricket fans was England's future captain R.W.V. Robins, who played one first team game against London Caledonians. He damaged his leg and never played for Woking again.

Epsom defeated Woking in the Preliminary round of the F.A. Cup, 5-2 after extra time after the first game had been drawn 1-1.

The first round of the Amateur Cup saw Woking just beaten 2-1 at Wimbledon before 4,000 spectators. Woking had battled through four qualifying rounds to reach the first round. Wellington Works, Guildford (Pinks), RASC (Aldershot) and Egham all of the County League were all defeated.

Wimbledon also proved to be a stumbling block in the Senior Cup but not before a hard fought 1-1 draw in the first game. The replay was lost 1-4. Carshalton Athletic (3-1) and Redhill (4-3) had been beaten in previous rounds.

Two easy wins 5-0 and 6-2 against P.O. Engineers and newly amalgamated Tooting & Mitcham United, gave Woking another chance in the Charity Shield Final. For the third successive year Woking had to be content with being runners-up as Sutton won comfortably 7-0.

Cowle and Buckmaster only missed two league and cup games with J. Francis and Lawrence playing over twenty league games.

Apart from Faggetter's goalscoring exploits, Francis scored 17 goals, Buckmaster 14 goals, and W.H. Lawrence scored 11 goals.

Woking's best home gate was the 1,900 achieved at the first game of the season against Oxford.

Only one point was gained away from home this being a 4-4 draw in the penultimate game. This was no doubt a contributory factor to Woking's poor league position.

1934 - 1935

There was a general improvement in the results for season 1934-35. D. Stevens, E. Searle and G. Eales all new additions to the team helped to improve the defence. F. Stockley came in at inside-forward and with Harry Hooker playing more games the forward line appeared to be better balanced.

Third from bottom was an improvement although the first three games were lost. Stockley scored his first goal for the club in a 3-2 victory at Wycombe and then repeated the feat in the 3-2 defeat of Ilford. A 3-3 draw at home to Oxford was an outstanding performance as their opponents finished runners-up to league winners Wimbledon.

Two goals from Hooker and one each from Stockley and Moulsdale gave Woking a double over Wycombe (4-3). Two thrashings by Dulwich, 8-3 at home and 6-2 away brought Woking up to the Christmas fixtures. Two wins out of four games in one week was satisfactory especially as Wimbledon, the eventual champions, were defeated by a Hooker goal at Kingfield on Boxing Day. This avenged a 5-1 drubbing in the reverse fixture the previous day.

A loss at home to bottom club Casuals 2-0, was followed by a 1-0 victory at home to Kingstonian and a draw at St. Albans in the penultimate fixture. A 5-1 drubbing of the same team in the final fixture of the season before the highest home league attendance, 2,300, enabled Woking to finish ahead of Casuals and Wycombe.

Guildford City defeated Woking 2-0 at the first F.A. Cup hurdle but goals from Stockley and Buckmaster gave Woking some revenge in the Surrey Combination Cup semi-final. The Final was lost 2-1 against Kingstonian.

In the Surrey Senior Cup competition, Hersham and London League side Streatham, were easily defeated 2-0 and 3-0 respectively. A magnificent semi-final at Wimbledon saw Woking defeat Dulwich 5-3. After being heavily defeated twice in the league this win was against all the odds, but a rare goal by Stevens and two from Abbott helped achieve the win. Unfortunately Kingstonian were again the stumbling block defeating Woking 2-0 in the final.

The Charity Shield was held over until the following season, Woking and Wimbledon needed a replay after a 2-2 draw but ran out of time.

Once again the Amateur Cup saw Woking battle their way through the qualifying competition only to lose in the first round 2-1 away to Athenian League side Bromley. Egham, Camberley, RASC and Hersham were comfortably defeated in the qualifying rounds. Harry Hooker was particularly successful with a total of six goals in the competition.

Lawrence and Buckmaster only missed two league games with Stevens and Searle only absent from three league and cup games.

Stockley topped the goalscoring lists with 19 goals although Hooker managed 15 from ten less games. Lawrence scored 10 with a useful 8 from Buckmaster and Moulsdale.

1935 - 1936

It would be very difficult to pick out too many highlights from season 1935-36. In retrospect it would be the debut and subsequent play of local goalkeeper Harry 'Tink' Medhurst. He came to the club just to complete some fitness training and had the occasional game on the left wing for the 3rd XI. During training he started to keep goal and it was found he had natural ability in this position. He learnt his trade through the 3rd XI and the reserves until he finally made his first team debut on the 5th October in the F.A. Cup against Sutton. The game ended 0-0 so it was a successful debut. He held his place for the rest of the season and then was snapped up by West Ham in November 1936.

For the first time since 1928-29 the opening league game was won. Goals by Lawrence and Hooker gave Woking a 2-1 victory over Tufnell Park.

Although Casuals defeated Woking 2-1 at Kingfield in the second game, a hat-trick by new forward H. Widmore gave Woking a 5-1 home victory over Wycombe. Unfortunately Widmore only played 11 games but he scored 10 goals which included a further hat-trick in the Amateur Cup victory 6-2 against Courage Sports at Alton.

Another local product Frank Preskett who had made his debut the previous season played in the early games with success but he turned professional in November for Plymouth.

From early November until early February only two league wins were recorded from twelve games. Two heavy reverses were 8-1 at eventual champions Wimbledon and a 7-3 defeat at home to Nunhead.

Wimbledon also defeated Woking 7-1 in the first round of the Senior Cup and 3-0 in the held-over semi-final replay of the Charity Shield. A loss, 3-0 in the league on Boxing Day, gave Wimbledon four wins over Woking during the season.

A rally in the last eight league games saw Woking climb to tenth place; only one game was lost with four victories. The defence which had leaked goals throughout the season only conceded eight goals in these eight games. G. Small came in as full back partner to Don Stevens and with Griffiths moving into centre-back there appeared to be more stability in defence. Buckmaster also came back into the side in the new year to re-form his partnership with Hooker.

Two rounds in the F.A. Cup were safely negotiated before Sutton won 4-2 after a 0-0 draw at Kingfield. A loss at RAMC (Aldershot) 3-0 in the Amateur Cup ended Woking's interest in both major cup competitions.

WOKING F.C. 1935

"Daily Mail" Souvenir.

Back Row, Left to Right: D. Stevens, W. Searle, C. E. Clarke (*Trainer*), C. Jarman (*Match Sec.*)
Middle Row: G. C. Eales, E. Searle, H. Medhurst, E. J. Cowle, H. Widmore, W. Lawrence.
Front Row: C. Simmons, F. Preskett, A. E. Griffiths (*Captain*), H. Hooker, W. H. ~~Mailsdale~~ Moulsdale, L. A. Knott (*Asst. Trainer*).

Woking F.C. 1935

<u>Back Row, left to right</u> D. Stevens, W. Searle, C.E. Clarke (Trainer), C. Jarman (Match Secretary)
<u>Middle Row</u> G.E. Eales, E. Searle, H. Medhurst, E.J. Cowle, H. Widmore, W. Lawrence
<u>Front Row</u> F. Preskett, A.E. Griffiths (Captain), H. Hooker, W.H. Moulsdale, L.A. Knott (Asst. Trainer)

Lawrence, Hooker and E. Searle played in the majority of the games with back-up from Medhurst, Eales, Stevens, Griffiths and Abbott. E. Stygal, Buckmaster, W.H. Moulsdale and G. Small came into the side late in the season but nevertheless played a strong role in Woking's late success.

Hooker scored 26 goals in 35 games, Buckmaster contributed ten in fifteen games, Lawrence struck 9 goals and the rest were evenly shared.

Only one more point was obtained compared to the previous season but fifth from bottom as against third from bottom represented some progress.

1936 - 1937

Season 1936-37 was very similar in performance to the previous campaign. The same number of points and the same tenth position achieved. More goals were scored but more were conceded.

Harry Medhurst played in the first six league games before leaving for West Ham, Peter West took over but was displaced by Sturt for 14 league matches. G. Small and Stevens were the full backs until Baldaro replaced Small from late February. E. Searle, Griffiths started in the half-back line and Lawrence started off as inside-forward but converted to half-back halfway through the season. Buckmaster did not miss a league game and although Hooker missed a number of games, new boy Lloyd Stone proved to be a prolific scorer.
F. Stockley and S. Carter played in the forward line for the last sixteen games.

The first three home games were won without conceding a goal. A 5-0 thrashing of Leytonstone, who finished third, was particularly pleasing. Unfortunately the first four away games were lost. A 3-3 draw at Casuals broke the sequence but his was followed by the first home defeat, 3-1 against Clapton.

Two hat-tricks by Stone in consecutive games gave Woking a 3-3 draw against Wimbledon and a 4-3 victory against the Casuals. This was followed by two heavy away defeats 7-3 at Wimbledon and 6-0 at Leytonstone. Four consecutive wins followed which included an excellent 2-1 home triumph against high riding Dulwich. The last four games were lost but two of these were against Kingstonian the champions and one against Nunhead the runners-up.

Camberley and Epsom were defeated 2-1 and 3-1 respectively in the F.A. Cup. W. Finlay who played only occasionally notched three of the five goals. A 3,000 crowd witnessed a 4-0 thrashing by Surrey Senior League Champions, Hersham, in the first qualifying round.

Hastings and St. Leonards defeated Woking 3-1 at the first stage of the Amateur Cup. Nunhead proved too strong winning 3-1 in the Surrey Senior Cup. A 5-4 victory against the Metropolitan Police in a replayed Charity Shield tie was in direct contrast to a dour 0-0 in the first game. A close defeat by Sutton prevented a final appearance.

Lloyd Stone top scored with 23 goals, Buckmaster and Hooker scored 9 each, Carter notched 7 and Stockley scored six time. Finlay scored six from only seven games.

1937 - 1938

Woking only just escaped from finishing in bottom place. It was a strange coincidence that the final two league games were against St. Albans City, who were one point ahead prior to these games. Lloyd Stone's four goals gave Woking a 4-1 victory at home and a Finlay goal secured a 1-0 win at St. Albans.

After losing the first two games, Woking defeated Dulwich 4-1 and Oxford 5-1. A draw at home to the eventual champions, Leytonstone, gave a false impression of how Woking would fare during the season. The next eleven games only yielded one win. It would be difficult to pinpoint the reason for the decline although the number of defensive alterations did not help the blend. Stone returned to the side in November and immediately started to score goals. Baldaro missed eleven games which necessitated Bill Lawrence moving into the full-back position. Two consecutive victories were achieved when Lawrence was switched to centre-back, although only Stone had the ability to score. In fact he contributed 18 goals out of 22 scored by Woking in the final sixteen games. He collected all four in the 4-2 victory over Tufnell Park and matched this in the home game against St. Albans.

Woking's problem was in defence where 72 goals were conceded in the 26 league games. Large defeats were 7-1 at Wycombe, 6-1 at Wimbledon and also Nunhead, and 5-1 at home to Clapton.

The cup campaigns were short-lived, the only victory being 3-1 away to Leyland Motors in the F.A. Cup. Nunhead hammered out a 6-1 thrashing in the following round. A massive attendance of 7,252 saw Dulwich gain revenge for the 4-1 defeat in no uncertain terms by 7-0.

Redhill ended Surrey Senior Cup hopes 3-0 and a poor performance in the Charity Shield gave P.O. Engineers an unlikely victory 2-1 at Kingfield.

Stevens played in all games with newcomer Hughes only missing one league match. E. Searle and Lawrence were rarely absent. H. Hooker only played two games before he left the club, Fred Buckmaster had already gone pre-season. To outweigh this forward loss Finlay only missed five league games, but his goalscoring touch deserted him, scoring only seven goals. Kittredge and Weller formed a useful left-wing pair. Baldaro, Knight, R. Gough and E. Fish made defensive contributions but not consistently enough. West, Dance and Wallage shared the goalkeeping spot.

Stone scored 18 in 18 games with D. Hughes being second highest scorer with nine goals. W. Finlay was the only other significant scorer with 7 goals. Season 1937-38 did not raise the blood pressure.

1938 - 1939

With a certain German dictator starting to utter threatening noises in Europe, season 1938-39 commenced.

Woking started with five consecutive losses, including a 2-1 F.A. Cup defeat at Nunhead. Lloyd Stone who scored in the opening game, left the club after the second game. Bob Reeves, a strong but raw talent took Stone's place, scoring at Nunhead on his debut and scoring again in his second game against Kingstonian. Unfortunately injuries restricted his appearances, but he averaged a goal every other game which was a good strike rate in a low scoring season.

Woking's first league victory come in spectacular style with a 5-1 thrashing of Wycombe, Reeves and Carter both scoring twice. The first and only league victory away from Kingfield was a 3-0 success at Casuals. J.V. Daley a new face struck twice.

Woking had eight home victories in thirteen starts; the best of these being a 2-1 success against Dulwich. Hobbs and Evans scored the goals. Ron Hobbs, who had played in the final four games of the previous season, only celebrated his 17th birthday at the beginning of this campaign. He would turn professional for Aldershot at the end of the war and play 170 times in 7 years.

Woking finished in 11th place in the league with twenty points. Only thirty-five goals were scored with fifty-six being conceded.

In the Amateur Cup, Tufnell Park were defeated 2-1 in the first round. A 3,000 crowd saw Wimbledon again beat Woking 3-1 in the second round.

D. Gough scored the goal which earned Woking a 1-1 draw against Dulwich in the Senior Cup. 6,291 saw Woking heavily defeated in the replay 7-0.

In the Charity Shield Walton withdrew from the competition but only after two cracking games. A 4-4 draw at Kingfield with Evans scoring three, was followed by a 3-3 draw at

Woking Reserves 1938 - 1939 Surrey Intermediate Cup Winners

Johnny Cowle holding the cup. Len Ledger seated second from right. Other well known players, second from left, back row R. Reeves, E. Baldaro, W.P. West and third from right, D. Potter.

Walton. Metropolitan Police overcame Woking easily 3-0 in the semi-final.

West and Wallage shared the goalkeeping position but H.W. Small and D. Stevens were the full-back partnership in every game.

R.E. Gough wore either number 4 or 5 in most of the games. Bill Lawrence missed some early games but played in 24 out of 35. Of the forwards, Hobbs only missed one cup game. Carter and Reeves played in the early games as did H.A. Evans.

In a season where goals were hard to come by, Reeves and Evans were joint top scorers with 7 goals. J Shepherd struck 5 goals in 13 appearances. Thirteen other players shared the rest of the goals.

1939 - 1940

Season 1939-40 started on time with Woking losing out at Wycombe 4-0. The final competitive game took place on 2nd September with an F.A. Cup tie at Egham. Woking duly won this by 12-0.

D. Gough, R, Reeves, G. Pinnock and R. Hobbs all scored hat-tricks. By this time players were being called up into the Armed Forces. Hitler marched into Poland, war was declared and all league competitions were cancelled by order of the Government.

Friendly matches were started at the end of September. As there was no distinction between amateurs and professionals Woking obtained the services of W.J. Price and F.M. Preskett for many of the games.

Competitive sport was encouraged by the Government to keep up the spirit of the population. Woking, therefore joined the Surrey Combination League playing sixteen matches. Of these, six were won and seven lost.

Guildford City who turned out their reserve side were defeated 11-1, W.H. Moulsdale scored eight of these which strangely enough were the only goals he scored during the season.

The Senior Cup Competition was also played for. Two goals by E.G. Hughes defeated Sutton 2-0. In the semi-final Wimbledon defeated Woking 3-1 after a 2-2 draw at Dulwich. Price scored all three goals.

The season ended on the 1st June with a 8-0 victory against Camberley.

Woking played 34 games winning twelve and losing sixteen. 94 goals were scored with 82 conceded.

Goalscorers were Potter 17, Price 16, Moulsdale 8, Hobbs and Preskett with 7 each.

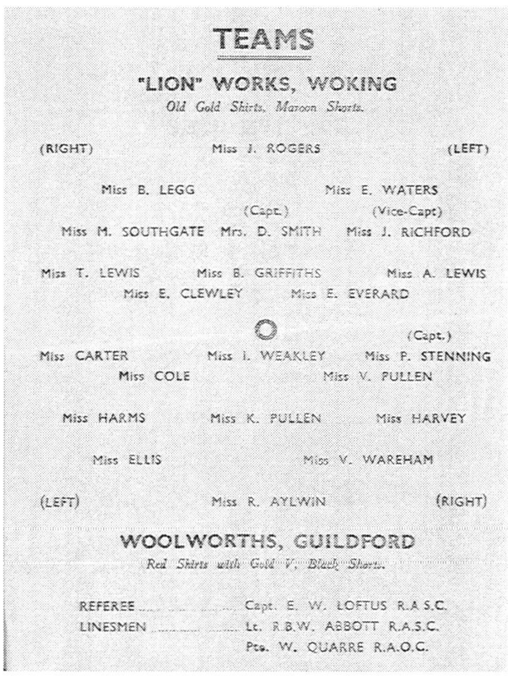

TEAMS

"LION" WORKS, WOKING

Old Gold Shirts. Maroon Shorts.

(RIGHT) Miss J. ROGERS (LEFT)

Miss B. LEGG Miss E. WATERS

(Capt.) (Vice-Capt.)

Miss M. SOUTHGATE Mrs. D. SMITH Miss J. RICHFORD

Miss T. LEWIS Miss B. GRIFFITHS Miss A. LEWIS

Miss E. CLEWLEY Miss E. EVERARD

O

(Capt.)

Miss CARTER Miss I. WEAKLEY Miss P. STENNING

Miss COLE Miss V. PULLEN

Miss HARMS Miss K. PULLEN Miss HARVEY

Miss ELLIS Miss V. WAREHAM

(LEFT) Miss R. AYLWIN (RIGHT)

WOOLWORTHS, GUILDFORD

Red Shirts with Gold V; Black Shorts.

REFEREE .... Capt. E. W. LOFTUS R.A.S.C.

LINESMEN .... Lt. R.B.W. ABBOTT R.A.S.C.

Pte. W. QUARRE R.A.O.C.

Programme

Ladies'

Football Match

in aid of

Red Cross and St. John Ambulance

(Woking and Guildford Funds)

"LION" WORKS, WOKING

(JAMES WALKER & CO. LTD.)

v

WOOLWORTH'S

(GUILDFORD BRANCH)

on the

WOKING FOOTBALL GROUND.

WEDNESDAY, APRIL 23RD. 1941

PRICE : ONE PENNY

An interesting wartime programme from 1941. Ladies' Football Match at Kingfield.

1940 - 1941

Many of the open spaces were being taken up by the armed forces to store vehicles and arms, so it was a bonus when once again football was to be played at Kingfield during season 1940-41.

Woking were invited to join the South Eastern Combination. Eight clubs made up the league which commenced on the 5th of October. Tooting were the visitors and despite a Potter goal, ran out convincing winners 3-1.

One of the interesting aspects about football during the war was that it was never certain that the team picked would be the one to turn out. Of the team that played against Tooting only five made it to the final game in May.

Forty-five players represented Woking in the fourteen combination games and six friendlies. Despite this ever changing scenario, Faulds, Reeves and J. Preskett played in every combination game. Jim Preskett brother of Frank would play an important role in Woking's post-war beginnings.

Woking recorded five wins and three draws from their fourteen combination games. The best win was a 5-1 victory at home to Nunhead with Faulds and Preskett scoring two goals each. Despite two goals from Preskett, Erith & Belvedere gave Woking their worst beating of the season 9-2.

Bob Reeves top scored with 10 goals followed by Jim Preskett with eight goals. Fred Pink, the flying winger of the late 40's and early 50's made his debut in the final game of the season. His greatest assets were his speed and unpredictability.

1941 - 1942

It was touch-and-go whether Woking competed during 1941-42. Money was scarce and the availability of Kingfield was again open to question. Nevertheless, the opening match, a friendly against an Army XI was played. Woking lost 2-1, although the result was immaterial; the main objective was to start the season.

Once again Woking played in the South Eastern Combination. Of the sixteen games played six were won and one was drawn.

Sutton were defeated twice including a remarkable 6-5 victory at Sutton. Dennis Smith scored three of the goals, Faulds went one better in the return 5-1 victory.

As expected with teams changing their personnel from one week to the next, some unusual results occurred. Tooting were defeated 1-0 at Kingfield but in the match the following week, Tooting won comfortably 10-0. Nine of Woking's players played in both games but Tooting turned out a very strong team in the second game. Heavy defeats were registered against Dulwich 9-1 and Erith & Belvedere 8-1.

In the South Eastern Combination Cup two goals from Reeves and Preskett helped to defeat Sutton 6-3 in the first round.

Friendlies were also completed on free Saturdays, mostly against the local Army barracks. Reeves scored six in a 9-1 win in one such encounter and a Navy XI were defeated 11-0, but not all friendlies were won easily. The London Fire Force came to Kingfield and triumphed 6-1.

Bob Reeves top scored with 11 combination and cup goals. Don Prett scored 6 in 16 games and Faulds scored 6 in 15 games.

Forty-three players turned out during the season, some at very short notice. Pre-war defender Doug Stevens played in ten league and cup games. Others who played regularly were R. Stuart (goalkeeper), D. Potter, R. Habgood and J. Underhill.

The last game was played at Kingfield on the 2nd May 1942. It was over three years before the 're-birth' of the club, once the war had ended in 1945.

New secretary Clarrie Jarman and treasurer Harry Goddard did their best to keep the club functioning, but the Government claimed the ground as a material store for the war effort. In 1945 the thirst for peace-time football was too great an obsession for any logical thought. Re-birth was inevitable.

Chapter 7

REVIVAL AND SURVIVAL - 1945 ONWARDS

As war ended and peace in Europe was declared the stranglehold and restrictions to the nation's culture were lifted, at least in the minds of the populace.

People were determined to enjoy themselves, to seek relief from the stresses and tensions of war times. This involved the cinema, radio, holidays and as a predominantly male preserve, football.

It was largely this desire that prompted the revival of Woking Football Club. The club had not functioned since 1941-42, there was a pre-war debt of £345 to consider and to secure the future a permanent home ground was a must.

Reviewing the situation logically, it was not financially viable to revive the football club but the burning desire after seven barren war years was too strong to worry about logic.

The basic problem was ready money The ground at Kingfield was available, albeit in a state of disrepair but cash was needed to purchase and repair the ground ready for the first peace time season.

Near the end of the war a "revival and survival of the Woking Football Club" meeting was held in Christ Church Halls. The Kingfield ground had been offered to Woking Council but they turned it down. Woking Football Club were given the option to purchase for £6,500 and it was decided to take up the option.

Carnivals and Charity matches were an acceptable means of raising money for the club in the early seasons after the war. The players, committee members and supporters joined together in dressing-up as shown in the two photographs.

An appeal to shareholders produced gifts to the club of over 1,000 shares. The club therefore now owned 1551 shares and raised approximately £600 by public subscription. This amounted to one-third of the purchase price and was used as a deposit.

By July 1946 a loan of £4,000 was raised through James Walker and Company Limited, the largest manufacturing company in Woking. The repayment costs were about £160 per year.

To offset some of this cost, the ground was let to the Lion Works Sports Association, (James Walker and Company Social Activities), at £75 per year, and the club would pay back £50 per year for ground maintenance. The supporters club paid the Football Club £50 per year for the use of the clubroom and car park. Therefore, the Football Club would need to find less than half the amount paid out in 1936-37. Financially this made good sense.

At this time, just after the war, a number of people were involved in the decision making and fund raising in order to provide top class amateur football for the benefit of the population of Woking.

Joe Steer organised a Carnival which finally reduced the mortgage to £2,900. Others played significant roles namely, J.H. Goddard, C. Jarman, F. Lewry, W.B. Davies and W.J. Dixon, but one man was recognised by his peers as the driving force behind the club's revival and the eventual purchase of the ground. Mr. L.A.'Gerald' Gosden had served the club in many capacities since 1932 and despite his ninety years "young" was still leading from the front in 1995, as president of the club.

Financial and voluntary support was given by the Supporters Club who were a thriving concern in 1945-46.

1945 - 1946

Although the only trophy won by Woking Football Club in 1945-46 was the Surrey Intermediate Charity Cup, which was retained by the Reserves, the first post-war season was highly successful.

Like the majority of football clubs in the post-war boom, Woking received better support with larger home attendances compared with the last full season prior the Second World War.

The creditable performance of the first XI was all the more noteworthy as matches had not been played since 1941-42.

When the season opened, the selectors had to start from scratch in a team building effort.

The Cardinals early successes - they only had two defeats prior to the new year - were largely due to the loyalty of the pre-war players who formed the nucleus of the team. These included Bill Lawrence (Captain), Peter West, Doug Stevens, Jim Preskett, Bob Reeves, Walker, Moulsdale and Doug Potter, while other 'old' players assisted the reserves.

A number of local players joined the club, therefore prospects for the future appeared bright. E. Freer joined from the Coldstream Guards. "Ginger" Smith still serving in the Royal Navy joined and later represented the Royal Navy against Malta.

The Cardinals achieved their best season in the Isthmian League since 1929-30. They secured the same number of points (27), to finish sixth, one place lower.

WE HAVE DONE OUR BEST

After five years of enforced inactivity the Supporters' Club is again rallying its forces to assist the W.F.C. in providing a return of first-class Amateur Football in Woking.

We have done our best to make ready for you this afternoon, but realised that much more work would have to be carried out before we consider the arrangements worthy of the best tradition of the Woking Football Club. Should, therefore, any arrangements for your comfort fall short of expectations we hope you will bear with us and appreciate the difficulties of material and labour. We hope, however, that full Club facilities will be available in the near future, and invite applications for membership.

The Annual Subscription is 2/6 per annum.

MEMBERS WANTED

THE WOKING FOOTBALL SUPPORTERS' CLUB
Welcome New Members
Licenced Club Facilities and other Amenities
Apply W. Carter, 3 Butts Road Woking
ANNUAL SUBSCRIPTION 2/6

ISTHMIAN LEAGUE — SAT., AUGUST 25th, 1945

WOKING F.C.
Cardinal and White

P. West
W. Lawrence (Capt.) R. Morgan
D. Potter J. Preskett G. Jones
R. Reeves D. Smith D. Moon E. Walker G. Cox

Referee : L. G. Aylott. Linesmen : H. Bish, D. J. Short.

A. Lihow A. Skelton K. Chambers L. Needham J. Westwood
D. Digby G. Donoghue R. Aspinell
L. Davey C. Brotherstone
R. A. Hill

LEYTONSTONE F.C.

Woking Football Club
OFFICIAL PROGRAMME

President : W. J. Dixon.
Hon. Sec. : C. Jarman.
Hon. Treasurer : J. H. Goddard.
Asst. Hon. Sec. : A. V. Gerhold.
Hon. Sec. (1st Team) : L. Ledger.
" (Reserves) : C. F. Andrews.

COUNCIL
G. Allen, J. Bond, W. Bryn Davies, L. Gosden, F. Lewry, A. V. Pearce, B. G. Ralph-Brown, J. Steer, T. Williams, F. G. Wakeford, P. West, C. Boeater F. Banister, S. Matthews, A. R. Waters, S. Sturt, F. C. Neve, Major C. H. May, R. H. Thorn, J. W. Fryer, W. Brooks, A. H. Preskett.

SUB-COMMITTEES
Selection Committee :
J. Bond, L. Gosden, T. Williams, P. West, C. Jarman, J. H. Goddard, A. V. Gerhold, C. F. Andrews W. Lawrence, L. Ledger.
General Committee :
W. J. Dixon, J. Bond, F. Lewry, W. Brooks, L. Gosden, A. V. Pearce, A. R. Waters, T. Williams, P. West, A. V. Gerhold, J. H. Goddard, C. Jarman, L. Ledger, W. Lawrence.
Finance Committee :
W. J. Dixon B. G. Ralph-Brown, F. Lewry, L. Gosden, W. Bryn Davies, J. Steer, J. W. Fryer, A. V. Gerhold, J. H. Gosden, C. Jarman.

Mr. W. J. DIXON.

NEXT MATCH
Woking v. Clapton
September 1st
(Away)

No 404

PRICE TWOPENCE

POST-WAR RADIO
That new RADIO You Require
Our Technical Expert and Knowledge is at your Service FREE
SURREY RADIO
AND ELECTRIC SERVICES
29 GUILDFORD ROAD - WOKING
Phone Woking 1554

First competitive Isthmian League match since 1939.
August 25th 1945 represented the first Saturday of peace time football.

The "Cardinals" 1945-1946
Left to right *Back Row* *L. Ledger (Hon 1st Team Sec), R. Morgan, G. Cox, J. Preskett, W.P. West, G. Jones, D. Stevens, E. Seavers (Trainer).*
Front Row *E.A. Walker, D. Moon, W. Lawrence, D. Potter, R. Reeves*

played representative games for both Surrey and the Isthmian League. Doug Stevens also played for both and represented the British Fire Service.

D. Moon, who scored a hat-trick in his Woking debut against Leytonstone in the first game of the season, notched ten goals in the same period.

Oxford who were the other pace makers and eventually finished runners-up, came to Kingfield just prior to Christmas. A hard fought 1 - 1 draw resulted before a then record home league attendance of 4,000.

Woking's Isthmian League record up to and including 29 December 1945, was played 15, won 8, drawn 6, lost 1.

A notable victory was achieved at Kingfield against the eventual league champions, Walthamstow Avenue, by 2 goals to 1.

Of the 39 league goals scored in this period Bob Reeves who was a fast and direct winger with a powerful finish contributed 18. This included five against Kingstonian in a 7-0 thrashing, and a hat-trick in a 5-1 victory away to Wimbledon the following week. Reeves,

Inevitably, the second half of the season disappointed with only two league victories from eleven games. One possible reason was that other clubs started to settle as players arrived back from the forces.

Nevertheless, Bob Reeves finished with 23 goals from 23 matches and a further ten in cup games, including a hat-trick against Epsom in an 8-1 F.A. Cup victory, gave him the honour of being Woking's highest scorer since Joe Perryman's 41 goals in 35 games in 1926-27.

Woking Reserves, a mixture of youth and experience - Winners of the Surrey Intermediate Charity Cup
Johnny Cowle standing fourth from the right with Stan Sturt second from the right.
Freddy Keefe sitting at exteme right, only sixteen years old, still watching the Cards today.

Some success was achieved in cup-ties. Two qualifying rounds were won in the F.A. Cup before Tooting came to Kingfield and won 2-1.

Wimbledon proved the stumbling block in the second round of the Amateur Cup. A 5-2 reverse came after Woking had triumphed 5-1 in the league just five weeks previously.

It is interesting to note that Wimbledon were something of a bogey side in cup ties. Previous to 1945-46 Woking had been defeated by Wimbledon in nine ties, their only success was in the Surrey Charity Shield of 1922-23. This would continue up to 1976-77 with Woking only winning four, Wimbledon being victorious 22 times and four draws.

Woking reached the final of the Surrey Senior Cup and in the process knocked out Tooting to gain revenge for losing in the F.A. Cup.

The Final was played at Kingstonian's ground against newly crowned Athenian League champions, Sutton, before an attendance of approximately 6,000. Sutton won the game with a single goal victory.

At the end of that first post-war season the ground purchase was finalised. Woking Football Club now held the freehold of the ground; the immediate future was therefore secured.

1946 - 1947

Unfortunately, the promise of 1945-46 was not reflected in the results or league position for 1946-47. It was a difficult season with snow and ice freezing out football during February and March.

Fourth from bottom with the lowest number of goals scored in the league and only 21 points, represented a very disappointing season. Wimbledon continued to be a thorn in Woking's side with two defeats in the league and defeats in the F.A. Cup and Surrey Senior Cup.

The season started poorly with an 8-1 defeat against the eventual champions, Leytonstone, and never really prospered after this reverse.

There were very few bright moments in a poor season although, once again, the champions-elect were defeated at Kingfield.

Bob Reeves, the club's leading scorer last term, spent most of the season in defence. This was surprising considering the lack of goals throughout the year.

Of the old guard Jim Preskett and Bill Lawrence had good seasons and of the "newcomers" Oliver Boxall, Dennis 'Ginger' Smith, Lou Wallace and Bill Short who had played for Football League side Gateshead showed the most promise. Jarvis joined from Erith and Belvedere, whilst goalkeeper Cousins joined Corinthian-Casuals.

Peter West who had lost much of his career due to the war was replaced in goal by Maurice Eastaff.

Jack Elliott, seventeen year old son of a former Woking player, made his debut against Tufnell Park in October, scored and played his last game versus Romford and scored. He then signed professional forms for Millwall. His short career with Woking lasted one month, five games and three goals.

Scoring was a problem throughout the season, eighteen different players found the net with Lou Wallace being the top marksman with only six goals. When this is compared with Bob Reeves' thirty-three goals the previous season, it was not difficult to establish the pressing need for a natural goalscorer.

Woking Rovers F.C. became the nursery club, for Woking in the late 40's and early 50's, under the administration of Fred Skilton, standing, end left, Phil Ledger standing third left and Geoff Hamm, first row, second right played for Woking and Wimbledon. Ron Rapley, George Burgin and Geoff Bonner also in the line-up still attend matches at Woking.

An interesting friendly was played against a Dutch First Division side HBS. The Crows as they were known, played at the Crows Nest wore all black with a yellow trim.

1947 - 1948

The scoring need was fulfilled in season 1947-48, Bill Wiles of the bandy legs and lack of speed was not the typical, ideal centre-forward, but his finishing power both with head and feet was second to none. His, was a natural in-built ability to find space and hit the target. Twenty-three goals in twenty-four games was a testimony to his skills.

He was ably supported in the forward line by Boxall, Wallace, Alfie Welland and Fred Pink. On his day 'Freddy' could destroy the strongest defence. He was lightning fast and direct with a vicious shot. Fortunately or unfortunately, depending on whose side you were on, Fred was erratic, sometimes the corner-flag was in more danger than the opponents goal. Nevertheless, Fred was an asset to Woking. Alfie Welland had joined the Cards from Guildford at the beginning of the season only to emigrate; setting sail for Canada in February. The Rev. Ron Cowley left for Dulwich.

One highlight which will be remembered by many supporters was a rare laying of the Wimbledon bogey in cup-ties. R Hewitt scored on his debut in the 1-0 victory at Plough Lane in the Surrey Senior Cup. This gave Woking a realistic chance of winning the trophy but Kingstonian had other ideas as they defeated the Cards 3-0 in the semi-final.

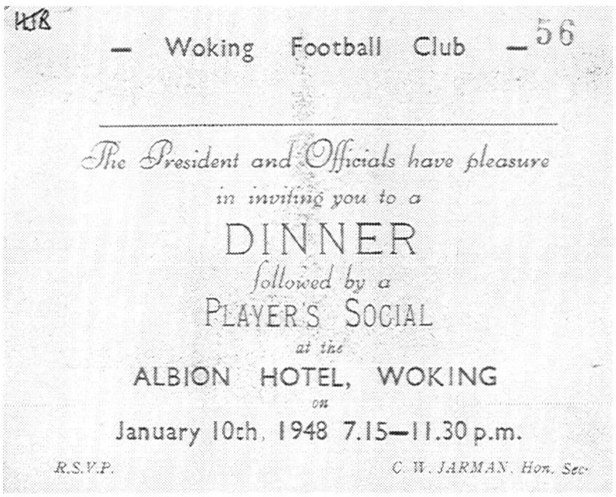
— Woking Football Club — 56

The President and Officials have pleasure in inviting you to a

DINNER

followed by a

PLAYER'S SOCIAL

at the

ALBION HOTEL, WOKING

on

January 10th, 1948 7.15—11.30 p.m.

R.S.V.P. C. W. JARMAN, Hon. Sec.

Mid-season dinner and social at the Albion Hotel, January 1948.

One sad event came when Bill Lawrence finally hung up his boots after eighteen years loyal service and nearly 300 competitive games. Bill had been a great servant to the club. In one of his last games for the club he actually scored a hat-trick in a 5-1 defeat of Ilford.

Kingfield played hosts to Surrey v Berks & Bucks with Reeves, Preskett and Wallace playing for the home county. Reeves and Wiles also represented Surrey v Hampshire. Soldiers Hewitt and Nugent, who joined at the beginning of the season, were posted away from the area in February. Unfortunately this was a fact of life with service players.

1948 - 1949

The AGM in July showed that the football club had a healthy balance of £1350. The ground purchase had been completed, however the previous poor season saw a drop of 300 Supporters Club members to 800. The supporters set to work planning for a new stand and club room at a cost of £6,500.

Since joining the Isthmian League in 1911, Woking had never won more matches in this competition than they achieved in 1948-49 but as only one match was drawn, they finished two points behind their record of 31 in 1927-28.

The number of goals scored was on a par with 1947-48 with four players sharing the main bulk of the goals.

Bill Wiles topped the list with 19 but newcomer, Joe Ballerino from Chertsey, equalled this total. Ginger Smith scored seventeen with Freddy Pink hitting the net 13 times.

Lou Wallace left to take up a teaching post on the Isle of Wight, whilst 18 years old Maurice Eastaff returned to sign amateur forms for Crystal Palace.

Tubby Braithwaite played in Spurs reserve side. He had already played for Gillingham, QPR first XI and the Royal Navy.

Six victories were obtained away from Kingfield which was by far the highest number since joining the league.

The defeat of Romford, just prior to the Essex club's appearance in the Amateur Cup Final, must be considered as the best performance of the season but a 1-0 victory at Dulwich, who were the eventual champions, was probably a better achievement.

A 4-2 victory at home to Wimbledon in late October ranked amongst the most satisfying with Ballerino notching up a hat-trick.

Five straight victories in February and March gave Woking a good chance of a top three place but three defeats in the last four matches ensured a mid-table position.

In the F.A. Cup two rounds were won including a 7-4 thriller at Corinthian League Carshalton, but losing by the odd goal in seven to the bottom club in the Athenian League, Redhill, ended any thoughts of glory.

The semi-final of the Surrey Senior Cup was lost in extra-time to bogey side Wimbledon before 7,000 spectators at Champion Hill, Dulwich.

One trophy was won when Kingstonian were defeated 3-0 at Richmond Road in the Surrey Combination Cup.

Preskett and Ballerino were selected for Surrey v Sussex. Alfie Welland returned from Canada in April. The last weeks of the season saw Villa chase Wiles and Orient chase Reeves for their services.

1949 - 1950

Unfortunately, the outstanding feature of 1949-50, was the number of players, many of first team standard, who left the club for various reasons.

The fashion was set at the very start of the season when Jim Preskett, the previous years captain, failed to find a place in the opening fixture. He immediately transferred his allegiance to Walthamstow Avenue and he performed with some success throughout the season. Jim, the youngest of eleven, including nine boys, was a local schools product who joined Woking just prior to the outbreak of the war. Once hostilities ceased, he made the centre-back spot his own, completing nearly 150 appearances in four seasons. During the war he had played for Walton and also Fulham.

There was a triple blow in January, with the loss of three first team men. Lou Wallace, who was making the journey from the Isle of Wight, decided to hang up his boots. The same week Joe Ballerino, who had quickly put himself among the leading goalscorers after he had regained his place a few weeks earlier, returned to his native Chertsey. Then "Tubby" Braithwaite, the regular left-back resigned because of a disagreement over team selection.

Early season form was good with only one point dropped in the first three games. This included the usual victory against the eventual champions, Leytonstone.

Unfortunately attendances up to December had been poor, therefore the club had to increase the entrance fee to one shilling.

The Cardinals at one period during the season built themselves a reputation for being a second half team. This became a necessary feature as the defence leaked so many early goals. Preskett and Braithwaite were sorely missed.

An excellent 6-4 home victory against Walthamstow, who had Jim Preskett in their line-up, included a hat-trick by Joe Ballerino.

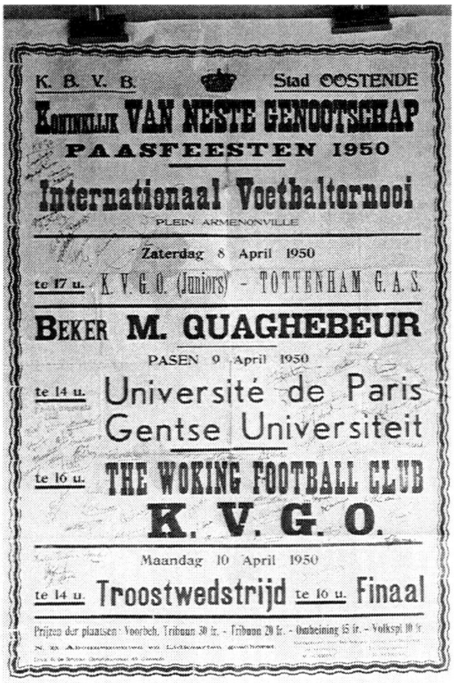

Ostend Easter Tour, 1950.
Woking won both games to win the Trophy.

Two weeks later, in the reverse fixture, Walthamstow, destroyed Woking by 9 goals to 1, not quite Woking's record Isthmian League defeat, as Oxford smashed Woking 11-2 back in season 1923-24. Nevertheless, revenge was no doubt very sweet for Wathamstow.

The final league position of 7th would have been bettered but for a poor defence which regularly leaked goals.

Five goals were conceded to Kingstonian, Dulwich, Clapton and Wimbledon with St Albans and Wimbledon (again), scoring six.

In the major cup competitions there were early exits in the F.A. and Amateur Cups. Progression to the semi-final of the Surrey Senior Cup was achieved but Kingstonian proved too strong and Woking were defeated 5-2.

The tussle with Guildford City before Woking relinquished their hold on the Surrey Combination Cup provided one of the best encounters of the season.

However, some silverware came to Kingfield, the cup brought back from Ostend following creditable performances in an Easter Tournament in which two victories were obtained from two matches. The Woking cup was won by defeating Guildford (Pinks) in a match to aid the finances of the old established amateur club, struggling to stay in the Surrey Senior League.

Once again Bill Wiles topped the goalscoring with 27 in 33 games. Fred Pink scored 16 and Joe Ballerino had scored 9 in 11 games when he left the club for Chertsey.

Of the newcomers, Nobby Clarke a local product, made an instant impact at wing-half. Although only five foot three inches in height, he covered every blade of the Kingfield turf during a game. He had been on amateur forms at West Bromwich Albion and Brentford.

The first Isthmian representative match was staged at Kingfield in March when the Isthmian League played the Royal Navy. 'Ginger' Smith scored one for the Isthmian League.

Maurice Eastaff represented Surrey in three games against Cornwall, Sussex and Kent. Reeves played in the Kent game whilst Smith was travelling reserve in one of the games. Reg Morgan represented the Isthmian League in their 5-1 drubbing of Nigeria at Ilford.

Caricatures of Woking players, as portrayed in the press, 30th September 1949

George Allen drawing the raffle prizes on match day.
Fred Skilton with hands in pockets obviously hasn't won!

Post-World War II - Ladies Catering Committee. The unsung heroines.

Chapter 8

CONSOLIDATION AND THEN GLORY: THE 1950'S

1950 - 1951

Woking have always relied on the youngster keen to gain a place in the leading amateur side of the district and on the good club man.

Season 1950-51 was no exception as both types of player served Woking well.

Apart from goalkeeper Maurice Eastaff who left the club pre-season there was an absence of resignations. Replacement Peter Towers was to be chased during the season by Derby County.

This was a season in which the club promoted young local talent and in so doing achieved results numbered amongst the best of the post-war period. Youngsters from local sides such as Woking Rovers could provide the nucleus for the future success of the club.

A notable newcomer to the side was diminutive Jimmy Wastell, the Royal Navy half-back. Although living a short distance from Leytonstone's ground, he signed for Woking as he was impressed with their playing style.

Geoff Hamm made the transition from local football with Woking Rovers to senior amateur football with Woking. He had a number of trials with professional clubs during the season.

It is interesting to note how Geoff came to join the club. He was cycling down Woking High Street during late summer and "bumped" into Bob Reeves. Bob, after establishing Geoff had no plans to join a club, persuaded him to try his luck with Woking and the rest, as we say, is history.

Another little known fact is that Geoff is the only Amateur International to have started 'life' in the Woking and District League. This record will now never be equalled.

League highlights included a victory at Wycombe on the dreaded slope of Loakes Park, the destruction of Tufnell Park 8-1 and 6-1 where Hamm and Wiles both scored four times in the respective games and Wimbledon were comprehensively beaten 3-0 at Kingfield.

Cup progress was minimal, although it was unfortunate in the F.A. Cup replay at Carshalton - Woking were leading 4-3 when the game was abandoned due to bad light. In the third game Woking lost 7-4 in extra time.

Coincidentally, Carshalton Athletic had been beaten 7-4 by Woking in the F.A. Cup two seasons previously.

In the Amateur Cup the journey to Shirley, Birmingham brought a slender victory against the Worcester Combination league works side, Jack Moulds Athletic. The pitch of the Robin Hood Stadium sloped away from the centre in all directions.

After having failed to win the second round meeting with Wimbledon before the best of the season attendance of 4,127, fate took a hand in the replay at Plough Lane where Woking fought back valiantly but in vain, despite an injury to goalkeeper Towers who was replaced in goal by Freddy Pink.

Redhill administered a 4-0 thrashing to Woking in the Surrey Senior Cup.

For the second year Woking were invited to the Easter Tournament at Ostend. Although the first game was won 5-4 against Ghent University, KVG smashed six goals without reply in the second game.

Eight players appeared in over 20 league games which indicated a certain stability throughout the season.

Bill Wiles, for the fourth season running, was the top goal scorer with 30 goals in 35 games. Bill Short celebrated his appointment as skipper with 15 goals, the same total as Freddy Pink. Geoff Hamm in his first season netted 10 times.

Morgan, Wastell, Hamm and Wiles all played for Surrey during the season. Morgan, Reeves and Eastaff received county caps at a Surrey F.A. presentation in recognition of their services. Pink and Short played for Surrey against London University at Tooting.

1951 - 1952

Season 1951-52 could be summed up in a few words "A good forward line but oh that defence!" Seventy-one goals conceded was the third highest in the league.

Two young full backs - Geoff Parsons and Ron Ellerby were introduced and took time to settle fully. These two youngsters had a great potential to be regular defenders for some years and would eventually solve some of the problems that were in this department for most of this season.

Individually, the defenders were never absolutely hopeless, but as a defensive unit they were sadly lacking.

One outstanding acquisition to the team was Freddy Keefe who came in as a deputy half-back and remained as a regular member of the team.

In November "Jock" Easton, a forward, joined. He was in the Military Police based at Inkerman Barracks.

The attack, apart from a bad spell in October and November when a goal was not scored in five consecutive games, did all that was asked of them.

As a respect to "Dad" Saunders, Woking's secretary for many years, black armbands were worn in November.

For the fifth time Bill Wiles was the leading scorer with 22 goals, Fred Pink and Geoff Hamm scored 18 and 12 respectively.

With one point less (27) from their 26 Isthmian League matches the Cardinals finished seventh, one place down on last season.

After losing the opening game against Walthamstow at Kingfield, Woking took on all Isthmian comers to their own ground and remained undefeated until the last match of the season when losing 5-4 to Corinthian Casuals.

It was a different story away from home, only eight points were gained out of a possible 26.

Once again the eventual champions tasted defeat at Kingfield. Leytonstone being on the wrong end of a 3-1 scoreline. Wimbledon, the runners-up were beaten by the same score at the same venue.

A creditable draw at Walthamstow in the penultimate game of the season probably cost Woking's hosts the championship, as they finished the season only one point adrift of Leytonstone.

Freddy Keefe, Freddy Pink and Alf Welland, three stalwarts of the early 1950's

Other highlights were an 8-1 thrashing of Wycombe in which all the forwards scored, including a Wiles hat-trick and a thrilling 5-5 at home to Kingstonian in the snow.

The major cup competitions produced very little for Woking. Having disposed of Epsom (where Geoff Hamm scored a hat-trick on his twenty-first birthday), and Dorking, Corinthian League runners-up Hounslow Town proved much too strong, destroying Woking 6-0 at Kingfield in the second qualifying round of the F.A. Cup.

One round of the Amateur Cup was won, but Marine (Crosby) of the Lancashire Combination, comfortably defeated Woking

3-0 in the second round. The dropping of leading scorer Bill Wiles for this game caused much controversy with the fans and the local press.

Quick exits were made in the Surrey Senior Cup and the Shield, and Guildford City were too powerful over both legs of the Surrey Combination Cup. Generally the season was a disappointment with more "downs" than "ups".

Nobby Clarke, awaiting a cartilage operation, played for an Anglo Welsh XI against Wales at Wimbledon.

In November new training lights were installed under the direction of "Tink" Medhurst. They were based on Chelsea's lights and enabled night training to be held at Inkerman Barracks.

1952 - 1953

Season 1952-53 commenced without Tufnell Park Edmonton, who were wooden spoonists for four consecutive seasons. They had been in continuous membership since 1919. Bromley and Barking from the Athenian League were elected as full members.

Two wins and a draw gave Woking a dream start to their league programme but they flattered to deceive as the next eight league games were lost. A mini-revival with five wins in the last eight games, including the usual defeat of the eventual champions Walthamstow, enabled Woking to climb to 12th place with 24 points from 29 games.

The old problem persisted, with Woking having the second worst defensive record in the league. Phil Ledger had replaced Peter Towers in goal but this had little effect on the number of goals conceded. Towers had left to join Guildford "Pinks". Joining the squad were J. McFetridge, an ex-Motherwell full-back billeted at Royal Military Police, Inkerman, 18 years old Ron Cox from Cove and John Ford (19) from Camberley.

Goals were shared equally among the forwards. Hamm and Pink scored 15, Welland slotted home 12, with Bill Wiles scoring 12 times in 16 games. This was Bill's final season with the club, the figures speak for themselves, over 130 goals in 170 plus competitive games spread over six seasons. Three times he scored four goals in a game.

Another military policeman was to make his mark, 27 year old bespectacled Ian Hart. Previously with Yeovil he also played rugby. He had already won Combined Services honours.

In the F.A. and Surrey Senior Cups swift exits were made with the 'old enemy' Wimbledon, being the victors both times.

Barnet from the Athenian League proved to be the stumbling block in the second round of the Amateur Cup. A replayed tie was lost 2-0 after a 3-3 thriller at Kingfield.

In this Coronation year the Surrey Senior Shield was won 2-1 against Banstead after defeating Sutton and Epsom in previous rounds. The last win in the final of this competition was in 1912-13.

A photocall prior the the 1953 Easter tour of the Channel Islands. Charlie Mortimore made his first appearance in a Woking shirt.

One young player, Bobby Edwards left pre-season for Chelsea and played in the first team. Also outgoing was Peter Pinhorn whose job at the bank took him to Jamaica.

In hindsight, the most significant event of the season was the addition of Charlie Mortimore, an England Amateur International, to the Easter tour of the Channel Islands. The three games against Jersey and Guernsey were duly won with Charlie scoring his first goal for Woking. Many more goals would be credited to him as the glory years unfolded.

Woking's February visit to Romford was fraught with travelling difficulties. Due to heavy fog locally, Woking never made it despite clear skies at Romford. Pink and Hamm played for Surrey with Hamm touring with Middlesex Wanderers and playing for the Isthmian League against the Athenian League.

1953 - 1954

Season 1953-54 really began before a ball had been kicked. The announcement was made, prior to the club's first trial match, that Charlie Mortimore, 25 year old England international centre-forward and his younger brother 18 year old John, had signed for Woking. Charlie had been a regular performer for Aldershot in the Football League Division 3 (South) for four seasons. He had twice led the England amateur international attack in 1950-51 and played three times on the right wing in 1951-52. After completing his training as a school teacher he went into the RAF. On being demobbed in 1949 he re-joined Aldershot. At the time he joined Woking he was employed as a schoolmaster at Cove Secondary School.

John was a regular member of Aldershot Reserves in the half-back line and played for England Youths in 1951-52.

The expectations of the season were never quite realised by the results, thirty points were gained with a final position of sixth. Lying in second place with 25 points and with seven matches to play at the end of February, it seemed this was to be Woking's year. Then the forward line, which had been described as being "among the most formidable in the country", lost its edge. Of the final seven league games Woking failed to score in four of them and only two were won. Injuries to key forwards did not help the cause. Charlie Mortimore, captain and mainspring of the side, badly injured a knee and as a result did not play for several weeks. Hamm, injured at St. Albans, missed four weeks. Defender Len Morris missed the last eight league games, with cartilage problems.

The reserves, drafted into the senior side, such as Alan Gibbs, Andy Cheyne, "Kipper" Killick and Ian Jones, came out with credit but the loss of high calibre players such as Mortimore and Hamm proved too great a strain.

Nevertheless, the improved style of football owed its origin to the outstanding successful tour of the Channel Islands at the end of the previous season. It was continued throughout the current season. Charlie Mortimore demonstrated his ability to get the best out of players like Hamm, Pink and Welland. Players such as John Mortimore and Alf Zimmer increased the skill factor in the team.

Charlie Mortimore set his standards by scoring in the first seven games. His final tally being 24 goals in 27 games.

Other main scorers were Alfie Welland with 11 and Alf Zimmer with 10 goals.

Two performances were outstanding. Walthamstow, the previous years league champions, were outplayed by, as quoted in the local paper, "Swift, pattern weaving football".

Leytonstone, one of the better teams in the post-war period, were well beaten in one of the best games of football seen at Kingfield.

Unfortunately, some poor performances were intermingled with the good, such as the 7-0 thrashing at Romford and the 3-2 loss at bottom club Oxford.

In the cups there were early exits in the F.A. Cup and the Surrey Senior Cup at the hands of Kingstonian and Wimbledon.

Two rounds were won in the Amateur Cup first against an unknown Bulford Utd then a revenge victory against Kingstonian. Charlie Mortimore scored five in these two games. Walton proved too strong in the next round, winning 3-1 at Stompond Lane before 5,935 spectators.

The final of the Surrey Senior Shield was reached for the second year running by defeating Walton 3-1 at Kingfield in the semi-final. With three reserves in the team the result was satisfying. Unfortunately, the final was lost against Kingstonian despite leading 1-0 at half-time with a Charlie Mortimore goal. The winner came in the last three minutes.

Progress had been made in the standard of football played, consistency was now required.

1954 - 1955

Season 1954-55 had some changes in personnel, Ron Newman, nineteen year-old ex-Fareham plus Hampshire County player, came in for Pink on the left wing. Fred had played just over 200 competitive games since season 1945-46 scoring 97 goals. On his day Fred could 'skin' the most accomplished of full backs.

Ron Newman joined from Newport IOW, but his career at Woking was all too brief as he signed professional forms for Portsmouth after completing just 18 games for Woking.

Vic Woodfield, an ex-England youth and Devon county player joined the Cards.

The careers of Reg Morgan and Len Morris came to an end during the season.

Phil Ledger and Bob Stratton a new signing from Cove, shared the goalkeeping spot throughout the season.

Ernie Clacey, the most awkward but certainly effective of defenders, played a few games, but his time would come.

Goals were scored with ease as Woking were the second highest scorers in the league but, unfortunately, the defence leaked nearly three goals per game, which ranked Woking as having the worst defensive record in the league.

The previous year's champions, Bromley, were beaten out of sight, 4-1 in the opening encounter of the season before 2,400 spectators. Defensive disasters occurred in the next three games, sixteen goals conceded and no points gained gave a poor start to the season.

Corinthian Casuals hammered Woking 7-4 at Kennington Oval to keep up an amazing scoring sequence. In three previous seasons Woking had been beaten 5-1, 5-2 and 7-2 in the league and 5-3 in the Surrey Senior Cup during 1951-52.

Romford 6 Woking 9 - 12 February 1955

This was the unbelievable scoreline in the Romford mud. Bob Stratton held onto the ball with John Mortimore and Ron Ellerby (3) looking on.

The games against Romford had to be seen to be believed. At Kingfield in November the Romford goalkeeper failed to turn up so chairman J. Parrish turned out. His portly figure belied his goalkeeping skills as he produced a series of amazing saves. It was only in the final minutes that

Woking scored two goals in a 4-4 draw. In February, Woking played at Romford in what was traditionally a high scoring game. A quagmire of a pitch did not help defenders. The half-time score was 4-4 and with five minutes left for play, both sides appeared to have settled for a 6-6 draw, which was remarkable in itself, but Woking rushed in three more goals to win by 9-6. Charlie and Geoff Hamm both scored hat-tricks.

Woking actually scored nine twice more during the season. A 9-1 thrashing of Wimbledon, albeit with a weakened side, came in the last home game of the season. Guernsey were beaten by the same score during the Easter tour where, once again, the three games were won.

Although the league position was only one place lower than the previous year there was a twelve point gap between Woking and the second placed club. Last season the gap was only three points, and the second place was under threat up to the last couple of games.

Woking's cup exploits were totally uninspiring. The F.A. Cup interest ended in a first ever visit to Dover, who were to become Kent League runners-up. Wycombe defeated Woking 4-0 in the second round of the Amateur Cup before a crowd of 7,350.

Dulwich accounted for Woking in the Surrey Senior Cup by the comfortable margin of 5-2. Guildford City, again, proved too strong in the Surrey Combination Cup, although the aggregate score of 7-4 was reasonably close.

Goalscoring was shared among the forwards with C. Mortimore, Hamm, Welland and Zimmer, scoring 23, 15, 15 and 12 respectively.

The season was a disappointing one as there was no apparent progress compared with the previous season, but individual players won plenty of representative honours. Morris, Parsons, Welland and Hamm (Surrey), John and Charlie Mortimore with Newman for Hampshire. John and Charlie for the Isthmian League. Charlie for Southern Counties, John Mortimore and Newman (FAXI). John Mortimore and Newman played in the Olympic squad and for England 'B' with Hamm as travelling reserve.

1955 - 1956

Season 1955-56 was without doubt the most successful for many years. The Surrey Senior Cup was finally won after a 29 year wait. It was as long ago as 1926-27 that a Woking captain last held aloft this cup.

History was made on the 27th December when Woking topped the Isthmian League table for the first time ever. This pinnacle of fame was extremely brief as three days later Woking disappointed a 2,500 crowd by losing at home to a middle of the table Oxford.

Fourth equalled the best ever league position achieved previously in 1927-28. Only goal average prevented Woking finishing in runners-up spot. It was all the more remarkable as in an appalling start to the season five of the first six games were lost. This was followed by an eight game unbeaten run (seven victories), which included a 5-1 thrashing of Wimbledon. A double over Christmas against the eventual runners-up Bromley put Woking on top, but three successive defeats finished off the dreams. A 3-1 victory over the runaway champions Wycombe at Loakes Park had to be the best performance of the season.

A new left wing Army partnership, Tony Redican from Basingstoke and Jack Harvey from Royal Engineers (Cove), performed well scoring 19 goals between them. Both were Hampshire County players but like the majority of forces players it was difficult to predict their permanency. Unfortunately their stay was all too brief, Redican 30 appearances with Harvey only completing 17 games. In the last two or three games of the season a new star emerged. Reg Stratton, a gangling, deceptively skilful schoolboy, played for the strollers, reserves and first team all within eight days. Coached by Charlie Mortimore at Cove School, Stratton would play a major role in the successes of the next few years.

Mervyn Gill, a goalkeeper from the RAF had played in Portsmouth's league team. He also played many games with John Mortimore in the RAF amateur side, and was then introduced to Woking. This stay was, however, brief, only 16 games before he joined Southampton.

Ernie Clacey played at centre-half for the majority of the season. In the Amateur Cup winning season he would take on a different role as the defensive wing half.

In October, Ken Turner, one of the best centre-halves Woking ever had, joined the club. His initial position was full-back. Although only five feet eight inches in height, his tremendous ability to read the game coupled with speed off the mark, compensated for his lack of inches. His move to centre-half in the following season was an inspired decision. Alf Welland returned in mid-November only to leave in January. Bill Wiles ex-Woking was now manager/coach at Farncombe and the famous Johnny Price was coach at Southern League side Yiewsley.

Folkestone defeated Woking in the preliminary round of the F.A. Cup after a drawn game at Kingfield. The Amateur Cup went the same way with Leytonstone progressing to the next round after a drawn first game.

Players and officials at the Annual Club Dinner 1955

Woking F.C. 1955 - 1956 - Winners of the Surrey Senior Cup and the Surrey Combination Cup.
Players only left to right Back Row G. Parsons, K. Turner, P. Ledger, R. Ellerby.
Centre Row F. Keefe, J. Mortimore, E. Clacey, A. Clarke.
Front Row R. Bond, R. Ford, C. Mortimore, G. Hamm, R. Stratton

Woking won the Surrey Senior Cup by defeating Tooting 1-0 in the final at Dulwich. 5,100 paid £488 for the privilege. The goal was scored by Robbie Ford who had joined late in the season and looked a class forward.

Victories over Surrey Senior League side Worcester Park, Corinthian Casuals and Kingstonian in the earlier rounds ensured a place in the final.

Charlie Mortimore scored hat-tricks against Worcester Park and Kingstonian and finished with 26 goals in 38 games. John Mortimore and Hamm found the net eleven times. The only other double figure scorer was Jack Harvey with 10.

On Good Friday, Charlie played for Aldershot in a league match and in early April John Mortimore played for the Football League champions, Chelsea.

Representative honours were achieved throughout the season. A change in County regulations meant that players could only represent the county of their club. This boosted Surrey with the Mortimores now available. However Hamm and Parsons secured places against Kent, Berks & Bucks and Middlesex. Hamm also played for Southern Counties and teamed up with the Mortimores for the South versus Schaffhausen (Switzerland) fixture. Isthmian League honours were gained by Hamm and Charlie. Ken Turner played for the FA XI.

Late in the season, Guildford City were beaten 4-1 at Kingfield with Reg Stratton scoring two, and so the Surrey Combination Cup found its place next to the Surrey Senior Cup.

One new venture was the first ever floodlit match for Woking when Yiewsley were visited on 22nd November 1955. The result being a 1-0 victory.

The performance of the side throughout the season gave cause for great optimism in the future. A few more pieces in the team jigsaw were required to change a good team into a great one.

1956 - 1957

The demands of Surrey probably cost Woking the championship in 1956-57. By playing county matches on Saturday key players were missing in crucial games. Two points were lost at Wimbledon during the final run-in to the end of the season. A below strength side fought gallantly throughout but finally lost 2-3. Prior to this loss six straight victories had been achieved. Wycombe, who had pulled away from the pack, held a massive points lead at one stage, but a combination of successive Woking victories and Wycombe's loss of form, no doubt due to players thoughts about a Wembley appearance in the Amateur

The successful line-up 1956 - 1957.
Isthmian League runers-up and Surrey Senior Cup winners.
Left to right *Back Row* *Geoff Parsons, Ken Turner, Ernie Clacey, John Burley, John Mortimore, Ron Ellerby.*
Front Row *Roy Littlejohn, John Hebdon, Charlie Mortimore, Geoff Hamm, Reg Stratton.*

Cup, reduced the deficit to one point.

Woking's defeat at fourth placed Oxford gave Wycombe some breathing space although the championship was only decided on the last day, with Wycombe playing in the morning.

Wycombe needed to defeat bottom placed Corinthian Casuals to win the league. Casuals put up a tremendous battle, actually leading 1-0 before two late goals secured Wycombe the title for the second year running.

Woking's forward line of Littlejohn, Hebdon, C. Mortimore, Hamm and Stratton was a powerful unit, all capable of scoring goals. This they did as 104 league goals were scored, four more than Walthamstow's record in 1945-46.

The new season opened with the Suez crisis hitting the pre-season trials. Charlie and John Mortimore were on holiday with a boys camp in Northern Ireland. However Woking lined-up new boys Mike Jacob, an ex-West Ham trialist and Devon County player from St. Austell and RMP Laurie Brown, ex-Lincoln City. Brown only managed three games for Woking but subsequently played 150 games for Arsenal and Spurs.

The season had started with Robbie Ford in the inside forward position but peculiarities with expenses payments in Scottish football cast doubts about his amateur status. This was very unfortunate as he had blended well into the side and was a class player. John Hebdon was drafted in and quickly established himself as a superb goal poacher. At the same time former Woking favourite, "Nobby" Clarke finally retired to concentrate on his new family, twins.

Clapton were thrashed 7-1 in the opening game of the season with Charlie bagging 5. St. Albans and Romford also perished 7-1 with Charlie scoring 4 and 5 respectively.

Six games were lost in the first fifteen but the turning point came against Wycombe. Just after half-time Wycombe were leading 5-0 then Woking started their own version of 'push and run'. At the end Wycombe were under the cosh but held out for a 5-3 win. For the rest of the season, when Woking had a full side, all-comers were beaten comprehensively.

In September the Mortimore brothers and Hamm played for the Isthmian League against the Athenians and later that month John Mortimore played again for the League versus Uganda at Dulwich. Mike Jacob was picked for the Army against the London F.A.

Reg Stratton, selected for England Youth Team, was the first Woking player to be so honoured since Billy Warnes played in all three international matches in 1930-31. In October the Olympic trials started with John Mortimore and Hamm representing the League against the Olympic XI before being selected for the England trial side playing Northern Counties.

Reg Stratton, who had a meteoric rise from Woking Strollers to Woking Reserves to Woking 1st XI, England Youth and Amateur International in a few short months during 1956 and 1957

Subsequently, honours were awarded to John Mortimore and Geoff Hamm who were given their first amateur international caps against Wales in February. Both players held their place for subsequent internationals and were joined by Charlie Mortimore and Reg Stratton for the summer tour.

Dulwich were beaten 2-1 in the preliminary round of the F.A. Cup but Kent League Tunbridge Wells proved too strong on the day in the next round.

Woking were one of the favourites to win the Amateur Cup, but Walthamstow had other ideas as they defeated Woking 3-2 in a replay at Kingfield in front of a crowd of 4,800.

Surrey Senior Cup retained 1956 - 1957 with a 4-2 victory over Wimbledon. The victory was obtained without the services of Charlie and John Mortimore, Geoff Hamm and Reg Stratton all on tour. Captain for the day, Geoff Parsons holding the cup, played at centre-forward and scored.

Woking defended the Surrey Senior Cup successfully, Tooting were hammered 5-1, Walton put up a great fight before losing 4-3. Sutton were dismissed 4-1 in the semi-final at Kingstonian's ground.

In the final at Crystal Palace, Woking by necessity, fielded a weak side, as the date coincided with the international tour. The Mortimores, Hamm and Stratton missed the final but with Geoff Parsons leading the attack and scoring, Woking defeated Wimbledon 4-2 after being behind in the first half. Players such as Dave Gamble deserved the winners medal after overcoming all the odds.

AMATEUR SELECTION COMMITTEE:

J. W. Bowers (Chairman)
E. W. Beetham
D. Follows
J. Glancey
L. J. Kingston
J. T. Stone
J. Taylor
H. W. Thompson
W. H. Webster

MEMBER OF INTERNATIONAL SELECTION COMMITTEE IN CHARGE:—
J. W. Bowers

TEAM MANAGER:—
F. N. S. Creek

ENGLAND XI (White shirts, blue knickers):—

Goalkeeper: M. J. Pinner (Pegasus)
Right Back: J. Harlow (Tooting & Mitcham)
Left Back: L. T. Farrer (Walthamstow Avenue) (Captain)
Right Half Back: J. Mortimore (Woking)
Centre Half Back: S. Prince (Walthamstow Avenue)
Left Half Back: H. E. Dodkins (Ilford)
Outside Right: L. Worley (Wycombe Wanderers)
Inside Right: L. Champelovier (Hayes)
Centre Forward: P. Thompson (R.A.F.)
Inside Left: J. Fletcher (Maidstone United)
Outside Left: G. Hamm (Woking)

Trainer: J. Jennings (Northampton Town)

Headquarters:
GREAT NORTHERN STATION HOTEL
PETERBOROUGH
(Telephone 3851)

Arrangements for Travel and Accommodation

ASSEMBLY. Players and Officials should make their own arrangements to travel so as to reach Headquarters by noon on Saturday, 16th February.

The main party travelling from London will assemble opposite the departure platform, Kings Cross Station at 10 a.m. on Saturday, 16th February. Train leaves at 10.20 a.m., due at Peterborough at 11.47 a.m.

Later trains for Members of Committee who are unable to travel with the main party are:—

Kings Cross	Peterborough
10.45	12.54
1.18	2.47

DISPERSAL. Players will be free to return to their homes immediately after the match. For those returning to London, seats have been reserved on the 6.13 p.m. train, due Kings Cross at 7.42 p.m. Dinner will be served en route. Reservations will be made at the Lancaster Court Hotel, Lancaster Gate, for those players unable to reach their homes on Saturday night.

ACKNOWLEDGEMENT. It is important that Players should acknowledge receipt of these arrangements stating:—

(a) Their fitness to play;
(b) Whether they will be travelling with the party from London, or reporting at Headquarters;
(c) Whether they will require Hotel accommodation in London on Saturday night.

PATRON:
HER MAJESTY THE QUEEN
PRESIDENT:
H.R.H. THE DUKE OF EDINBURGH, K.G., K.T.

Secretary.
SIR STANLEY ROUS, C.B.E., J.P.

Chairman of the Council:
A. DREWRY, ESQ. C.B.E., J.P.

Amateur International Match

ENGLAND
v.
WALES

To be played on the Ground of
Peterborough United F.C.
on
Saturday 16th, February, 1957

KICK-OFF 3 p.m.

Amateur International - England v Wales at Peterborough, February 1957.
John Mortimore and Geoff Hamm chosen to play. Billy Warnes in 1930 - 1931 was the last Woking Player to play for his country.

Woking reached the final of the Surrey Senior Shield but this was held over until the following season.

Twenty-one year old John Mortimore was named Player-of-the-Year by the News Chronicle. He had played for Chelsea against Arsenal on Christmas Day and the following Tuesday travelled to Old Trafford.

Charlie scored 39 in 34 games, Hamm had his best year scoring 27, Reg Stratton netted 14 and Hebdon 11. Alfie Welland who finally emigrated to Canada scored 10 goals.

The season was exceptional both for results and quality football, but the next season surpassed everything that had gone before.

1957 - 1958

Before the season 1957-58 had commenced, John Mortimore signed as a professional for Chelsea. This was a great loss to the side but it was expected that Mike Jacob, the utility player, would be able to fill the gap.

Phil Ledger joined Alton Town after being relegated to the "Strollers". Of the new players ex-Portsmouth Brian Naysmith failed to make the grade. Mick Sharpe a Singapore international only lasted a month before joining Wokingham.

After twelve games in the league, only four had been won, five games out of six had been lost away from home. Wimbledon and St. Albans happened to catch Woking on a good day and were hammered 5-1 and 6-1, respectively. Charlie had only scored three goals compared with twelve at the corresponding time last season. This probably said it all.

A 5-1 thrashing at home to Bromley in the F.A. Cup ended any thoughts of a run in this competition.

The Surrey Senior Shield held over from last season was duly won in September as Carshalton were hammered 5-0.

Jim Collingwood, a 23 year old P.T. instructor in the Royal Engineers (Cove) was introduced in November as wing-half. He had played for Loughborough College and the United Universities. He was awkward but very fit and his introduction coincided with a run of good results. The forward line suddenly came good, five goals at Wimbledon, seven against Clapton and a magnificent ten in the Surrey Senior Cup against Redhill. So impressive were they that Spurs regularly watched Roy Littlejohn. In January Phil Ledger resurrected his career with a move to Wimbledon. Chelsea signed on four Cards on amateur forms, Charlie, Stratton, Littlejohn and Hamm.

A slight hiccup at Corinthian Casuals was only a small blip and a week prior to the Amateur Cup tie versus Aveley, Wycombe the defending league champions were beaten 2-1 at Kingfield. The team were running into some decent form and Aveley were easily beaten 6-1 before 3,035 spectators. Hebdon and Hamm each scored a brace.

Woking had to visit Hendon in the second round of the Amateur Cup. Hendon were the top side in the Athenian League but Woking brushed them aside in a 3-1 victory before a crowd of 5,417. A Charlie Mortimore hat-trick ensured Hayes were beaten 5-1 at Kingfield in the 3rd round before a record attendance of 6,857. This match publicly showed Woking's friendship with Chelsea, as due to a strip clash with Hayes, Woking played in Chelsea blue.

Finchley, another Athenian League side, were to visit Kingfield in the next round. Prior to this, Wycombe were defeated 4-0 at Loakes Park with Charlie bagging a brace.

The tie with Finchley was played in pouring rain but 7,020 still packed into the Kingfield ground. Railway sleepers and raised scaffolding gave temporary terracing and the grass banks behind both goals afforded a precarious foothold for the Woking faithful. Queues started to form at 10 am Saturday morning despite some heavy early downpours. Early arrivals were given chairs by Clarrie Jarman.

The game itself seemed to be going Woking's way as they built up a 3-0 lead early in the second half. A goalkeeping error by John Burley allowed Finchley back in the game but the second goal in the last minute was not enough to prevent Woking winning through to the semi-final.

Before the semi-final against Barnet, Woking played two games which had unbelievable drama. In the league game at home to Leytonstone, Woking were totally lethargic for three-quarters of the game and found themselves 3-0 in arrears. Then, with seventeen minutes left on the clock, Charlie scored what was thought to be a consolation goal. Six minutes were left when Stratton scored the second and Charlie equalised in the next minute. Two minutes from the end Charlie pushed in the winner during a goal-mouth scramble. This amazing fight back was similar to that in season 1921-22. In an F.A. Cup tie Dorking stormed into a 3-0 lead. Woking scored three late goals and another three in extra-time. A 6-3 Woking victory at the end of extra time was as unlikely as the victory against Leytonstone, but football in never predictable.

Programme and stand ticket for the Amateur Cup Semi-Final at Fulham and stand ticket for the replay at Brentford.

The semi-final of the Surrey Senior Cup against Dulwich at Wimbledon a week before the Barnet game, looked to be a foregone conclusion. Dulwich Hamlet were bottom of the Isthmian League with only eight points from eighteen games. A hat-trick of Surrey Senior Cup Final victories looked easy but three missed penalties by Woking enabled Dulwich to complete an unlikely 2-1 victory.

A dramatic announcement came over the loudspeakers at Craven Cottage just before the semi-final against Barnet was due to start. Ken Turner would be missing from the Woking side. Delayed by the illness of his wife Ken was held up by the crowds and arrived a few minutes after the kick-off. So, at the last moment, the Cardinals were robbed of the services of the best uncapped centre-half in the South of England. Ernie Clacey moved across into Turner's position and turned in a faultless performance before 20,747 spectators who saw a fascinating game which ended in a 1-1 draw.

Two special trains took 1,100 Woking fans to Fulham and 83 coaches were required to convey the rest of the Kingfield army.

A crowd of 19,500 turned out for the replay at Brentford. This time Turner played and Woking dictated most of the play. Two Stratton goals and one from Charlie gave Woking a hard fought 3-2 victory. A dubious penalty had brought Barnet back in the game with half an hour remaining but the defence held firm to book their place in the final against Ilford, live on TV for the last time.

April 12, 1958, is a date that will be remembered by Woking fans as the day Woking won the Amateur Cup by defeating Ilford 3-0 at Wembley. For Charlie Mortimore, Woking's popular captain, the day was all the more significant because it was his 30th birthday. 71,000 fans paid £25,619 to see Woking score first in the 38th minute. Ilford then applied constant pressure on the Woking goal for the first 20 minutes of the second half. Two further goals in the 78th and 88th minutes gave Charlie and his men the coveted Amateur Cup.

Crowds jammed the streets around the vicinity of the Albion hotel awaiting the return of the players. A celebration dinner at the Cotteridge Hotel had been arranged, but first, the players joined their captain on the balcony to display the cup to the crowd. Bob Cumming (co-Author) remembers being driven around the town in an old Austin A30 decked out in Ilford colours by a family friend from Essex. Only friendly barracking and humorous comments were heard.

Amateur Cup Semi-Final 1958 against Barnet at Craven Cottage.
A diving header by Charlie Mortimore brilliantly saved by the Barnet goalkeeper.

Amateur Cup Final 1958..
The long walk from the dressing to the turf for the presentations.

Amateur Cup Final 1958
Charlie faces the Ilford goalkeeper against the background of an expectant crowd.

Amateur Cup Final 1958
Awaiting the presentation to the Lord Mayor of London

At the celebration dinner Charlie responded to the toast wearing a sports jacket and flannels. Evidently these had been worn on the day of each round, including the final.

It was not surprising that not one of the remaining eight league games was won. The players had reached the summit and anything after that was an anti-climax, four draws were obtained but a combination of weak sides and too many games in a short space of time gave easy victories to Bromley and St. Albans by 6-1 and 6-3 respectively.

Amateur Cup Final 1958
Reg Stratton scores Woking's second and killer goal despite the acrobatics of the Ilford defender.

Amateur Cup Final 1958
Charlie receives the cup from the Lord Mayor of London on his thirtieth birthday.

The final league position of 9th was not a true reflection of Woking's strength during the season.

Reg Stratton and Charlie Mortimore both scored 27 goals. Geoff Hamm scored 20, John Hebdon 17 (including 2 at Wembley), and Roy Littlejohn 15.

It is interesting to note that Ken Turner only missed the one game, the first semi-final against Barnet. As the season ended with eight games in sixteen days his fitness must have been remarkable.

A whole host of representative honours were won. Charlie Mortimore, Geoff Hamm and Roy Littlejohn played for England. Reg Stratton played for Middlesex Wanderers, Isthmian League, FA XI and Surrey. Geoff Parsons turned out for Surrey.

This season was a peak in Woking's history which was matched thirty-four years later when the Isthmian League Championship was won for the first time, and also in the memorable F.A. Trophy victories at Wembley in 1994 and 1995.

Amateur Cup Final Wembley Programme and Grand Stand ticket.

Amateur Cup Final 1958
The cup is Woking's after a hard fought victory.

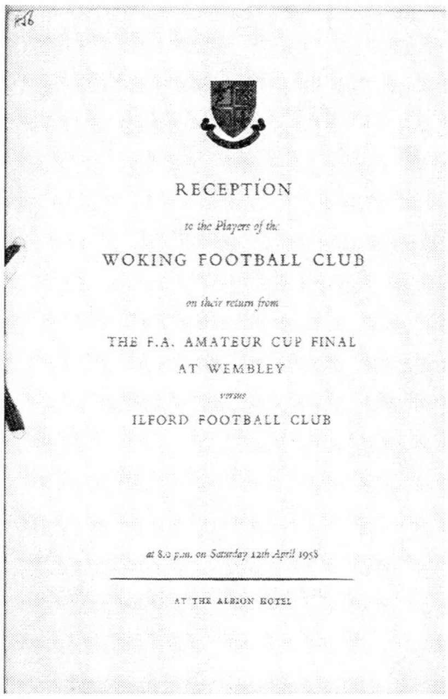

RECEPTION

to the Players of the

WOKING FOOTBALL CLUB

on their return from

THE F.A. AMATEUR CUP FINAL

AT WEMBLEY

versus

ILFORD FOOTBALL CLUB

at 8.0 p.m. on Saturday 12th April 1958

AT THE ALBION HOTEL

Amateur Cup celebration meal provided by Mr L.A. Gosden as a tribute.

THE PLAYERS

C. MORTIMORE*†
Captain
G. HAMM*†
Vice Captain
J. BURLEY
R. ELLERBY
G. PARSONS†
J. COLLINGWOOD
K. TURNER†
E. CLACEY†
R. LITTLEJOHN*†
J. HEBDON
R. STRATTON*
M. JACOB†
M. CASHMORE
R. TAYLOR

* International Honours † County Honours

Amateur Cup Final 1958
Winners reception at the Albion Hotel, Woking

Amateur Cup Final 1958
Back to the dressing room for a quiet celebration. Charlie with the appropriate nectar.

The winning Amateur Cup Final Team 1958

Left to right *Standing* *Bob Reeves (Team Manager), Jim Collingwood, Ernie Clacey, John Burley, Geoff Parsons, Ron Ellerby, Ken Turner, Bert Knott (physio).*
Seated *Roy Littlejohn, John Hebdon, Charlie Mortimore, Clarrie Jarman (Hon. Sec), Geoff Hamm, Mike Jacob (12th man), Reg Stratton*

At the celebrations outside the Albion Hotel with Charlie holding the Amateur Cup after the Wembley triumph in 1958.

1958 - 1959

Having reached the pinnacle in the 1957-58 season, Woking dropped back badly in season 1958-59, which came as a real anti-climax after two highly successful campaigns. Not one trophy came the way of the Cardinals, except for a share in the Alaway Brothers Memorial Trophy, held jointly with Middlesex Wanderers.

Geoff Parsons, a cultured full-back

The biggest blow to Woking's prospects came before the season opened when Geoff Hamm decided to transfer his allegiance to Wimbledon - and incidentally helped them to win the Isthmian League Championship. One of the strongest links in the attack was thus removed and never replaced adequately during the season.

Geoff Parsons who was also joining Wimbledon, changed his mind at the eleventh hour and decided to stay with Woking. Tony Pratt rejoined after a successful career at Hayes, along with Brian Stevens, the ex-Wealdstone goalkeeper. Neither could gain a regular first team spot.

That great utility player, Mike Jacob, was drafted into Geoff Hamm's position but his selection in the forward line was a waste of a talented wing-half.

Constant international calls against Wales, South Africa and France again robbed the Cardinals of their captain and centre-forward, Charlie Mortimore, at regular intervals, especially at the beginning of the season. Reg Stratton also received an international call-up for the match against Northern Ireland. Calls on players for Saturday representative games was beginning to create friction. This was very apparent with Surrey F.A., who flatly refused to play county games midweek.

Suitable deputies was never produced. Roy Littlejohn decided to assist Southampton Reserves, as much as possible, in order to ensure himself a regular club when he moved down that way during the summer.

One positive factor of the whole season was the emergence of Norman Cashmore as a first team player after a number of false starts.

The Cardinals league record had nothing to distinguish it apart from the fact that it was as level as it could be with 30 points from 30 matches and 66 goals for and against. They finished in eighth position.

There were very few league highlights. One unusual occurrence was during the visit to the "Spotted Dog" to play Clapton. It was realised there was no second kit in the bag. Woking, therefore had to play in an assorted selection of borrowed green shirts. A cracking game away to Wimbledon in late August, finished 5-4 in Wimbledon's favour. The result was somewhat unfortunate as in the last few minutes Reg Stratton scored from a penalty, but the referee ordered a retake which ex-Woking goalkeeper Phil Ledger saved. Nevertheless, it was an excellent recovery from 2-5 down. Charlie Mortimore claimed five goals in a 7-0 victory against Leytonstone and a then league record attendance of 4,100 witnessed Woking and Wycombe drawing 1-1. Ken Turner at last scored a goal for Woking against Bromley in a 3-2 victory, his very first, and although not known at the time, his only competitive goal.

It is best to draw a quick veil over the Amateur Cup. Woking were beaten in the first round 6-3 by Redhill, who were then bottom of the Athenian League.

The winning of the Amateur Cup the previous April secured exemption until the first round of the F.A. Cup, 18,141 paid £2,631 as Woking lost at Southampton 1-4.

Some success came in the Surrey Senior Cup. Molesey were blitzed 11-1 in the first round with Charlie scoring 6 and Bill Dowse (ex-Cove) who was making his first team debut scoring a cracking goal. Tooting were beaten 4-2 in the 2nd round with Charlie claiming a hat-trick. Walton were beaten by an own goal in the semi-final. Dulwich were the opponents in the final, played at Crystal Palace. Revenge for last years defeat at the semi-final stage was not to be as Dulwich proved too strong in a 4-1 defeat; two thousand Woking supporters who made the journey to Crystal Palace witnessed a disappointing display by Woking.

Twice Guildford City were beaten by superior football skill, once in the inaugural Surrey Invitation Cup, (Woking subsequently losing to Crystal Palace 4-1 in the final), and once in the first leg of the Surrey Combination Cup. The Southern League professionals made no mistake in the second leg giving their amateur neighbours a sound thrashing.

Player after player had been tried but the Cards were unable to find a successful penalty taker. Since that fateful day when three were missed against Dulwich in the Surrey Senior Cup semi-final, not one had been converted, fifteen in a row having been missed.

Charlie Mortimore topped the scoring with 28 goals, Reg Stratton managed 20, Mike Jacob scored 13 and John Hebdon 12.

Representative honours were once more plentiful. Charlie made six England appearances, played twice for the league and once for Surrey. Stratton played once for England and represented the F.A. Surrey and Isthmian League. Others to play for the County or the league were Littlejohn, Hebdon, Clacey and Parsons, who also turned out for the Southern Counties against the Northern Counties.

Stratton and Turner toured East Africa with the Middlesex Wanderers in June. The touring party played six matches organised by the Ugandan F.A.

Bob Reeves, team secretary, retired from that position as the season ended. He joined Woking in 1937 but the war cut six years from his career. In the first season after the war Bob scored 33 goals from the left-wing. He then became captain in 1947. When his playing days were over he took charge of the first team and was the leading 'back-room boy' in getting Woking to Wembley.

Chapter 9

A DECADE OF STRUGGLE - THE 1960'S

1959 - 1960

The dawn of the sixties produced very little for Woking Football Club. With the extra cash earned from the Amateur Cup Year and the successful league campaign the previous year, improvements were being carried out to the ground, namely, extra terracing, some covered, and pool baths for the dressing rooms.

Reg Stratton, as expected, signed professional forms for Fulham. Roy Littlejohn left the area and eventually turned professional with Southern League side Poole Town, Ernie Clacey and Ron Ellerby only played one game each during the season. The Amateur Cup winning side was inevitably breaking up. Time doesn't stand still.

Of the new players the most impressive was ex-Spurs youth and Fulham reserve George Harris, a nineteen year old outside left who could score goals. He ended the season as joint top scorer. Vic Reynolds a local boy from Westfield but an ex-Chelsea youth was a busy, workmanlike player who had a more than satisfactory season after stepping up from local football and was still only eighteen years old.

Reg Taylor, a twenty-one year old local product, replaced Ron Ellerby at right-back. It was a major disappointment when he left prior to season 1960-61 to join Kingstonian.

Ron Ellerby after 13 years with the club left in September and joined Staines. Ernie Clacey resigned with the intention of re-joining Wokingham Town.

After losing the first three league games heavily, Bill Dowse and Tony Ilsley, both Army players, were brought in to stiffen up the midfield. In November Matt Collins joined from Kingstonian to help pep-up the forward line. This brought about a mini-recovery with five games unbeaten during October/November. During this period two very good away draws were gained at Wycombe and Oxford. Points gained from visits to both clubs were always hard earned.

On Boxing Day, Kingstonian who at that time were second in the table were smashed 6-1 with John Hebdon and George Harris scoring two apiece.

Five consecutive games were lost in January including an early exit from the Amateur Cup against Aetolian League side, Ford United, who had just changed name from Briggs Sports and had beaten Leytonstone in the Essex Senior Cup three weeks earlier.

Redhill came to Kingfield for a Surrey Senior Cup tie and won handsomely 5-0 against a below par Woking side troubled by injuries.

Against all the odds, Woking then strung together a seven match unbeaten run in the league. This included a magnificent 4-2 victory at Plough Lane against last seasons league champions, Wimbledon. Two goals in the first five minutes took the game by the scruff of the neck and although Wimbledon pulled back from 3-0 to 3-2, George Harris then made it 4-2 late in the game.

Woking's inconsistency showed as the last four games were lost. What had promised to be a top six finish, finally ended in eleventh place.

Epsom, Dulwich and Kingstonian were all beaten 3-0 in the preliminary and qualifying rounds of the F.A. Cup and a 3-3 draw at Sutton promised more progress. Unfortunately Sutton won the replay easily 3-1.

Losses against supposedly inferior opposition in the Amateur Cup, Surrey Senior Cup and the Surrey Senior Shield ended Woking's interest in the cup competitions for another season.

George Harris topped the scoring list with 15 goals. Charlie Mortimore (14), John Hebdon (13) and Vic Reynolds (12) were not far behind.

John Burley in goal played in every game with John Hebdon, Charlie Mortimore and eighteen year old Vic 'Nobby' Reynolds only missing one league game. Ken Turner was once again the lynch-pin of the defence. Reg Taylor had finally made the right-back position his own. Newcomer Tony Ilsley from the Army, along with Bill Dowse, added some steel to the defence from midfield. Jim Collingwood and Mike Jacob played their part although long injuries restricted their appearances.

Representative honours were few; Charlie Mortimore and George Harris played for Surrey. Geoff Parsons the Isthmian League and Tony Ilsley for the Army. Matty Collins played in the Army Cup for REME in Germany.

The season was like the curate's egg, good in parts.

There were a number of promising youngsters such as George Harris, Vic Reynolds, Reg Taylor, Bill Dowse and Matt Collins who provided enough optimism to look forward to the future.

1960 - 1961

Season 1960-61 was very similar to the previous season, the same number of points (26) were gained and the final league position 13th was two positions below that achieved in 1959-60.

Unfortunately, two promising younger players had left the club prior to the start of the season. Reg Taylor who had made the right back position his own, decided to join Kingstonian. "Nobby" Reynolds who had successfully made the transition last season from local football to Isthmian football transferred his allegiance to Walton and Hersham.

In the Surrey Senior Cup Final, played at Woking in March, Walton and Hersham with Nobby Reynolds at inside forward comfortably beat Kingstonian 4-1. Reg Taylor plus Woking's Amateur Cup winner Jim Collingwood, played for Kingstonian.

A new look Woking side beat Ilford 2-1 in the opening fixture at Kingfield. Charlie Mortimore was playing for the Isthmian League against last seasons league champions, Tooting. His place was taken by another Amateur Cup favourite, John Hebdon, who scored one of the goals.

Michael Cashmore replaced Taylor at full-back. Younger brother Norman, moved back to wing-half with some success during the season. Ken Moody, another local product, played at centre-forward in the early games.

Geoff Parsons missed the early games due to a bone displacement in the foot and although he played another dozen matches his final game for Woking was on the 12th November at Clapton.

In a career spanning ten seasons, Geoff played over 300 league and cup games, represented Surrey many times, and was on the fringe of the England Amateur team more than once. He was an excellent club man and an example for all to follow.

Ken Turner once again had an excellent season, although reaching the veteran stage. He introduced a young seventeen year old wing-half from Wokingham, Rod Haider, who made his debut in the opening game at home to Ilford.

Early in the season, a professional coach was appointed. A forty-seven year old Scot, Bill "Jock" Gorrie, had previously played for Cowdenbeath and Reading Reserves.

One of the unsung heroes, physiotherapist Bert Knott, completed twenty-five years in the service of the club, having been appointed in 1935-36.

In a season with very few highlights, Charlie Mortimore still showed skills and maintained a goal scoring touch that was a great example to younger forwards.

In the league an excellent performance was produced at Corinthian Casuals in a 4-4 draw.

Casuals had previously won their four league games scoring nine goals without reply.

Mike Partridge, a full-back previously with Leytonstone added some maturity to the defence alongside Pat Finn who came into the side against Barking in November and kept his place for the season.

A young Pat Finn who made his debut in November 1960 and played his last game in February 1977. He was manager of Woking for a short spell at the end of 1976 - 1977 before being replaced by Fred Callaghan during October 1977.

Woking appeared to run out of steam in some games, losing early leads. In the game against Clapton in November, a 2-1 lead eventually ended as a 5-2 defeat. This was Clapton's first league win in thirteen games. At 2-1 Woking were reduced to nine players as both George Harris and goalkeeper John Burley were taken to hospital. Those remaining players found the handicap too much.

At league leaders Bromley, who were unbeaten after 14 games, Woking were leading 2-0 at half time but the final result ended 4-2 to Bromley.

The next game at home to Dulwich ended similarly with Woking storming into a 2-0 lead, and then being outplayed to finally lose 3-2.

A run of four straight league wins near the end of the season ensured a safe position in the league. Charlie found his scoring touch by notching eight goals in these games including a hat-trick against Maidstone.

During this run, a nineteen year old goalkeeper Brian Farris, took over from an injured John Burley and remained for a further nine seasons.

George Harris, in his second season with the club, scored regularly from the left wing, 26 goals in 37 games. Charlie managed 20 in the same number of games but no one else reached double-figures.

Wimbledon ended Woking's interest in the F.A. Cup and the Amateur Cup. The only consolation was that 3,928 people watched the second round Amateur Cup tie at Kingfield. Interest in the Surrey Senior Cup ended against Tooting after a replay.

Addlestone were despatched 3-1 in the first round of the Shield but Corinthian League club Dorking overcame their senior neighbours in the semi-final by the same 3-1 score.

Guildford City, the Southern League professionals, were beaten 3-2 at Joseph's Road in a vintage Woking performance. Woking were at the cross-roads, the old guard were moving on or retiring but with a few exceptions the youngsters were still learning.

Only George Harris won honours representing Surrey against Middlesex.

A free scoring winger, George Harris scored 40 goals in 68 appearances during seasons 1959 - 1960 and 1960 - 1961 for Woking. He then turned professional scoring 130 league goals in ten seasons with Newport, Watford, Reading and Cambridge.

1961 - 1962

The season opened amid letters and reports reflecting the growing concern over not paying players openly (shamateurism). Unfortunately the 'wealthy' clubs were creaming off the best players.

Nothing was won in season 1961-62 but success could be measured in the number of young players that made their mark in the first team. The experienced players such as Charlie Mortimore and Ken Turner ensured the youngsters transition, from, in some cases local football, was as smooth as possible.

Brian Farris who had come into the side at the latter end of last season did not miss a game and many times played brilliantly. John Burley, whom he replaced, finally resigned from the club after ten seasons. He had been a loyal member of the first team and played his part in winning the Amateur Cup in 1958. Norman Cashmore resigned after eight years at Kingfield to join Tooting and Mitcham. Matty Collins and Pat Finn left to join Kingstonian. As expected George Harris signed professional forms for Newport County.

Sixteen year old Ray Hyde, playing his first senior game away to Walthamstow, made club history by scoring the first goal of the new English football season within 20 seconds of the match starting.

Other players making their first team debuts in the first few matches were Dave Hirons, Peter Twitchen, "Bert" Williams and Johnnie Bangs, a prolific scorer whilst at Redhill, joined from Kingstonian.

Geoff Foulkes, a young stylish defender, did not quite fulfil his potential but nevertheless played with much skill.

When Johnnie Bangs did not live up to his reputation, twenty-year old Bruce Upton from Cobham replaced him at centre-forward, scored on his debut at Corinthian Casuals and ended the season with a final tally of 10 goals in 21 games. This included a hat-trick in a 5-1 win against Maidstone.

Another young player who played 19 games was Shaun Woods. He would play many more in the next seven seasons.

Unable to command a regular place, Mike Jacob a member of the 1958 squad left for Redhill.

Jim Collingwood, another member of the Amateur Cup Final side, returned to the club in December and stiffened up the defence during the successful run after the new year when Woking were not beaten in eight successive league games.

Compared with last season, Woking achieved one more point (27) and moved up from 13th to 10th. The forward line scored six less but the defence was eleven goals better. The finest performance in the league was the 2-1 home success against Walthamstow with Charlie scoring twice. Walthamstow were top of the league at this stage.

Another impressive victory was a 3-0 success at home to Tooting. Those old favourites Charlie Mortimore and John Hebdon scored the goals. Hebdon actually resigned to join Redhill early in the season but returned after Christmas.

Ernie Tindall, eventually, joined the club from Wokingham in December after a number of false starts. He scored on his debut away to Dulwich and was to be the main scorer throughout the rest of the 1960's.

The toughest victory of the season came at home to St. Albans, who quickly went 2-0 up in eight minutes. By the interval Woking were 4-2 in the lead with Charlie scoring a hat-trick, including two penalties. In the second half, against a very strong wind, only one goal was conceded in a final 4-3 victory.

Wimbledon provided the usual stumbling block in the cup. A 5-1 defeat at Plough Lane in the first qualifying round of the F.A. Cup did not tell the whole story. Woking were reduced to ten men when Ken Turner left the field with an injured ankle. The score at the time was 1-1.

Two victories in the F.A. Amateur Cup away to Corinthian Casuals and Eastbourne gave Woking a third round tie at home to Leytonstone. A best of the season attendance,

2,942 witnessed a hard fought 1-1 draw. In the replay a week later an equally hard fought affair saw Leytonstone win by the only goal of the game.

Woking and Tooting reached the final of the Surrey Senior Shield but, due to lack of time the tie would be played the following season. Alan Botley, another promising youngster, made his debut in the first round of the Shield and scored one of the goals in a 3-1 victory. Another goal in the 3-3 draw against Kingstonian gave Woking a replay chance which they duly won 2-1 at Richmond Road.

Towards the end of the season Johnny Bangs, Bob Stansbie and Bill Dowse all resigned for non-football reasons. John Mortimore was placed on the transfer list by Chelsea for a fee of £7,000. George Harris was transferred from Newport to Watford for £5,000. This proved to be a successful move as George scored over 50 league goals in only approximately 160 games. A good strike rate for a winger.

The achievements during the season were summarised in one of the Woking programmes as follows: "The confidence placed by the club in encouraging and fostering the younger players has been fully rewarded and the young senior side deserve great credit for the way they have played during the season".

1962 - 1963

Before the season 1962-63 commenced Rod Haider who had been thc regular wing-half for two seasons decided to join Kingstonian.

He believed that by joining Kingstonian he could further his career. With hindsight he was right, as Haider won every honour in the amateur game, including a record 65 international appearances for England, 10 at Kingstonian and 55 at Hendon.

Woking had a new chairman Ronald A.W. Cohen and a new president, the former chairman L.A. Gosden.

Prospects for the season looked good. A pre-season Netherlands tour, held to commemorate the 60th anniversary of the Heemstede Club was successfully completed. Three matches were won, one drawn and the decider lost. The runners-up cup plus two pennants and a decorated plate were brought back to Woking.

Optimism was high but eight league games without a win completed the worst start to the campaign for many years. The only success was an F.A. Cup victory against a Spartan League works side, Petters Sports.

Only Corinthian Casuals prevented Woking from being bottom of the league although when the teams met at the Oval in October, Woking were defeated 2-1. These were the only points gained by Corinthian Casuals in their first ten games.

Both Woking and Corinthian Casuals were still "true-blue" Amateur and with the changing face of amateur football players were difficult to keep. Clarrie Jarman again strongly defended the amateur code as the rest of non-league football looked for a more "open" situation and an end to under cover payments. Woking seemed to be a football factory, bringing young players to peak form only to lose them to more fashionable clubs with promises of extra expenses and hidden benefits.

The policy of bringing on the young players was in evidence against Corinthian Casuals. Seven players were 22 or under, Woods 18, Botley 18, Harrison (debut) 19, Foulkes 20, Bill Dowse 21, Farris 21 and Fitch 22.

Two draws were achieved in the first eight games, both 2-2's, one against Tooting at home and the other at Loakes Park versus Wycombe. Tooting finished third in the league so the draw was a good performance.

Bert French, a new signing, was one of the early successes. He was selected to represent Surrey against Sussex in December. This honour was fully merited.

Geoff Foulkes played the first thirteen games at centre-half but an injury against Maidstone brought back the evergreen Ken Turner, who played for the rest of the season.

Brian Finn, who in the future would set Woking's record number of competitive appearances at over 500, had left the club for Kingstonian only to return after a short period. He made his debut against

Wimbledon on 15th December 1962 and his final appearance was on 17th November 1973. His competitive edge was his greatest asset.

Only two league wins were completed in 1962 from eighteen games but the season was destined to last well into the cricket season. Woking's last game was played on the 29th May.

The winter was the severest since the big freeze after the second world war. It started snowing on Boxing Day, unfortunately not soon enough to abandon the game against Kingstonian which resulted in a 5-0 defeat.

January and most of February was a complete football whitewash, snow and ice remaining for weeks.

Woking made an unforgettable trip to Gloucester to play Lydbrook of the Gloucester Senior League in the Amateur Cup on 19th January. A combination of snowstorms and icy roads blocked out team and supporters alike. A night spent in a Church Hall resulted.

After countless postponements the game was finally played on the 23rd February with Woking winning 1-0. The only available ground being at AEI Ltd on the banks of the River Wye at Westbury-on-Severn.

On the 9th March the first league game was played since Boxing Day. Woking had a great 4-3 victory over Ilford, the current league leaders. Ernie Tindall hit a hat-trick including the winner in the last few minutes. The game was unusual as Bert French and two Ilford players were sent off. This was unheard of at that time.

Changes were made in the team over the last dozen games, some enforced. Bill Dowse resigned to join Basingstoke, his home town. Bob Billingsby came in at wing-half and a Woking Grammar school pupil, Brian Arnold, made a brilliant debut at home to Barking. He had a hand in all five goals.

In the last eight games five were won with one draw. With Jim Brennan, Bert French and Charlie Mortimore not available for the Easter Monday game at Maidstone a reshuffled cards triumphed 1-0. Nigel Wallington came in as left-back and held international winger Candy, and with Brian Farris having a brilliant game in goal, the points were secured with a Brian Arnold goal.

The final league position, 13th with 22 points, was poor considering the high hopes before the season started.

Charlie was top scorer with 24 league and cup goals. This included a club record of nine against Dorking in a 10-3 Surrey Senior Shield victory. Ernie Tindall scored 14 but no one else managed double figures, Brian Farris was ever-present with Ernie Tindall only missing one game and Bert French two games.

Brian Farris made his debut in 1960, he played over 430 competitive games before losing his place to Dave Collyer in 1970. A product of Woking's successful youth side, he replaced John Burley the 1958 Amateur Cup Final keeper.

The Surrey Senior Shield was won with a 4-1 victory over Petters Sports. Charlie and Bruce Upton scored two each.

Kingstonian ended Woking's interest in the Surrey Senior Cup with a 4-1 defeat. Wimbledon defeated the Cards 4-2 in the F.A. Cup and Walton beat Woking 2-1 in the Amateur Cup before 3,644 spectators.

Johnny Cowle resigned as reserve team secretary in November due to business and family commitments. He had joined the club in 1932 and played in the first team 1933 to 1938.

Attendance's dropped almost 50% which was not enough to self finance the club. The Progress Fund was keeping Woking Football Club alive which was not unique in football.

1963 - 1964

For the season 1963-64 the Isthmian League voted in the Athenian League sides Hendon, Sutton, Enfield and Hitchin. The first three named finished in the top five. There was no doubt now that the Isthmian League was the strongest Amateur League in the country and the increased number of matches required, meant most clubs were being encouraged to become equipped with floodlights.

Woking appointed Jack Elliott as manager, assisted by Charlie Mortimore on the coaching side. Chairman R.A. Cohen retired in September through ill health.

A relaxing bath after a tough game in 1963 - 1964.
A smiling Ernie Tindall, second from the right, must have scored.

Very little was achieved in a mediocre season with a fourth from bottom finish, the same as last year. The defence was poor, 88 goals conceded and the forward line only scored 44 goals.

The loss of Ken Turner at the back and the fact that Charlie Mortimore only played 15 league games, removed too much experience from basically a young side. Experienced campaigners, Jim Collingwood and Bert French gave of their best but it was a tough league.

The home form was more than adequate but only one away game against bottom of the table Clapton was won.

Brian Fuller, an exciting talent from the reserves and Brian S. Arnold signed from Alton Town, were brought in to strengthen the defence.

Brian Finn was played in an attacking role next to Ernie Tindall and young wingers Brian Arnold and Shaun Woods provided the crosses.

Two defeats in the first two games, with the defence leaking goals meant changes had to be made. French took over at centre-half with B.S. Arnold moving across to right back. Three successive home victories resulted with Tindall, Finn and Woods scoring the majority of the goals.

Unfortunately, the team found difficulty in settling down. Positional changes were made, which did not help the continuity of the side. Brian Arnold was tried at centre-forward. With his pace and strength the decision was not unreasonable, but it was soon established he was happier as a winger. Ted Pearce replaced Bob Billingsby in mid-field but it was a difficult position to fill. Brian Finn finally made the right side of midfield his own property.

Brian Farris played in all games, Woods, B.S. Arnold, Collingwood, Tindall, Finn, B. Arnold and French, all played 30 or more league games. Top scorer was Ernie Tindall with 13 league goals. No other player reached double figures.

Lennie Logan a local player from West End who played three games at centre-half, died in March under tragic circumstances. His potential would now never be realised.

Jack Elliott left the club due to the run of poor results and lack of confidence from the players. A selection committee was introduced until Charlie Mortimore was appointed chief coach in March.

Most of the good performances were achieved at home. Tooting, Kingstonian, Leytonstone, Walthamstow and Wycombe were all comprehensively beaten at Kingfield. The best performance away from Kingfield was a 2-2 draw with sixth-placed Oxford City.

A terrible spell in December resulted in five consecutive league games being lost by four clear goals, three 5-1 and two 4-0 defeats.

There was very little joy in Cup games. In the F.A. Cup, Dorking were beaten 3-2 which brought Guildford City to Kingfield in the first qualifying round. A tough battle in front of 2,300 resulted in a 2-0 defeat, but Guildford only made certain of victory in the closing minutes.

Croydon Amateurs, a Spartan League side, defeated Woking 4-2 for the second time in three years to end any thoughts of Surrey Senior Cup success.

In the F.A. Amateur Cup a 0-0 draw at Dagenham in which Tindall was stretchered off, then produced one of Woking's better performances in a 3-1 replay victory at Kingfield. Two goals from Dave Metherall and one direct from a corner by Brian Arnold gave Woking a relatively easy tie against Eastwood Town, of the Notts Alliance League.

A game in which Woking should have won comfortably resulted in a 2-1 defeat and ended any thoughts of cup glory for the season.

Wimbledon completed a hat-trick of league titles before moving on to the Southern League prior to achieving Football League status. Hendon, who finished runners-up, scored a magnificent 124 goals, a premier division record.

Woking had felt the power of Hendon's attack with defeats 6-1 at home and 5-1 away.

Despite the power of the top clubs, Clarrie Jarman signed an F.A. oath of allegiance to amateurism to reaffirm that Woking would not turn professional.

1964 - 1965

The man who first sold programmes for Woking Football Club when he was six years old in 1902, resigned as Hon. Secretary prior to the start of the 1964-65 season. Clarrie Jarman was elected to the club's committee in 1927. He had held the position of Hon. Secretary since 1941 and was one of the "gang of four" who restarted the club in 1945. He remained a trustee of the club for a time, and is still watching games in 1995.

Another great servant of the club, Mr J.H. Goddard, Hon. Treasurer for 22 years resigned at the same time.

Claude Elmer and John Francis succeeded the "old team" as Secretary and Treasurer.

The Progress Fund, which had been operating for one year, kept the club afloat, as the operational costs of running the club far outweighed the revenue through the turnstiles. The new floodlights were basically paid for by the Fund. Four 100 ft steel towers with 96 x 1500 watt lamps would light up Kingfield.

19th November 1964 was a milestone in the history of Woking Football Club; the floodlights were switched on. Marching bands greeted Chelsea, who were leaders of the 1st division of the Football League at the time. Household names now, such as George Graham and Terry Venables, played against Woking before 2,688 spectators.

Floodlight football at Woking was still a novelty and the players rose to the occasion in the first total floodlit league game a week later. Wealdstone were the visitors and at the end of the game Woking were the winners by 2-1 with Jimmy Martin scoring both goals. An all red strip was worn.

There were very few highlights in a disastrous season. Woking finished bottom of the league with only 18 points from 38 games. Seven games were won, all at home. Only three draws were obtained away from Kingfield. 113 goals were conceded, six goals were let-in five times, and although four goals were scored away to the eventual champions Hendon, unfortunately seven were conceded.

Jim Collingwood, the last remaining member of the 1958 Amateur Cup winning team still playing, stands next to Brian Finn and Brian Farris, who are first and second in the all-time list of competitive appearances

next few seasons but in 1964 his talent was raw and unhoned. Pat Finn played in the last dozen games. Jim Collingwood, the last link with the 1958 team, strove manfully to plug the defensive gaps but the legs were not what they were. In December Peter Davies, son of reserve team manager, Bill, rejoined Woking, but in February he suffered a facial fracture during which he lost a contact lens which he instinctively caught as he fell. Vic Reynolds, now playing in Australia, was selected for New South Wales against Russia and was certainly in-line for the Australian team.

Charlie Mortimore concentrated on coaching the team, only playing four league and cup games. His final tally of competitive games for Woking since 1953 totalled 362 with 250 goals. His strike rate was phenomenal. This, plus his overall skill and leadership qualities placed him as one of Woking's greatest ever players.

Thirty-eight players were used throughout the season in a desperate effort to stem the tide. Most were young and inexperienced. One famous name reappeared, that of Lintott. Colin, a distant relation of Evelyn, did not last too long, leaving the club after some "aggressive" performances.

Good football was always attempted but the team was basically not good enough, although Brian Fuller, Shaun Woods and Brian Farris gained representative honours with Surrey.

Fuller, Finn, Farris and Woods played most of the games. Tindall, the previous years top scorer only played in the first six games. Brian Arnold lost form and confidence and eventually left the club. Bert French only played in half the games before retiring. Shaun Woods finished with 13 goals but no one else managed double figures. John McBryde a fast, skilful, right-winger, with undoubted talent would come good in the

Guildford City dumped Woking out of the F.A. Cup 3-1 at Kingfield although this was one of Woking's better performances.

In the Amateur Cup, it took a replay after extra time before Bromley finally defeated Woking.

In the Surrey Senior Cup, local side Westfield, looked to have chances against their more illustrious neighbours, but even at their lowest Woking still had enough class to win comfortably 3-0. Leatherhead defeated Woking in the second round and also in the Surrey Invitation Cup. Both games went to replays after 2-2 draws. Charlie scored his final goal for Woking in the Invitation Cup.

A snap snow storm in March caused confusion. All local football was cancelled and notices were posted at the ground. The Woking players arrived at Kingfield and went home thinking the game at Dulwich was off. Only those living locally could be contacted to travel to Dulwich.

Woking Football Club had reached their lowest point for many years although results could only improve next season.

1965 - 1966

Having been unanimously re-elected to the Isthmian League, season 1965-66 had to be an improvement over the previous campaign. There was only one way up from rock bottom. The injection of new players in key positions came off. "Jock" Wood, from Addlestone, was a tower of strength at centre half. Ernie Tindall came back from Wokingham and provided the "punch" up-front with 24 goals in 31 league games. Graham Cooper a local lad, joined from Kingstonian.

Stuart McPhee from Wealdstone was an inspiration in midfield.

Brian Finn was re-elected captain. As always he gave 110% throughout the season.

A sad day for the club was the death of Les Cheeseman, who had only been recently elected Chairman of the Club. His larger than life personality would be sorely missed. A welcome bonus came in late September with a £3,500 grant towards the floodlights cost, from the Ministry of Education and Science.

Woking started the season with a 1-0 victory over Leytonstone. An Ernie Tindall goal defeated the eventual champions.

Roy Keeley, the nephew of Ronnie Rooke (whose stay at Woking was too brief, scoring 29 goals in 25 games during 1932-33 before turning professional with Fulham and winning a league championship medal with Arsenal), burst dramatically onto the scene. In the space of ten days he had scored a hat-trick for the 3rd XI, notched a pair for the seconds and scored two goals on his debut for the first team. Nineteen games and six goals later he was gone, as quickly as he had arrived. After losing his place he decided to join Cobham.

Brian Fuller who had emerged as a potentially great player resigned at the end of November and joined Enfield. This was a sign of the times with the more fashionable clubs offering "incentives" to the better players.

Woking's position in the league table tended to hover around mid-table for most of the season. Performances were erratic, a 3-1 lead against Tooting was lost in the second half in a 3-3 draw. A 7-1 defeat at Walthamstow, who actually finished below them was probably the poorest display of the season. A few weeks after this defeat Hendon, the champions were slaughtered 5-1 at Kingfield. Woking played some superb football even giving Hendon a goal start in 8 minutes. According to the newspaper of the day "the Hendon supporters applauded the Cardinals off the field at the end of one of the best games seen at Kingfield for a long time".

The bubble burst at Barking the following Saturday with a 6-0 defeat. Not one of the following eight league games was lost but only one of the final six games was won, 3-2 at Wealdstone, who had defeated Hendon at Wembley to win the Amateur Cup.

John Mortimore now at QPR, persuaded Chelsea to play Woking for his testimonial, 2,179 turned up to see Chelsea win 7-1.

In the F.A. Cup two rounds were safely negotiated. Addlestone perished 9-0 with John McBryde claiming 3 goals. Walton were beaten 4-0 but Guildford City proved too strong in a 6-0 defeat at Joseph's Road before 3,230. Walton gained revenge by winning 1-0 in the Surrey Senior Cup.

Once again Woking were defeated by supposedly lesser opponents when Eastern League Stowmarket won 3-2 in the 1st round of the Amateur Cup.

The final of the Surrey Senior Shield was reached by defeating Kingstonian 2-1 but Tooting were too strong winning 3-1.

Kingstonian reversed the result in the Surrey Invitation Cup beating Woking 4-2.

The Mithras Floodlit Cup gave Woking some success. Guildford City were beaten 1-0 over two legs which included a 0-0 at Joseph's Road. This was sweet revenge for the 6-0 F.A. Cup defeat. Horsham fell in the next round 5-4. In the quarter final first leg Cheshunt were defeated 1-0 on a pitch like a quagmire but nerves seemed to take over in a 4-2 home loss, so losing the tie 4-3 on aggregate.

Brian Finn played in every game. Pat Finn, Jock Wood, Shaun Woods and Stuart McPhee played in the majority. Ernie Tindall top scored with 27 goals in 45 matches but Graham Cooper and Eamonn O'Riordan were the only other players to score ten or more goals. Brian Farris unfortunately lost his confidence and was replaced by Harry Rose for the last dozen fixtures.

An invite to a Belgium tournament at Whitsun provided Woking with two trophies, for the most sporting team in the tournament and for the best player, John McBryde. One game was won and two games were lost.

Woking finished with 34 points and a final position of 12th. which was a satisfactory outcome.

Perhaps one of the seasons star turns was a black Labrador dog that regularly invaded the pitch and evaded his would be captors.

1966 - 1967

Season 1966-67 was reasonably successful, 11th place in the league was an improvement of one place over the previous season, with two extra points. An extra bonus was to reach the Surrey Invitation Cup Final but time prevented the final tie being played until the following season.

One sad occurrence was the death of Brian Fuller, the former Woking full back, who was killed in a motor cycle road accident during the summer. This was a tragic loss not only to his relatives, but to football, as he was on the verge of international honours.

Regulars from last season Pat Finn and Shaun Woods transferred to Kingstonian although Shaun returned to Woking later in the season. "Jock" Wood returned to former club Addlestone.

Ken Norgate from Alton, Alan Sexton a Physical Education teacher from Midhurst and "Jock" McIntyre from Tooting filled the defensive gaps. Unfortunately McIntyre was transferred to Glasgow by his employer, the Bank of Scotland, before the year was out. Gerry McDevitt took over at centre-half from McIntyre until he also left the Woking area in March, Roger Lewis from Merrow, the centre-half from the reserves played the rest of the games.

Harry Rose started as No.1 goalkeeper, but after four games Brian Farris regained the goalkeeping spot and held it for the rest of the season, despite the presence in the reserve team of Tony Hollins brother of Chelsea star John.

Brian Finn, elected captain once again, played his 100th consecutive first team game in a friendly against the Army. A suitably inscribed tankard, presented by the club chairman Mr S Tailford, marked the occasion.

Ernie Tindall had a tremendous season, scoring 42 league and cup goals, breaking Joe Perryman's record of 41 goals in season 1926-27. A great effort.

Woking had a good start to the season with a 2-2 draw at St. Albans, O'Riordan scoring both and a 3-2 win at Sandy Lane, Mitcham against Corinthian Casuals where Tindall notched a late winner. The bubble burst in the next game at home to Hendon. A 2-0 reverse before 1,095 spectators was a disappointment.

The first ten league games only produced two wins. Sutton and Tooting gave Woking a lesson in finishing by inflicting 5-1 defeats.

Ten goals from Tindall in the next nine games gave Woking five league wins moving them into a respectable mid-table position. He was aided by flying wingers Merrick Trevaskis, ex-Portsmouth and Johnny McBryde who had just signed amateur forms for Brentford.

In the next game Wycombe thrashed Woking 6-2 at Kingfield.

The very next week, playing second placed Tooting at Sandy Lane with seemingly very little chance, Woking gave an inspired performance with Peter Davies causing all sorts of problems in a 6-2 victory.

Woking continued to play well against the top teams, both Sutton, who finished champions and Enfield lost 2-0 at Kingfield, but only one win in the last eight league games prevented Woking from attaining a higher league position.

Victories were achieved in all the major cups. Hampshire League Basingstoke and Sussex League Littlehampton were defeated in the F.A. Cup before a surprising loss 2-1 at Horsham in the 3rd Qualifying Round.

A 6-1 aggregate victory over Horsham in the Mithras Cup gave Woking some revenge.

In the Amateur Cup an eight goal thriller at Alton Town ended 5-3 in Woking's favour. An excellent victory at Barking in the next round paired Woking with Southall. Despite going ahead with a Graham Cooper goal, Woking finally lost 2-1.

A hard fought "replay" victory 5-3 was achieved against local rivals Addlestone in the Surrey Senior Cup. Leatherhead proved too good in the second round with a 2-1 victory.

Woking reached the final of the Surrey Invitation Cup with three games all going to extra time, two against Met. Police and a 2-1 semi-final victory against Croydon Amateurs in which Tindall scored both.

A crowd of 1,700 watched Woking draw 0-0 at home to Maidenhead in the quarter-final of the Mithras Cup but unfortunately Maidenhead already held a 2 goal lead from the first leg.

Ernie Tindall topped the goalscoring with 42 goals. Graham Cooper had a fine season scoring 19 goals. O'Riordan was the only other scorer in double figures.

Johnny McBryde arguably the fastest winger in the league had a tremendous season providing Ernie with many crosses for his goals.

Brian Farris represented the F.A. and Surrey and Johnny McBryde toured with Middlesex Wanderers.

Another youngster with great potential made his debut late in the season. Trevor Waughman opened his account by scoring against Maidstone. Like many Woking youngsters he learnt his trade with Woking, played a couple of seasons and then moved to pastures new.

At the beginning of the year an award was made to a loyal servant, Fred Keefe, who completed 21 playing seasons. He was captain of the 'A' team this season.

Altogether a satisfactory if not spectacular season.

Unfortunately to save cash the reserve team would not function next season.

1967 - 1968

Although two trophies were won during season 1967-68 the overall performance of the team was poor. The club finished fourth from bottom with only eight league wins and twenty-four points. This was 12 points and six places below last seasons performance.

After the promise of the previous two seasons it was expected that results would improve further, but this did not occur.

Many friends were made in a short pre-season tour of Ireland, this despite losing both games to Cliftonville and Larne.

Regular first team players Graham Cooper and Ken Norgate left before the season proper started with John McBryde and Eamonn O'Riordan tendering their resignation during September.

Richard "Dinger" Elton who had joined in the final months of the previous season only missed one league game. Roger Lewis and Keith Scott had spells at centre-half before Christmas with Brian Oliver replacing Ken Norgate at full-back.

Trevor Waughman was a success in an otherwise lacklustre season. He scored 13 goals in partnership upfront with Ernie Tindall.

Brian Finn once again was ever present and played his 150th consecutive first team game in October.

The first trophy was won in September. Two goals by John McBryde, the winner in extra time, enabled Woking to defeat Tooting in the held over Surrey Invitation Cup Final. This was one of John's last games for Woking, as he left for Kingstonian in mid-September.

Two draws in the first five league games was not an ideal start to the season but two cracking midweek games against Wycombe briefly gave the team some confidence. Ernie Tindall bagged a pair in a 3-3 draw at Kingfield and Trevor Waughman did the same in a splendid 4-2 victory at Loakes Park. Two more wins followed but three consecutive 5-0 defeats albeit against the top three sides in the country, Enfield, Sutton and Hendon, showed the quality gap between the top sides and Woking. Nevertheless, Woking achieved four more wins before the new year, and draws away to St. Albans and Walthamstow who both finished in the top six, put them near a mid-table position.

Unfortunately only one win in the last thirteen games left Woking in the bottom four. Ninety goals against gave an indication of where most of the problems lay.

This lack of success led to the appointment in late March of Bill Mitchell a qualified F.A. Coach late of the Royal Navy, as Manager. Charlie Mortimore immediately resigned from his duties as Chief Coach. He was perhaps unlucky that the glory days overshadowed everything that came after. The youngsters that were drafted into the team were not quite ready for the big time.

Success in the Surrey Senior Shield gave Woking their second trophy. Wins against Addlestone and Kingstonian matched Woking against Athenian League side Leatherhead. New player Sammy Malcolmson scored a hat-trick in a 3-2 victory to lift the Shield.

Malcolmson emigrated some years later and represented New Zealand in the World Cup qualifying rounds.

Sammy Malcolmson, a Royal Navy player, scored a hat-trick in only his third game for the club to win the Surrey Senior Shield in 1967 - 1968. Some years later he emigrated to New Zealand and played in the World Cup qualifying round prior to the 1974 finals.

There were defeats at the first hurdle in the F.A. Cup, Amateur Cup, Surrey Senior Cup and Mithras Cup.

A new venture entered during the season was the participation in the Wycombe Midweek Floodlit League. Ten games were played against Wokingham, Maidenhead, Slough, Southall and Wycombe. Some success was achieved with five wins and one draw.

Ernie Tindall finished top scorer with 19 goals, with Trevor Waughman on 13.

Tindall and Stuart McPhee played for an F.A. XI against the Army during the season.

Alan Morton who was to play a part in the club's success in later years had played four games before being signed on pro forms by Crystal Palace. A £100 donation to Woking Club Funds was made in appreciation of help given in respect of the signing; £100 was useful money 25 years ago.

League attendances dropped from a total of 14,900 to 10,762 with a top attendance of 984. This represented a loss in revenue of nearly £500. Survival was even more dependent on the revenue from the Cardinals Progress Fund.

1968 - 1969

Season 1968-69 opened with a five match unbeaten run. This included a magnificent 3-2 victory at Sutton, who were among the strongest teams around at the time. Ernie Tindall came off the subs bench to smash home a late winner. The next home game against Oxford drew a crowd of 1,100. Despite pulling level after being 2-0 in arrears Woking then gave Oxford the points with a defensive error. True to form in recent years, Woking lost three league games in a row which effectively negated their good start.

New 'boy' Derek Godwin interrupted his holidays to travel back from Southend to play the opening game at St. Albans. This was the club spirit required by all the players.

Godwin had previous experience with Hendon, and was the current captain of the Royal Navy. It was unfortunate that both he and Sammy Malcolmson missed games because of Royal Navy and Combined Services representative football.

Two local players Gerry Carver and Ray Povey held their first team places throughout the season and with utility player John Moore providing cover for all defensive positions the nucleus of a good defence, which included established players such as Farris, Oliver, Elton and Sexton was in place.

Brian Finn, captain for the third season running, gave his usual 110% from midfield. His magnificent consecutive run of games tallied 216 before a business trip finally ended the sequence. He had been presented with a set of goblets after the Shield Final last season, to commemorate 200 consecutive games.

Ernie Tindall played his last game for Woking on the 9th December. His record over eight seasons speaks for itself, 134 goals in 269 appearances. A goal every other game is an excellent strike rate which places Ernie as one of Woking's best ever strikers.

A run of nine straight losses, which included being the first side to lose to Corinthian Casuals saw Woking tumble down the league.

Only one loss in seven matches helped to stop the rot but defeat in the last three games ensured only a final position of 5th from bottom, one place better than last year although the number of points ended one less.

Most of the season's action was reserved for the F.A. Cup. Three qualifying rounds were safely negotiated at the expense of Crawley, Addlestone and Wokingham. Wimbledon, then a Southern League side, provided the next opposition at Plough Lane, but in Woking's best performance of the season a 2-0 victory was achieved in front of 2,346.

Brentford away in the 1st round proved too tough an obstacle, but not before Woking had given the league side a few scares in a 2-0 defeat before 5,990 fans.

Early dismissals in all the other major cups was a great disappointment although Egham was brushed aside in a 6-0 victory only for Tooting in the next round of the Surrey Senior Cup to comprehensively defeat Woking 5-0 at Kingfield.

In the Wycombe Floodlit Cup, which had replaced the Floodlit League, Woking put up a great performance in defeating Slough 2-1 on aggregate, but in the next round Addlestone created a surprise by defeating Woking 2-0 after a 0-0 draw at Kingfield.

Waughman finished top scorer with 17 goals, Tindall managed 11 in 22 appearances with Carver being the only other double figure scorer. Brian Oliver who took over as an emergency centre-forward towards the end of the season led the line well scoring three goals.

The headline in the local newspaper in May read "Geoff Hamm returns to Woking F.C.". Geoff, who was managing local side Lion Sports agreed to help out the injury hit Woking reserve side by turning out with five other Lion Sports players.

One link with the past ended on 15th October when Harry Goddard, Woking's hon. treasurer for twenty years after the war, died.

BRENTFORD FOOTBALL CLUB

OFFICIAL PROGRAMME

Season 1968-69 **Price 9d.**

Football Association Cup
First Round

BRENTFORD
v.
WOKING

Saturday, 16th November, 1968

Kick-off 3.15 p.m.

Next Home Games

SATURDAY, 30th NOVEMBER, 1968	SATURDAY, 14th DECEMBER, 1968
BRENTFORD v. HALIFAX TOWN	BRENTFORD v. SWANSEA TOWN
Football League Div. IV	Football League Div. IV
Kick-off 3.15 p.m.	Kick-off 3.15 p.m.

GROUND: GRIFFIN PARK, EALING ROAD, BRENTFORD

It had taken 42 years for Woking to fight through the F.A. Cup qualifying rounds to the first round. Unfortunately Brentford of Division 4 were too strong, winning 2-0.

Chapter 10

MANAGERIAL CHANGES; AMATEUR - PROFESSIONAL PLAYER DISTINCTION REMOVED. THE 1970'S

1969 - 1970

Prior to the commencement of season 1969-70, Graham Cooper signed for Walton and Hersham, Trevor Waughman joined Sutton and Danny Godwin was posted to a distant base. Tim Binks a free-scoring forward signed from Waterlooville. John McCormack (27) and Derek Edwards (22) signed from Kingstonian. Micky Elliott joined from Guildford City.

Away to Enfield was the hardest start possible, as they had won the league for the last two seasons and completed a hat-trick of championships by the end of the season. A 1-0 defeat was therefore a moral victory.

The next four games were won with new boys, McCormack, Elliott and Binks scoring eight of eleven goals scored. As in the last few seasons, Woking then lost their way; five consecutive League games were lost without a goal being scored.

A major signing was the capture of Trevor Smith (26), captain of Hayes. He had represented Middlesex and the Athenian League and was a current Middlesex Wanderer recently touring Japan and Holland. He made his debut at home to Kingstonian on 9th September.

Ken Holder who had played 491 games for Tooting signed in October. He had represented the Army, Surrey, London, Isthmian League and Southern Counties. He made his debut at Oxford in a 2-2 draw against a side previously unbeaten at home. Goals from McCormack and Elliott gave Woking a hard earned point after being 2-0 down.

A long injury list during October and November did not help the side to settle into any rhythm. Alan Sexton, who had been a skilful performer over the last two seasons contracted glandular fever in November which put him out of action for three months.

Despite this Bill Mitchell released promising youngsters Johnny Folan, Brian Haddow, Tony Davies and Nigel Hall, much to the frustration of players and supporters alike keen to keep the talent of the future.

Just prior to Christmas, David Gale signed from Walton. He had played for Portsmouth Reserves and Wimbledon and was a proven goalscorer. He proved this by notching four goals in his third game against Clapton. Dave Leonard who had been a regular first team player for Sutton, signed for Woking in early December.

Woking now had quality players but the blend and consistency did not occur. Isolated performances gave an indication of this quality, a 7-1 thrashing of Clapton, a superb win 3-2 at Hendon after being two goals in arrears, and a 2-2 draw at home to Barking who at that time headed the league table. After this game the final seven matches were lost.

A final league position of 15th with only ten wins out of 38 games was poor fare considering the number of good players at the club.

In the F.A. Cup Chichester were beaten 4-1 with Tim Binks scoring twice. Binks scored his first hat-trick for the club in the next round against Addlestone in a 3-3 thriller but two goals from ex-player O'Riordan gave Addlestone a 2 nil victory in the replay.

Two cracking games against Walton in the first round of the Amateur Cup saw Woking lose 2-1 at Walton in the replay. McCormack's goal separated the sides until nine minutes from the end when Grondona equalised for Walton and three minutes from time Walton snatched an undeserved winner. A crowd of 2,200 had packed Kingfield to see the first game end goalless. This scoreline was entirely due to Woking's goalkeeper Brian Farris who stopped everything Walton threw at him.

Walton, who were becoming a bogey team to Woking also defeated them by a resounding 4-0 in the semi-final of the Surrey Senior Cup. Victories over Corinthian Casuals and Croydon gave Woking hope that the Senior Cup would be won but Walton prevented this dream being fulfilled.

A bright start was made in the Premier Floodlit League with three victories in four unbeaten games, but the next six games yielded only two draws. Despite a 3-1 victory at front runners Slough and two draws against Guildford City, Woking finished about halfway but it provided an opportunity to mix first team and reserve players in competitive fixtures.

Tim Binks finished top scorer with 23 goals, John McCormack scored 16 and Dave Gale claimed 10 in 24 games.

Woking Reserves won the Reserve Section pipping Leytonstone in the run in. This was their first championship win since 1936.

Amateur Cup Final favourite Geoff Parsons emigrated to Australia in February. Bill Mitchell was pushed 'upstairs' as a full-time general manager with no team responsibilities. Harry Hughes (40) was appointed team manager in May. He was a former captain of Bournemouth during their F.A. Cup exploits playing nearly 300 games for Bournemouth and Gillingham. Denny Rose joined him as coach/trainer. He had been a goalkeeper at Charlton and Alton and had developed a partnership with Hughes in non-league circles.

A great day for the social side of the club occurred with the opening of the new clubhouse (Cardinal Club) on 17th December. L A Gosden who had been in office since 1933 performed the opening ceremony. The cost approached £14,000 but it was a significant step forward.

1970 - 1971

Season 1970-71 was the most successful since 1957-58 with a top ten finish and runner-up in the Surrey Senior Cup. Harry Hughes in his first season as manager had made a good start. In October, Kingfield was chosen to host an amateur international match, England defeated Northern Ireland 1-0. Some years earlier Woking had hosted a Northern Ireland v Czechoslovakia youth international. A young Pat Jennings kept goal that day.

Prior to the season starting, the brightest prospect in the youth team, Billy Holmes, signed professional forms for Millwall. Players arriving in August were Dave Collyer, goalkeeper from Kingstonian, Ken Oram the RAF forward from Oxford City. Andy Christmas (18) ex-England Youth came from Bournemouth and Pat Finn rejoined from Kingstonian. John Hazell who came with a good pedigree had trouble settling into the side and finally left for Wealdstone in November. Woking continued their services connection by signing the diminutive Ken Heath from Oxford City and the Army. Alan Sexton left in the new year due to a move from the area.

Ken Oram, a prolific scorer from 1971 to 1977, was known as the gentleman of soccer. He played many times for the Royal Air Force.

Ken Oram heading the ball towards the goal, with Micky Elliott and Richard Elton (No 4) waiting for any rebounds. The earth mound and the covered structure in the background was removed in the 1990's ready for Conference football.

Brian Farris who made his first team debut in February 1961 finally played his last game in August 1970 after 15 years at the club and 437 first team competitive games. Collyer replaced him but Brian played again at Kingfield in Oxford's colours in late March.

Three wins and a draw in the first four league games gave Woking a dream start. This included a 3-2 win at Hendon in the opening game of the season. Two goals by Elliott and one by Binks repeated last seasons result.

A 3-0 defeat at Leytonstone marked the end of Farris's Woking career. Dave Collyer made the position his for the next four seasons and ranked among Woking's best ever keepers.

Action from a home league game is season 1970 - 1971. Richard Elton is just beaten to the ball. Dave Leonard looks on.

Oram and Binks looked to be a potent strike-force but knee problems kept Binks sidelined until he finally underwent a cartilage operation late in the season. Dave Gale only played intermittently and required an operation on his foot. Micky Elliott who had started strongly then had a long term injury and didn't appear in the first team until December. Dave Leonard was played in a more forward role with much success.

The Finn brothers played in every game (62) and formed an effective full back partnership. With Derek Edwards a commanding figure in central defence, defensively Woking had one of their best ever seasons.

Woking's away form was a revelation securing 8 victories, equalling the number of losses.

Major victories included the 3-2 victory at Hendon and the double over third placed St. Albans who only lost five league games all season.

Ninth place with 18 victories for 42 points represented a major improvement. Continuity helped the team's stability, as seven players played 32 or more league games.

Top scorer in his first season was Ken Oram with 20 goals, Tim Binks totalled 12 in 27 full games, with Dave Leonard claiming eleven goals.

One interesting scoreline was Woking's 5-0 defeat of Corinthian Casuals. Nothing spectacular in that, but three penalties were scored by different players, Christmas, Leonard and Oram.

Another match remembered by many was the home league match against Hendon. Dave Collyer was injured and the smallest man on the park, Ken Heath went into goal much to the amusement of the crowd.

Richard "Dinger" Elton and Andy Christmas both utility players had a role to play throughout the season filling many different positions due to injuries.

Who can jump the highest?
Oram (9) and Elton (4) do their best.

In the F.A. Cup, East Grinstead and Worthing were beaten fairly easily. An Oram goal gave Woking the lead at Crawley in the next round but the Cards finally faded to a 3-1 defeat.

Finchley, with the help of ex-Woking player Stuart McPhee defeated Woking 2-1 in the 1st round of the Amateur Cup.

Goalmouth action shows Ken Oram heading the ball over the bar in the Amateur Cup 1st Round away to Finchley, January 1971.
The game was lost 2-1. Other Woking players include No 4 Elton and in the background Leonard and Edwards.

This was after Woking had beaten Swaythling Athletic at the second attempt 2-1.

The Surrey Senior Cup provided Woking's best achievements in the cup competitions. Kingstonian were easily defeated 3-0 in the first round with Ken Oram slotting in two goals. Another Oram goal defeated Dulwich at Champion Hill. League leaders Sutton were beaten 1-0 in the semi-final with Trevor Smith notching the vital goal.

Mighty Walton proved too strong in the final at London Road, Redhill, defeating Woking 3-0. This was the beginning of the great era for the Swans.

Fourteen games were played in the Premier Floodlit League. Although only five games were won, young players were being blooded in the first team. Players such as Dennis Cheeseman and Hans Van den Berg gave much optimism for the future.

1971 - 1972

The improved playing record achieved in 1970-71 was not maintained in season 1971-72.

It was difficult to know the reason why, as the squad had changed very little. Geoff Chapple, a strong wing-half, signed from Alton Town and Alan Pentecost, whose pedigree involved Kingstonian, Sutton, Wealdstone and Oxford University missed very few games in his first season. Tim Binks had left the club and David Gale decided to return to Walton after losing his first team place in October.

Injuries reduced Dave Leonard's appearances to 18 league games. Basically the team did not perform consistently enough. This was highlighted by the fact that at no time during the season were two consecutive league games won. The final position of 14th was five places down on last season. Only eleven victories were gained.

The first three games produced no points and ten goals conceded.

The first win of the season came when Oxford City were heavily beaten 4-1 at Kingfield with Geoff Chapple making an impressive debut. The next game at home to Hendon produced a hard fought 1-1 draw. Two goals by Gale gave Woking a comfortable victory at Dulwich but the next five games produced only two draws.

This intermittent league form carried on throughout the season. Draws at Ilford and Sutton were the pick of the league results.

A good performance at Slough in the F.A. Cup gave Woking a home replay but Slough struck twice to end hopes of an F.A. Cup run.

Three victories in the Amateur Cup against Wembley, Alton and North Shields gave Woking a home tie against Blyth Spartans. Blyth had reached the third round of the F.A. Cup beating two league clubs before losing to Reading 6-1 after a replay. Three second half goals by Blyth disappointed a crowd of 2,116.

In the Premier Floodlight League the first four games yielded three wins and a draw but Woking flattered to deceive. From their fourteen games, six were won, five were lost and three were drawn. Guildford City were beaten twice. Against Horsham, Dave Collyer didn't arrive until after 20 minutes, Alan Pentecost went into goal until Dave came on.

Against all the odds Woking finally won the Surrey Senior Cup beating old rivals Walton 1-0. Despite having Pat Finn sent off Woking held on to an Alan Pentecost goal for three quarters of the game with ten men. Sutton had been defeated in the semi-final for the second successive year. Ken Oram scored all six Woking goals in the competition up to the final including a hat-trick against Corinthian Casuals in the first round.

Collyer, B. Finn, P. Finn and Pentecost played in all the league games with Smith only missing one. Oram was top scorer for the second year running with 23 goals in all competitions. Alan Pentecost scored 18 goals.

Brian Finn had a tremendous season and was a worthy winner of the Player of the Season award. Being the captain he led by example.

Winning the Surrey Senior Cup in the final match of the season gave the club and the players some reward for an indifferent season. It was fifteen years ago that the County Cup had last been won.

After 45 years association with various positions on the committee, Clarrie Jarman decided to retire as a Trustee of the club. He sold programmes at matches at the turn of the century and would no doubt support the team in the coming seasons. His contribution to the club could not be stated adequately in words alone.

MEMBERS OF THE PARTY

OFFICIALS

Member-in-Charge :
D. W. McKenzie (President and Chairman)
B. D. East (Vice-Chairman)
M. I. Whittingham (Hon. Secretary)

Team Manager : **K. C. Lister** (Leytonstone)
Trainer : **D. Jones** (Enfield)

PLAYERS

1	**A. Williams**	England and Enfield
2	**A. Jennings**	Hendon
3	**P. Deadman**	England and Hendon
4	**E. Powell (Captain)**	England and Wycombe W.
5	**J. Delaney**	England and Wycombe W.
6	**A. Phillips**	Wales and Hendon
7	**P. Wood**	St. Albans City
8	**J. Payne**	England and Enfield
9	**T. Bass**	England and Hendon
10	**J. Butterfield**	England and Enfield
11	**J. Baker**	England and Hendon
12	**A. Turley**	England and Enfield
13	**L. Pritchard**	England and Wycombe W.
14	**K. Jameson**	Hendon
15	**D. Collyer**	Woking

Colours: **Green, white and gold**

Headquarters :
Hotel Tamerici and Principe
Montecatini Terme, near Florence
(Telephone 71041 - 42 - 43)

SATURDAY 20th MAY 1972

Assembly
Players and Officials should make their own travelling arrangements in order to meet at BEA Air Terminal (Alitalia desk), Cromwell Road, S.W.7 (nearest Underground : Gloucester Road) by **not later than 10.00 hours.**

12.05 hrs. Depart from London Airport (Terminal 2) on Flight AZ 299 for Milan.

14.50 hrs. Arrive at Milan Airport. A motor coach will meet the party on arrival and convey them to the Hotel Tamerici and Principe, Montecatini Terme.

17.00 hrs. Arrive at Hotel Tamerici and Principe.

21.00 hrs. Dinner at the Grand Hotel Pace, Montecatini, as guests of the Italian Football Association.

SUNDAY 21 MAY 1972

10.30 hrs. Training Session. The programme for the afternoon will be announced at Headquarters.

19.30 hrs. Depart by motor coach for the ground at Monsummano.

21.00 hrs. Italian F.A. Amateur XI v Isthmian League XI.

MONDAY 22nd MAY 1972

14.00 hrs. Depart by motor coach for Milan.

16.30 hrs. Arrive at Milan Airport.

17.20 hrs. Depart from Milan Airport on Flight AZ 298.

19.10 hrs. Arrive at London Airport (Terminal 2).

Isthmian League Representative match, May 1972 in Italy. Dave Collyer, goalkeeper, was the only Woking player chosen.

1972 - 1973

Season 1972-73 looked to be the season of very little change, only Alan Pentecost of the first team squad left to join Kingstonian. Dave Collyer after a brief pre-season interlude at Hayes returned before the season commenced.

Leatherhead joined from the Athenian League to bring the division up to 22 teams.

The first fixture away to Bromley brought victory to Woking by 2-1. Injuries prevented Pat Finn and Geoff Chapple from playing.

Young players Cheeseman and Van den Berg came into the side and along with "Dinger" Elton gave Woking a winning start. Hans Van den Berg had been a member of the successful Rydens School squad that had reached the final of the individual schools U-18 competition. He was joined at Woking by others from the side, Rob Braithwaite and Phil Haddow.

Woking equipped themselves well in the first few games of the season. Midweek games against new club Leatherhead provided three points. Oram's goal at Leatherhead ensured a 1-1 draw and a full strength Woking side despatched the newcomers 2-0 at Kingfield.

Leatherhead, once they had found their feet proved to be a good side and at the end of the season they finished third.

Rob Braithwaite made his debut against Leatherhead. He was a calm and mature 21 year old, reminiscent of his father, who played for Woking for a number of seasons during the late 1940's.

Dave Leonard had a great start to the season scoring 10 goals in the first thirteen games but three losses in consecutive away games against Enfield, Walton and Kingstonian was enough for the management committee to sack the manager Harry Hughes and replace him with Trevor Smith as player manager. First team regular Stan Harding tended his resignation after hearing of the sacking.

Smith's first game in charge was in the F.A. Cup against Southern League Dartford. In a match of three doubtful penalties, the last one winning the game for Dartford 3-2, Woking's young team equipped themselves well against their semi-professional opponents.

The change in direction obviously worked well for Woking as only one game out of the next eight was lost. This included a 1-0 victory at home to eventual league runners-up Walton, and three consecutive away victories at Barking, St. Albans and Wycombe.

A victory at Loakes Park was very rare, but goals from Leonard and Oram and magnificent defending gave Woking a 2-1 success. Dave Collyer gave a marvellous performance in goal and was chaired off by the home team supporters.

The next six games yielded only one victory against bottom of the table Corinthian Casuals. Experienced striker John Grondona was signed from Maidenhead United in February. He had played 243 games for Walton scoring 128 goals. Although not fully match fit he scored four goals in the final eight games. His experience was invaluable at this time.

Woking's final league position was 15th one below last season but the points tally of 44 was 12 better than last year and the number of league victories increased from eleven to eighteen.

Before the loss at Dartford in the F.A. Cup third qualifying round victories were gained at Maidenhead United and new opponents Biggleswade Town.

In the Amateur Cup Woking lost at the first attempt away to Oxford by 2-1. In the earlier league fixture Woking had thumped the home team by four goals to one. The reverse happened in the first round of the Surrey Senior Cup. Three weeks earlier Woking had unluckily lost at Sutton in the league 1-0 but three goals by Oram and one each for Leonard and Edwards gave Woking a 5-1 success. Woking defeated Westfield 4-0 in the next round. This was a very local derby as Westfield's ground is no more than 150 yards from Kingfield. Strangely enough this was Westfield's only competitive visit across Kingfield Road to date.

Walton proved much too strong in the semi-final as Tooting were in the first round of the Surrey Senior Shield. Both games ended 3-1.

Leonard finished top scorer with 23 goals closely followed by Oram with 20. No other player managed double figures. Collyer played in all 51 first team matches, Leonard, B. Finn and Edwards only missed one each. Of the younger players Cheeseman, Braithwaite and Baker were the most successful.

In December, manager Smith appointed Pat Finn as assistant manager. Pat decided to concentrate on the managerial side and effectively hung up his boots, but because of injuries he actually returned to the side for the final seven games.

The season was barren as far as trophies were concerned but there was a good blend of experience and youth in the side and the success of the reserves in winning the Suburban League augured well for the future.

1973 - 1974

Season 1973-74 was the year sponsorship of the Isthmian League commenced. Rothmans put up prize money of £16,500. Sixteen new teams formed the new second division with promotion and relegation.

Three points for a win and one for a draw would be played for. Another innovation for the first time ever was the presentation of the Isthmian League trophy to last seasons champions Hendon.

New signings prior to the commencement of the season were Graham Cooper from Walton and Bob Underwood from Maidenhead. During August Dave Hutchins joined from Horsham and in September Dave Leonard and Dave Gale both quit the club and joined Sutton, Tony Roberts signed from Hayes and Nobby Reynolds who had been playing professionally in Australia signed as a permit player.

It was an eventful season, largely because of the power crisis floodlight games were not allowed during November. Training was completed on Sundays. On the 15th December, Woking played their 17th league game. Nearly three months later on the 9th March, Woking completed their 18th league game. Woking played nine consecutive cup games between these dates and by the seasons end, which finished on the 18th May twenty-two cup games had been played. Two ties went to three games and six other games required a replay. Twenty four league games were then played in 55 days.

In the first game of the season Bishop's Stortford were defeated 2-1 at Kingfield. This was in hindsight a good result as they finished in third place. The first ten league games yielded four wins and one draw but five wins in the next seven games put Woking in a mid-table position. Derek Edwards poached six goals from centre-half mainly from set pieces where he used his height and heading ability to good advantage.

Woking lost to Wycombe, the eventual champions twice in the space of four days once in the league and once in the F.A. Cup.

The three game saga in the F.A. Cup against Spartan league Farnborough preceded the Wycombe games. In the first two games Farnborough scored late equalisers but on neutral ground at Guildford goals from Oram and Grondona finally won the day. Farnborough were a team of ex-Cards who had blended into a good side.

At home to Walton, Woking were losing 2-1 but a late goal from Grondona gave Woking a 3-2 victory. Two late goals gave Woking the three points at home to Walthamstow by 2-1.

Vic 'Nobby' Reynolds, who played for Woking in 1959 - 1960 before emigrating to Australia. He made the national team before returning to play for the Cards in 1973 - 1974 and a few games in 1974 - 1975.

From the 23rd March to 2nd May 18 league games were played 12 were won and only two were lost. Wycombe the league leaders and eventual champions were beaten 1-0 at Kingfield. With three games being played each week even washing the kit was a problem.

Prior to this mad scramble to finish the season Brian Finn decided to leave the club for personal reasons. He had served the club well for many seasons, both as player and inspirational captain. Over 550 competitive 1st XI games including over 200 consecutively placed him in the record books at the top of the appearance table. His decision to join Sutton was a major disappointment in an otherwise successful season.

Graham Cooper took over as skipper for the remainder of the season.

Graham Cooper, one of the select number of players who wore the Woking colours over 250 times. This was spread over two spells, in the late 1960's and the mid 1970's.

Woking finally ran out of steam losing five of the final six games, although four of the games were against teams in the top four.

The final league position 7th was magnificent considering the backlog of games. The home record of W15, D3, L3 was among the best ever.

Young players Terry Molloy, Dickie Forbes, Malcolm Whatford, John Cassidy, Roger Steer and Micky Bennett all came into the side and played a part in the success.

In the Amateur Cup Woking beat Walthamstow 2-1 away. This was the first time Woking had defeated Walthamstow away. They had visited Walthamstow 29 times since 1945-46 without a victory. Strangely enough in March Woking won the league encounter also by 2-1.

Two hard fought victories after replays against Horsham and Aveley paired Woking with Ashington. The long trip to Northumberland proved fruitless as Ashington deservedly won 2-0. The home game against Aveley was the first "live" local radio broadcast.

A quick exit in the Surrey Senior Cup against Leatherhead followed although this was after a 2-2 draw at Kingfield.

Woking's first excursion into the London Senior Cup proved eventful. Nine games were played. Croydon, Redhill and Hoddesdon were each beaten at the second attempt but Walton defeated Woking at the third attempt. Even this third game was only decided in extra time.

Dave Collyer only missed two games and was selected by Middlesex Wanderers to tour Japan and Korea in June. Cooper, Edwards and Grondona also only missed two games.

Collyer and Tony Roberts were selected for the F.A. XI against London University.

Grondona topped the goalscoring with 28 goals, Oram scored 21 but no other player reached double figures.

The "Player of the Year" award was given to the team as a whole because of the overall performance of the side during the season.

At the end of the season Geoff Chapple decided to join Harry Hughes at Guildford and Dorking.

1974 - 1975

Prior to the first match of the season, Surrey F.A. chairman Bill Spong, presented Woking with a plaque to commemorate 75 years of membership. The final details for the formation of a limited company were completed in July. This was to ensure financial stability within the club.

There were a number of personnel changes in the close season which gave a certain unpredictability to season 1974-75. Chapple had already made his intentions clear by leaving at the end of last season for Guildford and Dorking but he was followed in August by Derek Edwards who also decided to join Harry Hughes and Brian Finn at Guildford.

Other first team regulars to leave were Underwood and Hutchins. Malcolm Whatford was a ready made replacement for Edwards and Micky Bell came from Hayes as replacement for Underwood. Trevor Waughman returned from Sutton and at midfield Brian Woozley was signed from Tooting. Dickie Forbes, John Cassidy and Roger Steer staked their claim in the first team. In fact Forbes and Steer signed contracts with the club in October. Malcolm Whatford became Woking's first professional when he signed in September to provide insurance for the future as scouts from Luton, Derby and Fulham hovered. The vastly experienced defender Adrian Hill joined in September from Kingstonian.

Malcolm Whatford became Woking's first contract professional in October 1974. He played over 200 games as a central defender between 1974 and 1978, before moving to Kingstonian.

Denny Rose the physio quit the club and joined Harry Hughes at Guildford.

Woking's strength the previous season had been their home record. This season the home record was poor, the first victory did not occur until the sixth game. Only 30 points were gained compared to last seasons' 48, although one of the eight victories was against second placed Enfield who only lost the championship on goal average to Wycombe.

A very poor spell between December and February saw Woking lose eight straight games, including the last seven without scoring a goal.

In an attempt to prevent relegation Smith signed defender Mick Rosser and attacker Cosham from Horsham and seasoned campaigner Ray Poole from Hendon. At this point Woking were second from bottom, but five straight wins and two draws pushed Woking towards their final position, 15th.

Steve Cosham was an instant success scoring 12 goals in fifteen league games.

In the F.A. Cup Kingstonian were defeated at the second attempt but in the next round Wokingham, who played in a division lower won 2-1. Sutton proved too strong in the first round of the F.A. Trophy. Early exits were made in the London Senior Cup and Surrey Senior Cup to Hounslow and Walton respectively.

In the Shield Dulwich were pipped at Kingfield by 2-1, goals coming from Oram and Whatford. Cosham and Steer scored two each in a 5-0 defeat of Egham. Lack of time prevented the final being held until next season. The Surrey Combination Cup Final was also reached with wins against London University, Farnborough and Hampton. Again the final was held over until the next season. Cosham scored two against Farnborough and a hat-trick against Hampton.

The largest gate of the season 2,000 plus witnessed the testimonial game against a Chelsea XI for Harry Medhurst. The result being a 4-3 win for Woking with the outstanding Cosham again scoring a hat-trick.

Cosham headed the goalscoring with 19 goals in 19 games. Grondona scored 12 and Oram 10. Whatford was the only ever present playing 53 games although Collyer only missed two games.

Collyer was deservedly awarded a touring place to Malaysia with Middlesex Wanderers.

1975 - 1976

Expectations were high for season 1975-76. Changes in the administration gave the club stability with the formation of a limited Company to manage the affairs.

Playing contracts were extended for Whatford, Steer, Cassidy and Forbes with Tony Roberts being offered a contract for the season.

For the first time Woking paid a transfer fee. £1,500 for Alan Morton was paid to Maidstone. Alan had played a few games for Woking in 1967-68 before signing professional forms for Crystal Palace. He moved on to Fulham and Ashford and then to Maidstone for whom he scored 105 goals. His pending attacking partnership with Steve Cosham was expected to be prolific.

Woking paid a transfer fee for the first time in 1975. £1,500 secured Alan Morton from Maidstone.

One regret before the season started was the winding-up of the supporters club due to the falling off of active support and transfer of activities to the Cardinal Club.

Other new signings were Peter Spittle a goalkeeper and Brian Roberts a midfielder both from Slough.

Disaster followed disaster as in the first ten league games only one point was gained. Even this was achieved in the last eight minutes at Dagenham when a 2-0 deficit was pulled back to 2-2 with goals from Morton and Ray Poole.

Only Clapton with zero points from nine games prevented Woking from reaching rock bottom.

The midfield was strengthened by signing Alick Brown ex-Wealdstone and Geoff Chapple returned from Guildford and Dorking.

Alick Brown made his debut at home to Ilford on 27th September. Dickie Vincent replaced Peter Spittle in goal. Goals by Cosham and Tony Roberts gave Woking their first league victory of the season. Only one game was lost in the next five. This included a 6-1 thrashing of Kingstonian. Unfortunately in the next six games only one point was gained. A Morton hat-trick enabled Woking to achieve a 3-3 home draw against Southall.

Trevor Smith was sacked with Pat Finn taking over until a manager was appointed. Despite all these internal problems managerless Woking defeated Oxford away 2-1. Both goals came from Alan Morton who was living up to his goalscoring reputation.

Tom Tranter was appointed manager/coach in December. He played for Woking in 1960 whilst a student teacher. For three years he was coach at Slough and preferred an attacking policy. He had been manager of Southall and was the current England Women's team manager and a senior lecturer at Borough Road College.

The next fourteen league games under Tranter produced eight wins, five draws and only one loss, a slender 1-0 defeat at Enfield. Derek Cottrell proved a good signing coming from Wycombe in January. Roger Steer was a revelation when moved to full back. Although three consecutive league games were then lost, a fine 3-1 win against Hendon in the last league game placed Woking in a respectable 14th position. Morton scored 24 league goals finishing top scorer in division one. Steve Cosham scored 16 league goals.

In cup games two finals held over from the previous season were played in August. The Southern Combination Cup was lost 2-0 to

Addlestone but the Surrey Senior Shield provided a 2-1 victory against Molesey. A fast and furious F.A. Cup replay was lost 5-3 to Wealdstone in extra time after holding a 3-1 lead with only 15 minutes of normal time left. Sutton knocked Woking out of two cups, the F.A. Trophy 4-2 at Kingfield and 3-1 in the semi-final reply of the Surrey Senior Cup. Goals by Forbes and Tony Roberts knocked Leatherhead out of the Surrey Senior Cup 2-0 in the first round.

Two goals by Cosham and one by Morton gained revenge for an earlier cup defeat in a 3-1 victory against Addlestone in the second round of the Surrey Senior Cup.

Hayes were defeated 3-0 in the new Rothmans Cup which was basically a league cup. Strikers Cosham and Morton shared the goals, a not uncommon feature during the season. A near reserve side lost at Chesham 3-0 in the second round.

Woking defeated Guernsey F.A. 6-1 in a friendly at Kingfield. To cement the good relations, an Easter Tour was arranged in Guernsey. The Victory Cup was won by Woking as both Guernsey sides were defeated 1-0.

Although the season did not live up to the initial expectations there were some successes, namely the continued skilful play of Malcolm Whatford and the attacking flair of Morton and Cosham.

Youth players were creating reputations in the reserves and Millwall were looking closely at young Paul McKinnon.

Alan Morton scored 34 goals and Steve Cosham 25. Graham Cooper, Ray Poole and Roger Steer were defensively strong but the goalkeeping was erratic throughout. It was only in the second half of the season that the midfield was strengthened, with Tony Roberts, Geoff Chapple and Derek Cottrell looking the best combination.

In December new club colours were introduced showing a broad white hoop on red shirts.

The change of manager improved results, as relegation looked a distinct possibility before Tommy Tranter's appointment. He also took the England Women's team to Rome to play Italy in aid of an earthquake fund and was granted an Audience with the Pope. Not many football managers have had this honour.

The line-up during season 1975 - 1976.
Left to right, Back Row A. Morton, R. Poole, M. Stratford, C. Norman, M. Whatford, S. Cosham, D. Cottrell.
Front Row R. Forbes, R. Steer, G. Cooper, A. Roberts, A. Brown.

1976 - 1977

Before season 1976-1977 had started two of the most successful players last season, Steve Cosham and Roger Steer left and joined Sutton. Geoff Chapple had also departed.

Alan Morton hooking the ball across the goal with the Kingfield crowd looking on optimistically. In 1976, the view across the Kingfield site was unrestricted. The second football pitch and the houses in the background are clearly seen.

New faces included goalkeeper John Overton from Sutton, Jim Godfrey from Wealdstone and midfielder Dave Alexander from Wycombe. Steve Hill from Slough replaced Cosham as Morton's strike partner.

The first game at home to champions Enfield provided a stern test from which a creditable 2-2 draw was achieved with Morton and Hill (on his debut) scoring the goals, Micky Stratford slotted in well at full-back.

Injuries deprived Woking of Poole, Cottrell, Tony Roberts and Morton but youngsters Alan Turner, Martin Bateman and Neil Brister came into the side and were rewarded with a 2-1 victory at Walthamstow .

The first twelve games produced five wins and three draws, including a 5-0 victory at home to Tooting. Only a 2-2 draw at Dulwich prevented a complete whitewash in the next 8 games. The defence which had looked strong early in the season conceded eleven goals in three games with the low point being a 5-0 thrashing at home to Dagenham.

A victory at Croydon stopped the losing sequence. Morton scored his first league goal for nearly three months. This was followed by a 2-1 victory at Bishop's Stortford.

Pat Finn's new signings.

Pat Finn, who had played nearly 250 games for Woking, became Manager in 1977. He is seen discussing tactics with the first team squad.

Successive defeats against Walthamstow, Barking, Tilbury and Kingstonian plunged Woking deep into the relegation zone. A great fight back at home to Leytonstone produced a 3-3 draw after being 3-0 down. Goals from Oram, Hill and Brown gave Woking a hard earned point in a bad tempered affair.

Three defeats, two at home followed this draw. In an attempt to improve results manager Tom Tranter was dismissed and replaced by Pat Finn. Steve Hill left the club and Graham Cooper retired from football. Rob Pollard and Henry Hill were signed by Finn and Steve Cosham who had not settled at Sutton re-signed for Woking.

A fine 1-0 victory at Leatherhead, followed by a 1-1 draw at Hayes gave Woking four precious points. Wycombe who were pushing Enfield hard for the title defeated Woking 3-0. Cosham scored his second goal on his return to gain a 1-0 victory at Southall. Tony Davies understudy to Dickie Guy at Wimbledon and Mick Preston made their debuts.

The journey to Dagenham provided Woking with a precious point against the 3rd placed side. This was a magnificent performance after the heavy defeat suffered earlier at Kingfield.

Two victories 2-0 and 1-0 respectively against Leatherhead and Slough gave Woking a realistic chance of avoiding the drop but the tension went right to the last game. A point at home to Hitchin was required to avoid relegation, Morton scored the goal in a 1-1 draw, so Woking finished four points above the second to bottom side Dulwich.

Some success, was achieved in the cups. In the F.A. Cup Burgess Hill were defeated 3-1, Croydon, Aveley and Slough were each dismissed after replays. A Steve Hill goal before 1,041 spectators brought victory over high flying Slough. A crowd of 2,266 watched Woking put up a gallant fight before losing 1-0 at Wimbledon in the first round.

First time exits occurred in the Trophy, Surrey and London Senior Cups Horsham, Tooting and Leyton-Wingate being the victors. In the Rothmans League Cup Maidenhead were thrashed 6-0 with Morton claiming a hat-trick and young Jim McMorran scoring twice, Wembley were dismissed 4-0 and St Albans were defeated 1-0 with a Dave Alexander goal in extra time. Hendon proved too powerful in the 4th round winning 2-0 at Kingfield.

Steve Hill scored 17 goals with Morton having a poor season only notching 11 goals. Dave

Alexander, Whatford, Poole, Brown and Cottrell were the mainstays of the team playing in 36 or more league games.

With the dismissal of Tom Tranter, Pat Finn had the unenviable task of keeping Woking in Division 1. This he achieved by signing key players Henry Hill, Mick Preston, Steve Cosham and Rob Pollard.

1977 - 1978

After the improvement late last season it was expected that season 1977-78 would be very successful. John Overton and Micky Stratford had moved across to Kingstonian but Roger Steer had rejoined from Walton and Micky Doig from the Army and Combined Services and Ian McGonagle from Crawley strengthened the squad.

Woking, as in previous seasons made their usual poor start. Injuries to key players Whatford and Preston did not help settle the team. Six defeats in the first seven games placed Woking in the relegation position. In an attempt to find a solution Pat Finn signed goalkeeper Frank Parsons from Staines. His debut match resulted in the first league victory at Bishop's Stortford 3-1. The improvement however did not materialise and it was no surprise when Pat Finn was sacked in October. Fred Callaghan who had played 294 games for Fulham and had managed Enfield to an Isthmian League championship was appointed as manager.

Alan Morton and Steve Cosham attacking Enfield's defence during season 1977 - 1978. The partnership produced 48 goals in the season.

His first game in charge was the 5-4 defeat at home to Dagenham. The game was eventful in that Cosham, after scoring had to go in goal to replace the injured Parsons. A 4-3 lead eventually ended in a victory for Dagenham. After 15 games in which only two were won Woking were locked firmly second from bottom.

Alan Morton and Steve Cosham, not too far away from the action

Woking's home record was appalling as the first home win didn't occur until the 10th game at Kingfield. Gradually Callaghan and Laurie Churchill, his newly appointed assistant started to achieve some good results. Three consecutive away victories at Carshalton, Croydon and Hayes gave Woking some breathing space.

The 6-3 victory at Croydon, with Morton coming back to form with a hat-trick, indicated Woking's improved form. The strike duo of Morton and Cosham started to score freely again.

Only two losses, which were close encounters with the top two, Enfield and Dagenham were the only blemishes in 20 league games from late October.

The final league position of 14th looked impossible after the first fifteen games. Once again managerial changes had performed the miracle.

Woking's best ever Trophy performance saw the first round reached for the first time. Steve Cosham's four goals out of six scored knocked out Witney, Bromley and Kingstonian. Gravesend and Northfleet survived a battering at Kingfield in a 0-0 encounter but a 2-0 defeat in the replay, ended Woking's interest in the Trophy.

Ilford, who had been relegated the previous season beat Woking 1-0 in a scrappy F.A. Cup tie and Enfield, who would complete a hat-trick of championships, knocked Woking out of the London Senior Cup 2-0.

Woking had a good 1-0 victory at Slough in the Hitachi Cup but a 2-1 loss after extra time at Boreham Wood ended the Cards interest in this competition.

Runners-up in the Surrey Senior Cup was a satisfactory but disappointing performance. Cosham who had scored in every round put Woking into the lead just before half-time but Tooting equalised on the hour and scored the winner in extra time. A fine 2-1 victory at high flying Leatherhead in the semi-final was arguably the best performance of the season.

Steve Cosham scored 25 goals closely followed by Alan Morton with 23. Derek Cottrell, the club captain played in every league and cup game with Morton only missing one.

Trevor Smith the former player and manager was appointed secretary and John Grondona became financial controller.

The DIY centre at West Byfleet sponsored the league game at home to Staines. This was Woking's first match sponsorship.

League sponsorship and sportsmanship awards were taken over by The Michael Laurie Surveyors Ltd with Radio Luxembourg providing cash for goal scoring awards.

A new second division was formed with the first division becoming the Premier division. The Isthmian League was now even more competitive.

Woking's first sponsored match - 23 August 1977.

1978 - 1979

During pre-season Kingfield started to bubble with enthusiasm and optimism for 1978-1979. Fred Callaghan signed John Love, Tony Field and Eggie James from Staines and Brendan O'Sullivan from Brentford. Tony Martin the QPR apprentice left back completed the jig-saw. The total assembly cost over £2,000.

Three regulars left the club, Malcolm Whatford to Kingstonian while Ian McGonagle and Alick Brown dropped down a division joining Walton and Hersham. Extra funding was provided by the new lottery scheme and club sponsors McEwan Ltd.

The four friendlies against Football League opposition were won but these counted for nothing, which was amply illustrated in the first league game at Hitchin that ended in a 1-0 defeat.

In the next nine games Woking achieved four victories and five draws, 21 goals were scored, of which Morton scored eight and James claimed six.

Eggie James, scorer of 67 goals in only 126 games, defending behind Micky Preston. Both played major roles in seasons 1978 - 1979 and 1979 - 1980.

goals were scored, with only champions Barking and runners-up Dagenham scoring more. In the F.A. Cup three qualifying matches were safely negotiated. Epsom & Ewell, Tunbridge Wells and Horsham were dispatched fairly comfortably. Margate who should have provided stiff opposition were thrashed 7-1 with Morton and James scoring hat-tricks.

The first round paired Barnet and Woking together. This stirred up memories of the two epic Amateur Cup semi-finals 20 years earlier.

Barnet who had Jimmy Greaves in their ranks provided a difficult barrier to overcome. It took three games before Woking triumphed 3-0 on neutral ground, Brentford. The first game at Barnet ended 3-3 amid much drama. Jimmy Greaves was sent off. Morton missed a penalty for Woking, Parsons in the Woking goal was pelted with coins by irate Barnet supporters and Barnet's equaliser came from a dubious

Les Barrett signed in September. He had played many games for Fulham and Millwall before signing for California Surfs in the American League.

By the end of October, although they had games in hand over most of the clubs above them Woking had slipped to 14th place. The number of cup games, which finally totalled 24 created a backlog of league fixtures which ensured a mad scramble to finish during March and April.

At the end of January twenty one league games were left to play. The strength of the squad was such that only 5 were lost. Walthamstow, for so long a bogey team, were thrashed 6-0 with Cosham netting four. Morton matched this when he scored all four in a 4-2 victory at Boreham Wood. A thirteen match unbeaten run ended, when a final match thriller at Dagenham saw Woking edged out 5-3.

A final position of 7th could have been bettered if the home form had been improved. Eleven of the twenty-one games ended as draws. A total of 79

John Adams, a wholehearted play-anywhere type of player.

penalty awarded in injury time to deny Woking the victory. The replay at Woking again ended 3-3 but this time after extra time. Barnet equalised three minutes from the end of extra time. So to the third meeting with Woking victorious.

Woking had never reached the second round before. Nerves were controlled in a 2-2 draw against a Swansea team at the top of Division 3.

A magnificent achievement. John Toshack had built his team around ex-Liverpool internationals, Tommy Smith and Ian Callaghan, but Woking fought back twice to take the game to Kingfield.

A crowd of 6,500 witnessed a magnificent game with Woking fighting back from 3-1 down. Les Barrett slammed in the equaliser three minutes from normal time. Two goals from Swansea in extra time won the game as tired legs finally gave out but all the accolades were for Woking.

It took four games before Woking finally defeated Waterlooville 1-0 in the 1st Qualifying round of the F.A. Trophy. Replays in the next two rounds against Bognor and Tilbury enabled Woking to progress into the first round proper. On the day Slough won 3-0 with very little trouble, this was a major disappointment as Slough had been defeated in the league 2-1 at Wexham Park.

Leatherhead ended the interest in the Surrey Senior Cup 2-1. This after Woking had thrashed Kingstonian 4-0 in the first round. In the London Senior Cup Letchworth and Staines were easily defeated but the champions elect Barking defeated Woking 3-1 in the third round.

Sixty five games were finally played during the season with 132 goals being scored. Morton topped the lists with 39 goals closely followed by James with 33. Cosham who played his last game against Boreham Wood on 27 March scored 17 goals. Field finished with 11 goals.

Frank Parsons missed only 3 games all season, John Love missed four and Tony Martin five.

The cups dominated the season, although the respectable league position was a great performance considering the backlog of fixtures at the end.

The squad assembled at the start of season 1978 - 1979, who under Manager Fred Callaghan reached the 2nd round of the F.A. Cup only losing after two epic games against Swansea.
From left to right, E. James, M. Preston, J. Love, F. Parsons, A. Morton, A. Field, T. Shrieves, S. Cosham, B. O'Sullivan, D. Alexander, D. Cottrell, R. Steer, A. Martin.

Micky Preston, a commanding central defender capped 13 times for England Amateurs whilst with Kingstonian. He played over 170 games for Woking between 1977 and 1980.

Dave Alexander who played over 220 games from 1976 to 1980. Basically a midfield general who still managed 37 goals during his Woking career.

John Love, a central defender of the 1978 - 1979 squad

Steve Cosham, an instinctive goal scorer, who scored 90 goals in only 170 appearances played from 1975 to 1979

Roger Steer had three spells at Woking, mainly during the middle to late 1970's. He started as a fast left-winger, but then converted to an overlapping full-back. He is one of the select band who played over 200 times for the Cardinals.

Chapter 11

NEAR EXTINCTION AFTER BEING CLOSE TO WEMBLEY. RELEGATION THEN CONSOLIDATION BEFORE SUCCESS - THE 1980'S

1979 - 1980

In March 1980 hopes were particularly high. Three semi-finals were waiting to be contested, with the twin towers of Wembley just a step away. Games in hand gave Woking a potential top four league position.

By the end of April the season had turned completely sour. All three semi-finals were lost. Manager Fred Callaghan had resigned just before the home leg of the F.A. Trophy against Dagenham to manage Football League side Brentford.

This shock resignation was no preparation for the vital first leg and it was no surprise when Dagenham wrapped up the tie 3-1 at Kingfield. Woking had their chances including a missed penalty by Field which would have levelled the scores. A 4-1 beating at Dagenham a week later knocked the stuffing out of Woking for the rest of the season. Only one league win in the last ten pushed Woking down into ninth position.

The bulk of the successful side of the previous season remained, one notable absentee being Cosham. Two newcomers at the start of the season were for different reasons destined not to play a complete season.

Mick Earls from Aldershot played half-a-dozen games before a bad knee injury virtually ended his career. Gary Rolph signed from Brentford, was thrown out of the club along with Adams for disciplinary reasons just prior to the Trophy 3rd round tie at Marine. Steve Adams a mid-season signing from Hillingdon was sorely missed. His midfield energy seemed to be Callaghan's last piece in the jigsaw. Once again Les Barrett returned from football American style to play a part in Woking's successes.

Despite having a number of niggling injuries which necessitated manager Callaghan playing, Woking hit the top of the table in mid-September. Excellent away victories at Walthamstow, Enfield and Sutton ensured this prime position.

Unfortunately a 6-3 defeat by lowly Croydon burst the bubble. Although two of the next three league games, were won, a run of six games without a league win finished Woking's championship hopes.

Woking proved their pedigree by beating Enfield, the eventual champions, for the second time, this time at Kingfield. Morton and James once again spearheaded a potent attacking force. Both scored 20 or more league goals.

Frank Parsons, an outstanding goalkeeper, who played over 170 games from 1977 to 1980.

Micky Preston tangling with the "enemy", with some support from Alan Morton.

Four goals from Eggie James smashed Boreham Wood 6-1 in the next round.

An interesting friendly against the Malawi National XI was played in September. An Eggie James hat-trick enabled Woking to clinch a 4-1 victory. Throughout the season John Love, Micky Preston and Tony Martin provided an effective defensive barrier around goalkeeper Frank Parsons. Tony Field, Dave Alexander and Derek Cottrell provided the "buzz" in midfield. Eggie James with 34 goals and Alan Morton with 29 goals were arguably the most potent duo in non-league football.

A total of 24 cup-ties equalled the number played in the previous season. Three successive away ties in the F.A. Cup produced victories against Corinthian-Casuals, Hounslow and Kingstonian before another away tie against Alliance Premier League side Wealdstone proved too much in a slender 1-0 loss.

A seventeen year old played at left back for Wealdstone. Stuart Pearce, who would play many seasons for Nottingham Forest and England, was at the start of a long career.

In the F.A. Trophy two Kent sides, Folkestone and Dover were beaten before visits to Ashington and Marine both resulted in hard fought 2-0 victories. A 3-1 quarter final victory at home to Barrow gave Woking their first ever Trophy semi-final which unfortunately was unsuccessful.

Two revenge victories against Wealdstone and Tooting paired Woking against Barking in the London Senior Cup semi-final. After a dour struggle a single goal was enough to defeat Woking.

Sutton defeated Woking 2-1 in the second round of the Surrey Senior Cup and went one better in a 3-1 success at Kingfield in a replayed Hitachi Cup semi-final. In the earlier rounds of the Hitachi Cup goals from Field and Alexander defeated Tooting once again.

Although there were no trophies on the Kingfield sideboard the quality football played throughout the season was a bonus for the supporters.

1980 - 1981

A dark cloud hung over Woking Football Club prior to the commencement of season 1980-81. Despite having one of the best ever playing seasons, expenses had increased dramatically. It was no secret that Woking had gambled on expensive players in the hope of getting to the top of the league and to Wembley. Unfortunately the gamble just failed. The final deficit was announced officially as approximately £40,000.

By the end of October the Chairman John Grondona and Trevor Smith the football secretary had tendered their resignations. It was a sad time for the club because both had been marvellous servants on the playing as well as on the management front.

At this time Grondona had been having "conversations" with Fulham Football Club regarding a link-up with Woking which would require Fulham leaving Craven Cottage and developing Kingfield to bring facilities up to Football League standard. This proposed merger did not come to fruition although talks continued for some months into the season. It was unfortunate that at this time, because of the unavailability of anyone to fulfil the administrative duties thc Reserve XI was withdrawn from the Suburban League.

Against this background of unrest and great change the new manager Bill Miller had to prepare a team for the new season. A new era was beginning with sponsorship starting to take effect. Berger Paints continued to sponsor the Isthmian League with rewards for all clubs.

was the hardest possible as the previous years champions Enfield came to Kingfield. In a hard fought encounter Woking fought like tigers but finally succumbed by the odd goal in three.

Of the new defenders Reg Leather and Dave Howitt linked up well with the "old boys" Martin and Barrett and a new face with the unpronounceable name Chukwuemeka Nwajoibi provided the flair up front with Field and Morton providing the experience.

Tony Martin on one of his many attacking runs from full back. He only scored one goal in his 237 games but he created many chances for his colleagues. In a Woking career spanning five seasons from 1979 to 1983, he would be many supporters choice as Woking's best ever left back.

At the end of November, Woking were a respectable tenth position in the league. Some famous heads had rolled at Kingfield; Dagenham, Slough, Sutton and Tooting were all beaten. In fact Slough the eventual champions were also held to a 1-1 draw at Slough.

Unfortunately some of the experienced players departed for pastures new although the transfer fees received were most welcome. Nwajiobi only played a handful of games in the new year because of his university studies in Wales. His potential however was recognised by Luton, for whom he played over 70 league games in the mid-80's. Of 18 league games played after Christmas only two were won. Manager Billy Miller signed on replacements for the departed players but only Roy Davies from Wimbledon looked the part. Woking finished their league campaign in bottom position.

Many of last seasons squad had left the club. Tony Martin, Les Barrett, Noel Fletcher, Tony Field, Alan Morton and Martin Black remained. Of these only Martin, Barrett and Black finished the season. Parsons who was in dispute with the club finally joined Slough in October for £2000. Morton joined Kingstonian in the new year for £1,500 and Noel Fletcher went to Addlestone for £1,000. Cash coming into the club was essential but the loss of these quality players left a void which was never totally filled with new players. Nevertheless it was known that relegation would be unlikely due to the loss of member clubs to the Alliance League, therefore financial solvency was the important factor. The first league game of the season

The new players performed well in the Surrey Senior Cup. Magnificent victories at Tooting, 3-0 with a brace of goals from Roy Davies and a hard fought 3-2 victory at home to Kingstonian gave Woking a semi-final against Metropolitan Police. After a 0-0 draw at Kingfield the other Nwajiobi namely Obi brother of Emeka scored two as did Martin Black. The final against Epsom and Ewell at Tooting proved to be an anti-climax with Epsom achieving a deserved 2-1 success. Very little progress was made in the other cups; Hendon ended Woking's F.A. Cup interest with a 4-1 defeat in the 2nd qualifying round. In the first round of the Trophy Sutton were too strong in a 1-0 defeat. The only hat-trick of the season by Morton helped defeat Corinthian Casuals 9-0 in the Hitachi Cup, a 4-3 win at St Albans in the next round indicated promise but Walthamstow put paid to this be defeating Woking 4-2 in the 3rd round.

Despite his departure in the new year, Morton top-scored with 18 goals in 39 league and Cup games. No other player managed 10 goals. Barrett, captain of the side only missed three league and cup games all season. With all the chopping and changing it was no surprise that 29 players were used. Despite finishing bottom of the league Woking actually made money over the season, approximately £14,000 was fed back into club funds. Such are the vagaries of football.

1981 - 1982

It was all change once again prior to season 1981-82, manager Billy Miller and assistant manager Graham Cooper were both sacked. This was probably no great surprise as they failed to build a team fit to compete against the top flight in non-league football, Woking's position in the Premier Division was solely due to the departure of Enfield and Dagenham into the Alliance League. Brian Caterer who had spent four successful years as Windsor and Eton's boss, was appointed Manager with Colin Lippiatt, his brother-in-law as assistant manager.

Of last seasons players only two remained, Martin Black and Steve Scrivens. Caterer and Lippiatt brought with them to Kingfield twelve ex-Windsor players - goalkeeper Kevin Mitchell, defenders John Mitchell, Gary Edwards, Colin Smith and Bob King, midfield men Ian Howard, Keith Beckett, and Jeff Chapman and strikers Ross McCulloch, Lance Cadogan, Joel Clark and Kevin Hill. Other newcomers who competed for first team places at the outset were Paul Holder from Kingstonian, Steve Palfrey from Maidenhead and experienced Lyndon Lynch from Hoddesdon.

Goals from Chapman, Lynch and Beckett gave Woking a great start to the season with a 3-0 victory at home to Walthamstow. This was followed by a hard fought midweek 0-0 draw at last season's champions Slough. The next three games produced only one point. A 2-1 victory at Tooting and a creditable 1-1 draw at Bishops Stortford stopped the rot. In the next

The above 1981 - 1982 squad comprised mainly ex-Windsor & Eton players, who followed the managerial team of Brian Caterer (extreme left) and Colin Lippiatt to Woking. Due to financial constraints only Colin Smith (seated extreme left), Kevin Hill (seated third left) and John Mitchell (standing third from right) played in the first and last games.

few weeks the manager released a number of players in an attempt to produce a winning team. Lynch, Beckett, Howard and King were released and Lance Cadogan, Tony Martin and Maurice Hepworth came into the side.

Maurice Hepworth who had played two league games for Sunderland made an immediate impact in midfield with his rugged, tough, no nonsense approach. Martin steadied the defence and Cadogan formed an excellent strike partnership with McCulloch. After ten games Woking were in an uninspiring mid-table position but by the end of November Woking were third in the table only losing two out of fourteen games. Lance Cadogan scored nine goals during this time. Excellent 0-0 draws were obtained away to Croydon and Wycombe followed by four straight victories including a superb 4-2 victory at home to Sutton. A brace of goals each by Cadogan and Hewitt accounted for the league leaders. Unfortunately financial problems oncc again came to the fore. The adverse weather conditions reduced potential income. The club therefore had to reduce payments to players to ensure expenditure matched income. Established first team players left the club, which resulted in a string of poor results. Not one game was won in the last fifteen league games. During this period relegation became a strong possibility. Seven straight losses during March and April plunged Woking into the bottom three. A 7-1 home loss against fellow strugglers Bromley was the lowest point in a disappointing end to a promising season.

Two away draws, both 2-2 at Billericay and Hitchin gave Woking a final margin of five points over second to bottom Harlow. Premier Division football was safe for another season. Progress in the major cups was minimal. Wick, a Sussex Senior side ended Woking's F.A. Cup progress with an unlikely 2-1 victory. Division 1 side Wembley produced a last minute goal to knock Woking from the Hitachi Cup in the first round. There were first round exits from the Surrey Senior Cup and the London Senior Cup with defeats by Kingstonian and Dulwich. In the F.A. Trophy Barking were defeated 2-1 in the 1st round. Goals by Cadogan and John Mitchell gave Woking a 2nd round home tie against Northern Premier League side Mossley who had unluckily lost 2-1 to Dagenham (Woking's conquerors in the Semi Final) in the 1980 Trophy Final.

A 0-0 draw gave Woking a second chance, but a combination of a long midweek journey to Manchester and a superior Mossley side resulted in a heavy 5-0 beating. Cadogan scored 14 goals in all competitive matches but no other player managed double figures. Kevin Hill only missed one game all season which was an achievement considering a total of 45 players were used in an increasingly frustrating season for the fans.

1982 - 1983

Following the disappointments of 1981-82 which saw the club plunge from third place in January to twentieth position in May a new management team was appointed prior to season 1982-1983. Dave Holloway was promoted to 1st Team Manager with Mick Garbutt as his assistant. Financial restraints meant that there was a heavy reliance on local talent. Of the side that played in the first game, the 0-0 draw at home to Bishop's Stortford only Martin Black remained from last years team. Another member of last years team Tony Martin returned from Hendon in September. Les Barrett who had left at the end of 1980-1981 re-signed from Slough. The mixture of local talent and experienced campaigners did not produce too many fireworks as the next five league games were lost with only two goals scored and Kent League side Chatham defeated Woking 2-1 after a replay in the preliminary round of the F.A. cup.

A Norman Rudd goal gave the Cards a deserved 1-1 draw at home to Slough but three consecutive league defeats placed Woking firmly in bottom place. A home victory against Wokingham with a Cassidy goal separating the two sides was purely a stay of execution. Five defeats in a row anchored Woking firmly in the relegation spot. Steve Finnieston the ex-Chelsea centre-forward came into the side in an attempt to

Martin Black a six foot defender, played approximately 200 games between 1978 and 1987. Rarely beaten in the air he was recognised for his many consistent performances.

Les Barrett, who scored 74 goals in 420 league games for Fulham as an attacking winger, played in the American Soccer League whilst playing over 170 games for Woking from 1978 to 1983, mainly at central defence.

provide the fire-power so desperately needed. Unfortunately the zip and pace had gone. Five games and one goal later Finnieston moved on. Three away victories against Sutton, Hitchin and Wokingham were interspersed with six home losses, five of them goal less. Tony Field returned to the club but despite scoring four goals he too disappeared after eleven games, joining Dulwich.

Players came and went in a vain attempt to produce a winning combination. At the end of the season forty-nine players had been used which was inevitable in the circumstances. The commitment of the team was never doubted only the quality necessary to survive in what was one of the most competitive leagues in the country. Cassidy, Barrett and Martin performed miracles in defence but a total of 30 goals scored in 42 league games was by far the lowest in the division.

Only the poor quality of Leatherhead, whom Woking defeated 2-1 in the second to last game of the season prevented Woking becoming the wooden spoonists for the second time in three seasons. Nevertheless a gap of 18 points from the team above them gave a good indication of Woking's league season. In the Surrey Senior Cup Leatherhead, bottom of the Isthmian League, defeated Woking 1-0 at Kingfield after a drawn first game. Barnet proved too strong in the Trophy. Epping were beaten 1-0 in the

Sponsorship in the 1980's. Three high kickers representing the Glass Centre, Horsell.

Hitachi Cup but despite outplaying hosts Hornchurch in the next round Woking were beaten 2-1. Woking's best performances of the season were reserved for the London Senior Cup. Four rounds were safely negotiated; this included a 1-0 victory at 4th placed Hayes.

The final was played at Champion Hill, Dulwich against Sutton. After a close affair Woking only just lost 1-0 to a side who had finished 5th in the league. The lack of finishing power was emphasised by the seasons leading scorer John Cassidy's five goals from a midfield position which highlighted one of the season's problems. Adie Cowler whose time would come made four league and cup appearances. Cassidy who would play a leading role in the clubs revival in a few years was ever present and as captain demonstrated many of the characteristics which came to the fore later in his career. Although relegation was a disaster for a club of Woking's potential, in hindsight it provided breathing space to rebuild. It can be said "the rest is history".

1983 - 1984

Season 1983-84 was a new adventure for Woking as they were playing, outside the Premier Division for the first time ever. Manager Dave Holloway had to rely heavily on a youth policy. For the first game at home to Oxford City new players Paul Holder, Tom Jones, Freddie Jones and Jezz Stagg fitted in well and single goal from Steve Bembridge won the game.

Unfortunately not one game was won out of the next seven and there were first game exits from the F.A. Cup and the Hitachi Cup. The loss in the F.A. Cup against Sussex County side, Hailsham was particularly embarrassing.

High kick action from John Cassidy in front of 'Moaners Corner'.

Maurice Cox who had played 60 times for Torquay in the 4th division joined the club in September. A proven goalscorer and a quality player Maurice scored on his debut in a 1-1 draw at home to Windsor and Eton. As Windsor eventually finished champions this was in hindsight a point gained. Windsor were managed by Geoff Chapple and Trevor Baron scored their equaliser. Both would play significant roles in the history of Woking Football Club. Incidentally Cox holds the record for the quickest goal in the Varsity matches,

The squad for season 1983 - 1984
Maurice Cox third from the left, back row, was a prolific scorer. Bill Dodgin third from the right took over the manager's role briefly the following season. Dave Holloway extreme right was the manager in 1983 - 1984.
Paul Jablonski front row, extreme left, gave many fine performances over the following few seasons. Terry Worsfold, third from the left, would have his moment of glory at West Bromwich in 1991.

scoring a goal within 20 seconds for Cambridge against Oxford University in the annual event at Wembley.

A series of erratic performances kept Woking in the bottom half of the table. A 7-0 victory at Hertford was an example of Woking's potential but no two games were the same. Cox scored four in this game which was matched later by Neil Gibson in a 5-1 victory at home to Metropolitan Police.

Tom Jones who looked a class player decided to return to Farnborough during November. He eventually moved into the Football League with some success playing over 150 games in midfield for Swindon Town and later represented Reading. Woking briefly threatened to climb into the promotion race with only one loss in eleven games but four straight defeats during March and April pushed Woking back into the pack. A final league position of 13th was an indication of the teams inconsistency. The one major success was the 21 league goals from Cox.

Other players who performed well during the season were Holder who didn't miss a game and Williams a hard running midfield player. Thirty-five players wore the Woking shirt during the season which was too many to achieve a reasonable blend.

There were first time exits in the F.A. Trophy and London Senior Cup against Hendon and Tooting. The only cup game won during a disappointing season was a first round Surrey Senior Cup tie against Merstham. Tooting ended Woking's Surrey Senior Cup interest with an easy 3-0 win in the following round. Woking relied heavily on the potential of youth plus a few experienced hands. This policy was necessary to survive as the average home attendance struggled to reach 175.

1984 - 1985

Saturday 4th May 1985 at 4.45 pm was probably the lowest point in Woking's history. After a great effort in the last month of the season Woking needed one point in their last game at home to St Albans to be certain of remaining in Division 1.

St Albans proved too strong scoring two in the first few minutes and finally defeating Woking 3-1. Unfortunately the three other sides Lewes, Basildon and Hornchurch who were all in danger, won, so relegating Woking into Division 2 South.

During the close season Dave Holloway had stepped down as team manager in favour of Bill Dodgin former manager of Fulham, Brentford and Northampton. Unfortunately his knowledge of non-league football was limited and the dependence to a large extent on local players was unsuccessful. Experienced players Cox, Black, Morton and Jablonski formed the basis of the side.

Five straight losses in the league and an F.A. Cup loss to Sussex County side Haywards Heath proved too much for Bill Dodgin, who resigned. Dave Holloway took over as caretaker Manager until Geoff Chapple was appointed on the 24th September. Coincidentally the first win was achieved on the following Saturday with a Lee Frost goal defeating fellow strugglers Clapton.

Three heavy losses followed before new personnel were drafted in for the home game against Hornchurch. Six new faces, goalkeeper I. Watson, defenders H. Richardson, A. Probert and K. Osnowski plus attackers R. Steer and P. Hampshire helped Woking to a narrow 3-2 victory.

At the halfway point in the season, after 21 games Woking were 2nd from bottom with five wins and two draws. Inconsistency was the main problem. The performances at Kingfield were poor. Since the Hornchurch game only one home game was won out of five compared with two wins and two draws out of six away from home.

Jeckyl and Hyde performances became the norm for Woking. It was not unusual for Woking to perform brilliantly in one half and put up an indifferent performance in the other half. A 3-1 lead at home to Bromley ended in a 5-3 defeat. Boreham Wood were 2-0 up at half-time but went home pointless after Woking smashed in four second half goals.. A 6-1 home loss against Walton was an unbelievably inept performance.

Geoff Chapple obtained the services of Ned Mataxa, a defender who was the current captain of Oxford University. He made his debut at home to Met Police in a 3-1 victory. A Morton hat-trick polished off Hertford 4-1 in the next home game and Woking had at last moved out of the bottom four. Two defeats both 3-2 against top of the table Kingstonian and bottom of the table Clapton put Woking back in trouble again. An impressive 3-2 victory at Wembley where Morton scored two and was then sent off, was followed by a 3-0

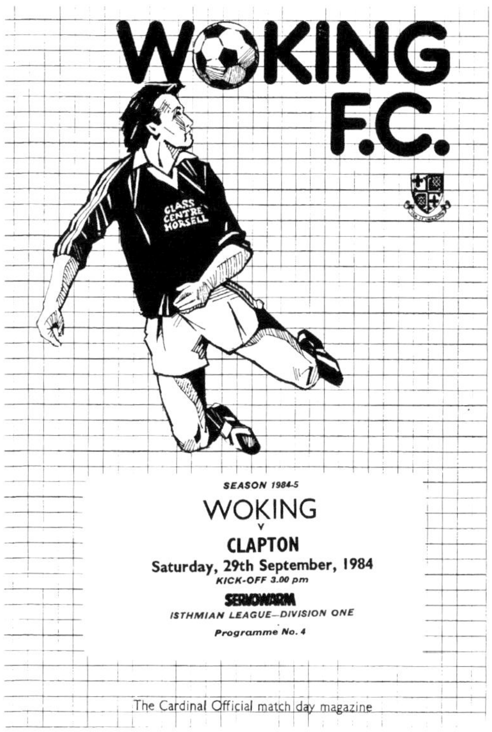

Programme cover: Geoff Chapple's first match as manager.

loss at home to a very strong Leatherhead side and a similar loss to the eventual champions, Farnborough.

Two new players arrived in an attempt to avoid relegation. Ian Stillwell a goalkeeper and Darren Watson, a classy full-back who had played for England under 19's.

With seven league games to play, the position was not good, but four straight away wins in eleven days looked to have saved the day. Hornchurch, Maidenhead, Aveley and

Basildon were all defeated. This left Woking two points clear of Hornchurch (who were in the final relegation position). Woking with three games at home and a game in hand should have been safe, but their poor goal average would be their downfall.

A hard fought 0-0 draw at home to Staines and a 2-1 victory at home to champions, Farnborough, should have been enough, but both Basildon and Hornchurch won leaving a point needed for safety from the last game.

Basildon and Hornchurch won their last games 1-0, so Woking were relegated because of their inferior goal difference. It was no consolation that 51 points was the highest ever for a relegated club.

Woking reached the 1st round of the F.A. Trophy. A total of eight games were played which included four replays. Lewes were beaten 3-1 at the Dripping Pan after a 1-1 draw at Kingfield. Epsom of the Premier Division were beaten 2-1 on their own patch. Aveley were dispatched 2-1 after a replay. Three epic games against Dulwich, (3rd in the Premier Division) were played with Dulwich finally winning 2-1 at Kingfield.

Tooting defeated Woking 1-0 after a replay in the 1st round of the Surrey Senior Cup after Woking had defeated Malden Vale 2-0 in the 5th qualifying round.

Forty-eight players represented Woking with Maurice Cox playing 49 out of 55, scoring 26 goals in the process. Martin Black played 48 and Alan Morton 47 with 20 goals. Adie Probert, Lee Frost and Paul Jablonski played 38 games.

A new era for Woking was about to commence from the basement of Division 2 (South) to Goodison, Everton in six seasons and the pinnacle of non-league football, the GM Vauxhall Conference in seven years.

1985 - 1986

The only way was up for Woking in the 1985-86 season. The basement had been reached in such a short time. Geoff Chapple was expected to stay in Division 2 South for only one season.

Of the previous season's unsuccessful side only Maurice Cox, Paul Jablonski, Adie Probert and Darren Watson remained. Addlestone's demise was Woking's gain as John Cassidy and Adie Cowler made the short trip to Kingfield. Justin Horner and Mark Dawber arrived from Virginia Water. Clive Youlton and Dave Lansley were brought in to score goals and back up Maurice Cox.

John Cassidy, a charismatic skipper who played a major role in the Chapple revival. He returned to Woking in 1985 - 1986 season after the demise of Addlestone. Three spells spanning fifteen years and 299 games ensured a prominent place in Woking's history.

The Isthmian League had new sponsors with Vauxhall Motors taking over for the next three years.

A 2-0 victory in the first game at Imber Court against Metropolitan Police with goals from Dawber and Lansley and victories against Eastbourne and Petersfield flattered to deceive. Banstead exposed the frailties in Woking's defence by scoring four before half-time. Clive Youlton scored twice in the second half to give some respectability to the scoreline. A 2-2 draw at leaders Whyteleafe in an ill-tempered game kept Woking in the top three, but 10 goals conceded in the next four games with only two points gained, seriously dented Woking's promotion hopes.

Two players were recruited from the Army in an attempt to plug the defensive holes, Chris Lomas, goalkeeper for the British Army plus Colin McDonald at centre-back.

November proved to be a fruitful month as 16 points were gained out of 18. This included an excellent 2-1 victory at Southall who were unbeaten prior to this.

After Woking had defeated Marlow 8-1 with hat-tricks from Cox and Lansley, Cox decided to join Kingstonian. In his two and a half seasons, he proved to be a consistent scorer with 66 goals in 107 league and cup games.

Woking's good run ended at Molesey in a 3-2 defeat. McDonald played his final game for Woking against Ruislip Manor on 18th January before being transferred to Shropshire with the Army. He also scored in a 4-0 victory. Fortunately, Trevor Baron signed from Windsor and Eton, so he immediately replaced McDonald at the centre of the defence. A cultured player, Baron would give many seasons service.

Bad weather prevented Woking playing any football in February, but a 3-2 reverse at Southwick in March, after surrendering a 2-0 lead proved to be the final loss of the season. New players, Morris, Woodley and Norman blended in perfectly. Eleven of the last 12 games were won but unfortunately Southwick and Bracknell did not crack under Woking's pressure. Woking finished 3rd behind these two clubs, but the nucleus of the side was beginning to take shape.

After a 3-1 victory at Ringmer in the F.A. Cup, Slough proved too much of an obstacle in the next round with a 5-1 demolition of Woking.

Maidenhead edged through in the first qualifying round of the F.A. Trophy, despite Woking leading 3-1 at half time, the final score was 5-4 in Maidenhead's favour.

In the Surrey Senior Cup, Camberley, with former Kingfield favourite Alan Turner, defended stoutly and finally pinched the game in the last two minutes. Four from Cox enabled Woking to defeat Vauxhall Motors 5-3 in the preliminary round but Uxbridge defeated Woking 2-1 in the next round of the A.C. Delco Cup.

The London Senior Cup Semi-final was reached with victories against Eton Manor 4-2, Darren Watson scored a brace of penalties to put Woking through after being 2-0 down. Hampton, Leyton-Wingate (Keith Morris hat-trick) and Haringey Boro' were all defeated. Wathamstow from the Premier Division duly knocked out Woking 3-0 in the Semi-final.

John Cassidy did not miss a game and Adie Cowler only missed three. Dave Lansley scored 23 league and cup goals during the season. Clive Youlton and Maurice Cox scored 18 goals each (although Cox left the club in January and only played 20 games). Mark Dawber who had played excellently throughout the season, scored 15 goals.

A total of 94 league goals were scored but unfortunately 45 were let through. Defensive lapses up to Christmas gave Woking too much leeway to make up, although the final margin was only three points. It was perhaps a blessing in disguise that Woking were not promoted, as a further season in the lower division enabled Chapple to hone his team for the seasons ahead.

1986-1987

The most significant action of season 1986-87 was the signing of Tim Buzaglo from local side, Weysiders. Buzaglo was a natural class player with an instinctive finish, who would become a household name after his hat-trick against West Bromwich Albion in the F.A. Cup of 1991.

The season did not start well, Banstead put up a ten man defence at Kingfield in the opening game and survived to a 0-0 draw. An incident packed second game at Marlow ended 5-3 in their favour. Woking missed two penalties and the defence leaked like the proverbial sieve. Nevertheless, Buzaglo opened his scoring account and Trevor Baron who had left in the close season, decided to return, although he only made the subs. bench for this game.

Three wins followed with no goals conceded and seven goals scored before a strong, physical Dorking side defeated Woking 2-0. Lloyd Wye, who had progressed from the youth side, finally made the number 4 shirt his own. Tim Buzaglo scored his first hat-trick in a 5-0 defeat of Petersfield. Peter Bonetti the ex-England goalkeeper and Chelsea's goalkeeping coach was persuaded to turn out

Peter Bonetti making one of many tremendous saves against Weymouth in the F.A. Cup.

for Woking in the absence of Chris Lomas. A blinding performance against Weymouth in the F.A. Cup was followed by a low-key league debut against Marlow. This last match was enough for Bonetti to call it a day, but the performance against Weymouth would remain as the best ever debut show.

Two home defeats running against Marlow and Feltham left Woking in 9th place after 12 games, 14 points behind leaders Marlow. Promotion looked a distant dream, but only one defeat in the next thirteen games pushed Woking into second place, 4 points behind Marlow. Forty goals were scored including 13 from Buzaglo and 10 from Lansley.

A rare defeat, which proved to be the last of the season, at Chertsey 3-2 on New Years Day was a minor irritation. A final run-in saw 13 wins and 3 draws with only 5 goals conceded. Three times Woking scored five without reply. The final five games had to be played in the space of ten days.

Promotion was developing into a three horse race between Marlow, Dorking and Woking. Dorking did Woking a favour by defeating Marlow in the penultimate game of the season. This result gave Woking a breathing space, Harefield were beaten 3-0 with a brace from Tim Buzaglo; this clinched promotion.

Whyteleafe provided the opposition on the final game, one point was required for the championship as Woking had the superior goal difference. A sloppy goal just after half time gave Whyteleafe a one goal lead. With fifteen minutes left it was fitting that Tim Buzaglo should notch the equaliser which won the Championship. Thirty-four league goals out of the 110 Woking scored was a good effort in his first senior season. He was ably backed up by Horner, Dawber (early in the season) and Lansley who all scored 10 or more league goals.

Continuity was the secret of Woking's success, eight players played 30 or more league games, with Cassidy being the driving force as captain.

The cup games provided some success. In the F.A. Cup, five rounds were safely negotiated which included the defeat of Weymouth by 1-0. Chelmsford were just too strong in the first round, although the game at Woking ended in a 1-1 draw. The replay ended 2-1 in Chelmsford's favour.

First time defeats came in the F.A. Trophy and the London Senior Cup. Bracknell were defeated 2-0 in the A.C. Delco Cup, but after a replay Leatherhead knocked out Woking 2-1.

Two excellent victories against premier division opponents, Croydon and Kingstonian ensured progress in the Surrey Senior Cup. Croydon were destroyed 6-1 with Tim Buzaglo netting four goals.

The final against Sutton at Imber Court proved to be very one sided. Sutton scored an early goal which effectively killed off the game. The final score 4-0 was a fair reflection of the play.

Champions of the Division and Cup Runners-up was a springboard for what was to follow.

Winners of Division 2 (South) in 1986 - 1987. The start of Chapple's march to the Conference. Tim Buzaglo (front row, second from right) scored 45 goals in 50 games.

1987 - 1988

Season 1987-88 was full of expectations. Prior to the start of the season, Colin Lippiatt had joined the club as assistant manager. Of the new playing arrivals, Paul Shrubb and Barry Blankley had vast Football League experience with Aldershot. Robert Tenkorang a 19 year old goalkeeper released by Fulham started as number one goalkeeper and Andy Parr a utility player and former youth international commenced on the right side of midfield.

In the first game the defence played poorly in a 3-2 loss at home to Kingsbury. Parr scored both goals but Tim Buzaglo away on holiday was badly missed. With Buzaglo back and scoring twice, Boreham Wood were blitzed 5-2 but the defence once again collapsed 4-0 to Wembley, two wins followed, but a loss 2-1 at home to Marlow gave Woking three wins and three losses in the first six games. Tenkorang was dropped and left the club. Replacement Ken Lavender broke his leg in the third game, Grant Lunn played a few games, Jezz Jukes had a run but was inconsistent. Fortunately Chris Lomas become available in the new year and played for the rest of the season. The younger of the Buzaglo brothers, Richard, made his mark as a fast, goalscoring winger.

Three wins in October was followed by a draw and two losses. Marlow, the top team in the division gained the double over Woking. They continued to be consistent and finally won the division with 101 points.

By Christmas, despite playing erratically, Woking were in third place but were nine points behind Marlow and eleven points behind Grays.

Mark Biggins was signed from Windsor & Eton for £2,000 and made an impressive Boxing Day debut in a 3-0 home victory against Oxford City. It was no coincidence that Woking remained undefeated for the next ten league games, which included a magnificent 1-0 victory at league leaders Grays. An unbelievable 2-1 loss at third from bottom Billericay effectively finished off Woking's promotion prospects. Marlow and Grays were worthy winners and runners-up respectively, with 101 and 100 points. Woking finished a clear third with 82 points, but never really threatened the top two. Woking's goalkeeping problems were resolved too late in the season and two injury bouts prevented Tim Buzaglo playing in ten league games. Nevertheless 20 goals in 32 league games was a reasonable if not spectacular return. Clive Youlton who came into the side mid-December, scored 11 in 18 league games. Richard Buzaglo scored 8 in 17 games and Trevor Baron who was the danger man at set pieces also scored 8.

Cassidy who played in every league and cup game was an inspirational captain.

The F.A. Cup replay at home to Windsor & Eton centred around two substitutions. Windsor were leading 3-0 and seemingly coasting, took off Mark Biggins whose brilliant play no doubt led to his subsequent transfer to Woking. Manager Chapple brought on Richard Buzaglo in a desperate bid to save the game. Three goals in the last ten minutes took the game into extra time. A rampant Woking smashed in three more goals to win a remarkable game 6-3. The younger Buzaglo scored twice as did Baron.

Banstead were defeated 1-0 after a replay but Thanet ended Woking's interest winning 2-0 after extra time in a third qualifying round replay.

Two premier division sides, Bognor and Basingstoke. were beaten 2-1 at Kingfield in the F.A. Trophy but Hendon defeated Woking 3-1 in the third qualifying round.

A poor performance in the Surrey Senior Cup against Croydon led to a 2-1 defeat at Kingfield.

Whyteleafe were defeated 3-0 in the A.C. Delco Cup but in the next round Barking ended Woking's interest 2-0 in extra time.

The season was basically one of consolidation and not trophy winning.

1988 - 1989

The disappointment felt by the committed supporters as Woking lost promotion in the very last game of 1988-89 was difficult to take. A win against an average Lewes side was required but a nervous Woking had problems containing the fast raiding Lewes forwards. Twice Woking fought back to draw level at 2-2 with fifteen minutes left. Despite constant pressure roared on by a 1,420 crowd, Lewes defence buckled and rode their luck. Basingstoke comfortably won their last game to gain promotion by one point.

Woking's home performance (five losses and six draws) cost them promotion. The only loss away from home occurred in the last game at Staines, who won the division with the victory against Woking. A penalty miss may have given Woking the extra points required, but it would be churlish to pinpoint one event in which promotion was lost.

Once again the season started with a home loss this time 2-1 to Uxbridge. The non-availability of Trevor Baron and Tim Buzaglo for this game was too much of a handicap although at Wembley in the next game, some superb football and a hat-trick by Terry Worsfold buried Wembley 5-0. Buzaglo returned from holiday before the next game at home to Hampton scored a brilliant winning goal after coming on as a substitute.

A win at Southwick was negated by the usual home loss against Bracknell. Mark Davis, a tough competitor came into the side after this and with an emerging Shane Wye forming an effective midfield unit with Biggins and Cassidy, the results started to improve. Of the thirteen league games played up to the end of the year 7 were won and 6 were drawn. Four of these draws, were at home.

Cassidy played his last game for Woking at the end of 1988. Unable to change his style to suit the coach's wishes, he decided to try pastures new.

A fine draw at Basingstoke in the new year was followed by two home losses. Four straight wins were again followed by a home draw and a home loss without scoring a goal. Nine straight wins looked to have achieved the desired promotion but the sting in the tail in the last home game provided total agony for the supporters, players and officials. The poor home form was a complete mystery.

Progress in all the cups gave Woking an extra 21 matches. In the F.A. Cup easy wins against Canterbury and Whyteleafe plus a hard fought victory in a replay against Molesey gave Woking a long trip to Exmouth in the fourth qualifying round. Despite being 1-0 down to an early Exmouth strike, Woking gradually started to control the game. An equaliser just before half time and two goals from Tim Buzaglo finally broke Exmouth's resistance in a 5-1 victory.

A home draw against football league side Cambridge United drew 2,614 to see Woking perform. Unfortunately goalkeeper Trevor Jones who was a bag of nerves, let through two early goals and despite a fightback after Shane Wye had reduced the deficit another two goals gave Cambridge a 4-1 victory.

The F.A. Trophy run to the third round saw Woking play three superb games. St. Albans of the Premier Division were hammered 4-1 in a replayed tie after Cowler had scored a late equaliser at Kingfield. After Sheppey had succumbed 2-0, Woking found themselves 2-0 down at Crawley. A tremendous hat-trick from Tim Buzaglo and a single strike from John Richardson gave Woking a thrilling 4-3 victory. It was Richard Buzaglo's two goals which destroyed Bromsgrove in a 3-2 thriller. A double strike from Worsfold defeated Weymouth for the second time in three seasons.

A long trip to Newcastle Blue Star, a heavy gluepot pitch cleared of snow by Woking supporters and the loss of Biggins through suspension proved too much of a handicap in a 2-0 loss.

In the Surrey Senior Cup, victories against Metropolitan Police, Leatherhead and Chertsey gave Woking a final appearance against Carshalton. A very poor defensive performance resulted in a 4-2 loss.

An injury riddled season for Tim Buzaglo did not help Woking's cause, as he only scored six league goals plus 9 cup goals. Terry Worsfold scored 21 goals in 35 league and cup games. Biggins, Shane Wye and Cowler all scored 10 or more goals.

Once again Woking had a goalkeeping problem using no fewer than five keepers during the season. Biggins and Lloyd Wye missed only two games with Baron playing in all bar four.

Woking had an excellent season in the league and cup but the cupboard was bare of trophies.

A dejected team after losing to Carshalton in the Surrey Senior Cup Final.

John Cassidy, Woking's captain, proudly displaying the Division 2 (South) trophy won in 1986 - 1987.

Chapter 12

F.A. CUP GLORY, DIADORA LEAGUE CHAMPIONS, GM VAUXHALL CONFERENCE - THE 1990'S FA TROPHY TRIUMPH

1989 - 1990

After the near miss of the previous season, promotion was the prime aim of season 1989-90. Progress in the cups would be a welcome bonus.

Andy Parr rejoined after one season with Chertsey. New defenders Stewart Mitchell and Andy Russell tightened up the back four. Mark Franks provided the crosses from the left and the strike pairing of Buzaglo and Mulvaney formed a prolific partnership with 80 league and cup goals.

Tim Buzaglo had been performing leg strengthening exercises throughout the summer in an attempt to prevent the niggling injuries that had caused him to miss 17 league and cup games last season.

A good start to the season was essential and this was achieved with six straight wins. The first defeat at Worthing, masterminded by old boy John Cassidy came in the thirteenth game.

Lewes, who had stolen that 2-2 draw to prevent promotion the previous season, were swamped 6-0 with Paul Mulvaney scoring a hat-trick.

Due to cup commitments Woking were only in 4th place at the end of December with an incredible eight games in hand over leaders Southwick. A Tim Buzaglo goal defeated Southwick but a 2-1 loss at home to the current leaders Wivenhoe before 1,150 spectators put Wivenhoe in control. A hard fought 0-0 at Dorking was a point gained, as four days earlier Dorking had knocked Woking out of the Surrey Senior Cup by a margin of 3-0. Boreham Wood provided the shock result in defeating Woking at Kingfield 2-1.

The response to this result was excellent as eight of the next nine games were won with only one goal being conceded. Buzaglo scored eleven goals in these nine games.

Two very hard away games followed at Metropolitan Police and Harlow. For once the defence were not at their best, nevertheless a 3-3 and 2-2 draw respectively was satisfactory. The championship depended on Wivenhoe but promotion was the prime aim. Promotion was achieved in the home game against Uxbridge. A Buzaglo hat-trick and two from Mulvaney gave Woking a 6-1 decisive victory. The last three games would decide the championship. Woking gained three victories to give them 98 points, but unfortunately Wivenhoe beat Worthing 3-1 to win the championship with 100 points. The introduction of Fred Callaghan as coach gave Woking consistency. The playing system formulated by Chapple, Lippiatt and Callaghan was based on the strengths of the players.

Mark Franks was given a specific role on the left-wing which included defensive as well as attacking duties.

Premier division football would be on show again after an absence of seven seasons.

In the F.A. Cup, progress to the second round was achieved with victories against Kingstonian 5-1, Southwick 4-1, Erith & B 5-0 after a 1-1- draw, 3-1 at Wokingham and a 2-1 victory at Slough. The thrashing of Kingstonian in their own backyard was arguably the most complete performance of the season. By a coincidence the second round draw again paired Woking with Cambridge United but this time away.

It was unfortunate that key defender, sweeper Cowler failed a last minute fitness test and Cambridge scored the important early goal whilst replacement Steve Moss was still finding his feet. Paul Mulvaney gave Woking an outside chance at 2-1 but a last minute goal gave Cambridge an undeserved two goal margin.

Four consecutive home draws in the F.A. Trophy helped Woking to reach the third round. Two goals from Mulvaney in each game helped defeat Fareham and midland-based Bromsgrove 5-1 and 3-0 respectively. Seaham Red Star from Co. Durham were finally defeated 3-1 in a hard fought encounter.

Buzaglo's late goal gave Woking a second chance at Bath but two soft goals conceded by on-loan keeper Julian Gray, saw Woking defeated by 2-1 in a bad tempered affair.

In the League Cup sponsored by A.C. Delco, the semi-final two leg stage was reached. In earlier rounds, two goals from Buzaglo helped destroy Tooting 5-1. Despite scoring first, Clapton were finally beaten 8-1 with a hat-trick from Buzaglo. Barking were defeated 3-0 after a 1-1 draw away. Kingsbury provided stiff resistance, 0-0 away and 2-1 at Kingfield. A 1-1 draw in the first leg semi-final at St. Albans should have given Woking a place in the final, but a muted performance at Kingfield enabled St. Albans to win 2-1.

Cobham were beaten 9-1 in the Surrey Senior Cup with Buzaglo grabbing a hat-trick. Epsom were just defeated 2-1 but Dorking's muscular efforts finished off Woking 3-0 in the semi-final.

Tim Buzaglo scored 49 league and cup goals including four hat-tricks, Paul Mulvaney was a perfect foil especially early in the season with 31 goals. Andy Parr scored 21 goals from midfield and Gary Hall scored 12 in 19 full games.

Sixty-four league and cup games were played during the season, including eight in 18 games during April and May. Fortunately injuries were few, so enforced changes were small. Nine players played 36 or more league games.

1990 - 1991

The number and importance of the cup-ties played in season 1990-91 no doubt prevented Woking making a serious assault on the championship at the end of the season. Nevertheless the achievements of the season, fourth place in the league, winning the Surrey Senior Cup and the A.C. Delco Cup, defeating second division West Bromwich Albion and frightening Division One Everton nearly to death in the F.A. Cup, made this season the best ever; certainly as far as media coverage was concerned.

It all started sedately on 18th August as Windsor & Eton, with their ten man defence, came to Kingfield and went away with a 0-0 draw.

Basingstoke and Staines were obliterated on their own grounds, 6-0 and 7-0 respectively. Midfielder Andy Parr snatched five goals in these two games. After five league games, Woking had not let through a single goal, the only points dropped were in the opening game. The home game against Carshalton changed all that. Within 36 minutes of the start Carshalton were leading 4-0. New goalkeeper, Tim Read cracked under the pressure along with his defensive colleagues. Two second half goals brought some respectability to the final score.

Nevertheless a 1-0 victory at Dagenham put Woking in top position. Three home victories followed including a fortunate 2-1 result against Enfield. Despite a disastrous 4-2 reverse at Kingstonian, four victories and a draw up to Christmas, kept Woking in the hunt for the title.

Dereck Brown, battling away against Everton.

During this period Woking began their F.A. Cup campaign which was to dominate the local and national sporting pages for a few weeks. Three Vauxhall Conference sides were defeated, Bath, Kidderminster (after three titanic games) and Merthyr Tydfil who had two players sent off during a 5-1 beating. Woking were drawn to play Second Division West Bromwich at the Hawthorns in the third round. On paper Woking had no chance, but West Bromwich were having a poor season and their confidence was at a low ebb. West Bromwich snatched a goal just before half time to seemingly settle the tie but lack of pace in the centre of their defence was exploited to the full by Tim Buzaglo. In fourteen minutes from the hour, Buzaglo had turned the tie on its head with a hat-trick of goals, substitute Terry Worsfold added a fourth before a late strike made the final score 4-2.

Unbelievably the Albion supporters chaired both Tim Buzaglo and Tim Read over to the home fans, a perfect ending to an unforgettable day. West Bromwich never recovered and were relegated at the end of the season. Manager Brian Talbot was sacked within 24 hours of the cup exit.

The dream ends. Woking players complete a lap of honour after the Everton game.

The fourth round draw paired Woking with mighty Everton. On police advice the game was switched to Goodison Park. 10,000 Woking supporters in a Sunday crowd of 34,724 made the day one to remember forever. Everton won by a slender margin of 1-0 but it was the Merseysiders who breathed a sigh of relief at the final whistle.

The atmosphere, as the Woking team completed their lap of honour was unbelievable, and the day must go down as the greatest in Woking's history. Everton manager Howard Kendall and his players stayed on the pitch to join in the applause.

After the hype and atmosphere created by the cup run, it was inevitable the league performances would suffer. Tim Buzaglo became a marked man and eventually fell foul of a diabolical tackle in the match against St. Albans. A cruciate ligament operation sidelined Tim for the remainder of the season and the whole of the 1991-92 campaign.

March proved to be the month when the title challenge started to slip away. Two draws and two defeats from six games proved to be costly as Redbridge Forest began to pull away at the top. Colin Caulfield had replaced an out sorts Tim Read in goal. New boy Richard Smart was brought in as Tim Buzaglo's replacement. The former Whyteleafe striker scored 7 goals in his ten league games.

Bradley Pratt goes close with a header against Everton.

With eleven league games left, Woking were eleven points behind leaders, Redbridge Forest; only a slim chance remained.

A below par performance at Hayes in a 4-1 thrashing finally finished the title challenge. A 1-0 victory, with a Richard Smart goal, prevented Redbridge Forest from taking the title until the following week. A 3-0 victory at home to Leyton-Wingate in the last league match of the season enabled Woking to hold on the fourth place.

The Surrey Senior Cup was won with an emphatic 3-0 victory over Kingstonian. Andy Parr made a triumphant scoring return to the side, but Lance Pedlar won the man of the match award with two outstanding goals.

Adie Cowler, club captain and Player of the Year, with the A.C. Delco Cup.

The 66th and last match of a magnificent season gave Woking a second trophy. Carshalton were defeated 2-1 in the A.C. Delco Cup Final. It was appropriate that Trevor Baron, who typified Woking's football skills, headed the winner.

Bradley Pratt, who had kept out Andy Russell for much of the season, played in 53 games and notched 12 goals. Adie Cowler played 62 games in his sweeper role. Tim Buzaglo who had such a sweet and sour season, was top scorer with 15 in 28 games. One player who made his mark in the cup ties against Kidderminster and Merthyr was Andy Clement, who only played eight games before joining Plymouth Argyle.

Attendances at Kingfield increased by 75% over the previous season, with a top league attendance of 2,376 against St. Albans. A crowd of 4,188 watched Woking defeat Merthyr in the F.A. Cup.

Ground improvements were already planned and cash set aside ready for the assault on the league title and the coveted Conference status.

1991- 1992

Following the magnificent achievements of 1990-91, season 1991-92 was viewed with great optimism. Unfortunately coach Fred Callaghan had joined Kingstonian along with striker Richard Smart. Other top Woking players were offered lucrative deals, which fortunately were not accepted. Derek Cottrell was appointed the new coach. Two ex-league players were signed up, George Friel a 20 year old striker from Reading and Laurence Batty, a goalkeeper from Fulham.

Kingfield had been transformed during the close season with new covered terracing behind the Kingfield Road goal, a relocated entrance with new turnstiles and new seating to both stands.

The pre-season friendlies were disappointing as the new striking partnership of Friel and Walkes (signed from Hampton) struggled to score. Victories at home to Carshalton by 3-0 and away to Kingstonian by 2-1, with Friel scoring in both plus a hard fought 0-0 draw at Chesham gave Woking a useful start to the league campaign.

Woking defeated Redbridge Forest 3-1 in the Isthmian Charity Shield with new signing Andy Perry causing havoc in the Redbridge defence. An early trophy was sign of things to come.

Adie being presented with the Charity Shield.

Half way through September, Woking reached the top spot of the Diadora League. A 2-1 defeat at home to Bromley in early September was followed by five consecutive victories. Steve Milton was signed "on approval" and immediately created a good impression in a 3-0 victory at Wokingham. Goalkeeper Batty scored an unbelievable goal in a 7-1 victory at Wivenhoe. His fly-kick that bounced over the stranded Wivenhoe goalkeeper overshadowed Friel's magnificent four goals.

Two second half goals completed the double over Carshalton and Steve Milton repaid some of his £15,000 transfer fee with a last minute winner at home to Grays.

Six unbeaten league games were played in October as the top spot was consolidated. Derek Cottrell had resigned as coach due to work pressures. Shane Wye returned from New Zealand to claim his midfield spot. Bradley Pratt replaced an injured Andy Russell and never lost his place.

November was significant in terms of the title. Fortunately exemption until the first round of the F.A. Cup enabled Woking to forge ahead with their league programme. By the end of November, Woking were 16 points clear of Enfield who nevertheless had five games in hand. Three games in November seemed to highlight Woking's destiny. Bottom club Bishops Stortford were leading a listless Woking by 1-0, when two goals in the last four minutes gave lucky Woking the points. A potentially difficult game at Hendon was surprisingly easy with Woking producing their best performance with a 5-0 victory.

The following Saturday 3,125 packed Kingfield for the visit of Enfield. At the end of 90 minutes a shell-shocked Enfield were blown away 5-0. In reviewing the season this was the point when Enfield knew they were only fighting for second place.

The squad that defeated Redbridge Forest in the Charity Shield.
Left to right Standing S. Mitchell, D. Brown, L. Wye, A. Russell, L. Batty, A Cowler.
Sitting A. Parr, T. Baron, M. Biggins, P. Mulvaney, P. Barrowcliffe, A. Perry.

Two victories at Staines and Aylesbury kept Woking on course up to the new year and although cup football then took over a number of weeks, the league championship remained the prime goal.

Twenty-one league games were played undefeated between losing at home to

Bromley on 3rd September and losing at home to Wokingham on 18th February. Eight straight wins followed with the league championship being won at Windsor and Eton on the 4th April with seven league games still to play.

The new league champions were welcomed by 3,073 supporters on the following Tuesday at home to Kingstonian. Old boy, Richard Smart threatened to spoil the party with a spectacular goal but three goals in the final half hour ensured the celebrations continued.

On the following Saturday, the official presentation of the championship trophy was made as Woking defeated Bishop's Stortford by 3-0.

Chapple and Lippiatt with the Diadora Trophy.

The Championship winning squad.
Left to right Standing Ted Hills, Bradley Pratt, Lol Batty, Trevor Baron, Stewart Mitchell, Steve Milton, Andy Parr, Francis Vines, Shane Wye. Seated Adie Cowler, George Friel, Lloyd Wye, Dereck Brown, Nick Collier, Mark Biggins.

As expected the final five games were somewhat of an anti-climax, two draws and three losses lay testament to this. Nevertheless 97 points and an 18 point margin over second place Enfield showed Woking's total dominance over the rest of the league.

Progress was made in all the cup competitions but the heights of the previous season were never matched.

In the F.A. Cup a hard fought victory over Windsor & Eton gave Woking a chance to show their teeth against Conference opponents. Yeovil attracted 4,250 to Kingfield and left a beaten side. George Friel scored a superb hat-trick, but Batty achieved the man of the match award with a magnificent display. Hereford came to Woking in the third round and defended for 90 minutes in a 0-0 draw. The replay went to extra time with Hereford finally winning against a tiring Woking.

A ground record of 5,801 saw Woking lose by the only goal at Adams Park to high flyers Wycombe in the second round of the F.A. Trophy. Enfield ended Woking's hopes of retaining the League Cup with a 2-0 victory at Kingfield in the quarter-final. The Surrey Senior Cup semi-final was lost by the same score to Carshalton.

The final of the Loctite Cup was reached, but a jaded Woking were beaten 2-0 by a strong Sutton side. The fading out in the last few weeks should not detract from a magnificent championship season.

Steve Milton, a skilful striker who contributed many goals in the Diadora Championship team 1991 - 1992.

Andy Parr, midfield utility player, 1987 to 1992, 47 goals in 177 games.

George Friel a prolific strike partnership with Steve Milton, 1991 - 1992, 37 goals in 56 appearances proved his worth.

George Friel scored 37 league and cup goals and his "twin" striking partner Steve Milton bagged 24 goals.

Trevor Baron played in all 62 games with Laurence Batty only missing one game. Like most successful seasons the balance of the team was rarely disturbed with incoming players slotting into the playing system easily. Although Batty was voted Player of the Season, Adie Cowler's captaincy and organisation throughout the season played a vital part in the success.

Another plus was the average league attendances which increased by 28% to an average of 1,881 at home.

The Vauxhall Conference would be a challenge which manager Geoff Chapple would no doubt relish.

Adie Cowler, captain and exceptional sweeper. Ideal for the Chapple system. 1986 to 1992, 342 games.

1992 - 1993

Season 1992-93, the first on the GM Vauxhall Conference nearly became a disaster before a ball had been kicked. The ground alterations stipulated by the Conference Ground Grading Committee had not been completed by the required date. Fortunately the grading committee had left a loophole which gave Woking a much needed extension thus enabling work to be completed by the due date. It was touch and go.

Manager Geoff Chapple decided that the majority of the championship side would not be good enough for the Conference. This was a drastic, and probably a brave move. The experience of Redbridge Forest in their first Conference season, when the first team squad was replaced after a few months, had a profound effect on Chapple's thinking.

Mark Biggins, an influential member of the Diadora championship winning side of 1992, one of Geoff Chapple's best ever signings.

Batty, Dereck Brown, Biggins and Baron survived the chop, although Baron lost his place after eleven games, the Wye brothers returned from New Zealand to play a part and the WBA hero, Tim Buzaglo, played some games but never really settled and finally was transferred to Marlow in March for £4,000.

The heroes of the previous season spread throughout the Diadora League. Interestingly enough very few of them set the league alight.

The replacements had mainly played league football. Kev Brown and Dave Puckett came

Trevor Senior, a big name signing for the inaugural Conference season 1992-93, in action against Brighton in the F.A. Cup.

from the defunct Aldershot. Richard Nugent arrived from Barnet. Robbie Carroll had Conference experience with Yeovil. Friel was swapped for Colin Fielder at Slough. Andy Clement returned from Plymouth and the prolific goalscorer Trevor Senior was signed on a free from Reading. Mark Fleming arrived from Farnborough.

Pre-season friendlies did not inspire any great confidence although Peter Beardsley gave great entertainment as Everton came to Kingfield, but 2,044 came to see Woking's first game in the Conference. A mediocre Stafford Rangers won at a canter 3-0. A Fleming penalty gave Woking a 1-0 midweek victory at Kettering. A good performance at home to Runcorn with Tim Buzaglo snatching two in a 4-0 victory and a 3-1 Biggins inspired victory at Kidderminster gave Woking three wins in five games.

Unfortunately the start was not maintained, the side leaked goals and the forward line lacked punch. Only one victory in nine games left Woking in a relegation situation. Trevor Senior scored his first league goal late in November.

The breaking-up of the Championship side seemed to be the wrong decision, but the midweek away game at Merthyr Tydfil changed Woking's season. Eighteen year old Tim Alexander was signed on loan from Barnet to replace Trevor Baron. A loyal servant, Baron had lost the vital edge in pace. Steve Milton came in to partner Senior. In appalling conditions two goals from Milton and from Senior gave Woking a 5-1 victory. Three victories and two draws in the next five games pushed Woking quickly up the table.

Scott Steele, a skilful forward who joined the club from Scottish football in 1992.

Tim Buzaglo, famed goalscorer, who became part of Woking's folklore in the late 1980's and early 1990's.

A record league gate of 4,911 on Boxing Day at home to eventual champions, Wycombe, was a test of Woking's new found confidence. Wycombe proved to be in a different class with a 3-0 victory.

Three victories followed without conceding a goal. A top six place was possible but the odd poor result prevented this. Kidderminster came to Kingfield and all the bad habits returned in a 5-1 defeat.

Richard Nugent returned in the next game at Wycombe. A rousing game before 5,000 ended 0-0. This was Tim Alexander's last game for Woking. His loan period was vital for Woking's survival.

Rob Peters on loan from Brentford also made a great impression in the last seven games. The last two home games against Farnborough and Stalybridge were won, but a one-nil defeat at Bromsgrove in the final game pushed Woking down to eighth place and gave Bromsgrove the runners-up spot.

After the first dozen games a final position of eighth was somewhat of a triumph and entirely satisfactory as the promoted sides from the South had a history of being relegated at the first attempt.

The Isthmian Charity Shield was retained as Grays were swamped 5-1. In the Drinkwise Cup, Welling defeated Woking 4-3 in a 2-legged tie.

Once again exemption to the first round of the F.A. Cup gave Woking a chance of some extra cash. A home tie against Nuneaton proved to be a thriller with 3,280 seeing Woking come back from 2-1 down to finally win with a Robbie Carroll 25 yarder in the last minute. An excellent 1-1 draw at Brighton in the second round with Shane Wye scoring the equaliser, gave Woking a second chance. A noisy crowd of 5,870 packed into Kingfield to see Senior give Woking an early lead. An equaliser before half time and a fluky rebound enabled Brighton to take their place in the third round at home to Portsmouth.

On an atrocious pitch at Sutton, Woking were easily defeated in the first round of the Trophy by 3-0.

Dorking defeated a lethargic Woking 2-0 at Kingfield in a replayed Surrey Senior Cup tie after a 2-2 draw at Dorking.

Trevor Senior top scored with 13 league and cup goals, Dave Puckett scored 12 goals and no one else managed more than six goals. Kevan Brown who had a poor start to his Woking career at full back moved into the centre of the defence and was so successful that he won Player of the Year and must have been on the England non-league short list.

Laurence Batty became Woking's first international since 1959, when he played against Finland and the Highland League.

Laurence Batty, Woking's top Conference keeper, with a young fan.

1993-1994

May 21st 1994 must surely go down as Woking's greatest day in their long history. Geoff Chapple's ten successful years as manager came to a magnificent climax as referee Durkin blew the final whistle at a very wet Wembley Stadium. Woking has won the F.A. Trophy 2-1 against fellow Conference opponents, Runcorn.

As Kevan Brown, captain supreme, raised the Trophy, 12,000 fans paraded a red sea of flags, hats, banners, shirts and scarves.

This triumph would not have been predicted at the start of the season as personnel changes did not immediately gel. Nugent, Fleming, Senior, Bushay and Carroll were released pre-season. Alexander, who had played a major role in the revival of 1992-93, signed pro-forms for Barnet. In came Gwynn Berry and Mark Tucker in defence.

Agboola, who had an outstanding football league pedigree, played a handful of games before a chronic back problem finished his season. Clive Walker had been released by Brighton, he chose Woking and although of mature years, he had a magnificent season. Two points and only one goal from the first five league games left Woking in 21st place. This included a 5-0 battering at newly promoted Dover, which shattered the confidence of the team. Jody Craddock, on loan from Cambridge, was brought into the defence. Lenny Dennis arrived from Sutton as strike partner to Clive Walker. Scott Steele shined in a free midfield role and raw talent Kevin Rattray from Tottenham district football, gave the midfield strength.

Macclesfield and Merthyr were defeated but a 6-2 thrashing at home to Halifax showed the brittleness of the Woking defence at that time.

A 3-0 home victory against top of the table Dover in atrocious conditions was the turning point. Fourteen league games without defeat included a 1-0 home victory against eventual champions Kidderminster and a fighting 3-2 success at Halifax after being 2-0 down in ten minutes.

Confidence returned and the return of the Wye brothers from New Zealand gave the

Surrey Senior Cup victory over Sutton United. Dereck Brown celebrating with the Cup.

Darran Hay scoring in the Surrey Senior Cup victory.

team a better balance. Clive Walker and Lenny Dennis couldn't stop scoring. Mark Tucker replaced Craddock and gained confidence in a winning side.

The team celebrating their victory over Sutton United.

A steady climb up the league table gave Woking a top four spot at the end of January. Back-to-back defeats at Telford and Kettering dashed Championship hopes. Kidderminster, despite a tremendous F.A. Cup run, finally won the league, although the vagaries of the Football League system prevented them taking up their rightful place in Division Three.

Despite being involved in the F.A. Trophy and losing key players, Lenny Dennis for the final two months of the season with a fractured cheekbone and Shane Wye returning to New Zealand, Woking finally managed a respectable third. The final three home games were played on consecutive days. It said much for the spirit of the side that two of these were won. There was an amazing match at Kingfield in which Woking were defeated 8-1 by Dagenham and Redbridge. Four days later Woking put up a defensive barrier in a 0-0 second leg semi-final F.A. Trophy at Enfield.

Little impression was made in the F.A. Cup; Weston-Super-Mare were beaten 1-0 in a replay after a 2-2 draw at Kingfield. In the 2nd round, a late penalty conceded at Kidderminster produced a 1-0 defeat.

Three fairly easy victories against Diadora opposition gave Woking a place in the final of the Surrey Senior Cup against bogey team, Sutton. Woking, with the F.A. Trophy Final in mind, played at half-pace for most of the game but goals by Tucker, Steele and Hay put to rest the Sutton bogey in a 3-1 victory.

Kevin Rattray (left) and Lenny Dennis (right) members of the successful 1993-94 squad.

Bashley were swept aside 4-2 in the first round of the F.A. Trophy with a brace of goals from Dennis and one-a-piece from Walker and Shane Wye. This was Shane Wye's last game before returning to New Zealand. A second half blitz by Dagenham & Redbridge could not prevent a 2nd round 2-1 victory to Woking. Woking's name appeared to be on the trophy, when Bromsgrove despite being twice in front, finally lost to a Barry Lakin goal five minutes from time. Kev Brown scored his first ever goal in this game and followed up with both goals in a 2-1 replay win at windswept Billingham Synthonia, the old ICI works team. Wembley was very close now, but Enfield proved to be very resilient with both legs of the semi-final being drawn. The replay at neutral Wycombe was very eventful with Enfield being reduced to ten men as early as the 13th minute. Two goals from Hay and one from Steele, gave Woking a final place for the first time in 36 years.

In the final against Runcorn, two goals before thirty minutes had elapsed, from Dereck Brown and Hay gave Woking control. a 74th minute penalty by Runcorn was only a consolation goal. Celebrations started early that day. As manager Geoff Chapple said at the celebration dinner, "what can one achieve now"?

Fifty-nine league and cup games were played, with Kevan Brown only missing one league game. He superbly marshalled a defence in which Clement (46 games), Berry (57 games), Tucker (40 games) and Lloyd Wye (36 games) played significant roles. Batty, although not as consistent in goal as in previous seasons, performed well in the Trophy semi-final and final. Scott Steele (52 games) found his best role behind the front two. Clive Walker had a magnificent season with 23 goals in 52 games. Dennis scored 13 in 27 games and in the final month a young talent on loan from Cambridge United, Darran Hay, made an immediate impact scoring 8 in 13 games. Colin Fielder (40 games) moved into a defensive midfield role late in the season. With Rattray (36 games) giving more midfield bite, this allowed Dereck Brown (57 games) to provide the midfield artistry.

Dereck Brown deservedly gained England non-league international honours against Guernsey, and on the Scandinavian tour came on as substitute against Finland U 21's and played a full game versus Norway U 21's.

The season was a triumph for manager Geoff Chapple, coach Colin Lippiatt and the players; third in the GM Vauxhall Conference, winners of the Surrey Senior Cup and winners of the F.A. Trophy.

Kevan Brown scoring a brilliant header against Bromsgrove during the F.A. Trophy run.

F.A. Trophy 1993/1994

Scott Steele and Lloyd Wye check out the Wembley turf.

Blazers and club ties prior to the real business of the day.

Introduction to Steve Coppell before kick-off.

Kevan Brown exchanges pleasantries with the Runcorn captain.

First blood to Woking as Dereck Brown celebrates the opening goal.

Darran Hay makes it two.

Celebration in front of the Woking hordes.

Kevan Brown leads the team out for the second half.

We've won the Trophy. Dereck Brown is submerged by Scott Steele and Kevin Rattray.

The Trophy is raised aloft from the Royal Box.

Celebration time.

Showing off to the fans.

Dereck Brown and Darran Hay with the Trophy.

Clive Walker and friend.

Andy Clement, Colin Fielder and Dave Puckett.

Team celebration on the pitch.

More celebrations in the dressing room.

A section of the crowd by the civic gates waiting for the F.A. Trophy bus to arrive.

Open -top coach tour of Woking after the victory in the F.A. Trophy Wembley Final 1994.

Geoff Chapple held aloft with the coveted F.A. Trophy.

A close-up study of the Trophy winners by Michael Hart. Under 18 prizewinner in the Woking Borough Council Photographic Competition 1994.

1994-1995

"What can we achieve now?" This was Geoff Chapple's memorable comment after Runcorn had been defeated in the F.A. Trophy Final at Wembley and third place in the Conference had been achieved last season.

At the end of the current season the question was answered, runners-up behind Macclesfield in the league and a last ditch victory against last season's champions Kidderminster to retain the F.A. Trophy. Only Scarborough had won the trophy twice running.

All this would have seemed impossible back in August. Financial restrictions were necessary to stabilise the club.

Andy Clement and Dave Puckett were released pre-season. Lee Tierling a 21 year old fullback released by Fulham claimed Clement's fullback position for the first half of the season. Darran Hay was brought back from Cambridge United on loan for the first three months of the season. He was finally signed for £15,000 at the end of March.

Another link with the West Bromwich, Everton F.A. Cup ties was severed with the transfer to Walton-and-Hersham of Dereck Brown. He had played a major role in Chapple's teams of the 90's but it was necessary to plan for the future. Lenny Dennis and Gwynne Berry also moved on. Tim Alexander returned from Barnet and Richard Newbery an exciting young talent arrived from Wokingham.

Defensive stability, together with a great team spirit and the magic ingredient of evergreen Clive Walker provided the essential mixture for a superb season. Walker won the Player of the Year award at the Conference end of season dinner/dance and with Chapple being awarded joint Manager of the Year, it was celebrations all round.

A 3-1 home loss to bogey team Halifax in the first game of the season was not the most auspicious start but five straight wins including victories at high flying Altrincham and newly promoted Stevenage, gave the season a kick-start.

The first trophy was won in September with a superb victory at Kidderminster in the Championship Shield. Making his midfield debut was Andy Ellis who had played for Barry Town in the European Cup-Winners Cup and also for the Welsh non-league international team. He was a talented player and formed an immediate rapport with Shane Wye.

Shane, who had first donned a Woking shirt in 1983, had probably played his final game. A two year player/coach contract awaited him in New Zealand, but he had the coveted F.A. Trophy winners medal and no doubt many memories.

Woking briefly topped the Conference table in September and at the end of October, but Macclesfield under Sammy McIlroy, put together a tremendous unbeaten run which looked to have the league won by January. Being turned down by the Endsleigh League had an immediate effect. From an unassailable position they started to lose. During the final weeks of the season the margin was reduced from 17 to 5 points.

Due to cup runs and cancellation, Woking played eight games in only two weeks. This probably decided the destiny of the championship.

Apart from winning the Trophy final the unbelievable 5-5 draw at Bromsgrove had to be the game of the season. The incident of the season was the abortive trip to Dover when a herd of marauding bulls loose on the fast lane of the motorway prevented players and spectators getting to the match. The football reporters had a field day with headlines such as "What a load of bullocks."

Nevertheless it was cup-tie football which produced the good and the not so good. the F.A. Cup tie at Barnet saw Woking storm into a 3-0 interval lead, only to be pegged back to a final 4-4 draw. Over 4,800 spectators witnessed Mark Tucker's winning goal in the replay. In contrast, the second round at lowly Marlow was an anticlimax with the home side winning in the final minute.

The most unbelievable result had to be the 6-1 thrashing at Chertsey in the Surrey Senior Cup. To their credit the players recovered to brush aside Chesham and Cheltenham in the Trophy.

A tricky away tie at form team Stevenage, hinged on the sending off of former Woking player, Richard Nugent. A 3-0 victory gave Woking the tie of the tournament at Macclesfield. It was the tale of two penalties, Walker scored and Macclesfield missed; end of story. In fact penalties scored and missed played a significant part during the season. Woking's goalkeepers (Batty 4, Read 1) saved the final five penalties of the season and Clive Walker blasted home his 16th consecutive penalty over two seasons. Surely both must be Woking records.

The magnificent Rushden and Diamonds stadium provided the venue for the semi-final. How Woking survived for only a 1-0 loss was a mystery but a 2-0 second leg victory at Kingfield with Walker scoring the winner meant a return to Wembley against the old foes, Kidderminster for the "friendly final".

A Scott Steele first minute goal and a winning header from Colin Fielder two minutes from the end of extra time, beat off the determined Kidderminster challenge. So it was Kevan Brown who proudly held the Trophy aloft once again. It was a memorable season for Kevan who also won his first caps for the England non-league side. Lol Batty also regained his England place.

Lol Batty, Mark Tucker, Colin Fielder, Kev Brown and Lloyd Wye formed an exceptional defensive unit throughout the season.

Lloyd has been part of the Woking scene for ten years, with the Trophy being his 435th competitive game. Only Brian Farris and Brian Finn have a greater number of appearances. It was fitting that the Supporters Club recognised Lloyd's commitment over ten years with the presentation of a commemorative trophy.

Kevin Rattray was unfortunate not to be a regular in midfield. When given his chance against Rushden in the second leg of the Trophy semi-final, he produced a match winning performance.

Darran Hay had an electric start to the season, claiming 13 goals in 14 games. He was immediately recalled by Cambridge United. On his return later in the season he never quite reached the same heights. A cameo role was played by on-loan Grant Payne from Wimbledon, who in his short spell created a lasting impression. John Crumplin, released by Brighton played the final dozen games. An instant success with the fans, he provided an extra dimension down the right.

The jewel however was Clive Walker, ably backed-up by will-of-the-wisp Scott Steele, who scored that fabulous opening goal at Wembley in 59 seconds. Clive surpassed his efforts of the previous season, not only scoring 25 goals but by his general play. He rightly won the Conference Player of the Year.

Wembley Stadium welcomes Woking Football Club.

F.A. Umbro Trophy 1994/1995

The Wembley team line-up.

The 'Cards' following - a sea of colour.

Kevan Brown - 2nd successive final as skipper.

Woking go ahead after 59 seconds with a wicked shot from Scott Steele.

The Wembley Scoreline.

Clive Walker fighting for possession.

Colin Fielder wraps up a fine match with the winning goal in extra-time.

Catch me if you can - I've just scored the winner.

Kevan Brown receives the F.A. Trophy 1995.

Colin Fielder - to the victor goes the spoils.

The scorer of the winning goal - the F.A. Trophy is mine.

A proud moment for the Wye brothers.

Reflecting on their successive win at Wembley.

Woking F.C. Skipper shows off the trophy.

Team members celebrate their victory on the open - top bus tour of the town.

Woking F.C. Sponsor OLC , John Lytle (Director) on the right of Geoff Chapple join in the town centre celebrations.

Wokings Junior 'Cards' join Geoff Chapple to learn all about being successful.

Chapter 13

MISCELLANY

Administrators and officials have been said to be a necessary evil. It would be true to say that results are achieved by the players on the field of play but is vital for effective administration of the club to have officials who are hard working, keen and above all efficient.

Ron Pook, born a year after the birth of Woking Football Club. Played at Bolton in 1908. Wearing the Centenary Pennant at the tender age of 101.

Nowadays, officials are a much more important factor. This is because the financial turnover of the club is large and run on the lines of a small business. The books have to balance.

Woking have always had an abundance of hard working officials with Cardinal Red running through their veins. Year in and year out they gave their time voluntarily.

In the early days Bert Robertson, a founder playing member was elected to the position of Hon. Secretary.

The surge of adrenaline at the formation of a new club provided the drive for the first couple of seasons. After this the enthusiasm of the officials was needed to maintain this drive.

Bert Robertson provided this energy along with President R.N. Stevens. The foundations had been well and truly laid.

E.T. Engall was the next Hon. Secretary to make his mark. He fought through a number of troughs, including season 1905-06 which was the poorest for many years. At this point in time Engall's main claim to fame was being involved in the record 16-0 defeat against New Crusaders. He actually played half the game in goal and it was reputed his bowler hat remained on throughout his stint as goalkeeper.

For a number of seasons there was the constant threat of losing the ground at Horsell. It was just prior to season 1907-08 that a permanent ground on the Hockering Estate was secured. The officials of the day had fought long and hard for this security.

It was the spur Woking needed and it was no coincidence that 1907-08 was arguably the best season so far. As well as superb results, the financial rewards were most welcome. This provided enough resources to build up the new ground and still maintain financial stability. E.T. Engall and his assistants, A. Wells and Tom Gloster, plus many others, ploughed their free time and more into improving the status of the club.

Clarrie Jarman and Leslie Gosden receiving a commemorative plaque from Woking Council Mayor in recognition of winning the Amateur Cup in 1958.

The F.A. Cup exploits of 1907-08 culminating in the game against top league side Bolton Wanderers, placed Woking to the forefront of amateur football. This one single outstanding season appeared to be sufficient for Woking to receive an invitation to join the Isthmian League from season 1911-12.

Financially, travelling expenses would be greater but it was expected that increased attendances would bring in a greater revenue. The turnover of the club had increased tenfold in fifteen years. This was pointed out at the annual meeting in September 1910, in 1895 income was £30 whereas in 1909 it was £336.

E.T. Engall's ten year reign as Secretary ended in 1911. After a short spell from F.G. Neville, E "Dad" Saunders commenced his 25 year mammoth stint. Elected as Hon. Secretary in 1913, he maintained his position until 1938.

Three Presidents served during Saunders' spell as Secretary, A.H. Godfrey (1913-19), T.C. Gloster (1919-23) and former Woking Captain and amateur international A.H. "Daisy" Bell (1923-42).

This longevity of officials is the norm at Woking. With this in mind it seems appropriate to mention Clarrie Jarman and Leslie Gosden in more detail, as their determination to provide the town with a football club to be proud of never wavered over many years.

Members of the Woking Football Club committee as perceived in the Woking Review, October 1958

Clarrie Jarman was a keen supporter of the Cardinals from an early age at the turn of the century. Whilst still at school, he spent his Saturday afternoons selling programmes at the match.

Before the 1914-18 war, he played for the Maybury School team. At that time "Dad" Saunders, Hon. Secretary and Treasurer of Woking Football Club was headmaster of Maybury School.

Clarrie turned out regularly for the Old Church Lad's Brigade team and when he joined the Army he played for the Battalion.

Although apprenticed to Skeet and Jeffes, like most of the young men, he enlisted as soon as war was declared. When the 7th Battalion, the Queens Regiment joined the front line, this signalled the end of Clarrie's Army career. On July 1st 1916, at the Battle of the Somme, a bad gunshot wound in his leg and a fortuitous fall into a shell hole, no doubt saved his life but nevertheless, the leg was amputated. Convalescence brought him back to Woking at Beechcroft, which then was the V.A.D. hospital.

In 1925, unhampered by his false leg, Clarrie set off for the Council Offices on his pedal cycle and applied for the job as School Attendance Officer, a job he held until retirement in 1961.

When Woking Football Club re-started after the First World War, Clarrie joined the Supporters Club, eventually becoming Secretary. In 1927 he was elected to the football club committee; two years later he became the club's Hon. Secretary. After the Second World War in 1945, he played a prominent role in the "revival and survival" of the club. Clarrie's proudest moment was recorded in 1958 when he witnessed the Amateur Cup Final triumph from the Royal Box.

Members of the 1958 Committee.
Standing Claude Elmer and Bob Reeves.
Seated Harry Goddard, Les Gosden and Clarrie Jarman.

He finally retired as Hon. Secretary in 1964 and became a trustee of the club. Clarrie's unstinting service, sustained during the bad times, ensured a unique place in the history of the football club.

At ninety-eight years of age he still enjoys his football, attending many home matches. Unfortunately he could not be present at Wembley in 1994 to witness the F.A. Trophy victory, but television provided all the action, bringing back memories of the Amateur Cup victory thirty-six years earlier.

Leslie Gosden was born on November 12th 1903, at Pirbright, the son of a builder who, against his fathers advice, trained as a bricklayer in order to continue the family tradition. He played football for Pirbright at junior level in his teenage years. Even then his administrative abilities were recognised as he became the club Secretary at just nineteen years of age. Before he was twenty his playing career was wrecked by a serious leg injury. Any loss on the playing side quickly became a gain behind the scenes as it gave "Gerald" the opportunity to concentrate on the administrative side, where his real interests lay.

During the early 1920's he worked with a number of Woking first team players, one of whom was Len Ledger, father of current club Chairman, Phil. With their encouragement he paid his first visit to watch Woking, then playing at Hobbs Meadow (close to the current site of Westfield F.C.). He was soon hooked on the football team which was to dominate over 65 years of his life. In 1930 he became a member of the club.

Early memories involved the travel arrangements to away games, with public transport being used. Steam train from Woking, then the underground (for London fixtures), followed a walk to the ground, carrying full kit. It's difficult to imagine today's players following a similar routine.

In the early 1930's "Gerald" was voted onto the committee. There wasn't the proliferation of responsibilities as seen now, only a Chairman, Vice-Chairman and a combined job Treasurer/Secretary. The administration was far less, as was the pressure to succeed.

During the Second World War his idea to offer the ground for recreational use by the troops billeted around the town, prevented it falling victim of being commandeered for agricultural purposes.

Phil Ledger, Woking goalkeeper in the 1950's.
A hard working, enthusiastic committee man,
seen writing out a team sheet in 1975.

After the war in 1945 he was the driving force behind the revival and survival of the club. Money was raised to ensure Kingfield Sports Ground was purchased ready for the re-start of senior amateur football. Leslie Gosden was formally voted in as Chairman, a position he held for over twenty years, before becoming President of the club, a position he still holds.

On the field one the club's finest days was the F.A. Amateur Cup success in 1958. He clearly remembers on that cold day in April being given a blanket by officials to help keep warm. That day was matched thirty-six years later when he watched the club he loved win the F.A. Trophy.

As well as his involvement at Kingfield, Mr Gosden was also President and founder of the Suburban League who played their inaugural season in 1971; he remains the League's patron.

Conference football at Woking was made possible by financial backing from Mr Gosden, who also supplied labour and resources to complete the ground improvements.

His success was not merely restricted to football but also featured in a successful business life. He became Director of a Construction company in the 1930's and built up an organisation responsible for the development of the Farnborough Air Show site. It was in connection with this work that he was awarded an MBE in 1977 for his efforts in promoting exports in relation to the air industry. Without the energy and drive of "Gerald" Gosden, sustained over sixty odd years, the club would have ceased to function in 1945.

Another member of the "gang of four" who revived the club in 1945 was Harry Goddard. Elected as treasurer in 1941 he held office unstintingly for over twenty years until retiring at the same time as Clarrie Jarman.

Son follows father is a common trend at Woking, Phil Ledger, a goalkeeper in the 1950's and the current Chairman followed his father, Len, who played at half-back in the 1920's before becoming a tireless committee member.

Paul Elmer, who worked long hours on the planning of the ground improvements essential to obtain Conference status, followed his father Claude, who was Hon. Secretary in the 1960's

Former Chairman, Ted Hills, played a major role in helping to save the club from extinction in 1980 when the finances were at rock bottom.

All the officials mentioned and many others too numerous to record, had one attribute in common, they had a passion for Woking Football Club.

* * * * * * *

Since the days in the late 1920's when refreshments were served at matches from a small counter under the stand, thousands of pounds of financial and material assistance have been given to the parent body by the Football Supporters Club.

Although Woking Football Club began its existence in 1887, it was not until 1925 that the Supporters' Club was formed. A group of soccer enthusiasts decided it was about time the supporters did something to assist the club materially. The Supporters' Club was formed mainly though the efforts of Mr J. Steer, who was Chairman for many years. Others who helped in its establishment were Messrs C. Barnes, G. Bullock, T. Talbot, C. Jarman, H. Burton, E.T. Trotman and W. Carter.

Join the Woking Supporter's Club. The enrolment form (early 1950's) portrays George Allen, a leading Supporter's Club committee member.

Harry Hughes, manager of Woking from 1970 to 1973.

The club's first efforts were concerned with raising money. They obtained an old Army hut used in the First World War for use as a clubroom. It was erected and decorated by voluntary labour. As there needed to be a right-of-way the clubhouse stood on stilts. Considering the clubhouse gave good value for forty-plus years, before the replacement by the Cardinal Club, a total cost of £40 was undoubtedly exceptional value.

Further money was raised at social evenings, concerts, raffles etc and £1,000 was donated towards the cost of a second stand. In the following years up to the Second World War, the penny on the ball competition and social events enabled the Supporters' Club to make average donations of £250 a year to the Football Club. This was quite a healthy sum at that time.

The Supporters' Club undertook the catering for players and supporters at all home matches, arranged coaches for away matches and did everything possible to secure financial stability for the parent club.

After the Isthmian League was suspended in 1939 the Cardinals played friendlies and competed in the Surrey Combination League. In 1942, when the Kingfield ground was taken over by the Government, the Supporters' Club also closed down for the duration of the war.

Following the war, the Football Club in co-operation with the Supporters' Club, agreed to purchase the Kingfield Sports Ground for £6,000. Over £500 was collected at the inaugural meeting and a carnival organised by Joe Steer raised £1,100. This amount, together with the issue of a number of £1 shares, put the club on a sound financial footing.

Having overcome the problem of the ground, the next big task was its preparation for the start of the 1945-46 season. The Supporters' Club accepted the job, working alongside members of the Football Club.

Everywhere was desolation. The grass was waist high in places; fences had been pulled down, or fallen down through dry rot. All windows of the stand and clubroom had been broken, paint was non-existent. Only two cups and six saucers remained intact in the clubroom. Within a few weeks the supporters led by S. Sturt and H. Preskett, had transformed the wilderness into something resembling a football ground.

In 1946 membership of the Supporters' Club reached 1,100, a record that has not yet been equalled. Another carnival was organised in 1949. A profit of some £300 was made, of which £100 was donated to the football club.

The Supporters' Club continued to raise money for the club throughout the 1950's. As expenses outstripped income the club relied on monies raised by the Tote. A substantial portion of the Tote profit was donated to the parent club to provide covered accommodation and terracing at the Kingfield end of the ground.

Trevor Smith, a former Woking player who managed the club from 1973 to 1976.

In the early 1960's the Progress Fund, organised by George Pavelin was born. The profits were responsible for the purchase and installation of the floodlights which were officially opened in November 1964 with a game against Chelsea Football Club.

Unfortunately, like most amateur clubs, Woking suffered both in playing standards and in a falling off of support. It was in the early 1970's that the Supporters' Club disbanded. The years of struggle finally took its toll.

Some twenty years later the Supporters' Club was reborn. A series of excellent seasons culminating in promotion to the Vauxhall Conference gave the necessary impetus for the rebirth. Keith Raymond was the prime organiser. Unfortunately he had to move to the North of England, but his initial enthusiasm was not wasted as Lynn Heywood, Andy Turner, Phil Davies, Alan Barnes and others ensured the Supporters' Club continued to thrive.

****

Woking have had their fair share of Managers/Coaches since World War II. Bob Reeves, a fine free-scoring winger whose career was curtailed by the war, was responsible for team affairs during the late 1950's. In those days the players tended to complete their own training schedule but nevertheless, Reeves fulfilled a vital role during the Amateur Cup success.

Tom Tranter, who managed Woking in 1976 - 1977.

Pat Finn, manager of Woking 1977 - 1978. He succeeded Tom Tranter.

Charlie Mortimore, one of Woking's finest and most successful player was appointed coach in 1963 and remained until 1968. Success was limited due to "shamateurism" with the best players tending to be poached by the top clubs. Woking could not compete, so heavy reliance was on young local talent. Charlie's teams always played attractive football; this was his legacy to the club.

Woking became the graveyard of managers; not may survived for more than a season. Bill Mitchell, Harry Hughes, Trevor Smith, Pat Finn and Tom Tranter all tried and failed in the 1970's.

Fred Callaghan who built a successful side in the late 1970's left to become manager of Brentford just prior to the F.A. Trophy semi-final in 1980. He returned as coach in the late 1980's and was a vital member of Woking's F.A. Cup run in 1990-91 before leaving to become manager of Kingstonian the following season.

Alan Humphreys took over from Fred as caretaker manger for the remainder of the season 1979-80. Billy Miller replaced him but was replaced by Brian Caterer and Colin Lippiatt (assistant manager) for 1981-82. Three quarters of the season was completed with some success before lack of money broke up the team and blunted their efforts. Dave Holloway tried his best for a couple of seasons before Bill Dodgin succeeded him, albeit very briefly.

Evelyn Henry Lintott proudly displaying his full England Shirt. He played for Woking between 1900 and 1908.

Geoff Chapple, who became manager in September 1984 provided essential stability to the club. In the ensuing decade he was without doubt the prime force behind the re-emergence of Woking Football Club.

As a youngster he excelled at football and athletics representing Surrey at cross-country and the mile. When a choice had to be made, he opted for football playing for Woking, Alton, Guildford City, Guildford & Dorking and Windsor & Eton.

Geoff Hamm in 1958, with the Amateur Cup and a selection of International and other representative caps.

An aggressive wing-half he made his Woking debut in August 1971 with a 4-1 victory against Oxford City. In two spells between 1971 and 1976 Chapple scored nineteen goals in 168 appearances. Amongst the honours he received were Hampshire County Cup and Surrey Senior Cup medals.

Double tragedy struck whilst playing for Windsor at Harefield. He collided with a team mate and suffered a fractured leg. Complications set in as a life threatening blood clot formed on a lung. At the same time as his leg fractured his father collapsed and died.

Returning to football, Geoff enjoyed four successful seasons in charge at Windsor, winning Division 2 (South) before taking over the manager's job at Kingfield. His first game in charge was on September 29th, 1984; a 1-0 victory at home to Clapton before 87 paying customers. Unfortunately not even Chapple could prevent relegation to Division 2 (South) of the Servowarm Isthmian League at the end of that first season.

Nevertheless a launching pad for almost a continuous success was about to start. Firstly with Bill Stoves and then latterly with Colin Lippiatt as assistants the following honours were achieved.

Champions Division 2 South	1986-87
Promoted to Premier Division	1989-90
Champions of Premier Division (promoted to Vauxhall Conference)	1991-92
Surrey Senior Cup Winners	1990-91, 1993-94
Surrey Senior Cup Finalists	1986-87, 1988-89
Surrey Charity Shield Winners	1987-88
AC Delco Cup Winners	1990-91
Isthmian Charity Shield Winners	1991-92, 1992-93
Loctite Cup Finalists	1991-92
4th Round F.A. Cup (after defeating WBA 4-2 in 3rd round)	1990-91
3rd Round F.A. Cup	1991-92.

His successful partnership with Colin Lippiatt culminated in a winning Wembley appearance with F.A. Trophy success in 1993-94 and successfully retaining the Trophy the following season.

On 1st April 1992, Geoff became Woking's first full time General Manager. He had previously combined the manager's role with his job as a financial consultant. He also found time to marry Sally and is the proud father of Lucy Jane born in 1993.

Woking Football Club have had many unsung heroes, but none more so than the physiotherapists who "patch-up" the injured for active service every Saturday. Bert Knott plied his trade from 1936 to 1963 and Barry Kimber the current physio, joined the club in 1975.

Barry Kimber being presented with his long service award by Geoff Chapple.

With all due respect to the many fine players who have given outstanding service to Woking Football Club, Evelyn Henry Lintott was arguably the finest footballer who ever wore their colours. He was born in a little village called Busbridge near Godalming, Surrey on 2nd November 1883, the son of Arthur Frederick and Eleanor Anne Lintott (nee Stacey).

Still in his teens when he played for the first XI he first made a name as a centre-forward. It was a bold - if fortunate stroke - when the committee, hard pressed for a centre-half, converted him to that position, as in the year previous he had scored some 60 goals out of about 90. Centre-half in those days was the key position in the team, the place for the hardest worker and it was because of his tremendous energy and untiring enthusiasm, that he was given his chance there. It was probably his best position, though he was to gain his greatest fame as a left-half.

Unfortunately his time with Woking Football Club lasted only a few years, for in 1905 he went to Exeter Training College and from that time on was, for a season or two only available for the Christmas matches. Yet he undoubtedly made his mark with Woking. For several years he was an automatic choice for Surrey County, who played him in any position in which it was felt the need was greatest.

While at Exeter, Evelyn played against Plymouth Argyle and Bob Jack, the Plymouth manager, signed him on as an amateur for the Southern League side. He did not, however, assist them for more than a match or two. In the summer of 1907, when to took up a teaching appointment at Willesden, Queens Park Rangers secured his signature on amateur forms. At the start of the season he was selected in the opening match at centre-half for the reserves. A day or two before the season opened however, Sammy Downing the club's left-half was injured; the question arose - could Evelyn play left-half? Strangely, considering the many positions in which he had played either for this club or county, he had never played there. Such was his versatility and confidence, not only did he make the position his own, only two months later, he was England's left-half against Ireland. Never before or since has a man played for England after such a short experience of first class football and of his particular position.

Evelyn played for England that season in all the three Internationals played in those days against Ireland, Wales and Scotland and he also played in the Amateur Internationals against Ireland, Holland, France, Belgium and Germany.

At the close of that season he signed for QPR as a professional. A few months later, he was surprisingly transferred to Bradford City then making a terrific fight to keep their place in the First Division.

He gained three more international caps that season against Ireland, Scotland and Hungary but, in the following season sustained a bad injury at Burnden Park, Bolton. His recovery was long delayed. It took even longer for him to regain his confidence and form. He just missed his place in the Bradford City team which won the cup in 1910-11.

It was not until he was transferred to Leeds City, that, in season 1913-14, he regained his form. He only just missed playing against Scotland - as centre-half - on a close vote by the selection committee.

He was an all-round athlete and immensely popular with the boys at Dudley Hill School, Bradford and previously at Maybury School, Woking, where he taught physical training.

Evelyn's football career ended when war was declared. He enlisted in the West Yorkshire Regiment (Leeds Pals) and gained a commission as a Lieutenant. On 1st July 1916 he was killed in the Battle of the Somme. It will be seen that his first class football career was tragically a very short one, although in the space of two years he established himself as the finest left-half in the first decade of this century.

Evelyn's four brothers all played for Woking Football Club with elder brother Stacey being the captain in the famous F.A. Cup tie at Burnden Park against Bolton Wanderers in 1908. Cuthbert was a high scoring forward who, because of business commitments, could only play occasionally.

Younger brothers Keith and Maurice played only a handful of games for Woking first team.

The second Woking player after Evelyn Lintott to represent his Country was A.H. "Daisy" Bell. A cultured full-back, who joined Woking after the demise of Addlestone in 1906, represented England Amateurs in 1909. He became captain of Woking and Surrey, earning the respect of all who new him. World War I ended his playing career but he served as President of the club from 1923 until his untimely death in 1942.

Richard Thorne-Thorne played occasionally for Woking , between 1921 and 1927. As with many other amateur players at that time, his services were spread across a number of teams. Nevertheless at the time he played for England against Wales in January 1922, he was representing Woking. A very fast wing-forward he played only twenty-four competitive games for Woking.

Season 1926-27 was a vintage year for Woking, winning the Surrey Senior Cup, battling through to the first rounds of the F.A. Cup and F.A. Amateur Cup, finishing a respectable fifth in the league. One of the reasons for the success was the legendary half-back line of Cartlidge, Payne and Briggs. Cartlidge and Briggs were capped for England and Scotland Amateurs respectively whilst Payne played in an England trial match.

Unfortunately the combination only lasted for the one season; Cartlidge moved on and Briggs only played occasionally due to his Army commitments.

Dereck Brown, a free transfer from Wembley in 1990. Played a significant role in Woking's successes, culminating in an England non-league call-up in 1994.

W.J. (Johnny) Price, also a member of the Surrey Senior Cup winning side of 1927, assisted Woking regularly for some seasons at inside-left and was one of the cleverest forwards the Cardinals ever had. Many representative honours came his way including playing for England Amateurs in 1928 against Ireland, Wales and Scotland. After leaving Woking to become a

England Amateurs on tour in 1957.
Four Woking players: kneeling, John Mortimore (first left), Charlie Mortimore, Geoff Hamm and Reg Stratton (fourth, fifth and six from the left).

professional with Fulham, Price was for some years, the idol of Craven Cottage. He toured South Africa with the full England team in 1929 playing in one of the three matches.

A bad knee injury whilst playing for Port Vale ended his professional playing career in 1938. Just prior to the outbreak of the Second World War he was appointed Woking's trainer. During the war years when professional and amateur players joined forces, he turned out for Woking in the Surrey Combination League.

In season 1930-31 Bill Warnes played three times for England scoring twice in a 5-0 victory against Wales. He turned professional playing many reserve games for Arsenal but his only first team game was in the amazing loss 2-0 against Walsall in the F.A. Cup. He was transferred to Norwich soon after this defeat.

Twenty-six years elapsed before a Woking player gained international recognition. John Mortimore and Geoff Hamm made their debut's against Wales in February 1957. They were also chosen along with Charlie Mortimore and Reg Stratton to tour Europe during May 1957.

All four played against Switzerland B with John and Charlie scoring in a 3-2 victory.

John Mortimore gained five caps before signing for Chelsea prior to season 1957-58. Geoff Hamm scored three times in ten internationals. He then signed for Wimbledon in the summer of 1958 gaining more caps during his time there.

Reg Stratton played twice for England Youths before gaining three caps for England amateurs. He scored twice in these three games before signing for Fulham in 1959.

Roy Littlejohn who had played once for England prior to joining Woking, played against Wales in November 1957 along with team mates Geoff Hamm and Charlie Mortimore.

Charlie Mortimore played fifteen times for England between 1957 and 1959 whilst with Woking, although he had won caps during his seasons with Aldershot.

It was thirty-four years before a Woking player once again wore an England shirt. Goalkeeper Laurence Batty played twice for the non-league international side in 1993 and won further caps in 1995.

Dereck Brown, who had been a consistent performer in a Woking shirt, deservedly achieved international recognition in 1994 against Guernsey, Finland and Norway.

International honours for Kevan Brown had been long overdue, but he finally made the England team in the 1994-95 season playing

Laurence Batty proudly wearing his England jersey in 1993. He was the first Woking player to achieve International honours for over thirty years.

against Wales, the Highland League and touring Gibraltar in the close season.

Woking have been well served throughout their long history by footballing brothers. Just prior to the turn of the century, the Ridler brothers E.H. and H.B. were automatic choices. Then it was the famous Lintott brothers, Evelyn, Stacey and Cuthbert who played a major role creating the club's high profile in the early years of the twentieth century.

The Cashmore brothers played for Woking between 1958 and 1961, Norman, a powerful forward played 64 games before turning professional with Aldershot. Michael a class defender played 32 times only, mainly due to the consistency of Ron Ellerby and Geoff Parsons. Eddie played mainly in the reserves with just a couple of first team games.

Other famous "pairs" included the Finns, Brian who made well over 500 appearances and brother Pat, as well as being an accomplished full-back also briefly managed the club in the late 70's.

Tim Buzaglo, who made the national headlines after his quick-fire hat-trick against West Bromwich was arguably Geoff Chapple's best ever signing, with 151 goals to his credit. His brother, Richard, a lightning quick left-winger played his part during the upsurge from the Diadora League's basement.

The Wye brothers, Lloyd and Shane, have been associated with Woking all their footballing careers. Lloyd has played over 400 first team games, being part of the Chapple revolution from the outset. Shane is fast approaching 250 appearances and has become one of the best playmakers in the Conference.

It was the Mortimore brothers who probably made the greatest impact on the Woking style of play and the success of the 1950's. Charlie had played in the Football League with Aldershot for a number of seasons and was an established England amateur international. John had played for Aldershot reserves and was an England youth international. The signing of both prior to the 1953-54 season was a major coup for the club.

Charlie Mortimore, a former schoolmaster at Cove County Secondary School, twice led the England Amateur attack in 1950-51 and played on the right wing in three internationals during 1951-52. He joined Aldershot in 1943 at the age of fifteen. In 1944 he played for Surrey Youth and Surrey ATC. Whilst completing his scholastic training at Loughborough College between 1945 and 1947, he assisted the Universities Athletic Union.

From college, he joined the Royal Air Force, and while stationed in the Bolton area during 1949, Charlie signed amateur for Bolton Wanderers. On demobilisation at the end of 1949, Charlie rejoined Aldershot and immediately won a place in the Division III (South) League side.

Charlie Mortimore, Geoff Hamm and Roy Littlejohn, toured Nigeria & Ghana with the F.A. during the summer of 1958. Ghana were thrashed 7-0, with Charlie netting two. This time the defender moves away with the ball.

Prior to joining Woking he scored 27 goals in 69 league games including a record haul; 5 in a 7-2 victory against Leyton Orient in a fixture played during February 1950.

Charlie was also a regular member of the Hampshire County side and when the County regulations were amended he played many times for Surrey.

At the start of his first season with Woking he was elected Captain, a position he held until his retirement. Charlie created a club record which still stands today, by scoring in his first seven competitive games.

He was recalled to the international

arena being picked against France in 1957 and played in the following nine international matches.

Winning the Amateur Cup in 1958 on his thirtieth birthday was his greatest triumph in a magnificent career. His scoring rate was exceptional notching 250 goals in 362 Woking games. He holds Woking's individual record by scoring nine goals against Dorking in a 10-3 Surrey Senior Shield victory in 1963.

After his playing days were over he was appointed Chief Coach at Woking, a position he held for five years before being relieved of the job. Although having the ability to produce good young players, the financial incentives were with more fashionable clubs. The unequal struggle proved to be too much in the end. Charlie remains a life member of the club and also for a time in the 1990's was Chairman of Farnborough Town F.C.

John Mortimore, six years younger than Charlie, was a regular member of the Aldershot reserve side at only eighteen years old. He experienced international football playing right-half for England Youths in season 1951-52. He also played for Hampshire Grammar Schools, the Army Cadet Force and Southern Command Cadet Force. In 1952-53 he captained Hampshire Youths.

Whilst playing for Woking he completed his national service with the Royal Air Force and qualified as a teacher. John played for the F.A. XI, the Isthmian League and Hampshire before making his debut for England Amateurs against Wales at Peterborough on February 16th 1957. He held his place, gaining a total of five caps.

Between 1953 and 1957 he played 130 games for Woking. This included winning the Surrey Senior Cup in 1956, thirty years after the previous victory. In his last season (1956-57), Woking finished runners-up in the Isthmian League scoring a record 104 goals and retained the Surrey Senior Cup. During this period, John played a couple of games in the Chelsea first XI before signing as a full-time professional prior to season 1957-58. He was immediately converted to centre-half.

His Chelsea career spanned eight seasons, 279 games and ten goals. He was "ever present" in the Second Division promotion team of 1962-63, lending invaluable experience to manager Tommy Docherty's youthful protégés. Before signing for Queens Park Rangers in September 1965 for an £8,000 fee, he gained a Football League Cup Winners medal.

A qualified F.A. coach, John held a position as player coach in his final season at Chelsea. When his playing days were over he coached at Sunderland from 1966 to 1968, before serving his managerial apprenticeship under Ted Bates at Southampton. He went to Greece twice as Manager/Coach to Ethnikos, was tempted home by Portsmouth but left because of board interference.

After reverting to teaching physical education, mathematics and geography he was recommended to Benfica by Allen Wade, the F.A.'s director of coaching. During his initial three seasons (1976 to 1979), the Portuguese championship was won once and runners-up was achieved twice.

A return to Southampton in 1979 as Assistant Manager/Coach, coincided with their best ever spell including Division I runners-up in 1983-84 and qualification for European competitions. A further spell at Benfica as Manager/Coach was exceptionally fruitful. the Portuguese Cup being won in 1985-86 and the Cup and League double the following season. He was know as Benfica's English Gentleman.

Two more moves followed, coach to Real Betis in Spain and Manager/Coach to Belenenses F.C., Lisbon, before in 1989 he returned to Southampton as assistant manager. He has remained there ever since where his organisational skills coupled with honesty, dignity and intelligence have been fully utilised.

Roy Littlejohn, Charlie Mortimore, Reg Stratton and Geoff Hamm, who gained amateur international caps in 1957 - 1958.

ROCKY THREE
TERROR TIM

WOWKING!
SALUTE 5,000-1 HEROES
£100,000 bonanza for Fred's heroes

EVERTON HERE WE COME
WOKING BACK TO HAPPINESS!

FA Cup Verdict
Rockafella!

BUZ OFF
Tim sinks sagging Baggies

WOKING ON AIR!

Woking's four-goal Cup blitz

SOCKER + + SOCCER SHOCKER + + SOCCER SHOCKER + + SOCC
BATMAN
Cricket ace Tim stumps Talbot in Cup stunner

SPECIAL ON THE GIANT-KILLERS OF THE CUP...
Roberts gave me a good kick, then we tore them apart. It was that easy!
–TIM BUZAGLO, WOKING'S HAT-TRICK HERO

'I still cannot believe I did it'
–TIM BUZAGLO

WOKING TALL

Woking wonders bank on Buzaglo

'Old Buz' is the wizard of Woking

Three-goal ace sinks West Brom
BUZAGLO'S WOKING ON WATER!
Cards blast giants out of FA Cup
WEST BROMWICH ALBION 2 WOKING 4

The Buzaglo boogaloo floors Talbot

Buzaglo fashions Woking's great day

Hitman from Gib is Woking goal hero

Talbot likely casualty after 'Buzaglomania' hits West Bromwich

Buzaglo cheered to the echo by rival supporters as non-League football triumphs in FA Cup
Woking's goal-scoring enigma

FA CUP THIRD ROUND
West Bromwich Albion 2, Woking 4
Fairytale with a deadly finish

Sporting headlines in the National Newspapers saluting Woking's giant killing act over West Bromwich Albion in the F.A. Cup

Tim Buzaglo celebrating the third goal at the Hawthorns.

Woking Football Club

President: MR. L. A. GOSDEN, M.B.E.

Kingfield Sports Ground
Kingfield
Woking
Surrey GU22 9AA
Woking (0483) 772470

Please reply to:

Honours

1st TEAM

F.A. Amateur Cup *Winners* 1957-58

Vauxhall - Opel League *Division Two South Champions 1986-7*

Surrey Senior Cup *Winners* 1912-13, 1926-7, 1955-6, 1956-7, 1971-2

Surrey Senior Shield *Winners* 1903-4, 1906-7, 1907-8, 1912-13, 1952-3, 1956-7, 1962-3, 1967-8, 1974-5

Surrey Invitation Cup *Winners* 1966-7

West Surrey League *Champions* 1895-6, 1897-8, 1904-5, 1907-8

Channel Islands Victory Cup *Winners* 1957-8, 1975-6

RESERVES:

Surrey Intermediate Cup *Winners* 1948-9 1958-9

Isthmian League *(Reserve Section) Champions* 1936-7, 1969-70

Suburban League *(Section A) Champions 1972-3* *(South) Champion 1987-8*

Suburban League Cup *Winners* 1972-3, 1975-6

Surrey Premier Cup *Winners* 1983-4, 1984-5

YOUTHS:

Servowarm Isthmian Youth Cup *Winners* 1982-3

Surrey County Shield *Winners* 1982-3

Southern Youth League *Champions* 1982-3

West Surrey Boys League *Champions* 1982-3

Southern Youth League Cup *Winners* 1983-4

FOUNDED 1889

CLUB COLOURS
Shirts — Red with White Trim
Shorts — White with Red Trim
Socks — Red with White Trim

Members of the Football Association Surrey County F.A., Vauxhall League and Suburban League

The giant killers' autographs

RECOLLECTIONS

By Martin Tyler

Thanks as much to Roger Sherlock's marvellous records as to my own childhood memories, I believe I was eight when I first watched Woking Football Club.

The circumstances were very clear in my mind. The Tyler family lived in Selsdon Road, New Haw. My father ran the Ironmongers in Station Approach, West Byfleet. None of my relatives has the slightest interest in football.

Martin Tyler, holding the F.A. Trophy, celebrates with the Woking players following their 1994 triumph.

Our neighbours, the Whites, had six children, one of whom, older than me, asked me whether I wanted to go with him to see Woking play. He took me on the bus from Woodham Lane to Kingfield and into a world which would become my life.

That day, in 1953, the Cardinals won 4-1 against Kingstonian and I was hooked. Until my own playing days interfered with my visits, I lived and breathed Woking F.C. and, even then, I found it hard to control my feelings.

In November 1971, I went through a schizophrenic experience of going to Kingfield not as a fan but as an opponent. I wore the number nine for Corinthian Casuals in an Isthmian League clash. The Woking side that day included a certain Geoff Chapple.

I wanted to win as I always did on the pitch. I vividly remember telling Brian Finn during the match that I watched him when I was a child and that he was surely far too old to stop us. Woking won 3-0, a defeat for me that I got over much quicker than any other. Once I'd arrived home, I entered the result in Woking records I kept for twenty years and which I've been delighted to pass on to help towards the accuracy of this marvellous publication.

I did dream of course that I would play at Kingfield in the cardinal and white halves, the club colours that mean so much to me and fans of my age. I trained with Woking briefly while I was at University, when Charlie Mortimore was manager, but no offer came. As a striker of limited ability, I can assure you the loss was mine and not Woking's!

In the fifties of course it was particularly wonderful to follow Woking, a thrilling team whose attacking adventurous style made so many games a marvellous spectacle, especially when watched through young eyes. I attended every game in the 1958 F.A. Amateur Cup run, travelling to Hendon, the semi-final at Fulham, the replay at Brentford and Wembley itself by special trains, a regular feature of the times. With my father always working in his shop on Saturdays, I was taken under the wing of the late Stanley Smith, a long-time Woking devotee whose son, Andy, was my pal at the Royal Grammar School, Guildford. One morning all of us arrived at Kingfield at nine o'clock for the Amateur Cup quarter-final against Finchley in 1958. The queues were enormous. The interest was massive. The game was typical of that era. Woking raced into a 3-0 lead but defending was not always a strong suit. It finished 3-2, nail-bitingly.

The Final could have gone the same way. John Hebdon's clean strike summed up a positive first half. We all suffered in the second half as Ilford were more inspired before Woking's attack clicked again. It was never as comfortable as 3-0 suggests.

The second half was live on BBC Television with full highlights that night. I had a lie down when I got home, asking my father to wake me up for the programme. I'm sure it was done with the best intentions but the call never came. I missed the re-run and didn't see the goals again for 33 years when Sky Sports screened some film footage from Movietone to preview the F.A. Cup tie against West Bromwich Albion, which turned out to be so memorable.

After such a high as 1958, the club's fortunes declined so quickly that being a fan was at best character-forming and at worst downright depressing. The era of "shamateurism" meant that, as Woking then didn't pay its team, a succession of promising players were whisked away by less scrupulous clubs. Geoff Hamm, Rod Haider and George Harris were just some of my favourites who accepted better offers, and who could blame them.

The struggles if anything intensified my love for the club. For a time Woking did not compete on level terms, so any success was special, and Charlie Mortimore's continued commitment emphasised the amateur spirit. I raced from school one spring evening to see his marvellous nine goal haul against Dorking; it would have been ten but for a brilliant save in the final minute.

So desperate was the club in the early sixties that they called for volunteers to re-paint the ground. Andy Smith and I joined the workforce which also included some of our heroes like Brian Farris, Shaun Woods and Geoff Foulkes. We slaved away on Sunday morning shifts, often in biting cold. As my wife will tell you, Kingfield is the only thing I've ever painted; for Woking I happily dropped my habitual reluctance for DIY.

The club rewarded us each with a season ticket for the 1963-64 season and, prior to that, invited Andy Smith and myself to travel to the F.A. Amateur Cup first round tie away to Gloucestershire, with the team! What a thrill. What an adventure.

This was the winter of '62-'63, still in the record books for its severity. We set off on the Saturday morning in January at 7.00 am. We returned at 7.00 pm on Sunday and not a ball had been kicked. The coach kept getting stuck in snowdrifts. All of us, including the team, had to dig a path through the worst of the weather. Why the match had not been called off, no one ever explained, but when we finally arrived at this tiny outpost in the West Country, daylight was fading fast and there were no floodlights. We turned straight round but ended up stranded for the night in Cheltenham.

The game was finally staged weeks later. Woking did win - 1-0 with a goal from Ernie Tindall; the same Ernie who must have been mystified to receive fan mail from Paris sent by the "French branch of the Ernie Tindall fan club" - in fact a group of us from the R.G.S. Guildford on our first trip aboard!

I had my lucky break into television in 1973 and since then, watching Woking has been a much rarer pleasure, but I've always kept in touch. My mother has sent me the local paper every week without fail, wherever my base has been.

After almost seventeen years with ITV, I took the plunge into satellite television in 1990. In the same year, now with a wife and two young children, I moved back to Surrey. Within months I found myself volunteering for extra F.A. Cup reporting duty as the famous "run" developed.

It was amazing how little had changed. I swear the paint I'd helped to put on in the early sixties was still the top coat and not too much of it was peeling. Phil Ledger and Paul Elmer were familiar faces in the boardroom. Above all, the character of the club remained intact. In the very competitive world of non-league football, Woking F.C. had retained its essential integrity.

What has happened since 1990 has been phenomenal. Geoff Chapple's place in this history is unique. From arguably the club's lowest point when he took over as manager in 1984, he has guided it to its highest.

I have been lucky enough to cover all the major football occasions around the globe, including the World Cup in the United States in 1994. There amongst the broadcasters on American television, was a former Woking player, Ron Newman, who later turned professional with Portsmouth and has had a distinguished coaching career in the United States. Yet during all these wonderful experiences, I have never been as emotional as on May 21st 1994, the F.A. Trophy Final - Woking's return to Wembley.

For all of us who had been there in 1958, it was an astonishing mixture of the present and past. To see my son, Adam, watching the game, was like a flashback to myself 36 years earlier. The return to the red and white halves, as I stressed, was a splendid omen for the superstitious amongst us. Five of the Amateur Cup heroes were there to lend there support - Geoff Hamm, John Burley, Roy Littlejohn, Jim Collingwood and Charlie, of course. The weather was very different - it had been a very sunny day on April 12th 1958 - but happily the outcome was the same.

As you may know, I did turn down the opportunity to commentate on the Final for Sky Sports. Ian Darke and Ray Clemence did a splendid job. Unfortunately my "friends" at work, unbeknown to the Tyler family, thrust us all into the limelight. I hope those shots didn't intrude too much into your enjoyment of the visual record of what was a splendid day. At least you could see how much I shared in the general suffering over that agonising final fifteen minutes until the final whistle brought such joy.

The performance of the team was worthy of such a splendid, if somewhat soggy, setting. Twenty-four hours later I returned to Wembley to commentate on the England international against Norway. Many of the stadium staff complimented the match as the year's best Cup Final. Many of the England squad had enjoyed the game on their hotel televisions the previous afternoon.

It seemed so appropriate that Dereck Brown scored one of the goals, someone who had helped the club rise through the ranks of the Diadora league. Those boom years of Tim Buzaglo, the clever defensive control and captaincy of Adie Cowler, the coaching flair of Fred Callaghan and the huge efforts of a pack of progressive players lifted the club to the level that culminated in the F.A. Trophy triumph and third place in the G.M. Vauxhall Conference.

By then of course, Geoff Chapple had changed his squad for Conference football, a controversial decision at the time but one which has been totally vindicated. No one could doubt the commitment to the cause of a different breed, the former full-time professionals. Clive Walker, Kevan Brown, Colin Fielder, Dave Puckett and others, far from looking down their noses at non-league football, worked tirelessly for their new employer.

The 1994-95 season pushed back the frontiers even further.

To finish runners-up in the Conference was a magnificent achievement in its own right, league placing always the best barometer of the quality of any side. The consistency was a great compliment to the appetite of players who had pushed themselves very hard the previous year.

To reach those heights and retain the F.A. Trophy was truly remarkable, a feat that will never be forgotten. Achieving success is difficult enough but sustaining it in such a competitive environment is much harder. Those hardships were shrugged aside by a magnificent Woking team, Colin Lippiatt's flair for coaching and of course Geoff Chapple's genius in management.

The defence of the Trophy started on a Tuesday night in January 1995 at home to Chesham United. The postponement from the

Saturday gave me the opportunity to go, and brought back painful memories. I'd been watching in 1959 on the only other occasion Woking had begun a national competition as holders after the F.A. Amateur Cup triumph.

The first round draw took Charlie Mortimore and company to Redhill who were bottom of the Athenian League with just seven points from sixteen games. Woking fielded the vast majority of the Cup-winning side but were humiliated by a 6-3 defeat. I sat in the stand in stunned silence. The shock was widely reported in the Sunday papers the following day.

Because of that, I was perhaps the most pessimistic person in the ground when Chesham came to Kingfield 36 years later, but I need not have worried. Woking won competently 3-0 and another Wembley adventure was underway.

Sadly, because of my commentating commitments, it was to be the only Trophy tie that season I could witness in the flesh but that did not lessen my excitement. As progress continued, I kitted out my family in yellow and black to represent me on May 21st, 1995.

Sky Sports again screened the Trophy Final live. This time I was not given the chance to pick up the microphone at Wembley, nor did I expect it. I was needed elsewhere, at Liverpool, for the pinnacle of the Premiership season as Blackburn went to Anfield to try to win the Championship.

Needless to say my pre-match thoughts were all about Wembley. I was virtually alone at Anfield when I saw on a monitor Scott Steele give the game such a splendid start. My shouts of joy echoed around the deserted stadium.

For an hour I was able to watch uninterrupted and I saw the Kidderminster equaliser. Then Liverpool and Blackburn players arrived and I had to go to the dressing rooms to collect the team information from Roy Evans and Kenny Dalglish. Someone told me it was extra time at Wembley.

The second period had just started when Andy Gray and I arrived at the commentary position so I was again thanks to my television screen, able to watch the Wembley story unfold. Like the majority of Woking fans, I was beginning to make my plans for the replay.

As the now-famous corner was won, I turned to Andy and said "We haven't won a ball in the air in either box all day". Two headers later the ball was nestling in the Kidderminster net and every Woking fan was in ecstasy. Even two hundred miles away from the scene of Colin Fielder's famous late winner, it was a fantastic feeling. Mind you it almost ruined my working relationship with Andy. I had to kiss someone and unfortunately for him he was the nearest!

Such wonderful progress clearly increased the possibility of a future place in the Football League. In sport nothing stands still. Ambition is admirable and essential but so too is financial wisdom. The sad experience of Maidstone United is one cautionary tale. Wimbledon offer a much more encouraging example.

Whatever happens my support is guaranteed. My thanks to Woking Football Club for fuelling my love for the world's most wonderful game.

It has been very frustrating at times. I well remember watching in tears while three penalties were wasted in a Surrey Senior Cup semi-final defeat In the late fifties! Yet all the bad times have been balanced out more and more by those three wonderful Wembley wins.

As always, "Come on you Cards!"

APPENDIX 1 ~ LEAGUE TABLES

1911-12

					Goals		
	P	W	D	L	F	A	Pts
London Caledonians	20	11	7	2	39	25	29
Ilford	20	11	3	6	37	24	25
Nunhead	20	10	5	5	36	30	25
Dulwich Hamlet	20	8	5	7	33	23	21
West Norwood	20	9	3	8	38	38	21
Clapton	20	7	5	8	37	37	19
Woking	**20**	**7**	**5**	**8**	**38**	**41**	**19**
Shepherd's Bush	20	5	6	9	39	49	16
Leytonstone	20	5	6	9	28	38	16
Oxford City	20	5	5	10	33	36	15
Tunbridge Wells	20	5	4	11	23	40	14

1912-13

					Goals		
	P	W	D	L	F	A	Pts
London Caledonians	20	14	5	1	38	12	33
Leytonstone	20	12	3	5	45	20	27
Nunhead	20	12	3	5	36	23	27
Clapton	20	7	7	6	23	20	21
Dulwich Hamlet	20	8	4	8	34	28	20
Woking	**20**	**7**	**5**	**8**	**33**	**40**	**19**
Oxford City	20	6	6	8	23	39	18
Ilford	20	6	5	9	27	37	17
Shepherd's Bush	20	5	5	10	26	38	15
Tunbridge Wells	20	5	4	11	22	36	14
West Norwood	20	3	3	14	23	37	9

1913-14

					Goals		
	P	W	D	L	F	A	Pts
London Caledonians	20	12	6	2	55	23	30
Nunhead	20	11	6	3	49	27	28
Ilford	20	11	4	5	52	35	26
Dulwich Hamlet	20	10	4	6	34	22	24
New Crusaders	20	10	3	7	40	30	23
Oxford City	20	10	0	10	42	42	20
Leytonstone	20	8	4	8	29	32	20
Clapton	20	8	3	9	29	27	19
Shepherd's Bush	20	7	2	11	24	46	16
West Norwood	20	4	3	13	27	47	11
Woking	**20**	**1**	**1**	**18**	**11**	**61**	**3**

1919-20

					Goals		
	P	W	D	L	F	A	Pts
Dulwich Hamlet	22	15	3	4	58	16	33
Nunhead	22	14	5	3	48	25	33
Tufnell Park	22	12	4	6	45	32	28
Ilford	22	13	1	8	63	42	27
Oxford City	22	12	3	7	63	51	27
London Caledonians	22	10	3	9	32	30	23
Leytonstone	22	8	3	11	50	43	19
Clapton	22	8	3	11	37	44	19
Civil Service	22	7	4	11	35	40	18
Woking	**22**	**6**	**3**	**13**	**36**	**42**	**15**
West Norwood	22	5	4	13	19	53	14
Casuals	22	3	2	17	20	88	8

1920-21

					Goals		
	P	W	D	L	F	A	Pts
Ilford	22	16	4	2	70	24	36
London Caledonians	22	13	5	4	45	16	31
Tufnell Park	22	14	3	5	43	24	31
Nunhead	22	12	5	5	53	33	29
Dulwich Hamlet	22	11	6	5	60	30	28
Oxford City	22	12	3	7	56	38	27
Leytonstone	22	8	6	8	36	29	22
Clapton	22	7	7	8	33	52	21
Civil Service	22	3	7	12	26	45	13
Woking	**22**	**3**	**5**	**14**	**16**	**43**	**11**
Casuals	22	3	3	16	31	87	9
West Norwood	22	2	2	18	17	65	6

1921-22

					Goals		
	P	W	D	L	F	A	Pts
Ilford	26	17	4	5	66	34	38
Dulwich Hamlet	26	14	8	4	65	24	36
London Caledonians	26	16	4	6	41	21	36
Nunhead	26	12	5	9	65	41	29
Clapton	26	13	3	10	51	46	29
Tufnell Park	26	10	7	9	44	39	27
Oxford City	26	12	2	12	48	47	26
Wycombe Wanderers	26	12	2	12	61	64	26
Civil Service	26	9	9	8	40	48	26
Woking	**26**	**10**	**6**	**10**	**39**	**49**	**26**
Leytonstone	26	9	6	11	41	48	24
West Norwood	26	8	5	13	43	57	21
Wimbledon	26	7	4	15	52	56	18
Casuals	26	0	2	24	25	107	2

1922-23

					Goals		
	P	W	D	L	F	A	Pts
Clapton	26	15	7	4	51	33	37
Nunhead	26	15	5	6	52	32	35
London Caledonians	26	13	7	6	43	26	33
Ilford	26	11	7	8	57	38	29
Casuals	26	12	5	9	68	51	29
Civil Service	26	9	10	7	39	36	28
Wycombe Wanderers	26	11	4	11	61	61	26
Dulwich Hamlet	26	9	7	10	60	44	25
Leytonstone	26	9	7	10	45	56	25
Tufnell Park	26	9	5	12	41	45	23
Wimbledon	26	10	2	14	49	50	22
Woking	**26**	**7**	**6**	**13**	**42**	**67**	**20**
Oxford City	26	6	5	15	45	68	17
West Norwood	26	5	5	16	25	71	15

1923-24

	P	W	D	L	Goals F	Goals A	Pts
St.Albans City	26	17	5	4	72	38	39
Dulwich Hamlet	26	15	6	5	49	28	36
Clapton	26	14	5	7	73	50	33
Wycombe Wanderers	26	14	5	7	88	65	33
London Caledonians	26	14	3	9	53	49	31
Civil Service	26	12	5	9	52	47	29
Casuals	26	13	1	12	65	55	27
Ilford	26	9	6	11	56	59	24
Nunhead	26	8	8	10	42	46	24
Wimbledon	26	8	4	14	43	62	20
Tufnell Park	26	8	2	16	38	53	18
Woking	**26**	**5**	**8**	**13**	**31**	**62**	**18**
Oxford City	26	7	2	17	53	74	16
Leytonstone	26	6	4	16	41	68	16

1926-27

	P	W	D	L	Goals F	Goals A	Pts
St.Albans City	26	20	1	5	96	34	41
Ilford	26	17	0	9	76	57	34
Wimbledon	26	15	3	8	72	45	33
Nunhead	26	11	8	7	51	33	30
Woking	**26**	**12**	**6**	**8**	**68**	**60**	**30**
London Caledonians	26	11	7	8	58	47	29
Clapton	26	11	4	11	58	60	26
Leytonstone	26	11	1	14	54	78	23
Dulwich Hamlet	26	9	4	13	60	58	22
Wycombe Wanderers	26	10	2	14	59	86	22
Tufnell Park	26	8	4	14	45	55	20
Oxford City	26	7	5	14	46	72	19
The Casuals	26	8	3	15	37	78	19
Civil Service	26	6	4	16	48	65	16

1924-25

	P	W	D	L	Goals F	Goals A	Pts
London Caledonians	26	18	5	3	76	36	41
Clapton	26	19	1	6	64	34	39
St.Albans City	26	16	2	8	69	39	34
Tufnell Park	26	11	4	11	47	41	26
Ilford	26	11	4	11	46	42	26
Leytonstone	26	12	2	12	55	63	26
The Casuals	26	12	1	13	55	58	25
Wycombe Wanderers	26	11	2	13	58	61	24
Civil Service	26	10	4	12	52	64	24
Nunhead	26	9	5	12	45	43	23
Wimbledon	26	10	2	14	50	54	22
Dulwich Hamlet	26	8	5	13	42	57	21
Oxford City	26	9	2	15	38	71	20
Woking	**26**	**5**	**3**	**18**	**33**	**67**	**13**

1927-28

	P	W	D	L	Goals F	Goals A	Pts
St.Albans City	26	15	5	6	86	50	35
London Caledonians	26	12	9	5	63	38	33
Ilford	26	14	4	8	72	54	32
Woking	**26**	**13**	**5**	**8**	**72**	**56**	**31**
Nunhead	26	13	2	11	57	54	28
Wimbledon	26	12	3	11	57	48	27
Leytonstone	26	13	1	12	53	56	27
Clapton	26	8	10	8	52	47	26
Dulwich Hamlet	26	8	9	9	56	49	25
The Casuals	26	8	8	10	54	58	24
Wycombe Wanderers	26	9	5	12	60	69	23
Oxford City	26	7	7	12	36	57	21
Civil Service	26	8	4	14	38	76	20
Tufnell Park	26	4	4	18	38	82	12

1925-26

	P	W	D	L	Goals F	Goals A	Pts
Dulwich Hamlet	26	20	1	5	80	49	41
London Caledonians	26	18	1	7	81	44	37
Clapton	26	14	4	8	64	50	32
Wycombe Wanderers	26	14	3	9	97	83	31
St.Albans City	26	12	6	8	76	54	30
Nunhead	26	13	4	9	49	43	30
Ilford	26	13	2	11	81	70	28
Leytonstone	26	12	1	13	75	63	25
Woking	**26**	**8**	**6**	**12**	**56**	**73**	**22**
Tufnell Park	26	8	5	13	36	53	21
The Casuals	26	8	4	14	48	61	20
Wimbledon	26	9	1	16	61	77	19
Oxford City	26	8	1	17	48	76	17
Civil Service	26	5	1	20	43	99	11

1928-29

	P	W	D	L	Goals F	Goals A	Pts
Nunhead	26	15	6	5	47	35	36
London Caledonians	26	15	4	7	65	33	34
Dulwich Hamlet	26	14	6	6	65	34	34
Wimbledon	26	9	10	7	66	54	28
Ilford	26	12	3	11	67	52	27
Clapton	26	11	5	10	60	55	27
Tufnell Park	26	11	5	10	58	55	27
St.Albans City	26	12	3	11	63	69	27
Leytonstone	26	11	3	12	56	79	25
Wycombe Wanderers	26	10	3	13	58	60	23
Oxford City	26	10	3	13	61	71	23
The Casuals	26	8	5	13	49	60	21
Woking	**26**	**8**	**3**	**15**	**39**	**65**	**19**
Civil Service	26	4	5	17	39	71	13

1929-30

	P	W	D	L	Goals F	Goals A	Pts
Nunhead	26	19	3	4	69	36	41
Dulwich Hamlet	26	15	6	5	74	39	36
Kingstonian	26	15	4	7	57	37	34
Ilford	26	16	1	9	84	60	33
Woking	**26**	**11**	**5**	**10**	**66**	**65**	**27**
Wimbledon	26	11	2	13	64	66	24
Wycombe Wanderers	26	10	4	12	49	52	24
The Casuals	26	8	7	11	50	51	23
Oxford City	26	10	3	13	45	60	23
St.Albans City	26	9	4	13	54	77	22
Clapton	26	8	4	14	47	57	20
London Caledonians	26	8	3	15	49	69	19
Leytonstone	26	8	3	15	48	68	19
Tufnell Park	26	6	7	13	35	54	19

1930-31

	P	W	D	L	Goals F	Goals A	Pts
Wimbledon	26	18	6	2	69	37	42
Dulwich Hamlet	26	12	9	5	51	39	33
Wycombe Wanderers	26	12	6	8	67	45	30
The Casuals	26	12	6	8	71	56	30
St.Albans City	26	11	7	8	67	66	29
Ilford	26	10	6	10	70	62	26
Oxford City	26	10	5	11	43	48	25
London Caledonians	26	8	8	10	43	53	24
Kingstonian	26	10	4	12	49	64	24
Tufnell Park	26	9	5	12	45	61	23
Nunhead	26	9	4	13	49	54	22
Woking	**26**	**9**	**4**	**13**	**56**	**63**	**22**
Clapton	26	7	4	15	62	75	18
Leytonstone	26	6	4	16	46	65	16

1931-32

	P	W	D	L	Goals F	Goals A	Pts
Wimbledon	26	17	2	7	60	35	36
Ilford	26	13	9	4	71	45	35
Dulwich Hamlet	26	15	3	8	69	43	33
Wycombe Wanderers	26	14	5	7	72	50	33
Oxford City	26	15	2	9	63	49	32
Kingstonian	26	13	3	10	71	50	29
Tufnell Park	26	9	7	10	50	48	25
Nunhead	26	9	7	10	54	61	25
The Casuals	26	10	4	12	59	65	24
Clapton	26	9	5	12	50	57	23
Leytonstone	26	9	3	14	36	61	21
St.Albans City	26	8	4	14	57	78	20
Woking	**26**	**6**	**5**	**15**	**44**	**64**	**17**
London Caledonians	26	2	7	17	24	74	11

1932-33

	P	W	D	L	Goals F	Goals A	Pts
Dulwich Hamlet	26	15	6	5	71	45	36
Leytonstone	26	16	4	6	66	43	36
Kingstonian	26	15	2	9	77	49	32
Ilford	26	14	0	12	60	58	28
The Casuals	26	12	2	12	48	36	26
Tufnell Park	26	11	3	12	51	51	25
St.Albans City	26	12	1	13	57	63	25
Clapton	26	10	5	11	51	65	25
Oxford City	26	9	6	11	49	54	24
Woking	**26**	**10**	**4**	**12**	**53**	**61**	**24**
Wycombe Wanderers	26	10	4	12	47	56	24
Nunhead	26	8	6	12	42	50	22
Wimbledon	26	8	5	13	55	67	21
London Caledonians	26	5	6	15	35	64	16

1933-34

	P	W	D	L	Goals F	Goals A	Pts
Kingstonian	26	15	7	4	80	42	37
Dulwich Hamlet	26	15	5	6	68	36	35
Wimbledon	26	13	7	6	63	35	33
Tufnell Park	26	14	5	7	55	50	33
Ilford	26	15	2	9	60	56	32
The Casuals	26	13	5	8	47	32	31
Leytonstone	26	13	3	10	55	48	29
Nunhead	26	10	5	11	48	44	25
London Caledonians	26	7	8	11	29	51	22
Wycombe Wanderers	26	9	2	15	57	60	20
St.Albans City	26	8	4	14	44	75	20
Oxford City	26	7	4	15	45	57	18
Clapton	26	5	6	15	35	62	16
Woking	**26**	**6**	**1**	**19**	**43**	**81**	**13**

1934-35

	P	W	D	L	Goals F	Goals A	Pts
Wimbledon	26	14	7	5	63	30	35
Oxford City	26	14	4	8	69	50	32
Leytonstone	26	15	2	9	49	36	32
Dulwich Hamlet	26	11	7	8	66	45	29
Tufnell Park	26	11	7	8	53	44	29
Kingstonian	26	11	6	9	44	40	28
Nunhead	26	10	7	9	35	34	27
London Caledonians	26	9	7	10	40	41	25
St.Albans City	26	9	6	11	61	80	24
Ilford	26	9	6	11	40	56	24
Clapton	26	7	7	12	46	48	21
Woking	**26**	**9**	**3**	**14**	**44**	**68**	**21**
Wycombe Wanderers	26	7	6	13	51	69	20
The Casuals	26	6	5	15	37	57	17

1935-36

					Goals		
	P	W	D	L	F	A	Pts
Wimbledon	26	19	2	5	82	29	40
The Casuals	26	14	5	7	60	45	33
Ilford	26	13	3	10	67	47	29
Dulwich Hamlet	26	10	8	8	64	47	28
Nunhead	26	11	6	9	51	40	28
Wycombe Wanderers	26	13	2	11	60	68	28
Clapton	26	11	5	10	42	46	27
Oxford City	26	11	4	11	60	58	26
St.Albans City	26	11	2	13	59	64	24
Woking	**26**	**9**	**4**	**13**	**43**	**62**	**22**
Tufnell Park	26	9	3	14	42	61	21
London Caledonians	26	9	3	14	35	52	21
Kingstonian	26	9	2	15	43	56	20
Leytonstone	26	7	3	16	34	67	17

1938-39

					Goals		
	P	W	D	L	F	A	Pts
Leytonstone	26	18	4	4	68	32	40
Ilford	26	17	4	5	68	32	38
Kingstonian	26	17	3	6	62	39	37
Dulwich Hamlet	26	15	5	6	60	32	35
Wimbledon	26	14	3	9	88	56	31
Nunhead	26	11	6	9	54	44	28
The Casuals	26	11	6	9	54	51	28
Clapton	26	12	2	12	69	61	26
Wycombe Wanderers	26	10	6	10	62	62	26
St.Albans City	26	8	5	13	44	50	21
Woking	**26**	**9**	**2**	**15**	**35**	**56**	**20**
Oxford City	26	4	4	18	44	84	12
Tufnell Park	26	4	4	18	33	87	12
London Caledonians	26	3	4	19	26	81	10

1936-37

					Goals		
	P	W	D	L	F	A	Pts
Kingstonian	26	18	3	5	63	43	39
Nunhead	26	17	3	6	77	32	37
Leytonstone	26	16	4	6	71	42	36
Ilford	26	14	5	7	86	39	33
Dulwich Hamlet	26	12	6	8	64	48	30
Wycombe Wanderers	26	10	5	11	55	52	25
Wimbledon	26	9	7	10	52	53	25
Clapton	26	10	5	11	42	51	25
The Casuals	26	10	3	13	46	58	23
Woking	**26**	**9**	**4**	**13**	**53**	**69**	**22**
Oxford City	26	8	5	13	56	89	21
St.Albans City	26	7	5	14	44	62	19
Tufnell Park	26	4	7	15	43	74	15
London Caledonians	26	5	4	17	26	66	14

1945-46

					Goals		
	P	W	D	L	F	A	Pts
Walthamstow Avenue	26	21	0	5	100	31	42
Oxford City	26	17	6	3	91	40	40
Romford	26	15	3	8	83	59	33
Dulwich Hamlet	26	14	2	10	63	59	30
Tufnell Park	26	12	4	10	70	55	28
Woking	**26**	**10**	**7**	**9**	**56**	**51**	**27**
Ilford	26	12	2	12	56	71	26
Leytonstone	26	11	3	12	61	75	25
Wycombe Wanderers	26	9	3	14	80	88	21
Wimbledon	26	7	6	13	52	72	20
Corinthian-Casuals	26	8	4	14	58	83	20
Clapton	26	8	3	15	51	62	19
St.Albans City	26	6	6	14	48	85	18
Kingstonian	26	6	3	17	48	86	15

1937-38

					Goals		
	P	W	D	L	F	A	Pts
Leytonstone	26	17	6	3	72	34	40
Ilford	26	17	3	6	70	39	37
Tufnell Park	26	15	2	9	63	47	32
Nunhead	26	14	3	9	52	44	31
Wycombe Wanderers	26	12	5	9	69	55	29
Dulwich Hamlet	26	13	3	10	57	46	29
Kingstonian	26	12	4	10	51	48	28
Clapton	26	9	6	11	49	53	24
Wimbledon	26	10	3	13	62	49	23
London Caledonians	26	9	4	13	44	55	22
Oxford City	26	7	7	12	35	71	21
The Casuals	26	8	3	15	51	74	19
Woking	**26**	**7**	**2**	**17**	**41**	**72**	**16**
St.Albans City	26	4	5	17	31	60	13

1946-47

					Goals		
	P	W	D	L	F	A	Pts
Leytonstone	26	19	2	5	92	36	40
Dulwich Hamlet	26	17	3	6	78	46	37
Romford	26	13	8	5	76	52	34
Walthamstow Avenue	26	13	4	9	64	37	30
Oxford City	26	12	6	8	70	51	30
Kingstonian	26	12	4	10	52	57	28
Wycombe Wanderers	26	9	8	9	63	62	26
Wimbledon	26	10	5	11	68	64	25
Ilford	26	7	7	12	66	78	21
Tufnell Park	26	8	5	13	45	69	21
Woking	**26**	**7**	**7**	**12**	**34**	**62**	**21**
Clapton	26	6	8	12	41	59	20
St.Albans City	26	7	5	14	47	79	19
Corinthian-Casuals	26	4	4	18	36	80	12

1947-48

	P	W	D	L	Goals F	Goals A	Pts
Leytonstone	26	19	1	6	87	38	39
Kingstonian	26	16	6	4	74	39	38
Walthamstow Avenue	26	17	3	6	61	37	37
Dulwich Hamlet	26	17	2	7	71	39	36
Wimbledon	26	13	6	7	66	40	32
Romford	26	14	1	11	53	47	29
Oxford City	26	10	5	11	50	68	25
Woking	**26**	**10**	**3**	**13**	**63**	**55**	**23**
Ilford	26	7	8	11	51	59	22
St.Albans City	26	9	2	15	43	56	20
Wycombe Wanderers	26	7	5	14	51	65	19
Tufnell Park	26	7	4	15	38	83	18
Clapton	26	5	4	17	35	69	14
Corinthian-Casuals	26	5	2	19	33	81	12

1948-49

	P	W	D	L	Goals F	Goals A	Pts
Dulwich Hamlet	26	15	6	5	60	31	36
Walthamstow Avenue	26	16	4	6	65	38	36
Wimbledon	26	15	4	7	64	41	34
Ilford	26	14	3	9	56	36	31
Oxford City	26	13	5	8	48	34	31
Leytonstone	26	12	6	8	49	41	30
Woking	**26**	**14**	**1**	**11**	**64**	**59**	**29**
Romford	26	11	3	12	47	54	25
Kingstonian	26	10	4	12	43	47	24
Corinthian-Casuals	26	11	2	13	47	59	24
Wycombe Wanderers	26	11	2	13	49	61	24
*St.Albans City	26	6	6	14	40	60	16
Clapton	26	5	5	16	32	61	15
Tufnell Park	26	1	5	20	28	70	7
(*2 points deducted, breach of rule)							

1949-50

	P	W	D	L	Goals F	Goals A	Pts
Leytonstone	26	17	5	4	77	31	39
Wimbledon	26	18	2	6	72	51	38
Kingstonian	26	16	3	7	59	39	35
Walthamstow Avenue	26	14	6	6	73	42	34
Dulwich Hamlet	26	14	3	9	60	47	31
St.Albans City	26	12	3	11	59	45	27
Woking	**26**	**10**	**6**	**10**	**60**	**71**	**26**
Wycombe Wanderers	26	9	7	10	51	52	25
Romford	26	10	4	12	45	49	24
Ilford	26	10	4	12	46	53	24
Clapton	26	8	6	12	51	59	22
Oxford City	26	6	6	14	35	54	18
Corinthian-Casuals	26	4	5	17	41	69	13
Tufnell Park	26	3	2	21	24	91	8

1950-51

	P	W	D	L	Goals F	Goals A	Pts
Leytonstone	26	20	3	3	72	26	43
Walthamstow Avenue	26	15	4	7	57	37	34
Romford	26	15	3	8	58	47	33
Wimbledon	26	13	5	8	58	39	31
Dulwich Hamlet	26	14	2	10	54	43	30
Woking	**26**	**11**	**6**	**9**	**65**	**55**	**28**
Ilford	26	12	4	10	44	45	28
Corinthian-Casuals	26	13	0	13	62	60	26
St.Albans City	26	11	4	11	32	36	26
Kingstonian	26	9	4	13	46	54	22
Wycombe Wanderers	26	8	3	15	46	64	19
Oxford City	26	7	4	15	47	65	18
Clapton	26	6	5	15	29	50	17
Tufnell Park Edmonton	26	4	1	21	24	73	9

1951-52

	P	W	D	L	Goals F	Goals A	Pts
Leytonstone	26	13	9	4	63	36	35
Wimbledon	26	16	3	7	65	44	35
Walthamstow Avenue	26	15	4	7	71	43	34
Romford	26	14	4	8	61	42	32
Kingstonian	26	11	7	8	62	48	29
Wycombe Wanderers	26	12	5	9	64	59	29
Woking	**26**	**11**	**5**	**10**	**60**	**71**	**27**
Dulwich Hamlet	26	11	4	11	60	53	26
Corinthian-Casuals	26	11	4	11	55	66	26
St.Albans City	26	9	7	10	48	53	25
Ilford	26	8	5	13	32	47	21
Clapton	26	9	2	15	50	59	20
Oxford City	26	6	3	17	50	72	15
Tufnell Park Edmonton	26	2	6	18	25	73	10

1952-53

	P	W	D	L	Goals F	Goals A	Pts
Walthamstow Avenue	28	19	6	3	53	25	44
Bromley	28	17	4	7	71	35	38
Leytonstone	28	14	6	8	60	38	34
Wimbledon	28	14	5	9	68	37	33
Kingstonian	28	13	6	9	62	50	32
Dulwich Hamlet	28	15	2	11	62	52	32
Romford	28	12	8	8	62	52	32
Wycombe Wanderers	28	14	2	12	54	62	30
St.Albans City	28	11	6	11	43	57	28
Barking	28	9	7	12	42	51	25
Ilford	28	10	4	14	59	57	24
Woking	**28**	**10**	**4**	**14**	**57**	**72**	**24**
Corinthian-Casuals	28	7	9	12	45	56	23
Oxford City	28	5	2	21	37	87	12
Clapton	28	2	5	21	27	71	9

1953-54

					Goals		
	P	W	D	L	F	A	Pts
Bromley	28	18	3	7	76	45	39
Walthamstow Avenue	28	13	7	8	55	30	33
Wycombe Wanderers	28	15	3	10	65	44	33
Ilford	28	11	10	7	48	44	32
Corinthian-Casuals	28	12	7	9	59	44	31
Woking	**28**	**13**	**4**	**11**	**54**	**58**	**30**
Leytonstone	28	12	5	11	58	48	29
St.Albans City	28	11	6	11	54	55	28
Dulwich Hamlet	28	11	6	11	55	57	28
Romford	28	11	5	12	57	54	27
Clapton	28	11	5	12	42	56	27
Barking	28	11	2	15	59	84	24
Kingstonian	28	8	7	13	59	71	23
Wimbledon	28	7	8	13	43	59	22
Oxford City	28	4	6	18	49	84	14

1954-55

					Goals		
	P	W	D	L	F	A	Pts
Walthamstow Avenue	28	21	1	6	80	38	43
St.Albans City	28	18	3	7	61	41	39
Bromley	28	18	2	8	66	34	38
Wycombe Wanderers	28	16	3	9	68	43	35
Ilford	28	13	5	10	64	46	31
Barking	28	15	1	12	55	51	31
Woking	**28**	**12**	**3**	**13**	**75**	**79**	**27**
Kingstonian	28	10	7	11	47	57	27
Leytonstone	28	10	4	14	35	51	24
Oxford City	28	10	3	15	43	74	23
Clapton	28	9	4	15	41	50	22
Wimbledon	28	10	2	16	48	62	22
Corinthian-Casuals	28	9	3	16	50	65	21
Dulwich Hamlet	28	7	5	16	48	60	19
Romford	28	4	10	14	43	73	18

1955-56

					Goals		
	P	W	D	L	F	A	Pts
Wycombe Wanderers	28	19	5	4	82	36	43
Bromley	28	12	7	9	54	43	31
Leytonstone	28	12	7	9	50	44	31
Woking	**28**	**14**	**3**	**11**	**62**	**60**	**31**
Barking	28	12	7	9	41	45	31
Kingstonian	28	12	6	10	67	64	30
Walthamstow Avenue	28	13	3	12	61	45	29
Ilford	28	10	8	10	44	52	28
Oxford City	28	10	7	11	48	55	27
Clapton	28	9	8	11	45	48	26
Wimbledon	28	12	2	14	51	62	26
Corinthian-Casuals	28	9	7	12	56	56	25
Dulwich Hamlet	28	9	6	13	55	67	24
Romford	28	9	6	13	42	55	24
St.Albans City	28	2	10	16	36	62	14

1956-57

					Goals		
	P	W	D	L	F	A	Pts
Wycombe Wanderers	30	18	6	6	86	53	42
Woking	**30**	**20**	**1**	**9**	**104**	**47**	**41**
Bromley	30	16	5	9	78	60	37
Oxford City	30	16	3	11	65	57	35
Ilford	30	12	8	10	59	65	32
Tooting & Mitcham United	30	10	11	9	53	48	31
Kingstonian	30	11	9	10	72	77	31
Walthamstow Avenue	30	11	8	11	48	46	30
Dulwich Hamlet	30	13	3	14	65	54	29
St.Albans City	30	13	3	14	62	71	29
Leytonstone	30	11	6	13	50	50	28
Clapton	30	9	9	12	48	59	27
Wimbledon	30	10	5	15	47	66	25
Romford	30	10	5	15	53	81	25
Barking	30	7	6	17	48	72	20
Corinthian-Casuals	30	7	4	19	46	78	18

1957-58

					Goals		
	P	W	D	L	F	A	Pts
Tooting & Mitcham United	30	20	6	4	79	33	46
Wycombe Wanderers	30	19	4	7	78	42	42
Walthamstow Avenue	30	17	5	8	63	35	39
Bromley	30	13	9	8	66	51	35
Oxford City	30	13	6	11	59	48	32
Leytonstone	30	13	6	11	49	48	32
Wimbledon	30	15	2	13	64	66	32
Corinthian-Casuals	30	12	8	10	62	68	32
Woking	**30**	**12**	**7**	**11**	**70**	**58**	**31**
Barking	30	10	6	14	49	61	26
St.Albans City	30	11	3	16	56	76	25
Clapton	30	8	9	13	42	65	25
Kingstonian	30	7	8	15	45	66	22
Dulwich Hamlet	30	7	7	16	49	64	21
Ilford	30	8	4	18	46	70	20
Romford	30	6	8	16	45	71	20

1958-59

					Goals		
	P	W	D	L	F	A	Pts
Wimbledon	30	22	3	5	91	38	47
Dulwich Hamlet	30	18	5	7	68	44	41
Wycombe Wanderers	30	18	4	8	93	50	40
Oxford City	30	17	4	9	87	58	38
Walthamstow Avenue	30	16	5	9	59	40	37
Tooting & Mitcham United	30	15	4	11	84	55	34
Barking	30	14	2	14	59	53	30
Woking	**30**	**12**	**6**	**12**	**66**	**66**	**30**
Bromley	30	11	7	12	56	55	29
Clapton	30	10	6	14	55	67	26
Ilford	30	10	6	14	46	67	26
Kingstonian	30	9	4	17	54	72	22
St.Albans City	30	8	6	16	53	89	22
Leytonstone	30	7	6	17	40	87	20
Romford	30	7	5	18	54	76	19
Corinthian-Casuals	30	7	5	18	44	92	19

1959-60

	P	W	D	L	Goals F	A	Pts
Tooting & Mitcham United	30	17	8	5	75	43	42
Wycombe Wanderers	30	19	3	8	84	46	41
Wimbledon	30	18	3	9	66	36	39
Kingstonian	30	18	3	9	76	51	39
Corinthian-Casuals	30	18	1	11	69	61	37
Bromley	30	15	6	9	74	46	36
Dulwich Hamlet	30	14	6	10	65	47	34
Walthamstow Avenue	30	11	11	8	48	38	33
Oxford City	30	10	10	10	57	57	30
Leytonstone	30	10	8	12	43	46	28
Woking	**30**	**10**	**6**	**14**	**54**	**61**	**26**
St.Albans City	30	10	6	14	50	65	26
Maidstone United	30	10	5	15	53	60	25
Barking	30	7	4	19	30	75	18
Ilford	30	5	6	19	34	86	16
Clapton	30	3	4	23	32	92	10

1960-61

	P	W	D	L	Goals F	A	Pts
Bromley	30	20	6	4	89	42	46
Walthamstow Avenue	30	20	5	5	87	38	45
Wimbledon	30	18	6	6	72	43	42
Dulwich Hamlet	30	17	4	9	71	59	38
Maidstone United	30	14	8	8	63	39	36
Leytonstone	30	15	6	9	46	34	36
Tooting & Mitcham United	30	14	3	13	69	51	31
Wycombe Wanderers	30	12	5	13	63	61	29
St.Albans City	30	12	4	14	45	72	28
Oxford City	30	10	7	13	59	59	27
Corinthian-Casuals	30	9	9	12	49	59	27
Kingstonian	30	10	6	14	55	61	26
Woking	**30**	**10**	**6**	**14**	**58**	**71**	**26**
Ilford	30	5	8	17	30	69	18
Barking	30	3	8	19	30	76	14
Clapton	30	3	5	22	25	77	11

1961-62

	P	W	D	L	Goals F	A	Pts
Wimbledon	30	19	6	5	68	24	44
Leytonstone	30	17	7	6	61	44	41
Walthamstow Avenue	30	14	8	8	51	31	36
Kingstonian	30	15	5	10	65	48	35
Tooting & Mitcham United	30	12	10	8	62	47	34
Oxford City	30	12	9	9	56	49	33
Wycombe Wanderers	30	12	7	11	57	51	31
Corinthian-Casuals	30	12	7	11	45	51	31
St.Albans City	30	10	9	11	55	55	29
Woking	**30**	**9**	**9**	**12**	**51**	**60**	**27**
Dulwich Hamlet	30	11	4	15	55	66	26
Barking	30	9	8	13	40	64	26
Ilford	30	7	10	13	50	59	24
Bromley	30	10	4	16	49	69	24
Clapton	30	6	8	16	45	67	20
Maidstone United	30	6	7	17	34	59	19

1962-63

	P	W	D	L	Goals F	A	Pts
Wimbledon	30	19	8	3	84	33	46
Kingstonian	30	18	8	4	79	37	44
Tooting & Mitcham United	30	17	8	5	65	37	42
Ilford	30	19	3	8	70	44	41
Walthamstow Avenue	30	14	7	9	51	44	35
Maidstone United	30	13	8	9	56	45	34
Bromley	30	12	10	8	57	51	34
Leytonstone	30	12	7	11	48	50	31
Wycombe Wanderers	30	10	10	10	56	61	30
St.Albans City	30	11	5	14	54	49	27
Barking	30	8	10	12	39	50	26
Oxford City	30	8	9	13	55	64	25
Woking	**30**	**8**	**6**	**16**	**42**	**66**	**22**
Clapton	30	7	4	19	30	71	18
Dulwich Hamlet	30	4	5	21	30	71	13
Corinthian-Casuals	30	4	4	22	28	71	12

1963-64

	P	W	D	L	Goals F	A	Pts
Wimbledon	38	27	6	5	87	44	60
Hendon	38	25	4	9	124	38	54
Kingstonian	38	24	4	10	100	62	52
Sutton United	38	23	5	10	99	64	51
Enfield	38	20	10	8	96	56	50
Oxford City	38	20	8	10	90	55	48
Tooting & Mitcham United	38	19	8	11	78	51	46
St.Albans City	38	14	12	12	62	63	40
Ilford	38	16	8	14	75	79	40
Maidstone United	38	15	8	15	65	71	38
Walthamstow Avenue	38	15	6	17	70	66	36
Leytonstone	38	14	8	16	66	71	36
Wycombe Wanderers	38	13	6	19	74	80	32
Hitchin Town	38	14	4	20	67	100	32
Bromley	38	11	8	19	64	75	30
Barking	38	10	9	19	48	69	29
Woking	**38**	**10**	**9**	**19**	**44**	**88**	**29**
Corinthian-Casuals	38	10	4	24	52	92	24
Dulwich Hamlet	38	6	12	20	47	97	24
Clapton	38	2	5	31	31	120	9

1964-65

					Goals		
	P	W	D	L	F	A	Pts
Hendon *	38	28	7	3	123	49	63
Enfield	38	29	5	4	98	35	63
Kingstonian	38	24	8	6	86	44	56
Leytonstone	38	24	5	9	115	62	53
Oxford City	38	20	7	11	76	50	47
St.Albans City	38	18	9	11	63	43	45
Sutton United	38	17	11	10	74	57	45
Wealdstone	38	19	6	13	93	68	44
Bromley	38	14	11	13	71	80	39
Tooting & Mitcham United	38	15	7	16	71	66	37
Hitchin Town	38	13	9	16	61	66	35
Walthamstow Avenue	38	15	5	18	63	82	35
Wycombe Wanderers	38	13	7	18	70	85	33
Corinthian-Casuals	38	13	7	18	56	77	33
Barking	38	10	8	20	58	80	28
Ilford	38	8	8	22	43	89	24
Maidstone United	38	8	6	24	49	86	22
Dulwich Hamlet	38	8	5	25	45	79	21
Clapton	38	8	3	27	43	91	19
Woking	**38**	**7**	**4**	**27**	**44**	**113**	**18**
*Championship determined by play-off (Rule 8 applied)							

1966-67

					Goals		
	P	W	D	L	F	A	Pts
Sutton United	38	26	7	5	89	33	59
Walthamstow Avenue	38	22	12	4	89	47	56
Wycombe Wanderers	38	23	8	7	92	54	54
Enfield	38	25	2	11	87	33	52
Hendon	38	20	9	9	64	37	49
Tooting & Mitcham United	38	19	10	9	76	60	48
Leytonstone	38	19	9	10	67	38	47
St.Albans City	38	16	12	10	59	45	44
Kingstonian	38	18	8	12	60	49	44
Oxford City	38	15	9	14	74	61	39
Woking	**38**	**13**	**10**	**15**	**65**	**71**	**36**
Wealdstone	38	13	8	17	72	73	34
Barking	38	11	12	15	56	61	34
Bromley	38	12	7	19	50	67	31
Clapton	38	10	8	20	49	92	28
Ilford	38	8	10	20	43	77	26
Corinthian-Casuals	38	9	7	22	45	68	25
Maidstone United	38	6	10	22	43	90	22
Hitchin Town	38	8	6	24	39	89	22
Dulwich Hamlet	38	3	4	31	33	107	10

1965-66

					Goals		
	P	W	D	L	F	A	Pts
Leytonstone	38	27	7	4	98	33	61
Hendon	38	27	5	6	111	55	59
Enfield	38	24	8	6	104	54	56
Wycombe Wanderers	38	25	6	7	100	65	56
Kingstonian	38	24	5	9	94	55	53
Wealdstone	38	20	6	12	90	64	46
Maidstone United	38	19	6	13	74	61	44
St.Albans City	38	19	5	14	57	56	43
Sutton United	38	17	7	14	83	72	41
Tooting & Mitcham United	38	16	7	15	65	58	39
Corinthian-Casuals	38	17	5	16	74	67	39
Woking	**38**	**12**	**10**	**16**	**60**	**83**	**34**
Walthamstow Avenue	38	12	9	17	81	75	33
Oxford City	38	10	9	19	49	72	29
Barking	38	10	7	21	51	72	27
Bromley	38	10	5	23	69	101	25
Ilford	38	7	10	21	50	84	24
Hitchin Town	38	6	8	24	57	118	20
Clapton	38	5	6	27	46	103	16
Dulwich Hamlet	38	5	5	28	30	95	15

1967-68

					Goals		
	P	W	D	L	F	A	Pts
Enfield	38	28	8	2	85	22	64
Sutton United	38	22	11	5	89	27	55
Hendon	38	23	6	9	90	36	52
Leytonstone	38	21	10	7	78	41	52
St.Albans City	38	20	8	10	78	41	48
Walthamstow Avenue	38	19	9	10	81	64	47
Wealdstone	38	19	8	11	80	45	46
Tooting & Mitcham United	38	19	5	14	57	45	43
Barking	38	17	8	13	75	57	42
Oxford City	38	17	4	17	59	58	38
Kingstonian	38	14	10	14	56	61	38
Hitchin Town	38	14	9	15	61	73	37
Bromley	38	12	10	16	58	80	34
Wycombe Wanderers	38	13	5	20	73	85	31
Dulwich Hamlet	38	10	7	21	39	66	27
Clapton	38	10	7	21	51	88	27
Woking	**38**	**8**	**8**	**22**	**50**	**90**	**24**
Corinthian-Casuals	38	7	10	21	40	80	24
Ilford	38	7	7	24	41	77	21
Maidstone United	38	3	4	31	26	131	10

1968-69

	P	W	D	L	Goals F	Goals A	Pts
Enfield	38	27	7	4	103	28	61
Hitchin Town	38	23	10	5	67	41	56
Sutton United	38	22	9	7	83	29	53
Wycombe Wanderers	38	23	6	9	70	37	52
Wealdstone	38	20	11	7	73	48	51
Hendon	38	22	5	11	69	47	49
St.Albans City	38	17	13	8	75	44	47
Barking	38	20	7	11	69	46	47
Oxford City	38	18	8	12	76	64	44
Tooting & Mitcham United	38	16	10	12	68	55	42
Leytonstone	38	18	4	16	71	53	40
Kingstonian	38	15	8	15	62	56	38
Walthamstow Avenue	38	10	10	18	47	71	30
Maidstone United	38	10	8	20	47	75	28
Clapton	38	10	7	21	52	76	27
Woking	**38**	**8**	**7**	**23**	**45**	**77**	**23**
Bromley	38	8	7	23	52	95	23
Dulwich Hamlet	38	6	9	23	31	77	21
Ilford	38	6	8	24	33	77	20
Corinthian-Casuals	38	2	4	32	23	120	8

1970-71

	P	W	D	L	Goals F	Goals A	Pts
Wycombe Wanderers	38	28	6	4	93	32	62
Sutton United	38	29	3	6	76	35	61
St Albans City	38	23	10	5	87	26	56
Enfield	38	24	7	7	67	24	55
Ilford	38	21	7	10	74	51	49
Hendon	38	18	11	9	81	37	47
Barking	38	20	4	14	89	59	44
Leytonstone	38	17	10	11	68	50	44
Woking	**38**	**18**	**6**	**14**	**57**	**50**	**42**
Walthamstow Avenue	38	14	11	13	63	52	39
Oxford City	38	13	10	15	51	48	36
Hitchin Town	38	12	9	17	46	60	33
Wealdstone	38	12	8	18	45	64	32
Tooting & Mitcham United	38	11	9	18	44	66	31
Kingstonian	38	11	8	19	53	71	30
Bromley	38	10	6	22	34	77	26
Dulwich Hamlet	38	7	10	21	30	66	24
Maidstone United	38	7	6	25	42	84	20
Clapton	38	5	7	26	33	101	17
Corinthian-Casuals	38	2	8	28	23	103	12

1969-70

	P	W	D	L	Goals F	Goals A	Pts
Enfield	38	27	8	3	91	26	62
Wycombe Wanderers	38	25	11	2	85	24	61
Sutton United	38	24	9	5	75	35	57
Barking	38	21	9	8	93	47	51
Hendon	38	19	12	7	77	44	50
St.Albans City	38	21	8	9	69	40	50
Hitchin Town	38	19	10	9	71	40	48
Tooting & Mitcham United	38	19	5	14	88	62	43
Leytonstone	38	17	7	14	57	41	41
Wealdstone	38	15	10	13	53	48	40
Oxford City	38	15	7	16	61	78	37
Kingstonian	38	13	9	16	55	57	35
Ilford	38	8	15	15	42	73	31
Dulwich Hamlet	38	8	12	18	46	66	28
Woking	**38**	**10**	**7**	**21**	**46**	**69**	**27**
Walthamstow Avenue	38	11	5	22	52	81	27
Clapton	38	9	7	22	45	87	25
Maidstone United	38	7	8	23	48	84	22
Corinthian-Casuals	38	6	3	29	30	99	15
Bromley	38	3	4	31	28	111	10

1971-72

	P	W	D	L	Goals F	Goals A	Pts
Wycombe Wanderers	40	31	3	6	102	20	65
Enfield	40	26	8	6	90	41	60
Walton & Hersham	40	24	8	8	69	25	56
Hendon	40	23	10	7	78	35	56
Bishop's Stortford	40	24	5	11	61	37	53
Sutton United	40	21	10	9	77	43	52
St.Albans City	40	23	4	13	74	47	50
Ilford	40	17	11	12	62	52	45
Barking	40	20	4	16	65	61	44
Hitchin Town	40	17	10	13	68	66	44
Bromley	40	16	10	14	67	64	42
Hayes	40	14	12	14	50	48	40
Oxford City	40	13	9	18	67	74	35
Woking	**40**	**11**	**10**	**19**	**52**	**58**	**32**
Kingstonian	40	10	12	18	49	59	32
Walthamstow Avenue	40	12	8	20	58	70	32
Leytonstone	40	11	8	21	48	68	30
Tooting & Mitcham United	40	6	9	25	38	93	21
Clapton	40	7	7	26	45	118	21
Dulwich Hamlet	40	4	12	24	35	81	20
Corinthian-Casuals	40	3	4	33	21	116	10

1972-73

	P	W	D	L	Goals F	A	Pts
Hendon	42	34	6	2	88	18	74
Walton & Hersham	42	25	11	6	60	25	61
Leatherhead	42	23	10	9	76	32	56
Wycombe Wanderers	42	25	6	11	66	32	56
Walthamstow Avenue	42	20	12	10	66	48	52
Tooting & Mitcham United	42	20	11	11	73	39	51
Sutton United	42	21	9	12	69	48	51
Kingstonian	42	20	10	12	60	49	50
Enfield	42	20	8	14	90	54	48
Bishop's Stortford	42	18	12	12	58	51	48
Hayes	42	19	8	15	69	42	46
Dulwich Hamlet	42	18	9	15	59	52	45
Ilford	42	18	9	15	61	59	45
Leytonstone	42	17	11	14	55	54	45
Woking	**42**	**18**	**8**	**16**	**61**	**56**	**44**
Hitchin Town	42	15	9	18	52	64	39
Barking	42	8	7	27	45	88	23
St.Albans City	42	5	12	25	34	76	22
Oxford City	42	6	7	29	30	101	19
Bromley	42	4	10	28	31	70	18
Clapton	42	3	11	28	31	100	17
Corinthian-Casuals	42	3	8	31	30	106	14

1974-75

DIVISION 1	P	W	D	L	Goals F	A	Pts
Wycombe Wanderers	42	28	11	3	93	30	95
Enfield	42	29	8	5	78	26	95
Dagenham	42	28	5	9	95	44	89
Tooting & Mitcham United	42	25	9	8	78	46	84
Dulwich Hamlet	42	24	10	8	75	38	82
Leatherhead	42	23	10	9	83	42	79
Ilford	42	23	10	9	98	51	79
Oxford City	42	17	9	16	63	56	60
Slough Town	42	17	6	19	68	52	57
Sutton United	42	17	6	19	68	63	57
Bishop's Stortford	42	17	6	19	56	64	57
Hitchin Town	42	15	10	17	57	71	55
Hendon	42	15	7	20	59	74	52
Walthamstow Avenue	42	13	9	20	56	62	48
Woking	**42**	**12**	**10**	**20**	**53**	**73**	**46**
Hayes	42	10	14	18	52	66	44
Barking	42	12	8	22	57	81	44
Leytonstone	42	12	7	23	42	61	43
Kingstonian	42	13	4	25	48	73	43
Clapton	42	12	4	26	46	96	40
Walton & Hersham	42	9	4	29	37	108	31
Bromley	42	6	3	33	25	110	21

1973-74

DIVISION 1	P	W	D	L	Goals F	A	Pts
Wycombe Wanderers	42	27	9	6	96	34	90
Hendon	42	25	13	4	63	20	88
Bishop's Stortford	42	26	9	7	78	26	87
Dulwich Hamlet	42	22	11	9	71	38	77
Leatherhead	42	23	6	13	81	44	75
Walton & Hersham	42	20	12	10	68	50	72
Woking	**42**	**22**	**6**	**14**	**63**	**55**	**72**
Leytonstone	42	20	9	13	63	44	69
Ilford	42	20	8	14	60	44	68
Hayes	42	17	14	11	65	43	65
Oxford City	42	15	16	11	45	47	61
Sutton United	42	13	16	13	51	52	55
Hitchin Town	42	15	10	17	68	73	55
Barking	42	14	12	16	57	58	54
Kingstonian	42	12	15	15	47	46	51
Tooting & Mitcham United	42	14	9	19	57	62	51
Enfield	42	13	11	18	50	57	50
Walthamstow Avenue	42	11	13	18	46	62	46
Bromley	42	7	9	26	37	81	30
Clapton	42	8	3	31	36	128	27
St.Albans City	42	4	7	31	30	92	19
Corinthian-Casuals	42	3	4	35	31	107	13

1975-76

DIVISION 1	P	W	D	L	Goals F	A	Pts
Enfield	42	26	9	7	83	38	87
Wycombe Wanderers	42	24	10	8	71	41	82
Dagenham	42	25	6	11	89	55	81
Ilford	42	22	10	10	58	39	76
Dulwich Hamlet	42	22	5	15	67	41	71
Hendon	42	20	11	11	60	41	71
Tooting & Mitcham United	42	19	11	12	73	49	68
Leatherhead	42	19	10	13	63	53	67
Staines Town	42	19	9	14	46	37	66
Slough Town	42	17	12	13	58	45	63
Sutton United	42	17	11	14	71	60	62
Bishop's Stortford	42	15	12	15	51	47	57
Walthamstow Avenue	42	14	11	17	47	60	53
Woking	**42**	**14**	**9**	**19**	**58**	**62**	**51**
Barking	42	15	6	21	57	70	51
Hitchin Town	42	13	11	18	45	57	50
Hayes	42	10	19	13	44	48	49
Kingstonian	42	13	8	21	53	87	47
Southall & Ealing Borough	42	11	9	22	56	69	42
Leytonstone	42	10	10	22	41	63	40
Oxford City	42	9	8	25	29	65	35
Clapton	42	3	3	36	19	112	12

1976-77

DIVISION 1	P	W	D	L	Goals F	Goals A	Pts
Enfield	42	24	12	6	63	34	84
Wycombe Wanderers	42	25	8	9	71	34	83
Dagenham	42	23	10	9	80	39	79
Hendon	42	19	10	13	60	48	67
Tilbury	42	18	13	11	57	49	67
Tooting & Mitcham	42	18	10	14	85	72	64
Walthamstow Avenue	42	19	7	16	61	55	64
Slough Town	42	18	9	15	51	46	63
Hitchin Town	42	19	6	17	60	66	63
Leatherhead	42	18	7	17	61	47	61
Staines Town	42	16	13	13	52	48	61
Leytonstone	42	16	11	15	59	57	59
Barking	42	16	9	17	63	61	57
Southall & Ealing Borough	42	15	8	19	52	64	53
Croydon	42	13	10	19	38	52	49
Sutton United	42	14	7	21	40	55	49
Kingstonian	42	13	7	22	45	60	46
Hayes	42	12	10	20	49	69	46
Woking	**42**	**11**	**12**	**19**	**47**	**61**	**45**
Bishop's Stortford	42	11	11	20	51	71	44
Dulwich Hamlet	42	11	8	23	52	68	41
Ilford	42	10	8	24	32	73	38

1978-79

PREMIER DIVISION	P	W	D	L	Goals F	Goals A	Pts
Barking	42	28	9	5	92	50	93
Dagenham	42	25	6	11	83	63	81
Enfield	42	22	11	9	69	37	77
Dulwich Hamlet	42	21	13	8	69	39	76
Slough Town	42	20	12	10	61	44	72
Wycombe Wanderers	42	20	9	13	59	44	69
Woking	**42**	**18**	**14**	**10**	**79**	**59**	**68**
Croydon	42	19	9	14	61	51	66
Hendon	42	16	14	12	55	48	62
Leatherhead	42	17	9	16	57	45	60
Sutton United	42	17	9	16	62	51	60
Tooting & Mitcham United	42	15	14	13	52	52	59
Walthamstow Avenue	42	15	6	21	61	69	51
Tilbury	42	13	11	18	60	76	50
Boreham Wood	42	13	10	19	50	67	49
Hitchin Town	42	12	11	19	59	71	47
Carshalton Athletic	42	10	16	16	49	69	46
Hayes	42	9	18	15	45	58	45
Oxford City	42	12	7	23	50	80	43
Staines Town	42	6	16	20	40	64	34
Leytonstone	42	8	7	27	36	75	31
Kingstonian	42	3	15	24	35	72	24

1977-78

PREMIER DIVISION	P	W	D	L	Goals F	Goals A	Pts
Enfield	42	35	5	2	96	27	110
Dagenham	42	24	7	12	78	55	79
Wycombe Wanderers	42	22	9	11	66	41	75
Tooting & Mitcham United	42	22	8	12	64	49	74
Hitchin Town	42	20	9	13	69	53	69
Sutton United	42	18	12	12	66	57	66
Leatherhead	42	18	11	13	62	48	65
Croydon	42	18	10	14	61	52	64
Walthamstow Avenue	42	17	12	13	64	61	63
Barking	42	17	7	18	76	66	58
Carshalton Athletic	42	15	11	16	61	63	56
Hayes	42	15	11	16	46	53	56
Hendon	42	16	7	19	57	55	55
Woking	**42**	**14**	**11**	**17**	**62**	**62**	**53**
Boreham Wood	42	15	8	19	48	65	53
Slough Town	42	14	8	20	52	69	50
Staines Town	42	12	13	17	46	60	49
Tilbury	42	11	12	19	57	68	45
Kingstonian	42	8	13	21	43	65	37
Leytonstone	42	7	15	20	44	71	36
Southall & Ealing Borough	42	6	15	21	43	74	33
Bishop's Stortford	42	7	8	27	36	83	29

1979-80

PREMIER DIVISION	P	W	D	L	Goals F	Goals A	Pts
Enfield	42	25	9	8	74	32	84
Walthamstow Avenue	42	24	9	9	87	48	81
Dulwich Hamlet	42	21	16	5	66	37	79
Sutton United	42	20	13	9	67	40	73
Dagenham	42	20	13	9	82	56	73
Tooting & Mitcham United	42	21	6	15	62	59	69
Barking	42	19	10	13	72	51	67
Harrow Borough	42	17	15	10	64	51	66
Woking	**42**	**17**	**13**	**12**	**78**	**59**	**64**
Wycombe Wanderers	42	17	13	12	72	53	64
Harlow Town	42	14	12	16	54	60	54
Hitchin Town	42	13	15	14	54	68	54
Hendon	42	12	13	17	50	57	49
Slough Town	42	13	10	19	54	71	49
Boreham Wood	42	13	10	19	50	69	49
Staines Town	42	14	6	22	46	67	48
Hayes	42	12	9	21	48	68	45
Leatherhead	42	11	11	20	51	60	44
Carshalton Athletic	42	12	7	23	48	78	43
Croydon	42	10	10	22	51	59	40
Oxford City	42	10	9	23	49	87	39
* Tilbury	42	7	11	24	41	90	30

* 2 points deducted

1980-81

PREMIER DIVISION					Goals		
	P	W	D	L	F	A	Pts
Slough Town	42	23	13	6	73	34	82
Enfield	42	23	11	8	81	43	80
Wycombe Wanderers	42	22	9	11	76	49	75
Leytonstone & Ilford	42	19	12	11	78	57	69
Sutton United	42	19	12	11	82	65	69
Hendon	42	18	10	14	66	58	64
Hayes	42	18	8	16	45	50	62
Dagenham	42	17	11	14	79	66	62
Harrow Borough	42	16	11	15	57	52	59
Bromley	42	16	9	17	63	69	57
Staines Town	42	15	9	18	60	61	54
Tooting & Mitcham United	42	15	8	19	49	53	53
Hitchin Town	42	14	10	18	64	62	52
Croydon	42	12	15	15	51	51	51
Dulwich Hamlet	42	13	12	17	62	67	51
Leatherhead	42	12	14	16	36	50	50
Carshalton Athletic	42	14	8	20	57	82	50
* Barking	42	13	12	17	58	72	49
Harlow Town	42	11	15	16	53	66	48
Walthamstow Avenue	42	13	7	22	50	81	46
Boreham Wood	42	10	13	19	46	69	43
+ Woking	**42**	**11**	**7**	**24**	**40**	**69**	**37**
* 2 points deducted + 3 points deducted							

1982-83

PREMIER DIVISION					Goals		
	P	W	D	L	F	A	Pts
Wycombe Wanderers	42	26	7	9	79	47	85
Leytonstone & Ilford	42	24	9	9	71	39	81
Harrow Borough	42	24	7	11	91	58	79
Hayes	42	23	9	10	63	41	78
Sutton United	42	20	8	14	96	71	68
Dulwich Hamlet	42	18	14	10	59	52	68
Slough Town	42	18	13	11	73	36	67
Bognor Regis Town	42	19	8	15	53	48	65
Tooting & Mitcham United	42	18	9	15	58	56	63
Billericay Town	42	17	10	15	54	51	61
Croydon	42	17	9	16	68	58	60
Hendon	42	18	6	18	68	61	60
Bishop's Stortford	42	17	9	16	61	58	60
Barking	42	14	14	14	47	55	56
Bromley	42	14	12	16	51	50	54
Carshalton Athletic	42	15	9	18	58	60	54
Wokingham Town	42	13	9	20	37	51	48
Walthamstow Avenue	42	12	11	19	48	64	47
Staines Town	42	12	11	19	62	79	47
Hitchin Town	42	11	9	22	49	77	42
Woking	**42**	**6**	**6**	**30**	**30**	**79**	**24**
Leatherhead	42	4	5	33	36	121	17

1981-82

PREMIER DIVISION					Goals		
	P	W	D	L	F	A	Pts
Leytonstone & Ilford	42	26	5	11	91	52	83
Sutton United	42	22	9	11	72	49	75
Wycombe Wanderers	42	21	10	11	63	48	73
Staines Town	42	21	9	12	59	46	72
Walthamstow Avenue	42	21	7	14	81	62	70
Harrow Borough	42	18	13	11	77	55	67
Tooting & Mitcham	42	19	10	13	58	47	67
Slough Town	42	17	13	12	64	54	64
Leatherhead	42	16	12	14	57	52	60
Hayes	42	16	10	16	58	52	58
Croydon	42	16	9	17	59	57	57
Barking	42	14	14	14	53	51	56
Hendon	42	13	13	16	56	65	52
Dulwich Hamlet	42	14	10	18	47	59	52
Bishop's Stortford	42	15	5	22	50	70	50
Carshalton Athletic	42	14	8	20	58	86	50
Billericay Town	42	11	16	15	41	50	49
Hitchin Town	42	12	11	19	56	77	47
Bromley	42	13	7	22	63	79	46
Woking	**42**	**11**	**13**	**18**	**57**	**75**	**46**
Harlow Town	42	10	11	21	50	73	41
Boreham Wood	42	8	13	21	47	58	37

1983-84

DIVISION 1					Goals		
	P	W	D	L	F	A	Pts
Windsor & Eton	42	26	7	9	89	44	85
Epsom & Ewell	42	23	9	10	73	51	78
Wembley	42	21	11	10	65	32	74
Maidenhead United	42	22	8	12	67	42	74
Boreham Wood	42	22	7	13	74	43	73
Farnborough Town	42	18	12	12	78	60	66
Hampton	42	18	12	12	65	49	66
Metropolitan Police	42	20	5	17	79	64	65
Chesham United	42	18	8	16	64	57	62
Tilbury	42	17	10	15	54	64	61
Leatherhead	42	15	10	17	67	56	55
Aveley	42	15	10	17	49	53	55
Woking	**42**	**16**	**7**	**19**	**66**	**73**	**55**
Hertford Town	42	15	9	18	56	73	54
Oxford City	42	14	9	19	57	56	51
Lewes	42	13	12	17	49	65	51
Walton & Hersham	42	13	10	19	52	70	49
Hornchurch	42	13	10	19	43	63	49
Kingstonian	42	13	9	20	47	67	48
Clapton	42	12	11	19	49	67	47
Cheshunt	42	12	8	22	45	64	44
Feltham	42	7	4	31	31	106	25

1984-85

DIVISION 1	P	W	D	L	Goals F	A	Pts
Farnborough Town	42	26	8	8	101	45	86
Kingstonian	42	23	10	9	67	39	79
+ Leatherhead	42	23	10	9	109	61	76
Chesham United	42	22	8	12	78	46	74
Wembley	42	20	10	12	59	40	70
St.Albans City	42	19	10	13	79	59	67
Tilbury	42	18	13	11	86	68	67
Bromley	42	18	9	15	71	65	63
Hampton	42	17	11	14	75	62	62
Staines Town	42	16	11	15	59	53	59
Maidenhead United	42	17	8	17	65	64	59
* Walton & Hersham	42	16	8	18	60	69	55
Aveley	42	16	7	19	62	78	55
Oxford City	42	14	12	16	62	53	54
Lewes	42	15	9	18	70	72	54
Basildon United	42	15	8	19	55	61	53
Boreham Wood	42	15	7	20	72	83	52
Hornchurch	42	15	6	21	55	74	51
Woking	**42**	**15**	**6**	**21**	**60**	**91**	**51**
Metropolitan Police	42	10	12	20	65	92	42
Clapton	42	5	11	26	50	124	26
Hertford Town	42	5	10	27	36	97	25

* 1 point deducted
+ 3 points deducted

1986-87

DIVISION 2 SOUTH	P	W	D	L	Goals F	A	Pts
Woking	**40**	**27**	**7**	**6**	**110**	**32**	**88**
Marlow	40	28	4	8	78	36	88
Dorking	40	24	12	4	78	30	84
Feltham	40	25	3	12	79	34	78
Ruislip Manor	40	22	10	8	85	47	76
Chertsey Town	40	18	11	11	56	44	65
Metropolitan Police	40	16	13	11	70	61	61
Chalfont St.Peter	40	17	10	13	60	55	61
Hungerford Town	40	14	14	12	55	48	56
Harefield United	40	14	14	12	53	47	56
Eastbourne United	40	15	10	15	72	59	55
Whyteleafe	40	12	15	13	52	63	51
Horsham	40	14	8	18	54	61	50
Egham Town	40	14	6	20	45	77	48
Camberley Town	40	13	3	24	62	89	42
Flackwell Heath	40	9	11	20	34	63	38
Banstead Athletic	40	7	15	18	44	61	36
Petersfield United	40	9	8	23	45	84	34
Molesey	40	7	12	21	37	89	33
Newbury Town	40	6	14	20	51	83	32
Southall	40	6	6	28	28	85	24

1985-86

DIVISION 2 SOUTH	P	W	D	L	Goals F	A	Pts
Southwick	38	25	8	5	86	34	83
Bracknell Town	38	24	9	5	80	23	81
Woking	**38**	**23**	**9**	**6**	**94**	**45**	**78**
Newbury Town	38	22	7	9	86	53	73
Whyteleafe	38	21	10	7	61	41	73
Molesey	38	21	8	9	59	39	71
Metropolitan Police	38	20	6	12	72	48	66
Southall	38	19	7	12	77	59	64
Dorking	38	18	10	10	70	57	64
Feltham	38	16	7	15	65	60	55
Banstead Athletic	38	15	8	15	60	66	53
Petersfield United	38	12	9	17	61	71	45
Hungerford Town	38	11	6	21	57	78	39
Flackwell Heath	38	11	6	21	46	72	39
Eastbourne United	38	9	8	21	51	81	35
Camberley Town	38	9	7	22	53	64	34
Egham Town	38	7	8	23	71	83	29
Horsham	38	6	10	22	33	74	28
Ruislip Manor	38	5	12	21	44	87	27
Marlow	38	6	5	27	47	108	23

1987-88

DIVISION 1	P	W	D	L	Goals F	A	Pts
Marlow	42	32	5	5	100	44	101
Grays Athletic	42	30	10	2	74	25	100
Woking	**42**	**25**	**7**	**10**	**91**	**52**	**82**
Boreham Wood	42	21	9	12	65	45	72
Staines Town	42	19	11	12	71	48	68
Wembley	42	18	11	13	54	46	65
Basildon United	42	18	9	15	65	58	63
Walton & Hersham	42	15	16	11	53	44	61
Hampton	42	17	10	15	59	54	61
Leatherhead	42	16	11	15	64	53	59
Southwick	42	13	12	17	59	63	51
Oxford City	42	13	12	17	70	77	51
Worthing	42	14	8	20	67	73	50
Kingsbury Town	42	11	17	14	62	69	50
Walthamstow Avenue	42	13	11	18	53	63	50
Lewes	42	12	13	17	83	77	49
Uxbridge	42	11	16	15	41	47	49
Chesham United	42	12	10	20	69	77	46
Bracknell Town	42	12	9	21	54	80	45
Billericay Town	42	11	11	20	58	88	44
Stevenage Borough	42	11	9	22	36	64	42
Wolverton Town	42	3	3	36	23	124	12

1988-89

DIVISION 1	P	W	D	L	Goals F	A	Pts
Staines Town	40	26	9	5	79	29	87
Basingstoke Town	40	25	8	7	85	36	83
Woking	**40**	**24**	**10**	**6**	**72**	**30**	**82**
Hitchin Town	40	21	11	8	60	32	74
Wivenhoe Town	40	22	6	12	62	44	72
Lewes	40	21	8	11	72	54	71
Walton & Hersham	40	21	7	12	56	36	70
Kingsbury Town	40	20	7	13	65	41	67
Uxbridge	40	19	7	14	60	54	64
Wembley	40	18	6	16	45	58	60
Boreham Wood	40	16	9	15	57	52	57
Leatherhead	40	14	8	18	56	58	50
Metropolitan Police	40	13	9	18	52	68	48
Chesham United	40	12	9	19	54	67	45
Southwick	40	9	15	16	44	58	42
Chalfont St.Peter	40	11	9	20	56	82	42
Hampton	40	7	14	19	37	62	35
* Worthing	40	8	10	22	49	80	32
Collier Row	40	8	7	25	37	82	31
Bracknell Town	40	8	6	26	38	70	30
Basildon United	40	6	7	27	34	77	25
* Two points deducted by League							

1990-91

PREMIER DIVISION	P	W	D	L	Goals F	A	Pts
Redbridge Forest	42	29	6	7	74	43	93
Enfield	42	26	11	5	83	30	89
Aylesbury United	42	24	11	7	90	47	83
Woking	**42**	**24**	**10**	**8**	**84**	**39**	**82**
Kingstonian	42	21	12	9	86	57	75
Grays Athletic	42	20	8	14	66	53	68
Marlow	42	18	13	11	72	49	67
Hayes	42	20	5	17	60	57	59
Carshalton	42	19	7	16	80	67	64
Wivenhoe Town	42	16	11	15	69	66	59
Wokingham	42	15	13	14	58	54	58
Windsor & Eton	42	15	10	17	48	63	55
Bishop's Stortford	42	14	12	16	54	49	54
Dagenham	42	13	11	18	62	68	50
Hendon	42	12	10	20	48	62	46
St.Albans	42	11	12	19	60	74	45
Bognor Regis	42	12	8	22	44	71	44
Basingstoke Town	42	12	7	23	57	95	43
Staines	42	10	10	22	46	79	39
Harrow Borough	42	10	8	24	57	84	38
Barking	42	8	10	24	41	85	34
Leyton-Wingate	42	7	7	28	44	91	28
Staines - 1 point by order of the League							

1989-90

DIVISION 1	P	W	D	L	Goals F	A	Pts
Wivenhoe Town	42	31	7	4	94	36	100
Woking	**42**	**30**	**8**	**4**	**102**	**29**	**98**
Southwick	42	23	15	4	68	30	84
Hitchin Town	42	22	13	7	60	30	79
Walton & Hersham	42	20	10	12	68	50	70
Dorking	42	19	12	11	66	41	69
Boreham Wood	42	17	13	12	60	59	64
Harlow Town	42	16	13	13	60	53	61
Metropolitan Police	42	16	11	15	54	59	59
Chesham United	42	15	12	15	46	49	57
Chalfont St.Peter	42	14	13	15	50	59	55
Tooting & Mitcham United	42	14	13	15	42	51	55
Worthing	42	15	8	19	56	63	53
Whyteleafe	42	11	16	15	50	65	49
Lewes	42	12	11	19	55	65	47
Wembley	42	11	10	21	57	68	43
Croydon	42	9	16	17	43	57	43
Uxbridge	42	11	10	21	52	75	43
Hampton	42	8	13	21	28	51	37
Leatherhead	42	7	10	25	34	77	31
Purfleet	42	7	8	27	33	78	29
Kingsbury Town	42	8	10	24	45	78	25*
* Nine points deducted							

1991-92

PREMIER DIVISION	P	W	D	L	Goals F	A	Pts
Woking	**42**	**30**	**7**	**5**	**96**	**25**	**97**
Enfield	42	24	7	11	59	45	79
Sutton United	42	19	13	10	88	51	70
Chesham United	42	20	10	12	67	48	70
Wokingham Town	42	19	10	13	73	58	67
Marlow	42	20	7	15	56	50	67
Aylesbury United	42	16	17	9	69	46	65
Carshalton Athletic	42	18	8	16	64	67	62
Dagenham	42	15	16	11	70	59	61
Kingstonian	42	17	8	17	71	65	59
Windsor & Eton	42	15	11	16	56	56	56
Bromley	42	14	12	16	51	57	54
St.Albans City	42	14	11	17	66	70	53
Basingstoke Town	42	14	11	17	56	65	53
Grays Athletic	42	14	11	17	53	68	53
Wivenhoe Town	42	16	4	22	56	81	52
Hendon	42	13	9	20	59	73	48
Harrow Borough	42	11	13	18	58	78	46
Hayes	42	10	14	18	52	63	44
Staines Town	42	11	10	21	43	73	43
Bognor Regis Town	42	9	11	22	51	89	38
Bishop's Stortford	42	7	12	23	41	68	33

1992-93

G.M. VAUXHALL CONFERENCE					Goals		
	P	W	D	L	F	A	Pts
Wycombe Wanderers	42	24	11	7	84	37	83
Bromsgrove Rovers	42	18	14	10	67	49	68
Dagenham & Redbridge	42	19	11	12	75	47	67 +
Yeovil Town	42	18	12	12	59	49	66
Slough Town	42	18	11	13	60	55	65
Stafford Rangers	42	18	10	14	55	47	59
Bath City	42	15	14	12	53	46	59
Woking	**42**	**17**	**8**	**17**	**58**	**62**	**59**
Kidderminster Harriers	42	14	16	12	60	60	58
Altrincham	42	15	13	14	49	52	58
Northwich Victoria	42	16	8	18	68	55	56
Stalybridge Celtic	42	13	17	12	48	55	56
Kettering Town	42	14	13	15	61	63	55
Gateshead	42	14	10	18	53	56	52
Telford United	42	14	10	18	55	60	52
Merthyr Tydfil	42	14	10	18	51	79	52
Witton Albion	42	11	17	14	62	65	50
Macclesfield Town	42	12	13	17	40	50	49
Runcorn	42	13	10	19	58	76	49
Welling United	42	12	12	18	57	72	48
Farnborough Town	42	12	11	19	68	87	47
Boston United	42	9	13	20	50	69	40
+ 1 Point deducted							

1994-95

G.M. VAUXHALL CONFERENCE					Goals		
	P	W	D	L	F	A	Pts
Macclesfield Town	42	24	8	10	70	40	80
Woking	**42**	**21**	**12**	**9**	**76**	**54**	**75**
Southport	42	21	9	12	68	50	72
Altrincham	42	20	8	14	77	60	68
Stevenage Boro.	42	20	7	15	68	49	67
Kettering Town	42	19	10	13	73	56	67
Gateshead	42	19	10	13	61	53	67
Halifax Town	42	17	12	13	68	54	63
Runcorn	42	16	10	16	59	71	58
Northwich Victoria	42	14	15	13	77	66	57
Kidderminster Harriers	42	16	9	17	63	61	57
Bath City	42	15	12	15	55	56	57
Bromsgrove Rovers	42	14	13	15	66	69	55
Farnborough	42	15	10	17	45	64	55
Dagenham & Redbridge	42	13	13	16	56	69	52
Dover Athletic	42	11	16	15	48	55	49
Welling Utd	42	13	10	19	57	74	49
Stalybridge Celtic	42	11	14	17	52	72	47
Telford United	42	10	16	16	53	62	46
Merthyr Tydfil	42	11	11	20	53	63	44
Stafford Rangers	42	9	11	22	53	79	38
Yeovil Town (-1pt)	42	8	14	20	50	71	37

1993-94

G.M. VAUXHALL CONFERENCE					Goals		
	P	W	D	L	F	A	Pts
Kidderminster Harriers	42	22	9	11	63	35	75
Kettering	42	19	15	8	46	24	72
Woking	**42**	**18**	**13**	**11**	**58**	**58**	**67**
Southport	42	18	12	12	57	51	66
Runcorn	42	14	19	9	63	57	61
Dagenham & Redbridge	42	15	14	13	62	54	59
Macclesfield Town	42	16	11	15	48	49	59
Dover	42	17	7	18	48	49	58
Stafford Rangers	42	14	15	13	56	52	57
Altrincham	42	16	9	17	41	42	57
Gateshead	42	15	12	15	45	53	57
Bath City	42	13	17	12	47	38	56
Halifax Town	42	13	16	13	55	49	55
Stalybridge Celtic	42	14	12	16	54	55	54
Northwich Victoria	42	11	19	12	44	45	52
Welling Utd	42	13	12	17	47	49	51
Telford Utd	42	13	12	17	41	49	51
Bromsgrove Rovers	42	12	15	15	54	66	51
Yeovil Town	42	14	9	19	49	62	51
* Merthyr Tydfil	42	12	15	15	60	61	49
Slough Town	42	11	14	17	44	58	47
Witton Albion	42	7	13	22	37	63	34
* Deducted 2 points.							

APPENDIX 2
FRIENDLY MATCHES INCLUDING OVERSEAS TOURS

Many of the early pre-West Surrey League friendlies have not been traced. The list will only include matches that have a result traced.

1887-88				
5 Nov	(H)	Chertsey	W	6-1 *
19 Nov	(H)	Weybridge Swifts	L	0-9
10 Dec	(A)	Chertsey	L	0-7
28 Jan	(A)	Weybridge Swifts	L	0-10 **
4 Feb	(A)	Tillingbourne	L	0-3
18 Feb	(A)	Weybridge Junior Rovers	L	2-3
3 Mar	(H)	Addlestone	L	2-3
10 Mar	(H)	Tillingbourne	D	1-1
Scorers: Railton, Eldridge, Mason 2, Tomlinson 3, O'Connor				

* also reported as 6-2 and 3-1
** also reported as 0-15

1889-90				
5 Oct	(H)	Addlestone	D	3-3
12 Oct	(H)	Chertsey	L	1-2
19 Oct	(A)	Castle School	D	0-0
26 Oct	(A)	Guildford WMC	L	0-1
2 Nov	(A)	Shere	L	1-5
9 Nov	(A)	Guildford	L	1-3
16 Nov	(H)	Weybridge Rose	W	5-1
23 Nov	(A)	Hersham	D	0-0
30 Nov	(H)	St.Georges College	W	4-1
28 Dec	(H)	Shalford	L	2-5
25 Jan	(H)	Hersham	W	7-0
22 Feb	(A)	Addlestone	D	3-3
8 Mar	(H)	Guildford	L	0-6
15 Mar	(A)	St.Georges College	L	0-4
12 April	(H)	Shere	D	1-1

1888-89				
6 Oct	(A)	Addlestone	L	0-1
13 Oct	(H)	Highfield House School (Chertsey)	L	0-1
20 Oct	(A)	Chertsey	L	0-6
24 Oct	(H)	Castle School	L	0-2
27 Oct	(H)	Tillingbourne	W	2-1
10 Nov	(H)	Guildford	L	1-4
24 Nov	(A)	Castle School	L	1-4
8 Dec	(H)	Caxton (Guildford)	W	4-3
15 Dec	(H)	Weybridge Swifts	W	1-0
12 Jan	(H)	Ditton	D	0-0
19 Jan	(H)	Chertsey	W	2-1
26 Jan	(H)	Weybridge Rovers	L	1-4
16 Feb	(A)	Shalford	L	0-4
2 Mar	(H)	Hersham	L	2-5
9 Mar	(A)	Guildford	L	1-3

1890-91				
27 Sep	(H)	Hersham	W	5-2
4 Oct	(A)	Addlestone	L	0-3
11 Oct	(H)	Shere	W	9-1
18 Oct	(H)	Shalford	W	5-2
1 Nov	(A)	Chertsey	L	3-4
15 Nov	(A)	Shalford Swifts	W	2-0
22 Nov	(A)	Castle School	W	2-1
13 Dec	(A)	Cobham Hawks	L	1-3
7 Feb	(H)	Caxton (Guildford)	W	7-4
14 Feb	(A)	Weybridge Swifts	L	3-4
21 Feb	(A)	Hersham	D	1-1
28 Feb	(H)	Shalford Swifts	W	5-0
14 Mar	(H)	Guildford	W	7-0

1891-92				
31 Oct	(A)	Hersham	L	3-4
7 Nov	(H)	Chertsey	W	3-2
14 Nov	(A)	Addlestone	L	2-4
21 Nov	(A)	Weybridge Rovers	W	7-2
5 Dec	(A)	Guildford	L	0-3
2 Jan	(H)	Addlestone	W	1-0
23 Jan	(A)	Stoke Pioneer	W	4-1
13 Feb	(A)	Caxton (Guildford)	W	3-2
5 Mar	(H)	Ripley	W	5-0
12 Mar	(A)	Shalford	W	4-0
Scorers: Laker, Heath.				

1892-93				
15 Oct	(H)	Addlestone	D	2-2
22 Oct	(A)	Ripley	L	2-6
29 Oct	(H)	Caxton (Guildford)	W	4-2
5 Nov	(A)	Chertsey	L	2-7
12 Nov	(H)	Stoke Pioneer	W	2-1
19 Nov	(A)	Chobham & District	W	4-0
3 Dec	(A)	Hersham	W	4-0
10 Dec	(H)	Weybridge 2nd XI	W	7-2
17 Dec	(A)	Caxton (Guildford)	D	0-0
4 Feb	(H)	Nine Elms	L	2-3
18 Feb	(H)	Chertsey	L	0-5

1893-94				
7 Oct	(H)	Ripley	W	3-0
11 Oct	(A)	Chobham	L	2-5
14 Oct	(A)	Stoke Rec	L	1-2
4 Nov	(H)	Aldershot	W	2-1
11 Nov	(H)	Chertsey	W	7-0
18 Nov	(H)	Hersham	W	1-0
25 Nov	(H)	Walton 2nd XI	W	7-4
2 Dec	(A)	Ripley	W	2-1
9 Dec	(H)	Cobham Hawks	W	1-0
16 Dec	(H)	Addlestone	W	3-2
20 Jan	(A)	Addlestone	L	2-3
27 Jan	(H)	Caxton (Guildford)	W	8-0
3 Feb	(A)	Cobham Hawks	W	3-2
10 Feb	(H)	Stoke Rec	W	3-1
14 Feb	(H)	St.Thomas Hosp 2nd XI	W	3-0
17 Feb	(A)	Hersham	L	0-2
10 Mar	(H)	Guildford 2nd XI	W	4-0
17 Mar	(A)	Chertsey	W	4-1
26 Mar	(A)	Addlestone	L	0-4

1894-95				
6 Oct	(A)	Cobham Hawks	W	3-2
13 Oct	(A)	Addlestone	W	2-0
20 Oct	(H)	Hersham	W	4-1
3 Nov	(A)	Ripley	L	2-3
7 Nov	(H)	St.Thomas Hosp 2nd XI	W	5-0
10 Nov	(A)	Chertsey	D	0-0
24 Nov	(A)	Aldershot	L	3-5
1 Dec	(H)	Cranleigh	W	6-0
8 Dec	(H)	Hermitage W.	W	4-0
15 Dec	(H)	Ripley	W	6-0
22 Dec	(A)	Weybridge Rose	L	1-2
29 Dec	(H)	Farncombe	W	1-0
26 Jan	(H)	Addlestone	W	2-0
23 Feb	(A)	Farncombe	W	6-0
9 Mar	(H)	Aldershot	W	6-1
6 April	(H)	Chertsey	W	4-0
15 April	(H)	Hermitage W.	W	8-1
Good Fri	(A)	Fareham	W	3-0

1895-96				
28 Sep	(H)	Weybridge	W	2-1
19 Oct	(H)	Hersham	W	6-2
2 Nov	(H)	Cobham Hawks	W	3-0
9 Nov	(A)	Godalming	W	2-0
16 Nov	(A)	Chobham	W	8-0
14 Dec	(A)	Farncombe	D	1-1
21 Dec	(H)	Ripley	W	3-0
4 Jan	(A)	Ripley	L	0-1
11 Jan	(A)	Cobham Hawks	W	3-0
25 Jan	(A)	Weybridge 2nd XI	W	9-0
29 Feb	(H)	Farncombe	W	5-1
21 Mar	(A)	Hersham	W	6-0
4 April	(H)	Hampton Ct & Molesey	W	3-2
6 April	(H)	Wandsworth	W	6-0
11 April	(H)	Godalming	W	4-0
Scorers: (known) F.P.Quinton 8, P.K.Allen 6, E.H. Ridler 6, F.Duffett 5, S.S.Mossop 5, E.Inwood 4, E. Laker 2, C.J.Bromfield 1,B.G.Popham 1, F.Heane 1.				

1896-97				
19 Sep	(H)	Borough Poly	W	2-0
17 Oct	(H)	Molesey	D	1-1
24 Oct	(A)	Ripley	W	8-3
7 Nov	(H)	Cobham Hawks	W	2-0
Unknown	(A)	Molesey	D	1-1
Unknown	(H)	The Queens Regt	L	1-4
Unknown	(H)	St.Michaels (Camberley)	W	2-1
26 Dec	(H)	Addlestone	W	3-0
2 Jan	(H)	Borough Poly	D	1-1
9 Jan	(A)	St.Michaels (Camberley)	W	3-1
30 Jan	(H)	Eastleigh	L	1-4
13 Feb	(H)	Ripley	W	3-0
6 Mar	(A)	Molesey	W	1-0
13 Mar	(A)	Godalming	L	0-1
10 April	(A)	Aldershot Comb.	W	2-0
Scorers (known) T.Denny 6, P.K.Allen 4, E.H.Ridler 3, F.Duffett 2, P.Hutton 2, B.G.Popham 1, F.J.Kemp 1, H.B.Ridler 1, A.Stansfield 1.				

1897-98				
18 Sep	(A)	Reigate Priory	L	1-4
25 Sep	(H)	Ewell	W	7-1
16 Oct	(H)	Vandals	W	5-2
23 Oct	(H)	Idlers	D	0-0
20 Nov	(H)	Queens Park	D	3-3
18 Dec	(A)	Chertsey	W	2-1
27 Dec	(H)	Addlestone	D	1-1
8 Jan	(A)	Ewell	L	2-3
15 Jan	(H)	Aldershot Comb.	W	2-1
5 Mar	(H)	Borough Poly	W	5-1
2 April	(H)	Eastleigh	W	8-1
11 April	(H)	Old Rossalians	L	0-2
23 April	(A)	Guildford	W	3-1
Scorers: A.Slater 9, A.Stansfield 6, P.K.Allen 6, F.P.Quinton 5, A.E.Reid 4, T.Denny 2, Croudace 2, E.H.Ridler 1, H.B.Ridler 1, P.Dalton 1, S.S.Mossop 1.				

1898-99				
17 Sep	(H)	Brookwood	L	0-2
24 Sep	(H)	Vandals	W	3-0
22 Oct	(H)	West Croydon	W	3-0
26 Nov	(A)	Kingston	L	0-5
10 Dec	(A)	Chertsey	W	3-0
24 Dec	(A)	Brookwood	L	1-5
31 Dec	(H)	Basingstoke	W	6-0
25 Feb	(H)	Brookwood	W	1-0
31 Mar	(A)	Guildford	L	2-5
2 April	(H)	Old Rossalians	D	3-3
Scorers: F.Butt 4, A.Slater 3, C.Fox 3, H.Denmead 2, Weaver 2, J.C.Stone 2, S.S.Mossop 1, Marriage 1, J.Duncan 1, G.Hutton 1, D.Keenan 1, H.Humphrey 1.				

1899-1900				
16 Sep	(H)	Muswell Hill	W	5-4
23 Sep	(H)	Croydon Wanderers	D	1-1
28 Oct	(A)	Brookwood	L	1-3
4 Nov	(H)	Leytonstone Ferndale	W	4-1
2 Dec	(H)	Brookwood	W	3-1
9 Dec	(A)	Weybridge	L	1-4
23 Dec	(H)	Guildford	W	2-0
26 Dec	(H)	Weybridge	D	2-2
30 Dec	(A)	Brookwood	W	2-1
20 Jan	(H)	Borough Poly	W	1-0
3 Mar	(A)	Holloway San.	L	1-4
13 April	(A)	Guildford	W	4-3
14 April	(A)	Basingstoke	W	4-3
16 April	(H)	Old Rossalians	W	4-1
Scorers: D.Keenan 9, Fred Butt 7, C.Fox 5, G.Hutton 5, F.P.Quinton 2, A.Slater 1, F.A.Drake 1, Dury 1, E.Farrow 1, H.Hunt 1, E.H.Lintott 1.				

1900-01				
8 Sep	(H)	Staines Albany	L	1-2
15 Sep	(H)	Croydon Wanderers	D	2-2
22 Sep	(H)	Leytonstone Ferndale	W	9-1
20 Oct	(H)	Royal Reserves	W	4-0
15 Dec	(A)	Brookwood	D	1-1
12 Jan	(H)	Croydon Wanderers	W	2-1
23 Feb	(H)	Borough Poly	D	2-2
9 Mar	(H)	Townley Park	W	2-1
16 Mar	(H)	South Farnborough	L	2-4
23 Mar	(H)	Brookwood	L	1-4
30 Mar	(H)	The Vulcans	W	2-1
5 April	(A)	Guildford	W	3-0
6 April	(H)	Addlestone	W	3-0
8 April	(H)	Old Rossalians	D	1-1
13 April	(A)	Staines Albany	L	1-6
20 April	(A)	Addlestone	L	1-5
Scorers: Fred Butt 12, G.Hutton 9, E.H.Lintott 4, F.A.Drake 3, F.P.Quinton 2, C.Fox 1, A.Heane 1, Ryde 1, G.F.Hawkins 1, D.Keenan 1.				

1901-02				
14 Sep	(H)	Putney	W	4-1
26 Oct	(H)	Norwood & Selhurst	W	3-1
9 Nov	(A)	Brookwood	D	2-2
7 Dec	(H)	West Ham Garfield	W	1-0
18 Jan	(H)	The Vulcans	L	1-3
25 Jan	(H)	Basingstoke	L	0-1
27 Mar	(A)	Guildford	W	6-0
28 Mar	(A)	Godalming	D	1-1
30 Mar	(H)	Crouch End Vampires	W	1-0
Scorers: Fred Butt 6, E.H.Lintott 5, G.Hutton 2, F.A.Drake 2,E.Dalton 1, W.Walker 1, A.Slater 1, J.B.Monk 1.				

1902-03				
13 Sep	(H)	Croydon Wanderers	W	4-2
20 Sep	(H)	Addlestone	W	2-1
4 Oct	(H)	Thornton Heath	W	4-0
1 Nov	(H)	Old Exonians	W	7-0
20 Dec	(H)	Grenadier Guards	D	3-3
26 Dec	(H)	Hampstead	W	5-2
27 Dec	(A)	Addlestone	W	2-1
3 Jan	(H)	The Vulcans	W	3-1
31 Jan	(H)	Addlestone	D	1-1
11 Feb	(H)	Sanatorium	D	1-1
4 April	(H)	Croydon Wanderers	L	1-4
10 April	(A)	Guildford	L	1-3
11 April	(H)	Weybridge	W	7-0
13 April	(H)	Kettering Ath.	W	9-1
Scorers: E.H.Lintott 19, Fred Butt 8, G.Hutton 5, F.A.Drake 4, F.S.Lintott 2, Frank Butt 2, Cox 2, C.W.Lintott 2, G.F.Hawkins 1, F.P.Quinton 1, J.B.Monk 1, Brice 1, White 1, Stare 1.				

1903-04				
12 Sep	(A)	West Norwood	L	1-5
3 Oct	(H)	Townley Park	L	1-2
26 Dec	(H)	Royal Marines	W	3-1
2 Jan	(H)	West Brixton	W	2-0
16 Jan	(H)	Croydon	W	3-0
12 Mar	(A)	Croydon	L	0-3
1 April	(H)	South West Ham	D	1-1
2 April	(H)	Army Service Corps	L	0-4
9 April	(H)	Alleyn	D	1-1
Scorers: E.H.Lintott 3, J.Kyle 2, C.W.Lintott 2, Waters 2, Firmin 1, Cottam 1, Frank Butt 1.				

1904-05				
10 Sep	(H)	City of Westminster	W	9-0
26 Dec	(H)	Richmond Ath	W	4-0
27 Dec	(A)	Oxford City	L	1-7
25 Feb	(H)	Richmond Ath	W	8-0
1 April	(H)	The Norsemen	L	1-3
22 April	(H)	Ilford Alliance	W	7-0
24 April	(H)	Croydon	W	5-0
Scorers: E.H.Lintott 13, G.Hutton 5, J.Kyle 4, Fred Butt 3, Viney 3, Stevens 2, Firmin 1, F.S.Lintott 1, C.S.Salisbury 1, Waters 1, Preston 1.				

1905-06				
9 Sep	(H)	Dulwich	L	1-8
16 Sep	(H)	Olympic	L	0-4
30 Sep	(H)	Croydon	D	0-0
14 Oct	(H)	Granville	W	7-3
26 Dec	(H)	Watford Clarendon	L	2-3
27 Dec	(H)	Plumstead	W	4-1
24 Feb	(H)	Alleyn	L	1-3
24 Mar	(H)	Old Citizens	W	4-2
7 April	(H)	City of Westminster	W	4-1
13 April	(H)	Croydon Wanderers	W	3-2
16 April	(H)	Civil Service	W	4-3
Scorers: G.Hutton 7, C.S.Salisbury 4, R.Pook 4, J.Kyle 4, A.V.Pearce 2, E.H.Lintott 2, R.Busfield 1, J.B.Monk 1, F.S.Lintott 1, S.J.Carter 1, A.M.Lintott 1, H.Stevens 1.				

1906-07				
22 Sep	(H)	2nd Lifeguards	W	5-0
20 Oct	(A)	Dorking	W	3-1
27 Oct	(H)	Sherwood Foresters	D	0-0
3 Nov	(H)	Townley Park	D	2-2
8 Dec	(A)	Weybridge	L	1-2
22 Dec	(H)	Parthians	W	2-0
5 Jan	(H)	Crouch End Vampires	D	1-1
23 Mar	(H)	Bowes Park	W	9-0
29 Mar	(A)	Guildford	W	3-0
Scorers: E.H.Lintott 8, R.Pook 6, G.Hutton 3, C.S.Salisbury 2, C.W.Lintott 2, A.V.Pearce 1, J.B.Monk 1, J.Kyle 1, F.S.Lintott 1, W.Waters 1.				

1907-08				
14 Sep	(H)	Clapham	L	2-3
21 Sep	(H)	Upton Park	W	5-3
28 Sep	(A)	Dorking	W	2-0
25 April	(H)	Guildford	W	7-1
Scorers: Kyle 4, Buck 3, Hutton 2, Salisbury 2, Johnson 1, Day 1, Shoesmith 1, J.B.Monk 1.				

1908-09				
5 Sep	(A)	Clapton	L	0-6
7 Nov	(H)	Guildford	W	3-2
14 Nov	(H)	Plumstead St.Johns	D	2-2
21 Nov	(H)	Foots Cray	L	2-3
26 April	(H)	Bolton W. 1,600	L	1-4
Scorers: Hill 3, J.B.Monk 1, Hutton 1, Gorringe 1, Tomlinson 1, Kyle 1				

1909-10				
4 Sep	(H)	Clapham	W	3-0
25 Sep	(A)	Hersham	W	9-0
1 Jan	(H)	Upton Park	W	4-0
25 Mar	(H)	Woking Wednesday	W	4-0
Scorers: Livesey 5, Hill 4, Swallow 3, Kyle 2, Shoesmith 2, Salisbury 1, Pearce 1, Johnson 1.				

1910-11				
3 Sep	(H)	Woolwich Poly	D	3-3
27 Dec	(H)	Surrey Wanderers	W	3-1
4 Feb	(A)	Farnham	W	4-3
Scorers: Swallow 2, Salisbury 2, Brooks 1, Ham 1, Shoesmith 1, Kyle 1, Alf Grove 1.				

1911-12				
2 Sep	(H)	East Lancs Regt	L	3-4
7 Oct	(H)	Godalming	W	8-0
26 Dec	(H)	South Farnborough	W	2-1
27 Dec	(H)	Surrey Wanderers	L	2-3
8 Jan	(H)	Ferencvarosi (Budapest)	L	2-3
24 Feb	(H)	London Caledonians	L	0-4
6 April	(H)	East Lancs Regt	L	2-4
8 April	(H)	South Farnborough	L	1-3
4 May	(H)	Kings Royal Rifles	L	1-2
Scorers: Humphreys 4, Swallow 4, Kyle 3, Shoesmith 2, Hartley 2, Ar. Grove 1, Salisbury 1, Ham 1, Croft 1, Bevan 1, Markwick 1.				

1912-13				
7 Dec	(H)	Dorset	D	5-5
26 Dec	(H)	Staines	L	0-1
8 Feb	(H)	South Farnborough	W	4-2
Scorers: Bell 3, Swallow 3, Pearce 1, Kyle 1, Ar. Grove 1.				

1913-14				
25 Oct	(H)	Hampstead Town	W	4-1
1 Nov	(H)	South Farnborough	W	6-2
15 Nov	(H)	Guildford Pinks	D	1-1
26 Dec	(H)	West London O.B.	D	1-1
14 Feb	(H)	East Ham	W	3-2
28 Feb	(H)	London Univ.	W	7-1
14 Mar	(H)	Shepherds Bush	L	2-3
13 April	(H)	Weybridge	L	0-2
18 April	(H)	Merton	W	2-1
Scorers: Kyle 8, Johnson 3, Ar.Grove 3, Crane 3, T.Smith 1, Swallow 1, Bedser 1, Jones 1, Bell 1, W.T.Knight 1.				

1914-15				
4 Sep	(H)	Nunhead	L	0-1
9 Jan	(H)	84th Comp. Royal Engrs	L	3-4
Scorers: Kyle 2, Halliday 1.				

1919-20				
13 Sep	(H)	Enfield	D	2-2
8 Nov	(A)	Kingstonian	W	3-1
22 Nov	(H)	Tufnell Spartan	W	4-0
26 Dec	(H)	Aldershot Town	W	6-0
21 Feb	(H)	Islington Town	W	5-0
20 Mar	(H)	Kingstonian	W	2-1
5 April	(H)	Guildford Pinks	W	2-1
Scorers: Gooch 4, Champion 4, Cockran 3, Filleston 3, Gowler 2, Kemp 2, Pearce 1, Wright 1, Salisbury 1, Hunter 1.				

1920-21				
20 Aug	(A)	Guildford Pinks	L	1-3
11 Dec	(A)	Hersham	L	1-2
18 Dec	(H)	Enfield	W	2-1
26 Dec	(H)	Ealing Ass.	W	4-1
28 Mar	(H)	Civil Service	L	1-2
2 April	(H)	Wood Green	D	1-1
16 April	(A)	Wimbledon	L	1-4
2 May	(A)	Guildford Pinks	L	1-4
Scorers: Gowan 3, Ar.Grove 2, Church 2, A.J.Hunt 1, Bell 1, Badcock 1, Sturt 1.				

1921-22				
26 Dec	(H)	Guildford Pinks	W	4-2
27 Dec	(A)	Guildford Pinks	L	0-3
17 April	(H)	Swansea Amateurs	D	1-1
Scorers: Tiller 2, Gowler 1, Salisbury 1, J.Martin.				

1922-23				
26 Dec	(H)	RAMC	W	2-0
27 Jan	(H)	Wood Green	D	2-2
2 April	(H)	Northern Nomads	L	1-5
Scorers: Briggs 2, C.Cook 1, Gibbs 1, J.Sturt 1.				

1923-24				
6 Oct	(H)	Leavesham Mental Hosp.	W	2-1
26 Dec	(H)	Carshalton	W	7-2
5 Jan	(H)	Guildford Pinks	W	3-0
29 Mar	(A)	Windsor & Eton	L	0-3
21 April	(H)	Botwell Mission	L	1-2
Scorers: (known) Harman 2, Briggs 1, Thayers 1, Gilbert 1.				

1924-25				
26 Dec	(H)	Westminster Bank	L	0-2
3 Jan	(A)	Guildford Utd	L	3-4
28 Feb	(H)	Bank of England	L	4-6
1 April	(H)	Guildford Utd	W	3-0
13 April	(H)	Cardiff & Dist.Lge	L	1-2
20 April	(H)	Fulham	D	0-0
29 April	(H)	Brentford	D	4-4
Scorers: (known) Thomas 3, Harman 3, Thayers 2, Stimson 2, Maidment 1.				

1925-26				
26 Sep	(H)	Bromley	D	3-3
26 Dec	(H)	Westminster Bank	W	4-2
9 Jan	(H)	Hanwell Town	W	5-1
13 Mar	(H)	Custom House	D	1-1
15 April	(H)	Swansea Corinthians	W	6-1
26 April	(H)	1st Bn. Scots Guards	W	3-1
Scorers: (known) Fitzgerald 4, Ledger 3, Woodards 3, Wheatcroft 2, Perryman 2,Wallis 1, Robinson 1, Ball 1, Price 1, Wharton 1.				

1926-27				
4 Sep	(H)	Leyton	L	2-6
3 Nov	(H)	Royal West Kent Rgmt	W	5-2
13 Mar	(A)	Ajax Sporting Club 8,000	L	2-5
15 April	(A)	Kolner Ballspiel Club (Cologne)	L	0-6
17 April	(A)	Sports & Spirl Verem Elberfield	D	3-3
18 April	(A)	Sportverein Union Krefeld	D	3-3
Scorers: (known) Price 4, Wheatley 1, Fitzgerald 1, Morrison 1.				

1927-28				
10 Dec	(H)	Epsom	L	2-6
9 April	(H)	Swansea Corinthians	W	4-3
Scorers: Long 1, Skelton 1, Maidment 1, Fitzgerald 1, Perryman 1, Moore 1.				

1928-29				
26 Sep	(H)	Fulham	L	0-5
27 Oct	(H)	Northampton Nomads	W	9-2
8 Dec	(A)	Redhill	D	2-2
23 Feb	(H)	London Univ	W	6-2
20 Mar	(H)	Fulham	W	2-1
30 Mar	(H)	Wimbledon	W	6-1
1 April	(H)	Rotherham Am.	W	6-1
13 April	(H)	Royal Warwick Regt	D	2-2
Scorers: (known) Perryman 10, Soper 5, Moore 5, Horton 3, Wills 1, J.S.Clifford 1, Westwood 1, Stimson 1, Chitty 1, F.Edwards 1.				

1929-30				
2 Oct	(H)	Fulham	D	2-2
21 April	(H)	Wrexham Amateurs	W	5-2
26 April	(H)	1st Bn Scots Guards (Windsor)	W	4-2
Scorers: Perryman 6, Moseley 2, Moore 2, E.C.Turner 1.				

1930-31				
1 Oct	(H)	Fulham	L	1-5
22 Nov	(H)	Army Wanderers	L	1-7
5 April *	(A)	Sportovini Klub Kladno (Prague) 12,000	L	1-2
6 April *	(A)	Sporting Club Anderlech tois	D	4-4
Scorers: Mason 2, Skipsey 2, May 2, Wilton 1. * Easter Tour of Belgium.				

1931-32				
26 Dec	(A)	Kingstonian	L	2-9
9 Jan	(H)	2nd Royal Warwick Rgmt	W	3-0
20 April	(H)	Fulham	L	0-3
Scorers: Udal 2, Warnes 2, S.Green 1.				

1932-33				
27 Dec	(H)	Cardiff Corinthians	W	5-3

1933-34				
26 Dec	(H)	Swindon Corinthians	W	3-2
Scorers: Hooker 1, G.E.Warnes 1, Faggetter 1.				

1934-35				
1 Dec	(A)	Epsom	W	4-2
30 Mar	(A)	Guildford C.	W	3-1
17 April	(A)	Hersham	L	1-2
27 April	(H)	HMS Excellent	W	7-3
Scorers: Stockley 5, Moulsdale 4, Hooker 3, Lawrence 1, Buckmaster 1.				

1935-36				
28 Mar	(H)	Oxford University	L	3-4
18 April	(H)	Fulham	D	2-2
Scorers: Stygal 2, Hooker 1, Buckmaster 1,Abbott 1.				

1936-37				
26 Dec	(H)	Streatham	W	3-2
10 April	(H)	RAMC (Aldershot)	L	3-5
26 April	(H)	West Ham	L	1-2
Scorers: Hooker 2, Buckmaster 1, Weller 1, Carter 1, Stockley 1, Stone 1.				

1937-38				
23 Oct	(H)	Oxford Univ	L	1-4
26 Dec	(H)	Swindon Victoria	W	4-1
Scorers: Finlay 2, Hooker 1, Hughes 1, Kittredge 1.				

1938-39				
17 Dec	(H)	Fulham	D	2-2
7 Jan	(A)	Hertford T.	L	0-1
Scorers: Barker 2.				

1945-46				
26 Jan	(A)	Golders Green	L	1-3
Scorers: Cox 1.				

1946-47				
29 Mar	(H)	Redhill	W	3-1
4 April	(H)	Woking & D.L'ge	D	3-3
5 April	(H)	HBS (Holland)	L	1-3
Scorers: Pink 2, Wride 2, Cowley 1, Boxall 1, Lawrence 1.				

1947-48				
29 Mar	(H)	U.A.U.XI	W	5-1
Scorers: Wiles 2, Reeves 1, Boxall 1, McBryde 1.				

1948-49				
18 April	(H)	Yorkshire Amateurs	W	2-1
4 May	(H)	Middlesex Wanderers	W	4-3
Scorers: (known) Welland 1, Pink 1, Ballerino 1.				

1949-50				
26 Dec	(A)	Worthing	D	1-1
18 Mar	(H)	Tooting	W	2-1
Easter Tour of Ostend		Ostend VG	W	6-2
		Ghent Univ	W	3-2
Scorers: (known) Wiles 4, Short 3, D.Smith 2, Boxall 1, Pink 1.				

1950-51			
Ostend Tour 25 Mar	Ghent Univ	W	5-4
26 Mar	KVG	L	0-6
Scorers: Wiles 2, Pink 2, Short 1.			

1951-52				
17 Nov	(H)	Oxford Univ	L	2-6
26 Dec	(H)	Eastbourne	W	2-0
5 April	(H)	Redhill	W	4-2
14 April	(H)	Taffs Well	W	4-1
Scorers: (known) Pratt 3, Pink 2, Wiles 2, Clarke 2, Welland 1.				

1952-53				
6 Sep	(H)	Guildford Res	W	5-1
18 Oct	(H)	Oxford Univ	W	4-2
3 April	(A)	Guernsey	W	5-2
4 April	(A)	Guernsey	W	3-1
6 April	(A)	Jersey	W	2-1
20 April	(H)	London All Stars	L	2-5
Scorers: Hamm 7, Pink 6, Wiles 3, Short 2, C.Mortimore 1, Phelan 1, Whitton 1.				

1953-54				
17 April	(H)	Clydach	W	4-1
Scorers: J.Mortimore 2, Jones 1, Hamm 1.				

1954-55				
5 Mar	(A)	Tooting	L	1-3
7 April	(A)	Guernsey	W	3-2
8 April	(A)	Guernsey B	W	9-1
10 April	(A)	Jersey	W	1-0
Scorers: Welland 3, Hamm 3, C.Mortimore 2, Edwards 2, Bond 1, W.Smith 1, Zimmer 1, J.Mortimore 1.				

1955-56				
22 Nov	(A)	Yiewsley 1st Floodlit Match.	W	1-0
31 Mar	(H)	Tonbridge	W	2-1
14 April	(H)	Hayes	W	6-1
Scorers: C.Mortimore 3, Bond 2, J.Mortimore 1, Redican 1, Hamm 1, Ford 1.				

1956-57				
19 April	(A)	Jersey	W	4-2
20 April	(A)	Jersey	W	2-0
22 April	(A)	Guernsey	W	2-0
Scorers: C.Mortimore 3, Welland 2, Clacey 1, Littlejohn 1, Parsons 1.				

1957-58
No friendlies played.

1958-59				
8 Sep	(H)	Middlesex Wanderers 1,850	D	1-1
4 April	(H)	Maidstone	W	5-1
Scorers: Stratton 3, Jacob 1, C.Williams 1, N.Cashmore 1.				

1959-60				
15 April	(A)	Guernsey	W	3-0
16 April	(A)	Guernsey	W	2-1
18 April	(A)	Jersey	D	2-2
Scorers: Reynolds 2, Hearman 2, N.Cashmore 2, Collins 1.				

1960-61				
1 May	(A)	Fleet	W	4-2
Scorers: Taylor 2, Hyde 1, C.Mortimore 1.				

1961-62				
18 Nov	(H)	Chelsea XI	L	2-3
31 Mar	(A)	Kingstonian	L	2-4
Scorers: (known) C.Mortimore 2, Gamble 1.				

1962-63			
Tournament in Holland			
17/19 Aug	TYBB Heemstede	W	4-0
Woking Finished Runners Up	Racing Club of Kiel (Belgium)	W	9-1
	HBC Heemstede	D	1-1
	Mindener Spielver (Germany)	W	3-1
	Leonidas (Rotterdam)	L	0-4
Scorers: C.Mortimore 6, Botley 3, Tindall 3, Upton 2, Brennan 1, Woods 1.			

1963-64				
24 August	(H)	HBC Heemstede	W	4-1
Scorers: Tindall 1, B.Finn 1, C.Mortimore 1, Woods 1.				

1964-65				
14 Nov	(H)	Carshalton	L	0-3
19 Nov	(H)	Chelsea Opening Floodlights 2,688	L	2-5
16 Feb	(H)	Aldershot	L	1-2
26 April		Woking 1965 3 Woking 1958 1		
Scorers: B.Finn 2, Woods 1, Petitt 1, Wooler 1, Jim Hebdon 1.				

1965-66				
7 Dec	(H)	Chelsea 2,179	L	1-7
7 Mar	(H)	Portsmouth	L	2-3
28 May		Standard Leige	L	0-1
29 May		Maastricht (Holland)	L	0-1
30 May		A.S Virtus D.B.Bolzano (Italy) Whitsun tournament in Belgium.	W	4-1
Scorers: McBryde 2, Tindall 2, O'Riordan 1, Wood 1, Cooper 1.				

1966-67				
13 Aug	(H)	Dorking	W	2-1
16 Aug	(H)	Ashford	W	6-3
22 Aug	(H)	Flushing (Holland)	W	4-1
19 Sep	(H)	Northerners (Guernsey)	W	7-1
22 Nov	(H)	The Army	D	2-2
31 Jan	(A)	Wokingham	L	1-3
1 April	(H)	Carshalton	D	1-1
10 April	(H)	Portsmouth XI	L	2-6
21 April	(H)	Blyth Spartan	W	5-1
Scorers: Tindall 10, Cooper 7, O'Riordan 5, B.Finn 3, Hyde 1, McBryde 1, Richardson 1, McPhee 1.				

1967-68				
31 July	(A)	Cliftonville	L	1-2
2 Aug	(A)	Larne	L	2-3
14 Aug	(H)	Ashford	W	2-1
6 Jan	(H)	Aldershot	L	1-6
5 Feb	(H)	The Army	L	1-4
Scorers: Tindall 2, O'Riordan 2, McBryde 1, B.Finn 1, Woods 1.				

1968-69				
1 Aug	(H)	Crystal Palace	L	0-3
10 Aug	(H)	Hemel Hempstead	L	1-2
24 Feb	(H)	The Army	D	2-2
5 April	(A)	Victoria (Hilversum) (Holland)	D	1-1
Scorers: Vooght 1, Palinski 1, Evans 1, Elton 1.				

1969-70				
25 July	(A)	Chichester	L	0-2
28 July	(H)	Waterlooville	W	3-0
2 Aug	(H)	Crystal Palace	L	1-2
5 Aug	(H)	Molesey	D	0-0
27 Jan	(H)	Basingstoke	W	3-0
1 April	(H)	Combined Services	D	1-1
Scorers: McCormack 4, Moore 2, Gale 1, Binks 1.				

1970-71				
1 Aug	(H)	Met. Police	W	3-2
5 Aug	(H)	Farnham	W	8-2
8 Aug	(H)	Luton	L	2-3
10 Aug	(H)	Fulham	W	3-2
23 Feb	(H)	RAF	D	0-0
8 Mar	(H)	British Army	W	2-1
11 May	(A)	Carshalton	W	2-1
5 June	(A)	A.C.Baleara (Ca'n Pastilla, Spain)	D	0-0
Scorers: (known) Oram 5, Elliott 4, Hazel 3, Robson 1, B.Finn 1, Leonard 1, Christmas 1.				

1971-72				
3 Aug	(H)	Redhill	W	3-1
5 Aug	(H)	Farnborough	L	1-3
7 Aug	(H)	Fulham	D	1-1
10 Aug	(H)	Basingstoke	D	1-1
7 Sep	(H)	Thorneycroft Ath.	D	0-0
Scorers: Elliott 2, Oram 2, Leonard 1, Patterson 1.				

1972-73				
29 July	(H)	Lancing	W	6-1
1 Aug	(H)	Basingstoke	L	0-1
5 Aug	(H)	Alvechurch	D	2-2
9 Aug	(A)	Addlestone	W	2-0
14 Oct	(H)	Finchley	W	2-0
20 Feb	(H)	RAF	W	5-0
28 April	(H)	BAC (Weybridge)	W	4-1
Scorers: Leonard 5, Grondona 3, Oram 2, Cheeseman 1 Smith 1, Van den Berg 1, Carney 1, Chapple 1, Baker 1, Elliott 1, P.Haddow 1, B.Finn 1.				

1973-74				
4 Aug	(H)	Wimbledon	D	1-1
7 Aug	(A)	Guildford C.	L	0-1
11 Aug	(H)	Horsham	D	1-1
Scorers: Grondona 1, Leonard 1.				

1974-75				
3 Aug	(A)	Southall	W	1-0
6 Aug	(H)	Bognor Regis	W	2-1
10 Aug	(H)	Fulham	D	3-3
13 Aug	(A)	Alton	D	1-1
24 Sep	(H)	Southall	W	2-0
7 Jan	(H)	Bracknell	W	3-0
11 Feb	(H)	St.Mary's College	W	2-0
18 Feb	(H)	Farnham	W	5-2
25 Feb	(H)	RAF	L	1-2
25 Mar	(H)	Chelsea	W	4-3
Scorers: Cosham 8, Grondona 5, Oram 4, Steer 2, Waughman 2, Cheeseman 1, Molloy 1, Forbes 1.				

1975-76				
2 Aug	(H)	Newport I.O.W.	W	2-1
4 Aug	(H)	Hillingdon B	W	2-1
9 Aug	(A)	Basingstoke	D	2-2
26 Jan	(H)	Guernsey	W	6-1
17 Feb	(H)	RAF	L	0-2
Easter Tour	(A)	St.Martins (Guernsey)	W	1-0
	(A)	Guernsey	W	1-0
Scorers: Morton 7, Hawkett 2, Bennett 1, Brister 1, Turner 1, McKinnon 1, A.Roberts 1.				

1976-77				
7 Aug	(A)	Waterlooville	L	3-5
13 Aug	(A)	Wokingham	D	0-0
17 Aug	(H)	Maidstone	W	2-1
16 Nov	(H)	Tottenham H	W	2-1
8 Feb	(H)	RAF	D	1-1
Scorers: Morton 2, Forbes 2, Alexander 1, Hill 1, A.Roberts 1.				

1977-78				
3 Aug	(A)	Swaythling Ath	W	1-0
6 Aug	(H)	Fulham	L	0-2
9 Aug	(H)	Lewes	W	2-0
13 Aug	(H)	Weymouth	D	1-1
16 Aug	(H)	Fleet	W	4-0
Scorers: Cosham 3, Morton 2, Brown 1, Cottrell 1, Alexander 1.				

1978-79				
4 Aug	(H)	Brighton	W	4-0
8 Aug	(H)	Brentford	W	3-0
12 Aug	(H)	Fulham	W	2-0
15 Aug	(H)	QPR	W	3-2
Scorers: James 7, Morton 3, Adams 1.				

1979-80				
4 Aug	(H)	Fulham	L	1-2
6 Aug	(H)	Aldershot	L	1-2
9 Aug	(A)	Chobham	W	3-1
11 Aug	(A)	Yeovil	L	1-3
14 Aug	(A)	Walton & H	W	2-0
18 Sep	(H)	Malawi	W	4-1
Scorers: James 4, Morton 3, Field 2, Yerby 1, Love 1, Rolph 1.				

1980-81				
26 July	(A)	Hungerford	W	1-0
2 Aug	(A)	Addlestone	W	1-0
5 Aug	(A)	Hillingdon B	D	1-1
9 Aug	(A)	Dartford	D	0-0
12 Aug	(H)	Waterlooville	W	2-0
6 Jan	(H)	Windsor & Eton	L	0-2
unknown	(H)	London Univ	W	2-0
Scorers: Morton 3, O.Nwajiobi 2, E.Nwajiobi 1, Scrivens 1.				

1981-82				
1 Aug	(H)	Wealdstone	L	0-2
4 Aug	(H)	Chelsea	D	2-2
6 Aug	(A)	Wokingham	W	2-1
8 Aug	(A)	Newbury	L	0-1
11 Aug	(H)	Brentford	L	0-3
19 Dec	(A)	Slough	D	2-2
26 Jan	(A)	Banstead	D	1-1
2 Feb	(H)	Chertsey	L	0-1
Scorers: Chapman 1, Lynch 1, Mitchell 1.				

1982-83				
7 Aug	(H)	Burnham	W	4-2
10 Aug	(H)	Southampton	D	2-2
14 Aug	(A)	Camberley	W	6-1
17 Aug	(A)	BAe (Weybridge)	W	2-0
13 Nov	(H)	R.S.Southampton	L	0-1
19 Mar	(H)	Millwall	L	0-2
22 Mar	(H)	Corinthian Casuals	L	0-2
Scorers: Franks 5, Francis 2, Davis 2, Hewitt 1, Black 1, Sorenson 1 Turner 1, Rudd 1.				

1983-84				
9 Aug	(H)	Millwall	W	3-2
13 Aug	(H)	Southampton	D	3-3
18 Aug	(H)	Aldershot	D	1-1
18 Oct	(H)	Croydon	L	0-2
25 Oct	(A)	Wycombe	L	1-4
20 Mar	(A)	Fleet	W	5-1
Scorers: Stagg 2, Jablonski 2, Ryan 2, T.Jones 1.				

1984-85				
7 Aug	(A)	Virginia Water	W	2-1
9 Aug	(A)	Chertsey	D	1-1
11 Aug	(A)	Newport I.O.W.	D	3-3
16 Aug	(H)	Wokingham	D	1-1
21 Aug	(H)	Fulham	L	1-2
18 Sep	(H)	Godalming	D	2-2
25 Sep	(H)	Hounslow	L	1-2
13 Nov	(H)	Southampton	L	0-2
4 Dec	(A)	Fleet	L	1-2
Scorers: Cox 3, Morton 3, Wilde 2, Black 1, Worsfold 1, K.Davies 2.				

1985-86				
3 Aug	(A)	Farnham	D	3-3
6 Aug	(A)	Westfield	W	3-2
10 Aug	(A)	Chobham	W	6-1
13 Aug	(A)	Ash	W	3-0
17 Aug	(A)	Thanet Utd	W	3-1
20 Aug	(H)	Hampton	W	3-1
24 Sep	(H)	Farnham	W	4-0
7 Oct	(A)	The Army	L	1-3
19 Nov	(H)	Wimbledon	L	0-9
17 Dec	(H)	Ash	W	3-2
Scorers: Lansley 8, Cox 7, Dawber 5, Youlton 4, McGranigan 2, Watson 1, Cowler 1.				

1986-87				
2 Aug	(A)	Dulwich	D	3-3
4 Aug	(A)	Ash	L	1-3
6 Aug	(H)	Farnham	W	2-1
9 Aug	(H)	AFC Bournemouth	W	2-1
12 Aug	(H)	Farnborough	W	3-1
Scorers: Sabourn 3, Dawber 2, T.Buzaglo 2, Cassidy 2, Black 1.				

1987-88				
1 Aug	(A)	Farnham	D	1-1
4 Aug	(A)	Cove	W	2-0
11 Aug	(H)	Met.Police	W	2-0
15 Aug	(H)	Alton	W	3-1
18 Aug	(A)	Ruislip Manor	D	2-2
24 Nov	(H)	Farnham	W	5-0
8 Dec	(A)	Carshalton	W	1-0
Scorers: Cowler 2, L.Wye 2, Edgar 2, Mitchell 2, Parr 2, Lickford 2, Cassidy 1, Kitchener 1, Harding 1.				

1988-89				
2 Aug	(A)	Cove	W	6-0
9 Aug	(A)	Farnham	L	1-2
13 Aug	(H)	Slough	W	3-1
Scorers: Miles 4, Worsfold 3, Cowler 2, Biggins 1.				

1989-90				
1 Aug	(A)	Farnham	W	2-0
5 Aug	(A)	Marlow	W	2-1
8 Aug	(H)	Carshalton	W	2-0
10 Aug	(A)	Cove	W	3-1
12 Aug	(H)	Tottenham H	L	1-3
14 Aug	(H)	Aldershot	W	4-2
24 Oct	(H)	Farnham	W	5-1
7 May	(H)	Aldershot	W	4-0
Scorers: S.Wye 7, Mulvaney 5, T.Buzaglo 5, Baron 1, Parr 1, Franks 1, Hall 1, L.Wye 1, MacLaren 1.				

1990-91				
28 July	(A)	Worthing	W	4-0
4 Aug	(A)	Bashley	W	3-1
7 Aug	(H)	Tottenham H	W	1-0
9 Aug	(A)	Cove	W	5-0
11 Aug	(A)	Farnham	W	2-1
14 Aug	(A)	Farnborough	L	0-1
11 May	(A)	Hitchin	L	0-1
Scorers: T.Buzaglo 7, Turkington 2, S.Wye 1, Biggins 1, Mulvaney 1, Pratt 1, Fearon 1, Davidson 1.				

1991-92				
27 July	(A)	Godalming	W	3-1
30 July	(A)	Corinthian Casuals	W	2-0
1 Aug	(A)	Cove	D	2-2
3 Aug	(A)	Andover	W	2-0
6 Aug	(A)	Leatherhead	W	1-0
8 Aug	(A)	Collier Row	W	6-0
10 Aug	(A)	Uxbridge	W	2-0
12 Aug	(H)	Northampton	D	0-0
13 Aug	(H)	Braintree	L	0-3
25 Sep	(H)	Southampton	D	1-1
2 Oct	(A)	Ruislip Manor	W	2-0
8 Oct	(H)	Godalming	W	3-0
21 April	(H)	Aldershot	W	2-0
30 April	(H)	Farnborough > C.Mortimore Trophy	L	2-3
8 May	(A)	Farnborough > C.Mortimore Trophy	W	2-1
Scorers: Mulvaney 3, L.Wye 3, Parr 3, Friel 4, Baron 3, Walkes 3, Biggins 2, Pratt 2, Mitchell 1, Pedlar 1, D.Brown 1, Milton 1, S.Wye 2.				

1992-93				
25 July	(A)	Southampton	D	2-2
27 July	(A)	Cove	W	3-2
29 July	(A)	Windsor & Eton	D	1-1
1 Aug	(H)	Everton 3,749	L	1-4
4 Aug	(A)	Kingstonian	W	5-0
6 Aug	(H)	Fulham 1,039	L	1-3
8 Aug	(H)	Brentford 1,258	L	1-2
12 Aug	(A)	Dorking	L	2-4
15 Aug	(H)	Aylesbury	L	2-3
17 Aug	(A)	Aldershot Town	D	0-0
13 Oct	(H)	Barnet	L	1-3
8 Feb	(H)	Kispest-Honved 1,168	W	2-1
23 Feb	(A)	Walton & H	D	0-0
16 Mar	(H)	Chelsea	D	1-1
Scorers: T.Buzaglo 7, Fleming 4, D.Brown 2, Biggins 2, Nugent 2, Senior 1, Baron 1.				

1993-94				
28 July	(A)	Camberley	W	2-0
31 July	(A)	Fareham	W	3-0
3 Aug	(A)	Walton & H	L	0-1
5 Aug	(H)	Fulham 1,549	W	2-0
7 Aug	(A)	Shoreham	W	4-1
10 Aug	(A)	Cove	D	0-0
14 Aug	(H)	Sutton	L	1-2
16 Aug	(H)	Molesey	W	3-1
Scorers: Puckett 6, Bushay 2, Steele 2, Biggins 2, Fleming 1, Salako 1, Del Brown 1.				

1994-95				
23 July	(A)	Hampton	W	4-0
27 July	(H)	Oxford Utd	D	0-0
30 July	(H)	Brighton	L	1-2
1 Aug	(H)	Fulham 1,087	W	1-0
3 Aug	(A)	Chesham	D	0-0
6 Aug	(H)	Crawley William Hill Trophy 1st Leg.	W	2-0
10 Aug	(H)	Cheltenham	L	0-3
13 Aug	(A)	Crawley William Hill Trophy 2nd Leg.	W	2-0
18 Feb	(H)	Arsenal 2,437	L	1-2
Scorers: Walker 3, Steele 2, French 1, Rattray 1, Tierling 1, Gorman 1, Payne 1.				

APPENDIX 3
WOKING CAREER RECORDS

Below are the career records for all competitive games since 1895-96 when Woking joined the West Surrey League. The year stated is the second half of the season i.e. 1904 relates to 1903-04. For ease of presentation the Floodlit League 1969-70,70-71 and 71-72 is shown under Cups. The years shown for each player represents the seasons played in the first team, which may differ from number of seasons with Woking.

PLAYER	SEASONS	LEAGUE		CUPS		TOTAL	
		APPS(sub)	GOALS	APPS(sub)	GOALS	APPS(sub)	GOALS
A							
Abbott A.W	1933-36,47	65	9	30	7	95	16
Adam J	1952	1	0			1	0
Adams J.C	1907-13	82	0	69	0	151	0
Adams J	1978-79,83	42 (4)	2	16	1	58 (4)	3
Adams S	1931	3	0			3	0
Adams S	1980,82	15	1	11	1	26	2
Agboola R	1994	6	0	1	0	7	0
Alexander D	1977-80	137 (10)	22	72 (4)	15	209 (14)	37
Alexander S	1912	5	2	4	2	9	4
Alexander T	1993,95	31 (2)	0	7 (1)	0	38 (3)	0
Allard O	1907	1	0			1	0
Allen P.K	1896-98	25	2	11	0	36	2
Amos A	1923	1	0			1	0
Anderson A.T	1926	7	0	7	0	14	0
Anderson J	1923	1	0			1	0
Andrews G	1926	1	0			1	0
Ansell J	1922	10	1			10	1
Archer H	1909	3	2	1	0	4	2
Arnold B	1963-65	46	4	10	3	56	7
Arnold B.S	1964-65	48	0	8	0	56	0
Arrow A	1984	3	0			3	0
Ashton A	1924-25	12	0	7	0	19	0
Atkins S	1985	12 (4)	4	8 (1)	3	20 (5)	7
Atkinson S.J	1896	4	1			4	1
B							
Badcock A.V	1921-25	32	9	8	1	40	10
Bailey A	1921	1	0			1	0
Baker M	1950	6	0			6	0
Baker J	1981	2	0			2	0
Baker J.W	1900	7	0	3	0	10	0
Baker S	1972-74	30 (8)	3	17 (4)	3	47 (12)	6
Baker S	1987-89	6 (1)	4	3	0	9 (1)	4
Baldaro E	1936-38,40,46-49	50	0	12	0	62	0
Baldwin	1906			1	0	1	0
Ball A.W	1925-26	13	0	7	2	20	2
Ballerino J	1949-50	33	21	10	7	43	28
Bangs J	1962	7	0	2	0	9	0
Banks J	1955	1	0	1	0	2	0
Banks W	1948	1	0			1	0
Barker C	1939-40	16	4	5	1	21	5
Barker R	1963-64	8	0			8	0
Barkshire C	1896	5	0			5	0
Barnett B	1969	0 (1)	0	0 (1)	0	0 (2)	0
Barnett D	1988	5	0			5	0
Barney A	1935	1	1			1	1
Baron T	1986-93	254 (3)	39	105	18	359 (3)	57
Barrett L	1979-81,83	113	3	62 (4)	5	175 (4)	8
Barrowcliff P	1991-92	0 (2)	0	1	1	1 (2)	1
Barrs J	1932	3	0			3	0
Bartlett S	1935	3	0	1	0	4	0

PLAYER	SEASONS	LEAGUE APPS(sub)	GOALS	CUPS APPS(sub)	GOALS	TOTAL APPS(sub)	GOALS
Bastine S	1989	0 (1)	0			0 (1)	0
Bateman D	1930-32	36	4	15	4	51	8
Bateman M	1977	2 (1)	0			2 (1)	0
Battrick T	1904	1	0			1	0
Batty L	1992-95	157	3	61	1	218	4
Bayley S.G	1932	1	0	2	0	3	0
Beadle A	1928-31	40	0	20	0	60	0
Beal P	1985	1	0	1	0	2	0
Beckett K	1982	7 (1)	1	3	1	10 (1)	2
Beckford W	1925	3	1			3	1
Bedser A	1911,13-14	12	0	2	0	14	0
Bell A.H	1907-14	124	3	92	2	216	5
Bell J.R	1932	1	0			1	0
Bell M	1975	30	0	5	0	35	0
Bembridge S	1984	2	1			2	1
Bennett G	1994	3	1	1	0	4	1
Bennett H.C	1913	5	2	6	10	11	12
Bennett M	1974,76	13 (4)	0	6 (1)	2	19 (5)	2
Benton J	1995	2	0	1	0	3	0
Berry G	1994-94	43 (3)	0	20	0	63 (3)	0
Berry L.B	1923	3	0	2	1	5	1
Beswick S.M	1931	2	1	1	0	3	1
Betts F.L	1924	2	0	1	0	3	0
Bettesworth R	1938	2	0	1	0	3	0
Bevan A	1912-13,20, 21	4	2	2	1	6	3
Bickford P	1983,85	13	1	4	0	17	1
Bickford S	1983-85	54 (1)	1	5	0	59 (1)	1
Biggins M	1988 to94	191 (14)	32	81 (8)	13	272 (22)	45
Billingsby R	1963-65	31	0	6	0	37	0
Binks T	1970-71	45 (5)	17	26 (2)	18	71 (7)	35
Birch W.G	1921	1	0			1	0
Bird G	1946	1	0			1	0
Black M	1979-85,87	146 (4)	5	44 (6)	5	190 (10)	10
Blankley B	1988	3	1	1	1	4	2
Blason W	1970-71	7 (4)	1	7 (2)	0	14 (6)	1
Blount K	1975-77	2 (2)	1	2	0	4 (2)	1
Blunden K	1928-37	71	13	31	5	102	18
Boardman S	1972			1	0	1	0
Bolton A.W	1930-31	9	10			9	10
Bonar E	1952	1	0			1	0
Bond R	1955-57	20	4	4	1	24	5
Bonetti P	1987	1	0	1	0	2	0
Booth A	1981	29	1	7	1	36	2
Booker W.E	1908	1	0			1	0
Botley A	1962-63	19	2	5	2	24	4
Bowey T	1920	1	0			1	0
Bowley M	1969-70	13 (1)	0	3 (1)	0	16 (2)	0
Bowtell S	1983	7	0	2	0	9	0
Boxall O	1947-50	94	13	28	8	122	21
Bradley E	1927	2	0			2	0
Bradshaw A	1931	4	0	1	0	5	0
Braithwaite A	1947-50	60	4	20	0	80	4
Braithwaite R	1973	28	1	8	1	36	2
Breach F	1909	2	0	1	0	3	0
Breeze C.H	1932	17	7	9	5	26	12
Brennan J	1962-63	26	2	12	3	38	5
Brice A	1898	8	1	7	1	15	2
Bridges G.E	1938	1	1			1	1
Briggs T.M.R	1923-29	64	13	26	3	90	16
Briggs W.A	1928	1	0			1	0
Briscoe E	1939	8	1	5	1	13	2
Brister N	1976-77	5 (2)	1			5 (2)	1
Bristowe E	1947	11	0	1	0	12	0
Broderick D	1993	3	0	0 (1)	0	3 (1)	0
Bromfield C.J	1896	3	1			3	1
Brooks R.A	1932	1	0			1	0

PLAYER	SEASONS	LEAGUE APPS(sub)	GOALS	CUPS APPS(sub)	GOALS	TOTAL APPS(sub)	GOALS
Brooks S	1995	0(1)	0			0 (1)	0
Brooks W	1902,11	4	1	3	0	7	1
Brown A	1976-78,82	107 (1)	8	33 (1)	4	140 (2)	12
Brown Del.	1994	2 (3)	0	0 (1)	0	2 (4)	0
Brown Der.	1991-95	144 (13)	12	61 (7)	3	205 (20)	15
Brown I	1979	4	0			4	0
Brown K	1993-95	116	1	40	3	156	4
Brown L	1957	3	0			3	0
Brown M.K	1933	2	0	3	0	5	0
Brown N	1970	5 (1)	1	3	1	8 (1)	2
Brown R.H	1904,08	1	0	1	1	2	1
Brown R.H	1937-38	11	0	5	0	16	0
Brown R.R	1926	1	0			1	0
Brown W.G.E	1936	1	0	1	0	2	0
Brownbill T.J	1931	1	1	1	2	2	3
Bruty M	1960	1	0			1	0
Buckmaster F	1932-37,46	131	34	67	24	198	58
Buck F	1908-09	11	15	4	1	15	16
Bullock I	1983	2	0			2	0
Bunyan W.J	1921	2	0			2	0
Burgess A	1923	1	0			1	0
Burley J	1954,57-61	131	0	52	0	183	0
Burrows J.E.T	1906-07	11	1	3	1	14	2
Burrows R	1906-07	12	0	3	0	15	0
Busfield R	1906	15	2	4	1	19	3
Bushay A	1993	12	2			12	2
Butcher G	1914			1	0	1	0
Butler A	1928-31	8	0	2	0	10	0
Butt Frank	1900-01,03- 04	16	1	2	0	18	1
Butt Fred	1899-09	111	26	60	15	171	41
Buzaglo R	1987-89,91,93	40 (5)	12	26 (3)	7	66 (8)	19
Buzaglo T	1987-91,93	157 (14)	104	67 (6)	47	224 (20)	151
Byrne L	1921	1	0			1	0
C							
Cable W	1928-29	14	0	9	0	23	0
Cadogan L	1982	29	12	6	2	35	14
Caeser J	1920	2	0	2	0	4	0
Caldwell H	1908	1	2	1	0	2	2
Callaghan F	1978-80	11 (2)	0	6 (1)	0	17 (3)	0
Callingham G	1934	1	0			1	0
Cann P	1983-84	4	0			4	0
Cappe Dr	1900	4	1	3	0	7	1
Carney M	1972-73	4 (1)	1	1	1	5 (1)	2
Carpenter D	1983	1	0			1	0
Carroll R	1993	11 (5)	2	3 (3)	2	14 (8)	4
Carter G	1974			0 (1)	0	0 (1)	0
Carter S.F	1936-39	39	11	8	1	47	12
Carter S.J	1906	10	1	1	0	11	1
Cartlidge A	1926-27	20	1	8	1	28	2
Cartwright H.C	1910-11	9	1	19	0	28	1
Carver G	1969-70	32 (2)	6	18 (1)	5	50 (3)	11
Casey D	1985	7	0			7	0
Cashmore E	1958,60	2	0			2	0
Cashmore M	1958-61	27	1	5	0	32	1
Cashmore N	1958-61	46	9	18	3	64	12
Cassidy J	1974-76,83,86-89	215 (3)	17	80 (1)	5	295 (4)	22
Caswell D	1947-48	3	2			3	2
Caulfield C	1989-91	58	0	22	0	80	0
Cawley P	1985	1	0			1	0
Challis W.H	1928	8	0			8	0
Champion P	1910			1	0	1	0
Chandler S	1983	15 (3)	3	4	1	19 (3)	4

PLAYER	SEASONS	LEAGUE APPS(sub)	GOALS	CUPS APPS(sub)	GOALS	TOTAL APPS(sub)	GOALS
Chapple G	1972-74,76,85	113 (3)	16	55	3	168 (3)	19
Chapman J	1928, 31-32	9	0	4	0	13	0
Chapman J	1982,87-88	16 (2)	6	10 (1)	0	26 (3)	6
Charlton J	1959	1	0			1	0
Chatterton A.H	1925			2	1	2	1
Cheeseman D	1972-75,78	89 (2)	4	31 (1)	2	120 (3)	6
Cheeseman S	1985	4	1	2	0	6	1
Chegwyn C	1968	6	2	5	0	11	2
Cherry R	1952			2	3	2	3
Chew J	1991			0 (1)	0	0 (1)	0
Cheyne A	1952-55	12	0	4	0	16	0
Chitty W	1930	17	4	9	2	26	6
Chown A	1958	1	1			1	1
Christie W	1920-21	34	0	7	0	41	0
Christmas A	1971-74	69 (1)	5	31 (1)	5	100 (2)	10
Christopher J	1933	1	0			1	0
Church A	1970	6 (1)	0	1	0	7 (1)	0
Church G	1921-22	13	1	2	0	15	1
Churchouse G	1982	2 (1)	0			2 (1)	0
Clacey E	1955-60	95	3	43	0	138	3
Clarke G	1913			1	0	1	0
Clarke J	1982	3 (3)	1	2 (1)	0	5 (4)	1
Clarke A	1950-57	125	7	50	3	175	10
Clarke E.C	1933-35	35	5	16	3	51	8
Clarke G	1900	2	0	1	0	3	0
Clement A	1991,93-94	57 (1)	5	20 (1)	2	77 (2)	7
Clifford J.S	1929	1	0			1	0
Clifford P.J	1923,25-29	36	0	22	0	58	0
Cockram A	1992	3	1	1	0	4	1
Cockram J	1948	1	0			1	0
Cockran G	1920	12	5	5	3	17	8
Coe A.P	1922-24	30	5	11	0	41	5
Cole J	1963	3	0			3	0
Coleman D	1993	6	1			6	1
Collier N	1992	9 (3)	2	8 (3)	0	17 (6)	2
Collingwood J	1958-60,62-65	132	1	48	0	180	1
Collins A.W	1931-35	33	1	19	0	52	1
Collins M	1985	12	1			12	1
Collins M	1960-61	38	5	12	3	50	8
Collis B	1953	4	0	1	0	5	0
Collyer D	1971-75	196	0	81 (1)	0	277 (1)	0
Collyer G	1924	1	0			1	0
Colman R.C	1922-23	5	0			5	0
Connaughton P	1969	1 (1)	0			1 (1)	0
Connolly A.J	1921	2	0			2	0
Constable S	1983	3	0	1	0	4	0
Cook A	1978	2	0	1	0	3	0
Cook C	1921	1	0			1	0
Cook J	1983 to84,89	29	0	9 (1)	0	38 (1)	0
Cooper G	1966-67,74-77	179 (2)	26	73	14	252 (2)	40
Cooper J	1981	28	1	11	1	39	2
Cosham S	1975-79	119 (4)	60	49 (2)	30	168 (6)	90
Cornell E.S	1930	1	0			1	0
Cottam R.R	1904-07	33	11	18	10	51	21
Cottrell D	1976-80	150 (5)	6	69	6	219 (5)	12
Cousins H	1946-47	2	0			2	0
Cowell N	1984	9 (3)	2	3	0	12 (3)	2
Cowle E.J	1933-38,46	71	0	36	0	107	0
Cowle P	1967,69	3 (1)	0			3 (1)	0
Cowler A	1983,86-92	233 (1)	9	109	7	342 (1)	16
Cowley R.A	1947	12	3	1	0	13	3
Cox C	1921	5	2			5	2
Cox G	1946-47	33	1	10	0	43	1
Cox M	1984-86	87	54	20	12	107	66
Cox R	1953	5	2	1	0	6	2

PLAYER	SEASONS	LEAGUE APPS(sub)	GOALS	CUPS APPS(sub)	GOALS	TOTAL APPS(sub)	GOALS
Craddock J	1994	7	2	1	0	8	2
Craddock S.E	1930-31	43	2	22	2	65	4
Crane H.J	1909-14,20 to24	174	8	110	4	284	12
Crawford A	1929	1	1			1	1
Crick H.E	1912-13	3	0	1	0	4	0
Croft S	1912			1	0	1	0
Crook A	1938	2	0			2	0
Cross N	1973	12	0	2	0	14	0
Crossley J	1903-04	7	0	8	0	15	0
Crossley S	1982	4	0			4	0
Crow E	1964-65	7	0	1	0	8	0
Crutchley C.J	1933-35	44	0	24	0	68	0
Crumplin J	1995	11 (1)	1	4	0	15 (1)	1
Crymble C	1921	2	0	1	2	3	2
Cunningham P	1977-78	4 (2)	1	1	0	5 (2)	1
D							
Dakin F	1976-77	8	0			8	0
Daley J.V	1939	14	3	2	0	16	3
Dalton E.H	1902-03	22	3	9	0	31	3
Dalton P	1898	8	7	7	2	15	9
Dance P	1938,40	13	0	3	0	16	0
Dando H.E	1906			1	0	1	0
Daniells H.W	1920	1	0			1	0
Daniels B	1909,11	13	16	4	0	17	16
Daniels L	1911			1	0	1	0
Daniels P	1978	9 (2)	0	4 (1)	0	13 (3)	0
Darcy G	1920	2	0	1	0	3	0
Darnell G	1978	2	0			2	0
Dashwood J	1952	1	0			1	0
Davidson L	1990-91	0 (1)	0	3	0	3 (1)	0
Davies A	1977-78	17	0	3	0	20	0
Davies B	1981	12	0	8	0	20	0
Davies G	1911	5	6	3	2	8	8
Davies I	1981	6	1	1	0	7	1
Davies K	1985	4	0			4	0
Davies L.J	1938-39	2	1	1	0	3	1
Davies L	1948	4	1	2	0	6	1
Davies P	1961,65-67	14	2	9	0	23	2
Davies R	1981	12	2	8	2	20	4
Davis H	1905-06	2	0	1	0	3	0
Davis M	1983,89-90	26 (1)	4	13 (3)	5	39 (4)	9
Dawber M	1986-87	44	22	19	6	63	28
Dawson P	1991	5 (5)	0			5 (5)	0
Day C.W	1904,09-10	22	3	6	2	28	5
Dearden K	1989	5	0	1	0	6	0
Debell D	1961	3	0	1	0	4	0
de Garis P	1995	1	0			1	0
Denmead H	1899	1	0			1	0
Dennis F	1982	2	0			2	0
Dennis L	1994-95	26 (9)	14	13 (1)	8	39 (10)	22
Denny T	1897,99-1900	16	5	1	0	17	5
Devereux M	1981			1	0	1	0
Devine J	1926	1	0			1	0
Devine S	1992	2 (1)	1	2	1	4 (1)	2
Dixon W	1981	9	1	2	0	11	1
Dixon I	1982-83	7 (1)	0	4	0	11 (1)	0
Docherty A	1984	19 (1)	0	3	0	22 (1)	0
Docherty W	1922	1	0			1	0
Dodd S	1987	1	0			1	0
Doe W	1921-22	7	3	2	2	9	5
Doig M	1978	11	1	1	0	12	1
Donovan C	1930	6	1	2	1	8	2
Dorkins E	1920-21	11	9	1	0	12	9

PLAYER	SEASONS	LEAGUE APPS(sub)	GOALS	CUPS APPS(sub)	GOALS	TOTAL APPS(sub)	GOALS
Dowse R	1962-63	18	0	3	0	21	0
Dowse W	1959-63	71	5	22	2	93	7
Drake C.E	1900-01,03	5	0	1	0	6	0
Drake F.A	1900-03	29	3	4	1	33	4
Drake J.F	1901	1	0			1	0
Drake P	1950	1	0			1	0
Drew	1911	1	0			1	0
Duckworth H	1911			1	0	1	0
Duff P	1985	2 (1)	1	2 (2)	1	4 (3)	2
Duffett F	1896	9	3			9	3
Duncan J	1899-00	8	1	1	0	9	1
Dunn J	1981	10	0	6	0	16	0
Dyason C	1926-27	4	0	1	0	5	0
E							
Eagles G	1983-84	5 (3)	1	2	0	7 (3)	1
Eales C	1946	5	0	1	0	6	0
Eales G	1935-36	38	1	23	1	61	2
Earls M	1980-81	5 (1)	0	1	0	6 (1)	0
East L	1934	7	6	6	3	13	9
Eastaff M	1947-50	72	0	24	0	96	0
Easton A	1952	9	6	4	1	13	7
Easton F.S	1905	14	1	9	1	23	2
Eastwood E	1921	1	0	1	0	2	0
Edwards A	1925-26	16	0	2	0	18	0
Edwards A	1934	4	0	2	0	6	0
Edwards A	1972,74	1	0	3	0	4	0
Edwards D	1970-74	186	12	90	4	276	16
Edwards G	1955-56	12	3	5	0	17	3
Edwards G	1982	5	0	1	0	6	0
Edwards R	1951-52	7	2	3	0	10	2
Edwards S.C	1925	7	0	8	0	15	0
Elkins	1968			1	0	1	0
Ellerby R	1952-53,55-60	104	1	39	0	143	1
Elliott J	1926-27	11	4	5	3	16	7
Elliott J	1947	5	3			5	3
Elliott M	1970-73,78	75 (5)	13	38 (1)	6	113 (6)	19
Ellis A	1995	26 (1)	3	12 (1)	1	38 (2)	4
Ellwood F	1906,11	7	0	3	0	10	0
Elmore J	1968	2	0	4	0	6	0
Elphick E	1903	2	0	2	1	4	1
Elsworth W.C	1924-25	28	0	9	1	37	1
Elton R	1967-73	176	7	90	0	266	7
Engall E.T	1906			1	0	1	0
Evans A	1927	5	5	1	0	6	5
Evans D	1969-71	8 (1)	1	4	0	12 (1)	1
Evans H.A	1939	15	4	3	3	18	7
Eyre E.B	1896-00	31	0	6	0	37	0
F							
Fabian M	1986	2	0			2	0
Faggetter S.H	1934	11	11	2	4	13	15
Farris B	1961-71	317	0	120	0	437	0
Farrow E	1898-00,04	5	0	5	0	10	0
Faulds M	1940	1	0	1	0	2	0
Fearon E	1990-91	18 (8)	8	6 (1)	3	24 (9)	11
Feeheely M	1965	1	0	1	0	2	0
Ferguson P	1981	3	0			3	0
Field A	1979-81,83	118 (2)	26	50 (4)	15	168 (6)	41
Field W	1937	1	0			1	0
Fielder C	1993-95	93 (6)	4	33 (2)	2	126 (8)	6
Filleston J	1920	2	0	3	1	5	1
Filmore A	1924,26	5	1			5	1
Finch J	1993	1	0			1	0
Finch F	1946	1	0	2	1	3	1

PLAYER	SEASONS	LEAGUE APPS(sub)	GOALS	CUPS APPS(sub)	GOALS	TOTAL APPS(sub)	GOALS
Finlay W	1937-38	24	10	10	3	34	13
Finn B	1963-74	393	35	175	15	568	50
Finn C	1968	2 (1)	1	1	0	3 (1)	1
Finn P	1961,65-66,71-73,77	165	3	77	2	242	5
Finn T	1977	0 (1)	0	1	0	1 (1)	0
Finnieston S	1983	5	1			5	1
Firmin C	1904-05	28	7	17	1	45	8
Fish E	1937-38	15	0	5	0	20	0
Fitch K	1962-64	55	2	23	0	78	2
Fitzgerald R.R	1926-31	52	44	13	7	65	51
Flack S	1990	1	0	1	1	2	1
Fleming D	1994	0 (2)	0	0 (1)	0	0 (3)	0
Fleming M	1993	28 (1)	5	5 (2)	0	33 (3)	5
Fletcher N	1980-81	32 (5)	4	16 (4)	3	48 (9)	7
Fletcher R	1968-70	36	1	15 (2)	2	51 (2)	3
Flippance J	1951	13	0			13	0
Folan J	1969-70	3 (1)	0	1 (1)	0	4 (2)	0
Foley M	1983	3	0			3	0
Forbes R	1974-77	53 (9)	2	17 (1)	3	70 (10)	5
Ford H	1913	1	0			1	0
Ford J	1953-54,57-58	22	4	3	1	25	5
Ford R	1956-57	18	9	7	1	25	10
Foulkes G	1961-63	25	0	3	0	28	0
Fox C	1899-01	20	2	4	0	24	2
Francis J	1934-35	23	9	15	8	38	17
Francis M	1983	10 (2)	0	5	0	15 (2)	0
Francis N	1969,71	3	0	3	0	6	0
Franks A	1929	2	0			2	0
Franks M	1983,90-91	73 (11)	10	32 (8)	2	105 (19)	12
Freeman W.G	1933	5	1	7	2	12	3
Freer E	1946	1	0			1	0
French A	1963-65	77	1	19	0	96	1
Friel G	1992	38 (2)	28	18 (2)	9	56 (4)	37
Frost L	1985	27	3	11	0	38	3
Fuller B	1964-66	79	0	15	0	94	0
Fuller S	1980-81	9 (2)	0	1	0	10 (2)	0
Furlonger K	1961	3	0			3	0
Furlonger R	1963	1	0			1	0
G							
Galbally W.C	1929-31	19	0	6	0	25	0
Gale D	1970-73	52 (3)	17	27 (2)	9	79 (5)	26
Gale T	1989	9	2	1	0	10	2
Gamble D	1955,57-58,61-63	10	2	4	3	14	5
Gammon A	1907	1	0			1	0
Gammon F	1922	1	0			1	0
Gary F	1929-31	32	0	7	4	39	4
Gaskin G	1965	2	0			2	0
Gibbons J	1899	5	1	1	0	6	1
Gibbs A	1921	1	1			1	1
Gibb A	1954	8	4	1	1	9	5
Gibbs C	1911			1	3	1	3
Gibbs F	1923	4	1	10	5	14	6
Gibbs S	1929,31,33	7	0	2	1	9	1
Gibson N	1938	1	0			1	0
Gibson N	1984	20	7	4	0	24	7
Giddings S	1977-78,85	6 (2)	1	5	0	11 (2)	1
Gilbert F.A	1924-26	23	8	8	1	31	9
Gill M	1956	13	0	3	0	16	0
Gillingham A.E	1899	1	0			1	0
Gillings A.E	1929	1	0			1	0
Girdler S	1995	1 (1)	0	0 (3)	0	1 (4)	0
Gladwin T	1906	3	2	1	0	4	2
Gloster G	1899	1	0			1	0

PLAYER	SEASONS	LEAGUE APPS(sub)	GOALS	CUPS APPS(sub)	GOALS	TOTAL APPS(sub)	GOALS
Goddard P.W	1931	1	0			1	0
Godding A	1947	2	1			2	1
Godfrey J	1977	11 (1)	3	7 (2)	1	18 (3)	4
Gooch E	1920-21	28	12	5	0	33	12
Godwin D	1969	26	0	10	0	36	0
Goodyear M	1959-60	6	3	1	0	7	3
Golden-Hann C	1940			1	0	1	0
Goslin T	1938	6	0			6	0
Gough D.A	1939-40	4	0	5	6	9	6
Gough R.E	1933-34,36-40	49	1	12	0	61	1
Gorringe S.B	1909	6	0	4	3	10	3
Gowan H.E	1920-22	28	1	6	1	34	2
Gowler H	1920-26	40	3	26	4	66	7
Graham F.E	1914	2	0			2	0
Graham J	1985-86	5 (1)	0	2	0	7 (1)	0
Grassam G	1956	3	0			3	0
Graves C	1904			3	0	3	0
Gray A	1994	7	2	2 (1)	0	9 (1)	2
Gray A	1929	2	1			2	1
Gray J	1990	6	0	5	0	11	0
Green G	1926	1	2			1	2
Green S.L	1932	1	0			1	0
Greene Dave	1993,95	8 (2)	4	1 (1)	2	9 (3)	6
Greene Den	1994	2 (1)	0			2 (1)	0
Greenwood H	1929-32	26	3	14	2	40	5
Griffin G	1921-23	71	0	32	0	103	0
Griffiths A.F	1934-37	62	1	31	0	93	1
Griffiths B.V	1923-26	23	2	6	0	29	2
Grondona J	1973-76	75 (1)	31	31	14	106 (1)	45
Grove Ar	1911-14,21	50	4	27	4	77	8
Gumbrell G	1938			1	0	1	0
Gummer J	1980	2	0			2	0
Gunstone J	1925,27	5	1			5	1
H							
Hadden	1953			1	0	1	0
Haddow G	1974			1	0	1	0
Haddow P	1973	2	0			2	0
Haider R	1961-62	57	7	17	1	74	8
Hall G	1990-91	14 (5)	10	12 (1)	7	26 (6)	17
Hamilton	1902	1	0			1	0
Hamm G	1951-58	190	81	71	37	261	118
Hammond P	1971	1 (1)	1	5 (1)	0	6 (2)	1
Hampshire P	1985	3	0	2	1	5	1
Hancock T	1960			1	0	1	0
Hann H	1914	1	0			1	0
Harding F	1930	2	0			2	0
Harding M	1988	1	0			1	0
Harding S	1971-73	49	3	37	0	86	3
Harman N.J	1923-27	65	15	41	19	106	34
Harper T.W	1946	4	0			4	0
Harris H.H	1931	4	0	1	0	5	0
Harris G	1960-61	52	34	16	7	68	41
Harrison H	1913	1	0			1	0
Harrison	1908	1	1	1	1	2	2
Harrison P	1963	2	0			2	0
Hart A	1914	2	0			2	0
Hart I	1953	15	0	7	0	22	0
Hartley J	1912	5	2			5	2
Harvey G.B	1929	9	1	1	0	10	1
Harvey J	1956	15	9	2	1	17	10
Harwars	1899	2	0			2	0
Hatcher N	1989	18 (2)	3	8	1	26 (2)	4
Hawkett G	1975-76	11 (2)	3	3	0	14 (2)	3
Hawkins C.E	1901,03-05	17	0	13	0	30	0

PLAYER	SEASONS	LEAGUE APPS(sub)	GOALS	CUPS APPS(sub)	GOALS	TOTAL APPS(sub)	GOALS
Hawkins G.F	1899-04	52	3	16	1	68	4
Hay D	1994-95	33	21	9	6	42	27
Hayden E	1957	2	1			2	1
Haylock P	1994	0 (1)	0			0 (1)	0
Hayward D	1965	3	0	1	0	4	0
Heane A	1900-01	6	1			6	1
Heane M	1900-01	11	0	2	0	13	0
Hearman P	1960-61	17	2	2	1	19	3
Heath K	1971	12 (2)	4	6 (1)	0	18 (3)	4
Heath W.H	1904-05	5	0			5	0
Hebdon Jim	1965	13	1	3	0	16	1
Hebdon John	1957-61	118	43	46	18	164	61
Hedgecock F	1907-08,10	2	0	3	0	5	0
Hennesey D	1979-80	0 (3)	0	0 (1)	0	0 (4)	0
Henshaw W	1947	4	0	1	0	5	0
Hepburn	1966	1	0			1	0
Hepworth M	1982,84	31	3	5	1	36	4
Heritage P	1994	3	0			3	0
Herrett V	1967	12	0	2	0	14	0
Hewitt H	1929-31	7	3	1	0	8	3
Hewitt R	1948	5	3	3	1	8	4
Hewitt T	1982-84	26 (5)	7	9 (1)	1	35 (6)	8
Higgs R	1971-72	6 (2)	1	19 (1)	6	25 (3)	7
Hill A	1975	15	0			15	0
Hill H	1977	11	0			11	0
Hill K	1982,87-88	66 (7)	7	20 (2)	1	86 (9)	8
Hill N	1929,31	3	0			3	0
Hill O.E	1933	3	0			3	0
Hill R	1909-11	21	10	27	15	48	25
Hill R	1968-69	24	2	17	2	41	4
Hill S	1977	23 (1)	10	13	7	36 (1)	17
Hindley G	1982	4	0			4	0
Hines M	1964	6	3			6	3
Hirons D	1962	12	0	6	0	18	0
Hislop C	1994	0 (2)	0	0 (2)	0	0 (4)	0
Hitchcock B	1932	7	0	2	0	9	0
Hobbs R	1938-40	31	2	9	4	40	6
Hodgeman E	1920	9	1	5	0	14	1
Hodges H.H	1914,21-22,24	16	0	7	0	23	0
Holder K	1970	24	0	18	0	42	0
Holder P	1982,84	21	4	4	0	25	4
Holdforth	1902	1	0			1	0
Hollingsworth A	1991	2 (1)	0	1	0	3 (1)	0
Hollingsworth F	1934	19	0	10	0	29	0
Holman A	1921	9	0	1	0	10	0
Holmes C	1983-84	22	0	5	0	27	0
Holmes W	1969-70	11 (2)	4	6	1	17 (2)	5
Holsgrove P	1988	3	0			3	0
Honey D	1993	1	0			1	0
Hook R	1976	3	0	1	0	4	0
Hooker H	1932-38	101	48	47	27	148	75
Hooker R	1934,37-38	2	0	2	1	4	1
Horne B	1993	1	0			1	0
Horner J	1986-88	78 (6)	17	20 (2)	2	98 (8)	19
Horton J	1929			1	0	1	0
Horton N	1984-85	3 (4)	1	5	0	8 (4)	1
Hough E	1934	1	0			1	0
Houghton T	1988	4 (1)	0			4 (1)	0
Hounsell J	1973	14	0	5	0	19	0
Howard I	1982,85	8	1	2	1	10	2
Howitt D	1981	23	0	6	0	29	0
Hughes A	1923,26	2	0	1	0	3	0
Hughes D	1938	25	6	6	3	31	9
Humphreyies W	1926			1	0	1	0

PLAYER	SEASONS	LEAGUE APPS(sub)	GOALS	CUPS APPS(sub)	GOALS	TOTAL APPS(sub)	GOALS
Humphreys A.W	1912	18	10	9	7	27	17
Hunt A	1921	1	0	1	1	2	1
Hunt H	1899-1901	3	0	1	0	4	0
Hunt J	1992	2	0			2	0
Hunter G.V	1920-21	6	1	2	0	8	1
Hutchins D	1974	32 (3)	5	11 (3)	0	43 (6)	5
Hutchins R.C.H	1934	4	0	2	0	6	0
Hutchinson G	1994	0 (1)	0			0 (1)	0
Hutton G	1899-10	139	73	63	15	202	88
Hutton P	1897	9	7			9	7
Huxley P	1976	2	0			2	0
Hyde R	1962-64,66-67	50 (1)	8	10	1	60 (1)	9
I							
Ilsley A	1960	27	1	10	1	37	2
Imison P	1975	6	0	5	0	11	0
Ingham P	1983-85	5	0	1	0	6	0
Inseal P.W	1922	20	1	7	1	27	2
Inwood F	1896-97	8	3			8	3
Ireland	1976	5	0	1	0	6	0
Ives W	1933,35	25	2	14	0	39	2
J							
Jablonski P	1984-87	113 (1)	8	40	0	153 (1)	8
Jacob M	1957-62	86	23	31	10	117	33
Jamel Z	1978	2 (1)	0			2 (1)	0
James C	1995			1 (3)	0	1 (3)	0
James E	1979-80	76 (3)	40	45 (2)	27	121 (5)	67
James H	1913	3	1	1	0	4	1
James K	1982-83	22	1	4	0	26	1
Jarvis G	1947	7	3	1	0	8	3
Johnson F.R	1931	1	0	1	0	2	0
Johnson J	1946	1	0	1	1	2	1
Johnson L.C	1908-12,14,20-21	57	5	43	7	100	12
Johnson R	1972	8	0	6 (1)	0	14 (1)	0
Johnstone A.E	1930	4	1	1	0	5	1
Jones	1899	1	0			1	0
Jones A	1928	1	0			1	0
Jones C	1984	11	2	2	0	13	2
Jones F	1984	4	0	3	0	7	0
Jones G	1987	3 (1)	0	0 (1)	0	3 (2)	0
Jones I	1954	5	1			5	1
Jones R	1957-61	24	1	6	0	30	1
Jones Tom	1984	15	2	3	0	18	2
Jones Trev	1989	15	0	15	0	30	0
Joyce A	1993	7	0	3	0	10	0
K							
Keefe F	1946,50-58	91	0	25	1	116	1
Keeley P	1963	1	0			1	0
Keeley R	1966	14	4	5	2	19	6
Keen J	1957	2	0			2	0
Keen N	1975	2 (1)	0			2 (1)	0
Keenan D	1900	6	5	2	0	8	5
Kemp F	1897-02	33	3	8	1	41	4
Kemp F	1920-21	5	0	4	0	9	0
Kelly P	1993	1	0			1	0
Kendrick S	1939	1	0			1	0
Kennedy J	1959	1	0			1	0
Kerbey S	1987	10 (1)	3	7	1	17 (1)	4
Kerr A.W	1921	2	0			2	0
Kerrins W	1990	1	0	0 (1)	1	1 (1)	1
Killick C	1951-56	30	0	10	0	40	0
Kimbell A.W	1926	1	0			1	0
King R	1982	9	0	3	0	12	0
Kingston W	1912			1	0	1	0

PLAYER	SEASONS	LEAGUE APPS(sub)	GOALS	CUPS APPS(sub)	GOALS	TOTAL APPS(sub)	GOALS
Kitchener K	1988			0 (1)	0	0 (1)	0
Kittredge A.V	1937-40	22	3	11	2	33	5
Knight A.E	1909-10			3	0	3	0
Knight B	1968	2	0	1	0	3	0
Knight H	1933-35,38-39	15	0	3	0	18	0
Knight H	1896-03	53	0	10	0	63	0
Knight P	1986	1	0			1	0
Knight S.W.J	1932	3	0	3	0	6	0
Knott F.G	1903-06	27	0	18	0	45	0
Kurn J	1948-49	4	0			4	0
Kyle J	1904-14	131	88	107	76	238	164
L							
Lakin B	1994	7 (6)	2	3 (1)	1	10 (7)	3
Langtree	1906	1	0			1	0
Lansley D	1986-88	47 (14)	36	18 (4)	9	65 (18)	45
Larcombe E	1907	2	2			2	2
Lavender K	1988	1	0	2	0	3	0
Lawes T	1906	2	0			2	0
Lawrence L	1904	1	0			1	0
Lawrence W.A	1902	1	0			1	0
Lawrence W.H	1902	1	0			1	0
Lawrence W.H	1930-39,46-48	205	30	79	15	284	45
Layton T.H	1913	9	0	6	0	15	0
Leahy K	1965	16	5	5	1	21	6
Leather R	1981	38	2	10	4	48	6
Ledger L	1922-27	30	3	7	1	37	4
Ledger P	1953-57	83	0	28	0	111	0
Lee R	1922	6	1	1	0	7	1
Lee S	1935	5	2			5	2
Lee V	1927	10	0	7	3	17	3
Lemoine H.M	1914	7	0	2	0	9	0
Leonard D	1970-74	111 (4)	30	53 (2)	10	164 (6)	40
Lester T	1925	1	0			1	0
Lewer A	1975-76	6 (1)	0	0 (1)	1	6 (2)	1
Lewis L.R	1913	9	3	10	6	19	9
Lewis R	1967-68	22	0	9 (1)	0	31 (1)	0
Lewry F	1906-07	6	0	2	0	8	0
Levy A	1981	11	0	8	1	19	1
Ley E	1959	2	1			2	1
Lickfold P	1986,88	5	0	1	0	6	0
Lintott A.M	1906	3	0			3	0
Lintott C	1965	8	0	2	0	10	0
Lintott E.H	1900-08	74	49	34	17	108	66
Lintott F.S	1901-09	104	3	61	0	165	3
Lintott K	1911	4	0			4	0
Littlejohn R	1957-59	52	18	24	9	76	27
Littlejohn P	1980	1 (1)	0			1 (1)	0
Livesley M	1910	1	0	2	0	3	0
Lloyd J.B.R	1939	4	0	3	0	7	0
Lockwood F.B	1930-32	41	4	22	2	63	6
Logan L	1964	3	0			3	0
Logan L	1985	2	0	2	0	4	0
Lomas C	1986-89	72	0	21	0	93	0
Long A.W	1911,14	10	2	1	0	11	2
Long C	1912-14	8	0	8	0	16	0
Long P	1928	3	2	4	0	7	2
Longhurst H.L	1924-25	14	2	6	1	20	3
Love J	1979-80	75	5	40 (1)	3	115 (1)	8
Love S.J	1912-14	39	2	21	0	60	2
Lovell M	1980	5	0	4	0	9	0
Lovett S	1965-66	4	0	1	0	5	0
Lucas H	1935	1	0	1	0	2	0
Lunn G	1988	3	0			3	0
Lusty J	1985	3	0			3	0

PLAYER	SEASONS	LEAGUE APPS(sub)	GOALS	CUPS APPS(sub)	GOALS	TOTAL APPS(sub)	GOALS
Luxton D	1947	9	1	2	0	11	1
Lynch A	1992	2 (2)	0	1	0	3 (2)	0
Lynch L	1982	6	2	1 (1)	0	7 (1)	2
M							
Mace A	1981-82	21	2	5 (1)	1	26 (1)	3
Maidment C.V	1923-29	99	7	38	7	137	14
Mailing J	1961	1	0			1	0
Malcolmson S	1968-69	13	3	9	5	22	8
Mallett A.E	1923	10	1	10	1	20	2
Mallinder E	1938	2	0	1	0	3	0
Mannering E	1912			1	0	1	0
Mapleson R	1978,83	15 (2)	1	4	0	19 (2)	1
Marciello L	1981	8 (7)	2	5	1	13 (7)	3
Marks C	1969	5 (1)	1	3	1	8 (1)	2
Marriage	1899	2	0			2	0
Martin A	1979-83	166	1	71	0	237	1
Martin C	1946	5	2	2	0	7	2
Martin G	1911	4	1			4	1
Martin S	1922-25	35	2	7	1	42	3
Martin J	1965-66	28	3	8	0	36	3
Masey A	1950-52	38	1	19	0	57	1
Mason G.W.H	1931-32	19	12	9	4	28	16
Mason L	1939	2	0	1	0	3	0
Mataxa N	1985	16	0			16	0
May H	1928-32	57	26	24	13	81	39
May P	1929	2	0	2	0	4	0
MacDonald	1985	1	0			1	0
MacFarlane A	1985	5	0	2	0	7	0
McBryde J	1965-68	82	6	36	13	118	19
McBryde M	1948	8	0	1	0	9	0
McCormack J	1960-61,70	32 (1)	11	19	5	51 (1)	16
McCulloch R	1982	28	6	6	0	34	6
McCollin A	1983	14	2	6	2	20	4
McDevitt G	1964-65,67	26	1	11	0	37	1
McDonald C	1986	12	1	2	1	14	2
McFetridge J	1953	10	0	5	0	15	0
McGonagle I	1978,82	31	0	12 (1)	0	43 (1)	0
McGranigan D	1986	10 (2)	5	4 (1)	0	14 (3)	5
McIntyre A	1967	20	0	7	0	27	0
McIsaac I	1989	2	0	2 (1)	1	4 (1)	1
McKay A	1929	1	0			1	0
McKercher R	1954-55	5	0	4	0	9	0
McKie G	1921	1	0			1	0
McKinnon P	1976-77	1 (1)	0	0 (2)	1	1 (3)	1
McLaren C	1990	2	0			2	0
McLeod D	1926			2	1	2	1
McMorran J	1977-78	9 (1)	1	1 (1)	2	10 (2)	3
McNiven J	1926	1	0			1	0
McPhee S	1966-68	92 (1)	5	39	2	131 (1)	7
McPherson G	1992	0 (2)	0			0 (2)	0
Medcalf W.M	1926	1	0			1	0
Medhurst H	1936-37	27	0	13	0	40	0
Medhurst G	1957			1	0	1	0
Meekings W.H	1928	1	0			1	0
Melville I	1983	15	0	3	0	18	0
Mepham J	1979,83,87-88	13	0	2	0	15	0
Metchick D	1978	7 (1)	0			7 (1)	0
Metherall D	1964	16	4	4	3	20	7
Middleton A	1939	1	0			1	0
Milburn D	1955	3	1	1	1	4	2
Miles A	1988-89	3	0	0 (1)	0	3 (1)	0
Miles H.C	1931			1	0	1	0
Miller D.A	1932	4	1	3	0	7	1
Mills A.E	1923	2	1			2	1

PLAYER	SEASONS	LEAGUE APPS(sub)	GOALS	CUPS APPS(sub)	GOALS	TOTAL APPS(sub)	GOALS
Mills R	1939	1	0			1	0
Milsom M	1984	16 (1)	3	2	1	18 (1)	4
Milton S	1992-93	32 (10)	18	15 (4)	8	47 (14)	26
Mitchell J	1982,87-88	97	15	26	4	123	19
Mitchell K	1982	35	0	8	0	43	0
Mitchell R	1937	1	0	1	0	2	0
Mitchell S.H	1913	2	0			2	0
Mitchell S	1990-92	117 (1)	7	57 (1)	10	174 (2)	17
Molloy T	1974-75	18 (5)	2	3 (1)	0	21 (6)	2
Monk H	1935	2	0			2	0
Monk H.M	1907-08	1	1	2	0	3	1
Monk J.B	1903-13	135	5	87	1	222	6
Monk W.H	1896-99,02	24	3	4	0	28	3
Montgomery L.E	1924-32	192	0	88	0	280	0
Moody K	1961	8	2	1	0	9	2
Moon D	1946	18	10	5	8	23	18
Moorcroft R	1968	4 (1)	1	4	1	8 (1)	2
Moore E	1928-31	61	14	26	10	87	24
Moore J	1966-70	68 (4)	1	31 (4)	2	99 (8)	3
Morah O	1994	1	0			1	0
Morgan P	1968	3 (2)	0			3 (2)	0
Morgan R	1946-55	159	4	58	0	217	4
Morris A.J	1913	1	0			1	0
Morris J	1965	1	0			1	0
Morris K	1986-87	36 (2)	13	15	10	51 (2)	23
Morris L	1947-55	170	3	53	0	223	3
Morrison W	1927	1	0			1	0
Mortimore C	1954-65,68	263	175	99 (1)	75	362 (1)	250
Mortimore J	1954-57	98	21	32	5	130	26
Morton A	1968,76-81,85,89	258 (3)	124	103 (5)	54	361 (8)	178
Moseley G.L	1930-33	30	7	15	7	45	14
Moss S	1989-90	25 (4)	0	10 (3)	1	35 (7)	1
Mossop S.S	1896-00,05	19	2			19	2
Moulsdale W.H	1935-36,46	34	7	18	3	52	10
Mulvaney P	1989-92	46 (23)	22	29 (6)	16	75 (29)	38
Murphy A	1993	2	0			2	0
Murphy M	1983	2	0			2	0
Musgrove M	1985	4	0	1	0	5	0
N							
Naysmith B	1958	1	0			1	0
Neil	1908			2	2	2	2
Nelson H	1990	2	0			2	0
Newbery R	1995	3 (5)	1	0 (1)	0	3 (6)	1
Newman D	1960,62	6	0	1	0	7	0
Newman R	1955	14	5	4	3	18	8
Newland M	1982	4	0			4	0
Norcott H.J	1922-26	88	1	46	1	134	2
Norgate K	1967	38	1	18	0	56	1
Norman C	1976	11	0	6	0	17	0
Norman D	1965	1	0			1	0
Norman S	1986	12	3			12	3
Norridge A	1903	1	1	1	0	2	1
Norridge G	1906			2	0	2	0
Norris E	1913	11	0	6	1	17	1
Nugent C	1948	5	0	1	0	6	0
Nugent R	1993	32	2	8	1	40	3
Nwajiobi E	1981	9 (1)	2	3	1	12 (1)	3
Nwajiobi O	1981	2	1	2	2	4	3
O							
O'Connor G	1910	3	0	3	0	6	0
O'Donnell J	1930-34	25	0	7	0	32	0
O'Flaherty D	1988	0 (1)	0			0 (1)	0
O'Gwynne R	1985			1	0	1	0

PLAYER	SEASONS	LEAGUE APPS(sub)	GOALS	CUPS APPS(sub)	GOALS	TOTAL APPS(sub)	GOALS
O'Riordan E	1965-68	67 (1)	16	31	9	98 (1)	25
O'Sullivan B	1979	28	0	19	0	47	0
Oliver B	1968-70	45 (1)	3	20 (2)	1	65 (3)	4
Olsen T	1929	1	0			1	0
Oram K	1971-77	160 (14)	62	66 (2)	37	226 (16)	99
Osborne R	1975	1	0	1	0	2	0
Osgood N	1932-33	30	1	21	1	51	2
Osnowski K	1985	8	0			8	0
Over C.H	1920-21	7	0	4	0	11	0
Overton J	1977	30	0	14	0	44	0
Owens R.D	1923-24	2	0			2	0
P							
Pacey D	1949	5	1			5	1
Paddon R	1965	8	1	2	0	10	1
Palfrey S	1982	7 (1)	0	1	0	8 (1)	0
Palin A.G	1922	4	0	2	0	6	0
Palinski G	1969-70,73-74	5 (3)	1	3	0	8 (3)	1
Pape A	1993	1	0			1	0
Paris S	1992	0 (1)	0			0 (1)	0
Parker B	1898-03	24	0	6	0	30	0
Parker D	1992	2	0	1 (1)	0	3 (1)	0
Parker W.S	1931	2	0	1	0	3	0
Parminter S	1995	1	0			1	0
Parr A	1988,90-92	123 (6)	33	46 (2)	14	169 (8)	47
Parsons F	1978-81	114	0	59	0	173	0
Parsons G	1952-61	225	5	84	3	309	8
Partridge M	1961	14	0	5	0	19	0
Patient N	1965-66	3	0	1	0	4	0
Pattison M	1972	1 (1)	0	1	0	2 (1)	0
Payne E	1927-28	47	4	23	3	70	7
Payne G	1995	6 (1)	4	4	1	10 (1)	5
Payne M	1985	2	0			2	0
Pearce A.V	1906-14,20-21	145	7	93	4	238	11
Pearce E	1963-65	17	2	1	0	18	2
Pearce T	1977-78	14 (3)	1	3 (1)	1	17 (4)	2
Pedlar L	1991	16 (4)	3	6 (2)	3	22 (6)	6
Pelham G	1946	1	0			1	0
Pelham L	1946	5	2	1	0	6	2
Pelham P	1928	3	1	1	0	4	1
Penny A	1925	1	0			1	0
Pentecost A	1972	39 (1)	11	21	7	60 (1)	18
People H	1924	4	1	5	1	9	2
Perrett G.R	1932-34	28	8	16	6	44	14
Perry A	1992	1 (9)	1	1 (1)	0	2 (10)	1
Perry F.C	1914	1	0			1	0
Perry A.O	1909-12	17	1	7	0	24	1
Perryman J	1926-30	64	60	34	32	98	92
Peters C.W	1924	2	0	1	0	3	0
Peters R	1993	7	0			7	0
Petitt D	1970-71	11 (1)	0	10 (1)	0	21 (2)	0
Petitt T	1965-67	31	9	5	2	36	11
Peto W	1899			1	0	1	0
Pickerman	1911			1	0	1	0
Pinhorn P	1951-53	22	4	7	1	29	5
Pink F	1946-54	155	72	55	25	210	97
Pinnock G	1940			1	3	1	3
Pipe D	1986	6	0	1	0	7	0
Pitts H	1932	1	0			1	0
Pitts R	1938	1	0			1	0
Phelan A	1952-53	3	2	1	0	4	2
Phillips	1976	1	0			1	0
Phillips A	1985	5	0			5	0
Phillips G	1980	1	0			1	0
Phillips H.J	1914,20-21	30	0	6	0	36	0

PLAYER	SEASONS	LEAGUE APPS(sub)	GOALS	CUPS APPS(sub)	GOALS	TOTAL APPS(sub)	GOALS
Plank C	1959	1	0			1	0
Pollard O	1911	1	1			1	1
Pollard R	1977-78	17 (1)	0	3	0	20 (3)	0
Pook R	1906-08	40	16	26	9	66	25
Pook S	1906	2	0	1	0	3	0
Poole R	1975-78	91 (1)	3	29 (1)	0	120 (2)	3
Pope C	1926-27	29	1	22	0	51	1
Pope S	1991	4	1	2	0	6	1
Popham B.G	1896-99	34	2	7	0	41	2
Porter T	1981	28	0	7	0	35	0
Potts A	1929	10	1	1	0	11	1
Potter D	1938-40,46	25	3	8	1	33	4
Povey R	1965-66,68-70	74 (1)	5	28	3	102 (1)	8
Powell	1968	0 (1)	0			0 (1)	0
Pratt A	1954-56,59-60	31	0	10	0	41	0
Pratt B	1990-92	80 (5)	17	43	3	123 (5)	20
Preskett F	1935-36	6	1	12	1	18	2
Preskett J	1946-49	100	11	31	6	131	17
Prestoe G	1932	3	2	1	1	4	3
Preston A	1905	2	0			2	0
Preston M	1977-80	119	8	55	3	174	11
Prett J	1949	4	1			4	1
Price W.J	1926-28	47	39	27	27	74	66
Probert A	1985-87	57 (1)	2	20 (1)	0	77 (2)	2
Puckett D	1993-94	42 (18)	14	13 (3)	3	55 (21)	17
Pugh H.J	1931			1	0	1	0
Pullen J	1940			1	0	1	0
Pullen W	1914	6	0	6	0	12	0
Q							
Quinton F.P	1896-03	67	31	20	10	87	41
Quirk T	1949,54-55	11	1	6	1	17	2
R							
Raggett A	1906	1	0			1	0
Rattray K	1994-95	45 (13)	9	13 (9)	5	58 (22)	14
Ravenscroft C	1995	0 (2)	0	2	0	2 (2)	0
Rayer R.A	1920-21	12	0	5	0	17	0
Read N	1951-53	13	0	4	0	17	0
Read T	1991-92,94-95	40 (3)	0	21	0	61 (3)	0
Redican T	1956	21	6	9	3	30	9
Reed M	1983-84	3	0	1	0	4	0
Reed T.W	1921	3	1	1	1	4	2
Reeder F	1947-48	5	3	1	0	6	3
Reeve E	1983	8	1	2	1	10	2
Reeves N	1983	9	0	1	0	10	0
Reeves R	1939-40,46-52	124	35	43	18	167	53
Reeves T	1977	0 (1)	0			0 (1)	0
Reid A.E	1898	5	2	5	1	10	3
Reynolds V	1960,74-75	58 (1)	11	12	4	70 (1)	15
Rhodes L	1983	2	0			2	0
Richardson D	1965-67	15 (1)	1	7	1	22 (1)	2
Richardson H	1985	16	0	11	0	27	0
Richardson Jim	1980	7	1			7	1
Richardson Jhn	1982,87-89	79 (6)	9	33 (1)	5	112 (7)	14
Richardson P	1985	15	6			15	6
Richardson S	1922	1	0	1	0	2	0
Richmond A	1911-12	2	0	1	0	3	0
Ricketts S	1947,49	2	1	1	1	3	2
Rickwood J.T	1939			1	0	1	0
Ridler H.B	1886-02	50	2	15	1	65	3
Ridler E.H	1896-98	28	12	7	0	35	12
Ritchie A	1986	3	1	1 (1)	0	4 (1)	1
Ritchie J	1979	16	1			16	1
Roberts A	1974-77	101 (5)	10	43 (3)	6	144 (8)	16

PLAYER	SEASONS	LEAGUE APPS(sub)	GOALS	CUPS APPS(sub)	GOALS	TOTAL APPS(sub)	GOALS
Roberts B	1976	8	0	2	1	10	1
Roberts B	1988	7	3	1	0	8	3
Roberts D	1978	7 (3)	2	2 (2)	1	9 (5)	3
Roberts K	1985	5	0	1	0	6	0
Roberts W	1932	1	0			1	0
Robbins M	1963	2	0	1	0	3	0
Robins R.W.V	1934	1	0			1	0
Robinson A	1961	2	0			2	0
Robinson N	1933	1	0			1	0
Robson P	1971	9 (1)	0	2	0	11 (1)	0
Roffe G	1993	2	0			2	0
Rogers A	1946	2	0			2	0
Rogers D	1914	1	1			1	1
Rolls E.A	1923	2	0	2	1	4	1
Rolph G	1980	22	4	8 (2)	4	30 (2)	8
Rooke R	1933	12	13	13	16	25	29
Roope G	1981	3	0			3	0
Rose H	1965-68	20	0	5	0	25	0
Rosser M	1975-76	34 (2)	1	11 (2)	0	45 (4)	1
Rowe E	1993	1	0			1	0
Rudd N	1983	4 (2)	1	3 (1)	0	7 (3)	1
Rundle E	1947	1	0			1	0
Russell A	1990-92	59 (2)	3	39 (3)	5	98 (5)	8
Russell R.J	1914	14	1	1	0	15	1
Ryan J	1982-84	16	2	3	0	19	2
Ryde	1901	1	0			1	0
S							
Sabourn N	1987	1 (1)	0			1 (1)	0
Salisbury C.S	1904-14,20-22	127	40	91	25	218	65
Salisbury H.C	1939	4	2			4	2
Sayers L	1956	1	0			1	0
Schofield D	1939	1	0	1	0	2	0
Scott K	1967-68	26	0	13 (1)	2	39 (1)	2
Scott R.N	1932	2	0	1	2	3	2
Scrivens S	1981-83	44 (4)	8	19	3	63 (4)	11
Seaman C	1946,50-51	3	0	3	0	6	0
Searle E	1935-39,46	108	6	46	2	154	8
Searle W	1934-35,37-38	26	0	9	0	35	0
Seddon C	1930-31	42	0	12	0	54	0
Senior T	1993	26 (5)	11	7 (2)	2	33 (7)	13
Sergeant C	1897	3	2			3	2
Sewell B	1927	5	0	8	1	13	1
Sex R	1928	1	0			1	0
Sexton A	1967-71	103	0	50	1	153	1
Shakespeare H	1921	2	0			2	0
Sharman S	1896,99-01	17	1	1	0	18	1
Sharpe M	1958	3	3			3	3
Shaw H	1930	2	0			2	0
Shaw J	1922-26	103	4	50	2	153	6
Shaw W	1966-67	2 (1)	0			2 (1)	0
Shepherd J	1939	8	4	5	1	13	5
Shepherd N	1987			0 (1)	0	0 (1)	0
Sherlock S	1926-29	24	1	9	0	33	1
Sherwood W.A	1921	1	0			1	0
Shires H.T	1933-34	8	0	1	0	9	0
Shodiende P	1982	2 (2)	0			2 (2)	0
Shoesmith C	1907-12	82	14	68	9	150	23
Shrieves T	1978-79	4 (3)	0			4 (3)	0
Shrubb P	1988-89	58 (1)	4	31	0	89 (1)	4
Shurville H	1910	2	0			2	0
Short W.J	1947-54	96	28	34	11	130	39
Simmonds E	1928,33	28	0	15	0	43	0
Simmonds G	1928	1	0			1	0
Simmons C	1936	2	0			2	0

PLAYER	SEASONS	LEAGUE APPS(sub)	GOALS	CUPS APPS(sub)	GOALS	TOTAL APPS(sub)	GOALS
Simmons M	1982,84	2	0			2	0
Sims T	1983	6	1			6	1
Sinclair F	1900,03	11	0	4	0	15	0
Skeet W.C	1909-14	27	0	18	0	45	0
Skelton W.E	1928	8	0	6	0	14	0
Skinner N	1976	8 (1)	1	1 (1)	1	9 (2)	2
Skipsey A	1931	3	2			3	2
Slater A	1898-00	23	14	9	3	32	17
Slater M	1968	6	0	1	0	7	0
Sleet A	1927,30	8	0	9	0	17	0
Small H.W	1936,38-40	32	1	9	0	41	1
Small G	1936-37	25	0	12	0	37	0
Smart R	1991	10	7			10	7
Smith C	1982	34	1	8	1	42	2
Smith D.A	1946-52	83	22	30	6	113	28
Smith F	1952	3	0			3	0
Smith F.E	1911-12,14,20-22	17	0	6	0	23	0
Smith G	1920-21	22	1	4	0	26	1
Smith M	1992	0 (4)	0	2 (2)	2	2 (6)	2
Smith P	1950	7	0	2	0	9	0
Smith R	1925	2	0	7	4	9	4
Smith T	1914	1	0	1	0	2	0
Smith T	1970-73	115 (2)	5	56	6	171 (2)	11
Smith W	1921	1	0			1	0
Smith W	1955	1	0			1	0
Smithers E	1939			1	0	1	0
Solomon G	1988			1	0	1	0
Soper W.G	1929	5	4			5	4
Sorenson M	1983	17	1	7	0	24	1
Souter G	1946,48	7	0	2	0	9	0
Soughton W	1913	4	3			4	3
Spittle P	1976,80	8	0	4	0	12	0
Spooner B	1913	1	0	1	0	2	0
Stagg J	1984	11	0	3	0	14	0
Stagg W	1984	0 (1)	0			0 (1)	0
Stansbie R	1962	3	0			3	0
Stare D	1901-02,04	3	1			3	1
Stebbings F.C	1925	1	0			1	0
Stedman M	1957-59	11	1	1	0	12	1
Steel D	1982	2 (1)	0			2 (1)	0
Steele S	1993-95	90 (13)	13	35	9	125 (13)	22
Steeple D	1928	1	0			1	0
Steer R	1974-76,78-79,85	154 (6)	7	56 (4)	4	210 (10)	11
Steer	1903	1	0			1	0
Stevens B	1959	1	0			1	0
Stevens D	1935-40,46-50	154	1	56	1	210	2
Stevens F	1905	1	0			1	0
Stevens W	1930	5	0	7	3	12	3
Stevenson R	1907-10	32	0	29	0	61	0
Steward C	1913	1	0			1	0
Stewart A	1902	2	0			2	0
Still F.M	1912-13	1	0	1	0	2	0
Stillwell C	1982	7	0	2	0	9	0
Stillwell I	1985-86	21	0	4	0	25	0
Stimson R.J	1923-26,29	38	6	12	14	50	20
Stocker A	1939-40,46-47	22	3	2	1	24	4
Stocker L	1930	1	0			1	0
Stockholm T	1965	1	0			1	0
Stockley F	1931,35,37	45	18	26	12	71	30
Stocks J	1922-23	42	0	25	0	67	0
Stone L.G	1937-39	43	38	12	4	55	42
Stratford M	1976-77	34 (1)	0	14	0	48 (1)	0
Stratford P	1982	6	0			6	0
Stratton Reg	1956-59	86	39	37	25	123	64

PLAYER	SEASONS	LEAGUE APPS(sub)	GOALS	CUPS APPS(sub)	GOALS	TOTAL APPS(sub)	GOALS
Stratton Bob	1955,58	18	0	4	0	22	0
Stubbs F.R	1932	2	0			2	0
Strudwick A	1903	3	0			3	0
Sturt F	1920-21	3	0			3	0
Sturt J	1920-22	7	0	4	4	11	4
Sturt S	1924-27,31-35, 37,39	91	0	39	0	130	0
Stygal E	1936-37	16	5	6	1	22	6
St.Hilaire M	1990	1 (1)	0			1 (1)	0
Sullivan L	1925-26	4	0			4	0
Sullivan N	1980	2	0	1	0	3	0
Summerfield H	1920-21	2	0			2	0
Sumners H	1926	1	0			1	0
Surey J	1985-86	25 (2)	3	5 (1)	0	30 (3)	3
Swain M	1983			2	0	2	0
Swallow H	1910-14	68	31	43	23	111	54
Swift K	1994	2 (2)	0	0 (2)	0	2 (4)	0
Symonds J	1933	1	0			1	0
T							
Tabert J.K	1930	3	0	1	0	4	0
Tambaro P	1983	4 (1)	0	1	1	5 (1)	1
Tann R.H	1931	1	0			1	0
Tanner R	1952	4	0	1	0	5	0
Taylor A.V	1913	3	0			3	0
Taylor C.H	1897-98	7	0			7	0
Taylor D	1953	1	0	1	0	2	0
Taylor J.H	1940	1	0			1	0
Taylor P	1961	5	0	1	0	6	0
Taylor R	1958-60	35	2	19	0	54	2
Teague A	1910			1	0	1	0
Tenkorang R	1988	6	0	7	0	13	0
Terry R	1982	5 (8)	2	1 (2)	0	6 (10)	2
Thayers H.H	1922-29	128	32	55	26	183	58
Thomas E.A	1925	11	13	3	3	14	16
Thomas W.J	1935			1	0	1	0
Thorne-Thorne R.J	1921-24,26-27	16	4	8	1	24	5
Threadgold W	1926			1	0	1	0
Threlkeld J	1961-64	16	5	6	1	22	6
Tierling L	1995	22 (5)	0	10	1	32 (5)	1
Timothy D	1995	1 (1)	0	1	0	2 (1)	0
Tindall E	1962-69	192 (2)	105	75	29	267 (2)	134
Tilley J	1922-24	14	4	9	3	23	7
Tilley J	1934,39	2	0			2	0
Todd E.J	1932	1	0			1	0
Tolfree H	1904-06	13	0	1	0	14	0
Tomlinson C	1935			1	0	1	0
Tomlinson R	1909,11-12	6	1	1	0	7	1
Tompkins J	1931-32	23	3	11	0	34	3
Towers P	1948,50-52	51	0	21	0	72	0
Trainer	1905	1	0			1	0
Tranter G	1963	1	0	1	0	2	0
Trevaskis M	1967-68	13 (1)	3	4	0	17 (1)	3
Triggs R.W	1931	2	0			2	0
Trinder D	1951			1	0	1	0
Tristram H	1939	4	0			4	0
Tucker M	1994-95	70	3	27	3	97	6
Tunnell A	1958	2	0	1	0	3	0
Turkington M	1983	5 (1)	0	1	0	6 (1)	0
Turner A	1976-78,85	46 (3)	0	21	0	67 (3)	0
Turner D	1983	1	0			1	0
Turner E.C	1930-32	3	0	1	0	4	0
Turner G.F	1922-30	181	4	91	4	272	8
Turner H.E	1931-34	81	0	44	0	125	0
Turner K	1956-64	204	1	75	0	279	1

PLAYER	SEASONS	LEAGUE APPS(sub)	GOALS	CUPS APPS(sub)	GOALS	TOTAL APPS(sub)	GOALS
Twine F	1927			1	0	1	0
Twitchen P	1962	5	1	1	0	6	1
U							
Udal G	1936			1	0	1	0
Udal P	1932-34	13	1	4	2	17	3
Ugle T	1947	1	0			1	0
Underwood R	1974	39	0	20	0	59	0
Undery H.E	1923	1	0			1	0
Upton B	1962-63	24	9	7	6	31	15
Urpeth L.W	1923-26,28	50	5	21	1	71	6
Urquhart H	1946	2	0	1	0	3	0
Urquhart W	1936	3	0			3	0
V							
Van den Berg H	1971-73	5 (1)	0	4 (3)	0	9 (4)	0
Varney G	1984-85	33	0	6	0	39	0
Viercant J	1929	1	0			1	0
Vincent E	1922,24,26	3	0	2	0	5	0
Vincent J	1932	2	0			2	0
Vincent R	1976	18	0	4	0	22	0
Vines F	1992	9 (2)	3			9 (2)	3
Viney T	1905			2	2	2	2
Voice	1900	1	0			1	0
Vooght A	1967-70	21 (2)	6	5 (1)	1	26 (3)	7
W							
Wakeley F	1920	8	6	1	0	9	6
Walker C	1994-95	75 (1)	35	30	13	105 (1)	48
Walker C	1923	3	2	1	1	4	3
Walker E.A	1939-40,46	18	2	5	2	23	4
Walker W.H	1900-04	38	0	11	1	49	1
Walkes R	1992	3 (2)	1			3 (2)	1
Wallace C	1989	1	0			1	0
Wallace L.M	1947-48,50	40	13	10	1	50	14
Wallage D	1938-39	22	0	4	0	26	0
Waller V	1926	1	0	4	0	5	0
Wallington N	1963-66	12	0	7	0	19	0
Wallis W	1924-27	31	1	19	2	50	3
Walters G	1926	1	0			1	0
Walton S	1986	7	0			7	0
Wand F	1929			1	0	1	0
Ward J	1911	3	0			3	0
Wardleworth J	1948-49	5	3	3	0	8	3
Ware W.J	1927	1	0			1	0
Warman D	1946	1	0			1	0
Warner M	1905,09-12	34	0	28	0	62	0
Warnes G.E	1930,34	3	0			3	0
Warnes W.H	1930-32	47	29	30	17	77	46
Warren R	1949-52	11	0	9	0	20	0
Wastell J	1951	15	0	4	0	19	0
Waterman J	1984	1	0			1	0
Waters A.R	1906-07,09,11	12	1			12	1
Waters J.T	1939	1	0			1	0
Waters W	1907			1	0	1	0
Watson C	1906	1	2	1	0	2	2
Watson D	1985-86	25 (1)	1	7	2	32 (1)	3
Watson I	1985	18	0	10 (1)	0	28 (1)	0
Watson J	1950	1	0			1	0
Watson R	1931	8	3	4	2	12	5
Waughman T	1967-69,75	97	25	40	14	137	39
Weaver	1899	5	1	1	0	6	1
Webb A	1972	1	0	1	0	2	0
Webb A	1983	5	0	4	0	9	0
Webb K	1952	1	0			1	0
Webster A	1897	3	0			3	0

SEASON 1897-1898

WEST SURREY LEAGUE

Date	Venue	Opponents	Result		Atten-dance	Taylor C.H.	Eyre, E.B.	Kemp, F.	Monk, W.H.	Popham, B.G.	Ridler, H.B.	Quinton, F.P.	Stansfield, A.	Slater, A.	Allen, P.K.	Ridler, E.H.	Knight, H.	Brice, A.	Dalton, P.	Mossop, S.	Parker, B.	Reid, A.E.	Farrow, E.
2 Oct	(A)	Godalming	W	4-2		1	2	3	4	5	6	7	9[2]	10	11[1]	8[1]							
9 Oct	(H)	Addlestone	W	6-1		1	2	3	4	5[1]	6	7	9[3]	10	11[1]	8[1]							
30 Oct	(H)	Guildford	L	1-5		1	3	2	4	5	6	7[1]	9[1]	10	11	8							
13 Nov	(H)	Chertsey o.g.	W	9-2				2		4	6	7[4]	9[1]	10[3]	11	1	3	5	8				
27 Nov	(H)	Walton	W	12-0			3	2[1]		4	6[1]	7[3]		10[1]	9[3]	1		5	8[3]	11			
11 Dec	(A)	Walton o.g.	W	13-0		1		2		4	3	7	9[5]	10[2]	6			5[1]	8[3]	11[1]			
5 Feb	(A)	Chertsey o.g.	W	4-0			2	3	4		6	8	9	10[3]				5	7		1	11	
12 Feb	(H)	Godalming	W	4-2			2	3		4	6	10[1]	9[1]	7		1		5	11			8[2]	
26 Feb	(A)	Guildford	W	1-0	2,000		3	2		4	6	7	9	10		1		5	8[1]			11	
19 Mar	(A)	Addlestone	W	3-1					7[1]	4	6	8[1]		11[1]			2	5	3	10		1	9
30 Mar	(Godalming)	Rest of League	L	0-3			2		4		6	8	9	10		1		5	3	7		11	
SURREY SENIOR CUP																							
6 Nov	1st R (H)	Kenley	W	3-0				2		4	6	7	8	10[2]	11	1	3	5	9[1]				
4 Dec	2nd R (H)	Guys Hospital	W	2-1			3	2		4	6	7	9	10	11	1		5[1]	8[1]				
22 Jan	3rd R (A)	Croydon Park	D	1-1			2	3		4	5[1]	10	9	7		1		6	11			8	
29 Jan	Rep (H)	Croydon Park	W	4-1			2	3		4	5	10	9[2]	7[1]		1		6	11			8	
19-Feb	S-F	(W'bridge) Surbiton Hill	D	0-0	1,500		3	2		4	6	7	9	10		1		5	8			11	
12-Mar	Rep	(W'bridge) Surbiton Hill	W	1-0				2	10	5	6	11	9	8		1		4	3			7[1]	
26-Mar	F	(Guildford) Weybridge	L	0-4					4	3	6	7	9	10		1		5	2			11	8
TOTAL APPEARANCES						**4**	**12**	**15**	**8**	**16**	**18**	**18**	**16**	**18**	**8**	**15**	**3**	**15**	**15**	**4**	**1**	**10**	**2**
GOALS SCORED								**1**	**1**	**1**	**2**	**10**	**14**	**13**	**5**	**2**		**2**	**9**	**1**		**3**	

SEASON 1898-1899

EAST & WEST SURREY LEAGUE

Date	Venue	Opponents	Result		Atten-dance	Popham, B.G.	Knight, H.	Eyre, E.B.	Gibbons, J.	Kemp, F.	Ridler, H.B.	Quinton, F.P.	Denmead, H.	Slater, A.	Butt, F.	Denny, T.	Shipton, F.	Gillingham, A.E.	Monk, W.H.	Weaver	Parker, B.	Sharman, S.	Harwar	Hutton, G.	Gloster, G.	Duncan, J	Lemon	Mariage	Cox, C.	Hawkins, G.F.	Mossop, S.	Farrow, E.	Jones	Peto, W.	Hunt, H.
1 Oct	(A)	Addlestone	W	3-1		1	2	3	4[1]	5	6	7	8	9[1]	10[1]	11																			
8 Oct	(H)	Godalming	L	0-3		1	2	3	8	5	6	7		9	10	11	4																		
15 Oct	(A)	Dorking	W	6-2		4	2	3	1	9[1]		10[1]		8[2]	7[1]	11	5[1]	6																	
5 Nov	(A)	Guildford	L	1-6		11		3	1	2	6	7		10	9[1]		5		4	8															
12 Nov	(A)	Kingston	L	2-4		10		3	4	2					9	8	5[1]				1	6	7	11[1]											
3 Dec	(A)	Camberley	L	1-3				2						8	7	6						5	3		1	4	9[1]	10	11						
17 Dec	(H)	Addlestone	L	0-5				3		9	6	7		10	11							5		1				8	4	2					
7 Jan	(A)	Godalming	L	2-5				3			6				10				4			5		1		8[1]	9[1]		7	2	11				
14 Jan	(H)	Dorking	W	3-1				3			6				10					8[1]		5[1]		1			9[1]		7	2	11	4			
28 Jan	(A)	Guildford	D	1-1				3			6			10	7					8		5		1		4	9[1]			2	11				
4 Mar	(H)	Camberley	L	0-1		9		2			6			11	8					10		5		1		4			7	3					
18 Mar	(A)	Kingston	L	0-3				3				7		10	8					9	1	5		11		4				2			6		
SURREY SENIOR CUP																																			
29 Oct	1st R (H)	Townley Park	L	1-2			2	3	4	9[1]	6			10	11	8	5																	1	7
SURREY CHARITY SHIELD																																			
4 Feb	1st R (A)	Guildford	L	1-4				3			6	7		10	11					8		5		1		4	9			2[1]					
TOTAL APPEARANCES						**6**	**4**	**14**	**6**	**7**	**10**	**7**	**1**	**11**	**14**	**6**	**5**	**1**	**2**	**6**	**2**	**9**	**2**	**8**	**1**	**6**	**5**	**2**	**5**	**7**	**3**	**1**	**1**	**1**	**1**
GOALS SCORED									**1**	**2**		**1**		**3**	**3**		**2**			**1**		**1**		**1**		**1**	**4**								

WEST SURREY LEAGUE

SEASON 1895-1896

Date	Venue	Opponents	Result		Atten-dance	Ridler, E.H.	Barkshire, C.	Eyre, E.B.	Sharman, S	Popham, B.G.	Ridler, H.B.	Bromfield, C.J.	Duffett, F.	Allen, P.K.	Atkinson, S.J.	Quinton, F.P.	Inwood, E.	Mossop, S.S.	Heane, F.	Knight, H.	Monk, W.H.	Stansfield, A.	Butt, F.	Wendover, E.	
5 Oct	(A)	Guildford	D	0-0		1	2	3	4	5	6	7	8	9	10	11									
12 Oct	(H)	Addlestone	W	2-1		1	2		8	5	6		3	7[1]	4	11	9[1]	10							
26 Oct	(A)	Walton	W	5-1		1			2	5	6	7[1]	3		4[1]	10[1]	9[2]	11	8						
30 Nov	(H)	Guildford o.g.	W	4-3		1		2	9	5	6	11	3	10[1]	4	7[1]		8[1]							
7 Dec	(A)	Addlestone	L	0-2		1		2	4	5	6			11		7	9	8		3					*sub played at No. 10*
18 Jan	(H)	Dorking	W	4-0		1	2			5	4		10[2]	11		7[1]		8		3	6	9[1]			
1 Feb	(H)	Walton	W	1-0		9	1	2		5	4		10[1]	11		7		8		3	6				
8 Feb	(H)	Godalming	2 points awarded to Woking - Godalming did not turn up																						
14 Mar	(A)	Dorking	W	1-0	600	1	3	2		5	4		11	10		7[1]		8			6		9		
28 Mar	(A)	Godalming	D	2-2		1		2		5	4		9	10		7[2]	8	11		3	6				
18 Apr		Rest of League	W	3-1		8[2]				5	6		3	10		7	1	11		2	4			9[1]	
Appearances						**10**	**5**	**6**	**5**	**10**	**10**	**3**	**9**	**9**	**4**	**10**	**5**	**9**	**1**	**5**	**5**	**1**	**1**	**1**	
Goals Scored						**2**						**1**	**3**	**2**	**1**	**6**	**3**	**1**				**1**		**1**	

WEST SURREY LEAGUE

SEASON 1896-1897

Date	Venue	Opponents	Result		Atten-dance	Inwood, E.	Eyre, E.B.	Knight, H.	Ridler, H.B.	Popham, B.G.	Monk, W.H.	Quinton, F.P.	Ridler, E.H.	Denny, T.	Allen, P.K.	Mossop, S.S.	Hutton, P.	Kemp, F.J.	Webster, A.	Sergeant, C.	Taylor, C.H.	
26 Sep	(A)	Godalming	W	2-1		1	2	3	4	5	6	7	8[1]	9[1]	10	11						
3 Oct	(H)	Addlestone	D	2-2		1	3	2	6	5	4	7	8[1]	9	11		10[1]					
10 Oct	(H)	Guildford	L	0-4		1		2	4	5	6	7	8	9	11		10	3				
31 Oct	(H)	Dorking	W	3-0				3	6	5[1]	4	7[1]	8[1]	9	11		10	2	1			
14 Nov	(A)	Walton	W	5-2				3	6	5	4	7[1]	8[2]	9[1]	11		10[1]	2	1			
28 Nov	(A)	Addlestone	W	3-0				3	6	5		7[1]	8[2]	9	11		10	2	1	4		
5 Dec	(H)	Walton	W	6-0								7[1]	8[1]	9	11[1]		10[3]		1			*Rest of team untraced*
6 Feb	(H)	Godalming	W	6-1			3	2	4	5		11	10	9[1]	7[3]		8[2]	6			1	
20 Feb	(A)	Guildford	L	1-4			3	2	6	5		7[1]	8	9	11		10			4	1	
27 Feb	(A)	Dorking	W	3-2			3	2	6	5	4		8	9[1]	11		10			7[2]	1	
Appearances						**3**	**5**	**9**	**9**	**9**	**6**	**9**	**10**	**10**	**10**	**1**	**9**	**5**	**4**	**3**	**3**	
Goals Scored										**1**		**5**	**8**	**4**	**4**		**7**			**2**		

PLAYER	SEASONS	LEAGUE APPS(sub)	GOALS	CUPS APPS(sub)	GOALS	TOTAL APPS(sub)	GOALS
Weedon	1911			1	0	1	0
Welland A	1948-57	170	46	64	20	234	66
Weller C.B	1937-38	27	5	10	1	37	6
Wells	1929	4	1	1	0	5	1
Wendover E.S	1896	1	1			1	1
Westwood F.W	1928-29	6	0	1	0	7	0
West G	1938	1	0			1	0
West W.P	1934-39,46-48	92	0	43	0	135	0
Wharton W	1926	8	0	1	0	9	0
Whatford M	1974-78	152	7	50	3	202	10
Whatley I	1931	1	0			1	0
Wheatcroft J	1926	18	8	6	6	24	14
Wheatley A	1973	0 (1)	0			0 (1)	0
Wheatley E	1927-29	56	14	31	9	87	23
Whelan A	1984	11 (1)	0	1	0	12 (1)	0
White C	1992	0 (1)	0	1	1	1 (1)	1
White J	1949,53	7	0	4	0	11	0
White T	1904			1	0	1	0
White W.J	1927-28	4	1	1	0	5	1
Whitton J	1953	7	4	3	1	10	5
Widmore H	1936	6	4	5	6	11	10
Wigley J	1965	1	0			1	0
Wilde M	1985	2	0	0 (1)	0	2 (1)	0
Wiley A	1903-04	7	0	5	0	12	0
Wiles W	1948-53	127	100	46	33	173	133
Wilmot C	1983			2	0	2	0
Williams C	1959-60	1	0	1	1	2	1
Williams P	1984	37	8	6	1	43	9
Williams R	1922	2	0			2	0
Williams R	1962-63	33	2	6	2	39	4
Williams S	1968	9	0	5	0	14	0
Wills A	1927-29	18	4	1	0	19	4
Wiltshire B	1963	1	0			1	0
Wiltshire T	1974	5 (1)	0	3 (1)	0	8 (2)	0
Withers E.V	1922-23,25	27	11	12	6	39	17
Withers F.R	1901	3	0			3	0
Wonham A	1982-83	5 (3)	0	2 (2)	1	7 (5)	1
Wood G	1966	35	6	14	3	49	9
Woodards C	1927	3	2			3	2
Woodbridge S	1985	3	0			3	0
Woodfield V	1955	3	2	1	0	4	2
Woodley D	1986	16	5	3	2	19	7
Woods S	1962-68	188	34	61	7	249	41
Woodward R.W	1912	1	0			1	0
Woolen M	1971	5	0	4	2	9	2
Wooler R	1964-66,68-70	35 (3)	5	9 (2)	0	44 (5)	5
Wooler P	1990	1	0			1	0
Woozley B	1975	10	0	3	0	13	0
Worsfold O	1906	2	0			2	0
Worsfold T	1983-85,89-91	92 (9)	24	26 (5)	8	118 (14)	32
Worsley D	1963	1	0			1	0
Wride E	1946-49,52	21	9			21	9
Wright W	1914,20	6	0	1	0	7	0
Wye L	1985-95	298 (9)	26	123 (5)	12	421 (14)	38
Wye S	1984-85,89-95	197 (6)	21	107	18	304 (6)	39
Y							
Yarham W.E	1913-14	15	0	13	0	28	0
Yates C	1987	8 (1)	3	2	0	10 (1)	3
Yerby D	1979-80	32 (6)	0	5	0	37 (6)	0
Youlton C	1986,88,91	41 (6)	25	10	6	51 (6)	31
Young R	1924	1	0			1	0
Z							
Zimmer A	1954-56	63	23	19	5	82	28

APPENDIX 4
APPEARANCES AND STATISTICS TABLES

Key to abbreviated information:

AB	-	Abandoned
AET	-	After extra time
Ex P	-	Extra Preliminary
F	-	Final
L	-	Leg
o.g.	-	Own goal
Pre/Prel	-	Preliminary
Q	-	Qualifying
Q-F	-	Quarter-final
R	-	Round
Rep	-	Replay
S-F	-	Semi-final
Square brackets [ ]	-	Number of goals scored
£	-	Gate receipts

SEASON 1912-1913

ISTHMIAN LEAGUE

Date	Venue	Opponents	Result	Attendance	Adams, J.C.	Layton, T.H.	Bell, A.H.	Taylor, A.V.	Crane, H.J.	Love, S.J.	Mitchell, S.H.	Swallow, H.	Harrison, H.	Bevan, A.	Salisbury, C.S.	Grove, Ar.	Bennett, H.C.	Still, F.M.	Skeet, W.C.	Kyle, J.	Lewis, L.R.	Pearce, A.V.	Yarham, W.E.	James, H.	Ford, H.	Norris, E.	Morris, A.J.	Monk, J.B.	Spooner, B.	Bedser, A.	Steward, C.	Soughton, W.	Long, C.	Clark, G.	Crick, H.E.
7 Sep	(A)	Tunbridge Wells	W 1-0		1	2	3	4	5	6[1]	7	8	9	10	11																				
14 Sep	(H)	West Norwood	W 4-2		1	2	3	4	5	6		8[2]			11	7	9[2]	10																	
21 Sep	(A)	Leytonstone	W 3-1	1,500		2	3	4	5	6		10[1]			11	7			1	8[2]	9														
19 Oct	(A)	London Caledonians	L 0-5		1	2	3		5	6		10			11	7	9			8		4													
9 Nov	(A)	West Norwood	W 2-1			2	3		5	6		10[1]				7				9	8	4	1	11[1]											
16 Nov	(H)	Leytonstone	L 0-4	1,300		2	3		5	6		10			11	7				9	8	4			1										
23 Nov	(H)	Clapton	L 0-3			2	3		5	6		10			11	7				9	8	4	1												
30 Nov	(A)	Dulwich	D 2-2	2,000			2		5	6[1]		10			11	7	9				8[1]	4	1			3									
14 Dec	(A)	Clapton	L 1-2			2	3		5	6		10(1)			11	7	9				8	4	1												
21 Dec	(H)	Nunhead	L 0-2				2		5	6	8	10				7	9					4	1	11			3								
11 Jan	(A)	Oxford	D 3-3				2		5	6		10(1)			11(1)	7				9	8(1)		1			3		4							
1 Feb	(H)	Oxford	W 3-0				3		5(2)	6		10[1]			11	7				9	8	4	1			2									
22 Feb	(H)	Dulwich	D 0-0				2		5	6		10			11	7				9		4	1			3			8						
15 Mar	(H)	Ilford	W 2-0				2		5	6		10			11	8				9[2]		4	1			3				7					
22 Mar	(A)	Shepherds Bush	W 5-1				2		5	6		10			11[1]	7				9[3]	8(1)	4	1			3									
12 Apr	(A)	Ilford	L 1-3				2		5	6		10			11	7				9[1]		4	1			3					8				
16 Apr	(H)	Shepherds Bush	D 1-1			2	3					10			11	7[1]				9		4	1			5		6				8			
19 Apr	(H)	Tunbridge Wells o.g	D 2-2				2		5	6		10			11	7				9		4	1			3						8[1]			
26 Apr	(A)	Nunhead	L 3-5				2		5	6		10				7				9[1]			1	11		3						8[2]	4		
30 Apr	(H)	London Caledonians	L 0-3				2			5		10			11					9		6	1			3				7		8	4		
F.A. CUP																																			
28 Sep	PR (H)	Cranleigh	W 5-0			2	3		5	6		10[2]			11		9[2]			7	8[1]	4	1												
12 Oct	1st Q (A)	West Norwood	W 4-1			2	3		5	6		10[2]			11	7				9	8[2]	4	1												
2 Nov	2nd Q (H)	Nunhead	L 1-2	1,500		2	3		5	6		10[1]			11		9		1	7	8	4													
F.A. AMATEUR CUP																																			
4 Jan	1st R (A)	Dulwich	L 0-5	only 10 men			2		5			10				4	9		1		8	6		11		3									
SURREY SENIOR CUP																																			
28 Dec	1st R (A)	Kingston	W 2-1	1,000		2	3		5			11[1]				7	9[1]				8	6	1					4						10	
18 Jan	2nd R (A)	Dorking AB	2-1	extra time			3		5	6		10			11[1]	7				9	8[1]	4	1										2		
25 Jan	Rep (H)	Dorking	W 3-1				2		5	6		10			11	7				9[1]	8[1]	4[1]	1			3									
15 Feb	S-F	Old Kingstonians	W 3-0				2		5	6		10[1]			11	7				9[1]	8[1]	4	1			3									
24 Mar	F	Metrogas £105	W 2-0	5,000			2		5	6		10			11[1]	7				9[1]	8	4	1			3									
SURREY CHARITY SHIELD																																			
5 Oct	1st R (H)	Camberley	W 4-0			2	3		5	6		10			11	7[1]	9[1]			8(2)		4	1												
26 Oct	2nd R (H)	Farnham	W 17-4			2			3	5		10[5]			11	7[1]	9[6]			8[2]		4[3]	1												6
8 Mar	S-F (H)	Guildford Pinks	W 7-1				3		5	6		10[1]			11[1]	7				9[4]		4	1			2[1]			8						
2 Apr	F (H)	Old Kingstonians	W 2-0	2,000			2		5	6		10[2]			11	7				9	8	4	1			3									
TOTAL APPEARANCES					**3**	**15**	**32**	**3**	**31**	**30**	**2**	**33**	**1**	**1**	**28**	**29**	**11**	**1**	**3**	**26**	**19**	**28**	**26**	**4**	**1**	**17**	**1**	**3**	**2**	**2**	**1**	**4**	**3**	**1**	**1**
GOALS SCORED									**2**	**2**		**22**			**5**	**3**	**12**			**20**	**9**	**4**		**1**		**1**						**3**			

SEASON 1911-1912

ISTHMIAN LEAGUE

Date	Venue	Opponents	Result	Atten-dance	Skeet, W.C.	Richmond, A.	Bell, A.H.	Monk, J.B.	Crane, H.J.	Johnson, L.C.	Shoesmith, C.	Woodward, R.W.	Hartley, J.	Swallow, H.	Grove, A.r	Perry, A.O.	Kyle, J.	Humphreys, A.W.	Warner, M.	Salisbury, C.S.	Alexander, S.	Love, S.J.	Adams, J.C.	Pearce, A.V.	Crick, H.E.	Smith, F.E.	Bevan, A.	Kingston, W.	Croft, S.	Mannering, E.	Still, F.M.	Long, C.	Tomlinson, R.	Long, A.W.
9 Sep	(A)	London Caledonians	D 1-1		1	2	3	4	5	6	7	8	9[1]	10	11																			
23 Sep	(A)	Ilford	L 0-4		1		3	4	5	6	7		10	11		2	8	9																
30 Sept	(A)	Dulwich	L 0-4		1		3	4	5	6	7			10			8	9	2	11														
21 Oct	(H)	Nunhead	L 4-5	1,000	1		3	4		7				10[1]			8	9[1]	2	11	5[2]	6												
28 Oct	(A)	Tunbridge Wells	D 1-1				3	4		7				10			8	9[1]	2	11	5	6	1											
4 Nov	(H)	Oxford	W 2-0	1,200			3	4		7				10			8[1]	9[1]	2	11	5	6	1											
11 Nov	(A)	Leytonstone	D 3-3				3	4	2	7				10[1]			8[2]	9		11	5	6	1											
18 Nov	(H)	Dulwich	D 1-1	850			3	4	2	7				10			8[1]	9		11	5	6	1											
2 Dec	(A)	Shepherds Bush	L 1-2		1		3	4	5	7				10			8	9[1]	2	11		6												
9 Dec	(H)	Tunbridge Wells	W 1-0	1,200	1		3	4	5	7				10			8	9[1]	2	11		6												
16 Dec	(A)	Nunhead	L 1-3				3	4	5				8	10			7[1]	9	2	11		6	1											
23 Dec	(H)	Clapton	W 2-1	1,000			3	4	5				7[1]	10	11		8	9[1]	2			6	1											
30 Dec	(A)	West Norwood	L 2-4			3	2		5				7	10[1]			8[1]	9	4	11		6	1											
17 Feb	(H)	Leytonstone	W 2-1		1		3	4	5		7			10[2]			8	9	2	11		6												
2 Mar	(A)	Oxford	W 1-0	only ten men			3				7			10	6		4	9[1]	2	11		5	1											
9 Mar	(A)	Clapton	D 3-3				3	4			7			10[2]	6		8	9	2	11[1]		5	1											
16 Mar	(H)	London Caledonians	L 2-4				3	4		6	7			10			8	9[1]	2	11[1]		5	1											
30 Mar	(H)	Ilford	W 2-1				3			6	7			8				9[1]	2	11[1]		5	1	4	10									
24 Apr	(H)	West Norwood	L 1-3				3		5		7			8				9[1]				6	1	4	11	2	10							
27 Apr	(H)	Shepherds Bush	W 8-0				3		5	11	7			8[2]					2			6	1	4	9[4]		10[2]							
F.A. CUP																																		
16 Sep	Prel (A)	Dorking	L 2-3		1		3	4	5	6	7			10[1]	8	2	9[1]			11														
F.A. AMATEUR CUP																																		
6 Jan	1st R (H)	Pokesdown	W 5-0		1		3		4	7				10			8[2]	9[1]	2	11	5[2]	6												
20 Jan	2nd R (A)	Redhill AET	W 2-1	2,000			3		5					10			8	9[1]	2	11[1]		6	1					4	7					
10 Feb	3rd R (H)	Eston United £32	L 2-4				3	4	5		7			10			8[1]	9[1]	2	11		6	1											
SURREY SENIOR CUP																																		
27 Jan	1st R (H)	Dulwich	L 1-4	1,600			3	4	5	7				10	11[1]		8		2	9			1	6										
SURREY CHARITY SHIELD																																		
14 Oct	1st R (H)	Walton	W 4-2		1		3	4	5	7				10			8[2]	9[1]	2	11	6[1]													
25 Nov	2nd R (H)	Camberley	W 4-1	900			3	4	5					10[1]			8[1]	9[2]	2			6	1							7	11			
23 Mar	S-F (A)	Guildford Pinks	D 1-1				3	4		6	7[1]			10			8	9	2	11		5	1											
13 Apr	Rep (H)	Guildford Pinks AET	D 1-1	1,600					3	4	7			10[1]			8	9	2	11	5	6	1											
17 Apr	2nd Rep (A)	Guildford Pinks	L 1-2		7						8							9			5	6	1			3	10[1]					2	4	11
OXFORD HOSPITAL CUP																																		
13 Jan	1st R (H)	Slough	L 2-3	1,200			3		5	4				10	7		8[1]	9[1]	2	11		6	1											
TOTAL APPEARANCES					**11**	**2**	**29**	**21**	**22**	**20**	**15**	**1**	**5**	**30**	**7**	**2**	**26**	**27**	**24**	**24**	**9**	**25**	**21**	**4**	**3**	**2**	**3**	**1**	**1**	**1**	**1**	**1**	**1**	**1**
GOALS SCORED											**1**		**2**	**12**	**1**		**14**	**17**		**4**	**4**				**4**		**3**							

SEASON 1910-1911

WEST SURREY LEAGUE

Date	Venue	Opponents	Result	Attendance	Skeet, W.C.	Cartwright, H.C.	Bell, A.H.	Perry, A.O.	Monk, J.B.	Johnson, L.C.	Shoesmith, C.	Crane, H.J.	Swallow, H.	Salisbury, C.S.	Adams, J.C.	Pearce, A.V.	Kyle, J.	Brooks, W.	Long, A.	Davies, G.	Ward, J.	Warner, M.	Drew	Martin, G.	Lintott, K.	Tomlinson, R.	Pollard, O.	Grove, Ar.	Smith, F.E.	Gibbs, C.	Hill, R.	Daniels, B.	Bedser, A.	Ellwood, F.	Waters, A.R.	Weedon	Pickerman	Richmond, A.	Duckworth, H.
10 Sep	(A)	Farncombe	L 1-2	10 men	1	2	3	4	5	6	7	8[1]	9	10																									
24 Sep	(H)	Old Kingstonians	D 2-2				3		5	6	7	2	10		1	4	8[1]	9[1]	11																				
15 Oct	(A)	Farnham	D 1-1				3	4	5	10	7	6			1	11	8[1]	9		2																			
22 Oct	(H)	Farnham	W 3-0				3	4	6		7	5	10	11	1		8			9[3]	2																		
5 Nov	(H)	Farncombe	W 8-1				3	4	6	11	7[1]	5	10		1		8[5]			9[2]		2																	
12 Nov	(A)	Godalming	W 1-0				3		4	6	7	5		11	1		8[1]	10		9		2																	
19 Nov	(A)	Cranleigh	D 1-1		1		3	4	6		7	5		11			8			10[1]		2	9																
26 Nov	(H)	Walton	W 5-1				3		4	6	7[1]	5	10[1]	11	1		9[2]					2		8[1]															
3 Dec	(A)	Guildford	L 0-2				3		4	6	7	5	10	11	1		9					2		8															
17 Dec	(A)	Hersham	W 2-1		1		3		4	6	7[1]	5	10[1]	11			9					2		8															
24 Dec	(A)	Walton	L 1-6		1		3		6	10	7[1]	5	11				9					2		8	4														
26 Dec	(H)	Kingston £19	W 3-0				3		4		7	5	10	9[2]	1	8[1]			11			2				6													
31 Dec	(A)	Camberley	L 4-5					2	4		7		8[2]	9[1]	1		5		11			3				6	10[1]												
25 Feb	(H)	Guildford	W 2-1				3		5	6	7		10		1	4	9		11[1]			2						8[1]											
18 Mar	(A)	Old Kingstonians	L 0-5		1			9	6		8	5	10	11								2				4		7	3										
15 Apr	(H)	Godalming	W 5-0		6						7		10[4]		1				4		3	2			5			11			8[1]	9							
17 Apr	(H)	Hersham	D 3-3								9		10[3]		1	5						2			4	6		11	3				7	8					
22 Apr	(H)	Cranleigh	W 3-1		1			2				5	10[2]						8[1]		9	3			6	4		11							7				
F.A. CUP																																							
17 Sep	Prel (H)	Hersham	D 1-1				3		5	6	7	9[1]	10	11	1	4						2										8							
Hersham scratched couldn't raise a midweek team.																																							
1 Oct	1st Q (A)	Old Kingstonians	L 2-7			4	3		5	10[2]	7	6		11	1		8	9		2																			
F.A. AMATEUR CUP																																							
7 Jan	1st R (A)	Clevedon	W 4-3				3	4	6		7	5	10[1]	9[3]	1			8	11			2																	
21 Jan	2nd R (A)	Wycombe	L 3-4	1,500			3	11	4	6	7	5	10[1]	9[2]	1		8					2																	
SURREY SENIOR CUP																																							
28 Jan	1st R (H)	Guards Depot	W 1-0				3		4	6	7	5	10	9	1		8[1]					2						11											
18 Feb	2nd R (A)	Farnham	W 2-0				3		4	6	7[1]	5	10		1	11	9[1]					2						8											
11 Mar	S-F	(Norbiton) Dulwich	W 2-1	1,600	1		3		5	7		4	10[1]	9[1]		6	8					2						11											
8 Apr	F	(G'ford) Old Kingstonians	D 0-0	2,000	1		3		6		7	5	10	9		4	8					2						11											
29 Apr	Rep	(G'ford) Old Kingstonians	L 1-2	2,000	1		3		6		7	5(1)	10	9		4	8					2						11											
SURREY CHARITY SHIELD																																							
8 Oct	1st R (H)	Walton	W 2-0				3	4	5	10	7[1]	6		11	1		8[1]	9		2																			
29 Oct	2nd R (H)	Guildford £23	D 2-2	1,000			3	4	6	10	7	5		11	1		8			9[2]		2																	
11 Feb	Rep (A)	Guildford	W 1-0				3		4	11	7	5	10	9	1		8[1]					2														6			
AET - not sure why a second replay.																																							
25 Mar	Rep (A)	Guildford	W 3-0		1			6	4		7	5[1]	10[1]	11		9	8[1]					2							3										
1 Apr	S-F	Old Kingstonians	L 0-1	2,000			3	6	4		7	5	10	11	1	9	8					2																	
OXFORD HOSPITAL CUP																																							
14 Jan	1st R (H)	Maidenhead	D 2-2	550			3		4	6	7	5	10	9[1]	1		8(1)					2						11											
4 Mar	Rep (A)	Maidenhead	L 3-4		1					6	7	4	10	11														8		9[3]							2	3	5
TOTAL APPEARANCES					**12**	**2**	**27**	**14**	**30**	**21**	**32**	**30**	**28**	**25**	**23**	**12**	**25**	**6**	**7**	**8**	**3**	**27**	**1**	**4**	**4**	**5**	**1**	**12**	**3**	**1**	**1**	**1**	**1**	**1**	**1**	**1**	**1**	**1**	**1**
GOALS SCORED										**2**	**6**	**4**	**17**	**10**		**1**	**16**	**1**	**2**	**8**				**1**			**1**	**1**		**3**	**1**								

SEASON 1909-1910

WEST SURREY LEAGUE

Date	Venue	Opponents	Result	Attendance	Skeet, W.C.	Cartwright, H.C.	Bell, A.H.	Pearce, A.V.	Day, C.W.	Crane, H.J.	Shoesmith, C.	Johnson, L.	Salisbury, C.S.	Livesey, M	Hutton, G.H.	Adams, J.C.	Perry, A.O.	Monk, J.B.	Kyle, J.	Hill, R.	Swallow, H.	O'Connor, G.	Warner, M.	Stevenson, R.	Shurville, H.	Hedgecock, F.	Champion, P.	Teague, A.	Knight, A.E.
11 Sep	(H)	Farncombe o.g.	W 4-2		1	2	3	4	5	6	7[1]	8	9[2]	10	11														
4 Dec	(A)	Cranleigh	W 2-0			2	3			6	7	10	11			1	4	5	8[2]	9									
18 Dec	(H)	Walton	W 4-0			2	3			6	7[1]	10	11			1	4	5	8[2]	9[1]									
26 Dec	(H)	Godalming	W 5-2			2	3	4		6	7	11	10[1]			1		5	8[3]	9[1]									
15 Jan	(H)	Cranleigh	W 6-0		1	2	3	4		6[1]	7	8[1]	11					5[1]	9[2]		10[1]								
29 Jan	(H)	Guildford	W 4-1	700		2[1]	3	4[1]			7	10	11			1	6	5	8[1]	9[1]									
19 Feb	(A)	Godalming	W 4-0		1	2	3	4		6		7	11[2]					5	8[1]	9[1]	10								
26 Feb	(A)	Old Kingstonians	L 0-1			2	3	6				7	11			1	4	5	8	9	10								
12 Mar	(H)	Old Kingstonians	W 3-1				3	4		6	7[1]	10[1]	11			1		5	8[1]	9		2							
28 Mar	(H)	Hersham	W 3-0	1,400				4	6		7					1			8[1]	9[1]	10[1]	3	2	5	11				
2 Apr	(A)	Hersham	L 0-2						6		7					1	4		8	9	10	3	2	5	11				
Woking couldn't fulfill their fixtures by the stipulated date.																													
F.A. CUP																													
18 Sep	Prel (H)	Godalming	W 5-0		1	2	3	4	11	6	7		10[2]					5	8[1]	9[2]									
2 Oct	1st Q (H)	Old Kingstonians	L 0-1			2	3	4		6	7		11	9				5	8	10						1			
Game awarded to Woking. Ineligible player.																													
16 Oct	2nd Q (A)	Summerstown	L 4-5	700		2	3[1]	4		6	7	11	10			1		5	8[2]	9[1]									
F.A. AMATEUR CUP																													
9 Oct	1st Q (H)	Farncombe	W 4-0		1	2	3	4		6	7		11	10				5	8[2]	9[2]									
23 Oct	2nd Q (H)	Clapham	W 3-1			2	3	4		6	7[1]	10	11			1		5	8[1]	9[1]									
6 Nov	3rd Q (A)	Farnham	W 2-0		1	2		4		6	7[1]	11	10					5	8[1]	9		3							
27 Nov	4th Q (H)	Old Kingstonians	W 5-1			2	3	4		6	7[1]	10[1]	11			1		5	8[3]	9									
8 Jan	1st R (A)	Nunhead	L 4-5	1,800		2	3	4		6	7	10	11[1]			1		5	8[2]	9[1]									
SURREY SENIOR CUP																													
22 Jan	1st R (H)	West Norwood *(played at*	D 2-2			2	3	4		6	7	10[1]	11			1		5	8	9[1]									
5 Feb	Rep (H)	West Norwood *Woking)*	W 2-0	500		2	3	4		6	7	10	11			1		5	8[1]	9[1]									
12 Feb	2nd R (H)	Kingston	W 3-0			2	3	4		6	7	10[1]	11			1		5	8[1]	9[1]									
5 Mar	S-F	(Guildford) Nunhead	D 0-0	2,000		2	3	4		6	7	10	11			1		5	8	9									
9 Apr	Rep	(Kingston) Nunhead	W 2-1	AET		2		4		6	7	10	11			1		5	8[1]	9[1]			3						
16 Apr	F	(Norbiton) Dulwich	D 0-0			2		4		6	7	10	11			1		5	8	9			3						
30 Apr	Rep	(Redhill) Dulwich	L 1-2	AET			3	4		6[1]	7	10	11			1		5	8	9			2						
SURREY CHARITY SHIELD																													
30 Oct	1st R (H)	Farnham £16	W 4-0	800		2	3	4		6	7	11	10[1]			1		5	8[1]	9[2]									
13 Nov	2nd R (H)	Walton	D 1-1		1	2	3	4		6	7	11			10			5	8	9[1]									
20 Nov	Rep (A)	Walton	L 0-2			2		4		6	7		11			1		5	8	9		3					10		
OXFORD HOSPITAL CUP																													
11 Dec	1st R (A)	Slough	W 2-1			2	3			6	7	10	11			1		5	8[2]	9								4	
19 Mar	S-F (H)	Upton Park	W 2-0				3	4		6	7[1]	11[1]				1		5	8	9	10	2							
23 Apr	F (A)	Windsor & Eton	L 0-3	2,000				4		6	7	10	11			1		5	8	9			2						3
TOTAL APPEARANCES					**7**	**26**	**25**	**28**	**4**	**28**	**30**	**26**	**28**	**3**	**2**	**24**	**5**	**29**	**31**	**30**	**6**	**6**	**6**	**2**	**2**	**1**	**1**	**1**	**1**
GOALS SCORED						**1**	**1**	**1**		**2**	**7**	**6**	**9**					**1**	**31**	**19**	**2**								

WEST SURREY LEAGUE

SEASON 1908-1909

Date	Venue	Opponents	Result	Attendance	Waters, A	Butt, Fred	Bell, A.H.	Pearce, A.V.	Monk, J.B.	Lintott, F.S.	Shoesmith, C.	Johnson, L.	Buck, F.	Crane, H.J.	Hutton, G.H.	Adams, J.C.	Stevenson, R.	Salisbury, C.S.	Kyle, J.	Archer, H.	Hill, R.	Perry, A.O.	Day, C.W.	Daniels, B.	Gorringe, S.B.	Warner, M.	Skeet, W.C.	Breach, F.	Lintott, C.W.	Tomlinson, R.	Knight, A.
12 Sep	(H)	Farncombe	W 4-3		1	2	3	4	5[1]	6	7[1]	8	9[1]	10	11[1]																
19 Sep	(H)	Farnham	D 1-1	800		8	3	4	5	6	7		9[1]		11	1	2	10													
10 Oct	(A)	Farnham	W 3-0			2	3	4	5	6	7[1]				10[1]	1		11	8[1]	9											
24 Oct	(H)	Cranleigh	W 4-3				3	4[2]	5	6	7				11	1	2			10	8[1]	9[1]									
31 Oct	(A)	Guildford *	L 2-3			10	3	4	5	6	7				11	1	2			8[2]		9									
28 Nov	(H)	Walton	W 2-1				3	4	5	6	7				11[1]	1	2		8		9[1]				10						
5 Dec	(A)	Kingston	D 2-2	1,000			3	4	5	6	7				11[1]	1	2				9[1]		8		10						
12 Dec	(A)	Farncombe	W 4-0				3	4	5	6	7					1	2				10		8[2]	9[2]	11						
26 Dec	(H)	Godalming £28	W 5-0	1,000			3	4	5	6	7			8[3]		1	2				10			9					11[2]		
2 Jan	(H)	Old Kingstonians	W 1-0				3	4	5	6	7				11	1	2				10		8	9[1]							
23 Jan	(A)	Walton	W 3-1				3	4	5	6	7			10	11	1	2						8	9[3]							
30 Jan	(A)	Cranleigh	W 4-2		11[1]		3	4	5	10	7					1	2		8[2]				6	9[1]							
13 Feb	(A)	Old Kingstonians	D 0-0				3	4	5	11	7			6		1			10				2	9	8						
20 Feb	(A)	Wimbledon	W 6-2					11	5	6	7[1]			4		1			8[1]				3	9[4]	10	2					
6 Mar	(A)	Chertsey	W 5-1					10	5	6	8[2]	7[2]		4							9[1]	11	2				1	3			
20 Mar	(H)	Guildford	W 2-1				3	4	5	6	7					1					9		2	8[2]	10				11		
27 Mar	(H)	Chertsey o.g.	W 6-0				3	4	5	6	7[1]			11		1			8[1]				2	9[3]				10			
3 Apr	(A)	Guildford	W 2-1	800		2	3	9	5	6	8			4		1		10[1]									11			7[1]	
9 Apr	(A)	Godalming	L 1-3	*only 10 men*				4	5	6	7[1]			8		1		3			10		2	9							
12 Apr	(H)	Wimbledon	D 0-0					4	5	6	7				11	1		3	8		10		2	9							
21 Apr	(H)	Kingston	L 0-6				3	4	5	6	7					1	2	11	8		10			9							
* To be replayed, Guildford played an unregistered player.																															
F.A. CUP																															
3 Oct	1st Q (A)	Summerstown	L 2-3	1,500		10	3	4		6	7				9[1]	1	5	11					8[1]			2					
F.A. AMATEUR CUP																															
9 Jan	1st R (A)	1st Bn. Leics. Regt. £19	L 1-2	1,400		3	2	4		6	7			8	11	1	5				9				10[1]						
SURREY SENIOR CUP																															
16 Jan	3rd R (A) played at Woking	Cranleigh o.g. £12	W 4-0	500			3	4		6	7				11	1	2				9		5[1]	8	10[2]						
27 Feb	4th R (H)	Guards Depot Caterham	L 0-2				3	11	5	6	7			4		1			8				2	9	10						
SURREY CHARITY SHIELD																															
17 Oct	1st R (H)	East Lancs. Regt.	L 0-2			9	3	4	5	6	7				11	1	2			10						8					
OXFORD HOSPITAL CUP																															
19 Dec	1st R (H)	Windsor & Eton	D 0-0				3	4	5	6	7				11	1	2		8		10			9							
6 Feb	Rep (A)	Windsor & Eton	D 1-1	1,000			2	4	5	6	7					1			8		10[1]			9	11						3
10 Mar	2nd Rep	(Oxford) Windsor & Eton	L 0-1				2	10	5	6	8	7				1					9		4						11		3
LYMPOSS CUP																															
28 Apr	(H)	Guildford	W 2-0				2	4	5	6	7[1]				11	1		10[1]	8		9							3			
TOTAL APPEARANCES					**2**	**8**	**26**	**30**	**27**	**30**	**30**	**3**	**2**	**11**	**16**	**28**	**16**	**8**	**12**	**4**	**17**	**3**	**16**	**16**	**10**	**3**	**2**	**3**	**3**	**1**	**2**
GOALS SCORED					**1**			**2**	**1**		**8**	**2**	**2**	**3**	**5**			**2**	**5**	**2**	**5**	**1**	**4**	**16**	**3**				**2**	**1**	

SEASON 1907-1908

WEST SURREY LEAGUE

Date	Venue	Opponents	Result	Attendance	Adams, J.C.	Butt, Fred	Bell, A.H.	Pearce, A.V.	Monk, J.B.	Lintott, F.S.	Shoesmith, C.	Kyle, J.	Salisbury, C.S.	Johnson, L.C.	Hutton, G.H.	Stevenson, R.	Pook, R.	Hedgecock, F.	Lintott, E.H.	Caldwell, H.	Booker, W.E.	Buck, F.	Harrison	Monk, H.M.	Neil	Brown
14 Dec	(H)	Walton	W 4-0		1	2	3	4	5	6	7	8[1]	9[3]	10	11											
26 Dec	(H)	Godalming	W 2-0		1	2	3	4		6	7	8	9[1]		11[1]	5	10									
28 Dec	(A)	Farncombe	W 4-1		1	2	3	4		6	7	8[2]	9[1]		11	5	10[1]									
4 Jan	(H)	Farncombe	W 1-0				3	4	5	6	7	8	11			2	10[1]	1	9							
18 Jan	(H)	Cranleigh	W 10-0		1	2	3	4	5[1]	6[1]	7[2]	8[1]			11[2]		10[1]			9[2]						
15 Feb	(H)	Chertsey	W 6-1		1		2	4	5	3	7	8[1]			11[2]		10				6	9[3]				
22 Feb	(H)	Fanham	W 3-0		1	2	3	4	5	6	7	8[2]			11		10					9[1]				
29 Feb	(A)	Walton	W 4-1		1		3	4	5	6	7	8[4]			11	2	10					9				
7 Mar	(A)	Chertsey	W 4-0		1		3	4	5	6		8[2]		7	11[1]	2	10					9[1]				
14 Mar	(A)	Cranleigh	W 6-0		1	2	3	4[1]	5	6	7	8[3]			11		10					9[2]				
28 Mar	(A)	Guildford	D 1-1		1		3	4	5	6	7	8[1]			11	2	10					9				
4 Apr	(A)	Farnham	W 7-0		1	2	3	4	5	6	7[1]	8[2]			11		10					9[4]				
17 Apr	(A)	Godalming	W 3-0	1,200	1	2	3	4	6		7				11	5	10					9[2]	8[1]			
DID NOT COMPLETE FIXTURES																										
29 Apr	(H)	Rest of League	W 1-0		1	2	3	4	6		7	8[1]			11	5	10					9				
F.A. CUP																										
5 Oct	1st Q (H)	Guildford	W 5-0	850	1	3		4		5	7	8[4]	9		11	2	10[1]							6		
19 Oct	2nd Q (H)	Nunhead	W 5-1		1	2	3	4		6	7	8[1]	9[1]		11	5	10[3]									
2 Nov	3rd Q (H)	Clapham	W 2-0	1,000	1	2	3	4		6	7	8[2]	9		11	5	10									
23 Nov	4th Q (A)	Maidstone o.g.	W 2-1	1,100	1		3	4	5	6	7	8[1]			11	2	10								9	
7 Dec	5th Q (H)	Oxford £28	D 2-2	1,200	1	7	3	4	5	6		8	9[2]		11	2	10									
12 Dec	Rep (A)	Oxford £51	W 2-1	2,500	1	7	3	4	5	6			9		11	2	10								8[2]	
11 Jan	1st R (A)	Bolton	L 0-5	15,659	1	7	3	4	5	6		8	9		11	2	10									
F.A. AMATEUR CUP																										
25 Oct	1st Q (H)	Kingston	D 0-0	1,000	1	2	3	4		6		8	10		11	5	7		9							
9 Nov	Rep (A)	Kingston	L 1-2		1	2	3	4		6	7	8	11			5	10									9[1]
SURREY SENIOR CUP																										
30 Nov	3rd R (A)	Leatherhead o.g.	W 5-0			7	2	4	5	6		8[1]	9		11[2]	3	10[1]	1								
25 Jan	4th R (A)	Dulwich	D 2-2		1	7	3	4	5	6		8[1]	9		11	2	10[1]									
1 Feb	Rep (H)	Dulwich £43	W 4-2	1,600	1	9	3	4	5	6	7	8[3]			11	2	10[1]									
21 Mar	S-F	(Guildford) Kingston	W 3-0		1	2	3	4	5	6	7	8[1]	11[1]				10					9[1]				
11 Apr	F	(Guildford) Nunhead	L 0-2	3,000	1	2	3	4	5	6	7	8			11		10					9				
SURREY CHARITY SHIELD																										
16 Nov	1st R (H)	Farnham	D 1-1		1	2	3	4		6	7	8[1]			11	5	10					9				
20 Dec	Rep (A)	Farnham	W 2-1			9	3	4	5	6	7	8[2]			11	2	10	1								
8 Feb	S-F (H)	Godalming £22	W 1-0	850	1	3		4	5[1]	6	7				11	2	10			9				8		
20 Apr	F	(Guildford) Dorking £80	W 2-1	3/4,000	1	2	3	4	6		7[1]				11	5	10			9			8[1]			
TOTAL APPEARANCES					**29**	**26**	**30**	**32**	**24**	**29**	**25**	**28**	**15**	**2**	**29**	**24**	**31**	**3**	**2**	**3**	**1**	**12**	**2**	**2**	**2**	**1**
GOALS SCORED								**1**	**2**	**1**	**4**	**37**	**9**		**8**		**10**			**2**		**14**	**2**		**2**	**1**

SEASON 1906-07

WEST SURREY LEAGUE

Date	Venue	Opponents	Result	Atten-dance	Adams, J.C.	Stevenson, R.	Bell, A.H.	Pearce, A.V.	Monk, J.B.	Lintott, F.S.	Shoesmith, C.	Pook, R.	Kyle, J.	Hutton, G.	Salisbury, C.S.	Burrows, R.	Allard, O.	Lintott, E.H.	Butt, Fred	Burrows, J.E.T.	Monk, H.	Larcombe, E.	Lintott, C.W.	Hedgecock, F.	Gammon, A.	Lewry, F.	Waters, A.R.	Walters, W.	Cottam, R.R.
6 Oct	(H)	Chertsey	W 6-1		1	2	3	4	5	6	7	8[2]	9[3]	10[1]	11														
13 Oct	(A)	Walton #	L 1-3		1	2		4	5		7	8	9	10	11[1]	3	6												
10 Nov	(H)	Walton	D 1-1		1	2	3	4	5	6	7	8	9[1]	10	11														
1 Dec	(H)	Haslemere	W 6-0		1	2	3[1]	4	5	11[1]	7	8[1]	9[2]	10[1]		6													
15 Dec	(A)	Godalming AB	D 1-1	83 mins	1	2	3	4	6		7	8	9	10[1]	11			5											
19 Jan	(H)	Kingston #	D 1-1		1	2	3[1]	4	6		7	8	9	10	11			5											
2 Feb	(H)	Farncombe	W 9-2		1		3	4	5		7[1]	10[3]		11[2]					2	6	8[1]	9[2]							
9 Feb	(A)	Kingston	W 2-0		1		3	4	5		7	10[1]	8[1]	11	9				2	6									
16 Feb	(A)	Farncombe	W 3-1		1		3	4	5	6	7	10	8	11					2				9[3]						
23 Feb	(H)	Godalming o.g	W 2-1			2		6	5	4		10	7	11[1]	9				3				8	1					
9 Mar	(A)	Godalming	D 1-1		1		3	4	5	6	7	8[1]	2	11	10							9							
13 Apr	(A)	Haslemere o.g.	W 11-1		1	2		4	5	6[1]		10[1]	8[2]		11			9[6]	3						7				
17 Apr	(H)	Kingston	L 0-1		1	2	3	4	5	6		10	8	11	9				7										
20 Apr	(A)	Walton	D 1-1		1	2	8	4	5	6	7	10			9[1]											3	11		
27 Apr	(A)	Chertsey	W 3-2		1	2	9[1]	6	5	4	7[1]	10		11[1]		8			3										
F.A. AMATEUR CUP																													
15 Sep	Ex Pr (H)	Kingston	D 1-1	1,100	1		3	10	4	6	7	8		9				5[1]										2	11
29 Sep	Rep (A)	Kingston AB ET	L 0-1	1,100	1	4	3	11	5	6	7	8	9	10												2			
3 Oct	2nd Rep	(G'ford) 'Kingston	L 2-3	400	1	4	3	11	5	6	7	8	9[1]	10[1]												2			
SURREY SENIOR CUP																													
24 Nov	3rd R (H)	Surbiton Hill	W 4-1		1	3	2	4	5	6	7[2]	8	9	10[1]	11[1]														
12 Jan	4th R (A)	Old Tiffinians	W 1-0		1	2	3	4	6		7	8	9[1]	10	11			5											
2 Mar	S-F	(G'ford) Clapham	L 0-1		1	2	3	4	6			10	7	11	9			5	8										
SURREY CHARITY SHIELD																													
17 Nov	1st R (A)	Kingston	W 2-0	500	1	2	3	4	5	6	7	8	9[1]	10	11[1]														
16 Mar	S-F (A)	Guildford	W 4-1		1	2	3	4	5	6		10[2]	8[2]	11	9				7										
1 Apr	F	(G'ford) Croydon o.g. £90	W 3-1	4,000	1	2	3	4	5	6			8[1]	11	10[1]			9	7										
TOTAL APPEARANCES					**23**	**19**	**21**	**24**	**24**	**17**	**18**	**23**	**20**	**22**	**17**	**3**	**1**	**7**	**10**	**2**	**1**	**2**	**2**	**1**	**1**	**3**	**1**	**1**	**1**
GOALS SCORED							**3**			**2**	**4**	**11**	**15**	**9**	**5**			**7**			**1**	**2**	**3**						

 # Void Games

SEASON 1905-1906

WEST SURREY LEAGUE

Date	Venue	Opponents	Result	Attendance	Davis, H.	Cottam, R.R.	Burrows, R.	Monk, J.B.	Busfield, R.	Burrows, J.E.T.	Kyle, J.	Salisbury, C.S.	Gladwin, T.	Hutton, G.	Butt, Fred	Knott, F.G.	Waters, A.	Watson, C.	Tolfree, H.	Ellwood, F.	Lintott, E.H.	Carter, S.J.	Pearce, A.V.	Lintott, F.S.	Pook, R	Lintott, C.W.	Worsfold, O.	Lintott, A.M.	Lewry, F.	Pook, S.	Lawes, T.	Langtree	Raggett, A.	Engall, E.T.	Norridge, G.	Dando, H.E.	Baldwin
21 Oct	(A)	Walton	L 2-3		1	2	3	4	5	6	7	8	9[1]	10[1]	11																						
28 Oct	(H)	Chertsey	W 3-2			5	3	4	8[1]	6	7	11	9	10[2]	2	1																					
11 Nov	(H)	Addlestone	W 3-2			5		4	3	6		11	9[1]	10	2	1	7	8[2]																			
9 Dec	(A)	Guildford	L 0-10			5	3	4	8	6		9		10	2		11		1	7																	
16 Dec	(A)	Godalming	W 1-0			2	8	4	3	6		9		10[1]					1		5	7	11														
23 Dec	(H)	Farncombe	W 6-0			2[1]		4						9[1]		1	11			6	5	7[1]	10	3	8[3]												
6 Jan	(A)	Weybridge	L 0-4	only 9 men			2					9		8			3		1			6	5	4	7												
13 Jan	(H)	Walton	W 7-0				3		2	11[1]		10[2]		9[3]			4		1		5[1]	7		6	8												
20 Jan	(A)	Chertsey	W 7-1			2		4[1]	3			10		9[4]					1		5	7	11[1]	6	8[1]												
27 Jan	(H)	Haslemere	L 2-3			5	3	4	2			10[1]		9[1]					1			7	11	6	8												
3 Feb	(A)	Addlestone	W 3-1			5	3	4	2	6		11[1]		9[1]					1			7			8	10[1]											
10 Feb	(H)	Kingston	D 3-3			5		4	2[1]	6		11		9[1]					1			7	10[1]		8		3										
3 Mar	(A)	Haslemere	L 0-4			5	3	4	2	6		11		9					1						8	10		7									
10 Mar	(H)	Guildford	D 1-1			5		4	2			11		9[1]					1			7	10		8			6	3								
17 Mar	(H)	Godalming	D 2-2			5		4	2			9[2]								10			11	1	8		7	6	3								
31 Mar	(A)	Farncombe	L 1-3			5		4	2					9[1]			11			1			10	6	8				3	7							
14 Apr	(A)	Weybridge	L 0-2					5						9			4			1	10		6	11	8				3	7	2						
21 Apr	(A)	Kingston	L 0-6	only 10 men				5	3								9			7		8		6					2		4	1	10				
F.A. CUP																																					
7 Oct	1st R (A)	New Crusaders	L 0-16			4	3		9	6	7	8		10	2					5														1	11		
F.A. AMATEUR CUP																																					
23 Sep	Prel (A)	Godalming	L 1-2		1	7	3		8[1]	6	2	9			10					11				4												5	
SURREY SENIOR CUP																																					
25 Nov	3rd R (H)	Croydon	L 1-3			5	3	4	8			9		10[1]	2	1				6		7															11
SURREY CHARITY SHIELD																																					
18 Nov	1st R (A)	Guildford	L 0-8			5		4	3	6		10	9		2	1		8												7					11		
TOTAL APPEARANCES					**2**	**18**	**12**	**18**	**19**	**12**	**4**	**18**	**4**	**18**	**8**	**5**	**8**	**2**	**10**	**9**	**5**	**11**	**10**	**10**	**12**	**2**	**2**	**3**	**5**	**3**	**2**	**1**	**1**	**1**	**2**	**1**	**1**
GOALS SCORED						**1**		**1**	**3**	**1**		**6**	**2**	**18**				**2**			**1**	**1**	**2**		**4**	**1**											

SEASON 1904-05

EAST & WEST SURREY LEAGUE

Date	Venue	Opponents	Result	Atten-dance	Knott, F.G.	Easton, F.S.	Hawkins, C.E.	Lintott, F.S.	Lintott, E.H.	Monk, J.B.	Kyle, J.	Butt, Fred	Cottam, R.R.	Hutton, G.	Firmin, C.	Salisbury, C.S.	Mossop, S.S.	Preston, A.	Warner, M.	Tolfree, H.	Heath, W.H.	Lintott, C.W.	Davis, H.	Trainer	Stevens, F.	Viney, T.
22 Oct	(H)	Guildford 'A'	W 6-3		1	2	3	4	5[2]	6	7	8	9[1]	10[2]	11[1]											
5 Nov	(H)	Kingston	W 5-3		1	5	3	6	9[2]	4	7[1]	2[1]		10	11[1]	8										
12 Nov	(A)	Farncombe o.g.	L 1-3		1	2	3	6	5	4	7	9			11	8	10									
10 Dec	(A)	Walton	W 4-2			2	3	4	5[1]	6	7	8[2]	9	10[1]	11			1								
17 Dec	(H)	Farncombe	W 2-1			2	3	4	5	6	7[1]	8	9	10[1]	11			1								
31 Dec	(H)	Godalming o.g.	W 4-0		1	2		4	5	6	7[2]	9[1]		10	11	8			3							
7 Jan	(A)	Guildford 'A'	W 10-1		1	3	5	4	9[3]	6	7[1]	2		10[3]	11	8[3]										
21 Jan	(A)	Godalming	W 3-0			2	5	4	9[1]	6	7	3		10[1]	11	8[1]				1						
28 Jan	(H)	Addlestone	W 6-0		1	3	5	4	9[1]	6	7[2]	2		10[2]	11	8[1]										
11 Feb	(A)	Kingston	D 1-1		1	3	7	6	5[1]	4	8	2	9	10	11											
18 Feb	(A)	Guildford	W 1-0		1	3		4	5	6	7[1]	2	9	10	11	8										
4 Mar	(H)	Walton	W 6-0		1	3[1]	5		9[1]	6	7	2	4	10[1]	11[2]	8[1]										
11 Mar	(H)	Guildford	W 3-0	1,200	1	3			5	6	7	2		10[1]	11	8[2]					4	9				
15 Apr	(A)	Addlestone	W 4-0			3	5	6	9	4	7			10[1]	11[1]	8[2]					2		1			
29 Apr	(H)	Rest of League	W 1-0	400	1		5			6	7	9		10[1]		8			3		4			2	11	
F.A. CUP																										
17 Sep	PR (H)	Guildford £27	W 4-1	1,150	1	2	3	4	5	6	7[2]	9[1]		8	11											10[1]
1 Oct	1st Q (H)	Croydon Wanderers	W 4-1		1	2	3	4	5[1]	6	7[2]	9		10	11											8[1]
15 Oct	2nd Q (A)	Southern United	L 1-8		1	2	3	4	5	6	7	8	9	10[1]	11											
F.A. AMATEUR CUP																										
24 Sep	PR (A)	Godalming	W 2-0		1	2[1]	3	4	5	6	8	9	7	10[1]	11											
8 Oct	1st Q (A)	Royal Engineers	W 3-1	2,000	1	2	3	4	5	6	7	8[1]	9[2]	10	11											
29 Oct	2nd Q (H)	Reigate Priory	L 0-1		1	2	3	4	5	6	7		9	10	11	8										
SURREY SENIOR CUP																										
3 Dec	1st R (H)	Reigate Priory	W 2-1		1		3	4	5	6	7	2	9[1]	10[1]	11	8										
14 Jan	4th R (A)	Dulwich	L 2-4				3	4	5	6	7[1]	2	9	10[1]	11	8				1						
SURREY CHARITY SHIELD																										
19 Nov	1st R (H)	Guildford	W 4-1		1	2	3	4	5	6	7	8[2]	9[1]		11	10[1]										
4 Feb	S-F (H)	Kingston	W 2-1	700	1	3	5	6	9	4	7[1]	2	8[1]	10	11											
18 Mar	F	Croydon £53	L 1-3	2,000	1	3	5	4	9[1]	6	7	2		10	11	8										
TOTAL APPEARANCES					**21**	**23**	**23**	**23**	**25**	**26**	**26**	**24**	**14**	**24**	**25**	**16**	**1**	**2**	**2**	**2**	**3**	**1**	**1**	**1**	**1**	**2**
GOALS SCORED						**2**			**14**		**14**	**8**	**6**	**18**	**5**	**11**										**2**

SEASON 1903-1904

EAST & WEST SURREY LEAGUE

Date	Venue	Opponents	Result	Attendance	Knott, F.G.	Hawkins, G.F	Walker, W.	Lintott, F.S.	Lintott, E.H.	Firmin, C.	Day, C.W.	Butt, Fred	Kyle, J.	Salisbury, C.S.	Hutton, G.	Tolfree, H	Wiley, A.J.	Cottam, R.R.	Brown, R.H.	Butt, Frank	Monk, J.B.	Farrow, E.	Crossley, J.	Hawkins, C.E.	Lintott, C.W.	Battrick, T.	Lawrence, L.	Heath, W.H.	Stare, D.	Graves, C.	White
26 Sep	(A)	Farncombe	W 3-2		1	2	3	4	5	6	7	8[1]	9	10[1]	11[1]																
17 Oct	(A)	Addlestone	L 1-2				3		5	6		2	8[1]		11	1	4	7	9	10											
24 Oct	(H)	Redhill	D 0-0		1		3		5	6	9	2	8		11			7		10	4										
7 Nov	(A)	Guildford	L 1-2		1		3	5	9	6		2	8[1]		11			7			4	10									
28 Nov	(A)	Walton	W 5-2				3	4	5	10	8	2	7		11[2]	1		9[3]			6										
5 Dec	(H)	Godalming	W 2-0		1		3	4	5	10		8	7[1]		11			9[1]			6		2								
12 Dec	(H)	Farncombe	W 2-1		1		3	4	5	10	8[1]	2	7[1]		11			9			6										
9 Jan	(A)	Godalming	W 5-2				3	4[1]	9[1]	10[1]	7	2	8		11[2]		1				6			5							
23 Jan	(A)	Redhill	L 0-3		1		3	4	5	10		2			11			7		8	6				9						
13 Feb	(A)	Kingston	L 1-2				3		5	11		2	7		10			9			6			4	8[1]	1					
20 Feb	(H)	Guildford	W 2-1		1		3	4	5	10		2	7		11			9[1]			6				8[1]						
27 Feb	(H)	Addlestone *	W 3-0		1		3	4	5	10[1]		2			11			9[1]			6				8[1]		7				
5 Mar	(H)	Walton	W 7-2		1		3	4	5		2	10[1]			11[1]			9[1]			6				8[4]			7			
19 Mar	(H)	Kingston 2 o.g.	W 7-0		1			6	5[2]	10	2	8	7[1]		11[1]			9[1]			4							3			
4 Apr	(H)	Addlestone	W 2-0		1			6	5	9		2			10			8[1]			4			3	7[1]				11		
		* Game replayed																													
F.A. CUP (ENGLISH CUP)																															
19 Sept	Ex P (A)	Bromley	L 0-5			2	3	5	9	6	7	10	8		11								1	4							
F.A. AMATEUR CUP																															
10 Oct	1st R (A)	Godalming	W 3-1		1		3	4	5	6		10	8[1]		11[1]			7[1]												2	9
31 Oct	2nd R (A)	Townley Park	L 0-4		1		3	4	5	10		2	8		11			9				6								7	
SURREY SENIOR CUP																															
14 Nov	2nd R (A)	Ewell	L 2-5		1		3	4	5	10		8[1]	7	11	9[1]						6		2								
SURREY CHARITY SHIELD																															
21 Nov	1st R (H)	East Sheen	W 3-0		1		3	4	5[1]	10[1]		8	7		11			9[1]			6		2								
6 Feb	S-F (A)	Guildford	W 2-1		1		3	4	5	10		2	7		11			9[2]			6				8						
23 Mar	F	(G'ford) Townley Park o.g.	W 3-2	2,000	1			4	5			2	7		11			9			6			3	10[2]					8	
		(After two periods of extra time)																													
TOTAL APPEARANCES					**17**	**2**	**19**	**19**	**22**	**20**	**8**	**22**	**18**	**2**	**22**	**2**	**2**	**18**	**1**	**3**	**17**	**2**	**4**	**5**	**8**	**1**	**1**	**2**	**1**	**3**	**1**
GOALS SCORED								**1**	**4**	**3**	**1**	**3**	**6**	**1**	**9**			**13**							**10**						

SEASON 1901-1902

WEST SURREY LEAGUE

Date	Venue	Opponents	Result	Atten-dance	Parker, B.	Dalton, E.	Hawkins, G.F.	Knight, H.	Kemp, F.J.	Lintott, F.S.	Quinton, F.P.	Lintott, E.H.	Butt, Fred	Drake, F.A.	Hutton, G.	Walker, W.	Stewart, A.	Monk, W.H.	Hamilton	Ridler, H.B.	Brooks, W.	Holdforth	Lawrence, W.	Stare, D.	Laker, E.
28 Sep	(H)	Godalming	W 2-0		1	2	3	4	5	6	7	8	9[1]	10	11[1]										
5 Oct	(A)	Guildford	L 0-2		1	3	2	4	5	6	7	8	9	10	11										
12 Oct	(H)	Addlestone	W 4-2		1	3[1]		2	4	5	7		9	10[1]	11[2]	6	8								
19 Oct	(A)	Kingston	W 4-3		1	3		2	4	6	7	8[1]	9[2]	10	11[1]	5									
16 Nov	(A)	Camberley	W 6-0		1	3	5	2		6		8[3]	9[2]	10[1]	11	4		7							
23 Nov	(H)	Brookwood	W 1-0		1	3	5	2		4		8	9	10	11[1]	6			7						
14 Dec	(A)	Godalming	W 4-0		1	3	5[1]	2			7[1]	10	9[1]	8	11[1]	4				6					
20 Dec	(H)	Guildford	L 0-2	750	1	3	5	2		4	7	8	9		11		10			6					
28 Dec	(A)	Addlestone	W 2-1			10	2			4		9[1]	6[1]			5		7		3	1	8	11		
4 Jan	(A)	Brookwood	D 1-1			3	7	2		4		9[1]	10		11	5		8		6			1		
22 Feb	(H)	Kingston	W 6-1		1	3	5	2		4	7	9[4]	8[1]		11	6		10[1]							
21 Mar	(H)	Camberley	W 5-0		1	3	5	2		4		9	10		8[2]	6		11[1]						7[1]	
SURREY SENIOR CUP																									
30 Nov	2nd R (H)	Barnes o.g.	W 4-2		1	3	5	2		4	7	8[2]	9	10	11	6[1]									
11 Jan	3rd R (A)	Redhill	W 4-1		1	3	7	2		5		9[3]	10[1]		11	4		8							6
1 Feb	4th R (A)	West Norwood	L 1-5		1	3	4	2		5	7	9[1]	8		11			10		6					
TOTAL APPEARANCES					**13**	**15**	**13**	**14**	**4**	**14**	**9**	**14**	**15**	**8**	**14**	**11**	**2**	**7**	**1**	**5**	**1**	**1**	**2**	**1**	**1**
GOALS SCORED						**1**	**1**				**1**	**16**	**9**	**2**	**8**	**1**		**2**							

SEASON 1902-1903

EAST & WEST SURREY LEAGUE

Date	Venue	Opponents	Result	Atten-dance	Strudwick, A.	Knight, H.	Dalton, E.	Lintott, F.S.	Hawkins, G.F.	Walker, W.	Monk, J.B.	Butt, Fred	Lintott, E.H.	Drake, F.A.	Sinclair, F.	Crossley, J.	Steer	Wiley, A.	Quinton, F.P.	Norridge, A.	Butt, Frank	Elphick, E.	Knott, F.G.	Parker, B.	Drake, C.E.	Hutton, G.	Hawkins, C.E.
27 Sep	(A)	Godalming	W 3-1		1	2	3	4	5	6	7	8[1]	9[1]	10												11[1]	
11 Oct	(H)	Guildford	L 1-3	750	1	2	3	4	5	6		8[1]	9	10	11				7								
18 Oct	(A)	Redhill	L 2-3		1		7	4	5	6		9	8[2]	10	3	2	11										
22 Nov	(H)	Godalming	W 3-1				2	4	5	6		8[1]	9		3			1	7			10				11[2]	
29 Nov	(A)	Addlestone	AB 3-2	83 mins			3	5	2	6		8	9[3]	10				1	7							11	4
10 Jan	(A)	Addlestone	W 3-1				3	4	5			8	9[2]	10	6	2		1	7							11[1]	
7 Feb	(H)	Kingston	W 2-0				3	4	5			8	9[1]	10	6	2		1	7	11[1]							
14 Feb	(H)	Addlestone	D 2-2				8[2]	4		6		10	9		3	2		1	7		5					11	
21 Feb	(A)	Kingston	W 3-1	(10 men)			3	5	2	4	7[1]	9	8[1]								1	6				10[1]	
14 Mar	(A)	Guildford	W 2-1				3	4	5			8	9[1]	10	6	2			7[1]				1			11	
21 Mar	(H)	Redhill	L 0-2					5	4		7	10	9	6	3	2			8				1			11	
SURREY SENIOR CUP																											
25 Oct	1st R (H)	Camberley	W 11-0				3	4	5	6		8[5]	9[3]	10[1]		2			7[2]					1		11	
15 Nov	2nd R (H)	Guildford	W 4-0				3	4	5	6		8	9[2]		2			1	7[1]			10[1]				11	
6 Dec	3rd R (H)	Ewell	W 3-2				3	4	5			8[1]	9		6	2		1	7			10				11[2]	
24 Jan	4th R (H)	Townley Park	L 1-3				3	4	5			8	9[1]	10	6	2		1	7							11	
SURREY CHARITY SHIELD																											
8 Nov	1st R (A)	Guildford	W 3-2				3	4	5	6		8[1]	9			2		1	7[1]	11						10[1]	
13 Dec	S-F	(G'ford) Weybridge	L 0-1				3	5	4			8	9		6	2		1	7						10	11	
TOTAL APPEARANCES					**3**	**2**	**16**	**17**	**16**	**10**	**3**	**17**	**17**	**10**	**12**	**11**	**1**	**10**	**14**	**2**	**2**	**4**	**2**	**1**	**1**	**14**	**1**
GOALS SCORED							**2**				**1**	**10**	**17**						**5**	**1**						**8**	

SEASON 1899-1900

EAST & WEST SURREY LEAGUE

Date	Venue	Opponents	Result	Atten-dance	Parker, B.	Hunt, H.	Eyre, E.B.	Sharman, S.	Hawkins, G.F.	Duncan, J.	Fox, C.	Quinton, F.P.	Butt, Fred	Slater, A.	Drake, F.A.	Knight, H.	Kemp, F.J.	Denny, T.	Clarke, G.	Butt, Frank	Heane, A.	Hutton, G.	Baker, J.W.	Heane, M.	Walker, W.	Ridler, H.B.	Keenan, D.	Dr. Cappe	Farrow, E.	Lintott, E.H.	Sinclair, F.	Voice	Mossop, S.S.	Drake, C.E.
30 Sep	(A)	Addlestone	L 1-5		1	2	3	4	5	6	7	8[1]	9	10	11																			
7 Oct	(H)	Godalming	D 4-4		1		3		4	5	7[1]		8[1]	10[1]	11	2	6	9[1]																
14 Oct	(A)	Dorking	W 1-0		1		3		6	5	7[1]		8	11	10	2			4	9														
18 Nov	(A)	Camberley	D 1-1		1		3		4		7		8			2	9[1]	10	5		6	11												
13 Jan	(H)	Camberley	L 0-1				3		2		7	8	11										1	4	5	6	9	10						
17 Feb	(H)	Addlestone	D 1-1				3		5		7		8			2							1	4		6	10	11[1]	9					
24 Feb	(H)	Guildford	W 1-0				3		5		7	10[1]	9			2						11	1	4		6				8				
10 Mar	(H)	Dorking	W 3-0				3		5		7	10[2]	8			2							1	4		6	9[1]	11						
17 Mar	(A)	Godalming	L 2-4				3		5		7	10[1]	8			2					4		1			6	9[1]	11						
24 Mar	(A)	Guildford	L 0-3				2		5		7	10	9								4		1						6		3	8	11	
31 Mar	(H)	Kingston	W 3-1				2		5			8[1]			10						11		1	4		6[1]	9[1]			7	3			
7 Apr	(A)	Kingston	W 3-2		1		2		5						4		6				11[1]	10					9[2]			8	3			7
SURREY SENIOR CUP																																		
11 Nov	1st R (A)	Wandsworth	D 1-1				3		4		7	8[1]	10			2			5				1			6		11	9					
Wandsworth scratched																																		
25 Nov	2nd R (A)	Alleyn College	W 4-3				3[1]		4		7	8[3]	10			2							1			6	5	11	9					
27 Jan	3rd R (H)	Weybridge	L 1-2				3		5			9[1]	8			2							1	4		6	7	11	10					
TOTAL APPEARANCES					**5**	**1**	**15**	**1**	**15**	**3**	**12**	**10**	**13**	**3**	**5**	**10**	**3**	**2**	**3**	**1**	**5**	**3**	**10**	**6**	**1**	**9**	**8**	**7**	**5**	**3**	**3**	**1**	**1**	**1**
GOALS SCORED							**1**					**11**	**1**	**1**			**1**	**1**			**1**					**1**	**5**	**1**						

SEASON 1900-1901

EAST & WEST SURREY LEAGUE

Date	Venue	Opponents	Result	Atten-dance	Parker, B.	Knight, H.	Hawkins, G.F.	Heane, M.	Butt, Frank	Sharman, S.	Fox, C.	Lintott, E.H.	Butt, Fred	Quinton, F.P.	Hutton, G.	Gloster, G.	Hunt, H.	Heane, A.	Kemp, F.	Lintott, F.S.	Drake, F.A.	Drake, J.F.	Walker, W.H.	Withers, F.R.	Stare, D.	Ridler, H.B.	Drake, C.E	Hawkins, C.E.	Ryde
29 Sep	(H)	Godalming	L 2-3		1	2	3	4	5	6	7	8[1]	9	10[1]	11														
6 Oct	(A)	Guildford	L 0-3			2		4	5	6	7	8	9	10	11	1	3												
13 Oct	(H)	Addlestone	L 1-2		1	2	6	4		5	7		8	9	10[1]		3	11											
3 Nov	(H)	Weybridge	D 1-1		1	2	4	6	5			8[1]	9		11				3		10								7
17 Nov	(H)	Brookwood	L 0-1		1	2	5	6			7	8	9	10	11				3	4									
24 Nov	(A)	Godalming	L 1-4		1	2	5	6	9[1]		7		8		11				3	4	10								
1 Dec	(A)	Camberley	W 2-1			2	7[1]						9[1]		11	1				4	8	3	5	6	10				
8 Dec	(H)	Guildford	D 2-2			2	5					7	9[2]	8	11	1			3	4	10		6						
22 Dec	(A)	Kingston	L 0-1			2	4		5			7	9	8	11				3		10		1			6			
29 Dec	(A)	Addlestone	L 2-5			2	7[1]		5			8[1]	9		11	1				4	10		6				3		
5 Jan	(H)	Kingston	W 4-2			2	7		5			8[1]	9[1]		11[2]						10		1	4		6	3		
19 Jan	(A)	Weybridge	L 1-5			2	4		5			8	9	7	11						10[1]		1	6			3		
16 Feb	(A)	Brookwood	D 3-3			2	3		5			8[1]	9[1]	7	11[1]					4			1				10	6	
2 Mar	(H)	Camberley	W 4-1		1	2	6		5			8[1]	9[3]	7	11				3		10		4						
SURREY SENIOR CUP																													
27 Oct	1st R (H)	Reigate Priory	D 2-2		1	2	3	4	5		7	8[1]	11	10[1]	9											6			
10 Oct	Rep (A)	Reigate Priory	L 1-2		1	2	4		5		7	8	9[1]		11				3		10					6			
TOTAL APPEARANCES					**8**	**16**	**15**	**7**	**12**	**3**	**7**	**13**	**16**	**10**	**16**	**4**	**2**	**1**	**7**	**6**	**10**	**1**	**8**	**3**	**1**	**4**	**4**	**1**	**1**
GOALS SCORED							**2**		**1**			**7**	**9**	**2**	**4**						**1**								

ISTHMIAN LEAGUE

SEASON 1913-1914

Date	Venue	Opponents	Result	Atten-dance	Skeet, W.C.	Long, C.	Bell, A.H.	Pearce, A.V.	Crane, H.J.	Pullen, W.	Grove, Ar.	Hart, A.	Soughton, W.	Swallow, H.	Salisbury, C.S.	Johnson, L.C.	Hann, H.	Love, S.J.	Bedser, A.	Kyle, J.	Russell, R.J.	Lemoine, H.M.	Killick, A.G.	Kent, T.R.	Duck, F.J.	Parker, H.G.	Smith, F.E.	Scothern, A.E.	Kew, H.J.	Jones, S.	Phillips, H.	Moreton, R.	Long, A.W.	Perry, F.C.	Hodges, H.H.	Smith, T.	Rogers, D.	Graham, F.E.	Wright, W.T.	Over, C.	Yarham, W.E.	Butcher, G.
13 Sept	(H)	London Caledonians	L 0-1		1	2	3	4	5	6	7	8	9	10	11																											
20 Sept	(A)	Nunhead	L 2-3		1	2	3			5	4[1]	9	8(1)	10	11	6	7																									
18 Oct	(H)	Shepherds Bush	L 0-3		1	2	3	4	5	9				10		11		6	7	8																						
8 Nov	(A)	West Norwood	L 0-7		1		3	4	5	2	11			10		6			7	9	8																					
22 Nov	(A)	Ilford	L 0-4			2	3	4	5		11					10		6	7	9	8	1																				
29 Nov	(A)	Dulwich	L 0-3				2		5	3	4			10		11		6	7	9	8	1																				
13 Dec	(A)	Clapton	D 1-1			4	3		5		6			10		11			7	9[1]	8	1	2	8																		
20 Dec	(H)	Clapton	L 0-2				3	4	5		6			10		11			7	9	8	1	2																			
27 Dec	(A)	Shepherds Bush	L 1-4		1		3	4	5		6					11			7	9				8[1]	2	10																
10 Jan	(A)	Oxford	L 1-7		1	4	3		5		7			10		11				9[1]	8				2		6															
24 Jan	(H)	Leytonstone	L 0-4	500	1		3	6	5		7					11					9			8		10		2	4													
31 Jan	(H)	Nunhead	L 0-2				3	6	5		10					11			7	9	8	1						2	4													
7 Feb	(H)	New Crusaders	L 1-2				3	4	5		6					11			7	9	8	1						2		10[1]												
21 Feb	(H)	Dulwich	L 1-4				2	4	5	6	7									9	8	1				10	3			11[1]												
7 Mar	(H)	Oxford	L 0-2				3		5		7					11				9	8							2	4	10	1	6										
21 Mar	(A)	London Caledonians	L 0-5				2		9		8					11				10	7						3		4		1	5	6									
28 Mar	(H)	Ilford	L 1-2					4	2		7					11				10	8[1]						3				1	5	6	9								
4 Apr	(H)	West Norwood	W 2-1				10	4	2		6[1]					11				8[1]	7						3				1	5			9							
23 Apr	(A)	New Crusaders	L 1-3				2		5		7									10	8						3				1		4			6	9[1]	11				
25 Apr	(A)	Leytonstone	L 0-1				2		5		7					11				10							3				1	4	6					8	9			
F.A. CUP																																										
27 Sep	Pre (A)	Kingston	D 2-2	1,500	1	2	3		5	4	7		8	10		11		6																						9[2]		
1 Oct	Rep (H)	Kingston	AB 2-1	extra time		2	3	4	5	6	11		7	10						8[2]																				9	1	
4 Oct	2nd Rep (H)	Kingston	L 1-2	AET		2	3	4	5	6	7			10[1]		11				9																				8	1	
F.A. AMATEUR CUP																																										
3 Jan	1st R (H)	1st Kings Royal Rifles	L 1-2	AET	1		2	4	6	5	7			11		10[1]				9	8						3															
SURREY SENIOR CUP																																										
6 Dec	1st R (A)	Metrogas	L 1-5	1,500		2	3	4	5	6	8[1]			10		11			7	9		1																				
SURREY CHARITY SHIELD																																										
11 Oct	1st R (H)	Royal Sussex Regt.	L 1-2	800	1	2	3	8	5					10		11		6	7	9[1]																						4
OXFORD HOSPITAL CUP																																										
17 Jan	1st R (A)	Marlow	L 1-2			4	2[1]	6	5	3	7					11						1				8										10				9		
TOTAL APPEARANCES					**10**	**12**	**26**	**18**	**26**	**12**	**25**	**2**	**4**	**14**	**2**	**23**	**1**	**5**	**11**	**22**	**15**	**9**	**2**	**3**	**2**	**4**	**8**	**4**	**4**	**3**	**6**	**5**	**4**	**1**	**1**	**2**	**1**	**2**	**1**	**4**	**2**	**1**
GOALS SCORED							**1**				**3**		**1**	**1**		**1**				**6**	**1**			**1**						**2**							**1**			**2**		

SEASON 1919-1920

ISTHMIAN LEAGUE

Date	Venue	Opponents	Result	Atten-dance	Phillips, H.J.	Bowey, T.	Smith, F.E.	Rayer, R.A.	Crane, H.J.	Caesar, J.	Over, C.H.	Darcy, G.	Cockran, G.	Gowler, H.	Hodgeman, E.	Christie, W.	Bevan, A.	Smith, G.	Pearce, A.V.	Sturt, J.	Filleston, J.	Johnson, L.C.	Kemp, F.	Gooch, E.	Wakeley, F.	Sturt, F.	Wright, W.G.	Summerfield, H.	Gowan, H.E.	Dorkins, E.	Hunter, G.V.	Knight, A.	Cook, A.F.	Daniells, H.W.	Salisbury, C.S.
6 Sep	(A)	Leytonstone	D 2-2	1,500	1	2	3	4	5	6	7	8	9[2]	10	11																				
20 Sep	(H)	Tufnell Park	L 1-3	1,000	1			3	2	5	7	8	9	4	11[1]	6	10																		
11 Oct	(A)	Nunhead	L 0-3		1		3	4			7				11	5		2	6	8	9	10													
25 Oct	(A)	Dulwich	L 1-2		1		3	6	5		7		9[1]	10	11			2	4				8												
1 Nov	(H)	Nunhead	L 0-1		1		3	4	5		7		9	10	11			2	6				8												
29 Nov	(H)	Clapton	L 1-2		1			4	3				10	5	11			2	6		9		8[1]	7											
6 Dec	(H)	West Norwood	L 0-1		1			4	3				9	8	11	5		2	6					7										10	
20 Dec	(H)	Casuals	W 5-0	1,000	1			4	2				10[1]	6	11	5		3	8					7[2]	9[2]										
10 Jan	(A)	Casuals	W 2-0		1			4	2				9	6		5		3	8			11[1]	10	7[1]											
17 Jan	(A)	Clapton	L 2-3		1			4	2				9[1]	6	11	5		3	8			7			10[1]										
24 Jan	(H)	London Caledonians	L 1-2		1			4	2				9	6		5		3	8					7	10[1]										11
7 Feb	(A)	Oxford	L 3-5	2,000	1				2					6		5		3	4					7	8[1]	9	10[1]								11(1)
14 Feb	(A)	Civil Service	L 0-2		1				2				8			5		3	4					7		9	10	6							11
28 Feb	(H)	Civil Service	D 0-0		1								9	2		5		3	4					7			10		6	8					11
6 Mar	(A)	Tufnell Park	L 1-2		1				2							5		3	4					7[1]	9		10		6	8					11
13 Mar	(A)	West Norwood	D 2-2		1				2							5		3[1]	4					7	9		10		6	8[1]					11
27 Mar	(H)	Ilford	W 3-1		1				2							5		3	4					7	9[1]				6	8[1]	10[1]				11
10 Apr	(H)	Oxford	W 4-2		1				2					10		5		3	4					7[2]					6	8[2]	9				11
17 Apr	(H)	Dulwich	L 1-2	2,000	1				2					10		5		3	4					7					6	8[1]	9				11
22 Apr	(A)	London Caledonians	W 3-1		1				2					10		5		3	4					7	9				6	8[2]					11[1]
24 Apr	(A)	Ilford	L 1-4		1				2					10		5		3	4					7					6	8[1]	9				11
28 Apr	(H)	Leytonstone	W 3-2		1				2					10		5		3	4					7[2]					6	8[1]	9				11
F.A. CUP																																			
27 Sep	Pre (A)	Guildford Pinks	D 1-1	3,000	1			3	2	5	7	8	9[1]	6	10	4																			11
1 Oct	Rep (H)	Guildford Pinks	L 2-11	1,500	1			2		5	7		9	6	11				4	10[1]	8[1]											3			
F.A. AMATEUR CUP																																			
18 Oct	2nd Q (H)	RAE Farnborough	L 1-5		1		3	6	5		7			10[1]	11			2	4		9		8												
SURREY SENIOR CUP																																			
13 Dec	1st R (H)	Metrogas	AB 2-3	ET	1			4	2				9[1]	8	11	5		3	6					7											10[1]
3 Jan	1st R (A)	Metrogas	L 2-4		1				2				10[1]	6		5		3	4			11	8[1]	7	9										
SURREY CHARITY SHIELD																																			
15 Nov	1st R (A)	Guildford Pinks	L 0-6				3	4	5		7		10	8	11			2	6		9												1		
TOTAL APPEARANCES					**27**	**1**	**6**	**16**	**25**	**4**	**9**	**3**	**17**	**23**	**14**	**21**	**1**	**24**	**25**	**2**	**5**	**4**	**6**	**18**	**9**	**2**	**5**	**1**	**9**	**9**	**5**	**1**	**1**	**1**	**14**
GOALS SCORED													**8**	**1**	**1**			**1**		**1**	**1**	**1**	**2**	**8**	**6**		**1**			**9**	**1**				**3**

ISTHMIAN LEAGUE

SEASON 1920-1921

Date	Venue	Opponents	Result	Atten-dance	Phillips, H.J.	Crane, H.J.	Smith, G.	Pearce, A.V.	Christie, W.	Gowan, H.E.	Thorne-Thorne, R.J.	Dorkins, E.	Connolly, A.J.	Crymble, C.	Eastwood, E.	Birch, W.G.	Salisbury, C.S.	Griffin, G.	Summerfield, H.	Hunt, A.	Gowler, H.	Reed, T.W.	Hodges, H.H.	Over, C.H.	Church, G.	Gooch, E.	Bunyan, W.J.	Kerr, A.W.	Shakespeare, H.	Rayer, R.A.	Gibbs, A.	McKie, G.	Sturt, F.	Johnson, L.C.	Doe, W.	Holman, A.	Grove, A r	Hunter, G.V.	Bailey, A.	Byrne, L.	Cox, C.	Smith, F.E.	Kemp, F.	Sturt, J.	Sherwood, W.A.	Badcock, A.V.	Cook, C.	Smith, W.	Bevan, A.F.
4 Sep	(H)	Leytonstone £40	D 1-1	1,500	1	2	3	4	5	6	7[1]	8	9	10	11																																		
11 Sep	(A)	Ilford	L 0-7		1	2	3	4		6	7	8	10	9		5	11																																
2 Oct	(A)	Oxford	L 0-3			2		4	5	6	7						11	1	3	8	9	10																											
23 Oct	(H)	Oxford	W 4-0			2		4	5	6							11	1			10[2]	8[1]	3	7	9[1]																								
30 Oct	(A)	Leytonstone	L 0-2			2		4	5	6	7						11	1			10		3	8	9																								
6 Nov	(A)	Tufnell Park	L 0-3	2,000		2		4	5	6							11	1			10		3			7	8	9																					
13 Nov	(H)	Clapton	L 1-2			2		4	5	6	7[1]						11	1			10		3				8		9																				
20 Nov	(H)	West Norwood	L 0-2			2		4	5	6							11	1			10		3			7		8	9																				
27 Nov	(A)	West Norwood	D 1-1			5		4	2									1				10	3							6	7[1]	8	9	11															
1 Jan	(A)	Civil Service	W 2-1			2		4		10[1]	7						11	1			6		3		5	9[1]									8														
15 Jan	(A)	Clapton	L 0-1			2		4		10	7							1			6				5	9									8	3	11												
22 Jan	(H)	London Caledonians	L 0-2			2		4	6	10							11	1					5			7									8	3		9											
29 Jan	(H)	Civil Service	L 1-3	1,000		2		4	6	11	7							1			10		5			9									8[1]	3													
5 Feb	(H)	Tufnell Park	L 0-1			2		4	5		9							1			6					7									8	3			10	11									
12 Feb	(A)	Casuals	D 1-1	200		2		4			8[1]						11	1			6		9		5	7										3					10								
19 Feb	(H)	Casuals	W 2-1			2		4	5	6								1					3		9	7[1]										11	8				10[1]								
26 Feb	(A)	Nunhead	L 0-2			2		4	5	6								1							9	7										11						3	8	10					
5 Mar	(H)	Nunhead	D 0-0			2		4	5	6							10	1			7				9											11						3		8					
12 Mar	(H)	Ilford	L 1-4			2		4	5	6							11	1			7				9											3					10[1]			8					
19 Mar	(A)	London Caledonians	L 0-2			2		4		6	7						11	1			8				5																	3			9	10			
20 Apr	(A)	Dulwich	L 0-2	4,000				4		3							11	1							5	8											7				2					10	6	9	
27 Apr	(H)	Dulwich	D 2-2	1,800		2		4	5	6								1			11		3			8[2]											7				9					10			
F.A. CUP																																																	
25 Sep	Prel (H)	Walton	W 4-2			2		4	5	6[1]	7[1]						11	1		9[1]	10	8[1]																				3							
9 Oct	1st Q (A)	Kingston	L 2-3	2,500		2		4	5	6	7						11	1			10[2]		3															9					8						
F.A. AMATEUR CUP																																																	
16 Oct	2nd Q (H)	Guildford Pinks £95	L 0-1			2		4	5	6					11		8	1			10		3			7												9											
SURREY SENIOR CUP																																																	
4 Dec	1st R (H)	Redhill	L 1-5			5		4	2	6							11	1			10		3			7									8(1)									9					
SURREY CHARITY SHIELD																																																	
18 Sep	1st R (H)	Camberley	L 2-3		1	2		4		5	7	8		9[2]			11				3																						6						10
OXFORD HOSPITAL CUP																																																	
8 Jan	1st R (H)	Wycombe	L 1-4	2,000		2				10	7						11	1			6		5		4	9									8[1]	3													
TOTAL APPEARANCES					3	27	2	27	20	25	15	3	2	3	2	1	20	25	1	2	21	4	16	2	12	15	2	2	2	1	1	1	1	1	7	10	4	3	1	1	5	4	3	4	1	3	1	1	1
GOALS SCORED										2	4			2						1	4	2			1	4					1				3						2								

ISTHMIAN LEAGUE

SEASON 1921-1922

Date	Venue	Opponents	Result	Attendance	Griffin, G.	Crane, H.J.	Smith, F.E.	Shaw, J.	Norcott, H.J.	Gowler, H.	Coe, A.P.	Thayers, H.H.	Withers, E.V.	Badcock, A.V.	Tilley, J.	Richardson, S.	Inseal, T.W.	Docherty, W.	Hodges, H.H.	Thorne-Thorne, R.J.	Turner, G.F.	Stocks, J.	Palin, A.G.	Salisbury, C.S.	Lee, R.	Sturt, J.	Ansell, J.	Gammon, F.	Church, G.	Williams, R.	Colman, R.	Doe, W.	Vincent, E.	Gowan, H.E.	Martin, S.	Ledger, L.
27 Aug	(A)	Ilford	L 2-4		1	2	3	4	5	6	7	8	9[1]	10[1]	11																					
3 Sep	(H)	West Norwood	W 1-0		1	2		4	5		7	8	9[1]	10	11	3	6																			
17 Sep	(A)	Dulwich	L 0-2		1	5					7	8	9	10	11			2	3	4	6															
8 Oct	(H)	Oxford	D 0-0	2,500	1	2		6	4		7	8		10	11		5					3	9													
22 Oct	(H)	Ilford	D 1-1	3,000	1	2		6	4		7	8	9				5				11[1]	3	10													
29 Oct	(A)	Leytonstone	W 1-0	3,000	1	2		6	4		7	9		10			5				11[1]	3	8													
5 Nov	(H)	Casuals	W 2-1		1	2		6	4		7	9[2]		10			5				11	3	8													
19 Nov	(A)	Wycombe	W 3-1		1	2		4	7			8[1]	9[1]	10	11[1]		5				6	3														
3 Dec	(H)	Wycombe	W 3-1	2,000	1	2		6	4		7	8[3]	9	10	11		5					3														
10 Dec	(A)	West Norwood	D 4-4		1	2		6	4		7[1]	8[1]		10[2]	11		5					3		9												
24 Dec	(A)	Casuals	W 2-1		1	2		6	9		7	8[1]		10	11[1]		5					3			4											
31 Dec	(H)	Tufnell Park	W 2-1		1	2		6	9		7	8[1]		10[1]	11		5					3			4											
21 Jan	(A)	London Caledonians	L 2-4		1	2		6	4		7[1]	8		10	11[1]		5					3				9										
28 Jan	(H)	Leytonstone	W 2-1	3,000	1	2		6	4		9	8[1]		10			5			7		3					11[1]									
4 Feb	(A)	Tufnell Park	W 2-1		1	2		6	4		9[1[	8					5			7[1]		3				10	11									
11 Feb	(A)	Oxford	L 2-5	2,000	1	2		6	7		9[1]	8		10[1]			5					3			4		11									
18 Feb	(A)	Wimbledon	W 2-1	5,000	1	2		6	4		7	8[1]	9	10[1]			5					3					11									
25 Feb	(A)	Civil Service	D 1-1		1	2			4	7		8[1]	9	10			5					3			6		11									
4 Mar	(H)	London Caledonians	L 0-1	3,000	1	4			6		7	8	9	10			5		2			3					11									
11 Mar	(H)	Clapton	L 2-4	2,000	1	2			4		7	8	9[1]	10[1]			5		3			6					11									
18 Mar	(A)	Nunhead	L 1-2		1	2			4		7	8	9	10			5					3			6[1]		11									
25 Mar	(H)	Civil Service	L 1-3	2,000	1	2			4		7	8	9	10			5[1]					3					11									6
1 Apr	(H)	Wimbledon	D 1-1		1	2			4			8	9	10[1]								3			6		11	7	5							
8 Apr	(A)	Clapton	L 0-2		1	2		6	4		7	8	9	10								3							5	11						
22 Apr	(H)	Nunhead	L 1-6		1	2		6	4		7			10								3				9				11	5	8[1]				
1 May	(H)	Dulwich	D 1-1	1,000	1			6	4		10	8	9	11								3									5	7[1]	2			
F.A. CUP																																				
10 Sep	Ex Pr (H)	Earlsfield	W 1-0	2,000	1	2		6				8[1]	9	10	11	3	5			7														4		
24 Sep	Pr (A)	Guildford United	D 2-2		1	2		6	4		7	8[1]	9	10	11[1]		5		3																	
28 Sep	Rep (H)	Guildford United AET	L 1-2	5,000	1	2		6	4		7	8	9[1]	10	11		5					3														
F.A. AMATEUR CUP																																				
1 Oct	1st Q (A)	Dorking AET	W 6-3		1	2		6	4[1]		7	8[3]	9[1]	10	11[1]		5					3														
15 Oct	2nd Q (A)	Guildford Pinks	L 1-2		1	2		6	4		7	8	9				5				11[1]	3	10													
SURREY SENIOR CUP																																				
17 Dec	1st R (A)	Nunhead	L 1-3		1	4		6	9		7	8		10[1]	11		5		2			3														
SURREY CHARITY SHIELD																																				
12 Nov	1st R (H)	Kingstonian	L 1-2		1	2		6	4		7	9		10	11		5[1]					3	8													
OXFORD HOSPITAL CUP																																				
14 Jan	1st R (H)	Slough Trading Co.	W 4-0	2,000	1	2		6	5	7		8[1]	9		11[1]							3			4	10[2]										
19 Apr	S-F (A)	Slough AET	L 1-2	4,500	1	2		6	4		7	8		10								3				9[1]			5						11	
TOTAL APPEARANCES					35	34	1	28	33	3	30	34	21	31	17	2	27	1	5	4	6	30	6	1	7	5	10	1	3	2	2	2	1	1	1	1
GOALS SCORED									1		4	18	6	9	6		2			1	3				1	3	1					2				

SEASON 1922-1923

ISTHMIAN LEAGUE

Date	Venue	Opponents	Result	Atten-dance	Griffin, G.	Crane, H.J.	Urpeth, L.W.	Norcott, H.J.	Shaw, J.	Turner, G.F.	Coe, A.P.	Thayers, H.H.	Griffiths, B.V.	Badcock, A.V.	Undery, H.E.	Stocks, J.	Amos, A.	Gowler, H.	Rolls, E.A.	Harman, N.J.	Mallett, A.E.	Briggs, T.M.R.	Gibbs, F.	Walker, C.	Ledger, L.	Stimson, R.J.	Berry, L.B.	Withers, E.V.	Martin, S.	Anderson, J.	Coleman, R.C.	Maidment, C.V.	Mills, A.E.	Clifford, P.J.	Burgess, A.	Owens, R.D.	Thorne-Thorne, R.J.	Hughes, A.
26 Aug	(H)	Tufnell Park	D 1-1	3,000	1	2	3	4	5	6	7[1]	8	9	10	11																							
2 Sep	(A)	Leytonstone	L 3-5	3,000	1	5	3	4	6	11	7	8[2]		10[1]		2	9																					
16 Sep	(A)	Ilford	L 1-7		1	5	3	4	6	11	7					2		8[1]	9	10																		
30 Sep	(H)	Civil Service	L 0-1	2,000	1	5	3	4	6	11	7	8				2			10	9																		
4 Nov	(H)	Wycombe	D 1-1		1	5	3	4	6	11		8				2				9	7	10[1]																
25 Nov	(H)	Oxford	W 4-2	2,000	1	5	3	4		11[1]		8[1]				2					7	6	9[1]	10[1]														
30 Dec	(H)	Clapton	L 1-2		1	5	3	4				9				2				8[1]			10		6	7	11											
6 Jan	(A)	Oxford	D 3-3	2,500	1	5	3	4								2		9		8[3]	7	6		10			11											
13 Jan	(H)	Ilford	L 2-7	2,000	1	5[1]	3	4				9				2				8	11[1]	6	10			7												
20 Jan	(A)	West Norwood	L 0-4		1	2	3	4	6			9								8	7	5	10				11											
10 Feb	(A)	Wimbledon	W 3-0	3,000	1	5	3		6			4				2				8	7	10[1]						9[1]	11[1]									
24 Feb	(H)	West 'Norwood	W 2-0		1	5	3	4	6			7				2				8		10[2]						9	11									
3 Mar	(H)	Dulwich	W 2-1	2,000	1	5	3	4	6			7[1]				2				8[1]		10						9	11									
17 Mar	(H)	Leytonstone	L 0-3	1,800	1	5	3	4	6			7				2				8		10						9	11									
24 Mar	(A)	London Caledonians	L 1-2	2,500	1	5	8	4	6	3		7				2						10						9[1]	11									
28 Mar	(A)	Clapton	L 0-1			5	3		6			9				2				8	7	10							11	1	4							
31 Mar	(A)	Casuals	D 0-0		1			4	6	3						2				8	7	10						9	11		5							
7 Apr	(A)	Tufnell Park	D 2-2		1	5		4	6	3		8				2					7	10[1]						9[1]	11									
14 Apr	(A)	Wycombe	L 4-9	4,000	1	5		4	6	3		8[2]	7			2						10[2]						9	11									
18 Apr	(A)	Civil Service	W 2-1		1	5		4	6	3		8	7			2						10[1]						9[1]	11									
25 Apr	(A)	Dulwich	L 1-6		1	5		4	6	3		8	7			2				11		10[1]										9						
26 Apr	(H)	Nunhead	L 0-2		1	2		4		3			7									10			6	8			11		5		9					
28 Apr	(H)	Casuals	W 4-1	1,500	1	2		4	5	3		8[1]	7									10[1]			6			9[2]	11									
2 May	(H)	London Caledonians	W 2-1		1	2		4	5	3		8[2]	7									10			6			9	11									
3 May	(A)	Nunhead	D 2-2		1									5						10	11			8[1]		7						6	9[1]	2	3	4		
4 May	(H)	Wimbledon	L 1-3		1	2		4	5	3		8	7									10			6			9[1]	11									
F.A. CUP																																						
9 Sep	Ex Pr (A)	RAMC £100	W 1-0	3,000	1	5	3	4	6	11	7	8				2			10[1]	9																		
23 Sep	Pr (A)	RAE (Farnborough)	W 3-1	1,500	1	5	3	4	6	11	7	8[1]				2			10	9[2]																		
7 Oct	1st Q (H)	Kingstonian	D 2-2	3,500	1	5	3	4	6	11[1]	7	9[1]				2		8		10																		
11 Oct	Rep (A)	Kingstonian	W 3-0	3,000	1	5	3	4	6	11		8[1]				2				10[1]	7		9[1]															
21 Oct	2nd Q (H)	Guildford United	L 0-1		1	5	3	4	6	11		8				2				9	7		10															
F.A. AMATEUR CUP																																						
14 Oct	2nd Q (A)	Guildford Pinks	W 2-1	3,800	1	5	3	4	6	11						2		8[1]		10	7[1]		9															
28 Oct	3rd Q (A)	Farnham U.B.	W 3-1	1,750	1	5	3	4	6	11		8[2]				2				9[1]	7		10															
18 Nov	4th Q (H)	RE (Aldershot)	W 1-0		1	5	3	4		11		8[1]				2				10	7		9		6													
9 Dec	1st R (H)	Erith & B after 68 mins	AB 1-1	3,000	1	5	3	4	6	11		8				2		7		10[1]			9															
16 Dec	1st R (H)	Erith & B	D 1-1	3,000	1	5	3	4	6			8				2				10	7		9				11[1]											
23 Dec	Rep (A)	Erith & B	L 1-6	3,000	1	5	3	4	6			8				2				10	7		9[1]				11											
SURREY SENIOR CUP																																						
2 Dec	1st R (A)	Livesey United	W 6-2		1	5	3	4				8[2]				2				11[1]	7	6	9[2]	10[1]														
17 Feb	2nd R (H)	Mitcham Wanderers	L 0-1		1	5	3		6	10		4				2				8	7							9										11
SURREY CHARITY SHIELD																																						
11 Nov	1st R (A)	Kingstonian	W 1-0	3,000	1	5	3	4	6			8				2				10	7	11	9[1]															
21 Apr	S-F (A)	Wimbledon	W 2-0		1	5		4	6	3		8				2				10						7[2]		9	11									
12 May	F	(W'don) Summerstown	L 1-6	5,500	1	5		4	6	3		8				2				10[1]						7		9	11									
OXFORD HOSPITAL CUP																																						
3 Feb	1st R (H)	Wycombe	W 2-1	2,000	1	5		4	6	3						2				8		10						9[1]	11[1]								7	
10 Mar	S-F (H)	Marlow	W 4-0	2,000	1	5	3	4	6			7				2				8		10[1]						9[3]	11									
TOTAL APPEARANCES					**43**	**42**	**31**	**40**	**36**	**29**	**7**	**37**	**8**	**3**	**1**	**37**	**1**	**5**	**4**	**33**	**20**	**24**	**14**	**4**	**6**	**6**	**5**	**17**	**18**	**1**	**3**	**2**	**2**	**1**	**1**	**1**	**1**	**1**
GOALS SCORED						**1**				**2**	**1**	**17**		**1**				**2**	**1**	**12**	**2**	**11**	**6**	**3**		**2**	**1**	**11**	**2**				**1**					

ISTHMIAN LEAGUE

SEASON 1923-1924

Date	Venue	Opponents	Result	Attendance	Montgomery, L.E.	Young, R.	Turner, G.F.	Norcott, H.J.	Filmore, A.	Shaw, J.	Griffiths, B.V.	Thayers, H.H.	Longhurst, H.L.	Harman, N.J.	Briggs, T.M.R.	Elsworth, W.C.	Crane, H.J.	Coe, A.P.	Tilley, J.	Urpeth, L.W.	Maidment, C.V.	Ledger, L.	Betts, F.L.	Gilbert, A.	People, H.	Martin, S.	Gowler, H.	Stimson, R.J.	Owens, P.D.	Collyer, G.	Wallis, W.	Peters, C.W.	Badcock, A.V.	Sturt, S.	Ashton, A.	Hodges, H.H.	Thorne-Thorne, R.J.	Vincent, E.
1 Sep	(H)	Wycombe	L 1-6	1,500	1	2	3	4	5	6	7	8[1]	9	10	11																							
8 Sep	(H)	Leytonstone	W 2-1		1		3	4		6	7[1]	8			10[1]	2	5	9	11																			
12 Sep	(H)	Nunhead	D 0-0		1		3	4		6	7	8			10		5	9	11	2																		
27 Sep	(A)	Nunhead	L 1-2		1		3			5		8		9[1]	10			7	11	2	4	6																
29 Sep	(H)	Ilford	L 2-3	2,000	1		3	4		6	7	8		9[1]	10	2	5		11[1]																			
27 Oct	(H)	Civil Service	D 1-1	1,600	1		3	4		5		8		10	6	2				11[1]			7	9														
3 Nov	(A)	Civil Service	L 3-6		1		3	4		5		8		9	6	2				11[1]			7	10[2]														
17 Nov	(A)	Leytonstone	L 0-1		1		3	4		5	7		9	8	6	2				11				10														
24 Nov	(A)	St. Albans	L 0-1		1		3	4		5	7			8	6	2	9			11				10														
8 Dec	(A)	Wycombe	D 2-2		1		3	4		5		7	9	8	6	2				11				10[2]														
15 Dec	(A)	Tufnell Park	L 1-3		1		3	4[1]		5		7	9	8	6	2				11				10														
22 Dec	(H)	Dulwich	W 1-0		1		3	4		5		7		9		2						6		10[1]	8	11												
19 Jan	(H)	Oxford	W 1-0		1		3	4		5	7	8		9	6	2									11[1]		10											
9 Feb	(H)	Wimbledon	D 1-1		1		3	4		5[1]		8		9		2						6		10	11			7										
23 Feb	(H)	Casuals	D 1-1		1		3	4		5[1]	7	8	10	9		2				11		6																
1 Mar	(H)	St. Albans	D 0-0		1		3	4		5	7	8		9		2				11		6		10														
15 Mar	(A)	Oxford	L 2-11		1		3	4		5		8		9[2]		2						6		10				7	11									
22 Mar	(H)	Tufnell Park	L 0-2		1		3			5		8		9		2				11		6		10	7		4											
5 Apr	(A)	London Caledonians	L 2-4		1		3	4		5	7[1]			9		2						6		10		11		8[1]										
10 Apr	(A)	Dulwich	D 0-0		1		3	5					9	8						2		6		10		11				4	7							
12 Apr	(A)	Casuals	L 1-5				3			5				8	6	2						4		10[1]		11		9			7	1						
14 Apr	(A)	Ilford	L 0-3				2	4		5	7		9							3		6		10		11		8					1					
26 Apr	(H)	Clapton	W 2-1		1			4		5			9			2				3		6		10		11		8[2]			7							
28 Apr	(A)	Clapton	L 2-6				3	4		5	7		9[1]							2[1]		6		10		11		8						1				
30 Apr	(A)	Wimbledon	D 1-1		1		3	4		6			9							2				10[1]		11		8			7				5			
3 May	(H)	London Caledonians	W 4-1				3	4		6			9[4]			2								10		11		8			7	1			5			
F.A. CUP																																						
22 Sep	Prel (A)	Wellington Wks	L 2-6		1		3	4		6[1]	7	8			10	9[1]	5										11									2		
F.A. AMATEUR CUP																																						
13 Oct	1st Q (H)	RASC (Ald'shot) AET	AB 2-1	1,500	1		3	4		5	7	8[1]		10[1]	6		2		11					9														
20 Oct	1st Q (H)	RASC (Ald'shot)	L 1-3		1		3	4		5		8[1]		10	6		2						7	9			11											
SURREY SENIOR CUP																																						
29 Dec	1st R (A)	Farnham U.B.	D 1-1		1		3	4		5		8		9		2						6		10	11[1]												7	
12 Jan	Rep (H)	Farnham U.B.	W 1-0				3	4		5		7		8	6	2								10[1]	11		9					1						
26 Jan	2nd R (A)	Wimbledon £134 AET	D 3-3	5,000	1		3	4		5	7	8 [1]		9[2]	6	2									11		10											
2 Feb	Rep (H)	Wimbledon	L 3-4	2,500	1		3	4		5	7	8		9[3]	6	2									11		10											
SURREY CHARITY SHIELD																																						
10 Nov	1st R (H)	Kingstonian	W 2-0		1		3	4		5			9	8[1]	6	2				11[1]				10				7										
16 Feb	S-F (H)	Summerstown	L 1-2		1		3	4		5	7	8[1]				2						6		9	11		10											
OXFORD HOSPITAL CUP																																						
19 Apr	1st R (H)	Cowley	L 0-4		1		5							8	10	2				3		6		9							7		11					4
OXFORD HOSPITAL CUP 1922-23																																						
15 Sep	Final (A)	Oxford	L 2-5	2,000	1		3	4		6	7	8[2]			10	2	5	9	11																			
TOTAL APPEARANCES					**32**	**1**	**36**	**33**	**1**	**35**	**18**	**25**	**12**	**27**	**22**	**28**	**8**	**4**	**6**	**18**	**1**	**16**	**3**	**26**	**9**	**9**	**8**	**10**	**1**	**1**	**6**	**3**	**2**	**1**	**2**	**1**	**1**	**1**
GOALS SCORED								**1**		**3**	**2**	**7**	**5**	**11**	**1**	**1**			**1**	**4**				**8**	**2**			**3**										

SEASON 1924-1925

ISTHMIAN LEAGUE

Date	Venue	Opponents	Result	Atten-dance	Montgomery, L.E.	Elsworth, W.C.	Turner, G.F.	Norcott, H.J.	Ashton, A.	Shaw, J.	Wallis, W.	Stimson, R.J.	Longhurst, H.L.	Gilbert, A.	Martin, S.	Lester, T.	Clifford, P.J.	Stebbings, F.C.	Edwards, S.C.	Maidment, C.V.	Gowler, H.	Smith, R.	Harman, N.J.	Thayers, H.H.	Thomas, E.A.	Urpeth, L.W.	Ledger, L.	Edwards, A.	Beckford, W.	Sturt, S.	Gunstone, J.	Briggs, T.M.R.	Badcock, A.V.	Penny, A.	Sullivan, L.	Griffiths, B.V.	Withers, E.V.	Chatterton, A.H.	Ball, A.W.
30 Aug	(A)	Clapton	L 1-8	5,000	1	2	3	4	5	6	7	8	9[1]	10	11																								
4 Sep	(A)	London Caledonians	L 0-1				3		5			8	9		11	1	2	4	6	7	10																		
10 Sep	(H)	London Caledonians	L 0-1	1,500	1		3	4	5		7	8	9		11		2		6			10																	
13 Sep	(A)	Nunhead	L 1-3		1		3	4	5		7	8[1]					2		11	9		6	10																
1 Nov	(H)	Wycombe	W 4-2		1		3	4	5		7						2		6	11			10	8	9[4]														
15 Nov	(H)	Tufnell Park	D 0-0		1			4	5	6							2		10	11			8	7	9	3													
22 Nov	(H)	Casuals o.g.	W 6-1		1		3	4		5	7	8					2		6	11				10[1]	9[4]														
6 Dec	(A)	St. Albans	L 2-5		1		3	4		5	7	8					2			11				10	9[2]		6												
13 Dec	(A)	Wimbledon	L 0-1	3,000	1		3	4	5	6	7	8					2			11				10	9														
20 Dec	(H)	Clapton	W 2-0		1		3	4	5			8[1]								7				10	9	2		6	11[1]										
27 Dec	(A)	Wycombe	D 1-1		1		3	4		5		8								7			10		9[1]	2		6	11										
10 Jan	(A)	Casuals	L 1-6		1		3		5		7	8								4			10		9[1]	2		6	11										
17 Jan	(H)	Civil Service	L 0-1		1		3	4	5		7	8								11				10	9	2		6											
31 Jan	(A)	Tufnell Park	L 1-3		1		3	4		6	7	10[1]								11			9	8		2		5											
7 Feb	(A)	Oxford	L 0-5				3			5	7	10					2		6	11				8	9					1	4								
21 Feb	(H)	Leytonstone	L 4-5	1,200	1		3	4		5[1]		8			11					7				10[2]	9[1]	2		6											
7 Mar	(A)	Civil Service	L 1-3			2	3			5		8[1]			11					7			9	10				6		1	4								
14 Mar	(H)	Ilford	W 1-0			2	3			5	7				11					9[1]				8						1	4	6	10						
21 Mar	(A)	Dulwich	D 2-2		1	2	3			5	7				11					10[1]			9	8							4[1]	6							
28 Mar	(H)	Nunhead	W 2-0	1.000	1	2	3			5	7	9			11[1]					10[1]				8				4				6							
4 Apr	(H)	St. Albans	L 0-1		1	2	3			5	7	9			11					10				8				4				6							
11 Apr	(A)	Leytonstone (o.g.)	L 3-5		1	2	3			5	7	9[1]								10				8[1]				4				6		11					
18 Apr	(A)	Ilford	L 0-6		1	2				5	7				11					10			9	8		3		4				6							
23 Apr	(H)	Oxford	L 0-1		1		3	6			7	8		10	11								4	9		2		5											
25 Apr	(H)	Wimbledon	L 1-3			2	3	4			7	10[1]			11								9	8				5		1		6							
28 Apr	(H)	Dulwich	L 0-3		1		3	4															9	8		10	6	5							2	7			11
F.A. CUP																																							
6 Sep	Ex Pr (A)	Camberley	W 5-1		1		3	4	5			8[1]	9[1]		11		2		6	7[2]		10[1]																	
20 Sep	Pr (H)	Wellington Wks	W 4-1		1		3	4	5		7	8[2]			11		2		6			10[2]															9		
4 Oct	1st Q (H)	Tooting Town	W 3-1	3,000	1		3	4	5		7	8[1]					2		6	11[1]		10[1]	9																
18 Oct	2nd Q (H)	Summerstown 23 mins	AB 0-0		1		3	4		5	7	8					2		6	11		10	9																
		Referee collapsed and died.																																					
22 Oct	2nd Q (H)	Summerstown	L 0-2		1		3	4		5	7	8					2		6	11		10	9																
F.A. AMATEUR CUP																																							
11 Oct	1st Q (H)	Royal Engineers	W 2-1		1		3	4	5		7	8[1]					2		6	11[1]		10																9	
25 Oct	2nd Q (A)	Farnham U.B.	L 1-3		1		3	5									2		6	11	4	10	8	7														9[1]	
SURREY SENIOR CUP																																							
29 Nov	1st R (A)	Reigate Priory	W 8-3		1		3	4	5	6		8[3]					2			7			10[2]		9[3]	11													
24 Jan	2nd R (A)	Weybridge	W 4-0		1		3		5	6	7	10[3]								11				8[1]	9	2		4											
14 Feb	3rd R (A)	Farnham U.B.	L 2-4		1		3	4		5	7	8[1]								11			9			2		6				10[1]							
SURREY CHARITY SHIELD																																							
8 Nov	1st R (A)	Kingstonian	L 1-2	4,000	1		3	4	5		7						2		6	11			8	10[1]	9														
TOTAL APPEARANCES					**32**	**9**	**35**	**26**	**17**	**21**	**27**	**29**	**4**	**2**	**14**	**1**	**18**	**1**	**15**	**31**	**2**	**9**	**19**	**23**	**14**	**13**	**2**	**16**	**3**	**4**	**4**	**8**	**1**	**1**	**1**	**1**	**1**	**2**	**1**
GOALS SCORED										**1**		**18**	**2**		**1**					**7**		**4**	**2**	**6**	**16**				**1**		**1**	**1**						**1**	

ISTHMIAN LEAGUE

SEASON 1925-1926

Date	Venue	Opponents	Result	Attendance	Montgomery, L.E.	Vincent, E.	Turner, G.F.	Edwards, A.	Shaw, J.	Gilbert, F.A.	Wallis, W.	Wheatcroft, J.	Perryman, J.	Sumners, H.	Ball, A.W.	Pope, C.	Maidment, C.V.	Anderson, A.T.	Harman, N.J.	Thayers, H.H.	Stimson, R.J.	Briggs, T.M.R.	Devine, J.	Brown, R.R.
29 Aug	(A)	Leytonstone	L 1-8		1	2	3	4	5	6	7	8	9[1]	10	11									
2 Sep	(H)	London Caledonians	W 1-0		1		2		5		7		9		11	3	4	6	8[1]	10				
5 Sep	(H)	Dulwich	L 1-2		1		2		5		7		9[1]		11	3	4	6	8	10				
10 Sep	(A)	London Caledonians	L 0-1		1		2		5		7					3	4	6		9	8	10	11	
12 Sep	(H)	Tufnell Park	L 1-4		1		2		5		7				11	3	4	6	8[1]			10		9
19 Sep	(H)	The Casuals	D 1-1	500	1		2		5		7[1]	8			11	3	4	6		10				
31 Oct	(A)	Tufnell Park	L 2-3		1		2		5			8[1]			11	3	4[1]			10				
7 Nov	(A)	Ilford	L 1-3		1		3		5			8			11		4	6	9					
14 Nov	(H)	Nunhead	D 1-1	1,600	1		2		5			8[1]			11	3	4	6	9	10				
21 Nov	(A)	The Casuals	D 1-1		1		2		5			8[1]			11	3	4		9	7				
28 Nov	(H)	Wimbledon	W 4-3		1	2			5			8				3[1]	4		9[1]	10				
12 Dec	(H)	Leytonstone	W 2-0	1,300	1		2		5			8				3	4			7				
19 Dec	(H)	Wycombe	L 3-5		1		3[1]		5			8			11		4		10	7				
2 Jan	(A)	Wimbledon	W 5-4	4,000	1		2		5						11	3	4			7		6		
16 Jan	(A)	Clapton	W 4-3		1		2		5			8				3	4			7				
30 Jan	(H)	Civil Service	W 4-0	2,000	1		2		5			8[2]			11	3	4			7				
6 Feb	(A)	Oxford	W 4-3	2,500	1				5	10[1]		8[2]					2		9[1]					
20 Feb	(A)	Wycombe	L 4-6		1		2		5			8[1]								7[1]				
27 Feb	(A)	Civil Service	D 1-1		1				5			8				3			9	7				
24 Mar	(H)	Clapton	L 1-2				2					8				3	4		10	7				
27 Mar	(A)	Nunhead	L 0-3		1							8				3			9	7				
3 Apr	(H)	Oxford	W 3-2				2		5[1]			10				3	4		8			6		
10 Apr	(H)	Ilford	D 3-3	2,000			2		5				10				4		9[1]	8[1]				
17 Apr	(H)	St. Albans	D 3-3		1				6							3	4		9[1]	8[1]				
24 Apr	(A)	St. Albans	L 0-4		1				6			10				3			4	8				
29 Apr	(A)	Dulwich	L 5-7		1		6	4					10[2]			3			8	7				
F.A. CUP																								
3 Oct	1st Q (A)	Wellington Wks	D 3-3		1		2		5		7[1]	8			11[1]	3	4	6	9	10[1]				
7 Oct	Rep (H)	Wellington Wks AET	AB 2-0		1		2		5		7	8[1]	9[1]		11	3	4	6	10					
12 Oct	2nd Rep (H)	Wellington Wks	L 1-3				2		5	4			8			3		6	9[1]					
F.A. AMATEUR CUP																								
10 Oct	1st Q (H)	Aldershot Trac.	D 2-2	2,000	1		2		5			8[1]			11	3	4	6	9	10[1]				
21 Oct	Rep (A)	Aldershot Trac.	W 3-2				3		5[1]						11		7	6						
24 Oct	2nd Q (A)	2nd Rifle Brigade	L 1-5		1		2		5						11	3	7	6						
SURREY SENIOR CUP																								
23 Jan	1st R (H)	The Casuals	W 6-1	1,000	1		2		5			8[3]			11[1]	3	4		10	7				
13 Feb	2nd R (A)	Kingstonian	L 2-4	6,000	1		2		5			8				3	4		9[2]	7				
SURREY CHARITY SHIELD																								
17 Oct	1st R (H)	Guildford Pinks	W 3-1		1	2	3		5						11		9[2]	6	8					
26 Apr	S-F (H)	Kingstonian	L 1-5		1		2		5			7[1]	10			3			8					
TOTAL APPEARANCES					**31**	**3**	**30**	**2**	**33**	**3**	**8**	**24**	**8**	**1**	**19**	**28**	**28**	**14**	**25**	**25**	**1**	**4**	**1**	**1**
GOALS SCORED							**1**		**2**	**1**	**2**	**14**	**5**		**2**	**1**	**3**		**9**	**5**				

Date	Opponents	Elliott, J.	Dyason, C.	Griffiths, B.V.	Filmore, A.	Ledger, L.	Sherlock, S.	Thorne-Thorne, R.J.	Woodards, C.	Price, W.J.	Wharton, W.	Fitzgerald, R.R.	Kimbell, A.W.	Urpeth, L.W.	Hughes, A.	Norcott, H.J.	Walters, G.	Green, G.	Waller, V.	Gowler, H.	Sturt,S.	Cartidge, A.	Sullivan, L.	Medcalf, W.M.	Andrews, G.	McNiven, J.	Threadgold, W.	Humphreyies, W.	Clifford, P.J.	McLeod, D.
29 Aug	Leytonstone																													
2 Sep	London Caledonians																													
5 Sep	Dulwich																													
10 Sep	London Caledonians																													
12 Sep	Tufnell Park																													
19 Sep	The Casuals	9																												
31 Oct	Tufnell Park	9		7	6																									
7 Nov	Ilford		2	7	10[1]																									
14 Nov	Nunhead	7																												
21 Nov	The Casuals				10	6																								
28 Nov	Wimbledon					11[2]	6	7																						
12 Dec	Leytonstone						6		9[1]	10[1]	11																			
19 Dec	Wycombe		2				6		9[2]																					
2 Jan	Wimbledon								8	10[1]		9[4]																		
16 Jan	Clapton					11	6		10[1]			9[3]																		
30 Jan	Civil Service	9[1]				10[1]							6																	
6 Feb	Oxford	7			4	6								3	11															
20 Feb	Wycombe					6					11			3		4	9	10[2]												
27 Feb	Civil Service	10[1]									11			2					4	6										
24 Mar	Clapton						6				11	9[1]									1	5								
27 Mar	Nunhead													6	11							5	2	4	10					
3 Apr	Oxford	7[1]							9[1]		11										1									
10 Apr	Ilford	7[1]				6					11			3							1									
17 Apr	St. Albans	7								10	11											5[1]	2							
24 Apr	St. Albans	7									11	9										5				2				
29 Apr	Dulwich											9[1]		11[2]								5	2							
F.A. CUP																														
3 Oct	Wellington Wks																													
7 Oct	Wellington Wks																													
12 Oct	Wellington Wks																			10	1						7	11		
F.A. AMATEUR CUP																														
10 Oct	Aldershot Trac.	7																												
21 Oct	Aldershot Trac.	9[1]														10			4		1								2	8[1]
24 Oct	2nd Rifle Brigade	9[1]																	4	10										8
SURREY SENIOR CUP																														
23 Jan	The Casuals					6			9[2]																					
13 Feb	Kingstonian					10	6							11																
SURREY CHARITY SHIELD																														
17 Oct	Guildford Pinks	7[1]																	4	10										
26 Apr	Kingstonian						6		9		11								4											
TOTAL APPEARANCES		**14**	**2**	**2**	**4**	**9**	**7**	**1**	**7**	**3**	**9**	**5**	**1**	**7**	**2**	**2**	**1**	**1**	**5**	**4**	**5**	**5**	**3**	**1**	**1**	**1**	**1**	**1**	**1**	**2**
GOALS SCORED		**7**			**1**	**3**			**7**	**2**		**9**		**2**				**2**				**1**								**1**

ISTHMIAN LEAGUE

SEASON 1926-1927

Date	Venue	Opponents	Result	Atten-dance	Montgomery, L.E.	Ware, W.J.	Pope, C.	Maidment, C.V.	Briggs, T.M.R.	Ledger, L.	Elliott, J.	Perryman, J.	Wheatley, E.	Price, W.J.	Sewell, B.	Sturt, S.	Turner, G.F.	Cartlidge, A.	Payne, E.	Thayers, H.H.	Thorne-Thorne, R.J.	Sleet, A.T.	Sherlock, S.	Wallis, W.	Harman, N.J.	Wills, A.	Evans, A.	Lee, V.	Fitzgerald, R.R.	Woodards, C.	Clifford, P.J.	Gunstone, F.	Dyason, C.	Morrison, W.	White, W.J.	Bradley, E.	Twine, F.
28 Aug	(A)	Leytonstone	L 3-6		1	2	3	4	5[1]	6	7	8	9[2]	10	11																						
11 Sep	(H)	Nunhead	L 0-1				3	7	6				9	10	11	1	2	4	5	8																	
16 Sep	(A)	London Caledonians	D 2-2	2,500			3		6			8[1]	9	10[1]	11	1	2	4	5		7																
22 Sep	(H)	London Caledonians	D 2-2				3	7	6			8	9[1]	10[1]	11	1	2	4	5																		
6 Nov	(H)	Leytonstone	W 4-2		1		3					9[2]	5	10[2]	11		2					4	6	7	8												
11 Dec	(A)	Ilford	L 3-5		1		3					9[2]	4	10			2		5				6			7	8[1]	11									
18 Dec	(A)	Wycombe	D 3-3		1		3							10			2		5	7		4	6				8[1]	11	9[2]								
25 Dec	(A)	Wimbledon	W 3-2	3,000	1		3	4	6					10			2		5								7	11	9[2]	8[1]							
27 Dec	(H)	Wimbledon	L 0-2	2,500	1		3	4				7					2		5				6				8	11	10	9							
8 Jan	(A)	Oxford	D 2-2		1			6						10[1]			3	4	5	7								11	8	9[1]	2						
15 Jan	(A)	Clapton	D 3-3		1			6				9[1]	4	10[1]				5	2[1]	7					8			11			3						
29 Jan	(H)	Civil Service	W 5-1	1,500	1			6	11			9[2]	8[1]	10[2]			3	4	5	7											2						
5 Feb	(A)	St. Albans	L 2-5		1			4				9[1]					3		5	8		6				7		11	10[1]		2						
19 Feb	(H)	Wycombe	W 5-1	2,000	1			7	6[1]					10			3	4	5	8[1]							9[3]		11		2						
26 Feb	(H)	Ilford	W 5-0	2,000	1			6				9[2]		10[2]			3	4	5	8[1]								7	11		2						
5 Mar	(H)	Tufnell Park	W 2-0		1			7	6			9[1]		10[1]			3	4	5	8									11		2						
12 Mar	(A)	Civil Service	W 4-2		1			6				9	5	10[1]			3			8[1]								7	11[2]		2	4					
26 Mar	(A)	Nunhead	L 0-8		1			7	6			9	5	10			3	4	2	8									11								
2 Apr	(H)	St. Albans	L 2-4	2,000+	1			4	6			9[2]		10			3		5	8						7			11				2				
6 Apr	(H)	Oxford	W 3-2	2,000+	1				6			9	8	10[2]			3		5				4			7[1]			11				2				
13 Apr	(H)	The Casuals	W 2-1									9[1]	4	10		1	3		5	8			6			7			11[1]		2						
23 Apr	(H)	Clapton	L 0-3	2,500	1				6			9	8	10			3	4	5	7									11					2			
27 Apr	(A)	The Casuals	D 1-1		1				3				9[1]	10			2	4	5							7		11							6	8	
30 Apr	(A)	Dulwich	W 3-1		1			6					9[2]	10			3	4	5	8						7[1]			11		2						
2 May	(A)	Tufnell Park	W 4-0		1			6	3				9[3]				2	4	5							7			11						10[1]	8	
4 May	(H)	Dulwich	W 5-1	2,500	1			6	3	11		9[2]		10[1]			2	4	5	7									8[2]								
F.A. CUP																																					
18 Sep	Prel (H)	Aldershot Tract.	W 4-1	3,000			3		6			8[1]	9	10[2]	11	1	2	4[1]	5		7																
2 Oct	1st Q (H)	RAMC	W 3-2	2,000	1		3	5	6			9[1]	8	10[1]	11[1]		2					4		7													
16 Oct	2nd Q (H)	Guildford United £179	W 2-0	5,481	1		3		6			9[2]	8	10	11		2	4	5					7													
30 Oct	3rd Q (H)	Thorneycroft Athletic	W 5-1	3,000	1		3		6			9[2]	8[2]	10[1]	11		2	4	5					7													
13 Nov	4th Q (H)	Leytonstone	W 3-0		1		3					9[1]	8[1]	10[1]	11		2	4	5				6	7													
27 Nov	1st R (H)	Charlton £373	L 1-3	5,593	1		3		6			9	8	10[1]			2		5	7			4					11									
F.A. AMATEUR CUP																																					
9 Oct	1st Q (H)	Godalming	W 5-2		1		3	5	6[1]			9	8[2]	10[2]	11		2					4		7													
23 Oct	2nd Q (H)	Eng. Civlian Staff	W 4-1		1		3			6[1]		9[1]	5	8[1]	10		2					4		7				11[1]									
20 Nov	3rd Q (A)	Addlestone	W 5-1	2,000	1		3					9	8	10[4]			2		5			4	6	7				11[1]									
4 Dec	4th Q (H)	RASC	W 7-0		1		3	4				9[2]	5	10[3]			2[1]			8			6	7[1]				11									
1 Jan	1st R (H)	St. Albans	L 1-4	3,500	1		3		6			9[1]		10			2	4	5							7	8	11									
SURREY SENIOR CUP																																					
22 Jan	1st R (A)	Epsom	W 8-3	2,000	1		3	7	6			9[7]		10			2	4	5	8								11[1]									
12 Feb	2nd R (H)	Farnham U.B.	W 5-1	2,000	1			7	6			9[2]		10[3]			2	4	5	8									11								3
19 Mar	S-F	(Kingston) Nunhead	D 3-3	5,500	1		3	4	6			9[1]	5	10			2			8[1]								7	11[1]								
9 Apr	Rep	(Dulwich) Nunhead	W 4-2	1,500	1			6[1]				9[2]	8[1]	10			3		5	7									11				2		4		
14 May	F	(Guildford) Redhill	W 3-0	7,000	1			6	3			9[1]	8[1]	10[1]			2	4	5	7									11								
SURREY CHARITY SHIELD																																					
25 Sep	1st R (A)	Redhill	L 1-3		1		3	4	6		7	8	9	10[1]	11		2		5																		
TOTAL APPEARANCES					38	1	23	27	27	3	2	35	30	40	13	5	41	23	35	23	2	7	10	9	2	9	6	17	21	3	10	1	3	1	3	2	1
GOALS SCORED								1	3	1		41	17	36	1		1	1	1	4				1		2	5	3	11	2					1		

ISTHMIAN LEAGUE

SEASON 1927-1928

Date	Venue	Opponents	Result	Atten-dance	Montgomery, L.E.	Turner, G.F.	Wheatley, E.	Sherlock, S.	Payne, E.	White, J.	Moore, E.	Fitzgerald, R.R.	Perryman, J.	Price, W.J.	Skelton, W.E.	Simmonds, E.	Maidment, C.V.	Pelham, P.	Beadle, A.	Clifford, P.J.	Steeple, D.	Simmonds, G.	Meekings, W.H.	Long, P.	Butler, A.	Cable, W.	Thayers, H.H.	Blunden, K.	Briggs, T.M.R.	Briggs, W.A.	Challis, W.H.	Sex, R.	Westwood, F.R.	Jones, A.	Chapman, J.	Wills, A.	Urpeth, L.W.	May, H.
27 Aug	(H)	Ilford	W 7-4	2,500	1	2	3	4	5	6	7	8[3]	9[1]	10[3]	11																							
7 Sep	(H)	London Caledonians	D 2-2		1	2		4	5[1]		7	8[1]	9	10		3	6	11																				
10 Sep	(A)	Oxford	W 5-4		1	2		6[1]	5		8	9[1]		10[2]		3	4	11[1]	7																			
15 Sep	(A)	London Caledonians	W 2-1		1		9[1]	6	5		7	8		10[1]		3	4	11		2																		
24 Sep	(H)	St. Albans	W 3-0	3,000	1	2		6	5		7	8	9[2]	10	11[1]	3	4																					
8 Oct	(A)	Wycombe	L 1-3		1	3	9	6	5		7	8		10	11[1]					2	4																	
15 Oct	(H)	Wycombe	D 1-1		1	3	9	6	5		7	8[1]		10	11		4			2																		
22 Oct	(H)	The Casuals	W 2-1	1,000	1	2	5	6			7	9[1]		10[1]	11	3	4					8																
29 Oct	(A)	Tufnell Park	L 0-2		1	2	8	6	5		7	9		10	11	3	4																					
12 Nov	(H)	Leytonstone	L 3-4		1	2	8[2]	6	5	9	7	11[1]			10		4						3															
19 Nov	(A)	Nunhead	L 1-3		1	3	8	6	5		7	11[1]		10			4			2				9														
3 Dec	(A)	Ilford	W 3-2		1	3	8	6	5		7	11		10[1]			4			2				9[2]														
17 Dec	(A)	Dulwich	L 0-2			3	4		5		2	8		10	11									9	1	6	7											
4 Feb	(A)	St. Albans	L 2-4		1	3	4		5		7	10[1]	9[1]							2						6	8	11										
11 Feb	(A)	The Casuals	D 2-2		1	3	4		5[1]		7	11		10[1]						2						6	8		9									
25 Feb	(H)	Wimbledon	W 2-1	3,000 -	1	3	4		5		8		9[1]	10[1]			7			2						6		11										
3 Mar	(H)	Civil Service	W 6-1		1	3	4		5[1]		7	10[1]	9[3]				11[1]			2						6	8											
17 Mar	(A)	Wimbledon	L 1-5		1	3	4		5		7	8[1]	9				11			2						6				10								
24 Mar	(A)	Clapton	D 1-1		1	3	4		5		7		9[1]	10			8			2						6					11							
7 Apr	(A)	Leytonstone	L 1-4			3					7		9[1]	10			4			2					1						11	5	6	8				
14 Apr	(H)	Tufnell Park	W 5-2		1	3	4[1]		5			8	9[1]	10[3]			7			2						6					11							
21 Apr	(A)	Civil Service	W 8-2		1	3	4		5		7	8[2]	9[2]	10[4]			6			2											11							
23 Apr	(H)	Dulwich	W 5-3		1	2	4		5			8	9[3]	10[2]			6														11				3	7		
25 Apr	(H)	Oxford	W 4-1	3,000	1	2	4		5			8[1]	9[1]	10[1]												6					11					7[1]	3	
28 Apr	(H)	Clapton	D 1-1		1	3	4		5		7	10	9							2						6					11					8[1]		
2 May	(H)	Nunhead	W 4-0	2,000	1	2	4		5				9[2]	10[2]												6	7				11						3	8
F.A. CUP																																						
17 Sep	Prel (H)	Weybridge	W 6-2	3,000	1	2	9[2]	6	5[1]		7		8[1]	10[2]		3	4	11																				
1 Oct	1st Q (A)	Guildford City £331	L 0-3	6,013	1	3	8	6	5		7	10	9		11		4			2																		
F.A. AMATEUR CUP																																						
31 Dec	1st R (H)	The Casuals	D 2-2	2,000	1	3	4		5[1]		7	8[1]		10	11					2				9		6												
7 Jan	Rep (A)	The Casuals	W 5-1	3,500	1	3	4		5[1]		7[1]	8		10[1]	11[2]					2				9		6												
21 Jan	2nd R (H)	London Caladonians	L 0-1	3,400	1	3	4		5		7	9		10	11					2				8		6												
SURREY SENIOR CUP																																						
28 Jan	1st R (H)	Mitcham Wanderers	W 2-0	2,000	1	3	4		5		7	11[1]	9	10[1]						2						6	8											
18 Feb	2nd R (H)	The Casuals	W 3-1	2,500	1	3	4		5				9[1]	10[1]			7			2						6	8[1]	11										
10 Mar	S-F	(Wimbledon) Nunhead	W 3-1	2,500	1	3	4		5		7	8[1]	9[1]	10[1]			11			2						6												
5 May	F	(Kingston) Dulwich	L 0-3	4,000	1	3	4		5				9	10	11		7			2						6	8											
SURREY CHARITY SHIELD																																						
3 Sep	1st R (A)	The Casuals	L 1-4		1	2	8	4	5		7	11[1]	9	10		3	6																					
SURREY BENEVOLENT CUP																																						
14 Jan	(A)	Guildford City	W 3-0		1	3	4		5		7[1]	9[2]		10	11					2				8		6												
TOTAL APPEARANCES					35	36	33	15	35	2	31	30	22	31	14	8	24	4	1	24	1	1	1	7	2	19	8	3	1	1	8	1	1	1	1	3	2	1
GOALS SCORED							6	1	6		2	21	22	28	4		1	1						2			1									2		

ISTHMIAN LEAGUE

SEASON 1928-1929

Date	Venue	Opponents	Result	Atten-dance	Montgomery, L.E.	Gary, F.	Turner, G.F.	Potts, A.	Wheatley, E.	Harvey, G.B.	Moore, E.	Franks, A.	Gray, A.	Wells, E.	Maidment, C.V.	Viercant, J.	Crawford, A.	Olsen, T.	May, H.	Beadle, A.	Clifford, J.S.	Greenwood, H.	Cable, W.	Wills, A.	Perryman, J.	Blunden, K.	Sherlock, S.	Thayers, H.H.	Clifford, P.J.	Westwood, F.W.	McKay, A.	May, P.	Briggs, T.M.R.	Galbally, W.C.	Fitzgerald, R.R.	Horton, J.	Gibbs, S.	Butler, A.	Soper, W.G.	Stimson, R.J.	Gillings, A.E.	Hewitt, H.	Hill, N.	Wand, F.
1 Sep	(H)	Civil Service	W 1-0	1,750	1	2	3	4	5	6	7	8	9[1]	10	11																													
5 Sep	(H)	London Caledonians	L 1-2	1,600	1		3	6	4	5		8			11	2	7[1]	9	10																									
8 Sep	(A)	St. Albans	L 2-3		1	2		6	4	5	7[1]		9		11[1]				8	3	10																							
13 Sep	(A)	London Caledonians	L 0-2		1	2	3		8	5					11							4	6	7	9	10																		
15 Sep	(A)	Ilford	L 0-4		1	2	3	4	8	5	7				11				10				6		9																			
22 Sep	(A)	Oxford	D 1-1	3,000	1	2	3	4		5	7			11					10			6		8	9[1]																			
29 Sep	(H)	Dulwich	D 3-3		1	3		8[1]		5	2			10[1]	11								6		9[1]		4	7																
13 Oct	(A)	Dulwich	L 0-4		1	2	3	4	10	5	8				11										9	6		7																
20 Oct	(H)	The Casuals	D 2-2	1,500	1	2	3		8	5[1]	10			11	4										9[1]	6		7																
17 Nov	(H)	Clapton	L 1-3	1,800	1		3		5		9				6				8						10[1]	11		7	2	4														
1 Dec	(A)	Leytonstone	L 2-3		1	3		4	5		2				6				8[1]					7	10[1]	11					9													
22 Dec	(H)	Nunhead	L 0-1	500	1	2	3	5	9										8					7	10							4	6	11										
25 Dec	(H)	Wimbledon	W 5-3	1,200	1	2	3	5			8				4									7	10[2]								6	11	9[3]									
26 Dec	(A)	Wimbledon	L 2-4		1	2	3		4		9								8[1]					7	10[1]	11						6	5											
29 Dec	(A)	Tufnell Park	L 1-3		1	2	3		9		4				6				8					7	10[1]								5	11										
5 Jan	(H)	Wycombe	W 1-0	700	1	2			4		9[1]				5				8	3					10	6								11			7							
12 Jan	(H)	Oxford	W 2-1		1	2	3		4		9				5				8						10[2]	6								11			7							
19 Jan	(A)	The Casuals	W 2-0	1,500	1	2	3		4		9[1]				5[1]				8						10	6								11			7							
2 Feb	(H)	Tufnell Park	L 0-5	500		2	3		4		9				5				8						10	6								11			7	1						
9 Feb	(H)	St. Albans	L 2-5	1,000	1	2	3		4		9[2]				5				8						10	6								11			7							
2 Mar	(H)	Ilford	L 2-4	2,000	1	2	3		4		9				5										10[1]	6								11					7[1]	8				
9 Mar	(A)	Civil Service	W 4-2		1	2	3				6				5				8															11					7[2]	4	9	10[2]		
16 Mar	(A)	Nunhead	W 2-1		1	2	3				6								8[1]						9[1]					5				11					7	4		10		
6 Apr	(H)	Leytonstone	W 1-0		1		3				6								8						9[1]					5				11					7	4		10	2	
20 Apr	(A)	Wycombe	L 1-7		1		3				6								8			4			9					5				11					7[1]			10	2	
24 Apr	(A)	Clapton	L 1-2		1	4	3				7								8[1]	2					9	6				5				11								10		
F.A. CUP																																												
10 Nov	4th Q (A)	Tooting Town	W 3-1	2,000	1		3		5		9[1]				6				8						10[1]	11[1]		7	2	4														
24 Nov	1st R (A)	Newport £175	L 0-7	3,000	1		3	4	5		9				6				8						10	11		7	2															
F.A. AMATEUR CUP																																												
15 Dec	1st R (A)	Barking	L 1-6		1	2	3		5		7				6				8[1]						10	11						4					9							
SURREY SENIOR CUP																																												
26 Jan	1st R (A)	Wimbledon	L 1-7		1	2	3		4		9								8						10[1]	6						5		11										7
SURREY CHARITY SHIELD																																												
3 Nov	1st R (A)	Wimbledon	L 2-5		1		3		5		8				4							6			10[2]	11		7	2							9								
SURREY COMBINATION CUP																																												
6 Oct	S-F (H)	Guildford City £102	L 1-4	2,955	1	2	3		4	5	8[1]			10	11								6		9			7																
TOTAL APPEARANCES					31	25	28	11	24	10	29	2	2	5	24	1	1	1	23	3	1	4	4	7	28	18	1	8	4	6	1	4	4	15	1	1	6	1	5	4	1	5	2	1
GOALS SCORED								1		1	7		1	1	2		1		5						18	1									3				4			2		

SEASON 1929-1930

ISTHMIAN LEAGUE

Date	Venue	Opponents	Result	Attendance	Montgomery, L.E.	Beadle, A.	Turner, G.F.	O'Donnell, J.	Craddock, S.E.	Greenwood, H.	Moore, E.	May, H.	Sayer, R.J.	Moseley, G.L.	Larking, J.	Sleet, A.T.	Lockwood, F.B.	Chitty, W.	Tabert, J.K.	Galbally, W.C.	Cornell, E.S.	Butler, A.	Johnstone, A.E.	Harding, F.	Warnes, W.H.	Stevens, W.	Hewitt, H.	Donovan, C.	Blunden, K.	Bateman, D.	Gary, F.	Seddon, C.	Bolton, A.W.	Fitzgerald, R.R.	Perryman, J.	Stocker, L.	Shaw, H.	Lawrence, W.H.	Jennings, G.	Harrison, D.	Turner, E.C.	Warnes, G.
31 Aug	(A)	Leytonstone	L 1-6		1	2	3	4	5	6	7	8[1]	9	10	11																											
4 Sep	(H)	London Caledonians	W 4-2	1,500	1	2	3		5			8[2]		9[1]		4	6	7[1]	10	11																						
12 Sep	(A)	London Caledonians	L 0-3		1	3			5		2			9		4	6	7	10	11	8																					
14 Sep	(A)	Oxford	L 1-4			3				5	2	8		9		4	6	7	10			1	11[1]																			
5 Oct	(H)	Wycombe	D 2-2	1,600			3		5					8[1]		4	6[1]	11				1	10	2	7	9																
19 Oct	(A)	Nunhead	L 0-3		1	2	3		5			8		9			6	11					10		7	4																
2 Nov	(A)	Clapton	L 1-3		1	2			5		9			8		7	6	11						3		4	10[1]															
30 Nov	(A)	St. Albans	L 3-5		1	3	2		5		9[1]			10			6	11[1]							7[1]	4		8														
7 Dec	(A)	Ilford	L 1-5		1	3	2		5		9[1]			10				7								4		8	6	11												
21 Dec	(H)	Nunhead	W 5-4				3		5					10			6	11				1			7[1]						2	4	9[1]	8[3]								
25 Dec	(A)	Wimbledon	W 4-2	3,000	1		3		5					10			6	11[1]							7			8			2	4	9[3]									
26 Dec	(H)	Wimbledon	W 6-2	3,000	1		3		5					10[2]			6	11							7[1]						2	4	9[2]	8[1]								
28 Dec	(A)	Dulwich	D 0-0		1		3		5					10			6	11							7			8			2	4	9									
4 Jan	(H)	Oxford	W 4-1	2,000	1		3		5					10			6	11							7[1]						2	4	9[1]	8[2]								
11 Jan	(H)	St. Albans	W 4-0		1	3			5		8[2]			10[1]			6	11							7						2	4	9[1]									
18 Jan	(H)	Leytonstone	W 5-1	2,000+	1		3		5		8[2]			10			6[1]	11							7[1]						2	4			9[1]							
1 Feb	(H)	Kingstonian	W 5-1	3,000+	1		3		5[1]		8			10			6	11[1]							7[2]			9[1]			2	4										
8 Feb	(A)	Wycombe	L 0-6		1		3		5		8			10			6	11							7			9			2	4										
8 Mar	(H)	The Casuals	W 3-1	3,000+	1	2	3		5		8[1]			10			6			11					7[1]							4			9[1]							
15 Mar	(H)	Tufnell Park	L 0-3	1,200	1	2			5		8			10			6			11									3			4				7	9					
22 Mar	(H)	Clapton	W 1-0	1,700	1	2	3		5		8[1]			10			6			11					7							4					9					
29 Mar	(A)	The Casuals	D 2-2		1	2	3		5[1]		8[1]			9									10		7				6	11		4										
5 Apr	(H)	Dulwich	D 4-4	2,000	1	2	3		5		8	9[1]		10[2]			6								7[1]					11		4										
10 Apr	(A)	Tufnell Park	D 1-1		1	2	3		5			9		10			6								8[1]					11		4										7
29 Apr	(H)	Ilford	W 9-3	2,000	1	2	3		5	10[3]		8[1]					6								7[1]					11		4			9[4]							
30 Apr	(A)	Kingstonian	L 0-2		1	2			5	6		8		7			10												3			4			9			11				
F.A. CUP																																										
21 Sep	Pr (H)	Mitcham Wanderers	L 1-2	2,000	1		3				7	8		9[1]		4	6						10			5					2								11			
F.A. AMATEUR CUP																																										
12 Oct	1st Q (A)	Hersham	W 5-1			3			5		6	8[1]		10[1]		4		11[1]				1			7	9[2]					2											
26 Oct	2nd Q (A)	RASC (Aldershot) AET	W 5-3		1	2	3[1]		5		9[2]	8[1]		10[1]			6	11							7	4																
9 Nov	3rd Q (H)	RAMC (Aldershot)	W 3-2	2,000	1	3	2		5		9[1]	8[1]		10[1]			6	11							7	4																
23 Nov	4th Q (A)	K.O.S.B.	W 3-2		1	3	2		5		9[1]	8		10			6[1]	11							7[1]	4																
14 Dec	1st R (A)	Hampstead Town	L 2-3	2,000			3		5		9			10			6	11				1			7[1]	4		8[1]			2											
SURREY SENIOR CUP																																										
25 Jan	1st R (A)	Whyteleafe	W 9-3		1	2	3		5		8[2]			10[1]		6		11[1]							7[1]						9[4]	4										
22 Feb	2nd R (H)	Nunhead AET	D 1-1	2.500	1	2	3		5		8			9			6	11							7[1]							4			10							
1 Mar	Rep (A)	Nunhead	L 1-2		1	2	3		5		8			10			6			11					7[1]							4								9		
SURREY CHARITY SHIELD																																										
7 Sep	1st R (H)	Egham	W 2-1	1,500	1	2	3		5[1]			8		9[1]		4	6	7	10	11																						
15 Feb	S-F (H)	Mitcham Wanderers	L 0-1		1		3		5		2			10			6	11							7			9				4									8	
SURREY COMBINATION CUP																																										
28 Sep	S-F (A)	Guildford City	L 2-4		1		3		5		7	8		9[1]		4	6			11						10[1]					2											
TOTAL APPEARANCES					**33**	**25**	**31**	**1**	**36**	**4**	**26**	**15**	**1**	**37**	**1**	**10**	**33**	**26**	**4**	**8**	**1**	**5**	**5**	**2**	**27**	**12**	**1**	**8**	**4**	**5**	**14**	**21**	**6**	**3**	**5**	**1**	**2**	**1**	**1**	**1**	**1**	**1**
GOALS SCORED							**1**		**3**	**3**	**15**	**8**		**14**			**3**	**6**					**1**		**16**	**3**	**1**	**2**			**4**		**8**	**6**	**6**							

SEASON 1930-1931

ISTHMIAN LEAGUE

Date	Venue	Opponents	Result	Attendance	Montgomery, L.E.	Beadle, A.	Hill, N.	Seddon, C.	Craddock, S.E.	Lockwood, F.B.	Warnes, W.H.	May, H.	Fitzgerald, R.R.	Watson, R.	Lawrence, W.H.	Gary, F.	Moseley, G.L.	Bateman, D.	Butler, A.	Bradshaw, A.	Turner, E.C.	Beswick, S.	Turner, H.E.	Mason, G.W.H.	Blunden, K.	Harris, H.H.	Greenwood, H.	Brownbill, T.J.	Sturt, S.	Moore, E.	Bolton, A.W.	Hewitt, H.	Stockley, F.S.	Triggs, R.W.	Tomkins, J.	Chapman, J.	O'Donnell, J.	Skipsey, A.	Collins, A.W.	Johnson, F.R.	Gibbs, S.	Parker, W.S.	Adams, S.	Goddard, P.W.	Tann, R.H.	Galbally, W.C.	Miles, H.C.	Pugh, H.J.	Whatley, I.
3 Sep	(H)	London Caledonians	L 0-3	2,000	1	2	3	4	5	6	7	8	9	10	11																																		
6 Sep	(A)	Ilford	W 5-4		1	3		4	5	6	7[3]		8	10		2	9[1]	11[1]																															
11 Sep	(A)	London Caledonians	W 1-0			3		4	5	6			8	10[1]			9	11	1	2	7																												
13 Sep	(A)	Kingstonian	L 2-6			2		4	5	6			8[1]	10			7	11	1	3		9[1]																											
11 Oct	(H)	Wycombe	L 0-1	2,000	1	3		4	5	6		8		10							7		2	9	11																								
25 Oct	(A)	Wimbledon	L 3-4		1	3		4	5	8[1]	7[1]			9									2	10[1]	11	6																							
1 Nov	(H)	Nunhead	W 4-2	1,800	1	3		4		6	7[2]	8[2]		10				11					2	9		5																							
8 Nov	(A)	St. Albans	D 4-4		1			4	5	6	7	8[1]		10[2]				11					2	9[1]		3																							
15 Nov	(H)	The Casuals	L 0-1		1	3		4	5	6		8						11					2	9		7																							10
29 Nov	(A)	The Casuals	W 2-1		1	3		4	5	6	7	8[1]						11[1]					2	9			10																						
6 Dec	(A)	Oxford	D 1-1		1	3		4	5	6	7	8											2		11		10	9[1]																					
20 Dec	(A)	Wycombe	L 1-4		1	3		4	5	6	7	8						11		2				9[1]			10																						
27 Dec	(H)	Leytonstone	L 1-2	1,500		3		4	5	6										7			2	10					1	8	9[1]	11																	
3 Jan	(H)	St. Albans	W 4-2	1,200	1	3		4	5		7	8[1]						11					2				6				9[1]		10[2]																
10 Jan	(H)	Oxford	W 3-1		1			4	5		7[2]	8						11					2				6				9		10[1]			3													
30 Jan	(A)	Clapton	L 4-8		1	3		7	5	4		8[2]						11					2	9[2]			6						10																
14 Feb	(A)	Leytonstone	D 2-2		1				5			8[1]						11[1]					2	9			6						10	7		3	4												
28 Feb	(A)	Dulwich	W 4-1	5,000	1	3		6			7[2]	8						11					2	9			5										4	10[2]											
21 Mar	(H)	Ilford	D 2-2	2,000	1	3		4	5			8						11				7	2	9[2]			6						10																
28 Mar	(H)	Dulwich	L 0-1	2,000	1	3		4	5			8						11					2	9			6						10	7															
11 Apr	(A)	Nunhead	L 1-2		1	3		6		4	7	8[1]						11					2										9		5			10											
15 Apr	(H)	Kingstonian	L 0-2			3		6		4		8												9					1						10				2	5	7	11							
18 Apr	(H)	Clapton	L 2-3		1			6			7[1]	8			11								2	9[1]											5	3	4	10											
27 Apr	(A)	Tufnell Park	W 3-1					6		5[1]	7	8[2]											2	11					1						10		4					8	3						
30 Apr	(H)	Wimbledon o.g.	L 2-3		1			6		10		8			7								2	9[1]	11		5										4						3						
2 May	(H)	Tufnell Park	W 5-2					6			7[1]	8[1]			11								2	9[3]			5		1														3	4	10				
F.A. CUP																																																	
18 Sep	Pr (H)	Whyteleafe Albion	W 5-1	2,000	1	3		4	5[1]	6[1]	7[1]		8	10[2]			9			2																										11			
4 Oct	1st Q (H)	The Casuals	W 4-0	2,000	1	3		4	5	6	7	8[1]		10									2		11[1]			9[2]																					
18 Oct	2nd Q (A)	Kingstonian £179	L 1-3	5,500	1	3		4	5	8				10	7								2	9[1]	11	6																							
F.A. AMATEUR CUP																																																	
13 Dec	1st R (H)	Cambridge Town	W 3-1	2,300		3		4	5	6	7[1]	8[1]						11					2	9			10[1]		1																				
17 Jan	2nd R (H)	Leyton £108	W 4-0	3,600	1	3			5	4	7	8						11[1]					2	9[1]			6						10[2]																
7 Feb	3rd R (H)	Portland £135	W 2-1	4,500	1	3		6	5	4	7	8[1]						11					2	9[1]									10																
21 Feb	4th R (A)	Clapton	W 1-0	5,000	1	3			5	4	7	8[1]						11				9	2				6						10																
7 Mar	S-F	(Ilford) Wycombe	L 0-3	7,300	1	3			5	4	7	8						11					2	9			6						10																
SURREY SENIOR CUP																																																	
23 Jan	1st R (A)	Kingstonian £120	L 1-5	5,000	1	3			5	4	7[1]	8											2	9			6					11	10																
SURREY CHARITY SHIELD																																																	
25 Sep	1st R (H)	Egham	L 2-3		1	3		4	5		7[1]			10										9			6[1]																			11	2	8	
SURREY COMBINATION CUP																																																	
14 Mar	1st R (H)	Guildford City £85	D 1-1	3,000		2			5	4	7	8						11						9[1]			6		1				10			3													
20 Apr	Rep (A)	Guildford City	D 2-2		1			6		5		8[1]											2													3	4				7[1]	9	*only nine men played*						
23 Apr	2 Rep (A)	Guildford City	L 2-4		1	3		6		4	7	8[2]											2	11									9		10					5									
TOTAL APPEARANCES					**31**	**31**	**1**	**33**	**29**	**30**	**26**	**31**	**5**	**12**	**5**	**1**	**4**	**22**	**2**	**5**	**2**	**3**	**30**	**27**	**6**	**5**	**19**	**2**	**6**	**1**	**3**	**2**	**14**	**2**	**5**	**5**	**6**	**3**	**1**	**2**	**2**	**3**	**3**	**1**	**1**	**2**	**1**	**1**	**1**
GOALS SCORED									**1**	**3**	**16**	**19**	**1**	**5**			**1**	**4**				**1**		**16**	**1**		**2**	**3**			**2**		**5**					**2**			**1**								

SEASON 1931-1932

ISTHMIAN LEAGUE

Date	Venue	Opponents	Result	Attendance	Sturt, S.	Roberts, W.	Turner, H.E.	O'Donnell, J.	Tomkins, J.	Greenwood, H.	Warnes, W.H.	May, H.	Breeze, C.H.	Scott, R.N.	Bateman, D.	Collins, A.W.	Knight, S.W.J.	Udal, P.	Barrs, J.	Brooks, R.A.	Bayley, S.G.	Lockwood, F.B.	Montgomery, L.E.
29 Aug	(A)	St. Albans	L 2-3		1	2	3	4	5	6	7	8[1]	9[1]	10	11								
2 Sep	(H)	London Caledonians	W 4-2	2,500	1			4	5	6	7[1]	8[1]	10[2]			2	3	9	11				
5 Sep	(A)	The Casuals	L 0-4		1		2		5	6	7	8	10				3	9	11	4			
10 Sep	(A)	London Caledonians	W 3-0				2		5	6	7[1]	8[2]	10				3	9	11		1	4	
10 Oct	(H)	Wimbledon	L 0-1						6			8		10	11	2		9				4	1
24 Oct	(H)	The Casuals	W 4-1	2,300			2	4	6		7	8	10[3]		11[1]	3							1
31 Oct	(A)	Ilford	D 1-1				2	4	10[1]	6	7				11	3		9					1
7 Nov	(H)	Clapton £60	W 4-1				2	4	6		7[2]	8[1]	9		11	3							1
14 Nov	(A)	Oxford	L 1-3				2		6	5	7	8	9[1]		11	3						4	1
28 Nov	(A)	Leytonstone	D 1-1				2	4	6									9					1
5 Dec	(H)	Dulwich	L 0-4		1		2	4	6				9		11								
19 Dec	(H)	Tufnell Park	L 1-2				3	4	6									9					1
2 Jan	(H)	Oxford	L 2-3				2	4	6		7[1]					3							1
16 Jan	(A)	Tufnell Park	L 1-2				2		5		7				11	3		9					1
6 Feb	(A)	Clapton	W 2-1		1		2		5	4	7		9										
20 Feb	(H)	Leytonstone	L 1-2		1		2		4[1]						11								
27 Feb	(H)	St. Albans	W 4-2	1,200			2	4	6[1]						11	3							1
5 Mar	(A)	Wimbledon	L 1-3				2	4	5				8			3							1
12 Mar	(A)	Wycombe	L 1-2	3,500	1		2	4	6				8		11	3							
19 Mar	(H)	Wycombe	D 1-1		1			4					8		11	2		9					
26 Mar	(A)	Kingstonian	L 1-6				2	4					8		11	3							1
28 Mar	(H)	Kingstonian	L 1-5		1		2	4					8		11	3							
9 Apr	(H)	Ilford	D 2-2	1,200	1		2	4			7		10										
16 Apr	(H)	Nunhead	D 3-3		1		2	4			7[1]		10		11								
28 Apr	(A)	Dulwich	L 0-5		1		2	4			7												
7 May	(A)	Nunhead	L 3-4		1		2	3					10					9[1]					
F.A. CUP																							
17 Sep	Pr (H)	Leyland Motors £70	W 5-0	2,300			2		6	5	7[1]	8[1]	10[2]		11		3	9			1	4[1]	
3 Oct	1st Q (H)	Sutton	L 1-4	2,600			2	4	6		7	8	10		11	3	5						1
F.A. AMATEUR CUP																							
12 Dec	1st R (A)	Maidenhead £95	L 0-4	2,800			2	4	6		7		9			3							1
SURREY SENIOR CUP																							
23 Jan	1st R (H)	Guildford Pinks	W 3-1	1,500	1		2		6	4	7[1]		8		11[2]	3							
13 Feb	2nd R (H)	Wimbledon	L 1-3	2,300	1		2		4		7[1]		9		11								
SURREY CHARITY SHIELD																							
12 Sep	1st R (H)	Dorking	D 3-3				2	4	5	6		8[1]			11[1]		3	9[1]					1
17 Oct	Rep (A)	Dorking	W 4-0	1,000				4	10	6	7[1]			8[2]	11	2		9[1]					1
21 Nov	S-F (H)	Camberley & Y	D 2-2				2	4	6		7[1]		9[1]		11	3							1
30 Nov	Rep (A)	Camberley & Y	W 4-3	1,418	1		2		6	4	7[2]		9[2]		11								
3 May	F	(Wimbledon) Nunhead	L 1-2		1		2	4			7		10										
SURREY COMBINATION CUP																							
24 Sep	(A)	Guildford City	L 1-4	3,950			2		5	6	7[1]		10		11	3		9			1	4	
TOTAL APPEARANCES					**17**	**1**	**33**	**25**	**29**	**13**	**24**	**11**	**26**	**3**	**24**	**20**	**6**	**14**	**3**	**1**	**3**	**5**	**17**
GOALS SCORED									**3**		**14**	**7**	**12**	**2**	**4**			**3**				**1**	

Date	Opponents	Chapman, J.	Osgood, N.	Turner, E.C.	Miller, D.A.	Buckmaster, F.	Hooker, H.	Perrett, G.R.	Lawrence, W.H.	Blunden, K.	Mason, G.W.H.	Stubbs, F.R.	Hitchcock, B.	Todd, E.J.	Green, S.L.	Vincent, J.	Prestoe, G.	Bell, J.R.	Moseley.G.	Pitts, H.
29 Aug	St. Albans																			
2 Sep	London Caledonians																			
5 Sep	The Casuals																			
10 Sep	London Caledonians																			
10 Oct	Wimbledon	3	5	7																
24 Oct	The Casuals		5		9															
31 Oct	Ilford		5			8														
7 Nov	Clapton		5		10[1]															
14 Nov	Oxford				10															
28 Nov	Leytonstone	3	5			8[1]	7	10	11											
5 Dec	Dulwich	3	5		10	8	7													
19 Dec	Tufnell Park		5			10	8[1]	11	7											2
2 Jan	Oxford	11	5			8[1]	9				10									
16 Jan	Tufnell Park					10	8[1]			6		4								
6 Feb	Clapton					10[1]	8[1]		11	6			3							
20 Feb	Leytonstone		5			10	8		7	6			3	9						
27 Feb	St. Albans		5			10[1]	8[1]		7	9[1]										
5 Mar	Wimbledon					10	7		11	9[1]		6								
12 Mar	Wycombe		5			10	7[1]			9										
19 Mar	Wycombe	3	5[1]			10	7			6										
26 Mar	Kingstonian		5			10[1]	7			6					9					
28 Mar	Kingstonian					9	7[1]			6			5			10				
9 Apr	Ilford		5			8[1]	11[1]			6			3				9			
16 Apr	Nunhead		5			8				6			3				9[2]			
28 Apr	Dulwich					8			11	6			3			10	9	5		
7 May	Nunhead					8	7[1]	11[1]		5			4		*only ten players*					
F.A. CUP																				
17 Sep	Leyland Motors																			
3 Oct	Sutton					9[1]														
F.A. AMATEUR CUP																				
12 Dec	Maidenhead		5		10	8				11										
SURREY SENIOR CUP																				
23 Jan	Guildford Pinks		5		9	10														
13 Feb	Wimbledon		5			10	8			6			3							
SURREY CHARITY SHIELD																				
12 Sep	Dorking								7										10	
17 Oct	Dorking	3	5																	
21 Nov	Camberley & Y		5		10	8														
30 Nov	Camberley & Y	3	5			10	8													
3 May	(Wimbledon) Nunhead		5			8	11			6			3				9[1]			
SURREY COMBINATION CUP																				
24 Sep	Guildford City					8														
TOTAL APPEARANCES		**7**	**22**	**1**	**7**	**26**	**18**	**3**	**8**	**16**	**1**	**2**	**9**	**1**	**1**	**2**	**4**	**1**	**1**	**1**
GOALS SCORED			**1**		**1**	**7**	**8**	**1**		**2**							**3**			

SEASON 1932-1933

ISTHMIAN LEAGUE

Date	Venue	Opponents	Result	Atten-dance	Sturt, S.	Turner, H.E.	Simmonds, E.	Crutchley, C.J.	Osgood, N.	Ives, W.	Hill, O.E.	Buckmaster, F.	Christopher, J.	Symonds, J.	Perrett, G.R.	Hooker, H.	Moseley, G.	Gough, R.	Brown, M.K.	Rooke, R.	Blunden, K.	Freeman, W.G.	Cowle, E.J.	Gibbs, S.	O'Donnell, J.	Clarke, E.C.	Shires, H.T.	Udal, P.	Collins, A.W.	Abbott, A.W.	Lawrence, W.H.	Robinson, N.	Knight, H.
27 Aug	(A)	Oxford	L 1-5		1	2	3	4	5	6	7	8[1]	9	10	11																		
31 Aug	(H)	Wimbledon	D 2-2	1,400	1	2	3	4	5	6	7	10[1]			11	8[1]	9																
7 Sep	(A)	Wimbledon	L 1-5		1	2	3	5		4	7	10[1]			11	8	9	6															
24 Sep	(H)	St. Albans	W 3-0	1,300	1	2	3	4	5	6		10			11	8[1]			7	9[2]													
15 Oct	(A)	Dulwich	D 2-2	6,000	1	2	3	4		6		8			10				7	9[2]	5	11											
29 Oct	(H)	Nunhead	W 4-3	1,500	1	2	3	4	5	6		8			10[1]	7[1]				9[1]		11[1]											
12 Nov	(H)	Clapton	D 1-1	1,500	1		3	4	5	6[1]		8			10	7				9		11	2										
3 Dec	(A)	Clapton	L 1-5		1	2	3	5		6		8			10[1]	7						11		9	4								
17 Dec	(H)	Wycombe	W 5-1	1,400	1	2	3	4	5	6		10[1]			8[1]	7				9[3]		11											
24 Dec	(A)	Nunhead	L 1-2		1	2	3	4		6		10			8	7[1]				9	5					11							
31 Dec	(H)	Leytonstone	W 3-1	2,000	1	2	3	4	5	6		10			11	7[1]				9[1]								8[1]					
28 Jan	(A)	Leytonstone	L 1-3		1	5	3	4				10			11	9[1]													2	7	8		6
4 Feb	(H)	Oxford	W 2-1		1	2	3	4	5			10[1]				7		6		9[1]						11					8		
11 Feb	(H)	London Caledonians	D 1-1		1	2		4	5	6		10				7				9			3			11					8[1]		
18 Feb	(A)	Ilford	L 0-1		1	2	3	4		6		10				7				9					8	11	5						
25 Feb	(A)	St. Albans	W 6-1		1	2	3	4		6		10				7				9[3]						11[1]	5				8[2]		
4 Mar	(H)	The Casuals	W 1-0	1,600	1	2	3	4	5	6[1]		10				7				9						11					8		
18 Mar	(H)	Tufnell Park	L 2-3		1	2	3	4		6		10			8	7[1]									9	11[1]	5						
25 Mar	(A)	Tufnell Park	L 0-4	1,500	1	2	3	4		6		10									9					11	5				8	7	
1 Apr	(A)	The Casuals	L 3-5		1	2	3	4	5	6		10				7					9[2]					11					8[1]		
8 Apr	(H)	Ilford	W 5-3	1,300	1	2		4	5	6		10[1]				7					9[3]		3			11[1]					8		
15 Apr	(A)	Kingstonian	W 3-1		1	2	3	4	5	6		10[1]				7					9[2]					11					8		
17 Apr	(H)	Kingstonian £94	W 2-1	3,000	1	2		4	5	6					10[1]	7					9		3			11					8[1]		
26 Apr	(H)	Dulwich	L 3-4	1,100	1	2	3	4		6					10[1]	7[1]					9					11[1]	5				8		
29 Apr	(A)	London Caledonians	L 0-3		1		3	4		6		10			8	7					9		2			11	5						
6 May	(A)	Wycombe	L 0-3		1	2		4	5	6		10			11						9		3			7					8		
F.A. CUP																																	
17 Sep	Pre (H)	Walton	W 5-3		1	2	3	4	5	6		10[1]			11[1]	8[1]			7	9[2]													
1 Oct	1st Q (H)	Met. Police	L 0-2	1,650	1	2	3	4	5	6		10			11	8			7	9													
F.A. AMATEUR CUP																																	
8 Oct	1st Q (A)	Basingstoke AET	W 4-2		1	2		4	5	6		10			11	8			7	9[4]									3				
22 Oct	2nd Q (A)	RAMC	W 1-0		1	2	3	4	5	6		8			10	7[1]				9		11											
5 Nov	3rd Q (H)	2nd Bn. Loyal Regt.	W 5-1	1,776	1	2	3	4	5	6		8			10[1]	7[1]				9[2]		11[1]											
19 Nov	4th Q (A)	RASC (Aldershot)	D 2-2		1	2	3	4	5	6		8			10	7				9[2]		11											
26 Nov	Rep (H)	RASC (Aldershot)	W 5-0	2,500	1	2	3	4	5	6		8				7				9[2]	10[2]	11[1]											
10 Dec	1st R (H)	London Caledonians	W 3-0	1,500	1	2	3	4	5	6		10[1]			8[1]	7				9[1]		11											
14 Jan	2nd R (A)	Slough	L 1-6	2,500	1	2	3	4	5	6		10			8	7				9[1]		11											
SURREY SENIOR CUP																																	
21 Jan	1st R (H)	Nunhead	L 0-1	1,300	1	2	3	4	5	6		10			8	7				9						11							
SURREY CHARITY SHIELD																																	
10 Sep	1st R (H)	Camberley & Y	W 2-1		1		3	4	5[1]	6		8			11	7	10			9[1]									2				
11 Mar	S-F (H)	Redhill £62 AET	W 4-3	2,100	1	2	3	4	5	6		10[1]			8[1]	7[1]				9[1]						11							
22 Apr	F (H)	Epsom £70	L 0-5	2.045	1	2	3	4	5	6		10				7					9					11					8		
SURREY COMBINATION CUP																																	
7 Jan	S-F (H)	Guildford City	L 0-2	3,000	1	2	3	4	5	6		10				7				9		11						8					
TOTAL APPEARANCES					**40**	**37**	**35**	**40**	**29**	**38**	**3**	**38**	**1**	**1**	**28**	**36**	**3**	**2**	**5**	**25**	**12**	**12**	**6**	**1**	**3**	**18**	**6**	**2**	**3**	**1**	**13**	**1**	**1**
GOALS SCORED									**1**	**2**		**10**			**9**	**12**				**29**	**9**	**3**				**4**		**1**			**5**		

SEASON 1933-1934

ISTHMIAN LEAGUE

Date	Venue	Opponents	Result	Attendance	Sturt, S.	Turner, H.E.	Cowle, E.J.	Crutchley, C.J.	Edwards, A.	Hollingsworth, F.	Lawrence, W.H.	East, L.	Udal, P.	Buckmaster, F.	Francis, J.	O'Donnell, J.	Gough, R.	Clarke, E.C.	Collins, A.W.	Callingham, G.	Abbott, A.W.	Blunden, K.	Griffiths, A.F.	Robins, R.W.V.	Hutchings, R.C.H.	Perrett, G.R.	Shires, H.T.	Hough, E.	Warnes, G.E.	Faggetter, S.H.	Hooker, R.	West, W.P.	Hooker, H.	Searle, W.	Knight, H.	Tilley, J.
26 Aug	(H)	Oxford	L 2-3	1,900	1	2	3	4	5	6	7[1]	8	9	10	11[1]																					
31 Aug	(A)	Dulwich	L 1-6		1	2	3	5				8	9	10	11[1]	4	6	7																		
2 Sep	(A)	Leytonstone	L 2-3		1	2	3	4	5		7	8[2]	9	10	11			6																		
6 Sep	(H)	Dulwich	L 1-4		1		3	4	5	6	8	9			11[1]			7	2	10																
9 Sep	(H)	Tufnell Park	W 4-2		1	2	3	4	5		8	9[3]		10[1]	11			6			7															
30 Sep	(H)	The Casuals	W 2-1	1,650	1		3	4		6	8	9[1]		10	11			7	2[1]			5														
14 Oct	(A)	Wycombe	L 0-4		1	2	3	4		6	8	9		10	11			7				5														
11 Nov	(A)	London Caledonians	L 0-4		1	2	3	4		6	8			10	9			11					5	7												
25 Nov	(H)	Wycombe	W 3-1		1	2	3	4		5	8			10[1]	9[1]			11							6	7[1]										
2 Dec	(A)	Kingstonian	L 0-3		1	2	3	7		4	8				9			11							6	10	5									
16 Dec	(H)	Leytonstone	L 0-3		1		3	4		5	8			10	11			7	2						6	9										
30 Dec	(A)	Ilford	L 1-4		1	2		4			8			10											6	11	5	3	7	9[1]						
6 Jan	(A)	Oxford	L 1-4		1	2					8			6				4				5	3			10			7	9[1]	11					
27 Jan	(H)	Clapton	W 5-1				3				8[1]			10	11[1]			4	2			5	6			7				9[3]		1				
10 Feb	(H)	London Caledonians	W 6-1	1,500			3			2	8[2]			10	11[2]			4				5	6			7[1]				9[1]		1				
24 Feb	(A)	Nunhead	L 0-3				3				8			10	11			4	2			5	6			7				9		1				
10 Mar	(H)	Ilford	L 1-4	1,600			3			2	8			10	11			4			7	5	6							9[1]		1				
17 Mar	(A)	Clapton	L 0-4				3			4	8			10	11				2			5	6							9		1	7			
31 Mar	(H)	St. Albans	W 5-4	1,500		4	3			6	8			10[2]	11				2		7	5								9[3]		1				
2 Apr	(A)	St. Albans	L 2-4				3			6	8			10[1]	11		4		2		7	5								9[1]		1				
7 Apr	(H)	Nunhead	L 2-4			2	3	4		6	8			10	11[1]						7	5										1	9[1]			
24 Apr	(A)	The Casuals	L 0-2				2	4		3				10	11			8			7	5	6							9		1				
25 Apr	(H)	Wimbledon	L 0-2			4	3			2				10	11						7	5	9									1	8	6		
28 Apr	(H)	Kingstonian	L 1-5				3	4		2				8				11[1]			7	10	6							9		1		5		
2 May	(A)	Wimbledon	D 4-4			5	3	4		2	7			10	11[1]						8	9[3]	6									1				
4 May	(A)	Tufnell Park	L 0-1		1		3	4		2				10			7				8	9	5												6	11
F.A. CUP																																				
16 Sep	Pre (H)	Epsom £61	D 1-1	1,760	1	2	3	4	5	6	8	9		10[1]	11						7															
20 Sep	Rep (A)	Epsom AET	L 2-5	2,000	1	2	3	4	5	6		8		10				11			7[1]	9[1]														
F.A. AMATEUR CUP																																				
7 Oct	1st Q (H)	Wellington Wks £48	W 4-2	1,450	1		3	4		6	8	9[2]		10[2]	11			7	2			5														
21 Oct	2nd Q (H)	Guildford Pinks	W 3-0	1,500	1	2	3	4		6		9		10[1]	11[1]			7				5											8[1]			
4 Nov	3rd Q (A)	RASC (Aldershot)	W 3-0		1	2	3	4		6	8			10	9[2]			11[1]				5											7			
18 Nov	4th Q (A)	Egham	W 2-1	1,500	1	2	3	4		6	8			10[1]	9			11[1]			7						5									
9 Dec	1st R (A)	Wimbledon	L 1-2	4,000	1	2	3	4		5	8[1]			10	9			11			7				6											
SURREY SENIOR CUP																																				
20 Jan	!st R (H)	Carshalton	W 3-1				3				8			10	11[2]			4	2			5	6			7[1]						1	9			
17 Feb	2nd R (H)	Redhill	W 4-1			5	3			2	8[1]			10[1]	11			4					6			7[1]						1	9[1]			
		***Redhill protest, game to be replayed.**																																		
3 Mar	Rep (A)	Redhill AET	W 4-3	2,500			3				8[1]			10[1]	11[1]			4	2			5	6			7						1	9[1]			
24 Mar	S-F AET	(Tooting) Wimbledon	D 1-1	3,000		4	3				8			10	11[1]				2			5	6			7						1	9			
14 Apr	Rep	(Tooting) Wimbledon	L 1-4			2	3	4			8			10	11						7[1]	5	6									1	9			
SURREY CHARITY SHIELD																																				
23 Sep	1st R (H)	P.O. Engineers £25	W 5-0	600	1		3			4	8[4]	9[1]		10	11			6	2		7	5														
13 Jan	S-F (H)	Tooting	W 6-2	1,200			3				8			10[1]	11[1]			6	2			5			4	7				9[4]		1				
21 Apr	F (A)	Sutton	L 0-7			2	3				8			10	11			4			7	5	6							9		1				
SURREY COMBINATION CUP																																				
28 Oct	S-F (A)	Guildford City	L 3-4	2,100	1	2	3	4		6		8		10[1]	9			11[1]				5											7[1]			
TOTAL APPEARANCES					**23**	**25**	**40**	**26**	**6**	**29**	**34**	**13**	**3**	**40**	**37**	**1**	**3**	**30**	**14**	**1**	**17**	**28**	**18**	**1**	**6**	**13**	**3**	**1**	**2**	**13**	**1**	**19**	**11**	**2**	**1**	**1**
GOALS SCORED											**11**	**9**		**14**	**17**			**4**	**1**		**2**	**4**				**4**				**15**			**5**			

ISTHMIAN LEAGUE

SEASON 1934-1935

Date	Venue	Opponents	Result	Atten-dance	West, W.P.	Stevens, D.	Cowle, E.J.	Bartlett, S.	Searle, W.	Searle, E.	Abbott, A.W.	Barney, A.	Lee, S.	Buckmaster, F.	Lawrence, W.H.	Lucas, H.	Stockley, F.	Eales, G.	Blunden, K.	Francis, J.	Hooker, H.	Monk, H.	Moulsdale, W.H.	Collins, A.W.	Ives, W.	Knight, H.	Clarke, E.C.	Crutchley, C.	Griffiths, A.F.	Sturt, S.	Thomas, W.J.	Preskett, F.	Tomlinson, C.
25 Aug	(A)	Kingstonian	L 2-3	3,500	1	2	3	4	5	6	7	8[1]	9[1]	10	11																		
29 Aug	(H)	Leytonstone	L 1-4	1,500	1		3	4	5	6	7		9	10[1]	11	2	8																
6 Sep	(A)	Leytonstone	L 0-3		1	2	3	8	4	6	7		9					5	10	11													
8 Sep	(A)	Wycombe o.g.	W 3-2	4,000	1	2	3		4	6	7		9	10	11[1]		8[1]	5															
15 Sep	(H)	Ilford	W 3-2	1,500	1	2	3		4	6	7		9[1]	10[1]	11		8[1]	5															
29 Sep	(A)	The Casuals	D 2-2		1	2	3		4	6[2]	7			10	11		8	5			9												
13 Oct	(H)	Oxford £47	D 3-3	1,600	1	2	3		4	6	7			10	11		8[2]	5[1]			9												
27 Oct	(A)	Ilford	L 0-2		1	2	3		4	6	7				11		8	5			10	9											
10 Nov	(H)	London Caledonians	L 0-2		1	2	3		4	6	7			10	11			5				9	8										
24 Nov	(H)	Wycombe	W 4-3		1	2	3		4	6	7			10			8[1]	5			9[2]		11[1]										
8 Dec	(H)	Dulwich	L 3-8	1,700	1	2	3		4	6				10[1]	7		8	5			9[2]		11										
15 Dec	(A)	Dulwich	L 2-6	3,000	1	2	3		4	6				10[1]	7		8	5			9[1]		11										
22 Dec	(H)	Nunhead	W 2-1		1	2			4	6	7			10	11[1]		8	5			9[1]			3									
25 Dec	(A)	Wimbledon	L 1-5		1	2			4	6				10	7		8				9[1]		11	3	5								
26 Dec	(H)	Wimbledon £62	W 1-0	2,000	1	2			5	6				10	11		8				9[1]			3		4	7						
29 Dec	(A)	Nunhead	L 0-3		1	2			5	6	8			10	11			4			9			3			7						
5 Jan	(A)	Tufnell Park	L 0-2		1	2			5	6	7			10	11		8				9			3				4					
19 Jan	(H)	Tufnell Park £40	W 4-1	1,200	1	2	3			4				7	11[1]		8[2]	5			9		10[1]						6				
16 Feb	(A)	Clapton	W 2-0			2				4				7	11[1]		8	5			9[1]		10	3					6	1			
23 Feb	(H)	Clapton	L 1-2			2				4	7			10	11		8[1]	5			9			3					6	1			
2 Mar	(A)	Oxford	L 0-6			2				6	4			7	11		8	5			9		10	3						1			
16 Mar	(H)	The Casuals	L 0-2			2	3			4				7	11		8	5			9		10						6	1			
23 Mar	(H)	Kingstonian	W 1-0	1,200		2	3				7[1]			10	8		9	5					11				4		6	1			
13 Apr	(A)	London Caledonians	L 2-3	800			3		6	4	7			10[1]	8		9[1]	5					11	2						1			
20 Apr	(A)	St. Albans	D 2-2			2	3			4	7[1]			10	8		9[1]		5				11						6	1			
22 Apr	(H)	St. Albans £75	W 5-1	2,300	1	2	3			4	7			10	8[2]		9[2]		5				11[1]						6				
F.A. CUP																																	
1 Sep	Ex Pr (H)	Guildford City	L 0-2	3,000	1		3	8	5	6	7			10	11	2												4			9		
F.A. AMATEUR CUP																																	
6 Oct	1st Q (A)	Egham	W 3-2		1	2	3		4	6	7			10	11[1]		8[1]	5			9[1]												
20 Oct	2nd Q (H)	Camberley	W 5-0	1,800	1	2	3		4	6	7[1]			10	11		8[2]	5			9[2]												
3 Nov	3rd Q (H)	RASC £62	W 2-1	1,950	1	2	3		4	6	7			10	11		8	5					9[2]										
17 Nov	4th Q (H)	Hersham £74	W 3-0	2.200	1	2	3		4	6	7			10	11[1]		8	5			9[2]												
12 Jan	1st R (A)	Bromley	L 1-2	3,000	1	2			5	6				10	11		8	4			9[1]		7	3									
SURREY SENIOR CUP																																	
26 Jan	!st R (H)	Hersham	W 2-0	1,000	1	2				4				7	11[2]		8	5			9		10	3					6				
9 Feb	2nd R (H)	Streatham	W 3-0	1,400		2				4				7	11		8[1]	5			9		10[2]	3					6	1			
6 Apr	S-F	(Wimbledon) Dulwich	W 5-3	4,000		2[1]	3			4	7[2]			10[1]	8		9	5					11[1]						6	1			
11 May	F	(Dulwich) Kingstonian	L 0-2	3,500	1	2	3			4	7			10	11			5	6				9									8	
SURREY CHARITY SHIELD																																	
22 Sep	1st R (H)	P.O. Engineers	D 0-0		1	2	3		4	6	7			10	11		8	5															9
2 Feb	Rep (H)	P.O. Engineers	W 1-0			2			4					7	11		8[1]	5			9		10	3					6	1			
6 May	S-F (A)	Wimbledon	D 2-2		1	2	3				7[1]			10[1]	11		9	5	6							4						8	
		Replay next season																															
SURREY COMBINATION CUP																																	
10 Apr	S-F (H)	Guildford City	W 2-1	1,200		2				4	7			10[1]	8		9[1]		5				11	3					6	1			
4 May	F (A)	Kingstonian	L 1-2	3,000	1	2	3			4	7			10	8		9[1]	5					11						6				
TOTAL APPEARANCES					**30**	**38**	**28**	**4**	**26**	**38**	**30**	**1**	**5**	**39**	**39**	**2**	**35**	**32**	**6**	**1**	**23**	**2**	**22**	**14**	**1**	**2**	**3**	**2**	**13**	**11**	**1**	**2**	**1**
GOALS SCORED						**1**				**2**	**6**	**1**	**2**	**8**	**10**		**19**	**1**			**15**		**8**										

ISTHMIAN LEAGUE

SEASON 1935-1936

Date	Venue	Opponents	Result	Attendance	West, W.P.	Stevens, D.	Cowle, E.J.	Searle, E.	Eales, G.	Griffiths, A.F.	Abbott, A.W.	Lawrence, W.H.	Widmore, H.	Hooker, H.	Moulsdale, W.H.	Blunden, K.	Preskett, F.	Medhurst, H.	Small, H.	Simmons, C.	Stygal, E.	Gough, R.	Small, G.	Urquhart, W.	Buckmaster, F.	Brown, W.G.E.	Carter, S.	Udal, G.	Baldaro, E.	Knight, H.
31 Aug	(H)	Tufnell Park	W 2-1	1,600	1	2	3	4	5	6	7	8[1]	9	10[1]	11															
4 Sep	(H)	The Casuals	L 1-2	1,600	1	2	3	4		6	7	8	9[1]	10	11	5														
14 Sep	(H)	Wycombe	W 5-1	1,700	1	2	3	4	5	6	7[1]		9[3]	10	11[1]		8													
19 Sep	(A)	The Casuals	D 1-1		1	2	3	4	5	6	7		9	10[1]		11	8													
28 Sep	(A)	Wycombe	L 1-5	1,400	1	2	3	4	5	6		7	9	10		11	8[1]													
19 Oct	(A)	Tufnell Park	W 3-0			2	3	4	5	6		8		9[2]	11		10	1	7[1]											
2 Nov	(H)	Kingstonian	L 0-2	1,600			3	2	5	6		8	9	10	11		4	1		7										
9 Nov	(H)	Ilford	L 2-3	1.300		9	3	2	5	6		8[1]		10[1]	11		4	1		7										
23 Nov	(A)	Kingstonian	L 2-3			2	3	4	5	6	7[2]	8		10	11	9		1												
14 Dec	(A)	London Caledonians	W 2-1			2	3	4	5	6	7	8		9[1]	10			1			11[1]									
20 Dec	(H)	Oxford	L 0-2	800		2	3	4	5	6	7	8		9	10			1			11									
25 Dec	(A)	Wimbledon	L 1-8			2	3	5			7	8		10[1]	6			1			11	4		9						
26 Dec	(H)	Wimbledon	L 0-3	1,000		2	3	5			7	8			10			1				6	4	9			11			
28 Dec	(A)	Dulwich	L 0-5			3					4	8		9	5			1	7		11	6	2	10						
11 Jan	(H)	Leytonstone	W 4-2	1,000		2	3	4	5	6	7[1]	8[1]		9[1]				1			11				10[1]					
18 Jan	(A)	Leytonstone	L 2-4			2	3	4	5	6	7	8[1]		9[1]				1			11				10					
1 Feb	(H)	Nunhead	L 3-7			2	3	4	5	6[1]	7	8						1			11[1]				10[1]	9				
8 Feb	(A)	Clapton	L 2-4			3		4	5	6	7[1]	8		9				1			11[1]		2		10					
15 Feb	(A)	Oxford	W 1-0			3		4	5	6	7	8		9[1]				1			11		2		10					
22 Feb	(H)	Clapton	D 1-1			3		4	5	6	7	8		9[1]				1			11		2		10					
7 Mar	(H)	Dulwich	W 3-1	1,500		3		4		5	7	8		9[2]				1			11	6	2		10[1]					
14 Mar	(H)	London Caledonians	W 1-0	1,600		3		4	6	5	7	8		9				1			11		2		10[1]					
4 Apr	(A)	Nunhead	D 2-2				2	4	3	5	7	8		9[1]	6			1			11[1]				10					
11 Apr	(H)	St. Albans	D 1-1	1,200			3	4	6	5	7	8		9[1]	11			1					2		10					
13 Apr	(A)	St. Albans	L 1-2				3	4		5	7	8[1]		9	6			1					2		10		11			
28 Apr	(A)	Ilford	W 2-1			3		4		5	7	8[2]		9	6			1			11		2		10					
F.A. CUP																														
7 Sep	Ex Pr (A)	Tooting	W 2-1		1	2	3	4	5	6	7	8	9[2]		11		10													
21 Sep	Pr (A)	Beddington Corner	W 4-0		1	2	3	4	5	6	7	11	9[1]	10[3]			8													
5 Oct	1st Q (H)	Sutton £69	D 0-0	2,200		2	3	4	5	6		7	9	10	11		8	1												
9 Oct	Rep (A)	Sutton	L 2-4				3	4	5	6				10[1]	11	9	8[1]	1					2					7		
F.A. AMATEUR CUP																														
12 Oct	1st Q (A)	Courage Sp'ts	W 6-2	500			3	4	5	6		7[1]	9[3]	10[2]	11		8	1					2							
26 Oct	2nd Q (A)	RAMC (Aldershot)	L 0-3			2	3	4	5	6		7	9	10	11		8	1												
SURREY SENIOR CUP																														
25 Jan	1st R (H)	Wimbledon	L 1-7			2	3	4		6	7	8		9	5			1			11				10[1]					
SURREY CHARITY SHIELD (1934-35)																														
11 Sep	S-F Rep	(H) Wimbledon	L 0-3	1,700	1	2		4		6	7	8		9	11	5	10												3	
SURREY CHARITY SHIELD																														
16 Nov	1st R (H)	Epsom	L 1-2				3	4	5	6	7	8		9[1]	11		10	1					2							
SURREY COMBINATION CUP																														
30 Nov	S-F (A)	Guildford City	L 1-3			2	3	4	5		7	8[1]		10				1			11					9				6
GUILDFORD CUP																														
4 Jan	(H)	Guildford Pinks	W 7-0			3		6	5		7	8		9[3]				1			11	4	2		10[4]					
HERSHAM CHALLENGE CUP																														
21 Mar	(H)	Hersham £41	W 3-0	1,400		3		4	6[1]	5	7	8		9[1]				1			11		2		10[1]					
TOTAL APPEARANCES					**8**	**31**	**28**	**37**	**29**	**33**	**30**	**35**	**11**	**35**	**24**	**6**	**14**	**30**	**2**	**2**	**18**	**5**	**15**	**3**	**15**	**2**	**2**	**1**	**1**	**1**
GOALS SCORED									**1**	**1**	**5**	**9**	**10**	**26**	**1**		**2**		**1**		**4**				**10**					

ISTHMIAN LEAGUE

SEASON 1936-1937

Date	Venue	Opponents	Result	Attendance	Medhurst, H.	Small, G.	Stevens, D.	Searle, E.	Griffiths, A.F.	Fish, E.	Weller, C.B.	Lawrence, W.H.	Hooker, H.	Buckmaster, F.	Stygal, E.	Stone, L.G.	Finlay, W.	Gough, R.	Searle, W.	West, W.P.	Sturt, S.	Stockley, F.	Carter, S.	Blunden, K.	Brown, R.H.	Baldaro, E.	Field, W.	Cowle, E.J.	Mitchell, R.	Kittredge, A.V.	Hooker, R.
29 Aug	(A)	Wycombe	L 2-4	3,000	1	2	3	4	5	6	7[1]	8	9	10	11[1]																
12 Sep	(H)	Oxford	W 2-0	1,000	1	2	3	4	5	6	7			10	11	8	9[2]														
10 Oct	(A)	Oxford	L 3-4	1,500	1	2	3	4	5		7[1]	8	9	10[1]		11[1]		6													
17 Oct	(H)	Tufnell Park	W 4-0	1,250	1	2	3	4[1]	5		7	8[1]	9]2]	10		11		6													
24 Oct	(A)	Ilford	L 0-2		1	2	3	4	5		7	8	9	10		11		6													
31 Oct	(H)	Leytonstone	W 5-0		1	2	3	4	5		7[1]	8		10[1]		11[2]	9[1]		6												
7 Nov	(A)	Tufnell Park	L 2-5			2	3	4	5		7	8[1]	9	10[1]		11			6	1											
14 Nov	(A)	The Casuals	D 3-3			2	3	4[1]	5		7	8	9[1]	10		11[1]			6	1											
28 Nov	(H)	Clapton	L 1-3			2	3	4	5		7	8	9	10[1]		11			6	1											
5 Dec	(A)	Nunhead	L 1-5			2	3	4	6		7	8		10		11[1]	9		5	1											
12 Dec	(H)	London Caledonians	D 1-1			3	2		6		7	4		10		8			5		1	9[1]	11								
19 Dec	(H)	Wycombe	W 3-2			3	2		6		7			10[1]		8		4	5		1	9[1]	11[1]								
2 Jan	(A)	Clapton	D 1-1			3	2	6			7	4		10		8					1	9	11[1]	5							
16 Jan	(H)	Ilford	L 2-4			3	2	4	5	6		7		10[1]		9[1]					1	8	11								
6 Feb	(H)	Wimbledon	D 3-3			3	2		6			4	7	10		9[3]					1	8	11		5						
20 Feb	(H)	The Casuals	W 4-3				2		6			4	7	10		9[3]					1	8	11[1]		5	3					
27 Feb	(A)	Wimbledon	L 3-7				2		6			4	7[1]	10		9[2]					1	8	11		5	3					
6 Mar	(A)	Leytonstone	L 0-6				2		6			4	7	10		9						8	11		5	3	1				
13 Mar	(H)	Dulwich	W 2-1				2	6	5			4	7	10		9					1	8	11[2]			3					
20 Mar	(A)	London Caledonians	W 2-0				2	6	5			4	7	10		9[2]					1	8	11			3					
27 Mar	(A)	St. Albans	W 4-2				2	6				4	7[1]	10[1]		9					1	8[1]	11[1]		5	3					
29 Mar	(H)	St. Albans	W 2-1	1,900			2					4	7[2]	10		9		6			1	8	11		5	3					
3 Apr	(A)	Kingstonian	L 0-3				2	6				4	7	10		9					1	8	11	5		3					
17 Apr	(H)	Nunhead	L 1-4				2	6	5			4	7	10		9[1]				1		8	11			3					
28 Apr	(H)	Kingstonian	L 0-1					6				4	7	10		9					1	8	11		5	2		3			
1 May	(A)	Dulwich	L 2-4					2		4			10	6		9[2]					1	8	11		5	3			7		
F.A. CUP																															
5 Sep	Ex Pr (A)	Camberley & Y	W 2-1	800	1	2	3	4	5	6	7			10	11[1]	8	9[1]														
19 Sep	Pr (H)	Epsom £64	W 3-1	2,000	1	2	3	4	5	6	7[1]			10	11	8	9[2]														
3 Oct	1st Q (A)	Hersham £58	L 0-4	3,000	1	2	3	4	5	6	7	8		10		11	9														
F.A. AMATEUR CUP																															
21 Nov	4th Q (A)	Hastings & ST.L	L 1-3	2,300		2	3	4	5		7	8	9[1]	10		11			6	1											
SURREY SENIOR CUP																															
23 Jan	1st R (A)	Nunhead 69 mins	AB 3-4			3	2		6			4		10[1]		9[2]		7			1	8	11		5						
30 Jan	1st R (A)	Nunhead	L 1-3				2		6			4	7	10		9[1]					1	8	11		5			3			
SURREY CHARITY SHIELD																															
26 Sep	1st R (H)	Met. Police	D 0-0	1,600	1	2	3	4	5		7	8		10		11	9	6													
9 Jan	Rep (H)	Met. Police	W 5-4			3	2	6				4				9[1]					1	8[2]	11[1]	5					7	10[1]	
13 Feb	S-F (A)	Sutton	L 0-1				2	6	5			4	7	10		9					1	8	11			3					
SURREY COMBINATION CUP																															
19 Apr	(H)	Guildford City £23	L 1-3	850			2	6	5		7	4	8	10[1]						1		9	11			3					
GUILDFORD CUP																															
24 Apr	(H)	Guildford Pinks	W 2-1					6				2	7[1]	10		9				1		8[1]	11		5	3					4
TOTAL APPEARANCES					**10**	**22**	**34**	**28**	**29**	**7**	**19**	**32**	**24**	**36**	**4**	**35**	**7**	**7**	**8**	**8**	**18**	**22**	**22**	**3**	**11**	**14**	**1**	**2**	**2**	**1**	**1**
GOALS SCORED								**2**			**4**	**2**	**9**	**9**	**2**	**23**	**6**					**6**	**7**							**1**	

SEASON 1937-1938

ISTHMIAN LEAGUE

Date	Venue	Opponents	Result	Attendance	West, W.P.	Stevens, D.	Baldaro, E.	Lawrence, W.H.	Brown, R.H.	Searle, E.	Hooker, H.	Hughes, D.	Finlay, W.	Pitts, R.	Carter, S.F.	Kittredge, A.V	Hooker, R.	Knight, H.	Gough, R.	Weller, C.B.	Davies, L.J.	Cowle, E.J.	Fish, E.	Stone, L.G.	Mallinder, E.	Bridges, G.E.	Dance, P.	Bettesworth, R.	Potter, D.	Goslin, T.	Crook, A.	Wallage, D.	Gibson, N.	Small, H.	Hobbs, R.	Gumbrell, G.	West, G.	Searle, W.
28 Aug	(A)	Clapton	L 1-3		1	2	3	4	5	6	7	8	9[1]	10	11																							
1 Sep	(H)	Dulwich	L 0-3		1	2	3	4	5	6	7	8	9			10	11																					
8 Sep	(A)	Dulwich	W 4-1		1	2	3	4		6		8[1]	9[1]			10[2]		5	7	11																		
11 Sep	(H)	Oxford	W 5-1	1,000	1	2	3		5	6		8[1]	9[1]			10			4	11[2]	7[1]																	
25 Sep	(H)	Leytonstone	D 2-2		1	2		5		6		8[1]	7[1]			10				11		3	4	9														
2 Oct	(A)	Wimbledon	L 1-6		1	2		4		6		8	7			10				11		3			5	9[1]												
9 Oct	(H)	The Casuals	D 2-2			3		2		6		8[1]	9[1]		11	10		5	4	7							1											
16 Oct	(A)	Oxford	L 0-3			3		2		6		8	9		11	10		5	4	7							1											
30 Oct	(H)	London Caledonians	W 3-2			3		2		6		8	9[1]					5		11					4		1	7	10[2]									
13 Nov	(A)	Wycombe	L 1-7			3		2		6		8[1]	9			10		5	7	11			4				1											
20 Nov	(H)	Kingstonian	L 0-1	1,200		3		2		6		10				8		5	7	11			4	9			1											
27 Nov	(A)	Ilford	L 2-4			3		2		6		10						5	7	11			4	9[2]			1		8									
4 Dec	(H)	Wimbledon	L 1-3			3		2		6		8						5	7	11			4	9[1]			1		10									
11 Dec	(A)	London Caledonians	L 0-1			3		2		6		10	7					5		11			4	9			1	8										
1 Jan	(A)	Leytonstone	L 0-3	2,000	1	2		5		6		8	7			10		3		11			4	9														
8 Jan	(H)	Wycombe	L 2-3		1	3	2	5		6		8	7			10				11			4	9[2]														
29 Jan	(H)	Tufnell Park	W 4-2	650		3	2	5		10		8			11								4	9[4]			1			6	7							
5 Feb	(H)	Nunhead	W 2-1			3	2	5		10		8	7		11[1]								4	9[1]			1			6								
19 Feb	(A)	The Casuals	L 2-4			3	2	5		10		8[1]	7		11								4	9[1]			1			6								
26 Feb	(A)	Nunhead	L 1-6			3	2	5		10		8	7		11[1]	6		4						9			1											
5 Mar	(A)	Kingstonian	L 0-1			2		5		6		8	7		11	10								9						4		1	3					
12 Mar	(H)	Clapton	L 1-5			3	2	5		6		10	7		11				4					9[1]					8			1						
19 Mar	(H)	Ilford	L 2-4			3		10		6			7						5					9[2]					4	8		1		2	11			
26 Mar	(A)	Tufnell Park	L 0-3			3		6				8							5					9					10	4	7	1		2	11			
16 Apr	(H)	St. Albans	W 4-1			3				6		8	7			10			5					9[4]					4			1		2	11			
18 Apr	(A)	St. Albans	W 1-0			3	2					8	9[1]			10			5										4			1			11		7	6
F.A. CUP																																						
4 Sep	Ex Pr (A)	Leyland Motors	W 3-1		1	2	3	4	5	6		8[1]	9		11	10[1]	7[1]																					
18 Sep	Pr (A)	Nunhead	L 1-6	2,000	1	2	3	4	5	6		8[1]	9			10				11	7																	
F.A. AMATEUR CUP																																						
15 Jan	1st R (A)	Dulwich	L 0-7	7,252	1	2	3	5		6		8	9			10		4		11																7		
SURREY SENIOR CUP																																						
22 Jan	1st R (A)	Redhill	L 0-3	2,000		3	2	5		6		7	9		11	10							4	8			1											
SURREY CHARITY SHIELD																																						
6 Nov	(H)	P.O. Engineers	L 1-2			3		2		6		8[1]	9					5		11					4		1	7	10									
SURREY COMBINATION CUP																																						
18 Dec	(A)	Guildford City	L 1-2			3	2	5		6[1]		8	7			10				11			4	9			1											
TOTAL APPEARANCES					**11**	**32**	**16**	**29**	**5**	**30**	**2**	**31**	**27**	**1**	**11**	**20**	**2**	**13**	**13**	**18**	**2**	**2**	**13**	**18**	**3**	**1**	**15**	**3**	**9**	**6**	**2**	**6**	**1**	**3**	**4**	**1**	**1**	**1**
GOALS SCORED										**1**		**9**	**7**		**2**	**3**	**1**			**2**	**1**			**18**		**1**			**2**									

ISTHMIAN LEAGUE

SEASON 1938-1939

Date	Venue	Opponents	Result	Attendance	Wallage, D.	Small, H.W.	Stevens, D.	Searle, E.	Kittredge, A.V.	Potter, D.	Hobbs, R.G.	Mason, L.	Stone, L.G.	Waters, J.J.	Carter, S.F.	Kendrick, S.	Sturt, S.	Daley, J.V.	Gough, R.E.	Reeves, R.	Middleton, A.	Salisbury, H.C.	Evans, H.A.	Davies, L.	Barker, C.	Knight, H.	West, W.P.	Lawrence, W.H.	Shepherd, J.	LLoyd, J.B.R.	Gough, D.A.	Briscoe, E.	Tristram, H.T.	Udal, P.	Mills, R.	Tilley, J.	Walker, E.A.	Schofield, D.	Stocker, A.	Rickwood, J.T.	Smithers, E.
27 Aug	(A)	Clapton	L 1-3		1	2	3	4	5	6	7	8	9[1]	10	11																										
31 Aug	(A)	Kingstonian	L 0-4		1	2	3	4	10	6	7	8	9		11	5																									
7 Sep	(H)	Kingstonian	L 1-3			2	3	4		10	7						1	5	6	8[1]	9	11																			
10 Sep	(H)	Leytonstone	L 0-2		1	2	3	4		6	7							5		9		11	8	10																	
17 Sep	(H)	Wycombe	W 5-1			2	3				7				11[2]			10	4	9[2]			8[1]		5	6	1														
24 Sep	(A)	Wycombe	L 0-2		1	2	3				7				11			10	4	9			8		5			6													
1 Oct	(A)	The Casuals	W 3-0		1	2	3				7				11			10[2]	4	9[1]			8		5			6													
8 Oct	(H)	Tufnell Park	W 1-0		1	2	3				7				11			10	4	9[1]			8		5			6													
15 Oct	(H)	Ilford	L 1-2		1	2	3		6		7				11[1]			10	4	9			8		5																
22 Oct	(H)	Nunhead	W 3-1		1	2	3	6			7				11			10[1]	4	9[1]			8		5[1]																
29 Oct	(A)	London Caledonians	L 0-2		1	2	3				7				11			10	4	9			8		5			6													
5 Nov	(H)	Wimbledon	L 1-4		1	2	3				7				11			10	4	9			8[1]		5			6													
12 Nov	(A)	Wimbledon	L 1-5			2	3	9			7				11			10	4				8[1]		5		1	6													
19 Nov	(A)	Nunhead	L 0-2			2	3	9			7				11			10	4				8		5		1	6													
3 Dec	(H)	Dulwich	W 2-1			2	3				11[1]							5	4				8[1]		9		1	6	7	10											
10 Dec	(A)	Dulwich	L 1-4			2	3				11							5	4				8		9[1]		1	6	7	10											
31 Dec	(H)	Clapton	W 2-1			2	3	10	4[1]		11								5				8		9		1	6	7[1]												
28 Jan	(A)	Ilford	L 2-5			2	3		4		11[1]								5	9			8				1	6	7[1]		10										
18 Feb	(A)	Leytonstone	L 1-4			2	3	4	10		11								5								1	6	7[1]		8	9									
4 Mar	(H)	The Casuals	D 1-1		1	2	3	4			11								5									6	7[1]	10	8	9									
11 Mar	(A)	Oxford	L 1-2		1	2	3	4			8								5	11					9[1]			6		10		7									
25 Mar	(H)	London Caledonians	W 2-1		1	2	3	4			8									11					9			6				7[1]	5	10[1]							
1 Apr	(H)	Oxford	W 2-1		1	2	3	4[1]			8											11[1]			9			6			10	7	5								
8 Apr	(A)	St. Albans	L 1-3	1,500	1	2	3				8								5			11[1]										7		9	4	6	10				
10 Apr	(H)	St. Albans	W 1-0		1	2	3			6	8								4										7			10	5					9	11[1]		
15 Apr	(A)	Tufnell Park	D 2-2			2	3	4[1]			8								7[1]								1	6	11			10	5	9							
F.A. CUP																																									
3 Sep	(A)	Nunhead	L 1-2		1	2	3	4	9	6	10	8						5		7[1]																				8	
F.A. AMATEUR CUP																																									
14 Jan	1st R (H)	Tufnell Park	W 2-1			2	3		4		11[1]								5	9			8				1	6	7[1]	10											
4 Feb	2nd R (H)	Wimbledon £96	L 1-3	3,000		2	3	4			11								5	9			8				1	6	7		10[1]										
SURREY SENIOR CUP																																									
11 Feb	1st R (H)	Dulwich	L 1-1			2	3	4	10		11								5						9		1	6			8[1]	7									
25 Feb	Rep (A)	Dulwich £191	L 0-7	6,291		2	3	4	10		11								5								1	6	7		8	9									
SURREY CHARITY SHIELD																																									
26 Nov	1st R (H)	Walton o.g.	D 4-4			2	3				11							9	4				8[3]		5		1	6	7	10											
18 Mar	Rep (A)	Walton	D 3-3		1	2	3	4[1]			8								5	11					9[1]			6		10		7[1]									
		Walton withdrew from the competition																																							
29 Apr	S-F (H)	Met. Police	L 0-3		1	2	3	10		6									4						5				7			8		9							11
WRIGHT HOSPITAL CUP																																									
6 May	(A)	Camberley & Y	L 2-3		1	2	3				10								4						5			6			8[1]	7						9	11[1]		
TOTAL APPEARANCES					**20**	**35**	**35**	**20**	**10**	**7**	**34**	**3**	**2**	**1**	**12**	**1**	**1**	**16**	**29**	**17**	**1**	**4**	**18**	**1**	**21**	**1**	**14**	**24**	**13**	**7**	**8**	**13**	**4**	**4**	**1**	**1**	**1**	**2**	**2**	**1**	**1**
GOALS SCORED								**3**	**1**		**3**		**1**		**3**			**3**	**1**	**7**		**2**	**7**		**4**				**5**		**3**	**2**		**1**					**2**		

SEASON 1939-1940

ISTHMIAN LEAGUE

Date	Venue	Opponents	Result	Attendance	Dance, P	Small, H.W.	Stevens, D.	Faulds, M.	Barker, C.	Potter, D.	Gough, R.E.	Hobbs, R.G.	Taylor, J.H.	Kittredge, A.V.	Stocker, A.	Golden-Hann, C.	Baldaro, E.	Pullen, J.W.	Pinnock, G.	Gough, D.A.	Reeves, R.	Walker, E.A.	Wallage, D.	Cowle, E.J.	Mills, R.	Griffiths, A.F.	Abbott, A.W.	Preskett, F.M.	Price, W.J.	Lawrence, W.H.	Dale, A.	Stuart, R.	Searle, E.	Blunden, D.	Moulsdale, W.	Hughes, E.G.	Flanagan, W.	Stone, L.G.	Buckmaster, F.	Hooker, H.	Smith, D.A.	White, L.	West, W.P.
26 Aug	(A)	Wycombe	L 0-4		1	2	3	4	5	6	7	8	9	10	11																											
F.A. CUP																																										
2 Sep	Ex Pr (A)	Egham	W 12-0					4			5	11[3]		6		1	2	3	7[3]	8[3]	9[3]	10																					
WAR DECLARED. FOOTBALL CANCELLED BY ORDER OF THE GOVERNMENT																																										
SURREY COMBINATION LEAGUE																																										
2 Dec	(A)	Hersham	L 2-3							9	4	11		6[1]									1	2	3	5	7	8[1]	10																	
9 Dec	(H)	Camberley & Y	W 4-2				3			6	5	11		4									1				7[1]	8[2]	10[1]	2	9													
23 Dec	(A)	Walton o.g.	W 2-0				2			6				4			11							3	9[1]		7	8	10			1	5											
25 Dec	(A)	Guildford City	L 0-3							9	5	11		6			2							3			7	8	10			1	4											
12 Jan	(H)	Cobham Avorians	L 0-2				2			6		11		4									1	3	9		7	8			5								10				
19 Jan	(A)	Epsom	L 1-5				3			4	5	11[1]					2						1					8	10		9	7		6									
24 Feb	(H)	Walton	D 0-0				3			4	2	11													10	5	7	8				1			6	9							
9 Mar	(A)	Leyland Motors	L 1-5							4	3	7		6												5			11	2		1			9	10	8[1]						
16 Mar	(H)	Guildford City	W 11-1				3			4[1]	5	11		6														7		8	2		1			9[8]	10[2]							
30 Mar	(A)	Cobham Avorians	D 2-2							4		11		6				3										7		8	2		1			5	10		9[2]					
6 Apr	(H)	Epsom	L 2-3				2				3	8		4													5	7		10			1		11[1]	6			9[1]					
13 Apr	(H)	Hersham	W 2-0				3				4	11		6									1			5	7[1]	8	10	2[1]					9								
20 Apr	(H)	Leyland Motors	L 1-2				2				3	9		6									1			4[1]	7	8	10					11	5								
24 Apr	(H)	Vickers	D 4-4				2				6[1]	8		4								7			3							1		11	5	9			10[3]				
15 May	(A)	Vickers	W 2-1							9[1]	3												7											1	2	6	5				10	4	8[1]	11	
1 Jun	(A)	Camberley & Y	W 8-0							9[2]	3	4													11[2]	6			8[1]			1	2		5				10[2]		7[1]		
SURREY COMBINATION CUP																																										
23 Mar	1st L (A)	Guildford City	L 0-3	1,000			2			6	3	11		4							9								8	7			1			5	10								
27 Apr	2nd L (H)	Guildford City	L 1-3				2			4	3	11											1			6	7	8[1]	10						5			9					
SURREY SENIOR CUP (EMERGENCY COMPETITION																																										
10 Feb	1st R (H)	Leyland Motors	Walk over																																							
2 Mar	2nd R (H)	Sutton	W 2-0				2			4	3	11		6													5	7	8				1			9	10[2]							
11 May	S-F	(Dulwich) Wimbledon £61	D 2-2	2,500			2			9	3	8															6	7	4	10[2]			1		11	5								
18 May	Rep	(Guildford) Wimbledon	L 1-3				2			6	3	11															4	7	8	10[1]			1			5			9					
FRIENDLIES																																										
23 Sep	(A)	Hersham	W 3-2		1			4		9[2]	5	11		6					7[1]	8		10		3									2											
30 Sep	(H)	Met. Police £12	L 1-2	500				4		9[1]	5	11		6			2		7	8				3																10				1
7 Oct	(H)	Wimbledon £19	W 5-3	750			3			9[2]	5	11						2										4	7	8[2]	10[1]	6															1
14 Oct	(H)	Hersham	W 3-1							9[1]	5	11		6		1	2					7		3		4		8[1]	10[1]															
21 Oct	(A)	Walton	W 8-0					4		9[3]		11[2]		6		1								3		5	7[2]	8	10[1]	2													
4 Nov	(A)	Tooting & Mitcham	L 2-5	2,500				4[1]		9		11		6		1		3		8				2		5	7		10[1]															
11 Nov	(H)	Walton	L 3-4				2			9[2]	5	11						3									4	7	8	10[1]			1	6										
18 Nov	(H)	Wealdstone	L 2-6				3			9	5	11		4		1	2											7[2]	8	10	6														
25 Nov	(A)	Wealdstone	L 1-5							9		8					2						1	3		5	7	4	10[1]	6		11											
16 Dec	(A)	Redhill	D 2-2				3			6	5			4			9						1		10		7	8	11[2]	2														
25 May	(A)	Oxford City	D 4-4				2			9[2]	3	8[1]													11	4			10[1]			1		6	5						7		
Appearances: League/Cup					1	1	16	2	1	18	20	21	1	16	1	1	4	2	1	1	2	3	7	4	6	11	15	14	16	5	3	15	4	6	15	7	1	4	4	1	2	1	
Goals Scored: League/Cup										4	1	4		1					3	3	3				3	1	2	4	5	1				1	8	4	1	3	5		2		
Appearances: Friendlies					1		5	4		11	8	10		7		4	6	2	2	3		2	2	6	2	7	7	7	9	5		3	2	1	1				1		1		2
Goals Scored: Friendlies								1		13		3								1								4	3	9																	

WAR COMPETITION

SEASON 1940-1941

SOUTH EASTERN COMPETITION

Date	Venue	Opponents	Result	Atten-dance	Golden-Hann, C.	Gough, R.E.	Faulds, M.	Warden, T.	Moulsdale, W.	Potter, D.	Ugle, T.	Hobbs, R.G.	Reeves, R.	Preskett, J.	Smith, D.A.	Stevens, D.	Mills, R.	Hughes, E.G.	Stuart, R.	Kittredge, A.V.	Pinnock, G.	Kunz, C.	Salmond, C.	Leigh, G.	Newman, N.	Smithers, E.	Barker, C.	Rolands, J.	Bannister, E.	Nichols, S.	Nichols, E.	Fitzsimmons, M.	O'Hara,T.	Fagence, K.	Merrett, J.	Sturt, S.	Jacobs, D.	Smith, J.	Griffiths, A.F.	Peters, H.	Mather, G.	Hynds, T.	Gayther, R.S.	Frankish, E.	Harrison, J.	Elliott, J.	Noves, S.V.	Smith, A.	Pink, F.
5 Oct	(A)	Tooting & Mitcham	L 1-3		1	2	3	4	5	6[1]	7	8	9	10	11																																		
12 Oct	(A)	Sutton	W 3-0		1	4	3		5	6	7	8	9[2]	10[1]	11	2																																	
26 Oct	(H)	Erith & B	D 1-1			5	3			6	7		9[1]	8	11	2		10	1	4																													
9 Nov	(A)	Dulwich	D 2-2				3			5	11		9[1]	10[1]		2		8	1		4	6	7																										
16 Nov	(A)	Walton	L 2-6				2			5	7		9	10[1]				8[1]	1			6		3	4	11																							
8 Feb	(H)	Sutton	L 3-5				3		5	6			9[1]	11		2					7									4	8[1]				10[1]	1													
22 Feb	(H)	Dulwich	L 3-4	400			3		5	6			9	10		2					7[1]				11						8[2]					1			4										
15 Mar	(H)	Tooting & Mitcham	L 2-5				3			6			9[1]	10		2					7[1]				11		5				8					1				4									
22 Mar	(A)	Nunhead	W 3-2			2	3[1]			5			9	11[1]							7[1]				8											1					4	6	10						
29 Mar	(H)	Nunhead	W 5-1			3	10[2]			5			9[1]	11[2]		2			1						7						8										4	6							
12 Apr	(A)	Erith & B	L 2-9				10			5	7		9	8[2]		2			11						4											1								3	6				
19 Apr	(H)	Walton	D 1-1				3			5			9[1]	11		2			1						7		4				8											6				10			
26 Apr	(A)	Epsom	W 4-2				3			5	7		4[1]	8	11	2			1																							6	10				9[3]		
3 May	(H)	Epsom	W 1-0				3			5	8		9[1]	4		2					7												10			1												6	11
FRIENDLIES																																																	
19 Oct	(H)	Army XI	L 2-7		1	2	3		5	6	7		9[2]	8	11		4	10																															
2 Nov	(H)	Army XI	L 2-3	*Team unknown*										[2]																																			
14 Dec	(H)	Walton	W 1-0				3			6			9	10	11	2			1		7[1]				4		5	8																					
25 Jan	(A)	Walton	L 2-3				5				7		9[2]			2			1			6							3	4	8	10	11																
1 Feb	(H)	Army XI	W 5-2				3			5			9[2]	10[1]		2		11[1]							6					4	7[1]			1	8														
15 Feb	(H)	Army XI	D 0-0						5	6						2	3					9			4					7	8					1	10	11											
Appearances: League					2	5	14	1	4	14	8	2	14	14	4	11		3	7	1	6	2	1	1	7	1	2			1	5		1		1	6			1	1	2	4	2	1	1	1	1	1	1
Goals Scored: League							3			1			10	8				1			3										3				1												3		
Appearances: Friendlies					1	1	4		2	4	2		4	3	2	4	2	2	2		1	2			3		1	1	1	3	3	1	1	1	1	1	1	1											
Goals Scored: Friendlies													6	3				1			1										1																		

WAR COMPETITION

SEASON 1941-1942

SOUTH EASTERN COMPETITION

Date	Venue	Opponents	Result	Atten-dance	Stuart, R.	Stevens, D.	Faulds, M.	Barker, C.	Potter, D.	Habgood, R.	Walker, E.A.	Evans, H.	Reeves, R.	Smith, D.A.	Pink, F.	Abbott, A.W.	Poole, G.	Preskett, J.	Prett, D.	Longley, E.	Gough, R.E.	Howe, E.	Ugle, T.	Underhill, J.	Oldham, G.	Unswood, J.	Sturt, S.	Messenger, F.	Wilson, D.	Lt. West	Beeson, T.	Cowle, E.J.	Cousins, H.	Kittredge, A.V.	Brant, C.	Warden, T.	Butt, A.	Smithers, E.	Stevens, E.	Cpl. Turner, G.	Lt. Hemmings, J.	Lt. Jackson	Coates, L.	Cpl. Nelson	Cpl. Hall	Bale, R.	Hogg, J.
20 Sep	(H)	Met. Police	L 1-5		1	2	3	4	5	6			9[1]	10		7	8	11																																				
4 Oct	(A)	Sutton	W 6-5		1	2	3	4	5			8[1]	6	9[3]		7[2]		10	11																														
11 Oct	(H)	Erith & B	L 1-3		1	2	3	4	5			8		9		7[1]		10	11			6																										
18 Oct	(A)	Epsom	L 1-2		1	2	10[1]			4		8	6	9					11	3	5		7																										
8 Nov	(H)	Sutton	W 5-1		1	3	9[4]		5	2		8	6			7		10	11[1]					4																								
15 Nov	(A)	Met. Police	L 0-6		1	3	9		5	2			6					10					7	4	8	11																						
22 Nov	(H)	Walton	L 1-2		1		9		5	3		8	6[1]			7		10	11	2				4																						
29 Nov	(A)	Dulwich	L 1-9		1	3	2		5				6					10	11					4			7	8	9		*Scorer unknown*																		
13 Dec	(A)	Walton	W 3-1				7		5	2		6	9[2]	8[1]				10	11					3									1	4													
20 Dec	(H)	Dulwich o.g.	W 6-2		1	2	7[1]		5	3		8	9[2]					10	11[2]					4										6													
17 Jan	(A)	Bromley	W 2-1		1				5	2		6	9[1]	7				10[1]	11	4				3											8													
21 Feb	(H)	Tooting	W 1-0		1	3	4			2			9			7		10	11[1]					5										6	8													
28 Feb	(A)	Tooting	L 0-10		1		6			2			9			7		10	11	3				5									8		4													
7 Mar	(A)	Erith & B	L 1-8						3			9[1]	8					10					5					7				1	6		2	4	11										
28 Mar	(H)	Bromley	L 1-2				8			2			9			7		10	11[1]					6									1						3	5		4						
2 May	(H)	Epsom	D 1-1						5			8	9[1]					10	11					6								2								4				7			1	3
SOUTH EASTERN COMBINATION CUP																																															
14 Feb	1st R (A)	Sutton	W 6-3		1	3	8		5	2			9[2]			7[1]		10[2]	11[1]	6				4																						
21 Mar	2nd R (A)	Erith & B	L 1-12		1		7			2			9						8[1]	10		6			4																	3	5	11					
FRIENDLIES																																															
13 Sep	(H)	Army XI	L 1-2		1	2	3	4	5	6	7	8	9	10	11			*Scorer unknown*																												
25 Oct	(H)	Navy Xi	W 11-0		1		9[4]		5	2		8[4]	6[2]			7		10	11[1]	3				4																						
6 Dec	(H)	London Fire Force	L 1-6		1		6		5	2		8		9					11					4	10					3	7[1]															
10 Jan	(H)	Army XI	W 5-2		1		7[1]		5	3[1]			9[1]	8				10[1]	11[1]		2			4										6													
14 Mar	(H)	Army XI	L 4-5		1					2			9[1]			8[1]		10	11[1]					5					7					6		4[1]			3							
11 Apr	(H)	Army XI	W 9-1						3			9[6]			7[2]		10	11[1]					5	8												4						1	2	6		
25 Apr	(H)	Army XI	D 3-3			3			5	2			9[1]			7		10[1]	11[1]					6															8			4			1	
Appearances: League/Cup					14	10	15	3	12	14		9	17	7		9	1	16	16	5	2	1	2	14	1	1	1	1	2			1	4	4	3	1	1	1	3	2	1	1	1			1	1
Goals Scored: League/Cup							6					1	11	4		4		4	6																												
Appearances: Friendlies					5	2	4	1	5	7	1	3	6	3	1	4		5	6	1	1			6	2				1	1	1			2		1	1		2			1	1	1	1	1	
Goals Scored: Friendlies							5			1		4	11			3		2	5											1					1												

ISTHMIAN LEAGUE

SEASON 1945-1946

Date	Venue	Opponents	Result	Attendance	West, W.P.	Morgan, R.	Lawrence, W.H.	Jones, G.	Preskett, J.	Potter, D.	Cox, G.	Walker, E.A.	Moon, D.	Smith, D.A.	Reeves, R.	Buckmaster, F.	Johnson, J.	Finch, F.	Keefe, F.	Stevens, D.	Urquhart, H.	Martin, C.	Moulsdale, W.H.	Rogers, A.	Pink, F.	Souter, G.	Pelham, G.	Freer, E.	Harper, T.W.	Searle, E.	Pelham, L.	Stocker, A.	Cowle, E.J.	Seaman, C.	Warman, D.	Wride, E.	Baldaro, E.	Eales, C.	Bird, G.	Cousins, H.
25 Aug	(H)	Leytonstone	W 3-0		1	2	3	4	5	6	7	8	9[3]	10	11																									
1 Sep	(A)	Clapton	L 0-3		1	2	3	6	5		4	8	9	10	11	7																								
15 Sep	(A)	St. Albans	D 1-1		1	2	3	6	5		4	8	9		11[1]		7	10																						
29 Sep	(A)	Wycombe	W 2-1		1	2	3	6	5		4	7	9[1]		11[1]	10			8																					
13 Oct	(A)	Corinthian Casuals	D 2-2		1		3	6	5		4	7	9[1]		11[1]	10				2	8																			
20 Oct	(A)	Kingstonian	W 2-0		1	2	8[1]	6	5		4	7	9		11[1]					3		10																		
27 Oct	(H)	Walthamstow	W 2-1		1	2	8	6	5		4	7	9[1]		11[1]					3		10																		
3 Nov	(A)	Tufnell Park	D 2-2		1	2	3	6	5	10	4	7	9		11[2]							8																		
10 Nov	(H)	Ilford	W 2-1		1	2		6	5[1]	10	4	7	9		11[1]					3			8																	
17 Nov	(H)	Wycombe	W 5-4		1	2		3	5	6	4	7[1]	9[2]		11[1]							10	8[1]																	
24 Nov	(A)	Leytonstone	D 2-2		1	2		6	5[1]	10	4[1]	7	9		11								8	3																
8 Dec	(H)	Kingstonian	W 7-0		1	2	8	6	5	10[1]	4	7	9[1]		11[5]					3																				
15 Dec	(A)	Wimbledon	W 5-1		1	2	8	6	5	10	4	7			11[3]					3		9[2]																		
22 Dec	(H)	Oxford	D 1-1	4,000	1	2	8	6	5[1]	10	4	7	9		11					3																				
29 Dec	(A)	Oxford	D 2-2		1	2	8	6	5	10	4		9[1]		11[1]					3	7																			
5 Jan	(H)	Tufnell Park	L 1-3		1	2	8	6	5	10	4		9		11[1]					3					7															
9 Feb	(H)	Dulwich	L 0-3		1		4	6	5			7	9		11					3						2	8	10												
16 Feb	(A)	Dulwich	L 0-2		1	2	8	6	5		4	7	9		11					3						10														
23 Feb	(H)	Clapton	W 2-1				7	6	5	10	4		9		11[2]					3			8						1	2										
9 Mar	(A)	Romford	L 2-5			2	9	6	5		4	7[1]			11					3									1		8[1]	10								
16 Mar	(H)	Corinthian Casuals	L 1-3		1	2	7		5														10	4								11	3	6	8	9[1]				
23 Mar	(A)	Ilford	L 3-4					6[1]	5		4															3			1		8[1]	11[1]				9	2	7	10	
30 Mar	(H)	Wimbledon	D 3-3				2	6	5		4				11[1]											3			1		8	10				9[2]		7		
13 Apr	(H)	St. Albans	W 4-1		1	2	3	6[1]	5[1]		4			10[1]																	8	11				9[1]		7		
20 Apr	(H)	Romford	L 2-4	3,000	1		2	6	5		4			8[1]	11[1]					3												10				9		7		
25 Apr	(A)	Walthamstow	L 0-1	3,000			2	3	5		4			10	11																8	6				9		7		1
F.A. CUP																																								
8 Sep	Prel (A)	Epsom	W 8-1		1	2	3	6	5		4	8[1]	9[2]		11[3]		7[1]	10[1]																						
22 Sep	1st Q (A)	Met. Police	W 4-1		1	2	3	6	5		4	7	9[2]		11[2]			10	8																					
6 Oct	2nd Q (H)	Tooting	L 1-2		1	2	3	6	5		4	7	9[1]		11	10					8																			
F.A. AMATEUR CUP																																								
19 Jan	1st R (H)	Finchley	W 2-1	2,446	1	2	8	6	5[1]	10[1]	4				11					3		9			7															
2 Feb	2nd R (A)	Wimbledon	L 2-5		1	2	8	6	5		10		9[1]		11[1]					3					7	4														
SURREY SENIOR CUP																																								
1 Dec	1st R (A)	Redhill	W 5-2		1	2	8[1]	6	5	10	4	7[1]	9[2]		11[1]					3																				
12 Jan	2nd R (H)	Tooting	W 3-0	2,660	1	2	8	6	5	10	4				11[2]					3		9			7[1]															
2 Mar	S-F	(G'ford) Cor. Casuals	W 2-1		1	2	7	6[1]	5	10	4				11[1]					3			9								8									
11 May	F	(Kingston) Sutton	L 0-1	6,000	1	2	8	6	5	10	4			9	11					3																		7		
TOTAL APPEARANCES					**30**	**28**	**31**	**34**	**35**	**16**	**33**	**21**	**23**	**6**	**32**	**4**	**2**	**3**	**2**	**20**	**3**	**7**	**6**	**2**	**4**	**5**	**1**	**1**	**4**	**1**	**6**	**7**	**1**	**1**	**1**	**6**	**1**	**6**	**1**	**1**
GOALS SCORED							**2**	**3**	**5**	**2**	**1**	**4**	**18**	**2**	**33**		**1**	**1**				**2**	**1**		**1**						**2**	**1**				**4**				

SEASON 1946-1947

ISTHMIAN LEAGUE

Date	Venue	Opponents	Result	Atten-dance	Cousins, H.	Lawrence, W.H.	Stevens, D.	Cox, G.	Morgan, R.	Stocker, A.	Pink, F.	Smith, D.A.	Wride, E.	Preskett, J.	Reeves, R.	Bristowe, E.	Abbott, A.W.	Luxton, D.	Godding, A.	Harper, R.W.	Jarvis, G.	Elliott, J.	Boxall, O.	Ugle, T.	Cowley, R.A.	Short, W.J.	Wallace, L.M.	Eastaff, M.	Baldaro, E.	Rundle, E.	Ricketts, S.	Henshaw, W.	Braithwaite, A.	Morris, L.	Reeder, F.	Caswell, D.	West, W.P.
31 Aug	(A)	Leytonstone	L 1-8		1	2	3	4	5	6	7	8	9	10	11[1]																						
7 Sep	(H)	Tufnell Park	W 2-1			3[1]		4	2	6		10		5	11	1	7	8	9[1]																		
14 Sep	(A)	Clapton	D 1-1			3		4	2	6		10		5	11[1]	1	7	8	9																		
21 Sep	(H)	Walthamstow	W 1-0			3		4	2	6		10[1]		5	11	1	7	8		9																	
28 Sep	(A)	Wycombe	L 2-5			3		4	2	6	11[1]	10		5		1	7	8[1]			9																
12 Oct	(A)	Tufnell Park	D 2-2			3			2	11		10		5[1]	6	1		4			9	7[1]	8														
19 Oct	(H)	Leytonstone	W 2-1			3		4	2	11[1]		10		5	6	1					9[1]	7	8														
26 Oct	(A)	St. Albans	L 0-3			3			2	11		10		5	6	1					9	7	8	4													
2 Nov	(H)	Corinthian Casuals	W 3-2			3		4	2	11		10		5	6	1					9[2]	7[1]	8														
9 Nov	(A)	Romford	L 1-5				3	4	2	11				5	6	1					9	7[1]	8		10												
16 Nov	(H)	St. Albans	W 4-0				3	4	2	6			8[1]	5	9	1							7[1]			10[1]	11[1]										
23 Nov	(H)	Wimbledon	L 2-6				3[1]			6		11	9[1]	5	4	1							7		8				2	10							
30 Nov	(A)	Dulwich	L 0-5				3							5	6						9		7		8	10	11	1	2							4	
7 Dec	(H)	Oxford	L 1-3			6			2			9		5	3			4					7		8	10[1]	11	1									
14 Dec	(A)	Ilford	L 2-3			5				6		9			3		7	4					8		10[1]		11[1]	1	2								
21 Dec	(H)	Dulwich	D 1-1			6						9		5	3		7	4					8		10[1]		11	1	2								
28 Dec	(A)	Walthamstow	L 1-2			6								5	3		7[1]	4					8		9	10	11	1	2								
11 Jan	(A)	Oxford	L 1-6				6		4					5	3		7						9		8	10	11[1]	1					2				
25 Jan	(H)	Clapton	D 0-0			6						8		5	3		7						4			10	11		2		9						1
8 Feb	(H)	Wycombe	L 1-2			6			2			8		5	3		7						4			10	11[1]					9					1
1 Mar	(A)	Kingstonian	D 0-0			6								5	3		7						4		8	10	11					9	2				1
15 Mar	(A)	Corinthian Casuals	W 2-0			6					11			5			7[1]						4		9[1]	8	10		2				3				1
22 Mar	(H)	Ilford	D 2-2			6[1]					11			5	3		7						4[1]		9	8	10						2				1
12 Apr	(H)	Kingstonian	D 1-1			6			7		11	10		5	3								4		9	8[1]							2				1
19 Apr	(H)	Romford	W 1-0			6			7			9		5	3								4			8	11[1]					10	2				1
26 Apr	(A)	Wimbledon	L 0-3			6			8					5	9								4				11					10	2	3	7		1
F.A. CUP																																					
5 Oct	1st Q (H)	Wimbledon o.g.	L 2-6			3		4	2	6		10		5	11[1]	1	7	8			9																
F.A. AMATEUR CUP																																					
18 Jan	1st R (A)	Hastings & St. L. £170	W 3-1	4,119		6			2			4		5[1]	3		7						8[1]			10	11				9[1]						1
1 Feb	2nd R (A)	Leytonstone	L 1-3	3,000		6			2			8		5	3		7[1]						4			10	11					9					1
SURREY SENIOR CUP																																					
4 Jan	1st R (H)	Wimbledon £99 AET	L 3-4	3,000		6			2					5[1]	3		7	4					9		8	10[1]	11[1]	1									
TOTAL APPEARANCES					**1**	**25**	**6**	**10**	**21**	**14**	**5**	**20**	**3**	**29**	**28**	**12**	**17**	**11**	**2**	**1**	**8**	**5**	**24**	**1**	**13**	**15**	**17**	**7**	**7**	**1**	**2**	**5**	**7**	**1**	**1**	**1**	**10**
GOALS SCORED						**2**	**1**			**1**	**1**	**1**	**2**	**3**	**3**		**3**	**1**	**1**		**3**	**3**	**3**		**3**	**4**	**6**				**1**						

SEASON 1947-1948

ISTHMIAN LEAGUE

Date	Venue	Opponents	Result	Attendance	West, W.P.	Morgan, R.	Braithwaite, A.	Boxall, O.	Preskett, J.	Lawrence, W.H.	Wallace, L.M.	Welland, A.	Smith, D.A.	Short, W.J.	Reeves, R.	Souter, G.	McBryde, M.	Caswell, A.	Baldaro, E.	Reeder, F.	Wride, E.	Pink, F.	Morris, L.	Banks, W.	Stevens, D.	Davies, L.	Nugent, C.	Hewitt, R.	Kurn, J.	Cockram, J.	Towers, P.	Wardleworth, J.	Wiles, W.	Eastaff, M.
30 Aug	(H)	Clapton	D 1-1		1	2	3	4	5	6	7[1]	8	9	10	11																			
3 Sep	(A)	Kingstonian	D 1-1	2,500	1		3	4	5	6	7	8	9[1]		11	2	10																	
6 Sep	(A)	Ilford	D 2-2		1		3	4	5		7	8	9		11	2	10	6[2]																
10 Sep	(H)	Kingstonian	L 0-1		1		3	4	5		7	8	9		11	2	10	6																
13 Sep	(A)	Wimbledon	L 2-5		1	3		4	5	6		8					10		2	7	9	11[2]												
11 Oct	(H)	St. Albans	W 3-2				3	4	5			8	10		6				2	7[1]		11[1]											9[1]	1
18 Oct	(A)	Dulwich	L 1-3	6,000			3	4				8		10	6		7		2			11[1]	5										9	1
25 Oct	(A)	Romford	L 1-6				3	4[1]		6		8		10			7		2				5	9	11									1
1 Nov	(H)	Wimbledon	L 1-3				3	7[1]	5		11	8		10	6				2				4										9	1
8 Nov	(H)	Walthamstow	W 3-2				3	7	5[1]			8			6				2				4			10[1]	11[1]						9	1
15 Nov	(A)	Corinthian Casuals	W 5-3				3	7	5			8			6				2				4			10	11[1]						9[4]	1
29 Nov	(H)	Oxford	W 5-1				3	7[1]	5			8[1]			6				2				4			10	11						9[3]	1
6 Dec	(A)	St. Albans	L 0-1				3	7	5			8			6				2		11		4			10							9	1
13 Dec	(H)	Romford	W 3-0				3	8	5	11		10			6				2	7[1]			4										9[2]	1
20 Dec	(A)	Oxford	L 1-2				3	8	5		7[1]	10			6				2			11	4										9	1
10 Jan	(A)	Wycombe	L 3-4				3		5		11	8			6				2	7[1]			4					10					9[2]	1
17 Jan	(H)	Corinthian Casuals	L 1-2				3	7	5			8	9		6				2				4				11	10[1]						1
24 Jan	(H)	Tufnell Park	W 7-2				3	9[2]	5[2]		11	8			6				2			7[1]	4					10[2]						1
31 Jan	(A)	Clapton	W 5-0					9	5			8[3]			6				2			7[2]	4				11	10	3					1
21 Feb	(H)	Dulwich	L 2-4			2	3	8	5		11				6							7[1]	4							10			9[1]	1
28 Feb	(H)	Ilford	W 5-1				3	8	5	11[3]	10[2]				6				2			7	4										9	1
6 Mar	(A)	Walthamstow	L 1-2				3	8	5		10				6				2			7	4								1	11[1]	9	
13 Mar	(A)	Tufnell Park	L 1-3			2	3[1]	8	5		10				6							7	4								1	11	9	
27 Mar	(H)	Wycombe	W 4-2			2	3	7[1]			8[1]				6		10						4		5						1	11[1]	9[1]	
3 Apr	(A)	Leytonstone	L 2-3			2	3	7	5		8				6		10						4								1	11[1]	9[1]	
24 Apr	(H)	Leytonstone	W 3-0	2,500		2	3	7[3]	5		8				6								4					10			1	11	9	
F.A. CUP																																		
20 Sep	Prel (H)	Leatherhead	W 2-0				3	4	5			8	9		10[1]	6			2	7		11[1]												1
4 Oct	1st Q (H)	Tooting	L 2-3			2	3	4	5	6		8	9		10							11											7[2]	1
F.A. AMATEUR CUP																																		
22 Nov	4th Q (H)	Hastings	L 1-4				3	7[1]	5			8			6				2				4			10	11						9	1
SURREY SENIOR CUP																																		
3 Jan	1st R (A)	Wimbledon	W 1-0				3	7	5		11	8			6				2				4					10[1]					9	1
7 Feb	2nd R (H)	Corinthian Casuals	W 2-0			2	3	8	5		11				6							7	4					10					9[2]	1
20 Mar	S-F	(Wimbledon) Kingston	L 0-3			2	3	8	5		7				6								4					10			1	11	9	
SURREY CHARITY SHIELD																																		
7 Apr	1st R (H)	Walton & H	W 4-1	***Team not traced***				[1]		[1]																							[2]	
SURREY COMBINATION CUP																																		
10 Apr	1st L (A)	Guildford	D 1-1	3,460		2	3	8	5						6		7						4			10					1	11	9[1]	
1 May	2nd L (H)	Guildford	L 1-4			2	3	7	5	10	8				6								4								1	11	9[1]	
TOTAL APPEARANCES					**5**	**12**	**32**	**33**	**31**	**8**	**19**	**23**	**8**	**4**	**32**	**4**	**9**	**2**	**20**	**5**	**2**	**13**	**26**	**1**	**2**	**6**	**6**	**8**	**1**	**1**	**8**	**8**	**24**	**21**
GOALS SCORED							**1**	**11**	**3**	**4**	**5**	**4**	**1**		**1**			**2**		**3**		**9**				**1**	**2**	**4**				**3**	**23**	

SEASON 1948-1949

ISTHMIAN LEAGUE

Date	Venue	Opponents		Result	Atten-dance	Eastaff, M.	Morgan, R.	Braithwaite, A.	Morris, L	Preskett, J.	Reeves, R.	Boxall, O.	Smith, D.A.	Wiles, W.	Ballerino, J.	Wardleworth, J.	Quirk, T.	Stevens, D.	Warren, R.	Pink, F.	Kurn, J.	Wride, E.	White, J.	Baldaro, E.	Ricketts, S.	Prett, J.	Short, W.	Pacey, D.	Welland, A.	
28 Aug	(H)	Leytonstone		L 2-3		1	2	3	4	5	6	7	8	9[2]	10	11														
11 Sep	(A)	Romford		W 6-4		1	2	3[1]	4	5	6	7[1]	8[1]	9[1]	10[2]		11													
9 Oct	(H)	Oxford		D 0-0		1	2		4	5		7	8	9	10		11	3	6											
23 Oct	(H)	Wimbledon		W 4-2		1	2		4	5		7	8	9[1]	10[3]		11	3	6											
30 Oct	(A)	Kingstonian		L 1-2		1	2		4	5		7	8[1]	9	10		11	3	6											
6 Nov	(H)	Walthamstow		L 2-5		1	2		4[1]	5	6		8	9	10		11	3		7[1]										
13 Nov	(H)	Corinthian Casuals		L 3-4		1	2		4	5			6[2]	9[1]	10		11			7	3	8								
20 Nov	(A)	Leytonstone		L 0-3		1	2		3	5		4	10	9	11					7		8	6							
27 Nov	(H)	Kingstonian		W 4-2		1			3	5		4	10[3]	9	11					7		8[1]	6	2						
4 Dec	(A)	Tufnell Park		W 3-2		1	2	3	6	5[1]		4	10	9	11					7[2]		8								
11 Dec	(A)	St. Albans		W 4-1		1	2	3	6	5		8	10	9	11[1]					7[3]			4							
18 Dec	(H)	Dulwich		L 1-4		1	2	3	4	5		8	10	9	11				6	7[1]										
1 Jan	(H)	St. Albans		W 1-0		1	2	3		5	11[1]	4	10	8	9					7			6							
22 Jan	(A)	Wimbledon		L 1-2		1	2	3		5		4	10	8	9				6						7[1]	11				
12 Feb	(H)	Tufnell Park	o.g	W 6-3		1			3	5[1]	11	4	10[1]	8[1]	9[2]					7			6	2						
19 Feb	(A)	Wycombe		W 3-1		1	2	3	5	6		4	10[1]	9[1]	8					7						11[1]				
26 Feb	(A)	Clapton		W 5-3		1	2	3	5	6		4	10[1]	9[4]						7						11	8			
5 Mar	(H)	Wycombe		W 4-2		1		2	5	6	3[1]	4	10	9	8[2]					7[1]						11				
12 Mar	(A)	Dulwich		W 1-0		1	2	3	5	6	11	4	10	9[1]	8					7										
26 Mar	(A)	Corinthian Casuals		L 2-4		1	2		5	6	11	4	10[2]	9	8					7	3									
2 Apr	(H)	Romford		W 3-1		1	2	3	5	11	6	4	10	9[1]						7[1]								8[1]		
9 Apr	(H)	Ilford		W 2-1		1		3	5	11[1]	6	4	10	9[1]						7	2							8		
16 Apr	(A)	Ilford		L 0-1		1	2	3		11	6	4	10	9						7			5					8		
28 Apr	(A)	Oxford		L 2-3		1		2	5	6	3	4	10	9	11[1]					7[1]								8		
30 Apr	(A)	Walthamstow		L 1-5		1		2	5	6	3	4	9[1]		11					7								8	10	
7 May	(H)	Clapton		W 3-1		1		3	5	11	6	4	10	9[2]	8[1]			2		7										
F.A. CUP																														
18 Sep	Prel (H)	Carshalton	AET	D 1-1	3,000	1	2	3	4	5[1]		7	8	9	10		11		6											
25 Sep	Rep (A)	Carshalton		W 7-4		1	2	3	4	5[2]		7[1]	8[2]	9	10[1]		11[1]		6											
2 Oct	1st Q (A)	Met. Police		W 2-0		1	2	3	4	5		7[1]	8	9	10[1]		11		6											
16 Oct	2nd ! (A)	Redhill		L 3-4	4,000	1	2		4	5		7	8[1]	9	10[2]		11	3	6											
F.A. AMATEUR CUP																														
15 Jan	1st R (H)	Kingstonian		W 3-1		1	2	3		5	11	4	10	8[1]	9[1]					7[1]			6							
29 Jan	2nd R (A)	Erith & B		L 0-4		1	2	3		5	11	4	10	8	9					7			6							
SURREY SENIOR CUP																														
8 Jan	1st R (H)	Sutton		W 1-0		1	2	3		5	11	4	10[1]	8	9					7			6							
5 Feb	2nd R (H)	Carshalton		W 2-1		1	2	3		5	11	4	10	8	9					7[2]			6							
19 Mar	S-F	(D'wich) Wimbledon		L 1-3	7,000	1		3	5	6	11	4	10	9	8[1]			2		7										
SURREY COMBINATION CUP																														
6 Apr	S-F (H)	Walton		W 4-1		1	2	3	5	11	6	4	10	9						7								8[1]		*other scorers unknown*
14 May	F (A)	Kingstonian		W 3-0		1	2	3		11	6	4	10	9[2]	8[1]				5	7										
TOTAL APPEARANCES						**37**	**29**	**27**	**29**	**37**	**21**	**35**	**37**	**36**	**32**	**1**	**10**	**7**	**10**	**27**	**3**	**4**	**10**	**2**	**1**	**4**	**1**	**6**	**1**	
GOALS SCORED								**1**	**1**	**6**	**2**	**3**	**17**	**19**	**19**		**1**			**13**		**1**			**1**	**1**		**2**		

SEASON 1949-1950

ISTHMIAN LEAGUE

Date	Venue	Opponents	Result	Attendance	Towers, P.	Morgan, R.	Braithwaite, A.	Boxall, O.	Morris, L	Reeves, R.	Pink, F.	Clarke, A.	Wiles, W.	Smith, D.A.	Drake, P.	Wallace, L.M.	Masey, A.	Eastaff, M.	Short, W.	Welland, A.	Baker, M.	Ballerino, J.	Stevens, D.	Smith, P.	Seaman, C.	Warren, R.	Watson, J.	Keefe, F.
27 Aug	(A)	Oxford	D 2-2		1	2	3	4	5	6	7[1]	8[1]	9	10	11													
3 Sep	(H)	Leytonstone	W 2-0			2	3	4	5	6	7[1]	8	9[1]	10		11		1										
10 Sep	(A)	Romford	W 3-1				3	4	5	6	7[1]	8	9[1]	10		11[1]	2	1										
24 Sep	(A)	Kingstonian	L 1-2		1	2	3	4	5		7	8	9			11			6	10[1]								
8 Oct	(A)	Leytonstone	L 0-3			2		4	5	6	7	8	9	10			3	1			11							
15 Oct	(H)	Walthamstow	W 6-4			2	3	4	5	6	7[1]		9[2]	10				1			11	8[3]						
22 Oct	(H)	Ilford	W 5-3			2	3	4	5	6[1]	7		9[1]	10[1]				1			11	8[2]						
29 Oct	(A)	Walthamstow	L 1-9			2	3	4	5	6	7		9[1]	10				1			11	8						
5 Nov	(H)	Kingstonian	L 3-5			2	3[1]	4	5	6	7[1]		9	10		11		1				8[1]						
12 Nov	(A)	Ilford	W 3-2					4	5	6	7[1]		9[2]	10		11	2	1				8	3					
19 Nov	(A)	Clapton	W 3-1			2		4	5	6	7[1]		9	10		11[1]		1				8[1]	3					
26 Nov	(H)	Tufnell Park	W 6-0			2	3[1]	4	5	6	7[1]		9[3]	10		11		1				8[1]						
3 Dec	(H)	Dulwich	D 2-2				3	4	5	6	7		9[1]	10		11[1]	2	1				8						
10 Dec	(A)	Dulwich	L 2-5			2	3	4	5	6[1]	7			9		11		1	10			8[1]						
17 Dec	(H)	Romford	D 2-2			2		4	5	6	7[1]		9[1]	10		11	3	1				8						
24 Dec	(A)	St. Albans	L 2-6					4		3	7	8[1]	9[1]	10		11	2	1					5	6				
7 Jan	(A)	Wycombe	L 0-2			2	3	8	5	6	7	4	9	11				1				10						
28 Jan	(A)	Corinthian Casuals	W 2-1			2		4	5	11	7	8	9[1]	10[1]			3	1						6				
4 Feb	(H)	Clapton	L 1-5					4[1]	5	11	7	8	9	10			2	1					3	6				
11 Feb	(H)	Oxford	D 2-2			2		4	5	11	7		9[2]	10			3	1	8					6				
25 Feb	(A)	Wimbledon	L 4-5					7	5	6	11		9[2]	10[2]			3	1	8					4	2			
11 Mar	(A)	Tufnell Park	W 2-0			2			5		7	10	9[1]				3	1	8[1]		11			4		6		
25 Mar	(H)	St. Albans	W 1-0					7	5	3	11	4	9[1]	10			2	1	8					6				
1 Apr	(H)	Corinthian Casuals	D 2-2			2			5	3	7	4	9	10[1]			6	1	8[1]		11							
26 Apr	(H)	Wycombe	D 1-1					11	5	3	7[1]	10	9				6	1								4	2	8
29 Apr	(H)	Wimbledon	L 2-6			2		11	5	3	7[2]	10	9				6	1	8							4		
F.A. CUP																												
17 Sep	Prel (H)	Met. Police	W 1-0			2	3	4	5	6	7	8	9	10[1]		11		1										
1 Oct	1st Q (H)	Epsom	L 1-2			2	3		5	6	7[1]	8	9	10		11		1	4									
F.A. AMATEUR CUP																												
14 Jan	1st R (A)	Barnet £283	L 1-3	4,430		2	3	4	5	11	7[1]	8	9	10			6	1										
SURREY SENIOR CUP																												
31 Dec	1st R (H)	Leatherhead £123	W 3-2	2,000		2		4[1]	5	6	7	8	9[2]	10		11	3	1										
21 Jan	2nd R (H)	Met. Police	W 2-0			2		4	5	11	7[1]	8	9[1]	10			3	1						6				
4 Mar	S-F	(Wimbledon) Kingston	L 2-5					7	5	6	11[1]		9	10[1]			3	1	8					4	2			
SURREY COMBINATION CUP																												
24 Apr	(H)	Guildford City £94	L 1-2	1,400		2		7	5	3	11	10	9[1]				4	1	8							6		
WOKING CUP																												
15 Apr	(H)	Guildford Pinks	W 5-1			2		7[2]	5	3	11	4	9[2]	10			6	1	8[1]									
TOTAL APPEARANCES					**2**	**25**	**15**	**31**	**33**	**32**	**34**	**21**	**33**	**29**	**1**	**14**	**21**	**32**	**12**	**1**	**6**	**11**	**4**	**9**	**2**	**4**	**1**	**1**
GOALS SCORED							**2**	**4**		**2**	**16**	**2**	**27**	**7**		**3**			**3**	**1**		**9**						

ISTHMIAN LEAGUE

SEASON 1950-1951

Date	Venue	Opponents	Result	Atten-dance	Towers, P.	Morgan, R.	Masey, A.	Clarke, A.	Morris, L	Short, W.	Welland, A.	Hamm, G.	Wiles, W.	Edwards, R.	Pink, F.	Warren, R.	Pinhorn, P.	Read, N.	Flippance, J.	Wastell, J.	Smith, D.A.	Keefe, F.	Seaman, C.	Trinder, D.	Killick,C.	Reeves, R.
26 Aug	(A)	Walthamstow	L 2-4		1	2[1]	3	4	5	6	7	8	9	10[1]	11											
9 Sep	(A)	Wycombe	W 4-3		1	2	3	4	5		7		9	10[1]	11[2]	6	8[1]									
23 Sep	(H)	Oxford	W 3-2			2		4	5	10[1]		8	9[2]		11			1	3	6	7					
30 Sep	(H)	Clapton	W 2-0			2		4	5	10[1]		8	9[1]		11			1	3	6	7					
7 Oct	(A)	Leytonstone	L 2-3			2		4	5	11		8[1]	10[1]		9			1	3	6	7					
14 Oct	(H)	Romford	L 2-4			2		4	5			8[2]	9	10	11			1	3	6	7					
21 Oct	(A)	Wimbledon	D 2-2		1	2		4	5	10[1]	7[1]	8	9		11				3	6						
28 Oct	(H)	Kingstonian	D 2-2		1	2		4[1]	5	10	7	8[1]	9		11				3	6						
4 Nov	(A)	St. Albans	D 1-1		1	2[1]		4	5	10	7	8	9		11				3	6						
11 Nov	(H)	Tufnell Park	W 8-1		1	2		4	5	10[2]	7	8[4]	9[1]		11[1]				3	6						
18 Nov	(A)	Dulwich	L 0-3		1	2		4	5	10	7	8	9		11				3	6						
25 Nov	(H)	Wycombe	D 2-2		1	2		4	5	10	7	8	9[2]		11				3	6						
2 Dec	(A)	Kingstonian	L 2-3		1	2		4	5	10	7	8	9[1]		11[1]				3	6						
9 Dec	(A)	Oxford	L 2-3		1		2	4	5	10	7	8	9[2]		11				3	6						
16 Dec	(H)	Leytonstone	L 2-3		1		3	4	5	10	7	8	9[1]		11[1]				2	6						
23 Dec	(H)	Wimbledon	W 3-0	1,103	1	2	3	4	5	10[1]	7[2]	8	9		11					6						
30 Dec	(A)	Romford	D 2-2		1	2	3	4	5	10[1]	7	8	9[1]		11							6				
10 Feb	(A)	Corinthian Casuals	W 2-1			2	3		5	6[1]	7	8	9[1]	10	11			1				4				
24 Feb	(A)	Clapton	W 4-1			2	3[1]		5	6	7	8[1]	9[2]		11		10	1				4				
3 Mar	(H)	St. Albans £55	D 2-2	1,500		2	3		5	10[1]	7		9		11[1]		8	1		6		4				
10 Mar	(H)	Dulwich (o.g.)	W 4-1		1		2		5	6	7	10	9[1]		11[2]		8					4	3			
17 Mar	(A)	Ilford	L 1-4		1	2	3	4	5	6	7	10	9[1]		11		8									
31 Mar	(H)	Corinthian Casuals	W 2-1		1	2	3	4[1]	5		7		9[1]	10	11		8					6				
7 Apr	(A)	Tufnell Park	W 6-1			2	3	4	5	10[1]	7		9[4]		11		8[1]	1				6				
14 Apr	(H)	Ilford	L 1-5		1	2	3	4	5	10	7		9[1]		11		8					6				
28 Apr	(H)	Walthamstow	W 2-1		1	2	3	4	5	6	7	10	9[1]		11[1]							8				
F.A. CUP																										
2 Sep	Ex Pr (H)	Carshalton £78	D 2-2	1,700	1	2		4	5	6	7		9[1]	10	11[1]		8									3
6 Sep	Rep (A)	Carshalton	AB 4-3		1	2	3		5	4[1]	7	8	9[2]		11[1]	6					10					
11 Sep	Rep (A)	Carshalton o.g. AET	L 4-7	(3-3 FT)	1	2			5	4[1]	7	8[1]	9		11[1]						10			6		3
F.A. AMATEUR CUP																										
13 Jan	1st R (A)	Jack Moulds Athletic	W 3-2		1	2	3	4	5	10[1]	7	8	9[1]		11[1]					6						
27 Jan	2nd R (H)	Wimbledon £233	D 1-1	4,127	1	2	3	4	5	10	7[1]	8		9	11					6						
3 Feb	Rep (A)	Wimbledon £298	L 2-3	5,800	1	2	3	4	5	10[1]	7	8	9		11[1]					6						
SURREY SENIOR CUP																										
6 Jan	1st R (A)	Redhill	L 0-4		1	2	3	4	5	10	7	8	9		11					6						
ADDENBROOKE HOSPITAL CUP																										
12 May	(A)	Cambridge C	D 1-1	5,000	1		2	4	5	6	7	10	9[1]		11		8						3			
SURREY COMBINATION CUP																										
13 Sep	(H)	Met. Police	L 2-4		1		2	8[1]	5	4[1]	7	10	9			6					11		3			
WOKING CUP																										
21 Apr	(H)	Guildford Pinks	W 4-1				2	4[1]	5	6	7[1]		9[1]	10	11[1]		8	1							3	
TOTAL APPEARANCES					**27**	**30**	**23**	**30**	**36**	**33**	**32**	**29**	**35**	**8**	**35**	**3**	**11**	**9**	**13**	**19**	**7**	**9**	**3**	**1**	**1**	**2**
GOALS SCORED						**2**	**1**	**4**		**15**	**5**	**10**	**30**	**2**	**15**		**2**									

ISTHMIAN LEAGUE

SEASON 1951-1952

Date	Venue	Opponents	Result	Attendance	Towers, P.	Morgan, R.	Masey, A.	Clarke, A.	Morris, L	Short, W.	Welland, A.	Pinhorn, P.	Wiles, W.	Hamm, G.	Pink, F.	Smith, D.A.	Reeves, R.	Edwards, R.	Smith, F.	Wride, E.	Dashwood, J.	Bonar, E.	Parsons, G.	Phelan, A.	Ellerby, R.	Easton, A.	Tanner, B.	Warren, R.	Cheyne, A.	Killick, C.	Adam, J.	Keefe, F.	Read, N.	Cherry, R.	Webb, K.
25 Aug	(H)	Walthamstow £107	L 1-4	1,900	1	2	3	4	5	6	7	8	9[1]	10	11																				
1 Sep	(A)	Ilford	W 1-0		1	2	3	4	5	6	7		9	10[1]		8	11																		
8 Sep	(H)	St. Albans £87	W 2-1	1,500	1	2	3	4	5	6	7[1]		9[1]		11	8		10																	
22 Sep	(H)	Oxford	W 4-2	1,700	1	2	3		5	4[1]	7[1]		9		11[2]		6		8	10															
6 Oct	(H)	Romford £116	D 2-2	2,050	1	2		4	5	6[1]	7		9[1]	10	11	8					3														
20 Oct	(A)	Oxford	L 0-4		1	2	3	4	5	6	7				11			10	8	9															
27 Oct	(A)	Wimbledon	L 0-6		1	2	3		5	4	7		9		11				8	10		6													
3 Nov	(H)	Ilford	D 0-0		1	2		4	5	6	7	8		10	11								3	9											
10 Nov	(A)	Tufnell Park	D 1-1		1			4	5	6	7	8	9[1]	10	11								3		2										
24 Nov	(A)	Clapton	W 3-1		1			4	5	6	7	11	9[2]	10									3		2	8[1]									
1 Dec	(H)	Wycombe	W 8-1		1		4		5[1]	6	7[1]		9[3]	10[1]	11[1]					8[1]			3		2										
8 Dec	(A)	Romford	L 1-5		1		4		5	6	7		9[1]	10	11					8			3		2										
22 Dec	(H)	Tufnell Park	W 3-1		1	2		4	5	6[1]	7		9[1]	10	11								3			8[1]									
5 Jan	(A)	Dulwich	L 2-6		1	2			5	6	7	8[1]		10	11					9[1]			3				4								
19 Jan	(A)	Wycombe	L 2-5		1	2		6	5	10	7		9	8	11[2]								3				4								
26 Jan	(H)	Kingstonian	D 5-5		1	2[1]			5	6	7[1]		9[1]	10	11[1]								3			8[1]	4								
2 Feb	(A)	St. Albans	L 2-4		1	2		6		3	7		9	10[1]	11[1]											8	4	5							
9 Feb	(A)	Kingstonian	W 2-1		1	2		4	5	6			9	10	7								3			8[2]			11						
16 Feb	(H)	Leytonstone	W 3-1		1	2		4	5	6[2]			9[1]	10	7								3			8			11						
23 Feb	(A)	Corinthian Casuals	L 2-7		1			4	5	6	8		9[1]	10	7[1]								3						11	2					
1 Mar	(A)	Leytonstone	L 1-3		1			4	5			8	9	10	11[1]								3							2	7	6			
8 Mar	(H)	Wimbledon	W 3-1		1	2			5	6	7[1]	8		10	11[2]								3									4			9
15 Mar	(H)	Dulwich	W 4-3		1	2			5	6[2]	7		9	10	11[1]								3			8[1]						4			
22 Mar	(H)	Clapton	W 3-1		1	2[1]			5	6	7		9	10	11[2]								3			8						4			
12 Apr	(A)	Walthamstow	D 1-1		1			6	5		7		9	10[1]	11								3	8	2							4			
23 Apr	(H)	Corinthian Casuals	L 4-5		1			6		5	7		9[2]	10[2]									3		2	8			11			4			
F.A. CUP																																			
15 Sep	Ex Pr (A)	Epsom	W 4-3		1	2	3	4	5	6	7[1]		9	10[3]	11	8																			
29 Sep	1st Q (H)	Dorking £100	W 5-1	1,750	1	2	3	4	5	6	7		9[2]	10[1]	11[2]	8																			
13 Oct	2nd Q (H)	Hounslow £185	L 0-6	3,250	1	2	3		5	4	7		9	10	11	8	6																		
F.A. AMATEUR CUP																																			
15 Dec	1st R (H)	Keynsham Town £115	W 3-2	1,900	1	2		4	5	6	7		9[1]	10[1]	11[1]								3			8									
12 Jan	2nd R (H)	Marine (Crosby)	L 0-3	3,900	1	2		6	5	10	7			8	11								3			9	4								
SURREY SENIOR CUP																																			
29 Dec	1st R (A)	Corinthian Casuals	L 3-5		1	2	6	4	5		7[1]	8	9[2]	10	11								3												
SURREY SENIOR SHIELD																																			
26 Apr	1st R (H)	Walton £100	L 1-4	1,800	1			6		5	7	8	9[1]	10	11								3		2							4			
SURREY COMBINATION CUP																																			
1 Oct	1st L (A)	Guildford City £137	L 0-3	1,772	1	2	3	4	5	6	7		9	10	11	8																			
7 May	2nd L (H)	Guildford City	L 1-6					8		6	7		9	10	11[1]								3			5				2		4	1		
WOKING CUP																																			
19 Apr	(H)	Guildford Pinks	W 4-1	***Team not traced***								8[1]																						9[3]	
ADDENBROOKE HOSPITAL CUP																																			
10 May	(A)	Cambridge C.	D 4-4		1			7		6[2]	11			10[1]									3		2	8[1]		5				4		9	
TOTAL APPEARANCES					**35**	**25**	**13**	**26**	**31**	**33**	**33**	**10**	**30**	**32**	**32**	**7**	**3**	**2**	**3**	**6**	**1**	**1**	**24**	**2**	**8**	**13**	**5**	**2**	**4**	**3**	**1**	**9**	**1**	**2**	**1**
GOALS SCORED						**2**			**1**	**9**	**7**	**2**	**22**	**12**	**18**					**2**						**7**								**3**	

SEASON 1952-1953

ISTHMIAN LEAGUE

Date	Venue	Opponents		Result	Attendance	Read, N.	McFetridge, J.	Parsons, G.	Keefe, F.	Morris, L.	Short, W.	Welland, A.	Pinhorn, P.	Cox, R.	Hamm, G.	Pink, F.	Wiles, W.	Clarke, A.	Killick, C.	Ledger, P.	Davies, B.	Hart, I.	Ford, J.	Morgan, R.	Phelan, A.	Ellerby, R.	Cheyne, A.	Collis, B.	Whitton, J.	White, J.	Taylor, D.	Hadden
23 Aug	(H)	Barking		W 4-2		1	2	3	4	5	6[1]	7	8	9[2]	10	11[1]																
27 Aug	(A)	Leytonstone		D 0-0		1	2	3	4	5	6	7	8	9	10	11																
30 Aug	(A)	Oxford		W 3-2		1	2	3	4	5	6	7	8[1]	9	10	11[2]																
3 Sep	(H)	Leytonstone		L 1-3		1	2	3	4	5	6	7[1]	8		10	11	9															
20 Sep	(H)	Wycombe		L 2-3		1	2	3			6	7[1]	8		10[1]	11	9	4	5													
4 Oct	(A)	St. Albans		L 1-2				3		5	6	7	8	9	10[1]	11		4	2	1												
11 Oct	(A)	Walthamstow		L 0-1				3		5	6	7	8	9	10	11		4	2	1												
25 Oct	(A)	Ilford		L 3-6				3		5	6	11[1]			10		9[2]	4	2	1	7	8										
1 Nov	(H)	Romford		L 2-3			3			5	6	7			10	11	9[1]	4	2	1			8[1]									
8 Nov	(A)	Corinthian Casuals		L 2-5			2	3		5	6	7			10[1]	11[1]	9	4		1			8									
22 Nov	(A)	Kingstonian		L 0-4			2	3		5	6	7			10	11	9	4		1			8									
29 Nov	(H)	Oxford		W 4-3			3			5	10[1]	7[1]			8[2]	11	9	4		1		6		2								
10 Jan	(H)	St. Albans		D 3-3			2	3		5	4[1]	7			8	11	9[2]			1		6	10									
17 Jan	(A)	Wimbledon		L 3-5				3		5	4	7[1]			8	11[1]	9[1]	10		1		6		2								
24 Jan	(H)	Ilford		W 4-0				3		2	4[1]	11			8[1]		9[2]	7	5	1		6	10									
31 Jan	(H)	Kingstonian		D 1-1				3		2	4	7			8	11[1]	9	10	5	1		6										
7 Feb	(A)	Dulwich		L 3-4				3		2	4[1]	7			8	11		6	5	1			10		9[2]							
14 Feb	(A)	Romford		L 2-7				3		2		7[1]			8	11[1]	9	4	5	1		6	10									
21 Feb	(H)	Dulwich		W 2-1				3	4	9	6[1]	7			8	11		10	5	1						2[1]						
7 Mar	(H)	Wimbledon		L 0-4				3	4		6	9						10	5	1		7	8			2	11					
14 Mar	(A)	Barking		W 2-0				3	6	4		9[1]			10[1]	11		8	5	1		7						2				
11 Apr	(H)	Clapton		W 3-1				3	4	2		7[1]			10[1]	11		8	5	1		6							9[1]			
18 Apr	(A)	Wycombe		W 2-1				3	4	2		7			10	11			5	1		6	8[1]						9[1]			
23 Apr	(A)	Clapton		D 0-0				3	4	2	5	8								1	7		10				11		9	6		
25 Apr	(A)	Bromley		L 0-6				3	4	2	10	11								1	7	6	8					5	9			
28 Apr	(H)	Corinthian Casuals		W 4-1					4	2		7			10[1]	11[1]				1		6	8[1]					5	9[1]		3	
29 Apr	(H)	Walthamstow		W 3-0					4	2		7			10[1]	11[1]		8[1]	5	1		6						3	9			
2 May	(H)	Bromley		L 3-4					4	2	3	7[1]			10	11[1]		8	5	1		6							9[1]			
F.A. CUP																																
13 Sep	Prel (H)	Dorking	£102	W 4-1	1,650	1	2	3			6[1]	11[1]	8		10[1]	9[1]		4	5		7											
27 Sep	1st Q (H)	Wimbledon	£155	L 1-2	2,500	1		3		5	6[1]	7	8	9	10	11		4	2													
F.A. AMATEUR CUP																																
15 Nov	4th Q (H)	Bexleyheath	£87	W 5-0	1,373		2	3		5	6	7[1]			10[1]	11	9[2]	4[1]		1			8									
13 Dec	1st R (H)	Barnet		D 3-3	2,500		2	3		5	10	7			8	11[1]	9[2]	4		1		6										
20 Dec	Rep (A)	Barnet		L 0-2	1,381		2	3		5	10	7			8	11	9	4		1		6										
SURREY SENIOR CUP																																
3 Jan	1st R (A)	Wimbledon		L 1-3			2	3	10	5		7			8[1]	11	9	4		1		6										
SURREY SENIOR SHIELD																																
28 Feb	1st R (A)	Sutton		W 1-0				3	4	2	6	9[1]			8	11		10	5	1		7										
28 Mar	S-F (H)	Epsom		W 3-1				3	6	4		7			10[2]	11[1]		8	5	1								2	9			
7 May	F (H)	Banstead		W 2-1					4	2	3	7				11		8	5	1		6	10[1]						9[1]			
SURREY COMBINATION CUP																																
21 Mar	1st L (H)	Guildford City	£138	L 1-4	2,338			3	4	2		7			10	11[1]		8	5	1		6							9			
22 Apr	2nd L (A)	Guildford City		L 0-5					4	2		7							5	1		6	10		9		11				3	8
CORONATION CUP																																
8 May	(A)	Walton		L 1-3	***Team not traced***											[1]																
TOTAL APPEARANCES						**7**	**15**	**32**	**20**	**36**	**29**	**39**	**9**	**6**	**34**	**33**	**16**	**29**	**23**	**32**	**4**	**22**	**15**	**2**	**2**	**2**	**3**	**5**	**10**	**1**	**2**	**1**
GOALS SCORED											**8**	**12**	**1**	**2**	**15**	**15**	**12**	**2**					**4**		**2**	**1**			**5**			

SEASON 1953-1954

ISTHMIAN LEAGUE

Date	Venue	Opponents		Result	Atten-dance	Ledger. P.	Morris, L.	Parsons, G.	Keefe, F.	Morgan, R.	Mortimore, J.	Welland, A.	Hamm, G.	Mortimore, C.	Zimmer, A.	Pink, F.	Killick, C.	Clarke, A.	Short, W.	Gibbs, A.	Burley, J.	Ford, J.	McKercher, R.	Cheyne, A.	Quirk, T.	Pratt, A.	Jones, I.
26 Aug	(H)	Dulwich		W 1-0		1	2	3	4		6	7	10	9[1]		11	5	8									
29 Aug	(A)	Wycombe		L 3-5		1	2	3	4		6	7	10	9[2]		11[1]	5	8									
5 Sep	(H)	Bromley		D 2-2		1	2	3	4			7	10	9[2]		11	5	8	6								
9 Sep	(A)	Dulwich		W 3-1		1	2	3	4	5		7	10[1]	9[1]		11[1]		6	8								
19 Sep	(H)	Walthamstow		W 3-0		1	2	3	4	5	6	7	10[1]	9[1]		11		8[1]									
26 Sep	(A)	Leytonstone		L 2-4		1	2	3	4	5	6	7[1]	10	9[1]		11		8									
3 Oct	(A)	Romford		L 0-7		1	2	3	4		6	7	10	9		11	5	8									
10 Oct	(H)	Wimbledon		L 2-3		1	2	3	4	5	6	7	10			11[1]		8		9[1]							
17 Oct	(A)	St. Albans		W 2-1		1	2	3	4	5	6		10	9	8[1]	11				7[1]							
24 Oct	(H)	Barking		W 6-4		1	2	3	4	5	6	7[1]	10[1]	9[2]	8[2]	11											
31 Oct	(A)	Clapton		D 2-2			2	3	4	5	6	7[2]	10	9	8	11					1						
7 Nov	(H)	Ilford		D 0-0		1	2	3	4	5	6	7	10	9	8	11											
21 Nov	(H)	Leytonstone		W 3-0		1	2	3	4	5		7	10	9[1]	8	11[2]		6									
28 Nov	(A)	Oxford		L 2-3		1	2[1]	3	4	5		7	10[1]		8	11		6				9					
5 Dec	(A)	Ilford		W 4-1		1	5	3	2		6	7[1]	10	9[2]	8[1]	11		4									
12 Dec	(H)	Oxford		W 4-3		1	2	3	4	5		7	10	9[1]	8[2]	11[1]		6									
26 Dec	(A)	Wimbledon		W 3-0		1	2	3		5	6	7	10	9[1]	8[1]	11[1]		4									
16 Jan	(H)	Romford	£129	W 1-0	2,400	1	2	3		5	6	7	10	9[1]	8	11		4									
6 Feb	(H)	Kingstonian		L 0-2		1	3		2	5	4	7	10	9	8	11		6									
20 Feb	(A)	Corinthian Casuals		L 1-5		1	5	3	2		6	7[1]	8	9	10	11		4									
27 Feb	(H)	St. Albans		W 4-1		1		3	2	5	6[1]		8[1]		10					9[1]			4	7	11[1]		
13 Mar	(A)	Barking		L 0-3		1		3	2	5	6	7			10					9			4	11		8	
20 Mar	(H)	Clapton		W 4-3		1		3	2	5	6				10[1]	11[1]		4		9[1]		8[1]					7
27 Mar	(A)	Kingstonian		W 1-0		1		3	2	5	6		8		10			4		9				11			7[1]
10 Apr	(H)	Wycombe		L 0-3				3	2	5	6	7	8		10			4		9	1						11
24 Apr	(H)	Corinthian Casuals		L 1-3		1		3	2		4	7	6	10	8[1]		5			9							11
28 Apr	(A)	Bromley		L 0-2		1		3	2	5	6	7	8	9	10			4									11
1 May	(A)	Walthamstow		D 0-0		1		3	2	5	6	7	8	9	10			4						11			
F.A. CUP																											
12 Sep	Prel (A)	Kingstonian		L 1-3		1	2	3	4			7	10	9[1]		11	5	6	8								
F.A. AMATEUR CUP																											
14 Nov	4th Q (A)	Bulford United	£60	W 4-1	1,200	1	5	3	4		6	7[1]	10	9[3]	8	11									2		
19 Dec	1st R (H)	Kingstonian		W 4-1	3,000	1	2	3		5	6	7[1]	10	9[2]	8	11[1]		4									
23 Jan	2nd R (A)	Walton		L 1-3	5,935	1	2	3		5	6	7	10	9	8[1]	11		4									
SURREY SENIOR CUP																											
9 Jan	1st R (H)	Wimbledon	£150	L 1-4	2,600	1	2	3		5	6	7[1]	10		8	11		4								9	
SURREY SENIOR SHIELD																											
13 Feb	1st R (H)	Surbiton		W 5-0		1	2	3		5	6	7[1]	10[3]	9[1]	8			4						11			
6 Mar	S-F (H)	Walton		W 3-1		1		3	2	5	6[1]	8[1]			10	11				9[1]			4	7			
8 May	F (H)	Kingstonian		L 1-2		1		3	2	5	6	7	8	9[1]	10			4						11			
TOTAL APPEARANCES						**34**	**26**	**35**	**30**	**27**	**30**	**32**	**33**	**27**	**27**	**27**	**6**	**27**	**3**	**9**	**2**	**2**	**3**	**7**	**2**	**2**	**5**
GOALS SCORED							**1**				**2**	**11**	**8**	**24**	**10**	**9**		**1**		**5**		**1**			**1**		**1**

SEASON 1954-1955

ISTHMIAN LEAGUE

Date	Venue	Opponents		Result	Atten-dance	Ledger, P.	Morris, L.	Parsons, G.	Keefe, F.	Morgan, R.	Mortimore, J.	Welland, A.	Hamm, G.	Mortimore, C.	Zimmer, A.	Newman, R.	Woodfield, V.	Clacey, E.	Banks, J.	Pratt, A.	Edwards, G.	Quirk, T.	Milburn, D.	Killick, C.	Stratton, Bob	Ellerby, R.	Cheyne, A.	McKercher, R.	Bond, R.	Smith, W.	Clarke, A.	Gamble, D.
25 Aug	(H)	Bromley		W 4-1	2,400	1	2	3	4	5	6[1]	7[1]	8[1]	9[1]	10	11																
28 Aug	(H)	Barking		L 1-4		1	2	3	4	5	6	7	8[1]		10	11	9															
4 Sep	(A)	Clapton		L 2-5		1	2	3	4		6	7	8	9[1]	10[1]	11		5														
15 Sep	(A)	Corinthian Casuals		L 4-7			5	3	2			7[1]	6	9	10[2]	11			1	4	8[1]											
18 Sep	(H)	Leytonstone		W 3-1		1	5	3	4		6	7[1]	8	9[1]	10[1]	11						2										
2 Oct	(H)	Ilford		W 3-1		1		3	6		5	7[1]	8		10[1]	11				4		2	9[1]									
9 Oct	(A)	Wimbledon		W 3-1		1		3	6		5	7	8[1]	9[2]	10	11				4		2										
16 Oct	(A)	Walthamstow		L 0-3		1		3	6		5	7	8	9	10	11				4		2										
23 Oct	(H)	Dulwich		W 3-2		1		3	6		5	7[1]		9	10	11[1]				4	8[1]			2								
30 Oct	(A)	Kingstonian		L 2-4		1		3	6		5	7	8		10[1]	11[1]				4			9	2								
6 Nov	(H)	Romford		D 4-4		1		3	4	2	5[1]	7	8	9[2]	10[1]	11															6	
13 Nov	(A)	St. Albans		L 1-5				3	6	2	5	7	4	9	10	11[1]					8				1							
20 Nov	(H)	Kingstonian	o.g.	W 6-2				2		5	6[1]	7	10[1]	9[1]	8[1]	11[1]				4					1	3						
27 Nov	(A)	Leytonstone		W 4-2				2		5	6	11[2]	8	9[1]	10	7[1]				4					1	3						
1 Jan	(A)	Bromley		L 0-5				3		5	6	7	8	9	10					4					1	2	11					
8 Jan	(H)	Wycombe		L 2-4				2		5	6	11	8	10			9[2]								1	3	7	4				
29 Jan	(H)	St. Albans		L 1-4				2		5	6	11	8	9	10										1	3		4	7[1]			
5 Feb	(H)	Corinthian Casuals		D 0-0				2	6	5	4		11	9	10						8				1	3			7			
12 Feb	(A)	Romford		W 9-6				2	6		4[1]		11[3]	9[3]	10[1]						8[1]			5	1	3			7			
19 Feb	(A)	Dulwich		L 1-2				2	6	5			11[1]		10		9				8				1	3		4	7			
12 Mar	(H)	Oxford		W 2-1				3	6	5	4	8[1]	11	9[1]	10					2					1				7			
19 Mar	(A)	Ilford		L 2-3				3	6	5	4	8	11[1]	9[1]	10					2	7				1							
26 Mar	(A)	Barking		L 1-5					4	5		7	11					6[1]		2	10		9		1	3				8		
2 Apr	(H)	Walthamstow		W 1-0		1		3	4		5	7[1]	11	9	10			6		2	8											
16 Apr	(H)	Clapton		W 4-0		1		3		5	4	7[1]	11[1]	9[2]	10					2	8										6	
30 Apr	(A)	Wycombe		L 0-3		1		3	4		5	10	11	9				6		2	8								7			
2 May	(H)	Wimbledon		W 9-1		1		3	4		5		11[3]	9[4]	10[1]			6		2	8								7[1]			
7 May	(A)	Oxford		D 3-3		1		3	4		5	8[1]	11[1]	9				6		2									7			10[1]
F.A. CUP																																
11 Sep	Prel (A)	Dover	£209	L 1-2	3,000		2	3	4	5	6[1]	7	8	9	10	11			1													
F.A. AMATEUR CUP																																
18 Dec	1st R (H)	St. Albans		W 2-1				2		5	6[1]	11	8	9	10	7[1]				4					1	3						
22 Jan	2nd R (A)	Wycombe		L 0-4	7,350			2	6		5	7	11	10	8		9								1	3		4				
SURREY SENIOR CUP																																
11 Dec	1st R (H)	Tooting		W 2-1				2		5	6[1]	11	8	9	10	7[1]				4					1	3						
26 Feb	2nd R (A)	Dulwich		L 2-5				2	6	5		7	11		10[1]						8		9[1]		1	3		4				
SURREY COMBINATION CUP																																
25 Sep	1st L (A)	Guildford City		L 2-4		1		3	6		5	7	8	9[1]	10	11[1]				4		2										
23 Apr	2nd L (H)	Guildford City	£66	L 2-3	1,100	1		3	6		5	8[2]	11	9	10					2	4								7			
ADDENBROOKE HOSPITAL CUP																																
14 May	(A)	Cambridge C.		W 7-2		1		3	4[1]			7[2]	11[1]	9[2]	10[1]			5		2	8							6				
TOTAL APPEARANCES						**18**	**6**	**35**	**28**	**19**	**31**	**32**	**35**	**30**	**32**	**18**	**4**	**7**	**2**	**22**	**15**	**5**	**4**	**3**	**16**	**13**	**2**	**6**	**9**	**1**	**2**	**1**
GOALS SCORED									**1**		**7**	**15**	**15**	**23**	**12**	**8**	**2**	**1**			**3**		**2**						**2**			**1**

SEASON 1955-1956

ISTHMIAN LEAGUE

Date	Venue	Opponents		Result	Attendance	Ledger, P.	Ellerby, R.	Gill, M.	Pratt, A.	Parsons, G.	Keefe, F.	Mortimore, J.	Clacey, E.	Welland, A.	Harvey, J.	Mortimore, C.	Zimmer, A.	Hamm, G.	Grassam, G.	Redican, T.	Killick, C.	Clarke, A.	Bond, R.	Turner, K.	Ford, R.	Sayers, L.	Stratton, Reg.	Edwards, G.
27 Aug	(A)	Barking		L 0-1				1	2	3	4	5	6	7	8	9	10	11										
31 Aug	(A)	Leytonstone		L 0-4				1	2	3	4	5	6	7	8	9	10	11										
3 Sep	(H)	Dulwich		L 1-2				1	2	3	4	5[1]		7	8	9	10		6	11								
17 Sep	(A)	Ilford		L 1-3				1	2	3	4	5	6	7	10[1]	9		8		11								
24 Sep	(H)	Romford		W 1-0		1			2	3	4	8[1]		7		9	10	11			5	6						
1 Oct	(H)	Walthamstow		L 2-6				1	2	3	4	8[1]		7		9[1]	10	11			5	6						
8 Oct	(A)	Clapton		W 2-1				1	2	3		4[1]			8[1]	9	10			11	5	6	7					
15 Oct	(H)	Kingstonian	£114	D 2-2	2,100			1	2	3		4			8[1]	9	10[1]	7		11	5	6						
22 Oct	(A)	Dulwich		W 4-3				1	2	3		4	5		8[1]	9[1]	10[1]	11		7[1]		6						
5 Nov	(H)	Leytonstone		W 2-0				1	2	3			5		8	9[2]	10	11	4	7		6						
12 Nov	(A)	Corinthian Casuals		W 5-4				1		3		4	5		8[2]	9[2]	10	11		7[1]		6		2				
19 Nov	(H)	Wimbledon		W 5-1				1		3		4[1]	5		8[1]	9	10[1]	11[2]		7		6		2				
26 Nov	(A)	Romford		W 3-1				1		3		4	5		8[1]	9[1]	10	11[1]		7		6		2				
3 Dec	(H)	St. Albans		W 4-3				1		3		4[1]	5		8	9[2]	10	11[1]		7		6		2				
17 Dec	(A)	Walthamstow		L 1-2		1				3		4	5		8	9	10[1]	11		7		6		2				
26 Dec	(H)	Bromley		W 2-1		1				3		4[1]	5		8	9[1]	10	11		7		6		2				
27 Dec	(A)	Bromley		W 2-1		1				3		4	5		8[1]	9	10	11		7[1]		6		2				
31 Dec	(H)	Oxford		L 2-3	2,500	1				3		4[1]	5			9[1]	10	11	8	7		6		2				
14 Jan	(A)	Wimbledon		L 1-2		1				3		4	5	8		9	10	11		7[1]		6		2				
4 Feb	(H)	Barking		L 1-3		1	3					4	5	8		9	10	11		7[1]		6		2				
11 Feb	(H)	Ilford		W 2-0		1				3		4	5			9[2]		10		11		6	7	2	8			
18 Feb	(A)	Oxford		D 3-3		1	3					4[1]	5			9		10[1]		11		6	7	2	8[1]			
3 Mar	(H)	Clapton		L 3-5		1	3					4[1]	5	7		9[1]		10[1]		11		6		2	8			
17 Mar	(A)	Wycombe		W 3-1		1	3					4	5			9[1]		10		11[1]		6	7	2	8[1]			
7 Apr	(H)	Wycombe	£117	D 2-2	2.100	1	3					4[1]	5			9[1]		10		11		6	7	2	8			
21 Apr	(A)	St. Albans		W 2-1		1	3					4	5			9		11[1]				6	7[1]	2	8	10		
26 Apr	(H)	Corinthian Casuals		W 4-1	1,500	1	3					4	5			9[1]		10[1]				6	7[1]	2	8[1]		11	
28 Apr	(A)	Kingstonian		L 2-4		1	3				4		5			9		10				6	7	2	8[1]		11[1]	
F.A. CUP																												
10 Sep	Prel (H)	Folkestone	£121	D 1-1	2,070			1	2	3[1]	4	5	6	7	10	9				11								8
14 Sep	Rep (A)	Folkestone	£180	L 1-2	3,200			1	2	3	4	5	6	7		9[1]		11							10			8
F.A. AMATEUR CUP																												
21 Jan	1st R (H)	Leytonstone	£146	D 0-0	2,447	1	2			3		4	5	8		9	10	11		7		6						
28 Jan	Rep (A)	Leytonstone	£120	L 0-2	1,877	1	2			3		4	5	8		9	10	7		11		6						
SURREY SENIOR CUP																												
10 Dec	1st R (A)	Worcester Park		W 7-1				1		3		4	5		8[1]	9[3]	10[1]	11[1]		7[1]		6		2				
7 Jan	2nd R (H)	Corinthian Casuals	£105	W 4-2	1,800	1				3		4	5	8[1]		9[1]	10[1]	11		7[1]		6		2				
10 Mar	S-F	(Walton) Kingston		W 4-1	5,000	1	3					4	5			9[3]		10[1]		11		6	7	2	8			
12 May	F	(Dulwich) Tooting	£488	W 1-0	5,100	1	3					4	5			9		10		11		6	7	2	8[1]			
SURREY COMBINATION CUP																												
25 Feb	1st L (A)	Guildford City	£194	D 2-2	2,121	1	3					4	5			9		10		11[1]		6	7[1]	2	8			
2 May	2nd L (H)	Guildford City	£130	W 4-1	2,327	1	3				2	4				9[1]		10[1]		7		6		5	8		11[2]	
TOTAL APPEARANCES						**22**	**14**	**16**	**12**	**26**	**10**	**36**	**32**	**14**	**17**	**38**	**23**	**35**	**3**	**30**	**4**	**32**	**11**	**24**	**13**	**1**	**3**	**2**
GOALS SCORED										**1**		**11**		**1**	**10**	**26**	**6**	**11**		**9**			**3**		**5**		**3**	

ISTHMIAN LEAGUE

SEASON 1956-1957

Date	Venue	Opponents		Result	Attendance	Ledger, P.	Ellerby, R.	Parsons, G.	Mortimore, J.	Clacey, E.	Clarke, A.	Bond, R.	Ford, R.	Mortimore, C.	Hamm, G.	Stratton, Reg	Turner, K.	Welland, A.	Burley, J.	Keefe, F.	Stedman, M.	Jacob, M.	Jones, R.	Brown, L.	Keen, J.	Gamble, D.	Hayden, E.	Littlejohn, R.	Medhurst, G.	Hebdon, J.	Ford, J.
17 Aug	(H)	Clapton		W 7-1		1	2	3	4	5	6	7	8[1]	9[5]	10	11[1]															
22 Aug	(A)	Bromley		L 2-4		1		3	4	5	6		8	9[1]	10[1]	11	2	7													
25 Aug	(A)	Walthamstow		L 1-3		1	2	3	4		6	7	8	9[1]	10	11	5														
29 Aug	(H)	Leytonstone		L 2-4		1		3[1]			6	7	8		10[1]	11	5			2	4	9									
1 Sep	(H)	Wycombe	£124	W 3-2	1,900		2	3			6	7	8[2]		10	11	5		1		4	9[1]									
15 Sep	(A)	Kingstonian		W 3-2			2	3	4		6		8	9[2]		11	5	7[1]	1	10											
29 Sep	(H)	Dulwich		W 1-0			2	3[1]			6				10	11	5	7	1	8	4	9									
6 Oct	(A)	Corinthian Casuals		L 2-3			2	3	4		6		8[1]	9	10[1]	11	5	7	1												
13 Oct	(A)	Ilford		W 5-1			2				6		8[1]	9[1]		11[1]	5	7[1]	1			10[1]	3	4							
20 Oct	(H)	Wimbledon		W 6-0	2,100		2	3	4[1]		6		8	9[1]	10[2]	11[2]	5		1			7									
27 Oct	(H)	Kingstonian	£156	W 4-1	2,400		2	3[1]			6[1]		8	9[1]		11	5	7[1]	1			10		4							
3 Nov	(A)	Clapton		L 1-2	600		2	3	4		6			9	10	11	5	7	1			8[1]									
10 Nov	(H)	Barking		W 4-1			2	3	4		6			9	10[1]	11[2]	5	7[1]	1			8									
17 Nov	(A)	St. Albans		L 0-1			2	3	4		6			9	10	11	5	7	1					8							
24 Nov	(H)	Romford		D 3-3			2	3	4[2]		6			9[1]	10	11	5	7	1			8									
1 Dec	(A)	Wycombe		L 3-5			2	3	4		6			9[2]	8	11	5	7	1			10[1]									
22 Dec	(H)	St. Albans		W 7-1			2	3	4	6				9[5]	10	11	5	7	1											8[2]	
26 Dec	(A)	Dulwich		W 6-3			2	3	4					9[1]	10[3]	11[1]	5	7	1						6					8[1]	
29 Dec	(A)	Leytonstone		W 1-0			2	3	4							11[1]	5	7	1						6	9	10			8	
5 Jan	(H)	Ilford		W 6-0	2,200		2	3	4	6				9[1]	10[2]		5	7[1]	1			11								8[2]	
1 Feb	(H)	Oxford		W 5-0			2	3	4	6				9[2]	10[1]		5	7[1]	1			11								8[1]	
8 Feb	(A)	Barking		W 5-2			2	3	4	6				9	10		5	7[1]	1			11[1]								8[3]	
15 Feb	(A)	Wimbledon		L 2-3			2			6						11[1]	5	7	1		4	9	3				10[1]			8	
22 Feb	(A)	Romford		W 7-1			2	3	4	6				9[4]	10[1]	11[2]	5		1									7		8	
2 Mar	(H)	Tooting	£206	W 5-0	3,000		2	3	4	6				9[1]	10[2]	11	5		1									7[1]		8[1]	
9 Mar	(H)	Corinthian Casuals		W 6-0	2,950		2	3	4	6				9[3]	10[3]	11	5		1									7		8	
16 Mar	(H)	Bromley	£217	W 3-1	3,200		2	3	4[1]	6				9[1]	10	11	5		1									7[1]		8	
6 Apr	(A)	Oxford o.g.		L 1-3			2	3	4	5				9	10	11			1		6							7		8	
15 Apr	(A)	Tooting		W 1-0			2	3	4[1]	6						11	5	7	1							10		8			9
4 May	(H)	Walthamstow		W 2-0			2	3	4	6				9[1]	10	11[1]	5		1							8		7			
F.A. CUP																															
8 Sep	Prel (A)	Dulwich	£376	W 2-1	4,500		2	3	4		6		8	9[1]	10	11	5		1			7[1]									
22 Sep	1st Q (A)	Tunbridge Wells	£177	L 0-3	2,029		2	3	4		6		8	9		11	5	7	1			10									
F.A. AMATEUR CUP																															
12 Jan	1st R (A)	Walthamstow		D 1-1	2,700		2	3	4	6				9	10[1]	11	5	7	1											8	
19 Jan	Rep (H)	Walthamstow		L 2-3	4,800		2	3	4	6				9	10[2]	11	5	7	1											8	
SURREY SENIOR CUP																															
15 Dec	1st R (A)	Tooting		W 5-1			2	3	4	6				9[1]	10[2]	11[2]	5	7	1											8	
26 Jan	2nd R (A)	Walton & Hersham		W 4-3	2,000		2	3	4	6				9[1]	10[2]	11	5	7	1											8[1]	
23 Mar	S-F	(Kingston) Sutton		W 4-1			2	3	4	6				9[1]	10[2]	11	5	8[1]	1									7			
11 May	F	(C. Palace) Wimbledon		W 4-2	4,500		2	9[1]		6							5		1	4		7[1]	3			11[1]		10[1]		8	
SURREY SENIOR SHIELD																															
30 Mar	1st R (H)	Leatherhead		W 2-1		1	2	3						9		11	5	7[2]		4	6	10						8			
27 Apr	S-F (A)	Kingstonian		W 2-0				3	4[1]	6				9[1]		11	5		1				2			10		7	8		
SURREY COMBINATION CUP																															
13 Apr	(A)	Guildford City		L 0-1			2	3	4	6				9	10	11	5	8	1									7			
TOTAL APPEARANCES						**5**	**38**	**39**	**33**	**22**	**18**	**4**	**12**	**34**	**31**	**37**	**39**	**27**	**36**	**5**	**6**	**18**	**4**	**3**	**2**	**5**	**2**	**12**	**1**	**17**	**1**
GOALS SCORED								**4**	**6**		**1**		**5**	**39**	**27**	**14**		**10**				**7**				**1**	**1**	**3**		**11**	

SEASON 1957-1958

ISTHMIAN LEAGUE

Date	Venue	Opponents		Result		Atten-dance	Burley, J.	Ellerby, R.	Parsons, G.	Jacob, M.	Turner, K.	Clacey, E.	Littlejohn, R.	Hebdon, J.	Mortimore, C.	Hamm, G.	Stratton, Reg	Gamble, D.	Ford, J.	Naysmith, B.	Tunnell, A.	Jones, R.	Stedman, M.	Collingwood, J.	Taylor, R.	Cashmore, N.	Cashmore, M.	Cashmore, E.	Chown, A.	Keefe, F.	Stratton, Bob	Sharpe, M.
24 Aug	(A)	Walthamstow		L	1-2		1	2	3	4	5	6	7	8	9[1]	10	11															
28 Aug	(H)	Bromley		D	1-1		1	2	3	4	5	6	7	8	9	10	11[1]															
31 Aug	(H)	Wimbledon		W	5-1		1	2	3	4	5	6	7[1]	8[1]	9[2]	10[1]	11															
14 Sep	(A)	Clapton		L	1-2		1	2	3	4[1]	5	6		8			11	7	9	10												
28 Sep	(H)	Corinthian Casuals		D	2-2			2	9[1]	10[1]	5	6	7	8				11			1	3	4									
5 Oct	(A)	Leytonstone		L	1-3			2	3	6	5		7	8	9	10	11[1]				1		4									
12 Oct	(A)	Barking		W	2-0			2	3	10	5	6	7	8			11						4								1	9[2]
19 Oct	(H)	Dulwich	£158	W	2-0	2,500		2	3	6	5		7	8	9	10[1]	11[1]						4								1	
26 Oct	(A)	Oxford		L	0-1			2	3	4	5	6	7	8		10	11														1	9
2 Nov	(H)	St. Albans	£130	W	6-1	2,500		2	3	4	5	6	7[1]	8[3]	9	10[2]	11														1	
9 Nov	(A)	Kingstonian		L	2-3			2	3	4	5	6		8			11[1]		7					10							1	9[1]
16 Nov	(H)	Romford	£116	L	1-3	1,900		2	3	4	5	6	7	8[1]	9	10	11														1	
23 Nov	(A)	Ilford		W	3-0		1	2	3[1]		5	6	7[1]	8	9	10[1]	11							4								
30 Nov	(H)	Oxford	£118	D	1-1	1,900	1	2	3		5	6	7	8	9	10[1]	11							4								
7 Dec	(A)	Wimbledon		W	5-2		1	2	3		5	6	7	8[1]	9[2]	10[1]	11[1]							4								
21 Dec	(H)	Clapton	£95	W	7-1	1,500	1	2	3		5	6	7	8[1]	9[2]	10[3]	11[1]							4								
28 Dec	(A)	Corinthian Casuals		L	2-4		1	2	3	7	5	6	8[2]		9	10	11							4								
4 Jan	(H)	Wycombe	£186	W	2-1	2,750	1	2			5	6	7[1]	8	9[1]	10	11							4			3					
1 Feb	(H)	Barking	£166	W	4-2	2,650	1	2	3	4	5	6	7[1]	8	9[1]	10[1]	11[1]															
15 Feb	(A)	Wycombe		W	4-0		1		3	11	5	6	7[1]	8[1]	9[2]	10								4	2							
1 Mar	(H)	Leytonstone		W	4-3		1		3		5	6	7	8	9[3]	10	11[1]							4	2							
29 Mar	(H)	Kingstonian	£216	W	1-0	3,000	1	2	3	10	5	6		8			11[1]		9					4		7						
17 Apr	(A)	Dulwich		L	0-2		1	2		7	5	6		8	9	10	11							4			3					
19 Apr	(A)	Romford		D	3-3		1	2		10	5	6[1]	8		9[1]		11[1]							4	3	7						
21 Apr	(H)	Tooting		D	1-1	3,000	1	2	3		5	6	7	8	9	10	11[1]							4								
23 Apr	(A)	Bromley		L	1-6		1				5		9	8			11		6					4	3	10		2	7[1]			
26 Apr	(H)	Walthamstow		D	2-2		1	2	3	9	5	6	7[1]	8			11[1]							4		10						
28 Apr	(H)	Ilford		D	2-2		1	2		7[1]	5	6		8			10		9			3				11[1]				4		
30 Apr	(A)	Tooting		L	1-3		1	2		8	5	6[1]		7			10		9			3				11				4		
3 May	(A)	St. Albans		L	3-6		1	2	4	8	5	6		7			11[3]		9			3				10						
F.A. CUP																																
7 Sep	Prel (A)	Kingstonian		W	5-3		1	2	3	4	5	6	7[1]	8[1]	9	10	11[3]															
21 Sep	1st Q (H)	Bromley	£215	L	1-5	3,126	1	2	3	4	5	6	7	8	9[1]	10	11				1											
F.A. AMATEUR CUP																																
11 Jan	1st R (H)	Aveley	£212	W	6-1	3,035	1	2			5	6	7[1]	8[2]	9[1]	10[2]	11							4			3					
25 Jan	2nd R (A)	Hendon	£354	W	3-1	5,417	1	2	3	4	5	6	7	8	9[1]	10	11[2]															
7 Feb	3rd R (H)	Hayes	£435	W	5-1	6,857	1	2	3	4	5	6	7[1]	8	9[3]	10[1]	11															
21 Feb	4th R (H)	Finchley	£445	W	3-2	7,020	1		3		5	6	7	8[2]	9	10[1]	11							4	2							
15 Mar	S-F	(Fulham) Barnet	o.g.	D	1-1	20,747	1	2	3	6		5	7	8	9	10	11							4								
22 Mar	Rep	(Brentford) Barnet		W	3-2	19,400	1	2	3		5	6	7	8	9[1]	10	11[2]							4								
12 Apr	F	(Wembley) Ilford	£25,619	W	3-0	71,000	1	2	3		5	6	7	8[2]	9	10	11[1]							4								
SURREY SENIOR CUP																																
14 Dec	1st R (H)	Redhill	£112	W	10-0	1,600	1	2	3[1]		5	6	7[2]	8[1]	9[2]	10[2]	11[2]							4								
18 Jan	2nd R (A)	Epsom		W	4-2		1	2			5	6	7[1]	8	9[1]	10[1]	11[1]							4			3					
8 Mar	S-F	(Wimbledon) Dulwich		L	1-2		1	2	3		5	6	7	8	9	10	11[1]							4								
SURREY SENIOR SHIELD SEASON 1956-57																																
4 Sep	F (A)	Carshalton		W	5-0		1		3	4	5	6	7	8[1]	9[2]	10[2]	11					2										
TOTAL APPEARANCES							**34**	**38**	**35**	**28**	**42**	**40**	**36**	**41**	**32**	**32**	**41**	**2**	**7**	**1**	**3**	**5**	**4**	**23**	**5**	**7**	**4**	**1**	**1**	**2**	**6**	**3**
GOALS SCORED									**3**	**3**		**2**	**15**	**17**	**27**	**20**	**27**									**1**			**1**			**3**

SEASON 1958-1959

ISTHMIAN LEAGUE

Date	Venue	Opponents	Result	Attendance	Burley, J.	Ellerby, R.	Parsons, G.	Collingwood, J.	Turner, K.	Clacey, E.	Littlejohn, R.	Hebdon, J.	Mortimore, C.	Jacob, M.	Stratton, Reg	Pratt, A.	Cashmore, N.	Ley, E.	Cashmore, M.	Taylor, R.	Jones, R.	Dowse, W.	Plank C.	Charlton, J.	Stevens, B.	Kennedy, J.	Stedman, M.	Goodyear, M.	Williams, C.
23 Aug	(H)	Romford	D 2-2		1	2	3	4	5	6	7[1]	8	9[1]	10	11														
28 Aug	(A)	Bromley	D 2-2		1	2	3	4	5	6	7	8	9[1]	10	11[1]														
30 Aug	(A)	Wimbledon	L 4-5		1	2	3	4	5	6	7[1]	8[1]	9[1]	10	11[1]														
6 Sep	(H)	Leytonstone £157	W 7-0	2,400	1	2	3	4	5	6	7	8	9[5]	10[2]	11														
10 Sep	(H)	Kingstonian	W 4-2		1	2	3	4	5	6	7	8	9[2]	10[1]	11[1]														
13 Sep	(A)	Clapton	L 1-3		1	2	3	4	5	6	7	8		10[1]	11	9													
20 Sep	(H)	Wycombe £250	D 1-1	4,100	1	2	3	4	5	6	7	8	9[1]	10	11														
27 Sep	(A)	Ilford	W 4-2		1	2	3	4	5	6	11[1]	7		10[1]			8[1]	9[1]											
4 Oct	(H)	Walthamstow	W 2-1	2,800	1	2		4	5	6	7[1]	8	9[1]	10	11				3										
11 Oct	(A)	St. Albans	L 0-3		1	2	3	4	5	6	7	8		10	11			9											
18 Oct	(H)	Ilford £184	L 1-2	2,500	1	2	3	4	5	6	7[1]	8	9	10	11														
25 Oct	(A)	Walthamstow	L 1-2		1	2	3	4	5	6	7[1]	10		9	11		8												
1 Nov	(H)	Bromley	W 3-2	2,300	1	2	3	4	5[1]	6		10		9	11[2]		8											7	
8 Nov	(A)	Corinthian Casuals	W 4-1		1	2	3	4		6		10[1]		9	11		8[1]			5								7[2]	
22 Nov	(H)	Barking £120	L 1-4	2,000	1	2	3	4	5		10	8	9		11												6[1]	7	
29 Nov	(A)	Oxford	L 1-6		1	2	3		5	6	7	8	9	10[1]	11						4								
6 Dec	(H)	St. Albans	W 2-0		1	2	3	6	5		7[1]	8	9[1]	10	11						4								
20 Dec	(H)	Oxford £100	D 2-2	1,600	1	2			5			8	9	10	11[1]				3		4[1]	6	7						
27 Dec	(A)	Dulwich	L 2-4		1	2	3			5	7	8[1]	9		11[1]		10				4	6							
3 Jan	(A)	Wycombe	L 0-4		1	2	3		5	6	7	8	9		11		10				4								
17 Jan	(A)	Barking	W 2-1		1	2	3		5	6	7	8[1]	9[1]	11	10							4							
24 Jan	(H)	Clapton £100	W 4-0	1,900	1	2			5	6	7	8[1]	9[1]	11[1]	10[1]				3			4							
31 Jan	(A)	Kingstonian	L 1-4		1	2			5	6	7	8	9		10[1]				3			4		11					
14 Feb	(A)	Leytonstone o.g.	D 2-2						5			8	9[1]	11	10					2	3	4			1	6		7	
21 Feb	(H)	Wimbledon £169	L 1-2	2,600	1		3		5	6	7	8[1]	9	11	10					2		4							
7 Mar	(H)	Corinthian Casuals £100	W 4-1	1,700	1		3		5	6		7[2]	9	10	11		8[1]			2		4[1]							
21 Mar	(A)	Romford	W 1-0		1		3		5	6		7	9	10	11[1]		8			2		4							
23 Apr	(H)	Dulwich	D 1-1	2,300	1		3	4	5		7		9	10[1]	11		8			2		6							
25 Apr	(H)	Tooting £80	W 4-3	1,500	1		3		5	6		7[1]	9[2]		11		8			2		10[1]					4		
29 Apr	(A)	Tooting	L 2-4		1			4	5	6		7	9[1]	10	11[1]		8		3	2									
F.A. CUP																													
15 Nov	1st R (A)	Southampton £2,632	L 1-4	18,141	1	2	3	4	5	6	7	8[1]	9	10	11														
F.A. AMATEUR CUP																													
10 Jan	1st R (A)	Redhill £200	L 3-6	2,500	1	2	3		5	6	7[1]	8[1]	9	10[1]	11						4								
SURREY SENIOR CUP																													
13 Dec	1st R (A)	Molesey £37	W 11-1	850	1	2	3		5		7	8[1]	9[6]	10[1]	11[2]						4	6[1]							
7 Jan	2nd R (H)	Tooting £212	W 4-2	3,100	1		3		5	6	7	8	9[3]	11	10[1]					2		4							
13 Mar	S-F	(Kingston) Walton o.g.	W 1-0	3,000	1		3		5	6		7	9	10	11		8			2		4							
13 Mar	F	(C. Palace) Dulwich	L 1-4	5,464	1		3	4	5	6		7	9	10	11[1]		8			2									
SURREY SENIOR SHIELD																													
21 Mar	1st R (H)	Walton £166	W 2-0	2,355	1		3	4	5	6			7		11[1]		8			2		10							9[1]
2 May	S-F (H)	Kingstonian	L 2-4		1	2	3	4				10	9		11[2]		8			5		6						7	
SURREY INVITATION CUP																													
15 Sep	1st R (A)	Guildford C. o.g. £180	W 3-1	2,110	1	2	3	4	5	6	7[1]	8	9	10	11[1]														
20 Apr	F (A)	Crystal Palace	L 1-4		1		3	4	5	6		7	9	10[1]	11		8			2									
SURREY COMBINATION CUP																													
11 Apr	1st L (H)	Guildford City £166	W 2-0	2,300	1		3	4	5	6		7	9	10[1]	11		8[1]			2									
4 May	2nd L (A)	Guildford City	L 1-4		1		3	4	5	6		7	9	10	11[1]		8			2									
ALAWAY CUP																													
8 Sep	(H)	Middlesex Wanderers	D 1-1	1,850	1	2	3	4	5	6	7	8	9	10[1]	11														
TOTAL APPEARANCES					**42**	**29**	**37**	**27**	**40**	**36**	**28**	**41**	**37**	**36**	**42**	**1**	**18**	**2**	**5**	**16**	**8**	**16**	**1**	**1**	**1**	**1**	**2**	**5**	**1**
GOALS SCORED									**1**		**9**	**12**	**28**	**13**	**20**		**4**	**1**			**1**	**3**					**1**	**2**	**1**

SEASON 1959-1960

ISTHMIAN LEAGUE

Date	Venue	Opponents		Result	Atten-dance	Burley, J.	Ellerby, R.	Parsons, G.	Collingwood, J.	Turner, K.	Jacob, M.	Hebdon, J.	Cashmore, N.	Mortimore, C.	Reynolds, V.	Williams, C.	Jones, R.	Goodyear, M.	Taylor, R.	Ilsley, A.	Dowse, W.	Newman, D.	Pratt, A.	Harris, G.	Cashmore, M.	Collins, M.	McCormack, J.	Cashmore, E.	Bruty, M.	Hearmon, P.	Clacey, E.	Hancock, T.
22 Aug	(A)	Ilford		L 1-5		1	2	3	4	5	6	7	8[1]	9	10	11																
26 Aug	(H)	Bromley		L 0-5		1		3	4	5	6	11	8	9	10		2	7														
29 Aug	(H)	Leytonstone		L 2-4		1		3	4	5	6	11[1]	8	9	10		2	7[1]														
2 Sep	(A)	Bromley		W 2-1		1		3		5	11[1]	7	8[1]	9	10				2	4	6											
12 Sep	(A)	Tooting		L 1-4		1		3		5	11	7	8[1]	9	10				2	6	4											
26 Sep	(H)	Clapton		D 1-1		1		3		5	11	7	8	9	10[1]				2	6	4											
10 Oct	(A)	St. Albans		D 2-2		1		3		5	11[1]	8		9[1]	10				2	6	4	7										
24 Oct	(H)	Wimbledon	£154	L 0-2	2,300	1					7	8		9	10				2	6	4		5	11	3							
31 Oct	(A)	Barking		W 1-0		1					7	8		9	10				2	6	4		5	11[1]	3							
14 Nov	(A)	Clapton		W 4-0		1		3		5	7[1]	8[1]		9[2]	10				2	6	4			11								
21 Nov	(H)	Ilford		W 2-0		1		3		5	7	8		9	10				2	6[1]	4			11[1]								
28 Nov	(A)	Wycombe		D 1-1		1		3		5		8[1]		7	10				2	6	4			11		9						
5 Dec	(A)	Oxford		D 2-2		1		3		5		8		7[1]	10				2	6	4			11[1]		9						
19 Dec	(H)	Wycombe		L 3-5		1		3		5		8[1]		7	10				2	6	4			11		9[2]						
26 Dec	(H)	Kingstonian	£150	W 6-1	2,050	1		3		5		8[2]		7[1]	10[1]				2	6	4			11[2]		9						
2 Jan	(A)	Maidstone		L 2-5		1		3		5	4	8[1]		7	10[1]				2	6				11		9						
16 Jan	(H)	Dulwich		L 1-3		1		3		5		8		7					2[1]	6	4			11		10	9					
23 Jan	(H)	Corinthian Casuals		L 0-1		1			4	5		8		7	10		2			6				11	3		9					
6 Feb	(A)	Dulwich		L 0-2		1				5				9	8		2			4				11	3	10		6	7			
13 Feb	(H)	Oxford		D 1-1		1			4	5		7		9	8				2	6				11[1]	3					10		
20 Feb	(H)	Barking		W 5-0		1			4	5		7		9[1]	8[2]				2	6				11[1]	3					10[1]		
27 Feb	(A)	Leytonstone		W 3-1		1		3	4	5		7		9	8[1]				2	6				11[2]						10		
5 Mar	(H)	Walthamstow	£105	D 1-1	1,700	1		3	4	5		7		9	8				2	6				11[1]						10		
12 Mar	(H)	Maidstone	£88	W 3-0	1,400	1		3	4	5		7[1]		9[2]	8				2	6				11		10						
19 Mar	(A)	Wimbledon		W 4-2		1		3	4	5		7[1]		9	8[1]				2[1]	6				11[1]		10						
26 Mar	(H)	St. Albans		W 3-0		1		3	4	5		7[1]		9[1]	8[1]				2	6				11			10					
9 Apr	(H)	Corinthian Casuals	£96	L 0-2	1,550	1		3	4	5		7		9	8		2			6				11		10						
11 Apr	(A)	Kingstonian		L 3-5		1		3	4	5		7		9[2]	8		2			6				11[1]		10						
28 Apr	(H)	Tooting		L 0-3		1		3		5		7		9	8				2	6	4			11						10		
30 Apr	(A)	Walthamstow		L 0-2		1		3	4	5		7	9		8				2	6				11						10		
F.A. CUP																																
5 Sep	Prel (H)	Epsom	£118	W 3-0	1,700	1		3		5	11	7	8[1]	9[1]	10[1]				2	4	6											
19 Sep	1st Q (H)	Dulwich	£154	W 3-0	2,275	1		3		5	11[1]	7[2]	8	9	10				2	4	6											
3 Oct	2nd Q (A)	Kingstonian		W 3-0		1		3		5	11[1]	8		9[1]	10[1]				2	6	4	7										
17 Oct	3rd Q (A)	Sutton		D 3-3		1		3			7[1]	8		9	10[2]				2	6	4		5	11								
21 Oct	Rep (H)	Sutton		L 1-3		1		3			7	8		9[1]	10				2		4		5	11							6	
F.A. AMATEUR CUP																																
9 Jan	1st R (A)	Ford United		L 0-2		1		3		5		8		7					2	6	4			11		9	10					
SURREY SENIOR CUP																																
12 Dec	1st R (A)	Met. Police		W 4-1		1		3		5		8[1]		7	10				2	6	4[1]			11[2]		9						
30 Jan	2nd R (H)	Redhill		L 0-5		1			4	5		8	10	7			2			6				11	3							9
SURREY SENIOR SHIELD																																
2 Apr	1st R (H)	Walton	£155	W 2-0	2,200	1		3	4	5				9	8				2	6[1]				11		10				7[1]		
2 May	S-F (A)	Dorking		L 0-4		1		3	4	5		7	9		8				2	6				11		10						
SURREY INVITATION CUP																																
23 Apr	(A)	Guildford City		D 1-1		1		3	4	5		7	9		8				2	6				11[1]						10		
TOTAL APPEARANCES						**41**	**1**	**34**	**18**	**37**	**17**	**39**	**12**	**38**	**38**	**1**	**7**	**2**	**33**	**37**	**21**	**2**	**4**	**31**	**7**	**15**	**4**	**1**	**1**	**8**	**1**	**1**
GOALS SCORED											**6**	**13**	**4**	**14**	**12**			**1**	**2**	**2**	**1**			**15**		**2**				**2**		

ISTHMIAN LEAGUE

SEASON 1960-1961

Date	Venue	Opponents		Result	Atten-dance	Burley, J.	Cashmore, M.	Jones, R.	Cashmore, N.	Turner, K.	Haider, R.	Hebdon, J.	Hearmon, P.	Moody, K.	Collins, M.	Harris, G.	Mortimore, C.	Partridge, M.	Mailing, J.	Taylor, P.	Jacob, M.	Finn, P.	Threlkeld, J.	McCormack, J.	Dowse, W.	Farris, B.	Foulkes, G.	Robinson, A.	Debell, D.	Furlonger, K.	Davies, P.	Gamble, D.	Parsons, G.
20 Aug	(H)	Ilford	£108	W 2-1	1,300	1	2	3	4	5	6	7[1]	8	9	10	11[1]																	
24 Aug	(H)	Corinthian Casuals		L 0-1	1,500	1	2	3	4	5	6		8	9	10	11	7																
27 Aug	(A)	Tooting		L 1-5		1	2	3	4	5	6	7	8		10	11[1]	9																
3 Sep	(H)	Bromley		L 1-4		1	2		4	5	6	8		9[1]	10	11	7																3
7 Sep	(A)	Corinthian Casuals		D 4-4		1	2		4	5	6	8[1]		9[1]	10	11[1]	7[1]																3
17 Sep	(H)	Clapton	£79	W 3-0	1,100	1	2[1]		4	5	6	8		9	10	11[1]	7[1]																3
24 Sep	(A)	Walthamstow		D 2-2		1	2		4	5	6[1]	10[1]		7	8	11	9																3
1 Oct	(A)	Wycombe		D 2-2		1	2	5			6	10	4	7	8	11[2]	9																3
8 Oct	(H)	Wimbledon		L 1-3		1	3	5	4		6		10	7	8	11	9[1]	2															
15 Oct	(A)	St. Albans		L 2-3		1	2	5	4		6	8	10		7	11[2]	9																3
22 Oct	(H)	Kingstonian	£106	L 1-3	1,400	1			4		6	8[1]	10			11	7	2	5	9													3
29 Oct	(A)	Dulwich		L 2-7		1			4	5	6	8			10	11[1]	7[1]	2		9													3
5 Nov	(H)	St. Albans	£76	W 4-2	800	1			4	5		8[2]			10	11[1]	7	2		9	6[1]												3
12 Nov	(A)	Clapton		L 2-5		1			4	5		8	10			11[2]	7	2		9	6												3
19 Nov	(H)	Barking	£70	D 1-1	800	1			4	5	6	8			10[1]		7	2		9		3	11										
26 Nov	(A)	Bromley		L 2-4		1			4	5	6	8			10	11[1]	7	2			9[1]	3											
3 Dec	(H)	Dulwich	£70	L 2-3	1,000	1			4	5	6	8			10	11	7	2			9[2]	3											
24 Dec	(A)	Kingstonian		L 0-2		1	2		4	5	6	10			11	7	9					3		8									
31 Dec	(H)	Oxford	£70	D 2-2	1,000	1			4[1]	5	6	8			10	11[1]	9	2			7	3											
7 Jan	(A)	Maidstone		W 2-0		1				5	6	8			10[1]	11	9[1]	2			7	3			4								
14 Jan	(H)	Leytonstone	£93	W 3-0	1,300	1			4	5	6	8			10	11[2]	9[1]	2			7	3											
28 Jan	(H)	Walthamstow	£113	L 1-3	1,500	1			4	5	6		8[1]		10	11	9	2			7	3											
11 Feb	(A)	Barking		D 2-2					4		6	7	8		10[1]	11[1]	9	2				3				1	5						
18 Feb	(A)	Oxford		L 2-3					4	5	6		8		10	11[2]	7	2				3				1		9					
25 Feb	(A)	Ilford		W 2-0					4	5	6				10	11	9[2]					3				1		8	2	7			
4 Mar	(H)	Maidstone		W 3-1					4	5	6				10	11	9[3]				8	3				1			2	7			
18 Mar	(H)	Wycombe	£80	W 4-2	1,100				4	5	6				10	11[2]	9[1]					3			8[1]	1			2	7			
8 Apr	(H)	Tooting o.g.		W 4-2			2		8[1]	5	6				10	11	9[2]					3			4	1					7		
11 Apr	(A)	Wimbledon		L 0-4			2		8	5	6				10	11	9					3			4	1					7		
15 Apr	(A)	Leytonstone		W 1-0			2		8	5	6					11[1]	9					3			4	1					7	10	
F.A. CUP																																	
10 Sep	1st Q (A)	Wimbledon		L 1-5		1	2		4	5	6	8		9	10[1]	11	7																3
F.A. AMATEUR CUP																																	
21 Jan	1st R (H)	Chichester	£202	W 6-2	2,344	1			4[1]	5	6	8[1]			10[1]	11	9[3]	2			7	3											
4 Feb	2nd R (H)	Wimbledon	£329	L 1-5	3,938	1			4	5	6	8			10	11	9[1]	2			7	3											
SURREY SENIOR CUP																																	
10 Dec	1st R (H)	Tooting	£97	D 2-2	1,100	1			4	5	6	8			10	11[2]	7	2			9	3											
17 Dec	Rep (A)	Tooting		L 0-3		1				5	6	8			10	11	7	2			9	3		4									
SURREY SENIOR SHIELD																																	
25 Mar	1st R (H)	Addlestone		W 3-1						5	6				10	11[2]	9[1]				8	3			4	1			2		7		
19 Apr	S-F (H)	Dorking		L 1-3			2		8	5	6				10[1]	11	9					3			4	1					7		
SURREY COMBINATION CUP																																	
31 Oct	(A)	Guildford City		W 3-2		1			4	5	6[1]	8[1]			10	11	7[1]	2		9													3
TOTAL APPEARANCES						**28**	**16**	**6**	**34**	**33**	**36**	**26**	**11**	**9**	**35**	**37**	**37**	**19**	**1**	**6**	**14**	**22**	**1**	**2**	**7**	**10**	**1**	**2**	**4**	**3**	**5**	**1**	**12**
GOALS SCORED							**1**		**3**		**2**	**8**	**1**	**2**	**6**	**26**	**20**				**4**				**1**								

ISTHMIAN LEAGUE

SEASON 1961-1962

Date	Venue	Opponents	Result	Attendance	Farris, B.	Jacob, M.	Hirons, D.	Dowse, W.	Turner, K.	Haider, R.	Hyde, R.	Mortimore, C.	Bangs, J.	Twitchen, P.	Williams, R.	Dowse, R.	Hebdon, J.	Foulkes, G.	Upton, B.	Woods, S.	Threlkeld, J.	Newman, D.	Stansbie, R.	Collingwood, J.	Fitch, K.	Tindall, E.	Brennan, J.	Botley, A.	Gamble, D.
19 Aug	(A)	Walthamstow	D 1-1		1	2	3	4	5	6	7[1]	8	9	10	11														
26 Aug	(H)	Ilford o.g.	D 2-2		1	2	3	4	5	6	7	8	9	10[1]	11														
30 Aug	(H)	Kingstonian o.g.	D 2-2		1	2	3	4	5		7	8[1]	9	10	11	6													
2 Sep	(H)	Tooting	L 1-5		1	2	3	4	5	6		8[1]	9	10	11		7												
16 Sep	(H)	Corinthian Casuals o.g.	L 2-3		1		3	4		6	7	10		8	11	2		5	9[1]										
20 Sep	(A)	Kingstonian	W 2-1		1			4	5	6[1]	7	8				2		3	9	10	11[1]								
23 Sep	(H)	Clapton £80	W 2-1	1,200	1		3	4	5	6	7	8				2			9[2]	10	11								
30 Sep	(A)	Leytonstone	L 0-2		1			4	5	6	7	8			11	2		3	9	10									
7 Oct	(H)	Bromley £90	L 1-2	1,300	1			4	5	6	7	8[1]			11	2		3	9	10									
14 Oct	(A)	Corinthian Casuals	D 2-2		1			4	5	6[1]	7	8[1]			11	2		3	9	10									
21 Oct	(H)	Walthamstow	W 2-1		1			4	5	6	7	8[2]			11	2		3	9	10									
28 Oct	(A)	Barking	D 1-1		1			4	5	6[1]	7	8			11	2		3	9	10									
4 Nov	(A)	Oxford	L 1-4		1			4	5	6		8			11	2		3	9	10		7[1]							
11 Nov	(H)	Wycombe £55	W 3-0	700	1			4	5	6		8			11	2		3	9[2]	10[1]		7							
25 Nov	(A)	Wimbledon	L 1-5		1			4	5	6	7	8[1]			11	2		3	9	10									
2 Dec	(H)	Leytonstone	L 1-3		1			4	5	6		8[1]			11	2		3	9	10		7							
9 Dec	(H)	Maidstone	W 5-1		1		3	4[1]	5	10[1]		8			11				9[3]			7	2	6					
16 Dec	(A)	Wycombe	L 1-3		1		3	10[1]	5	6		8			11				9			7	2	4					
23 Dec	(A)	Dulwich	L 1-3		1		3	4	5	6		8	7		11				9				2			10[1]			
30 Dec	(H)	Wimbledon £90	L 0-1	1,200	1		3	4	5	6			7		11					8					2	9	10		
6 Jan	(A)	Maidstone	W 3-2		1			4	5	6			7		11	3	8[1]								2	9[1]	10[1]		
27 Jan	(H)	Tooting £150	W 3-0	1,700	1		3		5	6		8[2]			11		7[1]		9					4	2		10		
10 Feb	(A)	Clapton	D 1-1		1		3		5	6		8			11		7		9					4	2		10[1]		
3 Mar	(H)	Barking £77	D 3-3	900	1				5	6[2]		8[1]			11	3	7							4	2	9	10		
17 Mar	(A)	Ilford	D 1-1		1			3	5	6		8			11[1]		7							4	2	9	10		
7 Apr	(A)	St.Albans	W 2-0		1			3	5	6		8			11					7[1]				4	2	9[1]		10	
14 Apr	(H)	St.Albans	W 4-3		1			3	5	6		8[3]			11					7				4	2	9[1]		10	
21 Apr	(A)	Bromley o.g.	D 2-2		1			3	5	6		8[1]			11					7				4	2	9		10	
26 Apr	(H)	Dulwich	L 1-3		1			3	5	6		8			11[1]					7				4	2	9		10	
5 May	(H)	Oxford	L 0-2		1			3	5	6		8								7				4	2	9		10	11
F.A. CUP																													
9 Sep	1st Q (A)	Wimbledon	L 1-5		1		3	4	5	6	7	8	9	10	11[1]	2													
F.A. AMATEUR CUP																													
20 Jan	1st R (A)	Corinthian Casuals	W 3-2		1		3		5	6		8[1]			11		7		9[1]					4	2		10[1]		
3 Feb	2nd R (A)	Eastbourne £256	W 1-0	3,000	1		3		5	6		8			11		7		9[1]					4	2		10		
17 Feb	3rd R (H)	Leytonstone £308	D 1-1	2,942	1		3		5	6		8			11[1]		7		9					4	2		10		
24 Feb	Rep (A)	Leytonstone £252	L 0-1	2,230	1		3		5	6		8			11		7		9					4	2		10		
SURREY SENIOR CUP																													
20 Jan	1st R (A)	Croydon AM	L 0-3		1		3	4	5	6			7		11		8								2	9	10		
SURREY SENIOR SHIELD																													
24 Mar	1st R (H)	Vickers o.g.	W 3-1		1			3	5	6		7								11				4	2	9	10[1]	8[1]	
28 Apr	S-F (H)	Kingstonian	D 3-3		1			3	5	6		8[1]								7				4	2	9		10[1]	11[1]
7 May	Rep (A)	Kingstonian	W 2-1		1			3	5	6	7	8												4	2	9[1]		10	10[1]
TOTAL APPEARANCES					**39**	**4**	**18**	**32**	**38**	**38**	**14**	**36**	**9**	**6**	**33**	**16**	**11**	**11**	**21**	**19**	**2**	**5**	**3**	**18**	**19**	**14**	**12**	**8**	**3**
GOALS SCORED								**2**		**6**	**1**	**17**		**1**	**4**		**2**		**10**	**2**	**1**	**1**				**5**	**4**	**2**	**2**

SEASON 1962-1963

ISTHMIAN LEAGUE

Date	Venue	Opponents	Result	Attendance	Farris, B.	Fitch, K.	French, A.	Dowse, W.	Foulkes, G.	Brennan, J.	Woods, S.	Tindall, E.	Upton, B.	Botley, A.	Williams, R.	Keeley, P.	Gamble, D.	Mortimore, C.	Hyde, R.	Turner, K.	Collingwood, J.	Harrison, P.	Worsley, D.	Barker, R.	Threlkeld, J.	Pearce, E.	Cole, J.	Robbins, M.	Wiltshire, B.	Furlonger, R.	Finn, B.	Wallington, N.	Billingsby, R.	Tranter, G.	Dowse, R.	Arnold, B.
25 Aug	(H)	Wimbledon	L 0-2		1	2	3	4	5	6	7	8	9	10	11																					
29 Aug	(A)	Clapton	L 2-4		1	2	3	4	5	6	7	9[1]		10		8	11[1]																			
1 Sep	(H)	Tooting	D 2-2		1	2	3	4	5	6	7	9[1]		10			11	8[1]																		
5 Sep	(H)	Clapton	L 2-4		1	2	3	4	5	6	8[1]	9		10[1]	11				7																	
15 Sep	(A)	Wycombe	D 2-2		1	7[2]	3	6	5	10	11	9						8		2	4															
29 Sep	(H)	Walthamstow	L 0-1		1	2	3	6	5	10	11	9		7				8			4															
6 Oct	(A)	Corinthian Casuals	L 1-2		1	2	3	6	5		11	10[1]		7				8			4	9														
13 Oct	(A)	St.Albans	L 0-5		1	2	3	6	5		11	10		8				9	7		4															
20 Oct	(H)	Dulwich	W 2-1		1	2	3	6	5		8[1]	10			11			9[1]	7		4															
27 Oct	(A)	Bromley	L 2-3		1	2	3	6	5		8	10			11			9[2]	7		4															
3 Nov	(H)	Ilford	L 0-1		1	2	3	6	5		10				11			8	7		4	9														
10 Nov	(A)	Leytonstone	L 2-4		1	2	3	4	5			9[1]			11			8	7[1]				6	10												
17 Nov	(H)	Maidstone £44	D 1-1	400	1	2	3	4	5	6		9						8	7					10	11[1]											
24 Nov	(A)	Oxford	D 3-3		1	2	3	4				9						8[2]	7[1]	5				10	11	6										
1 Dec	(H)	Corinthian Casuals	W 3-0		1	2	3			6		9[2]		10				8	7[1]	5	4				11											
8 Dec	(H)	St.Albans £50	L 0-1	600	1	2	3			6		9		10				8	7	5	4						11									
15 Dec	(A)	Wimbledon	L 0-4		1	2	3			6		9		10				8	7	5	4						11				8					
26 Dec	(H)	Kingstonian	L 0-5		1		3			10		9								5	6						11	2	4	7	8					
9 Mar	(A)	Ilford	W 4-3		1	2	3			6	11	9[3]						10	7[1]	5	4										8					
16 Mar	(H)	Oxford £61	D 1-1	600	1	2	3[1]			6	11	9						10	7	5								4			8					
27 Mar	(A)	Kingstonian	L 1-6		1		2				11	9[1]		8					7	5				10								3	4	6		
30 Mar	(A)	Walthamstow	L 0-1		1	2				6	11	9		8				10	7	5													4		3	
6 Apr	(H)	Barking	W 5-1		1	2	3			6	11[1]	9[2]		8[1]				10[1]		5													4			7
13 Apr	(A)	Tooting	L 0-4		1		3			6	11	9		8				10		5													4		2	7
15 Apr	(A)	Maidstone	W 1-0		1	2					11	6	9							5				8	10							3	4			7[1]
20 Apr	(H)	Leytonstone	W 2-0		1	2	3			10	11	6	9[1]							5					8[1]								4			7
27 Apr	(A)	Dulwich	D 1-1		1	2	3			10	11	6	9							5					8								4			7[1]
4 May	(H)	Wycombe	W 3-2		1	2	3			10	11[1]	6[1]	9					8[1]		5													4			7
11 May	(H)	Bromley	L 0-2		1	2	3			6	11	10	9					8		5													4			7
24 May	(A)	Barking	W 2-0		1		5				11	6	9					8[1]							10[1]							3	4		2	7
F.A. CUP																																				
8 Sep	Pre (A)	Petters	W 2-0		1	7	3	6	5		11	9		10				8[2]		2	4															
22 Sep	1st Q (A)	Wimbledon	L 2-4		1	7	3	6	5	10	11	9						8[2]		2	4															
F.A. AMATEUR CUP																																				
23 Feb	1st R (A)	Lydbrook	W 1-0		1	2	3			6	11	10[1]						9	7	5	4										8					
2 Mar	2nd R (H)	Walton o.g. £377	L 1-2	3,644	1	2	3			6	11	9						8	7	5	4										10					
SURREY SENIOR SHIELD																																				
30 Apr	1st R (H)	Farncombe	W 2-1		1	2	3			10	11	6	9[1]							5					8								4			7[1]
22 May	S-F (H)	Dorking	W 10-3		1	5					11	6	9[1]					8[9]							10							3	4		2	7
29 May	F	(Leatherhead) Petters	W 4-1		1		3				11	6	9[2]					8[2]		5					10								4		2	7
SURREY SENIOR SHIELD FINAL 1961-62																																				
19 Sep	(A)	Tooting	L 1-2		1	7	3	6	5	10[1]	11	9						8		2	4															
MICKY MAYES MEMORIAL CUP																																				
23 Mar	(A)	Carshalton	L 2-3		1	2	5				11[1]	9		8				10	7[1]									3					4	6		
SURREY SENIOR CUP																																				
27 Feb	(A)	Kingstonian	L 1-4		1	2	3			6	11	9						8	7	5	4										10[1]					
TOTAL APPEARANCES					**40**	**35**	**37**	**17**	**16**	**26**	**33**	**39**	**10**	**16**	**6**	**1**	**2**	**30**	**19**	**25**	**18**	**2**	**1**	**5**	**10**	**1**	**3**	**3**	**1**	**1**	**7**	**4**	**14**	**2**	**5**	**11**
GOALS SCORED						**2**	**1**			**1**	**5**	**14**	**5**	**2**			**1**	**24**	**5**						**3**						**1**					**3**

SEASON 1963-1964

ISTHMIAN LEAGUE

Date	Venue	Opponents	Result	Atten-dance	Farris, B.	Fuller, B.	French, A.	Collingwood, J.	Arnold, B.S.	Billingsby, R.	Arnold, B.	Mortimore, C.	Finn, B.	Tindall, E.	Woods, S.	Wallington, N.	Threlkeld, J.	Fitch, K.	Barker, R.	Turner, K.	Pearce, E.	Wooler, R.	Metherall, D.	Logan, L.	Hyde, R.	Hines, M.	Crow, E.	McDevitt, G.
28 Aug	(A)	Tooting	L 0-3		1	2	3	4	5	6	7	8	9	10	11													
31 Aug	(H)	Oxford	L 1-3		1	2		4	5	6	7		8[1]	9	11	3	10											
4 Sep	(H)	Tooting	W 2-0		1		5	6	3	4	9		10	8[1]	7[1]		11	2										
14 Sep	(A)	Maidstone	L 2-3		1	2		6	3	4	9		10[1]	8	7		11[1]	5										
18 Sep	(H)	Kingstonian	W 2-0		1		5	6	3	4	9		10	8[2]	11		7	2										
28 Sep	(H)	Leytonstone £70	W 4-0	900	1	2		6	3	4	7		9[1]	8[1]	11[2]			5	10									
2 Oct	(A)	Kingstonian	L 0-7		1	2		6	3	4	7		9	8	11			5	10									
5 Oct	(A)	St.Albans	D 0-0		1			6	3	4	7		9	8	11			2	10	5								
12 Oct	(H)	Hendon £141	L 1-6	1,500	1		5	6	3	4	7		8	9[1]	10		11	2										
19 Oct	(A)	Dulwich	D 0-0		1		5	10	3	6	9		4	8	11		7	2										
22 Oct	(A)	Wimbledon	L 0-3		1	2	5	6	3		7		9	8	11						4	10						
26 Oct	(H)	Walthamstow	W 3-1		1	2	5	6	3		7		9[2]	8	11[1]						4	10						
29 Oct	(A)	Wycombe	L 1-2		1	2	5	6	3		7		9	8	11[1]						4	10						
2 Nov	(A)	Bromley	L 1-4		1	2	5	6[1]	3			7	9	10	11						4		8					
16 Nov	(H)	Corinthian Casuals	W 2-1		1	2	5	6	3	8		7[1]		10[1]	11						4		9					
23 Nov	(H)	Wycombe	W 2-0		1	2	5	6	3		11	7		10[1]							4	9[1]	8					
30 Nov	(A)	Enfield	L 1-5		1	2	5	6	3		7	8[1]		10	11						4		9					
7 Dec	(H)	St.Albans	L 0-4		1	2	3		6			7	9	10	11[1]						4	8		5				
14 Dec	(A)	Walthamstow	L 1-5		1	2		4	3	6		7	9	10	11							8		5				
21 Dec	(H)	Sutton	L 0-4		1			4	3		7	8	9	6	11			2					10	5				
26 Dec	(A)	Sutton	L 1-5		1		5	6	3		7	8[1]	4	10	11			2					9					
28 Dec	(A)	Hitchin	D 3-3		1		5	6	3		7	8[1]	4	10	11			2					9[2]					
4 Jan	(H)	Clapton	W 2-0		1		5	6	3		7	8	4	10[1]	11[1]			2					9					
8 Feb	(H)	Maidstone	D 2-2		1		5	6	3		7		4	10	11			2					9[1]		8[1]			
15 Feb	(A)	Barking	D 0-0		1		5		3		7	10	4	6	11			2					9		8			
22 Feb	(A)	Hendon	L 1-5		1		5		3		7	8	4	6[1]	11			2					9			10		
29 Feb	(H)	Barking	W 3-0		1		5	6	3		7		4	9[1]	11[1]			2							8	10[1]		
7 Mar	(A)	Oxford	D 2-2		1		5	6	3		7		4	9[1]	11			2							8	10[1]		
14 Mar	(H)	Hitchin	L 1-2		1		5	6	3		7		4	9	11			2							8[1]	10		
21 Mar	(H)	Dulwich	D 0-0		1	2	5	6	3				4	9	11							10	7		8			
28 Mar	(H)	Bromley	W 1-0		1	2	5	6	3				4[1]	9	11							8			7	10		
30 Mar	(A)	Leytonstone	L 2-5		1	2	5	6	3				4[1]	9	11							8			7[1]		10	
4 Apr	(A)	Clapton o.g.	W 4-1		1	2	5	6	3		7		4	9[2]	11											10[1]	8	
11 Apr	(A)	Ilford	L 0-1		1	2	5	6	4		7		10	9	11	3											8	
18 Apr	(H)	Ilford	D 0-0		1	2	5	6	3		7		4	9	11								8				10	
23 Apr	(A)	Corinthian Casuals	D 2-2		1	2	5	6	3		7[1]	8[1]	4		11								10					9
25 Apr	(H)	Wimbledon	L 1-5		1	2		6	3		7	8	4	9	11								10[1]					5
2 May	(H)	Enfield	L 0-4		1	2	5	6			7		4	8	11	3							10					9
F.A. CUP																												
7 Sep	Pre (A)	Dorking	W 3-2		1		5	6		4	9[1]		10[1]	8	7	3	11[1]	2										
21 Sep	1st Q (H)	Guildford C. £248	L 0-2	2,300	1		5	6	3	4	9		10	8	11		7	2										
F.A. AMATEUR CUP																												
11 Jan	1st R (A)	Dagenham	D 0-0		1		5	6	3		7	8	4	10	11			2					9					
18 Jan	Rep (H)	Dagenham £103	W 3-1	1,000	1		5	6	3		7[1]	8	4		11		10	2					9[2]					
1 Feb	2nd R (A)	Eastwood T.	L 1-2		1		5	6	3		7	8[1]	4	10	11			2					9					
SURREY SENIOR CUP																												
25 Jan	1st R (A)	Croydon AM	L 2-4		1		5	6	3		7	8[1]	4		11			2					9[1]				10	
TOTAL APPEARANCES					**44**	**23**	**36**	**41**	**42**	**14**	**37**	**19**	**41**	**41**	**43**	**4**	**9**	**24**	**3**	**1**	**8**	**9**	**20**	**3**	**8**	**6**	**5**	**3**
GOALS SCORED								1			3	7	8	13	8		2					1	7		3	3		

SEASON 1964-1965

ISTHMIAN LEAGUE

Date	Venue	Opponents	Result	Attendance	Farris, B.	Fuller, B.	Arnold, B.S.	Finn, B.	Norman, D.	McDevitt, G.	McBryde, J.	Tindall, E.	Wigley, J.	Gaskin, G.	Woods, S.	Pearce, E.	Wooler, R.	Leahy, K.	Hayward, D.	Povey, R.	Arnold, B.	Wallington, N.	Martin, J.	French, A.	Lintott, C.	Collingwood, J.	Crow, E.	Rose, H.	Feeheely, M.	Hebdon, Jim	Petitt, T.	Billingsby, R.	Morris, J.	Paddon, R.	Stockham, T.	Finn, P.	Davies, P.	Richardson, D.	O'Riordan, E.	Patient, N.	Mortimore, C.	Lovett, S.
22 Aug	(A)	Barking	L 1-5		1	2	3	4	5	6	7	8[1]	9	10	11																											
27 Aug	(H)	Corinthian Casuals	W 3-2		1	2	3	4		5	7	8[1]			11	6[1]	9[1]	10																								
29 Aug	(H)	Clapton	L 1-3		1	2	3	4		5	7	8		10	11	6	9[1]																									
2 Sep	(A)	Corinthian Casuals	D 2-2		1	2	3	4		5	7	8			11[1]	6[1]	10		9																							
9 Sep	(A)	Tooting	L 0-4		1	2	3	4		5		8			11		10		9	6	7																					
12 Sep	(A)	Wycombe	L 1-6		1	2	3	4		5	7	6			11		10		9	8[1]																						
19 Sep	(H)	Dulwich	D 1-1		1	2		4		5	7				11	6	9[1]	10				3	8																			
23 Sep	(A)	Oxford	D 1-1		1	2	3	4		5	7				11	6	9	10					8[1]																			
26 Sep	(H)	Barking	L 1-3		1	2		4		5	7				11	6	9	10[1]					8	3																		
30 Sep	(A)	Hendon	L 4-7		1	2		4[1]							11[2]		9	8			7[1]		10	3	5	6																
3 Oct	(H)	Maidstone	W 1-0		1	2		4							11		9	8[1]			7		10	3	5	6																
5 Oct	(A)	Wealdstone	L 0-6		1	2		4							11		9	8			7		10	3	5	6																
10 Oct	(H)	Walthamstow	W 2-1		1	2		4							11[1]		9	8[1]			7		10	3	5	6																
14 Oct	(A)	Kingstonian	L 0-6		1	2		4							11		9				7		8	3	5	6	10															
17 Oct	(A)	St.Albans	L 0-6			2		4							11					10	7		8	3	5		9	1	6													
24 Oct	(H)	Kingstonian	L 1-3			2		4							11[1]		10						8	3	5	6	9	1		7												
31 Oct	(H)	Leytonstone	L 1-3			2		4												10[1]			8	3	6	5		1		7	9			11								
7 Nov	(A)	Clapton	L 0-2		1	2	3	4							8					10				5		6				7	9			11								
21 Nov	(H)	Hitchin	W 3-0		1	2		4							8[2]									3		6				7	9[1]	5	10	11								
26 Nov	(H)	Wealdstone	W 2-1	1,000	1	2		4							11					10			8[2]	3		6				7	9	5										
28 Nov	(H)	Enfield	L 0-1		1	2		4							7					10			8	3		6					9	5		11								
5 Dec	(A)	Bromley	L 3-6		1	2		4							8					10[2]				3		6				7	9	5		11[1]								
12 Dec	(H)	Tooting	W 1-0		1	2		4		5					7					8			10	3		6					9[1]			11								
19 Dec	(A)	Enfield	L 0-5		1	2	3	4		5					7					8			10			6								11	9							
26 Dec	(H)	Sutton	L 1-3		1	2		4		5					7					10[1]			8	3		6					9			11								
23 Jan	(A)	Ilford	L 0-2		1	2		4							11			9		8				5		6										3	7	10				
30 Jan	(H)	St.Albans	L 0-1		1	2									11	4		10		9				5		6										3	7	8				
6 Feb	(A)	Hitchin	L 0-5		1	2									11	4		10		9				5		6				8						3	7					
13 Feb	(H)	Ilford o.g.	W 4-0		1	2		4		5[1]	7							11[1]		9						6				8[1]						3		10				
2 Mar	(H)	Oxford	L 1-3	350	1	2		4[1]		5	7							11		9						6				8						3			10			
6 Mar	(A)	Dulwich	L 0-3		1	2		4		5	7									10						6				8	9					3			11			
13 Mar	(A)	Leytonstone	L 2-4		1	2		4			7				10			11[1]								6				8	9	5				3[1]						
20 Mar	(H)	Hendon	L 2-3		1	2		4			7[1]				10[1]			11								6				8	9	5				3						
27 Mar	(A)	Maidstone	L 1-2		1	2		4			7				10			8								6					9[1]	5				3				11		
3 Apr	(A)	Walthamstow	D 3-3		1		2	4[1]			7				11[1]		10									6					9[1]	5				3					8	
8 Apr	(H)	Bromley	L 0-3		1	6	2	4			7				11		10														9	5				3					8	
19 Apr	(H)	Wycombe	L 1-3		1	2		4[1]			7				11		10									6				8	9					3						5
29 Apr	(A)	Sutton	L 1-4		1	2		10		6	7				11								8			4					9[1]					3						5
F.A.CUP																																										
5 Sep	Pre (H)	Guildford	L 1-3		1	2	3	4		5	7	8[1]			11	6	10		9																							
F.A. AMATEUR CUP																																										
2 Jan	1st R (H)	Bromley o.g.	D 2-2		1	2		4		5					7			9		8[1]			10	3		6								11								
9 Jan	Rep (A)	Bromley AET	L 1-2		1	2		4		5					11[1]			9		8			7	3		6												10				
SURREY SENIOR CUP																																										
16 Jan	1st R (A)	Westfield o.g.	W 3-0		1	2		4							11			9		10[1]			7	5		6										3		8[1]				
20 Feb	2nd R (H)	Leatherhead	D 2-2		1	2		4		5	7				10[1]			11[1]		9						6				8						3						
27 Feb	Rep (A)	Leatherhead	L 0-2		1	2		4		5	7				10			11		9						6				8						3						
SURREY INVITATION CUP																																										
6 Apr	S-F (A)	Leatherhead	D 2-2		1	4	2	6		5	7				11[1]		10														9					3					8[1]	
12 Apr	Rep (H)	Leatherhead	L 1-2		1	2		4			7				11[1]		10									6					9					3					8	5
MITHRAS CUP																																										
8 Oct	1st R 1st L (A)	St.Albans	L 1-3			2		8[1]							11		9				7		10	3	5	4		1	6													
2 Nov	2nd L	(Guildford) St.Albans	W 2-1		1	2	3	4							8					10[1]					6	5				7	9[1]			11								
TOTAL APPEARANCES					**44**	**47**	**14**	**46**	**1**	**22**	**23**	**7**	**1**	**2**	**44**	**9**	**21**	**21**	**4**	**23**	**8**	**1**	**21**	**23**	**10**	**35**	**3**	**4**	**2**	**16**	**19**	**9**	**1**	**10**	**1**	**18**	**3**	**5**	**2**	**1**	**4**	**3**
GOALS SCORED								**5**		**1**	**1**	**3**			**13**	**2**	**3**	**6**		**8**	**1**		**3**							**1**	**6**			**1**		**1**		**1**			**1**	

ISTHMIAN LEAGUE

SEASON 1965-1966

Date	Venue	Opponents	Result	Attendance	Farris, B.	Fuller, B.	Finn, P.	Finn, B.	Lovett, S.	McPhee, S.	McBryde, J.	Tindall, E.	Petitt, T.	Cooper, G.	Woods, S.	Patient, N.	Wood, G.	Keeley, R.	Richardson, D.	O'Riordan, E.	Hyde, R.	Davies, P.	Povey, R.	Wallington, N.	Martin, J.	Wooler, R.	Rose, H.	Hepburn, R.	Shaw, W.	Moore, J.
21 Aug	(H)	Leytonstone £56	W 1-0	554	1	2	3	4	5	6	7	8[1]	9	10	11															
25 Aug	(A)	Wycombe	L 0-3		1	2	3	4	5	6	7	8	9	10		11														
28 Aug	(A)	St.Albans	L 1-5		1	2	3	4		6[1]	7	8	9	10	11		5													
30 Aug	(H)	Hitchin	W 4-1		1	2	3	4		6	7	8[1]		10[1]	11		5	9[2]												
11 Sep	(H)	Enfield	L 1-2	1,000	1	2	3	4		6[1]	7	8		10	11		5	9												
14 Sep	(A)	Dulwich	L 0-3		1	2	3	4		6	7	8		10	11		5	9												
23 Sep	(H)	Oxford o.g.	W 3-1		1	2	3	4			7	8[1]			11		5	9	6	10[1]										
25 Sep	(H)	St.Albans	L 0-3		1	2	3	4			7	8			11		5	9	6	10										
29 Sep	(A)	Oxford	W 2-1		1	2	3	4				8[2]			11		5	9	6	10	7									
7 Oct	(H)	Tooting	D 3-3		1	2	3	4		6[1]		8[2]			11		5	9		10		7								
9 Oct	(A)	Maidstone	L 0-3		1	2	3	4		6		8			11		5	9		10		7								
14 Oct	(A)	Sutton	L 1-2		1	2	3	4		6		8			11		5	9		10[1]	7									
16 Oct	(A)	Ilford o.g. £70	W 2-1	700	1	2	3	4		6					11		5	9[1]		8	7		10							
21 Oct	(H)	Sutton £103	D 2-2	1,010	1	2	3	4		6			9[1]		11		5	8		10[1]	7									
23 Oct	(A)	Walthamstow	L 1-7		1	2	3	4		6			8[1]		11		5	9		10	7									
30 Oct	(H)	Corinthian Casuals	W 3-1		1	2	3	4		6		8[1]	9[1]		11		5		10[1]			7								
6 Nov	(A)	Enfield	L 0-1		1	2	3	4		6			9		11		5		10	8		7								
13 Nov	(H)	Maidstone	D 3-3		1	2	3	4		6	7[1]	8	9		11[1]		5[1]		10											
20 Nov	(A)	Hitchin	D 3-3		1	2	3	4		6	7	8[1]			11[1]		5	9[1]	10											
27 Nov	(A)	Kingstonian	L 0-2		1		2	4		6	7	8		10	11		5	9						3						
4 Dec	(H)	Bromley	W 4-2		1			4		6	7	9[3]		10	11		5			8[1]				3	2					
11 Dec	(H)	Hendon	W 5-1		1		2	4[1]		6	7[1]	9		10[1]	11		5[1]			8[1]				3						
18 Dec	(A)	Barking	L 0-6		1		2	4		6	7	9		10	11		5			8				3						
26 Dec	(H)	Kingstonian	D 2-2		1		2	4		6	7	9[1]		10[1]		11				8				3		5				
22 Jan	(H)	Walthamstow	D 1-1		1		3	4		6	7	9[1]		10	11		5			8						2				
29 Jan	(A)	Clapton	W 3-2				3	4		6		9[1]		10[1]	11		5			8[1]	7					2	1			
5 Feb	(A)	Bromley	D 1-1				3	4		6		9[1]		10	11		5			8	7				2		1			
12 Feb	(H)	Clapton	W 2-1				3	4		6		9[2]		10	11		5			8	7				2		1			
19 Feb	(H)	Barking	W 5-1				3	4		6		9[4]		10	11[1]		5			8	7						1	2		
5 Mar	(A)	Leytonstone	D 1-1				3	4		6		9[1]		10	11		5			8	7				2		1			
12 Mar	(A)	Ilford	D 0-0				3	4		6	7	9		10	11		5			8						2	1			
19 Mar	(A)	Tooting	L 0-1				2	6			7	10	9	8			5				11				3		1		4	
25 Mar	(H)	Wycombe	L 1-3					4					9	10[1]	11		5		6	8	7				3	2	1			
2 Apr	(A)	Hendon	L 0-4		1		3	4		6	7	9		10			5						11		2					8
9 Apr	(H)	Wealdstone	L 2-5				3	4		6	7	9[1]		10	11		5[1]								2		1			8
23 Apr	(H)	Dulwich	D 0-0				3	4		6	7	9		10	11		5								2		1			8
26 Apr	(A)	Corinthian Casuals	L 0-3				3	4		6	7		9	10	11		5			8					2		1			
12 May	(A)	Wealdstone	W 3-2				3	4[1]		6	7		9	10	11[1]		5[1]			8					2		1			
F.A. CUP																														
4 Sep	1st Q (H)	Addlestone o.g.	W 9-0		1	2	3	4		6[1]	7[3]	8[1]		10[2]	11		5	9[1]												
18 Sep	2nd Q (A)	Walton	W 4-0		1	2	3[1]	4			7	8			11		5[2]	9[1]	6	10										
2 Oct	3rd Q (A)	Guildford C.	L 0-6	3,230	1	2	3	4				8			11		5	9	6	10	7									
F.A. AMATEUR CUP																														
1 Jan	1st R (A)	Stowmarket	L 2-3	850	1		2	4		6	7	9		10[1]	11		5			8[1]				3						
SURREY SENIOR CUP																														
15 Jan	1st R (A)	Walton	L 0-1		1		2	4		6	7	9		10	11		5			8				3						
SURREY SENIOR SHIELD																														
23 Jan	1st R (H)	Kingstonian o.g.	W 2-1				3	4				9[1]		10	11		5		6	8	7				2		1			
10 May	F (A)	Tooting	L 1-3				3	4		6	7[1]	9		10	11		5			8					2		1			
SURREY INVITATION CUP																														
13 Apr	1st R (H)	Carshalton	W 1-0				3	4		6	7	9		10[1]	11										2	5	1			8
28 Apr	S-F (H)	Kingstonian	L 2-4				3	4		6	7	9		10	11		5			8[2]					2		1			
MITHRAS CUP																														
18 Oct	1st R 1st L(H)	Guildford C. o.g. £132	W 1-0	1,353	1	2	3	4		6			9		11		5	8		10	7									
22 Nov	2nd L (A)	Guildford C.	D 0-0		1	2		4		6	7	8		10	11		5	9						3						
15 Dec	2nd R 1st L (H)	Horsham	W 1-0		1		2	4		6	7	9		10	11		5[1]			8				3						
22 Dec	2nd L (A)	Horsham	D 4-4		1		2	4		6	7[2]	9[1]		10	11		5			8[1]				3						
18 Jan	Q-F 1st L (A)	Cheshunt	W 1-0		1		3	4		6	7	9		10		11	5			8[1]						2				
25 Jan	2nd L (H)	Cheshunt	L 2-4		1		3	4[1]		6		9		10[1]	11		5			8	7					2				
TOTAL APPEARANCES					**37**	**24**	**50**	**53**	**2**	**45**	**34**	**45**	**13**	**37**	**48**	**3**	**49**	**19**	**11**	**36**	**16**	**4**	**2**	**10**	**15**	**8**	**16**	**1**	**1**	**4**
GOALS SCORED							**1**	**3**		**4**	**8**	**27**	**3**	**10**	**4**		**7**	**6**	**1**	**11**										

SEASON 1966-1967

ISTHMIAN LEAGUE

Date	Venue	Opponents	Result	Attendance	Rose, H.	Sexton, A.	Norgate, K.	Finn, B.	McIntyre, A.	Richardson, D.	McBryde, J.	O'Riordan, E.	Tindall, E.	Cooper, G.	Hyde, R.	McDevitt, G.	McPhee, S.	Farris, B.	Moore, J.	Shaw, W.	Cowle, P.	Petitt, T.	Herrett, V.	Vooght, A.	Trevaskis, M.	Davies, P.	Woods, S.	Lewis, R.	Waughman, T.	Elton, R.	Scott, K.
20 Aug	(A)	St.Albans	D 2-2		1	2	3	4	5	6	7	8[2]	9	10	11																
24 Aug	(A)	Corinthian Casuals	W 3-2		1	2	3	4		11	7	8	9[2]	10[1]	12	5	6														
27 Aug	(H)	Hendon £127	L 0-2	1,095	1	2	3	4	5		7	8	9	10	11		6														
30 Aug	(H)	Kingstonian	L 0-2		1	2	3	4	5		7	8	9	10	11		6														
6 Sep	(A)	Oxford	L 0-3			6	3	4	5		7	8	9	10				1	2	11	12										
10 Sep	(H)	Hitchin	W 2-0	600			3	4[1]	5		7	11[1]	10	8			6	1	2	12		9									
13 Sep	(H)	Oxford	D 2-2				3	4	5		7[1]	11	9	8			6	1				10[1]	2								
22 Sep	(A)	Sutton	L 1-5			10	3	4	5	11	7		9[1]	8			6	1	12				2								
24 Sep	(A)	Bromley	L 1-2			10	3	4	5	11	7[1]		9	8			6	1					2								
27 Sep	(H)	Tooting	L 1-5			10	3	4	5	12	7		9	8[1]			6	1				11	2								
4 Oct	(A)	Dulwich	W 4-1			6	3	4	5		7	8[2]	9[1]	10[1]			11	1					2								
8 Oct	(H)	Ilford	W 4-0			6	3	4	5		7	10	9[2]	8[2]			11	1					2								
11 Oct	(H)	Dulwich	W 3-0				3	4	5		7	10	9[2]	8			11[1]	1					2	6							
15 Oct	(A)	Clapton	L 0-3			6	3	4	5		7	10	9	8			11	1					2								
22 Oct	(H)	Wealdstone	D 1-1			6	3	4	5		7	10	9	8			11[1]	1					2								
29 Oct	(A)	Hitchin	W 4-0			6	3	4	5		7	10[1]	9[3]	8			11	1					2								
5 Nov	(H)	Bromley	D 1-1			6	3	4[1]	5		7	10	9	8			11	1					2								
12 Nov	(A)	Barking	D 1-1			6	3	4	5		7	10	9[1]	8			11	1					2								
15 Nov	(H)	Corinthian Casuals	W 2-1			2	3	4[1]	5		7	10	9[1]	8			6	1							11						
19 Nov	(H)	Wycombe	L 2-6			2	3	4[1]	5		7	10[1]	9	8			6	1							11						
26 Nov	(A)	Tooting	W 6-2			2	3[1]	4	5		7	10[1]	9[1]	8[2]			6	1								11[1]					
20 Dec	(H)	Sutton	W 2-0			2	3	4			7	10	9[1]	8[1]		5	6	1								11					
28 Dec	(A)	Kingstonian	L 3-5			2	3	4			7	10	9[1]	8[1]		5	6	1								11[1]					
21 Jan	(H)	Barking	D 1-1			2	3	4			7	10	9[1]	8		5	6	1								11					
4 Feb	(H)	Maidstone	W 4-1			2	3	4			7	10	9[3]	8[1]		5	6	1									11				
11 Feb	(H)	St.Albans	D 1-1			2	3	4[1]			7	10	9	8		5	6	1									11				
18 Feb	(A)	Ilford	L 0-2			2	3	4			7	10	9	8		5	6	1									11				
25 Feb	(A)	Leytonstone	D 0-0			2	3	4				8		9			6	1									10	5	7		
4 Mar	(H)	Clapton	W 3-1			2	3	4[1]			7	10	9[1]	8[1]			6	1									11	5			
11 Mar	(A)	Wealdstone	W 2-1			2	3	4			7	10[1]	9[1]	8			6	1									11	5			
18 Mar	(A)	Wycombe	L 1-2				2	4			7	10	9[1]	8			6	1									11	5		3	
27 Mar	(A)	Walthamstow	L 1-6			2	3	4			7	10	9	8			6	1									11[1]	5			
29 Mar	(H)	Enfield	W 2-0			2	3	4			7[1]	10	9[1]	8			6	1									11	5			
8 Apr	(A)	Enfield	L 0-2			2	3	4			7	10	9	8			6	1									11	5			
15 Apr	(H)	Leytonstone	D 1-1			2	3	4			7	10	9	8[1]			6	1									11	5			
29 Apr	(A)	Maidstone	D 2-2			2	3	4				10	9	8				1	6								11[1]	5	7[1]		
6 May	(H)	Walthamstow	L 2-4			2	3	4			7	10	9[1]	8[1]			6	1									11	5			
9 May	(A)	Hendon	L 0-1			2	3	4				10	9	8			6	1									11	5	7		
F.A. CUP																															
3 Sep	1st Q (A)	Basingstoke	W 2-1			2	3	4	5	11	7[1]	8	9	10[1]			6	1													
17 Sep	2nd Q (H)	Littlehampton	W 2-1				3	4	5	11	7		9	8[1]			6	1				10[1]	2								
1 Oct	3rd Q (A)	Horsham	L 1-2			11	3	4	5		7	8	9[1]	10			6	1					2								
F.A. AMATEUR CUP																															
10 Dec	4th Q (A)	Alton o.g.	W 5-3			2	3	4	5		7[1]	10[1]	9[2]	8			6	1								11					
14 Jan	1st R (A)	Barking	W 2-1			2	3	4			7	10	9[2]	8		5	6	1	12							11					
28 Jan	2nd R (A)	Southall	L 1-2			2	3	4			7	10	9	8[1]		5	6	1								11					
SURREY SENIOR CUP																															
3 Dec	1st R (H)	Addlestone	D 2-2			2	3	4	5		7	10	9[1]	8[1]			6	1								11					
31 Dec	Rep (A)	Addlestone	W 5-3			2	3	4			7	10[1]	9[2]	8[1]		5	6[1]	1								11					
7 Jan	2nd R (A)	Leatherhead	L 1-2			2	3	4			7	10	9[1]	8		5	6	1								11					
MITHRAS CUP																															
28 Nov	1st R 1st L (H)	Horsham	W 5-1	750		2	3	4[1]	5		7[1]	10	9[2]	8[1]			6	1								11					
12 Dec	2nd L (A)	Horsham	W 1-0			2	3	4	5		7	10	9[1]	8		6		1	11												
21 Feb	2nd R 1st L (A)	Redhill *Both legs*	D 0-0			2	3	4			7	10	9	8			6	1									11	5			
7 Mar	2nd L (H)	Redhill *at Woking*	W 3-0			2	3	4			7[1]	10[1]	9[1]	8			6	1									11	5			
21 Mar	3rd R 1st L (A)	Maidenhead	L 0-2			2	3	4			7	10	9	8			6	1									11	5			
4 Apr	2nd L (H)	Maidenhead	D 0-0			2	3	4			7	10	9	8			5	1	6								11				
SURREY INVITATION CUP																															
20 Apr	1st R (H)	Met.Police	D 1-1	AET		2	3	4[1]			7	10	9	8			6	1									11	5			
4 May	Rep (H)	Met.Police	W 4-3	AET		2	3	4			7[1]	10[1]	9[2]	8			6	1									11	5			
11 May	S-F (H)	Croydon AM	W 2-1	AET			2	4			7	10	9[2]	8			6	1										5	11		3
Final next season																															
APPEARANCES					**4**	**50**	**56**	**56**	**27**	**6**	**53**	**52**	**55**	**56**	**3**	**12**	**52**	**52**	**5**	**1**		**4**	**14**	**1**	**2**	**11**	**20**	**17**	**4**	**1**	**1**
SUBSTITUTE										**1**					**1**				**2**	**1**	**1**										
GOALS SCORED							**1**	**8**			**8**	**13**	**42**	**19**			**3**					**2**				**2**	**2**		**1**		

ISTHMIAN LEAGUE

SEASON 1967-1968

Date	Venue	Opponents	Result	Attendance	Farris, B.	Sexton, A.	Elton, R.	Finn, B.	Lewis, R.	McPhee, S.	McBryde, J.	Waughman, T.	Tindall, E.	O'Riordan, E.	Woods, S.	Carver, G.	Trevaskis, M.	Scott, K.	Oliver, B.	Slater, M.	Morgan, P.	Finn, C.	Morton, A.	Chegwyn, C.	Elmore, J.	Fletcher, R.	Moorcroft, R.	Malcolmson, S.	Williams, S.	Rose, H.	Povey, R.	Knight, B.	Vooght, A.	Hill, R.	Moore, J.	Crone, J.	Powell	Wooler, R.	Mortimore, C.
23 Aug	(A)	Corinthian Casuals	L 1-2		1	2	3	4	5	6	7	8	9[1]	10	11																								
26 Aug	(H)	Walthamstow	D 2-2		1	2	3	4	5	6	7		9[2]	8	11	10	12																						
28 Aug	(A)	Oxford	L 1-3		1	2	3	4	5		7		9	10	11[1]	8		6																					
2 Sep	(A)	Leytonstone	D 2-2		1	2	3	4	5		7		9	8[2]	10		11	6																					
9 Sep	(H)	Ilford	L 1-3		1	2	3	4	5	6	7		9[1]	8	10		11																						
12 Sep	(H)	Wycombe	D 3-3		1		3	4	5	6	11	7[1]	9[2]	8	10			2																					
19 Sep	(A)	Wycombe	W 4-2		1		3	4		6		7[2]	9		10[1]		11[1]	5	2														8						
23 Sep	(H)	Maidstone	W 5-2		1		3	4		6		7[1]	9[2]	12	10[1]		11[1]	5	2														8						
26 Sep	(H)	Dulwich	W 2-0		1		3	4		6		7	9		10[1]		11	5	2														8[1]						
30 Sep	(A)	Tooting	L 0-2		1		3	4		6		7	9		10		11	5	2														8						
2 Oct	(A)	Wealdstone	D 1-1		1	8	3	4		6		7	9		11[1]			5	2		10																		
7 Oct	(H)	Enfield	L 0-5		1		3	4		6		7	9		11			5	2	8	10																		
10 Oct	(A)	Sutton	L 0-5				3	4	5	6		7	9		11			2			8					10				1									
14 Oct	(H)	Hendon	L 0-5		1		3	4	5	6		7	9		8		11	2		10	12																		
17 Oct	(H)	Tooting	L 0-2		1	2	3	4	5			7	9		8		11	6		10	12																		
21 Oct	(A)	Maidstone	W 3-2		1	2	3	4	5	8		7	9[3]		11			6		10																			
28 Oct	(A)	Barking	L 2-5		1	8	3	4	5			7	9[1]		11			6	2	10		12[1]																	
4 Nov	(H)	Hitchin	W 3-2	440	1	10	3	4		6		7	9[1]				11[1]	5	2				8[1]																
11 Nov	(A)	Walthamstow	D 1-1		1	2	3	4		6		7[1]	9		10		11	5					8																
25 Nov	(A)	St. Albans	D 2-2		1	2	3	4		6		7	9[2]		10		11	5															8						
2 Dec	(H)	Oxford	L 0-3		1	2	3	4		6		7	9		11			5		10		8																	
9 Dec	(A)	Ilford	L 0-5		1	2	3	4		6		7	9		10			5				8		11															
16 Dec	(H)	St. Albans	L 0-2		1	4	3	8		6		7			10			5	2					11			9												
21 Dec	(H)	Wealdstone	W 3-0		1	2	9	4[1]		3		7			10			6						11[1]	5		8[1]												
27 Dec	(H)	Kingstonian	W 2-0		1		9[1]	4[1]		3		7			11			6	2						5	10	8												
27 Jan	(A)	Hendon	L 0-4		1		6	4		3			9		8			5	2					11		10			7										
3 Feb	(H)	Bromley	L 1-3		1		6	4		3			9[1]		11			5	2							10	12		7										
10 Feb	(A)	Clapton	L 2-4		1		5	4		3		7[1]			11			6	2					8[1]		10			9										
17 Feb	(A)	Bromley	L 0-1		1		5	4		12		9			11			3	2							10	8		7		6								
2 Mar	(H)	Clapton	L 1-3		1	2	5	4				9[1]			11				8							10			7		6	3							
9 Mar	(A)	Dulwich	L 1-2		1		5	4				9[1]							2							10			7			3	8	11	6		12		
16 Mar	(A)	Kingstonian	L 1-2		1	2	5	4				9							3					10		8			7		6			11[1]					
23 Mar	(H)	Corinthian Casuals	D 2-2		1	2	5	4				9							3							10			7		6			11[1]	8[1]				
30 Mar	(H)	Leytonstone	D 0-0		1	2	5	4				9	8						3							10			7		6		11						
6 Apr	(A)	Hitchin	W 1-0		1	2	5	4				9	8													10					6		7[1]	11	3				
27 Apr	(A)	Enfield o.g.	L 1-2		1	2		4				9	8						3												6		7	10	5	11			
4 May	(H)	Barking	L 0-2		1	2	5	4				9	8						3															10	11	7		6	
7 May	(H)	Sutton	L 2-4		1	2	5	4[1]				9[1]	8						3							10					6			11	7				
F.A. CUP																																							
16 Sep	1st Q (A)	Basingstoke	L 1-5		1		3	4	5	6	11	7	9	8	10[1]			2																					
F.A. AMATEUR CUP																																							
20 Jan	1st R (A)	Southall	L 0-2		1		9	4		3		7			10			6	2					11	5	12	8												
SURREY SENIOR CUP																																							
30 Dec	1st R (A)	Sutton	L 0-2		1	2	9	4		3		7			11			6	12						5	10	8												
SURREY SENIOR SHIELD																																							
26 Mar	1st R (H)	Addlestone	D 1-1	AET	1	2	5	4				9							3								10[1]		7		6		12	11	8				
1 Apr	Rep (A)	Addlestone	W 5-2	AET	1	2	5	4				9[1]	8[1]						3							10					6		7	11[1]	12[2]				
23 Apr	S-F (H)	Kingstonian	W 2-1		1	2	5	4[2]				9	8				11		3									10			6				12	7			
14 May	F	(G'ford) Leatherhead	W 3-2		1	2	6	5				9	8						3							10		11[3]							7			4	
SURREY INVITATION CUP 1966-67 FINAL																																							
6 Sep	F	(Walton) Tooting	W 2-1	AET	1	2	3	4	5	6	7[2]		9	8	10		11	12																					
MITHRAS CUP																																							
1 Nov	1st R 1st L (A)	Horsham	W 2-1		1	10	3	4[1]	12	6		7	9		11			5	2				8[1]																
28 Nov	2nd L (H)	Horsham	L 0-2	AET	1	2	3	4		6		7	8		10		11	5															9						
WYCOMBE FLOODLIT LEAGUE																																							
24 Oct	(H)	Wokingham	W 3-1		1	8	3	4[1]	5			7[1]	9[1]		11			6	2	10																			
14 Nov	(H)	Maidenhead	L 1-2		1	2	3	4		6		7	9		10		11	5[1]					8																
4 Dec	(A)	Slough	L 0-3		1	2	3	4		6		7	9		10			5				8		11															
3 Jan	(A)	Southall	D 2-2		1			4					9[1]		11[1]			5	2						6	10	8		7			3							
29 Jan	(A)	Wycombe	L 0-3		1		6	4		3		8	9					5	2					11	7	10													12
13 Feb	(H)	Wycombe	W 2-0		1		5	4		3		9[1]			11			10[1]	2					8		12			7		6								
26 Feb	(A)	Wokingham	L 0-1		1	2		4				9	5		11			10	3					8					7		6								
5 Mar	(A)	Maidenhead	W 3-0		1	2	5	4[1]				9[1]			10				3							8			7		6			11[1]					
8 Apr	(H)	Slough	W 2-1		1	2	5	4[2]				9	8						3												6			11	10	7		12	
30 Apr	(H)	Southall	W 1-0		1	2	5	4				9	8						3									7[1]			6			11	10	12			
APPEARANCES					57	39	55	58	14	34	8	50	44	8	42	2	15	38	36	7	3	3	4	11	6	19	8	3	14	1	16	3	11	12	10	4		2	
SUBSTITUTE									1	1				1			1	1	1		2	1				2	1						1		2	1	1	1	1
GOALS SCORED								10			2	13	19	2	7		3	2				1	2	2			2	4					2	4	3				

SEASON 1968-1969

ISTHMIAN LEAGUE

Date	Venue	Opponents	Result	Attendance	Farris, B.	Oliver, B.	Elton, R.	Godwin, D.	Moore, J.	Sexton, A.	Finn, B.	Carver, G.	Vooght, A.	Tindall, E.	Malcolmson, S.	Povey, R.	Wooler, R.	Hill, R.	Holmes, W.	Francis, N.	Fletcher, R.	Marks, C.	Evans, D.	Bowley, M.	Palinski, G.	Folan, J.	Barnett, B.	Cowle, P.	Connaughton, P.	Waughman, T.
17 Aug	(A)	St. Albans	D 2-2		1	2	3	4	5	6	7	8	9[2]	10	11															
20 Aug	(H)	Tooting	D 1-1		1	2	3	4	8	6	7		9[1]		11	5	12													10
24 Aug	(H)	Bromley o.g.	W 5-2	500	1		3	4	8	6	7[2]		9		11[1]	5		2												10[1]
27 Aug	(A)	Sutton	W 3-2		1		3	4	8	6	7[1]	11		12[1]		5		2	9[1]											10
31 Aug	(A)	Walthamstow	D 0-0		1	2	3	4	8	6	7	12	9			5			11											10
3 Sep	(H)	Oxford	L 2-3	1,100	1	2	3	4	8	6	7		9[1]		11[1]	5														10
7 Sep	(H)	Ilford	L 2-3	730		2	3[1]	4	8	6	7		9	12[1]	11	5				1										10
11 Sep	(A)	Wycombe	L 0-4		1	5	3	4	12	6	7				11			2	9		8									10
14 Sep	(A)	Bromley	W 4-0		1	5	3	4		6	7	8[1]		9	11[1]			2												10[2]
28 Sep	(H)	Barking	L 1-2		1	5	3	4	12	6	7	8		9[1]	11			2												10
1 Oct	(H)	Corinthian Casuals	W 4-1		1	12	3		4	6	7	8		10[3]		5		2			11									9[1]
9 Oct	(A)	Wealdstone	L 1-2		1	2	3		4	6		8	12	10		5	7[1]				11									9
12 Oct	(A)	Enfield	L 1-4		1		3	4	12	6	7	8		9[1]	11	5		2												10
15 Oct	(A)	Oxford	L 0-3		1	2	3		4	6	7	8	11	10		5	12													9
22 Oct	(H)	Hendon	L 1-3		1		3		4	6	7	8		10[1]		5	11	2												9
26 Oct	(H)	Hitchin	L 1-2		1		3	4		6	7	8		10	11	5		2												9[1]
9 Nov	(A)	Leytonstone	L 0-3		1		3	4	5	6	7	8		10	11			2												9
23 Nov	(H)	Kingstonian o.g.	W 2-1		1		3	4		6	7	8		10	11	5		2												9[1]
30 Nov	(H)	Maidstone	W 1-0		1		7	3	4		6	8[1]		10	11	5		2												9
7 Dec	(A)	Barking	L 0-6		1		4	3		6	7	8		10		5		2				11								9
4 Jan	(H)	Enfield	L 0-6	615	1		6	3	4		7	8	9			5		2				11								10
11 Jan	(H)	Wycombe	L 2-3	450	1		3	4		6	7[1]	11	8			5		2				10[1]								9
25 Jan	(A)	Hendon	L 0-3		1		3	4		2	6		9					5	11			10								8
1 Feb	(H)	Clapton	L 0-2	350	1		3	4	8	6	7					5		2	11			12		10						9
6 Feb	(A)	Corinthian Casuals	L 1-2		1		3		2	6	7[1]	11	12			5			9				8	10						4
8 Feb	(A)	Tooting	L 3-4		1		3		4	2	6	8[1]	11			5						9	7							10[2]
1 Mar	(A)	Dulwich	L 0-1		1		3	4	2	6	7	12				5					8		9		11					10
8 Mar	(A)	Maidstone	L 0-1	500			9	5	2	4	8					6	10		11	1						3	12			7
15 Mar	(H)	Walthamstow	D 0-0	300	1		5	6	2	4	10	8				3							11					9		7
22 Mar	(A)	Ilford	W 2-0		1			4	2	6	10	8[1]				5	12						11	3				9		7[1]
29 Mar	(A)	Kingstonian	L 0-2		1				2	4	10	8				6							11	5		3		9		7
1 Apr	(H)	Sutton	D 1-1	800	1	9	5		2	4	10	8				6							11[1]	12		3				7
11 Apr	(H)	Dulwich	W 2-1	430	1	9[1]	5		2	4	10	8[1]				6							11	3						7
19 Apr	(A)	Clapton	D 1-1		1	9[1]	5	6	2	4	8	11				3					10									7
25 Apr	(H)	St. Albans	D 0-0		1	9	5	6	2	4	8	7				3					10								11	
30 Apr	(H)	Wealdstone	L 2-3		1	9[1]	5		2	4	8	11[1]				6					10		12	3						7
3 May	(H)	Leytonstone	L 0-1		1	9	5		2	4	8	11				6					10			3						7
10 May	(A)	Hitchin	L 0-2		1	9	5		2	4	8	11				6					10		3						12	7
F.A. CUP																														
21 Sep	1st Q (H)	Crawley o.g.	W 2-1	1,114	1	5	3	4	12	6[1]	7	8		9	11			2												10
5 Oct	2nd Q (H)	Addlestone	W 5-2	1,128	1	12	3		4	6	7	8[1]		10[1]		5		2			11[1]									9[2]
19 Oct	3rd Q (H)	Wokingham o.g.	W 3-2	1,130	1		3	4	10	6	7	8[1]			11	5	12	2												9[1]
2 Nov	4th Q (A)	Wimbledon	W 2-0	2,346	1		3	4		6	7	8		10[1]	11	5		2												9[1]
16 Nov	1st R (A)	Brentford	L 0-2	5,990	1		3	4		6	7	8		10	11	5		2												9
F.A. AMATEUR CUP																														
14 Dec	1st R (H)	Leytonstone	L 0-1	850	1		3	4		6	7	8		10	11	5		2												9
SURREY SENIOR CUP																														
21 Dec	1st R (A)	Egham	W 6-0		1		5	3	4	8	6	11[1]	7[1]					2				10[1]								9[3]
22 Feb	2nd R (H)	Tooting	L 0-5	587	1		3	4	5	2	6	11									7	9	8							10
SURREY SENIOR SHIELD																														
9 Apr	1st R (A)	Redhill	L 1-3	AET	1	10[1]	3		2	6	7	8				4							11	5		12				9
MITHRAS CUP																														
6 Nov	1st R 1st L (H)	Horsham	D 2-2	600	1	5	3		4	6	7	8	11	10[1]				2												9[1]
11 Nov	2nd L (A)	Horsham	L 0-1		1		3		4	6		8		10		5	7	2	9		11									
WYCOMBE FLOODLIT CUP																														
19 Nov	1st R 1st L (H)	Slough	W 2-0		1		3	4		6	7	8[1]		10	11[1]	5		2												9
9 Dec	2nd L (A)	Slough	L 0-1		1		3	4	11	6	7	8		10		5		2												9
28 Jan	2nd R 1st L (H)	Addlestone	D 0-0	408	1		3	4	8	6	7	12				5		2	11			10								9
4 Mar	2nd L (A)	Addlestone	L 0-2				3		2	6	7	11	9			4				1	8					5	12			10
APPEARANCES					**50**	**20**	**51**	**36**	**39**	**51**	**51**	**42**	**14**	**22**	**19**	**43**	**4**	**29**	**9**	**3**	**13**	**8**	**11**	**8**	**1**	**4**		**3**	**1**	**50**
SUBSTITUTE						**2**			**4**			**3**	**2**	**2**			**4**					**1**	**1**	**1**		**1**	**2**		**1**	
GOALS SCORED						**4**	**1**			**1**	**5**	**10**	**5**	**11**	**4**		**1**		**1**		**1**	**2**	**1**							**17**

ISTHMIAN LEAGUE

SEASON 1969-1970

Date	Venue	Opponents	Result	Attendance	Farris, B.	Moore, J.	Bowley, M.	Edwards, D.	Povey, R.	Fletcher, R.	Sexton, A.	Elliott, M.	Oliver, B.	Finn, B.	McCormack, J.	Binks, T.	Elton, R.	Church, A.	Wooler,R.	Blason, W.	Smith, T.	Gale, D.	Petitt, D.	Brown, N.	Holder. K.	Palinski,G.	Leonard, D.	Holmes, W.	Evans, D.	Carver, G.	Vooght, A.	Schofield, M.	Folan, J.
9 Aug	(A)	Enfield	L 0-1		1	2	3	4	5	6	7	8	9	10	11																		12
12 Aug	(H)	Dulwich	W 2-1	565	1	2	3	4	5	6	7	8[1]	9	10	11[1]																		
16 Aug	(H)	Maidstone	W 4-1		1	2	3	5	4	6		7		8[1]	11[1]	9[2]	10																
19 Aug	(H)	Corinthian Casuals o.g.	W 2-0	590	1	2		5	4	6		7		10	11	9[1]	3	8		12													
23 Aug	(A)	Clapton	W 3-0	152	1	2		5	4	6		7[1]		10	11[1]	9[1]	3		8														
26 Aug	(A)	Tooting	L 0-2		1	2		5	4	6		7		10	11	9	3		8														
30 Aug	(H)	Hitchin	L 0-1		1	2	10	5	4	6	8	7			11	9	3																
2 Sep	(A)	Sutton	L 0-4		1	2		5	4	6	8			10	11	9	3													7			
9 Sep	(H)	Kingstonian	L 0-2	891	1	2		5	4		8	7		10	11		3			9	6												
13 Sep	(A)	Bromley	L 0-1		1	2		5	12		8	7		4	11	9	3				6									10			
16 Sep	(A)	Corinthian Casuals	W 1-0		1	2		5			8	7		4		9	3			6								11[1]		10			
30 Sep	(H)	Tooting	L 1-4		1	6		5	3		2	12		7		10[1]	4			9	8							11					
4 Oct	(H)	St. Albans	L 0-2		1	2		5	3			9		4	11	10					8			7				12		6			
11 Oct	(A)	Oxford	D 2-2		1	2		5			8	9[1]		4	11[1]		3				6		12	7	10								
18 Oct	(A)	Walthamstow	L 1-3		1	2		5[1]				9		4	11		3	12	10				6	7	8								
25 Oct	(H)	Ilford	D 1-1	434	1	2		5				12		4	11	9		3			10		6	7[1]	8								
28 Oct	(H)	Sutton	L 0-1		1	2	3							4	11	9	5				10		6	12	8	7							
1 Nov	(A)	Maidstone	W 1-0		1	2	3							4	9[1]	11	5				10			6	8	7							
8 Nov	(H)	Leytonstone	W 1-0		1	2		5				7		4	9[1]	11	3				10		6		8	12							
15 Nov	(A)	Barking	L 0-5		1	2		5				7		4	9		3				10		6		8			11					
22 Nov	(A)	Ilford	D 2-2		1			5		6		7		4	9		3[1]	2			10				8	11[1]							
29 Nov	(H)	Bromley	W 2-0		1	2		5		6		7		4	9[1]	11[1]	3				10				8								
6 Dec	(H)	Wycombe	D 1-1	567	1	2		5				7		4	9	11[1]	3				6				8		10						
27 Dec	(A)	Kingstonian	D 1-1		1			5				9	2	4		11[1]	3				6	7			8		10						
3 Jan	(H)	Wealdstone	L 0-1		1	2		5				9		4		11	3				6	7			8		10						
10 Jan	(H)	Clapton	W 7-1		1			5		6[1]				4		11	3	2			10	9[4]			8		7	12[2]					
7 Feb	(H)	Oxford	D 2-2		1			5		6				4	7	11[2]	3				10	9			2		8						
28 Feb	(A)	Wealdstone	L 3-4		1			5		7				4	10[2]	11	3[1]				6	9			2		8						
10 Mar	(A)	Hendon	W 3-2		1			5				11		4	10[1]		3	2			6	9[2]			7		8						
14 Mar	(A)	Dulwich	L 1-3		1			5		6		9		4	11[1]	12	3				10	7			2		8						
21 Mar	(H)	Barking	D 2-2		1	2		5[1]	4							11[1]	3				8	9	10		7		6						
24 Mar	(A)	Wycombe	L 0-3		1	2		5						4	9	11	3				10	7			6		8						
28 Mar	(A)	Leytonstone	L 0-1		1	2		5	3			7			12	11			4		10	9				6					8		
30 Mar	(H)	Walthamstow	L 2-3		1	2		5	3			8			9	11			4		6[2]	7			10								
10 Apr	(H)	Hendon	L 1-3		1			5				7	2	4	11		3[1]				6	9			10		8						
18 Apr	(A)	St. Albans	L 0-5		1			5				12	2	4		11	3				8	7	6		10		9						
25 Apr	(H)	Enfield	L 0-1		1			5	3					4		11	6	2				9	8		10		7						
1 May	(A)	Hitchin	L 0-3		1			4					2	3		10	5				8	9			7			11	6				
F.A. CUP																																	
6 Sep	Prel (H)	Chichester	W 4-1		1	2		5	4		8	7		10	11[1]	9[2]	3													6[1]			
20 Sep	1st Q (H)	Addlestone	D 3-3		1	3		5			2			8	9	10[3]	4				6							11		7			
25 Sep	Rep (A)	Addlestone	L 0-2		1	3		5			2	9		8		10	4				6							11		7			
F.A. AMATEUR CUP																																	
13 Dec	1st R (H)	Walton	D 0-0	2,200	1	2		5				7		4	9	11	3				10		6		8								
20 Dec	Rep (A)	Walton	L 1-2	1,600	1		12	5				7	2	4	9[1]	11	3				6				8						10		
SURREY SENIOR CUP																																	
31 Jan	1st R (A)	Corinthian Casuals	W 4-1		1			5		6				4	7[1]	11[2]	3				10	9[1]			2		8						
21 Feb	2nd R (H)	Croydon	W 3-0		1			5[2]		6				4	7[1]	11	3				10	9			2		8						
7 Mar	S-F (A)	Walton	L 0-4		1			5		6				4	10	11	3				7	9			2		8						
PREMIER FLOODLIT LEAGUE																																	
8 Oct	(A)	Crawley	W 2-1		1	2						9		4	11	10[2]	5	3			8		6	7									
14 Oct	(H)	Wokingham	W 3-2		1	2		5[1]				9		4	11		3				10[1]		6	7[1]	8								
3 Nov	(A)	Guildford City	D 1-1	1,387	1	2		5				7		4	9	11[1]	3						6	10	8								
11 Nov	(H)	Redhill	W 2-0		1	2		5				9		4	10[1]		3				8		6		7			11[1]					
18 Nov	(A)	Walton	L 0-1		1	2		5				7		4	9		3			12	10		6		8			11					
25 Nov	(H)	Guildford City	D 0-0		1	2		5				7		4	9		3				10		6		8	11							
2 Dec	(H)	Slough	L 2-3		1	2		5				7[1]		4	9	11[1]	3				6		12		8		10						
9 Dec	(A)	Addlestone	D 0-0		1	2	5	4						3		10				11	6				7		8			9			
11 Feb	(A)	Redhill	L 0-1		1			5		6				4	7		3			11	10	9			2		8						
24 Feb	(H)	Crawley	L 1-2		1			5		6[1]				4	7	11	3				10	9			2		8						
2 Mar	(A)	Wokingham	W 4-1		1	2	3		5			7[1]		4	11						6	9[2]			10		8[1]						
18 Mar	(A)	Slough o.g.	W 3-1		1	2		5	3			9		4		11[1]						7[1]	10		6		8						
23 Apr	(H)	Walton	L 0-2		1			5				11	2	4		10	3					9	6		8		7						
30 Apr	(H)	Addlestone	L 0-1					5				8		4		11	3				6	9			2		7		10			1	
TOTAL APPEARANCES					**59**	**41**	**8**	**56**	**18**	**19**	**12**	**40**	**8**	**56**	**45**	**44**	**51**	**7**	**5**	**5**	**45**	**24**	**17**	**8**	**42**	**5**	**24**	**8**	**2**	**8**	**2**	**1**	
SUBSTITUTE							**1**		**1**			**3**			**1**	**1**		**1**		**2**			**2**	**1**		**1**		**2**					**1**
GOALS SCORED								**5**		**2**		**5**		**1**	**16**	**23**	**3**				**3**	**10**		**2**		**1**	**1**	**4**		**1**			

ISTHMIAN LEAGUE

SEASON 1970-1971

Date	Venue	Opponents	Result	Atten- dance	Farris, B.	Finn, B.	Finn, P.	Edwards, D.	Christmas, A.	Smith, T.	Leonard, D.	Robson, P.	Binks, T.	Elliott, M.	Hazell, J.	Petitt, D.	Elton, R.	Collyer, D.	Gale, D.	Blason, W.	Harding, S.	Woolen, M.	Coxon	Heath, K.	Hammond, P.	Francis, N.	Van den Berg, H.	Cheeseman, D.	Higgs, R.	Long, G.	Brown, P.	Sexton, A.	Evans, D.	Payne, M.	Holt, P.	Davies, A.	Lennon, D.	Oram, K.
15 Aug	(A)	Hendon	W 3-2		1	2	3	4	5	6	7	8	9[1]	11[2]																							10
18 Aug	(H)	Tooting	D 1-1		1	2	3	4	5	6	7	8	9[1]	11	10	12																						
22 Aug	(H)	Ilford	W 3-1		1	2	3	5		6	7	8	11[1]	10[1]		4																					9[1]
25 Aug	(A)	Dulwich	W 2-1		1	2	3	4		6	7	8	9	11	12[1]	5																					10[1]
29 Aug	(A)	Leytonstone	L 0-3		1	2	3	4	11	6	7	8	9				5																				10
1 Sep	(H)	Sutton	L 1-2			2	3	5	4	8	7				10		6	1	11[1]																			9
8 Sep	(A)	Kingstonian o.g.	W 3-2			2	4	3	7[1]	8	5		10				6	1	11[1]																			9
12 Sep	(A)	Hitchin	L 0-2			2	3	5	4	8	7	12					6	1	10	11																		9
15 Sep	(H)	Corinthian Casuals	W 5-0			2	3	5	6[1]	8	7[1]				11		4	1	10[2]																			9[1]
23 Sep	(A)	Oxford	D 1-1			9	2	4		6	8		11				5	1	10		3																	7[1]
26 Sep	(H)	Walthamstow	L 0-1			6	2	5	4	7	8		11						1	9			3	12																10
3 Oct	(A)	Ilford	L 0-3			2	3	5		7	8		11				6	1	9		4																	10
6 Oct	(H)	Dulwich o.g.	W 2-1			2	3	5	4	7[1]	10	6	11						1				8																	9
13 Oct	(A)	Sutton	L 1-2			2	3	4	5	7	8	11	12				6	1				9																	10[1]
17 Oct	(H)	Barking	D 2-2			4	3	5[1]	6[1]	7	8	2	11						1	10																			9
24 Oct	(A)	Tooting	L 0-1			2	3	5	6	7	8		12				4	1	10			11																	9
31 Oct	(H)	Hitchin	W 1-0			2	3	5			7[1]	8					4	1	11	10		6																	9
7 Nov	(H)	Bromley	W 4-0			2	3	5		7	11		12				4	1	10[2]	6				8[1]															9[1]
14 Nov	(A)	Barking	L 1-4			2	3	5	8	6	7		12				4	1	11					9[1]															10
21 Nov	(H)	Leytonstone	D 1-1			2	3	5	4	6	7		11						1	10	12				8[1]															9
12 Dec	(A)	Walthamstow	D 1-1			2	3	4	8	6	7		11[1]	10			5	1			9																		
19 Dec	(H)	St. Albans	W 2-1			2	3	5	6[1]	7[1]	10		11				4	1						8															9
2 Jan	(H)	Maidstone	W 1-0			2	3	5	6	7	8		11				4	1		12				10															9[1]
30 Jan	(A)	Clapton	W 4-2			2	5		7	9	8		6[2]	10			3	1			4				12[1]														11[1]
6 Feb	(H)	Wealdstone	L 1-2			2	3	5	6	7	8			10			4	1						11															9[1]
9 Feb	(H)	Wycombe	L 0-2			2	3	5	6	9	12		8	10			4	1			7																	11
20 Feb	(A)	Bromley	W 1-0			2	3	4	8	6	10[1]						7	1			5			11															9
27 Feb	(H)	Enfield	D 0-0			2	3	5		7	10			11			4	1			6			8															9
6 Mar	(A)	Corinthian Casuals	W 5-1			2	3	5[1]	8	6	9[3]			11			7	1			4			10[1]																
13 Mar	(A)	Maidstone	W 1-0	321		2	3	5	8		10			11			7	1			4			6															9[1]
20 Mar	(H)	Oxford	W 2-0			2	3	5	7		10[1]			11			6	1			4			8															9[1]
29 Mar	(A)	Wycombe	L 0-2			2	3	5		6	10			11			7	1			4						8	12											9
3 Apr	(H)	Kingstonian	W 2-0			2	3	5		7	10			11[2]			6	1	8		4																	9
10 Apr	(H)	Clapton o.g.	W 4-0			2	3	5	7	8	10[1]			11			6	1			4[2]			12															9
13 Apr	(A)	Wealdstone	L 0-3			2	3	5	7	6	11			10			8	1			4			12															9
17 Apr	(H)	Hendon	L 1-3			2	3	5		8	10			11			6	1		12[1]	4			7															9
23 Apr	(A)	Enfield	L 0-3			2	3	5	10	6	7			11					8	9	4					1												
7 May	(A)	St. Albans	W 1-0			2	3	5		6	9							1	11[1]		4				7		8											10
F.A. CUP																																						
5 Sep	Pr (H)	East Grinstead	W 2-0			2	3	5	4	6	7		11[1]				8	1	10[1]																			9
19 Sep	1st Q (A)	Worthing	W 2-0			2	3	4			7		9[2]				8	1	11		6											5							10
10 Oct	2nd Q (A)	Crawley	L 1-3			2	3	6	4	7	9		11				8	1	12			5																	10[1]
F.A. AMATEUR CUP																																						
28 Nov	4th Q (A)	Swaythling	D 0-0			2	3	5	4	7	8		10				6	1						11															9
5 Dec	Rep (H)	Swaythling	W 2-1			2	3	5		6	7		12	11[1]			4	1	8					10															9[1]
9 Jan	1st R (A)	Finchley	L 1-2			2	3	4		8	9		12[1]	11			5	1			6			7															10
SURREY SENIOR CUP																																						
16 Jan	1st R (H)	Kingstonian	W 3-0			2	3	5		7			11[1]	10			4	1			6			8	12														9[2]
13 Feb	2nd R (A)	Dulwich	W 1-0			2	3	5	4	7			11	8					1			6			9															10[1]
27 Mar	S-F (H)	Sutton	W 1-0			2	3	5	7	8[1]	10			11			6	1			4			12															9
1 May	F	(Redhill) Walton & H	L 0-3			2	3	5	7	8	11			9			6	1			4																	10
PREMIER FLOODLIT LEAGUE																																						
20 Oct	(H)	Horsham	W 4-1			4	3	5	6[1]	7			11[1]						1	9			10[2]			8						2									
26 Oct	(A)	Wokingham	L 0-1			2	3	5		6		4	11				10		7			8									1									9
3 Nov	(H)	Kingstonian	W 2-1			2	3	5			7[1]	11					4	1	8	10		6																	9[1]
10 Nov	(A)	Addlestone	L 1-3			2	3	4	7	6			9						1	11[1]	10	8														5					
17 Nov	(H)	Crawley	L 1-2			2	3	5	11	6[1]	7			9			4	1						8					10										
24 Nov	(A)	Leatherhead	D 4-4			2	3	5	11	6[1]	8[1]			7			4	1	10	12																			9[2]
22 Dec	(H)	Wokingham	W 3-1			2	3	5	6[2]					10			4			7	11				8					1							12		9[1]
12 Jan	(H)	Leatherhead	L 2-3			2	3	4			6		10	8					1			5				7				11[2]										9
3 Feb	(A)	Redhill	L 1-2			2	3		6	10	8			11[1]			5	1			4				7														9
17 Feb	(A)	Horsham	W 2-1			2	3	5	4[1]		7			11[1]		6		1	10	8	9																		
2 Mar	(A)	Kingstonian	D 0-0			2	3	4	7	6	9			11			8	1			5						12	10												
11 Mar	(H)	Addlestone	W 1-0			2	3	5	7	8	12[1]			10			6	1	11		4								9									
22 Mar	(H)	Redhill	D 0-0			2	3	5	8	7	9			10			6		11		4					1	12											
22 Apr	(A)	Crawley	L 0-1			2	3											11		8	7	4				6	1	10							5	9		12	
TOTAL APPEARANCES					5	62	62	59	43	53	53	11	27	33	3	3	47	52	28	9	32	9		18	6	3	3	1	3	2	1	1	1	1	1			50
SUBSTITUTE													2	1	6		1	1			1	4			1	3	2		2	1									1	1	
GOALS SCORED								2	8	5	11		12	8	1				9	1	2	2		4	1				2										20

ISTHMIAN LEAGUE

SEASON 1971-1972

Date	Venue	Opponents	Result	Attendance	Collyer, D.	Finn, B.	Finn, P.	Elton, R.	Edwards, D.	Smith, T.	Leonard, D.	Pentecost, A.	Elliott, M.	Oram, K.	Gale, D.	Christmas, A.	Cheeseman, D.	Johnson, R.	Chapple, G.	Harding, S.	Higgs, R.	Pattison, M.	Baker, S.	Webb, A.	Boardman	Van den Berg, H.	Edwards, A.	Carney, M.
14 Aug	(H)	St. Albans	L 1-3		1	2	3	4	5	6	7	8	9	10[1]	11	12												
17 Aug	(A)	Tooting	L 0-2		1	2	3		5	6	7	8	10	9	11	4												
21 Aug	(A)	Walthamstow	L 3-5		1	2	3		5	10	7[1]	8[1]	11	9[1]			4	6										
24 Aug	(H)	Oxford	W 4-1		1	2	3	4	5[1]	12		8[2]	10	9[1]	11	6			7									
28 Aug	(H)	Hendon	D 1-1		1	2	3	4	5	8	12	7	10	9[1]	11	6												
31 Aug	(A)	Dulwich	W 2-0		1	2	3	4	5	6	11	8	10		9[2]	7												
4 Sep	(A)	Bromley	L 1-2		1	2	3	4	5	8	6	7[1]	11	9	10													
11 Sep	(H)	Hitchin	D 2-2		1	2	3	6	4	12	8[1]	7	11[1]	10		9				5								
14 Sep	(A)	Walton	D 0-0	1,400	1	2	3		4	8		7	11	9	10			6		5								
25 Sep	(A)	Leytonstone	L 0-1		1	2	5			6	7	8	11	9	10			4		3								
28 Sep	(H)	Sutton	L 1-4		1	2	3	5[1]			12	6	8	9			7	10		4				11				
2 Oct	(H)	Bishops Stortford	W 3-1		1	2[1]	3	8		6		7[1]	10[1]	9	12		11	5		4								
5 Oct	(A)	Kingstonian	D 1-1		1	2	3[1]	6	5	7		8	10	9			4	11										
9 Oct	(H)	Ilford	D 1-1		1	2	3	4	5	7		12	8	9[1]	10		11	6										
13 Oct	(A)	Oxford	W 2-1		1	2	3	4	5	7		6[2]	10			8	11		9									
16 Oct	(A)	Enfield	L 0-1		1	2	3	5	4	6		7	10	12		11	8		9									
23 Oct	(H)	Clapton	W 4-1		1	2	3	4	5	8		10[1]	11	9[1]			6[1]		7[1]									
26 Oct	(H)	Wycombe	L 0-4		1	2	3	4	5	8		10	11	9			6		7									
30 Oct	(A)	Barking	W 2-0		1	2	3[1]	4	5	6		10	11	9[1]			7	8										
2 Nov	(H)	Hayes	L 0-1		1	2	3	4	5	7		8	10			11	6					9						
6 Nov	(H)	Leytonstone	W 4-0		1	2	3	4	5	7		8[1]	10[2]	9[1]		11			6									
13 Nov	(A)	Hendon	L 0-2		1	2	3	4	5	6		10	11	9					7	8								
16 Nov	(H)	Corinthian Casuals	W 3-0		1	2	3	4	5	6		9[1]	11	10					8[1]	7[1]								
27 Nov	(H)	Enfield	L 1-4		1	2	3	8	4	6		10	11	9[1]					7	5								
4 Dec	(H)	Walton	L 0-1		1	2	3	8	4	6		10	11	9					7	5								
11 Dec	(A)	Wycombe	L 0-1		1	2	3	6	5	7	12	11	10						8	4	9							
18 Dec	(H)	Walthamstow o.g.	D 1-1		1	2	3		5	6	8	11	12	9					7	4	10							
1 Jan	(A)	Corinthian Casuals	D 1-1		1	2	3	5		8	9	11		10[1]		6			7	4	12							
22 Jan	(A)	Ilford	D 1-1		1	2	3	4[1]	5	6	8	10		9					7	11	12							
5 Feb	(H)	Dulwich	W 2-0		1	2	3	6	5	7	8	10		9[2]						4	11							
26 Feb	(A)	Sutton	D 1-1		1	2	3		4	7	10	11				6	5		9		8[1]	12						
4 Mar	(A)	Clapton	W 3-1		1	2	3		4	7[1]	10[1]	11		9		6	5		8[1]									
11 Mar	(H)	Tooting	L 1-2		1	2	4		5	8	9	10[1]		11		3	6		7									
18 Mar	(A)	Hayes	L 1-2		1	2	3			6		8		9[1]		5			7	4	10		11					
1 Apr	(A)	Bishops Stortford	L 0-1		1	2	3		5	6	8	11		9					7	4	10							
8 Apr	(A)	St. Albans	L 1-2		1	2	3	11	5	6		8		9[1]			10		7	4								
11 Apr	(H)	Bromley	L 0-1		1	2	3	7		6	9	11		10			5		8	4								
15 Apr	(H)	Barking	W 1-0		1	2	3	5		6	8	11	10	9[1]			12		7	4								
21 Apr	(H)	Kingstonian	L 1-3		1	2	3	5		6	8[1]	9	10				11		7	4								
29 Apr	(A)	Hitchin	D 2-2		1	2	3	6	4	8	7	10		9[1]					11[1]	5								
F.A. CUP																												
18 Sep	1st Q (A)	Slough	D 1-1		1	4	3			8		7	10	9	11[1]	2		6		5								
21 Sep	Rep (H)	Slough	L 0-2		1	4	3		5		11	8	12	9	10	2		7		6								
F.A. AMATEUR CUP																												
20 Nov	4th Q (A)	Wembley	W 2-0		1	2	3	7	4	6[1]		11	8[1]	10					9	5								
8 Jan	1st R (H)	Alton	W 3-1	621	1	2	3		4	6	11	8[1]		9					7	5	10[2]							
29 Jan	2nd R (H)	North Shields	W 1-0	1,341	1	2	3	4	5	6	7	10[1]		9						8	11							
19 Feb	3rd R (H)	Blyth Spartans	L 0-3	2,116	1	2	3	5	4	6	8	9		10					7		11							
SURREY SENIOR CUP																												
15 Jan	1st R (H)	Corinthian Casuals	W 3-0		1	2	3	4	5	6	11	8		9[3]					7		10							
12 Feb	2nd R (H)	Carshalton	W 1-0		1	2	3	7	5	6	8	10		9[1]						4	12	11						
25 Mar	S-F (H)	Sutton	W 2-1	830	1	2	3		5	6	8	10		9[2]					7	4	11							
5 May	F	(Kingston) Walton	W 1-0	2,000	1	2	3	7	5	6	11	10[1]		9			12		8	4								
PREMIER FLOODLIT LEAGUE																												
10 Nov	(A)	Redhill	W 2-1		1		3					9[2]	11				2		7	4	8			5	6	10		
23 Nov	(H)	Leatherhead	W 1-0		1	2		3	4	10			11			8	6	12	7	5	9[1]							
29 Nov	(A)	Tooting	D 0-0			2	3	5			9	11	10			7			8	6	4						1	
14 Dec	(H)	Guildford City	W 1-0		1	2	3	5		6	11	8		9					7[1]	4	10							
22 Dec	(A)	Horsham	L 0-3		12	2		5	4	7	8	1	11	10		3		6			9							
28 Dec	(H)	Walton	L 1-2		1	2	3	4	5	6	12	8	11	9[1]					7		10							
17 Jan	(A)	Guildford City	W 3-1		1	2	3	6	4		7[1]			11		8[1]		10		5	9[1]							
25 Jan	(H)	Dulwich o.g.	W 1-0		1	2	3	4	5	7	9	10				6		8			11							
1 Feb	(H)	Horsham	L 1-3		1	2	3		5	6	9	7[1]				10		8		4			12			11		
8 Feb	(H)	Redhill	L 0-2		1	2	3	6	5	8	7	11		9						4	10							
14 Mar	(H)	Tooting	W 3-1		1	2	3	11		8[1]		10[1]					6		7	5	9		4[1]			12		
21 Mar	(A)	Leatherhead	L 1-2		1	2	3	5			11	9		12			6[1]		8	4	10					7		
28 Mar	(A)	Walton	D 0-0			2	3	5	4	9	11	10					8		7	6							1	
25 Apr	(A)	Dulwich	D 1-1		1	2	3	4			10		11				6		7	5			9					8[1]
TOTAL APPEARANCES					61	63	62	48	49	55	37	60	36	48	11	22	23	14	39	40	22	2	3	2	1	3	2	1
SUBSTITUTE					1					2	4	1	2	2	1	1	2	1			3	1	1			1		
GOALS SCORED						1	2	2	1	3	5	18		23	3	1	2		5	1	5		1					1

ISTHMIAN LEAGUE

SEASON 1972-1973

Date	Venue	Opponents	Result	Attendance	Collyer, D.	Finn, B.	Christmas, A.	Edwards, D.	Smith, T.	Elton, R.	Leonard, D.	Cheeseman, D.	Oram, K.	Elliott, M.	Van den Berg, H.	Baker, S.	Chapple, G.	Harding, S.	Braithwaite,R.	Gale, D.	Finn, P.	Carney, M.	Haddow, P.	Hounsell, J.	Cross, N.	Wheatley, A.	Grondona, J.	Palinski, G.
12 Aug	(A)	Bromley	W 2-1		1	2	3	4	5	6	7[1]	8	9[1]	10	11	12												
15 Aug	(H)	Wycombe	L 0-2		1	2	5	4	6		9	3	10	11	8	12	7											
19 Aug	(H)	St. Albans	W 2-0		1	2	3	4	6	10	8[1]	5	9		11	7[1]												
22 Aug	(A)	Leatherhead	D 1-1		1	2	3	4	6	7	8	5	10[1]			9	11											
26 Aug	(A)	Hitchin	L 1-2		1	2	3	5	6	8	11[1]	4	9	10	7													
29 Aug	(H)	Leatherhead	W 2-0		1	2[1]		4	6		11[1]	10	9				7	5	8		3							
2 Sep	(H)	Clapton	D 1-1		1	2		4	7		10	6	9[1]	12			11	5	8		3							
5 Sep	(A)	Oxford	W 4-1		1	2[1]		5	7		10[1]	6		9[1]			11	4	8[1]		3							
9 Sep	(A)	Ilford	L 0-1		1	2		5	10	9	11	8					6	4	7		3							
12 Sep	(H)	Hayes	D 2-2		1	2		5	7		10[1]	6	9[1]				11	4	8		3							
19 Sep	(A)	Dulwich	L 1-4		1	2		5	7		10[1]	4	9				11	6	8		3							
23 Sep	(H)	Leytonstone	W 3-2		1	2	11	4	6		8[2]	12	9			10	7[1]	3	5									
26 Sep	(H)	Oxford	W 2-1		1	2	3	5	6		9		8			11[1]	10[1]	4	7									
30 Sep	(A)	Enfield	L 0-1		1	2	3	5	11	7	9	10				12	8	4	6									
3 Oct	(A)	Walton	L 0-2		1	2	3	5	7		10	9			11		8	4	6									
10 Oct	(A)	Kingstonian	L 0-2		1	2	3		8		9	5	10				7	4	6	11								
24 Oct	(H)	Walton	W 1-0		1	2	11	4			8[1]	5	10			9	7		6		3							
28 Oct	(A)	Barking	W 2-1		1	4		5			11[1]	6	10[1]			9	7		2		3	8						
31 Oct	(H)	Kingstonian	D 3-3		1	2		5			8	6				9	7[2]		4		3	11[1]	10					
4 Nov	(H)	Bromley	W 3-0		1	4		5			11	6	10[2]			9	7[1]		2		3			8				
7 Nov	(H)	Sutton	L 1-2		1	4		5			10	6	11			9[1]	7		2		3			8				
11 Nov	(H)	Enfield	W 2-1		1	4		5			11[1]	6	10[1]		12	9	7		2		3			8				
18 Nov	(A)	St. Albans	W 3-1		1	2[1]		5			9[1]	6	11[1]			10	7		4		3				8	12		
21 Nov	(A)	Wycombe	W 2-1		1	2		5			9[1]	6	10[1]			11	7		4		3			8				
25 Nov	(H)	Hendon	L 0-3		1	4		5			9	6	11			8	7		2		3			10				
28 Nov	(A)	Tooting	L 1-4		1	4		5			11	6				9	7		2	10[1]	3	12		8				
23 Dec	(A)	Sutton	L 0-1		1	4	8	5		3	11	6	10			7				9					2			
30 Dec	(H)	Corinthian Casuals	W 3-0		1	4[1]		5[1]		3	11	6	9			8	7[1]			10					2			
6 Jan	(A)	Walthamstow	L 0-1		1	4	6	5		3	8					11	10			7			9		2			
20 Jan	(H)	Bishops Stortford	L 1-3		1	4		5		3	9		10[1]			8	7			11				6	2			
27 Jan	(A)	Corinthian Casuals	W 3-1		1	4		5		3	10[1]	7[1]	11[1]			8				9		6			2			
3 Feb	(H)	Dulwich	D 1-1		1	4		5		3	9	6				8				10[1]		11		2	7			
17 Feb	(A)	Clapton	D 0-0		1	4	7	5			11	6	9			8			2	10					3		12	
24 Feb	(H)	Tooting	W 3-2		1	4[1]	8[1]	5			7	6	10			12			2	11					3		9[1]	
3 Mar	(H)	Ilford	L 0-2		1		2	5			7	6	9			8				11				4	3		10	
10 Mar	(H)	Walthamstow	W 2-1		1	4	7	5			11[1]	6[1]	10			8								2	3		9	
24 Mar	(A)	Leytonstone	W 3-0		1	4		5			11[1]	6	9			8	7							2	3		10[2]	
3 Apr	(H)	Barking	W 5-0		1	4		5			11[1]	6	9[3]				7		8		3			2			10[1]	12
7 Apr	(A)	Bishops Stortford	D 0-0		1	4		5			11	6	9			12	7		8		3			2			10	
10 Apr	(A)	Hendon	L 0-1		1	4		5			11	6	9				7		8	10	3			2				
21 Apr	(H)	Hitchin	D 0-0		1	4		5			11	6	9			8	7		2	12	3						10	
24 Apr	(A)	Hayes	L 1-4		1	4		5			11	6	9			8	7[1]		2	12	3						10	
F.A. CUP																												
16 Sep	1st Q (A)	Maidenhead	W 1-0		1	2		5	11		10[1]	8	9				6	4	7		3							
7 Oct	2nd Q (A)	Biggleswade	W 2-0		1	2	3	5	11		10[1]	8	9				6	4	7[1]									
21 Oct	3rd Q (A)	Dartford	L 2-3		1	4	2	5			11[1]	8	10			9	7		6		3[1]							
F.A. AMATEUR CUP																												
9 Dec	1st R (A)	Oxford	L 1-2		1	2	6	4				10				8[1]	9		5	11	3			7				
SURREY SENIOR CUP																												
13 Jan	1st R (A)	Sutton	W 5-1		1	4		5[1]		3	11[1]		10[3]			8	7			9				6	2			
10 Feb	2nd R (H)	Westfield	W 4-0		1	4		5			11[1]	6	9[1]			8	7		2	10[2]					3			
31 Mar	S-F (H)	Walton	L 1-3		1	4		5			11	6	10[1]			9	7		8		3			2				
SURREY SENIOR SHIELD																												
17 Apr	1st R (H)	Tooting	L 1-3		1	4		5			11	6				8	7		9	12	3			2			10[1]	
SURREY COMBINATION CUP																												
12 Apr	(A)	Tooting	L 1-4		1	4		5			10	6				9[1]	7	3	8	11				2				
TOTAL APPEARANCES					**51**	**50**	**20**	**50**	**18**	**13**	**50**	**46**	**40**	**4**	**5**	**33**	**41**	**14**	**36**	**16**	**26**	**4**	**2**	**19**	**14**		**9**	
SUBSTITUTE												**1**		**1**	**1**	**5**				**3**		**1**				**1**	**1**	**1**
GOALS SCORED						**5**	**1**	**2**			**23**	**2**	**20**	**1**		**5**	**7**		**2**	**4**	**1**	**1**					**5**	

ISTHMIAN LEAGUE

SEASON 1973-1974

Date	Venue	Opponents	Result	Atten-dance	Collyer, D.	Christmas, A.	Underwood, R.	Finn, B.	Edwards, D.	Cooper, G.	Chapple, G.	Cheeseman, D.	Oram, K.	Grondona, J.	Leonard, D.	Bennett, M.	Hutchins, D.	Palinski, G.	Baker, S.	Reynolds, V.	Roberts, A.	Blount, K.	Cassidy, J.	Edwards, A.	Steer, R.	Wiltshire, T.	Molloy, T.	Forbes, R.	Whatford, M.	Carter, G.	Haddow, G.
18 Aug	(H)	Bishops Stortford o.g.	W 2-1		1	2	3	4	5	6	7	8	9[1]	10	11	12															
21 Aug	(A)	Leatherhead	L 1-3		1	2	3	4	5	6[1]	7	8		10	11		9	12													
25 Aug	(H)	Clapton	W 2-0		1	2	3	4	5	6	7	8	12	9[2]	11		10														
28 Aug	(A)	Tooting	L 0-1		1	2	3	4	5	6	7	8	9	10	11		12														
5 Sep	(A)	Oxford	D 2-2		1	2	3	4	5[1]	6[1]	7	8	9	10			11														
8 Sep	(A)	Corinthian Casuals	W 3-0		1	2	3	4	5[1]	6	7[1]		9[1]	10			11		8												
11 Sep	(H)	Oxford	L 1-3		1	2	3	4	5	6	7	8	9	10[1]			11														
2 Oct	(A)	Wycombe	L 2-3		1		3	4	5	6	7	2	9[2]	10						8	11										
9 Oct	(A)	Sutton	L 0-2		1	2	3	4	5	6	7		9	10						8	11										
16 Oct	(H)	Tooting	W 2-1		1		3	2	5	4	7			9[1]		11	10[1]			8	6										
27 Oct	(A)	Leytonstone	L 1-4		1		3	2	5	4	7			9		11	10[1]		12	8	6										
3 Nov	(H)	Walthamstow	W 2-1		1		3	2	5	4	7			9		11	10[1]			8	6[1]										
6 Nov	(H)	Leatherhead	L 0-4		1		3	2	5	4	7			9		11	10			8	6		12								
13 Nov	(H)	Sutton	W 2-1				3	2[1]	5	4		7		9[1]		11	10			8	6			1							
24 Nov	(H)	Barking	W 2-0		1		3		5	4	7	2	12[1]	9		11	10			8	6[1]										
8 Dec	(H)	Walton o.g.	W 3-2		1		3		5[1]	4	7	2	11	9[1]			10		12	8	6										
15 Dec	(A)	Clapton	W 4-1		1		3		5[1]	4	7	2[1]	10[1]	9		11				8[1]	6										
9 Mar	(A)	Walthamstow	W 2-1		1		3		5[1]	4	6	2	8[1]	9			12				7				10	11					
23 Mar	(H)	Leytonstone	W 3-2		1		3		5	4	7[2]	2	10	9[1]			8								11	6					
26 Mar	(H)	Wycombe	W 1-0		1	6	3		5	4	7	2	8	10[1]			9								11						
28 Mar	(A)	Hayes	D 0-0		1	2	3		5	4				9		12	8			7	11					6	10				
30 Mar	(A)	Barking	L 0-2		1				5	4	7	2	9				11			6	3				10	12	8				
1 Apr	(A)	Kingstonian	W 1-0		1		3		5	4	7	2	9	10			12				6				11		8[1]				
4 Apr	(H)	Bromley	W 2-1		1		3		5	4	7	2		9[1]			10[1]			8	6				11						
6 Apr	(H)	Hitchin o.g.	W 2-1		1		3		5	4	7	2	8	9[1]			11				6						10				
9 Apr	(A)	Enfield o.g.	D 2-2		1		3		5	4	7	2		9[1]			10		12	8					11	6					
11 Apr	(H)	Kingstonian	W 1-0		1		3		5	4[1]	7	2	10	9						8					11			6			
13 Apr	(A)	Ilford	L 0-3		1	8	3		5		7	2	10	9			4								12	6	11				
15 Apr	(H)	Enfield	D 1-1		1		3		5	4	7	2	10	9						8					11[1]			6			
17 Apr	(H)	Hayes	D 0-0		1		3		5	4		2	10	9			7		6	11					8		12				
19 Apr	(H)	St. Albans	W 2-0		1		3		5	4	7	2		9			10[1]				8						11[1]		6		
23 Apr	(A)	Bromley	W 4-0		1		3		5[1]	4[1]	7	2	10	9[2]			8			6					11						
25 Apr	(A)	St. Albans	W 3-0		1				5	4	7	2		9[2]		12	10		3	8	6[1]						11				
27 Apr	(A)	Hitchin	W 2-0		1		3			4	7	2		10[1]			9			8[1]	6						11		5		
30 Apr	(H)	Dulwich o.g.	W 2-1		1		3		5	4	7	2		9[1]			10			8	6						11				
2 May	(H)	Corinthian Casuals	W 3-1	620	1		3		5	4		2	10[1]	9[1]							8				11			7	6[1]		
7 May	(A)	Dulwich	L 0-2		1		3		5	4		2	10	9			7			8	6						11	12			
9 May	(A)	Hendon	L 0-2		1		3		5	4				9			10			8	6				7		11	12	2		
11 May	(H)	Ilford	L 0-2		1		3		5	4	7	2	12	9			10				6						11	8			
14 May	(H)	Hendon	D 1-1		1		3		5	4[1]	7	2	10	9			8				6						11				
16 May	(A)	Walton	L 1-2		1					3	6	2	8[1]	9			11				5				7		10		4		
18 May	(A)	Bishops Stortford	L 1-2		1		3		5	4	6	2	10			9	8				7				11[1]		12				
F.A. CUP																															
1 Sep	Prel (H)	Tonbridge	W 2-1		1	2	3	4	5	6	7	11	9[2]	10	8																
15 Sep	1st Q (A)	Farnborough	D 2-2		1	2	3	4[1]	5	6	7[1]		9	10			12		11				8								
18 Sep	Rep (H)	Farnborough	D 2-2		1	12	3	4[1]	5	6	7	2	9	10[1]			11		8												
24 Sep	2nd Rep	(G'ford) Farnborough	W 2-1	855	1		3	4	5	6	7	2	9[1]	10[1]				11		8											
6 Oct	2nd Q (A)	Wycombe	L 0-1		1	2	3	4	5	6	7		9	10						8	11									12	
F.A. AMATEUR CUP																															
12 Jan	1st R (A)	Walthamstow	W 2-1		1		3		5	4	7[1]	2	10[1]	9			8				6				11						
26 Jan	2nd R (A)	Horsham o.g.	D 2-2	1,301	1		3		5		7	2[1]	10	9			8		4		6				11						
2 Feb	Rep (H)	Horsham	W 3-2		1		3		5	4	7	2	9[2]	10[1]			8				6				11						
16 Feb	3rd R (A)	Aveley	D 1-1		1		3		5	4	7	2	9[1]	10			12				6		8		11						
23 Feb	Rep (H)	Aveley	W 2-0		1		3		5	4	7	2	9[1]	10							6[1]				11	8					
2 Mar	4th R (A)	Ashington	L 0-2	1,900	1		3		5	4	7	2	8	9			11				6				10	12					
SURREY SENIOR CUP																															
19 Jan	1st R (H)	Leatherhead	D 2-2		1		3		5	4	7	2	10[2]	9					12		6				11	8					
16 Mar	Rep (A)	Leatherhead	L 0-1		1		3		5	4	7	2	9	8							6				10	11					
LONDON SENIOR CUP																															
22 Sep	1st Q (H)	Croydon	D 1-1		1	2		3	5	4	7		10	9[1]			11				6		12								8
29 Sep	Rep (A)	Croydon	W 1-0		1		3	8	5	4[1]	7	2	10	9				11			6										
13 Oct	2nd Q (A)	Redhill	D 1-1		1		3	2	5	4	7			10		11	9		12		6		8[1]								
20 Oct	Rep (H)	Redhill	W 3-0		1			2	5	4	7			10[2]		11[1]	9		3		6	12	8								
10 Nov	3rd Q (H)	Hoddesdon	D 1-1				3	2	5	4	7	8		9[1]		12	11		10		6			1							
17 Nov	Rep (A)	Hoddesdon	W 2-1		1		3	2	5	4	7	8		9[1]		11[1]	10		12		6										
1 Dec	1st R (A)	Walton AB	D 1-1	70 mins	1		3		5	4[1]	7	2	10	9		11	12		8		6										
22 Dec	1st R (A)	Walton	D 1-1		1		3		5	4	7	2	10[1]	9		11			8		6				12						
29 Dec	Rep (H)	Walton	L 2-3	AET	1		3		5	4	7	2	10[1]	9[1]			6		8						12		11				
TOTAL APPEARANCES					**62**	**15**	**59**	**25**	**62**	**62**	**58**	**51**	**53**	**62**	**5**	**13**	**43**	**2**	**13**	**25**	**44**		**4**	**2**	**23**	**8**	**15**	**4**	**5**		**1**
SUBSTITUTE						**1**							**3**			**4**	**6**	**1**	**4**			**1**	**2**		**3**	**2**	**2**	**2**		**1**	
GOALS SCORED								**3**	**6**	**7**	**5**	**2**	**21**	**27**		**2**	**5**			**2**	**4**		**1**		**2**		**2**		**1**		

SEASON 1974-1975

ISTHMIAN LEAGUE

Date	Venue	Opponents	Result	Attendance	Collyer, D.	Cheeseman, D.	Bell, M.	Cooper, G.	Whatford, M.	Forbes, R.	Roberts, A.	Woozley, B.	Oram, K.	Waughman, T.	Steer, R.	Reynolds, V.	Grondona, J.	Cassidy, J.	Molloy, T.	Imison, P.	Hill, A.	Osborne, R.	Blount, K.	Keen, N.	Lewer, A.	Cosham, S.	Rosser, M.	Poole, R.	Hawkett, G.
17 Aug	(H)	Tooting	L 1-2		1	2	3	4	5	6	7	8	9	10[1]	11	12													
21 Aug	(A)	Oxford	W 3-1		1	2[1]	3	4	5	7		6		10	11	8[1]	9[1]												
24 Aug	(A)	Dagenham	L 1-2		1	2	3	4	5	6	7	8	9[1]	10	11														
27 Aug	(H)	Hayes	D 1-1		1		3	4	5	7	6[1]	8	9	10		11		2											
31 Aug	(H)	Walthamstow	D 0-0		1	2	3	4	5	7		8	9	10		6			11										
3 Sep	(A)	Leatherhead	D 3-3		1	2[1]	3	4[1]	5	6		7	9	10[1]		11				8									
7 Sep	(A)	Enfield	L 0-1		1	2	3	4	5	6		8	9	10		7				11									
10 Sep	(A)	Kingstonian	W 3-1		1	2	3	4	5[1]	6		8	12	10[1]		7	9[1]			11									
21 Sep	(H)	Slough	D 3-3		1	2	3	4	5	11		7	9	10[1]			8[2]				6								
1 Oct	(A)	Hayes	L 0-2			2	3	4	5		8	7		10			9		11		6	1							
8 Oct	(H)	Kingstonian	L 0-1		1	2	3	4	5	8	7		12	10	11		9				6								
15 Oct	(A)	Sutton	L 0-2		1	2	3	4	5	8	10			7	11		9				6		12						
19 Oct	(H)	Clapton	W 3-2		1	2[1]	3	7	5	6	11			10[1]	8		9[1]				4								
26 Oct	(H)	Oxford	W 2-1		1	2	3	7	5[1]	6	11[1]			10	8		9				4								
2 Nov	(A)	Ilford	L 2-6		1	2	3	7	5	6	11[1]		9	10[1]	8			12			4								
9 Nov	(A)	Bromley	D 0-0		1	2	3	7	5	6	11		12	10	8		9				4								
12 Nov	(H)	Leatherhead	D 1-1		1	2	3	7	5	6			11	10	8		9[1]		12		4								
16 Nov	(H)	Dulwich	L 0-2		1	2	3	7	5		6		11	10	8		9		12		4								
19 Nov	(H)	Sutton	W 2-1		1	2	3	7	5		8			10	6[2]		9	4	11										
23 Nov	(H)	Walton o.g.	W 2-0		1	2	3		5	12	6			10	8		9[1]	4	11		7								
7 Dec	(A)	Barking	L 1-2		1	2		7	5	11	6			10	8		9[1]	4	12		3								
21 Dec	(A)	Tooting	L 0-2		1	12	2		5	11	6			10	8		9	7		3	4								
28 Dec	(H)	Dagenham	L 0-3		1		2	12	5	11	6			7	8		9	10		3	4								
4 Jan	(A)	Walthamstow	L 0-3		1		2	6	5	10	11			7			9	8		3	4			12					
4 Feb	(H)	Wycombe	L 0-4		1	2	3	4	5		6		9	10				7						11	8				
8 Feb	(A)	Clapton	L 0-1		1	2	3	4	5		6		9				10	7						11	8				
15 Feb	(A)	Leytonstone	L 0-1		1	2	3	7	5	6			12		11		9	4							8	10			
22 Feb	(A)	Hendon	L 0-3		1		2	7	5	6	11				8		9	4								10	3		
1 Mar	(H)	Bromley	W 4-1		1			7	5[1]	6	8		9[2]		11			2								10[1]	3	4	
4 Mar	(A)	Wycombe	L 0-3		1	6	2	7	5	8					11		9									10	3	4	
15 Mar	(A)	Bishops Stortford	D 2-2		1	11		7	5	6	8		9[1]		12			2								10[1]	3	4	
22 Mar	(A)	Hendon	L 1-4		1	11		7	5	6			9		8[1]			2								10	3	4	
29 Mar	(H)	Hitchin	L 1-2		1	8		7	5	6			9[1]		10		11	2									3	4	
8 Apr	(A)	Dulwich	D 1-1		1			7	5	11	6		9		8			2								10[1]	3	4	
12 Apr	(H)	Enfield	W 2-1		1		7		5	8	6				11		9	2								10[2]	3	4	12
15 Apr	(H)	Barking	W 2-0		1			7[1]	5		6		12		8		9	2								10	3	4	11[1]
19 Apr	(A)	Walton	W 4-1		1			7	5		6		9[1]		8			2								10[2]	3	4[1]	11
22 Apr	(A)	Slough	W 1-0		1			7	5		6		9		8			2								10	3	4	11[1]
25 Apr	(H)	Leytonstone	W 3-1		1		2	7	5	12	6		9		8											10[2]	3	4	11[1]
29 Apr	(H)	Bishops Stortford	D 1-1		1			7	5	12	6		9		8			2								10[1]	3	4	11
8 May	(A)	Hitchin	L 1-3		1			7	5		6				8		9	2					12[1]			10	3	4	11
10 May	(H)	Ilford	D 2-2		1			7	5		6				8		9	2								10[2]	3	4	11
F.A. CUP																													
14 Sep	1st Q (H)	Kingstonian	D 2-2		1	2	3	4	5	6		7	8	10[1]			9[1]			11									
17 Sep	Rep (A)	Kingstonian	W 2-1		1	2	3	4	5	6[1]	12	7	8	10			9[1]			11									
5 Oct	2nd Q (A)	Wokingham	L 1-2		1	2	3	4	5		8	7	12[1]	9			10		11	6									
F.A. TROPHY																													
30 Nov	3rd Q (A)	Sutton	L 0-3		1	2		7	5	6	11			10	8		9	4		3									
LONDON SENIOR CUP																													
28 Sep	1st Q (A)	Hounslow	L 1-2			2	3	4	5	6	8		10[1]	11		7	9		12			1							
SURREY SENIOR CUP																													
11 Jan	1st R (H)	Walton	L 0-1		1	2	3	4	5	6	8		9	11			10	7											
SURREY SENIOR SHIELD																													
1 Apr	1st R (H)	Dulwich	W 2-1		1			7	5[1]	11	6		9[1]		8			2								10	3	4	
3 May	S-F	Egham	W 5-0		1			7[1]	5		6		9		8[2]			2								10[2]	3	4	11
SOUTHERN COMBINATION CUP																													
2 Dec	1st R (H)	London University	W 2-0		1	2		7	5	6			9[1]	10[1]	8			4	11	3									
18 Mar	2nd R (H)	Farnborough	W 4-1		1	7			3	9	8[1]				6		10[1]	2							12	11[2]	5	4	
5 May	S-F (H)	Hampton	W 4-1		1			7	5		6				8		9[1]	2								10[3]	3	4	11
TOTAL APPEARANCES					**51**	**35**	**35**	**48**	**53**	**37**	**39**	**13**	**28**	**32**	**37**	**7**	**34**	**30**	**6**	**11**	**15**	**2**		**2**	**3**	**19**	**19**	**18**	**9**
SUBSTITUTE						**1**		**1**		**3**	**1**		**6**		**1**	**1**		**1**	**4**				**2**	**1**	**1**				**1**
GOALS SCORED						**3**		**3**	**4**	**1**	**4**		**10**	**8**	**5**	**1**	**12**						**1**			**19**		**1**	**3**

ISTHMIAN LEAGUE

SEASON 1975-1976

Date	Venue	Opponents	Result	Atten-dance	Spittle, P.	Lewer, A.	Rosser, M.	Poole, R.	Whatford, M.	Roberts, B.	Cooper, G.	Steer, R.	Morton, A.	Cosham, S.	Hawkett, G.	Roberts, A.	Cassidy, J.	Phillips	Hook, R.	Ireland	Brister, N.	Oram, K.	Turner, A.	Forbes, R.	Bennett, M.	Vincent, R.	McKinnon, P.	Grondona, J.	Brown, A.	Chapple, G.	Skinner, N.	Dakin, F.	Norman, C.	Blount, K.	Stratford, M.	Huxley, P.	Cottrell, D.
16 Aug	(H)	Dulwich	L 0-2	500	1	2	3	4	5	6	7	8	9	10	11	12																					
19 Aug	(A)	Southall	L 1-5		1			4	5		7	8	9[1]	10	11	6	2	3																			
23 Aug	(A)	Dagenham	D 2-2					3[1]	5	7	8		9[1]	10		6	2		4	11						1											
26 Aug	(H)	Staines	L 0-1			8		3	5		7	6	9		12		2		4	11		10				1											
30 Aug	(H)	Enfield	L 1-2		1			3	5	6	7	8	9[1]	10	11		2		4																		
2 Sep	(A)	Kingstonian	L 1-3		1			4	5		3	8	9[1]	10			2			7			6	11	12												
6 Sep	(A)	Hitchin	L 1-2				3	4	5			8	9				2			6		12	7		11	1		10[1]									
9 Sep	(H)	Sutton	L 0-1		1		3	4	5	6	7	8	9				2			11		12			10												
20 Sep	(A)	Ilford	L 1-2		1		3		5	11	7	8	9[1]	10		6	2						4														
23 Sep	(H)	Tooting	L 2-4		1		3[1]		5	4	7	8[1]	9	10		6	2								11												
27 Sep	(H)	Ilford	W 2-0				3		5	7	4	2	9	10[1]		6[1]									11	1			8								
4 Oct	(A)	Barking	L 0-1				3		5	7	4	2	9	10	11	6										1			8								
12 Oct	(H)	Clapton	W 2-0			12	3		5		4	2	9[1]	10[1]		6									11	1			8	7							
18 Oct	(A)	Leytonstone	W 1-0		1	11	3	5			4	2	9	10		6						12							8	7[1]							
21 Oct	(A)	Sutton	D 1-1				3	5	11		4		9[1]	10		6	2									1			8	7							
28 Oct	(H)	Kingstonian	W 6-1				3	4[1]	5		6		9[1]	10[2]			2							11[2]		1			8	7							
1 Nov	(H)	Barking	L 0-3				3	4	5		6		9	10			2							11		1			8	7	12						
4 Nov	(A)	Tooting	L 0-2				3	4	5		6	2	9	10			12							8		1				7	11						
8 Nov	(A)	Slough	L 1-4				3	4	5		8	2	9	10		6										1			12	7	11[1]						
11 Nov	(H)	Southall	D 3-3				3	4	5			2	9[3]	10		6										1			8	7	11						
15 Nov	(H)	Hayes	L 0-1				3	4	5			2	9	10		6													8	7	11	1					
18 Nov	(A)	Staines	L 0-1				3	4	5		12	2	9	10		6													8	7	11	1					
22 Nov	(A)	Oxford	W 2-1					2	5		4	6	9[2]	10															8	7	11		1	3			
13 Dec	(H)	Dagenham	W 2-1					3	5		4	2	9[1]	10		6[1]										1			8	7	11						
20 Dec	(A)	Enfield	L 0-1				12	3	5		4	2	9			6										1			8	7	11				10		
27 Dec	(H)	Hitchin	W 2-1				3	4	5			2	9[1]	10[1]		6								11		1			8	7							
10 Jan	(H)	Walthamstow	W 3-1				12	4	5		3	2	9[2]	10[1]		6								11									1			7	8
24 Jan	(A)	Walthamstow	D 1-1				6	4	5		3	2	9	10		12								11						7[1]			1				8
31 Jan	(A)	Clapton	W 5-1					4	5		3	2	9[2]	10[3]		6								11		1			8								7
7 Feb	(H)	Oxford o.g.	W 4-0					4	5		3	2	9[3]	10		7								11		1			8	12							6
10 Feb	(H)	Leatherhead o.g.	D 2-2					4	5		3	2	9	10[1]		6								11		1				8							7
14 Feb	(A)	Leatherhead	W 1-0					4	5		3	2	9	10		6													8[1]	12			1			11	7
28 Feb	(A)	Wycombe	D 1-1					4	5[1]		3	2	9	10		6								11					8	12			1				7
6 Mar	(H)	Leytonstone	D 1-1					4	5		3[1]	2	9			10								11					8	6			1				7
13 Mar	(A)	Hendon	D 0-0					4	5		3	2	9	12		10								11					7	6			1				8
16 Mar	(A)	Hayes	W 2-1					4	5		3	2	9[1]	10[1]		11								12					8	6			1				7
27 Mar	(H)	Bishops Stortford	W 1-0					4	5		3	2	9			6						10[1]		11						7			1				8
30 Mar	(A)	Dulwich	L 0-1					4	5		3	2	9			6								11						8			1		10		7
3 Apr	(H)	Slough	L 0-3					4	5		3	2	9	10		6								11					8				1		12		7
6 Apr	(H)	Wycombe	L 1-2						5		3	2	9	10[1]							6		4	11					8			1					7
23 Apr	(A)	Bishops Stortford	D 2-2					4	5		3		9	10[2]		6								11					8			1			2		7
27 Apr	(H)	Hendon	W 3-1					4	5		3	2	9[1]	10[2]										11					8			1			6		7
F.A. CUP																																					
13 Sep	1st Q (A)	Wealdstone	D 1-1		1		3	4	5	6[1]	7	8	9	10			2			11																	
16 Sep	Rep (H)	Wealdstone	L 3-5	AET	1		3		5		7	8	9[1]	10[2]		6	2						4		11												
F.A. TROPHY																																					
29 Nov	3rd Q (H)	Sutton	L 2-4				3	2	5		4	6				7[1]						10		11			12[1]		8				1	9			
LONDON SENIOR CUP																																					
25 Oct	1st R (H)	Redhill	W 3-1				3	4	5				9[2]	10[1]		6	2							11		1			8	7							
6 Dec	2nd R (A)	Hitchin	D 1-1				3		5		4	2		10		6						9				1			8[1]	7	11						
9 Dec	Rep (H)	Hitchin	W 2-1				3		5		4	2	11	10		6						9				1			8[1]	7	12[1]						
3 Jan	3rd R (A)	Enfield	L 1-3				12	4	5		3	2	9[1]	10		6								7					8				1		11		
SURREY SENIOR CUP																																					
17 Jan	1st R (A)	Leatherhead	W 2-0				8	4	5		3	2	9	10		6[1]								11[1]						7			1				
24 Feb	2nd R (H)	Addlestone	W 3-1					4	5		3	2	9[1]	10[2]		6								11					8	7			1				
20 Mar	S-F (A)	Sutton	D 2-2					4	5		3	2	9	10[1]		6								11[1]					8	7			1				
23 Mar	Rep (H)	Sutton	L 1-3				12	4	5		3	2	9	10[1]		6								11		1			8	7							
ROTHMANS CUP																																					
9 Mar	(H)	Hayes	W 3-0					4	5		3	2	9[2]	10[1]		11								12					8	6			1				7
25 Mar	(A)	Chesham	L 0-3	*Team not traced*																																	
SOUTHERN COMBINATION CUP																																					
8 Oct	1st R (H)	Virginia Water	W 5-1			[1]							[2]	[1]		[1]																					
SOUTHERN COMBINATION CUP SEASON 1974-75																																					
21 Aug	F	Addlestone	L 0-2	*Team not traced*																																	
SURREY SENIOR SHIELD SEASON 1974-75																																					
28 Aug	F	(Walton) Molesey	W 2-1		1			3	5	6	7	8[1]	9[1]	10	11		2		4																		
TOTAL APPEARANCES					**11**	**3**	**26**	**46**	**54**	**10**	**49**	**49**	**53**	**46**	**5**	**40**	**16**	**1**	**4**	**6**	**1**	**5**	**5**	**26**	**6**	**22**		**1**	**34**	**29**	**9**	**5**	**17**	**2**	**5**	**2**	**17**
SUBSTITUTE						**1**	**4**				**1**			**1**	**1**	**2**	**1**					**3**		**2**	**1**		**1**		**1**	**3**	**2**				**1**		
GOALS SCORED						**1**	**1**	**2**	**1**	**1**	**1**	**2**	**34**	**25**		**5**						**1**		**4**			**1**	**1**	**3**	**2**	**2**						

SEASON 1976-1977

ISTHMIAN LEAGUE

Date	Venue	Opponents	Result	Attendance	Overton, J.	Stratford, M.	Cooper, G.	Poole, R.	Whatford, M.	Cottrell, D.	Alexander, D.	Brown, A.	Morton, A.	Hill, S.	Roberts, A.	Forbes, R.	Godfrey, J.	Reeves, T.	Bateman, M.	Turner, A.	Brister, N.	McMorran, J.	Oram, K.	McKinnon, P.	Pearce, T.	Blount, K.	Dakin, F.	Pollard, R.	Finn, P.	Hill, H.	Cosham, S.	Davies, A.	Preston, M.	Cunningham, P.	Giddings, S.	Finn, T.
21 Aug	(H)	Enfield	D 2-2		1	2	3	4	5	6	7	8	9[1]	10[1]	11																					
24 Aug	(A)	Staines	L 0-1	660	1	2	3	4	5	6	7	8	9	10	11	12																				
28 Aug	(A)	Hitchin	L 0-2		1	2	3	4	5	6	7	8	9	10	11																					
31 Aug	(H)	Kingstonian	W 2-0		1	2	3	4	5	6	7[1]	8	9	10[1]	11																					
4 Sep	(H)	Bishops Stortford o.g.	L 1-2		1	2	3	4	5	6	7	8		10	11		9	12																		
7 Sep	(A)	Sutton	W 2-1		1	2	3	4	5	6	9	8		10[1]	11		7[1]		12																	
11 Sep	(A)	Walthamstow	W 2-1		1	2	3		5		6	8[1]		10			9		7	4	11[1]															
14 Sep	(H)	Croydon	L 0-1		1	2	3	4	5		7	8		10			9		11	6	12															
21 Sep	(A)	Tooting	D 1-1		1	2	3	4	5	6	7	8		10[1]			12			9	11															
25 Sep	(A)	Barking	W 2-1		1	2	3	4	5		7	8		10[1]			6[1]			9	11															
28 Sep	(H)	Tooting	W 5-0		1	11	3	2	5[1]		7[1]	8[1]	9[1]	10			6[1]			4																
6 Oct	(H)	Staines	D 1-1		1	2	3	6	5		7[1]	8	9	10			11			4																
19 Oct	(H)	Sutton	L 0-2		1	7	3	2	5		6	8	9	10	12		11			4																
13 Nov	(A)	Wycombe	L 0-1		1	2	3	4	5	6	7	8	9	10			11					12														
23 Nov	(A)	Slough	L 2-4		1	2	5	3	4	6	7	8		10[1]	11[1]							9														
27 Nov	(A)	Dulwich o.g.	D 2-2		1	2	3	4	5	6	7	8		10[1]	11					12		9														
4 Dec	(H)	Dagenham	L 0-5		1	2	3	4	5	6	7	8	12	9	11		10																			
11 Dec	(H)	Dulwich	L 0-2		1	2	3	4	5	6	7	8	9		11		10			12																
18 Dec	(A)	Enfield	L 0-1		1	8	3	4	5	6	7		9		12	11				2			10													
20 Dec	(A)	Croydon o.g.	W 2-0		1	7	3	4	5	6	12	8	9[1]		11					2			10													
1 Jan	(A)	Bishops Stortford	W 2-1		1	2	3	4		6	7	8[1]	9		11					5			10[1]													
3 Jan	(H)	Tilbury	D 2-2		1	8	3	4	5	6	7[1]		9[1]							2			10	11												
8 Jan	(H)	Walthamstow	L 1-3		1	2	3		5	6	7	8		9[1]	11					4			10	12												
22 Jan	(H)	Barking	L 2-3		1	2	3	4	5	6	7	8	9	10[1]	11[1]										12											
29 Jan	(A)	Tilbury	L 0-2		1	8	3	4	5	6	7		9	10	12					2					11											
1 Feb	(A)	Kingstonian	L 0-1		1	8	3	4	5	6	7	9		10						2					11											
5 Feb	(H)	Leytonstone	D 3-3		1	8	3	4	5	6	7	9[1]		10[1]						2			12[1]		11											
12 Feb	(A)	Ilford	L 0-1		1	11	3	4		6	7	8		10						2			9		12	5										
15 Feb	(H)	Southall	L 1-2		1	8	3	4	5	6	7	9	10							2			11[1]													
19 Feb	(H)	Hendon	L 2-4		1	11	3	4	5	6	7		9	12						2			10[1]		8[1]											
26 Feb	(A)	Leatherhead	W 1-0					4		5	6		8							12			10		9		1	2	3	7	11[1]					
5 Mar	(A)	Hayes	D 1-1					4		5	6[1]		11							3			9		8		1	2		7	10					
12 Mar	(H)	Wycombe	L 0-3					4		5	9	6	11							3			12		8		1	2		7	10					
19 Mar	(A)	Southall	W 1-0					12	3	8	6	5	11										9					2		7	10[1]	1	4			
22 Mar	(H)	Hayes	D 2-2						3	6	8	5	9												12			2		7	10[1]	1	4	11[1]		
2 Apr	(A)	Dagenham	D 0-0					5	3	10	6	8	11			12												2		7		1	4	9		
9 Apr	(H)	Ilford	D 0-0						3	6	9	5	11			12									8			2		7	10	1	4			
16 Apr	(A)	Hendon	D 1-1					5	3	6	8[1]	2	9												11					7	10	1	4			
23 Apr	(H)	Leatherhead	W 2-0					5	3	6		2	11[1]								12				8					7	10[1]	1	4		9	
25 Apr	(H)	Slough	W 1-0					5	3	6	11[1]	2	9												8					7	10	1	4			
30 Apr	(A)	Leytonstone	L 0-1					5	3	6	11	2	9								7				8						10	1	4			12
7 May	(H)	Hitchin	D 1-1					5	3	6	11	2	9[1]												8					7	10	1	4	12		
F.A. CUP																																				
18 Sep	1st Q (H)	Burgess Hill	W 3-1	318	1	2	3	4	5[1]	6	7	8[1]	12	10[1]	11					9																
9 Oct	2nd Q (A)	Croydon	D 0-0		1	6	3	2	5		7	8	9	10			11			4																
12 Oct	Rep (H)	Croydon	W 2-0	462	1	6	3	2	5		7	8	9[1]	10[1]			11			4																
23 Oct	3rd Q (A)	Aveley	D 1-1		1	6	3	2	5		7	8	9	10[1]	12		11			4																
26 Oct	Rep (H)	Aveley o.g.	W 4-0	402	1	2	3		5	6	7	8	9[1]	10[1]	12		11[1]			4																
6 Nov	4th Q (H)	Slough	D 0-0	813	1	2	3	4	5	6	9	8	12	10	11		7																			
9 Nov	Rep (A)	Slough	W 1-0	1,041	1	2	3	4	5	6	7	8	9	10[1]	11		12																			
20 Nov	1st R (A)	Wimbledon	L 0-1	2,266	1	2	3	4	5	6	7	8	9	10	11		12																			
F.A. TROPHY																																				
30 Oct	1st Q (A)	Horsham	L 0-1	500	1	2	3		5	6	12	8	9	10	7		11			4																
SURREY SENIOR CUP																																				
15 Jan	1st R (A)	Tooting	L 1-2		1	2	3	4	5[1]	6	7	8	9	10	11										12											
LONDON SENIOR CUP																																				
16 Oct	1st R (H)	Leyton-Wingate	L 1-2		1	6	3	2	5	8	7	12[1]	9	10			11			4																
ROTHMANS CUP																																				
14 Dec	1st R (A)	Maidenhead	W 6-0		1	8	3	4	5	6	7[1]		9[3]			11				2		10[2]		12												
25 Jan	2nd R (H)	Wembley	W 4-0		1	2	3	4		6[1]	11		9	10[1]	8[1]					5					7[1]											
29 Mar	3rd R (A)	St. Albans	W 1-0	AET				5	3	6	9[1]	8											10					2		7		1	4	11		
12 Apr	4th R (H)	Hendon	L 0-2					12	3	6	8	11	9			10									5	2				7		1	4			
SURREY CENTENARY CUP																																				
22 Feb	(H)	Merstham	W 1-0		1		3	4		6	7		9	10[1]						2					8				5							11
TOTAL APPEARANCES					**44**	**43**	**44**	**50**	**51**	**49**	**55**	**48**	**42**	**36**	**21**	**3**	**18**		**2**	**30**	**4**	**3**	**12**	**1**	**16**	**2**	**3**	**8**	**2**	**13**	**11**	**11**	**11**	**3**	**1**	**1**
SUBSTITUTE								**2**			**2**	**1**	**3**	**1**	**5**	**3**	**3**	**1**	**1**	**3**	**2**	**1**	**2**	**2**	**4**									**1**		**1**
GOALS SCORED									**3**	**1**	**9**	**6**	**11**	**17**	**3**		**4**				**1**	**2**	**4**		**2**						**4**			**1**		

SEASON 1977-1978

ISTHMIAN LEAGUE

Date	Venue	Opponents	Result	Atten-dance	Davies, A.	Pollard, R.	Preston, M.	Brown, A.	Cook, A.	Cheeseman, D.	Doig, M.	Cottrell, D.	Alexander, D.	Cosham, S.	Morton, A.	Cunningham, P.	Jamel, Z.	Whatford, M.	Steer, R.	Mapleson, R.	Turner, A.	Pearce, T.	McMorran, J.	Darnell, G.	Parsons, F.	Poole, R.	Roberts, D.	McGonagle, I.	Callaghan, F.	Daniels, P.	Giddings, S.	Metchick, D.	Adams, J.	Elliott, M.	Shrieves, T.
20 Aug	(A)	Tooting	L 0-2		1	2	3	4	5	6	7	8	9	10	11																				
23 Aug	(H)	Staines	L 2-4		1	2	3	6	5	4	7	8[1]	9[1]	10	11	12																			
27 Aug	(H)	Enfield	L 0-2		1	6	3	2			8	7	12	11	10	9	4	5																	
30 Aug	(A)	Kingstonian	L 1-3		1	6		4				8	11	10	9[1]		5	3	2	7															
6 Sep	(H)	Croydon	D 0-0		1			5		12		7	8	10	11			3	2		4	6	9												
10 Sep	(H)	Hitchin	L 0-1		1	6		5				7	9	10	11			3	2	12	4		8												
13 Sep	(A)	Leatherhead	L 1-4		1	6		5				7	8	10[1]	9			3	2	12			11	4											
17 Sep	(A)	Bishop Stortford	W 3-1			12		5			6[1]	7		10	9[1]			3	2	8			11[1]	4	1										
24 Sep	(H)	Walthamstow	L 0-1					2			8	7	12	9	10			3	5	6	4		11		1										
27 Sep	(A)	Sutton	L 0-1			6		2				7	8	9	10		12	3	5				11		1	4									
1 Oct	(A)	Barking	W 3-1			6		2			8	7	11[1]	9[1]	10			3[1]	5						1	4									
8 Oct	(A)	Staines	L 0-1			7		2			8	6	9	10	11			3	5						1	4									
11 Oct	(H)	Kingstonian	L 0-1					2			7	6	8	9	10	11		3	5						1	4									
22 Oct	(H)	Dagenham	L 4-5			8	4[1]	2			7	6	12	10[1]	9[1]			3	5						1		11[1]								
25 Oct	(H)	Leatherhead	L 0-3	700	1		5	2			8	6	7	10	9			4									11	3							
29 Oct	(A)	Charshalton o.g.	W 2-1				4	8				7	6	11[1]	10			5	2						1		9	3	12						
5 Nov	(A)	Croydon o.g.	W 6-3				4	7				6	8	10[2]	11[3]			3	2						1		9	5							
15 Nov	(H)	Sutton	L 1-2				4	8				6	7		9			5	2				10		1		11[1]	3							
19 Nov	(A)	Hayes	W 3-0				4	8				6	7[1]	10[2]	9			5	2						1			3	11						
26 Nov	(H)	Barking	W 4-1				5	4			2	8	9	11[2]	10[2]						7				1			3	6						
17 Dec	(A)	Walthamstow	D 3-3				3	8[1]				7[1]	9	11	10[1]			4	6						1		12	5		2					
7 Jan	(A)	Hitchin	D 1-1				4	9				7	8	11	10[1]			5	2						1		12	3		6					
4 Feb	(A)	Tilbury	W 1-0				5	9				7	8	10	11[1]			6	2		3				1		12	4							
11 Feb	(H)	Leytonstone	D 0-0				5	7				9	8	11	10			4	2		3				1			6							
18 Feb	(A)	Dagenham o.g.	L 1-2				4	7				8	9	10	11			5	2		6				1			3		12					
21 Feb	(H)	Wycombe	D 1-1				5	7				9[1]	8		10			6	12		3				1		11	4		2					
25 Feb	(H)	Carshalton	D 1-1				5	7				8[1]	9	11				6			2				1		10	4		3	12				
28 Feb	(H)	Slough	W 3-1				4[1]	9				7	8	10[2]	11			5	2		6				1			3							
11 Mar	(A)	Slough	W 1-0				4					8[1]	9	11	10			5	7		2				1			3		6					
18 Mar	(H)	Hayes	W 2-1									9	8	11	10[1]			5	2		3				1			6	12	4	7[1]				
25 Mar	(A)	Wycombe	D 0-0				4	9				8	7	10	11				2		6				1			5		3		12			
1 Apr	(H)	Southall	D 1-1				4	9				7		11[1]	10				2		5				1			6		3		8	12		
4 Apr	(A)	Boreham Wood	W 1-0				3	9				7	6		10[1]				4						1			5				8	11	2	
6 Apr	(A)	Enfield	L 2-3				3	9				6	7[2]	12	10				2						1			5				8	11	4	
8 Apr	(H)	Tilbury o.g.	W 2-0				3	9				6	7[1]	11	10				2						1			5				8	12	4	
11 Apr	(H)	Hendon	L 1-2				3	8				7	6	9	10[1]				2						1			5		12			11	4	
15 Apr	(A)	Southall	D 2-2				4	9				8	7	10	11[2]				3		2				1			6					12	5	
18 Apr	(A)	Leytonstone	D 1-1				3	7				6	9	10	11[1]				2						1			5				8	12	4	
22 Apr	(H)	Tooting	W 3-2				4	8				6	7		10[3]				2						1			5				9	11	3	12
25 Apr	(A)	Hendon	D 1-1				3	7[1]				6	8		10				2		4				1			5					11		9
1 May	(H)	Boreham Wood	L 0-2					8				6			9				7		5				1			3		2	12		10	4	11
4 May	(H)	Bishops Stortford	W 4-1				5[1]	8				6	7	10[2]	9[1]				2						1			3				11		4	12
F.A. CUP																																			
3 Sep	Prel (A)	Ilford	L 0-1		1	2		6	11			7	8	9	10			4	5		3		12												
F.A. TROPHY																																			
15 Oct	1st Q (A)	Witney	W 2-0			7		2			8	6	10	11[2]	9			4	3						1	5		12							
12 Nov	2nd Q (H)	Bromley	W 3-1				4[1]	8				6	7	10[1]	9			5	2						1		11[1]	3							
3 Dec	3rd Q (A)	Kingstonian	W 1-0				5	6				8	7	11[1]	10			4	3						1			9	2						
14 Jan	1st R (H)	Gravesend & N	D 0-0				5	9				7	8	11	10			4	3		2				1		12	6							
17 Jan	Rep (A)	Gravesend & N	L 0-2				3	9				7	8	11	10			4	2		5				1		12	6							
LONDON SENIOR CUP																																			
10 Dec	1st R (A)	Enfield	L 0-2				4	8				6	7	10	9				2						1	5		3	11						
SURREY SENIOR CUP																																			
31 Dec	1st R (A)	Croydon	W 2-0				4	9				7	8	10[2]	11			5	6						1			3		2					
28 Jan	2nd R (H)	Kingstonian	W 3-0				5	8				7[1]	9	11[2]	10			6	2		3				1			4							
4 Mar	S-F (A)	Leatherhead	W 2-1				4	9				7	8	11[1]	10[1]			5	2		6				1			3		12					
27 Mar	F	(Leatherhead) Tooting	L 1-2	AET			5	9				8	7	11[1]	10				2		4				1			6		3					
HITACHI CUP																																			
7 Mar	1st R (A)	Slough	W 1-0				4					7	8		10[1]			5	11		3				1			6	12	2	9				
14 Mar	2nd R (A)	Boreham Wood	L 1-2	AET			4					8	9[1]	11	10			5	7		2				1			6		3					
SURREY CENTENARY CUP																																			
1 Nov	S-F (H)	Dulwich	L 0-1				4	6				7	8	10	9			3	2						1		11	5							
TOTAL APPEARANCES					**9**	**12**	**42**	**52**	**3**	**2**	**12**	**56**	**50**	**48**	**55**	**2**	**2**	**39**	**49**	**3**	**25**	**1**	**7**	**2**	**47**	**6**	**9**	**40**	**4**	**13**	**2**	**7**	**6**	**9**	**2**
SUBSTITUTE						**1**				**1**			**3**	**1**		**1**	**1**		**1**	**2**			**1**				**5**	**1**	**3**	**3**	**2**	**1**	**4**		**2**
GOALS SCORED							**4**	**2**			**1**	**6**	**7**	**25**	**23**			**1**					**1**				**3**				**1**				

ISTHMIAN LEAGUE

SEASON 1978-1979

Date	Venue	Opponents	Result	Attendance	Parsons, F.	O'Sullivan, B.	Morton, A.	Martin, A.	Love, J.	Preston, M.	Cottrell, D.	Steer, R.	Field, A.	Adams, J.	James, E.	Alexander, D.	Cosham, S.	Barrett, L.	Shrieves, T.	Callaghan, F.	Black, M.	Yerby, D.	Brown, I.	Ritchie, J.	Mepham, J.	Hennesey, D.
19 Aug	(A)	Hitchin	L 0-1		1	2	9	3	4	5	6	7	8	10	11	12										
22 Aug	(H)	Sutton	D 3-3		1	2	9[1]	3	4[1]	5	6		8		11	7	10[1]									
26 Aug	(H)	Carshalton	W 3-2		1	2	9[2]	3	4	5	6		8	10	11[1]	7										
28 Aug	(H)	Oxford	W 4-1		1	2	9[1]	3	4	5	6	12[1]	8	10	11[2]	7										
2 Sep	(A)	Croydon	W 3-1		1	2	9	3	4[1]	5	6		8	10[1]	11[1]	7										
5 Sep	(A)	Kingstonian	W 3-1		1	2	9[1]	3	4	5	6		8[1]		11[1]	7	10									
9 Sep	(H)	Leytonstone	D 2-2		1	2	9	3	4	5	6		8		11[1]		10[1]	7								
12 Sep	(H)	Slough	D 0-0	1.120	1		9	3	4	5	6	2		8	11		10	7								
19 Sep	(H)	Hendon	D 2-2		1		9[2]	3	4	5	6	2			11		10	7	8							
23 Sep	(H)	Walthamstow	D 1-1		1		9[1]	3	4	5	6	2	8		11		12	7		10						
26 Sep	(A)	Sutton	L 0-3		1		9	3	4	5	6	2	8		11		12	7		10						
30 Sep	(A)	Tilbury	L 1-2		1		9	3	4	5	6	2	8		11[1]		10	7								
3 Oct	(A)	Slough	W 2-1		1	2			4	5	6		8	9[1]	11	7	10[1]	3								
10 Oct	(H)	Kingstonian	W 2-0		1	2		3	4[1]	5	6		8	9	11[1]	7	10									
24 Oct	(H)	Dagenham	L 3-4	830	1	2	9[1]	3	4	5	6		12		11	7	10[2]	8								
28 Oct	(A)	Barking	L 0-1		1	2	9	3	4	5	6		12		11	7	10	8								
18 Nov	(H)	Boreham Wood	W 1-0		1		9	3	4	5	6	2	11			7	10[1]	8	12							
21 Nov	(A)	Hendon	W 2-1		1		9		4		6	2	8	11	12[1]		10[1]	3	7		5					
9 Dec	(H)	Hitchin	W 3-1		1	2	9[2]	3	4				6	8	11	7	10[1]	5								
23 Dec	(H)	Croydon o.g.	W 3-1	350	1	2	9	3	4		6		7[1]	8	11		10	5[1]								
26 Dec	(H)	Leatherhead	D 0-0	800	1	2	9	3	4	5	6	7	10	8				11								
31 Jan	(A)	Carshalton	W 4-0		1	2	9[1]	3	4	5	6		8[1]		11	7[1]	10[1]					12				
3 Feb	(A)	Walthamstow	W 6-0		1	2	9[1]	3	4	5	6		8		11	7[1]	10[4]					12				
6 Feb	(A)	Dulwich	L 1-4		1	2	9[1]	3	4	5	6	12	8		11	7						10				
24 Feb	(H)	Barking	L 2-3	423	1	2	9	3	4	5[1]	6		8		11[1]	7	10					12				
27 Feb	(A)	Leytonstone	D 2-2		1		9	3	11	5	6		8[2]			7	10					2	4			
6 Mar	(A)	Leatherhead	L 0-2		1		9	3	4	5	6		8		12	7	10					2		11		
10 Mar	(A)	Wycombe	L 1-3		1		9	3	4	5[1]		6	8		12	7	10					2		11		
13 Mar	(H)	Tilbury	D 2-2		1	2		3		5			8		11[2]	7	10					6	4	9		
20 Mar	(H)	Dulwich	D 1-1			2	12	3		5			8		11	7[1]	10					6	4	9	1	
24 Mar	(A)	Hayes	D 1-1			2	12		3	5			8		11[1]	7	10					6	4	9	1	
27 Mar	(A)	Boreham Wood	W 4-2		1		10[4]		3	5			8		11	7	6				4	2		9		12
3 Apr	(H)	Hayes	D 1-1		1	2	9	3		5			8		11[1]	7					4	6		10		12
7 Apr	(H)	Staines	W 2-0		1		9[1]	3	6	5			8		11	7					4	2		10[1]		
10 Apr	(A)	Staines	W 3-1		1		10	3	6	5			8		11[2]	7[1]					4	2		9		
16 Apr	(H)	Tooting	D 2-2		1	7	10[1]	3	6	5	12		8		11[1]						4	2		9		
21 Apr	(A)	Oxford	W 2-0		1		10[1]	3	4	5	6		8		11[1]	7						2		9		
24 Apr	(H)	Wycombe	D 1-1		1	2	10	3	4	5	6		8[1]		11	7								9		
26 Apr	(A)	Enfield	D 1-1		1	2	9	3	4	5	6		8		11	7[1]								10		
28 Apr	(H)	Enfield	W 1-0		1	2	10[1]	3	4	5	6		8		11	7								9		
3 May	(A)	Tooting	W 1-0		1	2	10[1]	3	4	5	6		8		11	7						12		9		
5 May	(A)	Dagenham	L 3-5		1	2	10[1]	3	4	5	6		8		11[2]	7						12		9		
F.A. CUP																										
16 Sep	1st Q (H)	Epsom & Ewell	W 3-1		1		9[2]	3	4	5	6	2		8	11[1]		10	7								
7 Oct	2nd Q (A)	Tunbridge Wells	W 2-0		1	2		3	4	5	6		8	9[1]	11[1]	7	10	12								
21 Oct	3rd Q (H)	Horsham	W 5-2		1	2	9[1]	3	4	5	6		12		11[1]	7[1]	10[1]	8[1]								
4 Nov	4th Q (A)	Margate	W 7-1	1,092	1	2	9[3]	3	4	5	6	12	10		11[3]	7[1]		8								
25 Nov	1st R (A)	Barnet	D 3-3	2,023	1		9		4[1]	5	6	2	8[1]		11[1]	7	10	3								
28 Nov	Rep (H)	Barnet AET	D 3-3	3,523	1	2	9[1]	3	4		6		8		11	7[1]	10[1]	5								
5 Dec	2nd Rep	(Brentford) Barnet	W 3-0	2,950	1	2	9[2]	3	4		6		12	8	11[1]	7	10	5								
16 Dec	2nd R (A)	Swansea	D 2-2	7,174	1	2	9	3	4[1]		6[1]			8	11	7	10	5								
19 Dec	Rep (H)	Swansea AET	L 3-5	6,500	1	2	9[1]	3	4		6		12[1]	8	11	7	10	5[1]								
F.A. TROPHY																										
14 Oct	1st Q (H)	Waterlooville	D 2-2		1	2		3	4	5	6		8	9	11[2]	7	10	12								
18 Oct	Rep (A)	Waterlooville o.g.	D 3-3	AET		2	9[1]	3	4	5	6		8		11	7	10	12[1]							1	
30 Oct	2nd Rep (A)	Waterlooville	D 0-0	AET	1	2	9	3	4	5	6		12		11	7	10	8								
6 Nov	3rd Rep (H)	Waterlooville o.g.	W 1-0		1	2	9	3	4	5	6		10		11	7		8								
11 Nov	2nd Q (A)	Bognor	D 1-1		1		9[1]	3	4	5	6	2	10		11	7	12	8								
14 Nov	Rep (H)	Bognor	W 2-0	1,024	1	2	9[1]	3	4	5	6		10		11	7	12	8[1]								
2 Dec	3rd Q (H)	Tilbury	D 0-0		1	2	9	3	4		6		8		12	7	10	11			5					
11 Dec	Rep (A)	Tilbury o.g.	W 1-0		1	2	9	5	4				8	6	11	7	10	3								
13 Jan	1st R (A)	Slough	L 0-3	937	1	2	9	3	4	5	6		8		11	7	10	12								
SURREY SENIOR CUP																										
30 Dec	1st R (H)	Kingstonian	W 4-0	800	1		9	3	4	5	6[1]	2	8[1]	7		12	10[2]	11								
13 Feb	2nd R (A)	Leatherhead	L 1-2		1	2	9[1]	3	4	5	6		8		11	7	10				12					
LONDON SENIOR CUP																										
20 Jan	1st R (H)	Letchworth	W 3-0		1	2	9	3	4[1]	5	6		8[1]		11[1]	7	10									
10 Feb	2nd R (H)	Staines	W 4-1		1	2	9[1]	3		5	6	12[1]	8	4	11[1]	7[1]	10									
3 Mar	3rd R (A)	Barking	L 1-3		1	2	9	3	4	5	6	7	8		11[1]	12	10									
HITACHI CUP																										
9 Jan	1st R (A)	Dulwich	L 1-3		1		9	3	4	5	6	2	8[1]		11	12	10	7								
TOTAL APPEARANCES					63	47	59	61	62	57	55	16	56	20	58	51	44	30	2	2	7	13	4	16	3	
SUBSTITUTE							2				1	4	6		4	4	4	4	1		1	5				2
GOALS SCORED							39		6	2	2	2	11	3	33	9	17	5						1		

ISTHMIAN LEAGUE

SEASON 1979-1980

Date	Venue	Opponents	Result	Atten-dance	Parsons, F.	Yerby, D.	Martin, A.	Earls, M.	Preston, M.	Love, J.	Rolph, G.	Field, A.	Morton, A.	Callaghan, F.	James, E.	Alexander, D.	Black, M.	Fuller, S.	Hennesey, D.	Cottrell, D.	Fletcher, N.	Littlejohn, P.	Barrett, L.	Adams, S.	Sullivan, N.	Lovell, M.	Richardson, J.	Gummer, J.	Phillips, G.	Spittle, P.
18 Aug	(H)	Dagenham	D 0-0		1	2	3	4	5	6	7	8	9	10	11	12														
21 Aug	(H)	Tilbury	W 3-2		1	2	3	4	5	6	7	8[1]	9	10	11[2]															
25 Aug	(A)	Walthamstow	W 4-2		1	2	3	4	5	6[1]	10	8	9[2]		11[1]	7														
27 Aug	(A)	Enfield	W 1-0		1	2	3	4	5	6	10	8	9[1]		11	7	12													
1 Sep	(H)	Hendon	W 3-1		1	2			5	4	10	8[1]	9	6	11[2]	7		3	12											
4 Sep	(H)	Hitchin o.g.	D 1-1		1	2	3		5	4	10	8	9	6	11	7														
8 Sep	(A)	Oxford	W 3-0		1	2	3		5	4	10[1]	8	9[1]	6	11	7[1]				12										
11 Sep	(A)	Tooting	L 0-3		1	2	3		5	4	10	8	9	6	11	7				12										
22 Sep	(H)	Leatherhead	W 3-0		1	2	3		5	4	10[1]	8	9[1]		11[1]	7				6										
25 Sep	(A)	Sutton	W 3-0		1	2	3		5	4	10	8	9[1]		11[2]	7				6										
29 Sep	(H)	Dulwich	D 1-1		1	2	3		5	4	10[1]	8	9		11	7				6										
1 Oct	(A)	Croydon	L 3-6		1	2	3		5	4	10	8	9		11[3]	7	12			6										
9 Oct	(H)	Wycombe	D 0-0		1	2	3		5	4	10	8	9		11	7				6										
13 Oct	(H)	Slough	W 4-0	540	1	2	3		5[2]	4	10	8	9[2]		11	7				6	12									
16 Oct	(A)	Hayes o.g.	W 3-0		1	2	3		5	4	10	8[1]	9[1]		11	7				6	12									
23 Oct	(H)	Boreham Wood	L 2-3		1	2	3		5	4	10	8	9[1]		11[1]	7				6	12									
27 Oct	(H)	Barking	D 0-0		1	2	3		5	4	10	8		6	11	12					7	9								
5 Nov	(A)	Dagenham	D 2-2		1	2	3		5		10[1]	8	9[1]		11		4						6	7						
10 Nov	(H)	Walthamstow	L 0-1		1		3		5	2	10	8	9		11	12	4						6	7						
17 Nov	(A)	Barking	L 3-4		1	12	3		5	2		8[1]	9		11[1]	10	4						6[1]	7						
24 Nov	(A)	Hendon	L 0-3		1	2	3		5	4	10	8	9		11	12							6	7						
27 Nov	(H)	Enfield	W 2-1		1		3		5	2		8	9[1]		11	10	12				7[1]		6	4						
4 Dec	(A)	Hitchin	L 1-3		1		3		5	2		8	9		11[1]	10					7	12	6	4						
8 Dec	(H)	Oxford o.g.	W 5-1		1		3		5	2		8[1]	9[1]		11[1]	10				12	7		6	4[1]						
15 Dec	(H)	Carshalton	W 7-0		1		3		5	2		8[2]	9[3]		11[1]	10				12[1]	7		6	4						
26 Dec	(A)	Staines	D 1-1		1		3		5	2		8	9[1]		11	7				4	12		6	10						
1 Jan	(H)	Staines	L 2-3		1		3		5	2		8[1]	9[1]		11	7				4			6	10						
5 Jan	(A)	Leatherhead	W 1-0		1		3		5	2	8		9[1]		11	7				10			6	4						
16 Feb	(A)	Wycombe	D 1-1	609			3		5	6	2	8	9		11[1]					4	7			10	1					
26 Feb	(H)	Hayes	W 2-1				3	12	5	2[1]		8[1]	9		11		10			4	7		6		1					
8 Mar	(H)	Harlow	W 3-1		1		3			2		8[2]			11	10[1]	5			4	7		6			9				
22 Mar	(H)	Harrow	W 2-1		1		3		5			8	9[1]		11	10[1]				4	7		6			2				
25 Mar	(A)	Dulwich	L 0-1		1		3		5			8	9		11	12	2				7					4	6	10		
4 Apr	(H)	Croydon	D 1-1		1				5			8	9		11[1]		10			4	7		6			2	3			
5 Apr	(A)	Tilbury	D 0-0		1				5			8	9		11		10			4	7		6			2	3			
7 Apr	(A)	Harlow	D 1-1		1		2		5			8	9[1]				10			4	7		6				3	11		
22 Apr	(H)	Sutton	L 1-3		1				5	2		8[1]			11	10	9			4	7		6				3			
24 Apr	(A)	Boreham Wood	W 3-2		1		3		5	2		8	9[1]		11[1]	10				4	7[1]		6							
26 Apr	(A)	Slough	D 2-2		1		3		5	2		8	9[1]		11	7[1]				4	10		6							
28 Apr	(A)	Harrow	D 2-2				3		5[1]	2		8	9			7	10[1]			4			6				11		1	
1 May	(A)	Carshalton o.g.	L 1-2		1		3		5	2		8	9		11	7	10			4			6							
3 May	(H)	Tooting	L 1-3		1				5	2		8	9		11[1]	7	10			4			6				3			
F.A. CUP																														
15 Sep	1st Q (A)	Corinthian Casuals	W 6-1		1	2	3				10[1]	8	9[2]	4	11[1]	7[2]	5		12	6										
6 Oct	2nd Q (A)	Hounslow	W 3-2		1	2	3		5	4	12	8[1]	9[1]	10	11[1]	7				6										
20 Oct	3rd Q (A)	Kingstonian	W 2-0		1	2	3		5	4	10[1]	8	9		11	7[1]				6	12									
3 Nov	4th Q (A)	Wealdstone	L 0-1		1	2	3		5		10	8	9	6	11	7	4													
F.A. TROPHY																														
1 Dec	3rd Q (H)	Folkestone	W 2-1	561	1		3		5	2		8[1]	9		11[1]	10					7		6	4						
12 Jan	1st R (H)	Dover	D 0-0	555	1		3		5	2		8	9		11	7				4			6	10						
21 Jan	Rep (A)	Dover	W 1-0	677			3		5	2		8	9		11[1]	7				4			6	10						1
9 Feb	2nd R (A)	Ashington	W 2-0	1,340	1		3		5	2		8	9		11[1]	7				4			6	10[1]						
23 Feb	3rd R (A)	Marine	W 2-0	851	1		3		5	2		8	9		11		10			4[2]	7		6							
15 Mar	4th R (H)	Barrow	W 3-1	1,787	1		3		5			8[1]	9		11[1]	10	12			4	7[1]		6			2				
12 Apr	S-F 1st L (H)	Dagenham	L 1-3	2,087	1		3		5[1]	2		8	9		11	10				4	7		6							
19 Apr	S-F 2nd L (A)	Dagenham	L 1-4	2,723	1		3		5	2		8	9		11[1]	7				4			6				10			
LONDON SENIOR CUP																														
19 Jan	1st R (H)	Epsom & Ewell	W 2-1		1		3		5	2	9	8[2]			11	7				4			6	10						
5 Feb	2nd R (H)	Wealdstone	W 3-0		1		3		5	2		8	9		11[2]	7[1]				4			6	10						
1 Mar	3rd R (A)	Tooting	W 2-1		1		3		5	2		8	9		11	10[2]				4	7		6							
29 Mar	S-F (A)	Barking	L 0-1		1		3		5			8	12		11	10	2			4	7		6			9				
SURREY SENIOR CUP																														
29 Dec	1st R (A)	Banstead	W 1-0		1		3		5	2	12	8	9		11[1]	10					7		6	4						
26 Jan	2nd R (H)	Sutton	L 1-2		1		3		5	2	11[1]	8	9		12	7				4			6	10						
HITACHI CUP																														
30 Oct	1st R (H)	Kingstonian	W 2-1		1	2	3	4	5	12	10	8[1]	9[1]	6	11	7														
11 Dec	2nd R (A)	Tooting	D 1-1		1		3		5	2	9[1]	8			11	10					7		6	4						
18 Dec	Rep (H)	Tooting	W 2-1		1		3		5	2		8[1]	9		11	10[1]					7		6	4						
12 Feb	3rd R (A)	Boreham Wood	W 6-1				3		5		2	8	9[1]		11[4]	7[1]				4	12		6	10	1					
4 Mar	S-F (A)	Sutton	D 1-1		1				5[1]	3		8	9		11	10	12			4	7		6			2				
18 Mar	Rep (H)	Sutton	L 1-3		1		3		5			8	9[1]		11	10	12			4	7		6			2				
TOTAL APPEARANCES					**61**	**24**	**60**	**5**	**64**	**53**	**30**	**65**	**61**	**11**	**63**	**53**	**17**	**1**		**42**	**27**	**1**	**42**	**23**	**3**	**9**	**8**	**2**	**1**	**1**
SUBSTITUTE						**1**		**1**		**1**	**2**		**1**		**1**	**5**	**6**		**2**	**4**	**6**	**1**								
GOALS SCORED									**5**	**2**	**8**	**19**	**29**		**34**	**12**	**1**			**3**	**3**		**1**	**2**						

ISTHMIAN LEAGUE

SEASON 1980-1981

Date	Venue	Opponents	Result	Atten-dance	Porter, T.	Howitt, D.	Martin, A.	Dixon, W.	Leather, R.	Barrett, L	Fletcher, N.	Field, A.	Morton, A.	Scrivens, S.	Booth, A.	Black, M.	Nwajiobi, E.	Parsons, F.	Cooper, J.	Roope, G.	Fuller, S.	Ferguson, P.	Dunn, J.	Davies, R.	Davies, B.	Mace, A.	Levy, A.	Davies, I.	Baker, J.	Nwajiobi, O.	Devereaux, M.	Earls, M.	Marciello, L.
16 Aug	(H)	Enfield	L 1-2		1	2	3	4	5	6	7	8	9[1]	10	11	12																	
19 Aug	(A)	Carshalton	L 1-2		1		3	4[1]	5	6	7	8	9	10	11	2																	12
23 Aug	(A)	Boreham Wood	L 1-2		1	2	3	4	5	6	7[1]	8	9	10	11																		
30 Aug	(A)	Barking	W 3-1		1	2	3	4	5	6	7	8	9[1]	10[1]	11		12[1]																
2 Sep	(H)	Staines	L 0-3		1	2	3	4	5	6		8	9	10	11		7																
6 Sep	(H)	Dagenham	W 3-1		1	2	3	4	5	6		8[1]	9[1]	10	11[1]		7																
9 Sep	(A)	Slough	D 1-1		1	2	3	4	5	6		8[1]	9	10	11		7																
16 Sep	(A)	Sutton	L 1-3		1	2		3	5	6	8		9[1]	10	11	4	7																
20 Sep	(A)	Leytonstone-Ilford	W 3-1			2		3	5	6	12	8	9[1]	10[1]	11	4[1]	7	1															
27 Sep	(H)	Barking	D 1-1		1	2	3		5		6	8	9	10	11	4	7[1]																12
30 Sep	(H)	Hayes	W 1-0		1	2	3		5			8	9[1]	10	11	4	7		6														
11 Oct	(A)	Dulwich o.g.	L 2-3			2			5	3	7	8	9	10[1]	11	4			6	1													
14 Oct	(A)	Wycombe	L 0-4			2			5	3	7	8	9	10	11	4			6	1	12												
18 Oct	(A)	Walthamstow	W 1-0			2			5	6		8	9[1]	10	3	4			7	1													11
25 Oct	(H)	Croydon	D 1-1		1	2			5	6		8	9	10[1]	3	4			7														11
28 Oct	(H)	Carshalton	L 1-2		1	2			5[1]	6		8	9	10	3	4			7													11	
1 Nov	(A)	Hendon	W 2-0		1	2			5	3	7	8	9[1]	10[1]	11	4			6														
4 Nov	(A)	Staines	L 0-1		1	2			5	3	7	8	9	10	11	4			6														
8 Nov	(A)	Bromley	L 0-5		1				5	3	7	8	9	10		4			6		2												11
11 Nov	(H)	Slough	W 2-0		1	2	3		5	6		8	9[1]	10	11	4[1]			7														
15 Nov	(H)	Harlow	L 0-1		1	2	3		5	6		8	9	10	11	4			7														
22 Nov	(A)	Hitchin	L 1-3		1	4	3		5	6		8[1]	10	11		9			7			2											
25 Nov	(H)	Sutton	W 2-1		1	2	3		5[1]	6		8	9[1]	10	11	4			7														
29 Nov	(H)	Tooting	W 2-0		1	2	3		5	6		8	9[1]		11				7[1]		10	4											12
2 Dec	(A)	Hayes	L 0-1		1		3		5	6		8	9	10	11				7		4												2
6 Dec	(H)	Harrow	L 1-2		1	2	3		5	6	10[1]	8	9		11				7		4												12
9 Dec	(A)	Tooting	L 0-2		1		3		5	6	10	8	9		11	4					2												7
13 Dec	(H)	Walthamstow	W 1-0		1		3		5	6	7	8[1]	9		11	4					10	2											12
16 Dec	(H)	Wycombe	L 0-4		1		3		5	6	7	8	9		11	4	10				2												12
27 Dec	(H)	Leatherhead	L 1-2		1		3		2	6			9	10	11	5	8		4		7												12[1]
3 Jan	(A)	Leatherhead	D 0-0				3		2	6	11		9	10		5			4				1	7	8								
31 Jan	(H)	Boreham Wood	L 1-2				3		5	6				11		9			4				1	10[1]	8	2	7						
7 Feb	(A)	Dagenham	L 0-4				3		2	6				12	11	8			9				1	10	4	5	7						
21 Feb	(A)	Harrow	D 0-0				3			9				11		5							1	10	6	2	7	8					4
7 Mar	(A)	Croydon	L 1-2				3			8						5			4				1	10	6	2	7	11[1]	9				
14 Mar	(H)	Hendon	D 0-0				3			2						8			4				1	10	6	5	7	11	9				
28 Mar	(A)	Harlow	L 1-3				3			2				11		8			6				1	10	4	5	7			9[1]			
4 Apr	(H)	Hitchin	L 0-1		1		3		5	2				11		9			6					10	4		7			8			
18 Apr	(H)	Leytonstone-Ilford	L 1-4		1				5	3				11		9[1]			6		12			10	4	2	7	8					
23 Apr	(H)	Dulwich	D 1-1						5	3				11		9			6				1	10[1]	4	2	7	8					
25 Apr	(H)	Bromley	W 1-0						5	3				11					6				1	10	4	2	7	8					9[1]
2 May	(A)	Enfield	L 1-3						5	3				11[1]		8			6				1	10	4	2	7						9
F.A. CUP																																	
13 Sep	1st Q (H)	Tring	W 2-1		1	2		4	5	6	12	8[1]	9	10	11	3[1]	7																
4 Oct	2nd Q (A)	Hendon	D 1-1		1	2			5	3	12	8	9[1]	10	11	4	7		6														
7 Oct	Rep (H)	Hendon	L 1-4			2				3	7	8	9	10	11	4			6[1]		5										1		
F.A. TROPHY																																	
10 Jan	1st R (H)	Sutton	L 0-1		1		3		2	6	7		9	10	11	5			4														8
SURREY SENIOR CUP																																	
24 Jan	1st R (H)	Tooting	D 0-0				3		5	2				11		9			4				1	10	8		7						6
27 Jan	Rep (A)	Tooting	W 3-0				3		5	2				11		9[1]			4				1	10[2]	8		7						6
28 Feb	2nd R (H)	Kingstonian	W 3-2				3			9				11		5[1]			8				1	10	6	2[1]	7						4[1]
21 Mar	S-F (H)	Met. Police	D 0-0				3			2				9		8			6				1	10	4	5	7	11					
26 Mar	Rep (A)	Met. Police	W 4-1		1		3			2				11		8[2]			4					10	6	5	7			9[2]			
20 Apr	F	(Tooting) Epsom & E	L 1-2		1				5[1]	3				11		9			6					10	4	2	7			8			
LONDON SENIOR CUP																																	
17 Jan	1st R (A)	Farnborough	W 2-1				3			2			9[2]	11		5			4				1	10	8		7						6
14 Feb	2nd R (H)	Carshalton	L 2-3				3		5[1]	6				11		9			4				1	10	8	2	7[1]						
HITACHI CUP																																	
25 Aug	1st R (H)	Corinthian Casuals	W 9-0		1	2	3	4	5[1]	6	7[2]	8[2]	9[3]	10[1]	11	12																	
23 Sep	2nd R (A)	St. Albans	W 4-3			2	3		5[1]		6	8	9	10[1]	11[1]	4	7[1]	1															
18 Nov	3rd R (H)	Walthamstow	L 2-4		1	2	3		5	6	7	8	9[1]	10[1]	11	4																	
TOTAL APPEARANCES					**35**	**29**	**39**	**11**	**48**	**54**	**21**	**34**	**39**	**49**	**36**	**46**	**12**	**2**	**39**	**3**	**9**	**3**	**16**	**20**	**20**	**15**	**19**	**7**	**2**	**4**	**1**	**1**	**13**
SUBSTITUTE											**3**			**1**		**2**	**1**				**2**												**7**
GOALS SCORED								**1**	**6**		**4**	**7**	**18**	**9**	**2**	**8**	**3**		**2**					**4**		**1**	**1**	**1**		**3**			**3**

ISTHMIAN LEAGUE

SEASON 1981-1982

Date	Venue	Opponents	Result	Attendance	Mitchell, K.	Mitchell, J.	Edwards, G.	Chapman, J.	Smith, C.	King, R.	Hill, K.	Howard, I.	McCulloch, R.	Lynch, L.	Beckett, K.	Kinkaid, L.	Scrivens, S.	Shodiende, P.	Clark, J.	Palfrey, S.	Cadogan, L.	Holder, P.	Stratford, P.	Martin, A.	Adams, S.	Terry, R.	Hepworth, M.	Newland, M.	Hindley, G.	Hewitt, T.	Hurt, T.	Churchouse, G.	Wonham, A.	Dixon, I.	Crossley, S.	Stillwell, C.	Mace, A.	Dennis, F.	Cosham, G.	Richardson, J.	Steel, D.	Brown, A.	McGonagle, I.	Ryan, J.	May	Simmons, M.	Black, M.	James, K.	Taylor, M.
15 Aug	(H)	Walthamstow	W 3-0		1	2	3	4[1]	5	6	7	8	9	10[1]	11[1]	12																																	
18 Aug	(A)	Slough	D 0-0		1	2	3	4	5	6	7	8	9	10	11		12																																
22 Aug	(H)	Boreham Wood	D 1-1		1	2	3	4	5	6	7	8	9	10[1]	11		12																																
25 Aug	(H)	Staines	L 0-2		1	2	3	8	5	6	7		9	10	4		12	11																															
29 Aug	(A)	Dulwich	L 0-1		1	2	3	4	5	6	7	8	9	10	11			12																															
8 Sep	(A)	Tooting	W 2-1		1	2[1]		4	5	6	7	3	9	10	11			12	8[1]																														
12 Sep	(A)	Bishops Stortford	D 1-1		1	2[1]		4	5	6	7	3	9		10			11	8	12																													
15 Sep	(H)	Wycombe	W 2-1		1	2		4[1]	5	6	7	3[1]	9		12					8	10	11																											
26 Sep	(H)	Croydon	L 2-4		1	2		4	5	6	7[1]	3	9[1]						12	8	10	11																											
29 Sep	(A)	Staines	L 1-3			2			5		7		9[1]							8	10	11	1	3	4	12																					6		
3 Oct	(H)	Hitchin	D 2-2		1	2			5		7		9						12	8	10[1]	11[1]		3	4																						6		
10 Oct	(A)	Hayes	D 2-2		1	2			5		7[1]		9							8	10	11		3	6	12[1]																					4		
13 Oct	(H)	Harrow	W 5-2		1	2[1]		12	5		7		9[1]								10[2]	8		3		11	4[1]																				6		
17 Oct	(A)	Barking	W 2-0		1	2		8	5		7		9[2]							3	10					11	4																				6		
20 Oct	(H)	Slough	D 1-1		1	2[1]			5		7		9								10	8		3		11	4																				6		
24 Oct	(H)	Hendon	L 1-2		1				5		7		9						12	2	10	8		3		11	4[1]																				6		
31 Oct	(H)	Dulwich	W 1-0		1				5		7		9								10	8		3[1]		12	4	2	11																		6		
3 Nov	(H)	Tooting	L 2-4		1				5		7[1]		9								10[1]	8		3		12	4	2	11																		6		
7 Nov	(A)	Croydon	D 0-0		1				5		7		9						2		10	8		3		11	4			12																	6		
10 Nov	(A)	Wycombe	D 0-0		1				5		7		9								10	8		3			4	2	11																		6		
14 Nov	(H)	Harlow	W 2-0		1				5		7[1]		9								10[1]	8		3			4	2	11	12																	6		
21 Nov	(A)	Bromley	W 3-2		1	2			5		7		9[1]								10[1]	8[1]		3			4				11																6		
24 Nov	(H)	Carshalton	W 4-1		1	2			5		7										10[1]	8[1]		3		12[1]	4			11[1]	9																6		
28 Nov	(H)	Sutton	W 4-2		1	2			5		7		9								10[2]	8		3			4			11[2]																	6		
30 Nov	(A)	Harrow	L 1-2		1	2			5		7[1]		9								10	8		3		12	4			11																	6		
5 Dec	(A)	Carshalton	L 0-1		1	2			5		7		9								10	8		3		12	4			11																	6		
2 Jan	(H)	Leatherhead	W 2-0		1	2			5		7		9								10[1]	8[1]		3		12	4				11																6		
20 Feb	(H)	Bishops Stortford	D 0-0		1	2							9								10	11		3			4					8	12				5										6	7	
27 Feb	(H)	Hayes	L 0-3		1	2					11		9								10	8		3			7					4	12				5											6	
6 Mar	(H)	Barking	D 0-0		1	2					7										10									11			9	3	4		5										6	8	
9 Mar	(A)	Leatherhead	L 0-3		1	2					7										10			3						11		12				9	5	6									4	8	
13 Mar	(A)	Hendon	D 3-3		1	2					7										10			3						11						9[2]	5	6	12[1]								4	8	
16 Mar	(A)	Sutton	L 0-3		1	2					7										10						4			11						9	5		12	8							6	3	
20 Mar	(H)	Leytonstone-Ilford	L 2-4		1	2					12										10[2]			3			5			11						9				7	4						6	8	
23 Mar	(A)	Boreham Wood	L 0-1		1	2			5		7													3			4			11						9			10		8						6		
27 Mar	(A)	Harlow	L 1-3		1	2			5[1]		7													3			4			11			9		8	10					12						6		
30 Mar	(H)	Bromley	L 1-7			2			5		7													3						11				12	4	10						8[1]				1	6		9
3 Apr	(A)	Walthamstow	L 1-5			2			5		10[1]												1	8						11					4		6					7	3				9		
10 Apr	(H)	Billericay	L 0-2								7												1	2						10			9	8			5					4	3	11			6		
17 Apr	(A)	Billericay	D 2-2			2			6		7												1	3						10[1]			9				5[1]					4		8	11				
24 Apr	(A)	Hitchin	D 2-2			2			5		7										10		1							11[1]							9[1]			8		4	3				6		
1 May	(A)	Leytonstone-Ilford	L 1-2			2			6		7										9		1	3			4[1]			10							5					8		11					
F.A. CUP																																																	
5 Sep	Prel (H)	Newport IOW £170	W 1-0	285	1	2	3	4	5[1]	6	7		9	12	10		11					8																											
19 Sep	1st Q (A)	Wick £77	L 1-2	188	1	2		4	5	6	7	3	9		11[1]				12	8	10																												
F.A. TROPHY																																																	
19 Jan	1st R (H)	Barking £183	W 2-1	283	1	2[1]			5		7		9								10[1]			3		12	4			11	8																6		
6 Feb	2nd R (H)	Mossley £443	D 0-0	519	1	2			5		7		9						8		10			3			4			11																	6		
10 Feb	Rep (A)	Mossley £774	L 0-5	975	1	2			5		7								11		10	8		3		9	4																				6		
SURREY SENIOR CUP																																																	
30 Jan	1st R (H)	Kingstonian	L 1-3		1	2[1]			5		7		9								10	8		3		14	4			12	11																6		
LONDON SENIOR CUP																																																	
13 Feb	1st R (A)	Dulwich	L 2-3	AET	1	2			5												10[1]			3			4[1]			11			9	8			12										6	7	
HITACHI CUP																																																	
31 Aug	1st R (A)	Wembley	L 1-2		1	2		4	5	6	7	11[1]	9	10	8							3																											
TOTAL APPEARANCES					43	43	6	13	42	12	47	10	34	7	10		1	2	5	8	35	25	6	34	3	6	27	4	4	20	5	2	5	3	4	7	11	2	1	3	2	6	3	3	1	1	35	8	1
SUBSTITUTE								1			1			1	1	1	3	2	4	1						10				3		1	2	1			1		2		1								
GOALS SCORED						6		2	2		6	2	6	2	2				1		14	4		1		2	4			5						2	2		1			1							

ISTHMIAN LEAGUE

SEASON 1982-1983

Date	Venue	Opponents	Result	Attendance	Melville, I.	Sorenson, M.	Dixon, I.	Francis, M.	Foley, M.	Black, M.	Franks, M.	Cassidy, J.	Davis, M.	Mapleson, R.	Turner, D.	Hewitt, T.	Webb, A.	Cowler, A.	Rudd, N.	Reeves, N.	Cook, J.	Barrett, L.	Rhodes, L.	Ryan, J.	Bickford, S.	Martin, A.	Wonham, A.	Murphy, M.	Bickford, P.	Cann, P.	Carpenter, D.	Finnieston, S.	Chandler, S.	Reed, M.	Adams, J.	Bullock, I.	Field, A.	Sims, T.	Bowtell, S.	McCollin, A.	Mepham, J.	James, K.	Scrivens, S.	Tambaro, P.	Worsfold, T.	Holmes, C.	Constable, S.	Ingham, P.	Eagles, G.	Turkington, M.	Reeve, E.	Swain	Wilmott, C.
21 Aug	(H)	Bishops Stortford	D 0-0		1	2	3	4	5	6	7	8	9	10	11																																						
24 Aug	(A)	Carshalton	L 0-3		1	2	3	4	5	6	7	8	9	10		11																																					
28 Aug	(A)	Bromley	L 0-2			2	3			6	7	4	9	8		11	1	5	10																																		
11 Sep	(A)	Walthamstow	L 2-5				3	4		6	7	8[1]	9	10[1]		11	1		12	2	5																																
14 Sep	(H)	Sutton	L 0-1			2		4		6	7	5	9	10			1	8				3	11																														
18 Sep	(A)	Barking	L 0-3			2		4		6		5		10			1	8	9			3	11	7	12																												
25 Sep	(H)	Slough	D 1-1			2		4		6		8		10			1		11[1]			5		7		3	9																										
2 Oct	(H)	Hitchin	L 1-2		1			4				8		10					9	2	6	5		7		3	12	11[1]																									
5 Oct	(A)	Wycombe	L 0-1	464	1			4				6		10					12	2		5		7		3	9	11	8																								
9 Oct	(A)	Tooting	L 1-2		1				5	6		8		4						2		11				3					7	9[1]	10																				
12 Oct	(H)	Wokingham	W 1-0		1	4	11	12		6		8[1]								2		5				3						9	7	10																			
16 Oct	(A)	Hendon	L 0-2		1			4		6		8								2		5		11		3						9	12	10	7																		
19 Oct	(A)	Hayes	L 1-3		1					6	7	8		10						2		5			4	3						9	11[1]																				
23 Oct	(H)	Walthamstow	L 0-1		1	4				6	7	8		10						2		5				3						9	11																				
30 Oct	(H)	Harrow	L 0-2		1					6	7	8								2		5				3							11		9	4	10																
6 Nov	(A)	Leatherhead	L 1-2		1			12		6	7	8										5				3							11		9	2	10[1]	4															
9 Nov	(A)	Sutton	W 2-1		1						7[1]	8									2	5				3			11				9		6		10	4[1]															
20 Nov	(H)	Barking	L 0-1		1						7	8									2	5				3			11				9		6		10	4															
27 Nov	(H)	Billericay	L 0-2					11			7	8									2	5				3							9		6		10	4	1														
4 Dec	(A)	Hitchin	W 2-1								7	6									2	5				3			11				9		8		10[2]	4	1														
11 Dec	(H)	Bognor	L 0-2								7	6									2	5				3			11				9		8		10	4	1														
18 Dec	(A)	Wokingham	W 2-0							9		6									2	5			4	3			11				12[1]		8		10[1]		1	7													
27 Dec	(H)	Staines	L 2-3							9		8									2	5[1]			4	3							11[1]		6		10		1	7													
1 Jan	(A)	Staines o.g.	L 1-5							9		6									2	5			4	3			11				12		8		10		1	7													
4 Jan	(H)	Leytonstone-Ilford	D 1-1			4						6[1]									2	5				3			11				9		8		10		1	7				12									
22 Jan	(A)	Slough	L 0-3								4	6									2	5				3							9		8					7	1	10	11										
25 Jan	(H)	Carshalton	L 0-1			2					4	6										5				3							9		8					7	1	10	11										
29 Jan	(A)	Dulwich	D 1-1		1	2[1]					4	6										5				3									8					7		10	11	9									
5 Feb	(H)	Bromley	W 2-1		1	2					4	6										5				3									8					7		10[1]	11[1]	9									
19 Feb	(H)	Tooting	L 1-2			2					4	6[1]										5				3									8					7	1	10	11	9									
22 Feb	(H)	Dulwich	L 0-2			2					4	6										5				3														7	1	10	11	9	8								
26 Feb	(A)	Billericay	D 2-2			2					7	6										5				3														9[2]		10			11	1	4	8					
5 Mar	(H)	Hendon	L 1-4			2						6										5				3														9		10	7		11	1	4	8	12[1]				
12 Mar	(A)	Harrow	L 0-2									6										5				3									8					9		2	11		10	1	4		7	12			
26 Mar	(A)	Leytonstone-Ilford	L 0-2								7	6									5					3									8							2	11		12	1			10	4	9		
4 Apr	(A)	Croydon	L 1-4			2				7		6										5				3														8			11[1]		10	1				4	9		
9 Apr	(H)	Wycombe	L 0-2							5		6				11						3			2										8										10	1			7	4	9		
12 Apr	(H)	Croydon	L 1-2							7		6				11[1]						5				3									8							2			10	1			12	4	9		
16 Apr	(A)	Bognor	D 0-0							7		6				11						5				3									8							2			10	1			12	4	9		
19 Apr	(H)	Hayes	L 1-2							7		6				12[1]					5	3		10	2										8							4			11	1					9		
23 Apr	(H)	Leatherhead	W 2-1									6[1]									5	11			2	3									8							4			10	1			7		9[1]		
30 Apr	(A)	Bishops Stortford	L 0-2									6				11					5				2	3				1					8							4			10				7		9		
F.A. CUP																																																					
4 Sep	Prel (H)	Chatham	D 0-0			5	3	4		6		8		10		11	1		7								12																									2	9
7 Sep	Rep (A)	Chatham	L 1-2			5	3	4		6	7[1]	8	9	10			1		12																																	2	11
F.A. TROPHY																																																					
15 Jan	1st R (H)	Barnet	L 0-2		1	4				11	12	6				7					2	5				3			10				9		8																		
SURREY SENIOR CUP																																																					
8 Jan	1st R (A)	Leatherhead	D 0-0			4						6									2	5				3			11				9		8		10		1	7													
11 Jan	Rep (H)	Leatherhead	L 0-1			4						6									2	5				3			11				9		8		10		1	7													
LONDON SENIOR CUP																																																					
18 Jan	1st R (H)	Epsom	W 2-1		1			11		8		6									2	5[1]				3							9[1]	10						7					4								
15 Feb	2nd R (H)	Croydon	W 1-0		1	2					4	6										5				3									8					7		10	11	9[1]									
8 Mar	3rd R (A)	Hayes	W 1-0									6										5				3									8					9[1]		2	11		10	1	4		7				
2 Apr	S-F (H)	Boreham Wood	W 2-1							2		6										5				3									8					9[1]			7		10	1				4	11[1]		
7 May	F	(Dulwich) Sutton	L 0-1									6				11					4	5				3									8							2			10	1			7		9		
HITACHI CUP																																																					
30 Aug	1st R (A)	Epping	W 1-0			2	3	4		6	7	8		10		11[1]	1	5	9								12																										
28 Aug	2nd R (A)	Hornchurch	L 1-2					4		6		8		10			1		11	2		5		7		3	9[1]																										
TOTAL APPEARANCES					**18**	**24**	**8**	**15**	**3**	**29**	**25**	**54**	**6**	**16**	**1**	**11**	**9**	**4**	**7**	**10**	**21**	**45**	**2**	**7**	**8**	**43**	**3**	**2**	**11**	**1**	**1**	**5**	**19**	**3**	**32**	**2**	**13**	**6**	**9**	**20**	**4**	**18**	**13**	**5**	**15**	**13**	**4**	**2**	**7**	**6**	**10**	**2**	**2**
SUBSTITUTE								**2**			**1**					**1**			**3**						**1**		**3**						**3**											**1**	**1**				**3**	**1**			
GOALS SCORED						**1**					**2**	**5**		**1**		**3**			**1**			**2**					**1**	**1**				**1**	**4**				**4**	**1**		**4**		**1**	**2**	**1**					**1**		**2**		

SEASON 1983-1984

ISTHMIAN LEAGUE - DIVISION 1

Date	Venue	Opponents	Result	Attendance	Holmes, C.	Powell, D.	Jones, F.	Stagg, J.	Cook, J.	Black, M.	Jones, T.	Worsfold, T.	Ryan, J.	Holder, P.	Bembridge, S.	Jablonski, P.	Williams, P.	Bickford, S.	Cox, M.	Hewitt, T.	Dummer, I.	Waterman, J.	Cann, P.	Stagg, W.	Cowell, N.	Eagles, G.	Horton, N.	Varney, G.	Jones, C.	Whelan, A.	Arrow, A.	Gibson, N.	Docherty, A.	Reed, M.	Milsom, M.	Wye, S.	Hepworth, M.	Ingham, P.	Simmons, M.
20 Aug	(H)	Oxford	W 1-0		1	2	3	4	5	6	7	8	9	10	11[1]																								
23 Aug	(H)	Epsom & Ewell	L 1-2		1	2		4	5	6	7	8	9	10	11	3[1]																							
27 Aug	(A)	Tilbury	D 0-0		1	2	8	4	5		7		9	10		3	6	11																					
10 Sep	(H)	Windsor & Eton	D 1-1		1			4	2	6	7	8		10		3	5		9[1]	11																			
13 Sep	(H)	Leatherhead	L 1-2		1			4	2	6	7	8		10[1]		3	5		9	12	11																		
17 Sep	(A)	Clapton	L 1-3		1			5	3		7	8		10		4	6	2	9[1]			11																	
20 Sep	(H)	Hampton	L 0-1				3	4			7	8		10		6	5	2	9	11			1																
24 Sep	(A)	Cheshunt	L 0-5				3	4			7	8	11	10		5	6	2	9	12			1																
1 Oct	(H)	Clapton	W 2-1		1			4	6		7	8	11[1]	10[1]		3	5	2	9																				
8 Oct	(A)	Hertford	W 7-0		1			4	6		7[1]	8[1]	11[1]	10		3	5	2	9[4]																				
11 Oct	(A)	Met. Police	L 1-2		1			4	5		7	8	11	10[1]		3	6	2	9					12															
22 Oct	(H)	Feltham	W 3-0		1	4			5		7[1]	8		10[2]		3	6	2	9						11														
29 Oct	(A)	Wembley	L 0-2		1	4			5		7	8		10		3	6	2							11	9													
5 Nov	(H)	Boreham Wood	L 0-3			4			5		7	8		10		3	6	2	9				1		11		12												
12 Nov	(H)	Aveley	L 1-3			2					7	8		10		3	6	5	9[1]						11			1	4	12									
15 Nov	(H)	Lewes	W 1-0			2						8		10		3	6[1]	5	9						11	7		1	4										
19 Nov	(A)	Kingstonian	W 2-1			2						8		10		3	6	5	9						11[2]	7			4		1								
22 Nov	(A)	Epsom & Ewell	L 1-2			2						8		10		3	6	5	9[1]						11	7			4		1								
26 Nov	(A)	Oxford	L 1-3			2						8		11		3	6	5	9[1]						12	7			4		1	10							
3 Dec	(A)	Feltham	L 0-2			2						8		11		3	6	5	9						7				4			10							1
10 Dec	(H)	Maidenhead	W 2-1			2						8[1]		10		3	6	7	9[1]									1	4			11	5						
24 Dec	(A)	Farnborough	L 0-4			2						8		11		3	5	4									12	1	7				6	9	10				
2 Jan	(H)	Farnborough	D 2-2			2						8		11[1]		3	6	5	9						12			1	4[1]			10			7				
10 Jan	(A)	Walton & Hersham	W 3-0			2						8		11		3		5	9[1]									1	4[1]			10	6		7[1]				
14 Jan	(H)	Hertford o.g.	W 3-2			2						8		11[1]		3		5	9[1]						12			1	4			10	6		7				
21 Jan	(A)	Boreham Wood	L 0-5			3						8		11				5	9						4			1		2		10	6		7				
24 Jan	(H)	Met. Police	W 5-1			3								11		4	8	5	9[1]									1		2		10[4]	6		7				
4 Feb	(A)	Hornchurch	W 3-1									4		11		3	8	5	9[2]									1		2		10	6		7[1]				
18 Feb	(H)	Chesham	W 5-2			3						4		11[2]		10	8[1]	5										1		2		9[2]	6		7	12			
25 Feb	(A)	Aveley	W 5-2			2						4		11[2]		3	8	5	9[2]									1				10[1]	6			7			
3 Mar	(H)	Cheshunt	W 2-1									4		11		3	5[1]	6	9								8[1]	1		2		10			7				
6 Mar	(A)	Leatherhead	D 1-1			3						4		11		12	8[1]	5	9									1		2		10	6		7				
10 Mar	(H)	Wembley	W 2-1			3								11			8[1]	5	9[1]									1		2		10	6		7		4		
13 Mar	(A)	Lewes	L 1-3			3								11[1]		4	8	5	9								6	1		2		10	12		7				
17 Mar	(H)	Kingstonian	L 0-2			2								11			8	5	9									1		3		10	6		7		4		
3 Apr	(H)	Tilbury	L 0-1			2								11		3	8	5	9									1				10	6			7	4		
7 Apr	(A)	Windsor & Eton	L 0-2									7		11		2	4	5	9									1		3		10	6				8		
9 Apr	(A)	Maidenhead	D 3-3			2						4		11		3	10[2]	5	9[1]									1					6		7		8		
14 Apr	(H)	Walton & Hersham	D 2-2			3						4		11		10[1]	9	5										1		2			6		7[1]		8		
21 Apr	(A)	Chesham	W 2-1			2						7		11		3	8	5	9[2]									1					6		10		4		
23 Apr	(H)	Hornchurch	D 0-0			2						7		11		3	8	5	9									1				10	6		12		4		
28 Apr	(A)	Hampton	L 1-2			2						7		11		3	8[1]	5	9									1				10	6				4		
F.A. CUP																																							
3 Sep	Prel (A)	Hailsham	L 1-2		1	2	8	4	5		7		9	10		3	6[1]			11						12													
F.A. TROPHY																																							
17 Dec	3rd Q (A)	Hendon	L 0-2			2						9		8		3	4	5	10						7			1				11	6						
LONDON SENIOR CUP																																							
17 Jan	1st R (A)	Tooting	L 1-4			2						8		11		3		5							9			1	4			10	6		7[1]				
SURREY SENIOR CUP																																							
13 Dec	4th Q (H)	Merstham	W 3-0			2						9		8[2]		3	6	5	10[1]						7	12		1	4			11							
28 Jan	1st R (A)	Tooting	L 0-3			3								11		5	8	4	9									1		2		10	6		7				
HITACHI CUP																																							
30 Aug	1st R (H)	Met. Police	D 0-0		1	2	8	4	5		7		9	10		3	6			11																			
6 Sep	Rep (A)	Met. Police	L 0-2		1		8	4	5	6	7			10		3	9									11												2	
TOTAL APPEARANCES					**14**	**37**	**7**	**14**	**15**	**5**	**18**	**39**	**9**	**49**	**2**	**44**	**43**	**42**	**38**	**4**	**1**	**1**	**3**		**12**	**6**	**2**	**28**	**13**	**12**	**3**	**24**	**22**	**1**	**18**	**2**	**9**	**1**	**1**
SUBSTITUTE																**1**				**2**				**1**	**3**	**2**	**2**			**1**			**1**		**1**	**1**			
GOALS SCORED											**2**	**2**	**2**	**14**	**1**	**2**	**9**		**22**						**2**		**1**		**2**			**7**			**4**				

SEASON 1984-1985

ISTHMIAN LEAGUE - DIVISION 1

Date	Venue	Opponents	Result	Attendance	Varney, G.	Bickford, S.	Black, M.	Ingham, P.	Bickford, P.	Wye, S.	Morton, A.	Roberts, K.	Woodbridge, S.	Wilde, M.	Cox, M.	Horton, N.	Jablonski, P.	Worsfold, T.	Wye, L.	Surey, J.	Logan, L.	Musgrove, M.	Turner, A.	Cheeseman, S.	Davies, K.	Payne, M.	O'Gwynn, R.	Frost, L.	Watson, I.	Richardson, H.	Probert, A.	Steer, R.	Hampshire, P.	Osnowski, K.	Giddings, S.	Howard, I.	Atkins, S.	Duff, P.	Graham, J.	Richardson, P.	Beal, P.	MacDonald	MacFarlane, A.	Collins, M.	Lusty, J.	Cawley, P.	Mataxa, N.	Casey, D.	Stillwell, I.	Phillips, A.	Watson, D.	Chapple, G.
25 Aug	(A)	Tilbury	L 2-5		1	2	3	4	5[1]	6	7	8	9	10	11[1]	12																																						
28 Aug	(H)	Lewes	L 0-2		1	2	6	4	7	8	5	11			9		3	10																																		
1 Sep	(H)	Chesham	L 1-4		1	2	3	4	7		10	8	9		11	12	5	6[1]																																		
8 Sep	(A)	Hertford	L 1-2		1		5[1]		6		4	11	7	10	9		3	8	2	12																																
11 Sep	(H)	Maidenhead	L 0-2		1	7	6		4		9	11					3	8	2	10	5																															
22 Sep	(A)	Boreham Wood	L 1-4		1		6				8						3	4				2	5	7[1]	9	10	11																											
29 Sep	(H)	Clapton	W 1-0		1	7	5										3	4		11		2	6	9	10			8[1]																								
2 Oct	(A)	Leatherhead	L 1-5		1	7[1]	5				8						3	4	12	11		2	6	9	10																											
6 Oct	(A)	Staines	L 1-4		1		4				7				9		3[1]	6			5	2		11	10			8																								
13 Oct	(H)	Hornchurch	W 3-2				5				8[1]				9[1]		6[1]						2						1	3	4	7	10	11																		
16 Oct	(H)	Aveley	L 0-1				5				8				9		6											11	1	3	4	2	10		7																		
27 Oct	(A)	Walton & H'sham	D 0-0				5				8				9		6						2					11	1	3	4		10		7																		
30 Oct	(H)	Bromley	L 3-5			2	5				7[2]				10														6	1	3	4				11	8	9[1]														
3 Nov	(A)	Hampton	W 2-1			2	5				8				10[2]		7											6	1	3	4					11	9														
10 Nov	(A)	Oxford	L 0-2				4				5				10		2											7	1	3				6	11	8	9	12														
17 Nov	(H)	Tilbury	W 3-1				5				7				10[2]		6											11	1	3	4	2				8	9[1]														
1 Dec	(A)	St. Albans	D 3-3				5				7				10[2]		6												1	3	4	2					9[1]		8	11												
8 Dec	(A)	Chesham	L 0-4				5				9				10														7	1	3	4	2							8		6	11										
1 Jan	(A)	Lewes	W 1-0				5				9				10		6											7	1	3	4	2					8	11[1]														
5 Jan	(H)	Walton & H'sham	L 1-6				5				9				10[1]		6											7	1	3	4	2					8	11	12														
26 Jan	(H)	Kingstonian	L 0-3				5				8				10		6											7	1	3	4	2					12		11				9									
2 Feb	(H)	Boreham Wood	W 4-2				5				12				10[2]		6											7	1	3	2						9		11	8[2]			4									
23 Feb	(A)	Met. Police	D 1-1				4				11				10[1]		6												1	3	2	7								8			5	9								
2 Mar	(H)	Wembley	L 0-2												10		6			11								7		3	5	2								8			4	9	1							
5 Mar	(H)	Basildon	W 3-2												10[1]		6			11[1]								7		3	5[1]	2								8			4	9	1							
9 Mar	(A)	Bromley	L 1-3								9						8			6								7			4	2		5			12			11[1]				10	1	3						
12 Mar	(H)	Met. Police	W 3-1								9[1]				10					11								7	1		4[1]	2		3						6[1]				8			5					
16 Mar	(H)	Hertford o.g.	W 4-1								9[3]				10					11								7	1		4	2		3						6				8			5					
19 Mar	(A)	Kingstonian	L 2-3				5				9[1]				10[1]															1		4	6		3			11							8			2	7				
23 Mar	(A)	Clapton	L 2-3				4				9[1]				10[1]				7							2			1			6		5			8							11			3					
26 Mar	(H)	Hampton	D 2-2				5				9[1]				10[1]																	4	8		3			6											2	7	1	11		
30 Mar	(A)	Wembley	W 3-2				5				9[2]				10		6			11								7[1]			4	8																	2		1		3	
2 Apr	(H)	Leatherhead	L 0-3				4				9				10		6			11								7				2								3				8			5		1			
6 Apr	(A)	Farnborough	L 0-3				5								10		6											8			4	7					12			9				11			2		1		3	
13 Apr	(H)	Oxford	D 1-1												10					8								7			3	2					9[1]			6				11			4		1		5	
16 Apr	(A)	Hornchurch	W 2-0				5								10[1]					11											4	2													9[1]			6	7	1	8	3	
20 Apr	(A)	Maidenhead	W 1-0				5				9				10					11								7			6	2								8									4		1		3	
23 Apr	(A)	Aveley	W 1-0				5				9				10[1]					11								7			4	2								8									6		1		3	
27 Apr	(A)	Basildon	W 3-2				5				9[1]				10[1]					11								7[1]			4																			2	8	1	6	3	
30 Apr	(H)	Staines	D 0-0				5				9				10					11								7			4						12													2	8	1	6	3	
2 May	(H)	Farnborough	W 2-1				5				9				10[1]	7				11													2								3[1]									4	8	1	6		
4 May	(H)	St. Albans	L 1-3				5				9[1]				10					11								7				2								6									4	8	1		3	
F.A. CUP																																																				
15 Sep	1st Q (A)	Haywards Heath	L 0-2		1	7	9		4		5	11		12			3	8	2		6			10																															
F.A. TROPHY																																																				
20 Oct	1st Q (H)	Lewes	D 1-1				5				8				9		6											11	1	3	4	2	10[1]		7																		
23 Oct	Rep (A)	Lewes	W 3-1				5				8[1]				9[2]		6						2					11	1	3	4		10		7																		
24 Nov	2nd Q (A)	Epsom & Ewell	W 2-1				5				7				10[1]		6											11	1	3	4	2				8[1]	9	12														
15 Dec	3rd Q (A)	Aveley	D 2-2				5				8[1]				10														7	1	3	4	2			6	11	9[1]	12														
18 Dec	Rep (H)	Aveley	W 2-1				5				8				10[1]		6											7	1	3		2				9	11[1]			4										
12 Jan	1st R (A)	Dulwich	D 0-0				5				8				9	11	6											7	1	3	4	2					10														
22 Jan	Rep (H)	Dulwich	D 3-3	AET			5				8[2]				10	11	6											7	1	3	4	2					9[1]														
24 Jan	2nd Rep (H)	Dulwich	L 1-2				5				8				10[1]	11	6											7	1	3	4	2					9														
SURREY SENIOR CUP																																																				
22 Dec	5th Q (H)	Malden Vale	W 2-0				5				8[1]				10		6												1	3	4	2			7		9[1]	11														
31 Jan	1st R (H)	Tooting	D 1-1				9								10[1]	8	6											7	1	3	4	2					12		11				5									
5 Feb	Rep (A)	Tooting	L 0-1				1								10	8	6											7	12	3	4	2					9		11				5									
HITACHI CUP																																																				
9 Oct	2nd R (A)	Whyteleafe	L 1-5		1						11[1]				9		3	6			5	2	4	7				8																								10
TOTAL APPEARANCES					11	9	48	3	6	2	46	6	3	2	49	6	38	10	4	18	4	5	7	6	4	2	1	38	28	27	38	36	5	8	8	6	20	4	6	15	2	1	7	12	3	1	16	7	12	5	9	1
SUBSTITUTE													1			1		2			1	1									1								5	3	1													
GOALS SCORED						1	1		1		20				26		2	1		1				1				3			2		1			1	7	2		6				1									

ISTHMIAN LEAGUE - DIVISION 2

SEASON 1985-1986

Date	Venue	Opponents	Result	Attendance	Stillwell, I.	Pipe, D.	Cowler, A.	Probert, A.	Fabian, M.	Horner, J.	Dawber, M.	Graham, J.	Youlton, C.	Lansley, D.	Cassidy, J.	McGranigan, D.	Knight, P.	Cox, M.	Watson, D.	Ritchie, A.	Wye, L.	Surey, J.	Jablonski, P.	Lickfold, P.	Lomas, C.	McDonald, C.	Woodley, D.	Morris, K.	Baron, T.	Walton, S.	Norman, S.	Jukes, J.
24 Aug	(A)	Met. Police	W 2-0		1	2	3	4	5	6	8[1]	9	10	11[1]	7	12																
27 Aug	(H)	Egham	D 1-1			2	3	4	5	6	8		9	11	7		1	10[1]														
31 Aug	(H)	Eastbourne	W 2-1		1	2	3			6	9			10	4	7[1]		11	5	8[1]												
4 Sep	(A)	Petersfield	W 2-1		1	2	4	12			8		11[1]	10	3	6		9[1]	5	7												
10 Sep	(A)	Banstead	L 2-4		1	2	4			11	7		8[2]	9	5			10	3		6											
14 Sep	(H)	Feltham	W 4-0		1	2	4			11	7		8[1]	9[1]	5			10[2]	3		6											
21 Sep	(A)	Whyteleafe	D 2-2		1		4	6			7		8	9[2]	5			10	12		3	2	11									
2 Oct	(A)	Ruislip Manor	L 0-3		1		4	5			7		12	9	6			10	3	8		2	11									
12 Oct	(A)	Newbury	D 3-3		1		4			6	7		11[1]		5	9[1]		10[1]			3		8	2								
19 Oct	(A)	Bracknell	L 0-2				4			8	7			9	6			10			3		11	2	1	5						
22 Oct	(H)	Banstead	D 2-2				3			12	7		11	9	5	6		10[2]					8	2	1	4						
26 Oct	(H)	Horsham	W 4-1				2				6[1]		11	9[1]	3	8		10[2]	5				7		1	4						
6 Nov	(H)	Southwick	W 1-0				2	4		6			11	9	7			10[1]			3		8		1	5						
9 Nov	(H)	Bracknell	D 0-0				2	4					11	9	7	12		10			3	6	8		1	5						
12 Nov	(A)	Southall	W 2-1				2	4					11[1]	9[1]	6	7		10	3				8		1	5						
16 Nov	(A)	Marlow	W 8-1		1		2	4						10[3]	7	6[2]		11[3]	5		9		8			3						
23 Nov	(H)	Dorking	W 4-1				2	4		10				9[3]	6	8			3		5	11[1]	7		1							
30 Nov	(H)	Flackwell Heath	W 2-0				2	4		10				9[1]	6[1]	8			3			11	7		1	5						
7 Dec	(A)	Molesey	L 2-3				2	4		10[1]				9	6	8[1]			3			11	7		1	5						
10 Dec	(H)	Hungerford	W 5-1				2	4		10			8[1]	9	6[2]				3		11[1]	12[1]	7		1	5						
1 Jan	(H)	Petersfield	D 3-3				2	4			10[1]		8[1]	9[1]	6				3		5	11	7		1							
11 Jan	(A)	Eastbourne	W 5-1				2	4			6[1]			11[1]	7				5[1]		12		9[1]		1	3	8	10[1]				
18 Jan	(H)	Ruislip Manor	W 4-0				2	4			7		12[1]	9[1]	6						3		8[1]		1	5[1]	11	10				
26 Jan	(A)	Feltham	D 1-1				2				7		8	10	6				5		3		11		1			9[1]	4			
8 Mar	(A)	Hungerford	D 1-1				2	3			6[1]			11	7				5				8				9	10	4	1		
15 Mar	(A)	Southwick	L 2-3				2	4			7[1]			9[1]	6								8		1		11	10	5		3	
18 Mar	(A)	Flackwell Heath	W 4-0				2	4			7[2]			9	6								11[1]				8	10[1]	5	1	3	
22 Mar	(H)	Marlow	W 4-0				2	4			7		12	9[1]	6								11[1]				8	10[1]	5[1]	1	3	
25 Mar	(H)	Southall	L 1-2				2	4			7		12[1]	9	6						3		11				8	10	5	1		
29 Mar	(A)	Dorking	W 2-1				2	4					7	9	6						3		11		1		8[1]		5		10[1]	
3 Apr	(H)	Whyteleafe	W 1-0				2				7		11[1]	9	6						4		3		1		8		5		10	
8 Apr	(H)	Newbury	W 5-1				2				7		10[2]	9[1]	6[1]						3		11				8[1]		5	1	4	
12 Apr	(H)	Molesey	W 1-0				2				7		10	9[1]	6						3		11		1		8		5		4	
15 Apr	(A)	Egham	D 2-2					4			7		10[1]	9	6						3		11				8[1]		5	1	2	
19 Apr	(H)	Camberley	W 1-0				2	4			7[1]		10	12	6						3		11		1		8		5		9	
23 Apr	(A)	Horsham	W 5-1				2	4			7[2]		10	12	6						3		11		1		8[1]		5		9[2]	
26 Apr	(H)	Met. Police	W 1-0					4		11	7		10	12	6						3		2		1		8[1]		5		9	
29 Apr	(A)	Camberley	W 3-2					4		11	7[1]		12	10	6						3		2				8		5[2]	1	9	
F.A. CUP																																
7 Sep	1st Q (A)	Ringmer	W 2-1		1	2	4				7[1`]		8[1]	9[1]	5	11		10	3		6	12										
28 Sep	2nd Q (H)	Slough	L 1-5		1		4	5			7		8[1]	9	11			10	3	12		2	6									
F.A. TROPHY																																
5 Oct	1st Q (H)	Maidenhead	L 4-5		1		4	5		12	7[1]		8[1]	9	11[1]			10[1]			3	2	6									
SURREY SENIOR CUP																																
21 Dec	5th Q (H)	Camberley	L 1-2				10	4			7		8[1]	9	6	12			3		5	2	11		1							
LONDON SENIOR CUP																																
3 Dec	3rd Q (H)	Eton Manor	W 4-2				2	4		10				9[1]	6	8			3[2]		12	11	7			5[1]						1
21 Jan	1st R (A)	Hampton	W 1-0				2	4			7		8	9[1]	6					5	3		11		1			10				
6 Mar	2nd R (H)	Leyton-W	W 4-0				2	4			7			9	6				3				8		1		11[1]	10[3]	5			
13 Mar	3rd R (A)	Haringey B	W 2-1				2	4			7			9	6				3				11		1		8[1]	10	5[1]			
5 Apr	S-F (A)	Walthamstow	L 0-3				2	4			7		10	9	6						3		11		1		8		5			
A.C. DELCO CUP																																
17 Sep	Prel (H)	Vauxhall M	W 5-3		1		4	12			7[1]		8	9	5	6		10[4]	3			2	11									
15 Oct	1st R (A)	Uxbridge	L 1-2				3			6	7		11		5[1]	9		10					8	2	1	4						
TOTAL APPEARANCES					**13**	**7**	**46**	**34**	**2**	**16**	**39**	**1**	**31**	**44**	**49**	**14**	**1**	**20**	**23**	**4**	**28**	**12**	**42**	**4**	**27**	**14**	**19**	**11**	**18**	**7**	**12**	**1**
SUBSTITUTE								**2**		**2**			**5**	**3**		**3**			**1**	**1**	**2**	**2**										
GOALS SCORED										**1**	**15**		**18**	**23**	**6**	**5**		**18**	**3**	**1**	**1**	**2**	**4**			**2**	**7**	**7**	**4**		**3**	

SEASON 1986-1987

ISTHMIAN LEAGUE - DIVISION 2

Date	Venue	Opponents	Result	Attendance	Lomas, C.	Cowler, A.	Probert, A.	Black, M.	Jablonski, P.	Dawber, M.	Kerbey, S.	Cassidy, J.	Richardson, J.	Morris, K.	Buzaglio, T.	Baron, T.	Horner, J.	Wye, L.	Sabourn, N.	Hill, K.	Jones, G.	Lansley, D.	Mitchell, J.	Bonetti, P.	Dodd, S.	Baker, S.	Yates, C.	Jukes, J.	Mepham, J.	Chapman, J.	Shepherd, N.	Buzaglio R.
16 Aug	(H)	Banstead	D 0-0		1	2	3	4	5	6	7	8	9	10	11	12	14															
19 Aug	(A)	Marlow	L 3-5		1	2	5	4	3	7[2]	8	6	11	9	10[1]	12																
23 Aug	(A)	Met. Police	W 3-0		1	2		4	3	7	8	6	11	9[1]	10[1]	5[1]																
2 Sep	(H)	Chertsey	W 1-0		1	2	3		5	6	7[1]	8	9	11	10	4																
6 Sep	(A)	Ruislip Manor	W 3-0		1	2			5	6	7[1]	8	9[1]	10	11[1]	3		4	12													
9 Sep	(A)	Dorking	L 0-2		1	2			3	7	8	6	11		10	5		4	9	12	14											
17 Sep	(A)	Petersfield	W 5-0		1	2			5	6[1]	7		8	10[1]	11[3]	3		4		9		12										
20 Sep	(H)	Harefield	W 3-1		1	2			3	7[2]	8[1]	5	6	9				4		11												10
18 Oct	(H)	Chalfont St. Peter	D 1-1		1				3	7[1]		6	8	9	10	5		4		11			2									
22 Oct	(A)	Feltham	W 3-0		1				3	7		6	8[1]	9[1]	10[1]	5		4		11			2									
28 Oct	(H)	Marlow	L 1-2						3	7		6	8	9[1]	10	5		4		11		12	2	1								
1 Nov	(H)	Feltham	L 0-2		1				3	7		6	8	9	10	5		4		11		12	2									
8 Nov	(A)	Molesey	W 3-1		1	3			11	7[2]		6[1]	8		10	5	9	4					2									
22 Nov	(H)	Newbury	W 5-0		1	3			11	7		6[1]	8	9	10[2]	5	12[1]	4				14[1]	2									
25 Nov	(H)	Dorking	D 3-3		1	3			11			6	8	9[1]	10	5[1]	7[1]	4		14		12	2									
29 Nov	(A)	Chalfont St. Peter	W 3-1		1	5			9	6[2]		8	7	11		3	10[1]	4					2									
2 Dec	(A)	Camberley	W 1-0		1				3			6	11	10	12	5	8			7	4	9	2[1]									
6 Dec	(H)	Hungerford	L 2-4		1				3			6	8	9	10[2]	5	11			7	4		2									
9 Dec	(A)	Egham	W 5-0		1	3						6	8		10[2]	5[1]	11	4		7		9[2]	2									
13 Dec	(H)	Met. Police	W 5-0		1	5						7	8		11[2]	4	9	3		6		10[3]	2									
16 Dec	(H)	Camberley	W 8-1		1	5						7	8		11[3]	4	9[1]	3		6[1]		10[2]	2[1]									
20 Dec	(A)	Eastbourne	D 0-0		1							7	10			3	11	4		6	5	9	2		8							
27 Dec	(H)	Horsham	W 5-1		1							6	8		10[2]	5	11	3		7		9[2]	2			4[1]						
1 Jan	(A)	Chertsey	L 2-3		1							6	8		10	5	11	3		7		9	2[1]			4[1]						
24 Jan	(H)	Ruislip Manor	W 4-0		1	3						6	8	9	10[2]	5	11[1]	4		7						2[1]						
31 Jan	(A)	Flackwell Heath	W 2-1		1	3					2	6	8	9	10[1]	5[1]	7	4									11					
21 Feb	(H)	Southall	W 5-0		1	3[1]					7	6	8[1]	9[1]	10[1]	5	11[1]	4					2									
7 Mar	(H)	Petersfield	W 3-0			3[1]						6	8	9[1]	10	5[1]	11	4		7			2					1				
11 Mar	(A)	Horsham	W 5-0			3						6	8	9[1]	10[2]	5	11[2]	4		7			2						1			
14 Mar	(H)	Whyteleafe	D 1-1			3					12	6	8	9	10	5[1]	11	4		7			2						1			
17 Mar	(H)	Eastbourne	W 2-0			3						6	8	9	10	5	11[1]	4					2				12[1]		1	7		
31 Mar	(A)	Banstead	W 2-0		1	3						6	8		10	5	11[1]	4		7			2				9[1]					
11 Apr	(A)	Southall	W 2-0		1	3						6[1]	8		10[1]	5	11	4		7			2				9					
14 Apr	(H)	Flackwell Heath	W 2-0		1	3						6	8	12	10[2]	5	11	4		7			2				9					
18 Apr	(A)	Newbury	W 3-1		1	3						6	8[1]	12	10	5	11	4					2				9			7[2]		
23 Apr	(H)	Egham	W 4-0			3						6[1]	8	9	10[1]	5	11	4					2						1	7[2]		
25 Apr	(H)	Molesey	W 5-0		1	3						6	8	9[1]	10[1]	5[1]	11[2]	4					2							7		
28 Apr	(A)	Hungerford	D 1-1		1	3						6		9	10	5	11	4		7			2				8[1]					
30 Apr	(A)	Harefield	W 3-0		1	3						6		9	10[2]	5	11	4		7			2[1]				8					
2 May	(A)	Whyteleafe	D 1-1		1	3						6		9	10[1]	5	11	4		7			2				8					
F.A. CUP																																
30 Aug	Prel (A)	Horndean	W 3-2	153	1	2	3		5		7[1]	8[1]	9	10	11	4[1]				6												
13 Sep	1st Q (A)	Lancing	W 4-2	137	1	2			3	7[1]	8		6	9[1]	10[2]	5		4		11												
27 Sep	2nd Q (H)	Hastings	W 4-0	256	1	2		14	3	7	8	6	10[1]			5		4		11		9[3]									12	
11 Oct	3rd Q (H)	Crawley	W 3-1	403	1	2			3	7[1]		6	8	9[2]	10	5		4		11												
25 Oct	4th Q (H)	Weymouth	W 1-0	1,029					3	7[1]		6	8	9	10	5		4		11			2	1								
15 Nov	1st R (H)	Chelmsford	D 1-1	1,411	1	3			11	7		6	8	9	10	5	14	4				12[1]	2									
17 Nov	Rep (A)	Chelmsford	L 1-2	2,660	1	3			11	7		6	8	9[1]	10	5		4				12	2									
F.A. TROPHY																																
4 Oct	1st R (H)	Tooting	L 0-1	205	1	2			3	7	8	6	10			5		4		11		9										
SURREY SENIOR CUP																																
10 Jan	5th Q (H)	Malden Vale	AB 0-0			3						6	8		10	5	11	4		7		9	2					1				
2 Feb	5th Q (H)	Malden Vale	W 4-1		1	3						6	8[1]	9[1]	10[2]	5	11	4		7						2						
7 Feb	1st R (H)	Banstead	W 4-2		1	3						6	8	9[1]	10[1]	5	7[1]	4					2[1]				11					
28 Feb	2nd R (A)	Croydon	W 6-1		1	3[1]						6	8[1]	9	10[4]	5	11	4		7			2									
21 Mar	S-F (H)	Kingstonian	W 1-0		1	3						6	8		10[1]	5	11	4		7			2				9					
20 Apr	F	(Met. Police) Sutton	L 0-4		1	3						6	11	9	10	5	8	4		12			2							7		
LONDON SENIOR CUP																																
27 Jan	1st R (H)	Fister	L 1-4			3						6	8[1]	7	10	5	11	4		12		9				2		1				
A.C. DELCO CUP																																
26 Aug	Prel (H)	Bracknell	W 2-0		1	2	4		3		8	6	11	9[1]	10[1]	5				7												
23 Sep	1st R (H)	Leatherhead	D 2-2	AET	1	2			5	6	7	3	8					4		9[1]		10[1]										11
30 Sep	Rep (A)	Leatherhead	L 1-2		1	2			3	7	8	6	10			5		4		11	12	9[1]										
TOTAL APPEARANCES					**49**	**48**	**5**	**3**	**29**	**24**	**17**	**56**	**55**	**40**	**50**	**54**	**34**	**50**	**1**	**37**	**3**	**13**	**38**	**2**	**1**	**5**	**10**	**3**	**4**	**5**		**2**
SUBSTITUTE								**1**			**1**			**2**	**1**	**2**	**3**		**1**	**4**	**2**	**7**					**1**				**1**	
GOALS SCORED						**3**				**13**	**4**	**5**	**8**	**16**	**45**	**8**	**13**			**2**		**16**	**5**			**3**	**3**			**4**		

SEASON 1987-1988

ISTHMIAN LEAGUE - DIVISION 1

Date	Venue	Opponents	Result	Attendance	Tenkorang, R.	Mitchell, J.	Baron, T.	Wye, L.	Cowler, A.	Blankley, B.	Shrubb, P.	Cassidy, J.	Richardson, J.	Lansley, D.	Parr, A.	Horner, J.	Buzaglo, T.	Buzaglo, R.	Chapman, J.	Lavender, K.	Lomas, C.	Lunn, G.	Hill, K.	Holsgrove, P.	Jukes, J.	Baker, S.	Kitchener, K.	Harding, M.	Lickfold, P.	Roberts, B.	O'Flaherty, D.	Youlton, C.	Biggins, M.	Mepham, J.	Houghton, T.	Barnett, D.	Soloman, G.	Miles, A.
22 Aug	(H)	Kingsbury	L 2-3		1	2	3	4	5	6	7	8	9	10	11[2]	12																						
29 Aug	(A)	Boreham Wood	W 5-2		1	2[1]	3	4	5	6[1]	8	7	9[1]		10		11[2]																					
5 Sep	(A)	Wembley	L 0-4		1	2	3	4	5	6	8	7	9	14	10	12	11																					
8 Sep	(A)	Walthamstow	W 3-0		1	2[1]	5	4	3		7	6[1]	11		9	8	10[1]																					
19 Sep	(H)	Lewes	W 4-3		1		3	4			5	7	8	9[1]	6	12	10[2]	11[1]	2																			
6 Oct	(H)	Marlow	L 1-2		1	2	5	4			3	6	11		9	8		10[1]	7																			
17 Oct	(H)	Billericay o.g.	W 3-1	404		2	5[1]	4			3	6	10	9	7[1]	8		11	12	1																		
20 Oct	(H)	Chesham	W 2-0			2	5	4			3	6[1]	11	9[1]	7	8		10			1																	
24 Oct	(A)	Stevenage	W 2-0			2	5[1]	4			3	6	11	12	7	8	9[1]	10				1																
27 Oct	(A)	Staines	D 3-3			2	3[1]	4			5	7	9	12	6	8	10[1]	11[1]				1	14															
3 Nov	(A)	Walton & Hersham	L 0-2			2	5	4			3	6	11	12	7	8	10	9				1	14															
7 Nov	(A)	Marlow	L 0-3			2	5	4			3	6	11	12	9	7	10						14	8	1													
10 Nov	(H)	Southwick	W 4-0			2			3			6	11		4	7[2]	10[1]	9						8	1	5[1]												
14 Nov	(A)	Basildon	W 3-0			4[1]			5			6			3	8	10	9[2]					7	2	1			11										
17 Nov	(H)	Wolverton	W 6-0			2[1]		4	3		8[1]	6			11	7	10[3]	9[1]							1	5												
28 Nov	(A)	Bracknell	L 2-3			2	12	4	3[1]			6			7	8	10[1]	9							1	5			11									
1 Dec	(A)	Leatherhead	D 0-0			2	5	4	3			6			9	8	10						7		1	12			11									
5 Dec	(H)	Walton & Hersham	W 2-0			2	5	4	3		10[1]	6[1]			7	8	9								1					11	12							
12 Dec	(A)	Wolverton	W 3-1			2	5	4	3		11	6			7	8[1]	10								1					9[1]		12[1]						
15 Dec	(A)	Uxbridge	W 1-0			2	5[1]	4	3		11	6			7	8									1					9		10						
19 Dec	(H)	Staines	L 0-2			2	5	4	3		11	6			7	8							12		1					9		10						
26 Dec	(H)	Oxford	W 3-0			2	5	4	3[1]			6			7	11														9[2]		10	8	1				
2 Jan	(A)	Kingsbury	W 4-2			2	4	3[1]	5			8			6	9[1]														11		10[2]	7	1				
16 Jan	(A)	Worthing	W 2-0			2	5[1]	4	3			6			7	11	9[1]				1											10	8					
23 Jan	(H)	Wembley	W 3-0			2[1]	5	4[2]	3			6			7	11	10				1											9	8					
13 Feb	(H)	Grays	D 1-1			2	4		5			8	9		6[1]		10	11			1												7		3			
20 Feb	(A)	Chesham	D 1-1			2[1]	5		3		12	8	9		10	6	11	14			1												7		4			
23 Feb	(H)	Leatherhead	W 1-0			2	4				5	8			6[1]	9	10				1									11			7		3			
27 Feb	(A)	Grays	W 1-0			2	3	4			5	8			6	9	11[1]	10			1												7					
1 Mar	(H)	Uxbridge	W 4-3			2[1]	4	3			5	8[1]			6[1]	9	11	10[1]			1												7					
5 Mar	(H)	Walthamstow	W 4-2			2	3	4			5	8			6	9	11[2]															10[2]	7	1	12			
12 Mar	(H)	Stevenage	D 1-1			2	5[1]	4			3	6			7	11	10	12			1											9	8					
19 Mar	(A)	Billericay	L 1-2			2		4			3	6			7	11		10			1											9[1]	8		5			
22 Mar	(A)	Lewes	W 3-1				5	4	3		2	6		9[2]	12	11		7							1							10[1]	8					
26 Mar	(H)	Hampton	L 2-3				5	4	3		2	6		9[1]	12[1]	8	10				1											11	7					
29 Mar	(H)	Basildon	W 3-1				3	4	5		2[1]	8		14[1]		6	11	9			1											10[1]	7					
2 Apr	(A)	Hampton	W 2-0				3	4	5		2	8				9	11[1]				1											10[1]	7			6		
9 Apr	(A)	Oxford	W 4-2				3[1]	4	5[1]		2	8				9	11				1											10[2]	7			6		
12 Apr	(H)	Boreham Wood	W 2-0				3[1]	4	5		2	8				9	11[1]				1											10	7			6		
16 Apr	(H)	Worthing	D 1-1				3	4	5		2	8				9	11[1]				1											10	7			6		
23 Apr	(A)	Southwick	D 1-1				3	4	5		2	8			12	9	11[1]	14							1							10	7			6		
30 Apr	(H)	Bracknell	L 1-2				5	4	3		2	6			7	11	10	12[1]							1							9	8					
F.A. CUP																																						
12 Sep	1st Q (A)	Windsor & Eton	D 0-0		1	2	3	4	5		7	8	9		10	6	11																					
15 Sep	Rep (H)	Windsor & Eton	W 6-3	AET	1		3[2]	4	5		2	8	9	10	6[1]	7	11[1]	14[2]	12																			
26 Sep	2nd Q (A)	Banstead	D 0-0		1	2	3	4			5	8	9		10	7		11	6																			12
29 Sep	Rep (H)	Banstead	W 1-0		1	2	3	4			5	8	9		10[1]	6		11	7																			
10 Oct	3rd Q (A)	Thanet	D 1-1			2	5	4			3	6	11	12	9	8[1]		10	7	1																		
13 Oct	Rep (H)	Thanet	L 0-1	AET		2	5	4			3	6	11	12	9	8		10	7	1																		
F.A. TROPHY																																						
3 Oct	1st Q (H)	Bognor	W 2-1		1	2	3	4			5	8[1]	9		10	7		11[1]	6								12											
31 Oct	2nd Q (H)	Basingstoke	W 2-1			2[1]	5	4			3	6	11		7[1]	8	9	10							1													
21 Nov	3rd Q (A)	Hendon o.g.	L 1-3			2		4	5		8	7			9	6	11	10							1	3												
SURREY SENIOR CUP																																						
9 Jan	1st R (H)	Croydon	L 1-2			2	4	3	5			8			6	9	12													11		10[1]	7	1				
A.C. DELCO CUP																																						
25 Aug	Prel (A)	Whyteleafe	W 3-0		1	2	3	4[1]	5	6[1]	7	8	9		10[1]		11																					
22 Sep	1st R (A)	Barking	L 0-2	AET	1		3	4			5	8	6	11	10	7		12	2																		9	
TOTAL APPEARANCES					**13**	**42**	**48**	**49**	**33**	**4**	**43**	**54**	**25**	**8**	**46**	**48**	**37**	**24**	**8**	**3**	**16**	**3**	**2**	**3**	**15**	**4**		**1**	**2**	**8**		**19**	**22**	**4**	**4**	**5**	**1**	
SUBSTITUTE							**1**				**1**			**8**	**3**	**3**	**1**	**6**	**2**				**4**			**1**	**1**				**1**	**1**			**1**			**1**
GOALS SCORED						**8**	**10**		**3**	**2**	**3**	**5**	**1**	**6**	**11**	**5**	**21**	**11**								**1**				**3**		**12**						

ISTHMIAN LEAGUE - DIVISION 1

SEASON 1988-1989

Date	Venue	Opponents	Result	Atten-dance	Lomas, C.	Shrubb, P.	Baker, S.	Wye, L.	Cowler, A.	Moss, S.	Cassidy, J.	Biggins, M.	Richardson, J.	Miles, A.	Worsfold, T.	Jones, T.	Baron, T.	Buzaglo, R.	Bastine, S.	Buzaglo, T.	Wye, S.	Davis, M.	Hatcher, N.	Jukes, J.	Morton, A.	Dearden, K.	Cook, J.	Gale, T.	Mulvaney, P.	McIsaac, I.	Caulfield, C.	Wallace, C.
20 Aug	(H)	Uxbridge	L 1-2		1	2	3	4	5	6	7	8	9	10	11[1]																	
27 Aug	(A)	Wembley	W 5-0			2[1]		4	5		8	7	6	11	10[3]	1	3[1]	9	12													
30 Aug	(H)	Hampton	W 2-1	374		2		3	5		8	7	6[1]	11	10	1	4	9		12[1]												
3 Sep	(A)	Worthing	D 1-1	314		2		3	5		8	7	6		10[1]	1	4	9		11	12											
6 Sep	(A)	Southwick	W 2-0			2		4	5		8	7	12		10[2]	1	3	9		11	6											
10 Sep	(H)	Bracknell	L 1-2			2		4	5		8	7[1]	6		10	1	3	9		11	12											
8 Oct	(H)	Boreham Wood	W 4-1			2		4	5	12	8	7	14			1	3	9[1]		11[1]	6[1]	10[1]										
19 Oct	(A)	Chesham	W 5-0			5		3		2	8	7[1]				1	4	9		10[2]	6[1]	11[1]										
1 Nov	(A)	Hitchin	D 1-1			2		4[1]		5	8	7				1	3	9		10	6	11										
5 Nov	(A)	Walton & Hersham	W 3-1	393		2		4[1]	5		7	8				1	3	9[1]		11[1]	6	10										
8 Nov	(A)	Lewes	W 2-0			2		4[1]	5		7	8[1]				1	3	9		10	6	11										
12 Nov	(H)	Worthing	W 3-1	752		2		4	5	14	8	7[1]	12			1	3[1]	9		11[1]	6	10										
26 Nov	(H)	Staines	D 1-1			2		4	5	12	8	7[1]				1	3	9		11	6	10										
29 Nov	(H)	Kingsbury	W 1-0			5		4		2	8	7	9		12	1	3			11	6	10[1]	14									
10 Dec	(H)	Hitchin	D 1-1			5		4		2	7	8	9			1	3			11	6[1]	10										
17 Dec	(A)	Bracknell	D 0-0			5		4		2	8	7	9				3				6	11	10	1								
20 Dec	(H)	Met. Police	D 1-1			5		4[1]		2	8	7	9				3				6	10	11	1								
27 Dec	(H)	Collier Row	W 3-1			6		4	5	2	8	7	9				3[1]			11	12	10[1]	14[1]	1								
31 Dec	(H)	Chalfont St. Peter o.g.	D 2-2			6		4[1]	5	2	8	7	14				3	9			12	10	11	1								
2 Jan	(A)	Basingstoke	D 1-1	753				4	5	2		8	6		12		3	9[1]			7	10	11	1								
10 Jan	(H)	Wembley	L 0-1			5		3		2		8	6		12		4	9			7		11	1	10							
21 Jan	(H)	Chesham	L 0-2			5		4		2		7					3	9		11		10	6		12	1	8					
28 Jan	(A)	Hampton	W 2-0			5		4		2		8[1]	12		11[1]		3	9				10	6			1		7				
11 Feb	(A)	Met. Police	W 2-1			5		4	12	2		8	11		10		3				6					1		7[2]	9			
28 Feb	(H)	Southwick	W 1-0			2		3	5			7			10[1]		4	9		12	8					1			6	11		
4 Mar	(A)	Boreham Wood	W 3-2			2		4[1]	5			8[1]	12		10		3			11	7[1]					1		6	9			
11 Mar	(H)	Wivenhoe	D 0-0						5	2		6	8		10	1	4			11	7							3	9			
18 Mar	(H)	Walton	L 0-1			2			5			6	8							10	7	4						3	9	11	1	
21 Mar	(A)	Uxbridge	W 4-0					4	5	2		8	9[1]		11		3			12	7[2]	10	6[1]								1	
25 Mar	(A)	Basildon	W 2-1					4[1]	5[1]			8	9		11		3			12	7	10	6					2			1	
1 Apr	(A)	Collier Row	W 2-0					4	5	2		8			11[2]		3			10	6		7						9		1	
4 Apr	(A)	Wivenhoe	W 3-0					4	5	2		8	11		9[1]		3			10	6[1]		7						12[1]		1	
8 Apr	(H)	Basingstoke	W 3-0	1,032				4	5[1]	2		8	9		10[1]		3			11	7		6[1]								1	
11 Apr	(A)	Leatherhead	W 1-0					4[1]	5			8	9		10		3			11	2	7							12		1	6
15 Apr	(A)	Chalfont St. Peter	W 3-1					3	5			8[1]	9[1]		11[1]		4				7		6					2	10		1	
18 Apr	(A)	Kingsbury	W 1-0					3	5			7	9[1]		11		4				8		6					2	10		1	
22 Apr	(H)	Leatherhead	W 2-1					4[1]	5[1]			8	9		10		3				7		6					2	11		1	
29 Apr	(A)	Staines	L 1-0	1,122				4	5	2		8	9		10		3			11	7		6								1	
2 May	(H)	Basildon	W 1-0					4	5	2		8[1]			9		3			10	6	12	11						7		1	
6 May	(H)	Lewes	D 2-2	1,420				4	5[1]	2		8			10[1]		3			11	7		9						6		1	
F.A. CUP																																
17 Sep	1st Q (H)	Canterbury	W 3-0	280		2		4	5		8	7[1]			10	1	3	9[1]		11[1]	6											
1 Oct	2nd Q (A)	Molesey	D 1-1			2		3	5		8	7	10			1	4[1]	9		11	6											
4 Oct	Rep (H)	Molesey	W 1-0	357		2		3	5[1]		8	7			10	1	4	9		11	6											
15 Oct	3rd Q (A)	Whyteleafe	W 2-0	395		2		4	5[1]		6	7				1	3	9		11[1]	6	10										
29 Oct	4th Q (A)	Exmouth	W 5-1	937		2		4	5[1]		7	8				1	3	9[1]		11[2]	6	10[1]										
19 Nov	1st R (H)	Cambridge United	L 1-4	2,614		2		3	5	14	7	8	12			1	4	9		11	6[1]	10										
F.A. TROPHY																																
24 Sep	1st Q (H)	St. Albans	D 1-1	308		2		4	5[1]		3	8	6		10	1		9		11	7											
27 Sep	Rep (A)	St. Albans	W 4-1	318		2		4	5[1]		8	7			11	1	3[1]	9		10	6[2]											
22 Oct	2nd Q (A)	Sheppey	W 2-0	205		5		4		2[1]	7	8			10	1	3	9		11[1]	6											
3 Dec	3rd Q (A)	Crawley	W 4-3	528		5		4		2	8	7	9[1]			1	3			11[3]	6	10										
14 Jan	1st R (A)	Bromsgrove	W 3-2	916		5		4		2		8				1		11[2]		10	6[1]	9	7		12		3					
4 Feb	2nd R (H)	Weymouth	W 2-1	660		5		4		2		8			10[2]		3	11			6	9	7	1								
25 Feb	3rd R (A)	Newcastle B.S.	L 0-2	653		2		4	5	12					10	1	3	9		11	7	8	6							14		
SURREY SENIOR CUP																																
7 Jan	1st R (H)	Met. Police	W 2-1			6		4	5	2		8[1]					3[1]	9			7		10	1	11		12					
24 Jan	2nd R (A)	Leatherhead	D 0-0			5		4		2		8			10		3	9		11		7	6	1	12							
14 Feb	Rep (H)	Leatherhead	W 4-1			2		3	5			8			10[2]		4	9			7[1]		6	1						11[1]		
21 Feb	S-F (A)	Chertsey	W 1-0			6		3	5	2					11[1]		4	9		12	8					1		7		10		
27 Mar	F	(Walton) Carshalton	L 2-4					4	5	2		7	9		12	1	3			11	8	10[1]	6[1]									
A.C. DELCO CUP																																
13 Sep	1st R (A)	Whyteleafe	W 3-0			2		4	5[1]		8	7			10[1]	1	3	9		11[1]	6											
22 Nov	2nd R (A)	Petersfield	W 2-0			2		4	5		8	7			10	1	3[1]	9			6	11[1]										
13 Dec	3rd R (A)	Carshalton	L 0-2			5		4		2	8	7	9				3				6	11	10	1								
TOTAL APPEARANCES					1	46	1	59	45	31	32	59	29	3	35	30	57	36		39	51	31	26	11	2	6	2	10	11	4	13	1
SUBSTITUTE									1	5			7		4				1	5	4	1	2		3		1		2	1		
GOALS SCORED						1		9	10	1		11	5		21		7	7		15	12	7	4					2	1	1		

ISTHMIAN LEAGUE - DIVISION 1

SEASON 1989-1990

Date	Venue	Opponents	Result	Atten-dance	Caulfield, C.	Mitchell, S.	Cowler, A.	Russell, A.	Baron,T.	Wye, S.	Biggins, M.	Parr, A.	Buzaglo, T.	Worsfold, T.	Hall, G.	Moss, S.	Franks, M.	Mulvaney, P.	McLaren, C.	Wooler, P.	Davis, M.	Wye, L.	St.Hilaire, M.	Kerrins, W.	Pratt, B.	Gray, J.	Flack, S.	Nelson, H.	Fearon, E.	Davidson, L.
19 Aug	(A)	Croydon	W 2-0	394	1	2	3	4	5	6	7	8	9	10[1]	11[1]	14														
26 Aug	(H)	Walton & Hersham	W 3-1	515	1	2	3	4	5[1]	6		7	9[1]	8	10		11	12[1]												
30 Aug	(A)	Chesham	W 4-2	517	1	2		4	5	6	7	8[1]	10[2]			3	11	9[1]												
5 Sep	(A)	Leatherhead	W 2-0	385	1	2		4	5	6	7[1]	8	9			3	11	10[1]												
9 Sep	(H)	Kingsbury o.g.	W 3-0		1	2		4	5	6	7	8[1]	10			3	11	9[1]												
23 Sep	(H)	Harlow	W 4-0		1	2	3	4	5	6		8	9[1]		10[3]		11		7											
26 Sep	(A)	Southwick	D 1-1		1	2	3	4	5[1]	6		8	9		10		11		7											
7 Oct	(A)	Wivenhoe	W 2-1	611	1		3	4	5	6[1]		8	10				11	7[1]		2	9									
4 Nov	(A)	Boreham Wood	W 4-0		1	2	3	4	5	6		7	10[2]		9			8[2]				11								
7 Nov	(H)	Lewes	W 6-0	850	1	2	3	4	5		6[1]	7	10[1]		8[1]			9[3]				11								
11 Nov	(A)	Chalfont St. Peter	D 1-1	620	1	2	3	4	5	8	6	7[1]	10		12			9				11								
25 Nov	(A)	Uxbridge	W 3-2	407	1	2	3	4	5	6[1]	8	7[1]	10				11	9[1]				14	12							
28 Nov	(A)	Worthing o.g.	L 1-2		1	2	3	4	5	6	8	7	10					9				11								
16 Dec	(H)	Whyteleafe	L 0-1		1	2	3	4		6	12	7	10				14	9				11	8	5						
26 Dec	(A)	Tooting	D 2-2		1	2	3	4	5	6	8	7[1]	10		12		11	9[1]												
30 Dec	(A)	Lewes	W 3-0		1	2	3	4		6	8	7	10[2]		5[1]		11	9												
6 Jan	(A)	Kingsbury	W 3-1		1	2	3	4	5	6	8	7[1]	10		12		11[1]	9[1]							14					
20 Jan	(A)	Walton	D 1-1	778		2	3	4	5	6	8		10		7[1]		11	9							12	1				
23 Jan	(H)	Wembley	W 2-1			2	3	4	5	6	8		10[1]				11	9							7[1]	1				
27 Jan	(H)	Chesham	W 1-0			2[1]	3	4	5	6	8		10					9				11			7	1				
10 Feb	(H)	Purfleet	W 4-0	862		2[1]	3	4	7	6	8		10[3]					9				11			5	1				
17 Feb	(H)	Southwick	W 1-0	997		2	3	4	7	6	8		10[1]					9				11			5	1				
3 Mar	(H)	Wivenhoe	L 1-2	1,150		2	3	4	5	6	8	11[1]	10		7			9								1				
10 Mar	(A)	Dorking	D 0-0		1	2	3	4	5		8	6					11	9									7	10		
13 Mar	(H)	Met. Police	W 1-0		1	2	3		5		8	6					11	9[1]							4			10	7	
17 Mar	(H)	Boreham Wood	L 1-2		1	2	3	4	5[1]	7	8	6	10				11	9							12					
24 Mar	(A)	Hampton	W 1-0		1	2	3	4	5	6	8	7	10				11	9[1]												
29 Mar	(H)	Hitchin	W 3-0		1	2	3	4	5	6	8[1]	7	10[1]									11							9[1]	
31 Mar	(H)	Leatherhead	W 6-0		1	2	3	4	5[1]	6	8	7[1]	10[2]				14	12[1]				11							9[1]	
5 Apr	(H)	Tooting	W 2-0		1	2	3	4	5	6	8	7	10[1]									11							9[1]	
7 Apr	(A)	Whyteleafe	D 0-0		1	2	3	4	5	6	8	7	10					12				11							9	
10 Apr	(A)	Purfleet	W 1-0		1	2	3	4	5	6	8	7	10[1]				12	9				11								
12 Apr	(A)	Wembley	W 3-0		1	2	3	4	5	6	8	7	10[2]				14					11			12				9[1]	
14 Apr	(H)	Chalfont St. Peter	W 4-1		1	2	3	4[1]	5	6	8	7	10[2]				12[1]					11							9	
19 Apr	(H)	Dorking	W 3-0		1	2	3	4[1]	5	6	8	7	10[2]									11							9	
21 Apr	(A)	Met. Police	D 3-3		1	2[1]	3	4	5	6	8	7[1]	10[1]									11							9	
23 Apr	(A)	Harlow	D 2-2		1	2	3	4	5[1]	6	8	7[1]	10				11												9	
26 Apr	(H)	Hampton	W 2-0		1	2	3	4	5[1]	6	8	7	10[1]				11												9	
28 Apr	(H)	Uxbridge	W 6-1	1,136	1	2	3		5	6	8	7	10[3]				11	9[2]				12[1]			4				14	
1 May	(H)	Croydon	W 5-0	855	1	2	3	4	5[1]	6	8	7[2]	10[2]				11	9				14							12	
3 May	(H)	Worthing	W 2-1		1	2	3	4	5	6	8[1]	7[1]	10				11	9												
5 May	(A)	Hitchin	W 3-1		1	2	3	4	5	6[1]	8	7	10				11[1]	9											12[1]	
F.A. CUP																														
16 Sep	1st Q (A)	Kingstonian	W 5-1	706	1	2	3	4	5	6	8[1]	7[1]	9[2]		10[1]		11													
30 Sep	2nd Q (H)	Southwick	W 4-1	629	1	2	3	4[1]	5	6		8[1]	10				11	7[2]			9									
14 Oct	3rd Q (A)	Erith & B	D 1-1	503	1	2	3	4	5	6		8	10		7		11	9			12[1]									
17 Oct	Rep (H)	Erith & B	W 5-0	731	1	2	3	4[1]	5	6		8[1]	10[1]		7[1]			9				11[1]								
28 Oct	4th Q (A)	Wokingham	W 3-1	1,084	1	2[1]	3	4	5	6		7	10[1]		8[1]			9				11								
18 Nov	1st R (A)	Slough	W 2-1	2,182	1	2	3	4	5	6	8	7	10[1]				11	9[1]				14								
9 Dec	2nd R (A)	Cambridge United	L 1-3	3,477	1	2		4	5	6	12	7	10		8	3		9[1]				11								
F.A. TROPHY																														
2 Dec	3rd Q (H)	Fareham	W 5-1	641	1	2	3	4	5	6[1]		7	10		8[1]		11	9[2]				12[1]								
13 Jan	1st R (H)	Bromsgrove	W 3-0	913	1	2	3	4	5	6	8	7	10[1]				11	9[2]												
12 Feb	2nd R (H)	Seaham R.S.	W 3-1	1,211		2[1]	3	4	7	6	8		10[1]					9[1]				11			5	1				
24 Feb	3rd R (H)	Bath	D 1-1	1,507		2	3	4	7	6	8		10[1]					9				11			5	1				
27 Feb	Rep (A)	Bath	L 1-2	1,099		2	3	4	7	6	8		10					9				11[1]			5	1				
A.C. DELCO CUP																														
12 Sep	1st R (A)	Tooting	W 5-1	273	1	2	3	4	5	6[1]	8	7[1]	9[2]	12	10[1]		11				14									
13 Nov	2nd R (H)	Clapton	W 8-1	492	1	2[1]	3	4	5	6[1]	12	7[1]	10[3]		8		11	9[1]			14[1]									
12 Dec	3rd R (A)	Barking	D 1-1	221	1	2	3	4	5	6	12	7	10		8			9[1]				11								
23 Dec	Rep (H)	Barking	W 3-0	342	1	2	3	4	5	6[1]	8	7[1]	10				11	9[1]												
15 Mar	4th R (A)	Kingsbury	D 0-0	240	1	2		4	5		8	7					11	9				3			10					6
22 Mar	Rep (H)	Kingsbury	W 2-1	599	1	2[1]	3	4	5	6	8	7[1]	10				11	9												
27 Mar	S-F 1st L (A)	St. Albans	D 1-1	610	1	2	3	4	5	6	8	7	9[1]				11	10												
2 Apr	S-F 2nd L (H)	St. Albans	L 1-2	1,168	1	2	3	4	5	6	8	7[1]	10					9				11								
SURREY SENIOR CUP																														
3 Jan	1st R (H)	Cobham o.g.	W 9-1		1	2	3	4	5	6[1]	8[1]	7	10[3]			12	11[1]	9[1]						14[1]						
19 Feb	2nd R (A)	Epsom & Ewell	W 2-1			2	3	4		6[1]	8	7			9		11								5	1	10[1]			
6 Mar	S-F (A)	Dorking	L 0-3			2	3	4	5		8	6	10				11	9							7	1				
TOTAL APPEARANCES					**54**	**64**	**60**	**63**	**62**	**60**	**51**	**57**	**61**	**2**	**19**	**4**	**38**	**48**	**2**	**1**	**2**	**26**	**1**	**1**	**12**	**11**	**2**	**2**	**11**	**1**
SUBSTITUTE											**4**			**1**	**3**	**2**	**5**	**3**			**3**	**5**	**1**	**1**	**4**				**3**	
GOALS SCORED						**7**		**4**	**7**	**9**	**6**	**21**	**49**	**1**	**12**		**4**	**31**			**2**	**4**		**1**	**1**		**1**		**5**	

ISTHMIAN LEAGUE PREMIER DIVISION

SEASON 1990-1991

Date	Venue	Opponents	Result	Atten-dance	Read, T.	Mitchell, S.	Cowler, A.	Pratt, B.	Baron, T.	Wye, S.	Parr, A.	Biggins, M.	Fearon, E.	Buzaglio, T.	Wye, L.	Mulvaney, P.	Pope, S.	Franks, M.	Pedlar, L.	Brown, D.	Russell, A.	Hollingsworth, A.	Clement, A.	Hall, G.	Worsfold, T.	Caulfield, C.	Dawson, P.	Smart, R.	Davidson, L.	Buzaglio, R.	Barrowcliff, P.	Chew, J.	Youlton, C.
18 Aug	(H)	Windsor & Eton	D 0-0	1,023	1	2	3	4	5	6	7	8	9	10	11	14																	
21 Aug	(A)	Basingstoke	W 6-0	905	1	2[1]	3	4	5	6	7[3]	8		10[2]			9	11															
25 Aug	(A)	Staines	W 7-0	736	1	2	3	4[1]	5	6	7[2]	8	12[1]	10	14[1]		9[1]	11[1]															
1 Sep	(H)	Hayes	W 4-0	1,067	1	2	3	4	5	6	7	8[1]	10[2]			12[1]	9	11															
8 Sep	(A)	Wokingham	W 2-0	783	1	2[1]	3	4	5	6	7	8[1]	10			12	9	11															
22 Sep	(H)	Carshalton	L 2-4	1,084	1	2	3	4[1]	5	6[1]	7	8	14	10		9		11															
25 Sep	(A)	St.Albans	W 2-1	937	1	2	3	4	5	6		8	14	10	7	9		11[2]															
2 Oct	(H)	Bishops Stortford	D 0-0	1,026	1	2	3	4	5	6		8	9	10	7	12		11	14														
6 Oct	(A)	Grays	D 1-1	778	1	2	3	4	5	6[1]		8	14	10	7	12		11	9														
13 Oct	(H)	Aylesbury	W 3-1	1,548	1	2	3	4	5	6		8		10[1]	11[1]				9[1]	7													
15 Oct	(A)	Dagenham	W 1-0	840	1	2	3	4	5[1]	6		8		10	11				9	7													
20 Oct	(A)	Staines	W 5-1	1,334	1	2[1]	3	4[2]	5	6		8[1]		10[1]	11	14		12	9	7													
23 Oct	(H)	Marlow	W 4-1	1,544	1	2		4[1]	5	6		8	9	10	7	14[2]		11[1]		12	3												
30 Oct	(H)	Enfield	W 2-1	1,713	1	2	3	4	5			8[1]		10	11[1]				9	7		6											
3 Nov	(A)	Kingstonian	L 2-4	2,507	1	2	3	4[2]	5	6		8	12	10	11	9				7													
10 Nov	(H)	Harrow	W 4-0	1,246	1	2	3	4[1]	5[2]	6[1]		8	10		11	9		12		7				14									
24 Nov	(H)	Redbridge F	D 0-0	1,595	1	12	3	4	5	6		8			11			14	9	7			2	10									
15 Dec	(A)	Barking	W 1-0	353	1	2	3	4	5	14		8		10[1]	11			12	9	7			6										
22 Dec	(H)	Hendon	W 2-0	1,402	1	2	3	4	5	6		8[1]		10[1]	14			11		7				9									
26 Dec	(H)	Wokingham	W 4-0	1,501	1	2	3	4	5	6		8[1]		10[3]	11			9		7													
29 Dec	(A)	Enfield	L 0-2	1,268	1	2	3	4	5	6		8		10	11	14		9		7					12								
19 Jan	(H)	Basingstoke	L 0-2	1,871	1	2	3	4		6		8			5			9	14	7		11		12	10								
2 Feb	(H)	St.Albans	W 2-0	2,367	1		3	4		2		8		10	6	14		11		7[1]	5	12			9[1]								
16 Feb	(H)	Dagenham	W 1-0	1,773	1	2	3	4	5	6		8	9			14		11[1]		7					10								
23 Feb	(A)	Aylesbury	W 3-2	1,542	1	2	3	4		6					8			11		7	5			10[2]	9[1]								
2 Mar	(H)	Grays	D 1-1	1,816	1	2	3	4[1]		6				12	8			11		7	5			10	9								
9 Mar	(A)	Marlow	D 1-1	897	1	2	3	4		6		14			8	12		11		7	5			10[1]	9								
16 Mar	(A)	Bishops Stortford	L 0-2	593		2	3	4		6		14			8	10		11		7	5				9	1	12						
23 Mar	(H)	Bognor	W 3-0	1,552		2	3	4		6		14			8[1]			11	12[1]	7	5				9	1		10[1]					
26 Mar	(A)	Leyton-Wingate	W 4-0	395		2	3	4		6		14				12		11[1]	10	7[1]	5				9[2]	1	8						
30 Mar	(A)	Hendon	L 1-3	731		2	3	4			6				5			11	12	7[1]					9	1	8	10					
4 Apr	(A)	Wivenhoe	D 4-4	519		2	3	4[1]		6[1]	7	8			5			11	10							1	14	9[2]					
6 Apr	(A)	Barking	D 0-0	1,455		4	3		5	2	7				11			12	10	8						1	6	9	14				
8 Apr	(A)	Carshalton	D 2-2	756		2	3	4	5[1]	6	8				11				10	7						1		9[1]					
13 Apr	(A)	Harrow	W 1-0	785		2	3	4	5	6	8				11			12	10[1]	7					9	1	14						
16 Apr	(A)	Hayes o.g.	L 1-4	554		2	3	4	5	6	9				8				10	7					14	1				11			
20 Apr	(H)	Wivenhoe	W 1-0	1,187	1	2	3	4	5	6	9				8			11	10	7					14[1]								
23 Apr	(H)	Kingstonian	D 0-0	1,681	1	2	3	4	5	6	9				8				11	7					14			10					
27 Apr	(A)	Redbridge F.	W 1-0	828	1	2	3	4	5	6	8							11	9	7					12		14	10[1]					
29 Apr	(A)	Bognor	W 2-0	320	1	2		4[1]	5	6	7				8			11							9		3	10[1]					
2 May	(A)	Windsor & Eton	L 1-2	575	1	2		4	5	6	9				8[1]	12		11		7							3	10					
4 May	(H)	Leyton-Wingate	W 3-0	1,048	1	2[1]	3	4	5		8				6[1]	10		11		7	14						12	9[1]					
F.A. CUP																																	
27 Oct	4th Q (H)	Bath	W 2-1	2,029	1	2	3	4	5	6		8	14	10	11[1]	9		12		7[1]													
17 Nov	1st R (H)	Kidderminster	D 0-0	3,249	1	2	3	4	5	6		8	10		11	9		12		7			14										
21 Nov	Rep (A)	Kidderminster AET	D 1-1	2,827	1		3	4	5[1]	6		8			11	9		12		7	2		10										
26 Nov	2nd Rep (A)	Kidderminster	W 2-1	3,015	1	8	3	4	5			9		10	11					7	2[1]		6[1]										
8 Dec	2nd R (H)	Merthyr Tydfil	W 5-1	4,188	1	2	3	4	5	9		8[3]		10[1]	11[1]					7			6										
5 Jan	3rd R (A)	West Bromwich Albion	W 4-2	14,516	1	2	3	4	5	6		8		10[3]	11			9		7					12[1]								
17 Jan	4th R (A)	Everton	L 0-1	34,724	1	2	3	4	5	6		8		10	11	12		9		7													
F.A.TROPHY																																	
12 Jan	1st R (A)	Kettering	L 0-2	4,421	1	2	3	4	5	6		8		10	11			9	14	7					12								
PREMIER INTER-LEAGUE CUP																																	
4 Sep	Q Rd (H)	Wivenhoe	L 0-2	997	1	2	3	4	5	6	7	8	10				9	11															
A.C.DELCO CUP																																	
11 Sep	1st R (A)	Egham	W 2-0	864	1	2	3	4	5	6		8[1]	10[1]	14			9	11											7				
11 Dec	2nd R (A)	Bishops Stortford	D 3-3	359	1		3	4	5	9		8		10[1]	11	14[2]		12		7	2		6										
13 Dec	Rep (H)	Bishops Stortford	W 2-1	512	1	2			5	7		8[1]	10		3	9		11	14	12	4[1]		6										
18 Dec	3rd R (A)	Marlow	W 3-1	569	1	2	3	4	5[2]	9		8		10[1]		12		11		7			6										
21 Feb	4th R (A)	Molesey	W 2-1	812	1	2	3	4	5	6		10			11[1]	14		12		7					9								
12 Mar	S-F 1st L (H)	Dagenham	W 2-1	1,413		2[1]	3	4		6					8	10		11		7	5				9[1]	1					8[1]		
18 Mar	S-F 2nd L (A)	Dagenham	D 1-1	700		2	3	4		6					8[1]			11	10	7	5				9	1							
6 May	F	(Kingston) Carshalton	W 2-1	2,292	1	2	3	4	5[1]	6	14	8			11	9[1]		12	10	7													
LOCTITE CUP																																	
20 Dec	1st R (H)	Bognor	W 4-1	552	1		3			6					5[1]	10		11	8[1]		4	7		9[2]					2			12	
19 Feb	2nd R (H)	Leyton-Wingate	L 0-1	168	1	2	3	4	5	6			10			8		11	9	7													
SURREY SENIOR CUP																																	
15 Jan	1st R (H)	Tooting	W 4-0	1,743	1	2	3	4	5	6[1]			8[2]					11	10	7	12			14									9[1]
29 Jan	2nd R (H)	Walton & Hersham	W 2-1	2,079	1		3	4[1]	5	6		8		10	11[1]	14		9		7	2				12								
5 Mar	S-F (H)	Whyteleafe	D 2-2	1,216	1	2[1]	3	4		6				10	8[1]			12		7	5			11	9								
14 Mar	Rep (A)	Whyteleafe	W 2-1	800		2	3	4	5	6[1]		11			8	10				7	12[1]				9	1				14			
1 Apr	F	(Sutton) Kingstonian	W 3-0	2,871		2	3	4		6	9[1]	8			5			11	10[2]	7						1							
APPEARANCES					**53**	**60**	**62**	**63**	**51**	**61**	**20**	**43**	**13**	**28**	**52**	**15**	**6**	**42**	**22**	**50**	**17**	**3**	**8**	**7**	**17**	**13**	**5**	**10**	**2**	**1**	**1**		**1**
SUBSTITUTE						**1**				**1**	**1**	**4**	**6**	**1**	**3**	**18**		**13**	**6**	**2**	**3**	**1**	**1**	**3**	**8**		**5**		**1**	**1**		**1**	
GOALS SCORED						**6**		**12**	**8**	**6**	**6**	**11**	**6**	**15**	**13**	**6**	**1**	**6**	**6**	**4**	**3**		**1**	**5**	**7**			**7**			**1**		**1**

SEASON 1991-1992

ISTHMIAN LEAGUE PREMIER DIVISION

Date	Venue	Opponents	Result	Atten-dance	Batty, L.	Mitchell, S.	Cowler, A.	Russell, A.	Baron, T.	Parr, A.	Brown, D.	Biggins, M.	Walkes, R.	Friel, G.	Wye, L.	Mulvaney, P.	Barrowcliff, P.	Perry, A.	Hunt, J.	Milton, S.	Pratt, B.	Cockram, A.	Wye, S.	Parker, D.	Smith, M.	White, C.	Collier, N.	Lynch, A.	McPherson, G.	Devine, S.	Vines, F.	Paris, S.	Read, T.
17 Aug	(H)	Carshalton o.g.	W 3-0	1,402	1	2	3	4	5	6	7	8[1]	9	10[1]	11	12	14																
20 Aug	(A)	Kingstonian	W 2-1	2,071	1	2	3	4	5	6	7	8	9[1]	10[1]	11	12	14																
24 Aug	(A)	Chesham	D 0-0	1,299	1	2	3	4	5	6	7	8	9	10	11			12															
31 Aug	(H)	Dagenham	W 3-1	1,374	1	2	3	4[1]	5	6	7	8		10[1]	11[1]	9		14															
3 Sep	(H)	Bromley	L 1-2	1,521	1	2	3	4	5	6	7	8		10[1]	11	12		9															
7 Sep	(A)	Wokingham	W 3-0	1,080	1	2	3	4	5	6[1]	7	8		10[1]	11			12		9[1]	14												
14 Sep	(H)	Hayes	W 4-1	1,434	1	2	3	4	5[1]	6		8[1]	14	10[2]	11			12	7	9													
21 Sep	(A)	Wivenhoe	W 7-1	393	1[1]	2		4	5	6		8	14	10[4]	3			12	11	9[2]		7											
28 Sep	(A)	Carshalton	W 2-0	893	1	2		4	5	6		8		10[1]	11					9	3	7[1]											
5 Oct	(H)	Grays	W 1-0	1,689	1	2	3	4	5	6		8		10	11			12		9[1]	7												
12 Oct	(A)	Dagenham	D 0-0	883	1		3		5	2	7	8		10	11	14				9	4		6										
15 Oct	(H)	Basingstoke	W 5-0	1,701	1	2	3		5	6		8		10[2]	11	14		12		9[3]	4		7										
19 Oct	(H)	Harrow B.	W 2-0	1,451	1		3		5	7		8		10[1]	11			12[1]		9	4		6	2									
26 Oct	(A)	St.Albans	D 1-1	828	1		3		5	2	7	8		10	11[1]			14		9	4		6										
29 Oct	(A)	Marlow	W 3-0	1,020	1	2	3		5		7	8[2]		10[1]	11					9	4		6										
2 Nov	(H)	Staines	D 2-2	1,209	1		3		5[1]	2	7	8		10	11					9	4[1]		6										
5 Nov	(H)	Sutton	W 1-0	2,327	1	2	3		5		7	8		10	11					9	4		6[1]		14								
9 Nov	(A)	Bishops Stortford	W 2-1	723	1	2	3		5[1]	7[1]		8		10	11					9	4		6		12	14							
23 Nov	(A)	Hendon	W 5-0	751	1	2	3		5[1]	14	7[1]	8[2]		10[1]						9	4		6		12		11						
30 Nov	(H)	Enfield o.g.	W 5-0	3,125	1	2	3		5	8	7			10[2]	12					9[1]	4[1]		6		14		11						
21 Dec	(A)	Staines	W 2-0	1,410	1	2			5[1]		7	8		10	3					9[1]	4		6				11						
28 Dec	(A)	Aylesbury	W 4-0	2,165	1[1]	2	3		5	14	7	8		10	12					9[1]	4[1]		6				11[1]						
18 Jan	(H)	Chesham	W 2-1	2,305	1	2	3		5		7	8		10[1]						9[1]	4		6				11						
25 Jan	(A)	Bromley	W 2-0	1,545	1	2	3		5	12	7	8		10[1]	6					9[1]	4							11					
8 Feb	(A)	Hayes	D 2-2	1,148	1	2	3		5		7	8		10[2]						12	4		6				11	9					
15 Feb	(A)	Basingstoke	W 3-0	1,578	1	2	3		5	8[1]	7			10						9	4[1]		6				11[1]	12	14				
18 Feb	(H)	Wokingham	L 0-1	1,871	1	2	3		5	8	7			10						9	4		6				11	12	14				
22 Feb	(H)	Wivenhoe	W 2-0	1,953	1		3		5	2	7	8			11					9[2]	4		6							10			
29 Feb	(A)	Grays	W 2-0	1,012	1		3	12	5	2	7[1]	8		10						9	4		6[1]				11						
7 Mar	(H)	Bognor	W 3-1	1,608	1	2	3		5	8[1]	7[1]				11					9	4		6							10[1]			
14 Mar	(H)	St. Albans	W 4-1	1,912	1[1]	2	3		5	8[1]	7[1]	14		10[1]	11					9	4		6										
17 Mar	(H)	Windsor & Eton	W 2-0	1,952	1	2	3		5	7		8		10	11[1]					14	4		6[1]							12	9		
21 Mar	(A)	Harrow	W 3-1	1,139	1	2	3		5[1]	7	12	8		10[1]	11					14	4		6[1]								9		
28 Mar	(H)	Aylesbury	W 2-1	2,218	1	2	3		5	7		8		10	11					12[1]	4		6				14				9[1]		
4 Apr	(A)	Windsor & Eton	W 3-0	1,184	1	2	3		5	8	7	14		10[1]	11					12[1]	4		6								9[1]		
7 Apr	(H)	Kingstonian	W 3-1	3,073	1	2	3		5	8[1]	7			10[2]	11						4		6								9		
11 Apr	(H)	Bishops Stortford	W 3-0	2,396	1	2	3		5	6[2]	7	8		10	11					12	4[1]						14				9		
14 Apr	(A)	Bognor	D 1-1	580	1	2	3		5	6	7	8[1]		10	11						4						12				9		
18 Apr	(A)	Sutton	L 0-2	1,658	1	2	3		5	6	7	8		12	11					10	4										9	14	
25 Apr	(H)	Hendon	D 1-1	1,629	1	2	3		5	7	8	14		10	11					9	4		6								12[1]		
28 Apr	(H)	Marlow	L 0-1	1,283	1	2	3		5	7	12	8		10	11					14	4		6								9		
2 May	(A)	Enfield	L 0-1	1,182	1	3		4	5	8	7	9		14						11		10	6	2							12		
F.A. CUP																																	
16 Nov	1st R (A)	Windsor & Eton 69 Mins	AB 1-1	2,640	1	2	3		5[1]		7	8		10	11					9	4		6										
26 Nov	1st R (A)	Windsor & Eton o.g.	W 4-2	2,537	1	2[1]	3		5		7	8		10[1]						9[1]	4		6				11						
7 Dec	2nd R (H)	Yeovil	W 3-0	4,250	1	2	3		5	8	7			10[3]						9	4		6				11						
4 Jan	3rd R (H)	Hereford	D 0-0	4,753	1	2	3		5		7	8		10						9	4		6				11						
14 Jan	Rep (A)	Hereford AET	L 1-2	8,679	1	2	3		5		7	8		10						9	4[1]		6				11						
F.A.TROPHY																																	
11 Jan	1st R (H)	Wembley o.g.	W 4-2	2,087	1	2	3		5	12	7	8		10[1]						9[1]	4[1]		6				11						
1 Feb	2nd R (A)	Wycombe	L 0-1	5,801	1	2	3	4	5		7	8		10	11					9			6				12						
ISTHMIAN CHARITY SHIELD																																	
26 Aug	(H)	Redbridge Forest AET	W 3-1	1,397	1	2	3	4	5[2]	6	7	8[1]		10	11	12		9															
ISTHMIAN LEAGUE CUP																																	
10 Sep	1st R (A)	Barton R.	W 3-1	404	1	2	3	4	5[1]	6[1]	7	8		10[1]	11			12		9													
19 Nov	2nd R (H)	Rainham	W 4-1	944	1		3		5	2	7	8		12						14[1]	4		6		9[2]	10[1]	11						
18 Dec	3rd R (A)	Chesham	W 2-1	574	1	2[1]	3		5	8	7			10[1]	12					9	4		6		14		11						
11 Feb	4th R (H)	Enfield	L 0-2	1,578	1	2	3		5		7			10	8					9	4		6				12	11					
SURREY SENIOR CUP																																	
7 Jan	1st R (H)	Walton & Hersham	W 6-1	1,455	1		3		5[1]	7	12	8[1]		10	11					9[3]	4		6[1]	2	14								
28 Jan	2nd R (A)	Kingstonian o.g.	W 3-2	1,352	1[1]	2	3	4	5		7	8		10[1]	11					9			6										
3 Mar	S-F (H)	Carshalton	L 0-2	1,629	1			12	5	2	7	8		10	3					9	4		6				11						
LOCTITE CUP																																	
20 Jan	2nd R (H)	Walton & Hersham o.g.	W 2-1	1,274				3	5	2	7	8		10	11[1]					14	4		6		9		12						1
26 Feb	3rd R (A)	Chesham	W 5-2	793	1		3		5	2	7[1]	8[1]		14	11					9[2]	4		6							10[1]			
10 Mar	4th R (H)	Yeading	W 1-0	1,063	1	12		2	5	11	7	8		10[1]	3					14	4		6							9			
31 Mar	S-F (A)	Harrow	W 2-0	780	1	2[2]	3		5	8	7	12		10	11					9	4		6										
5 May	F (Hayes)	Sutton	L 0-2	1,935	1	2		4	5	8	7	9		10	3					12		11	6	14									
APPEARANCES					**61**	**50**	**54**	**18**	**62**	**46**	**50**	**50**	**3**	**56**	**46**	**1**		**2**	**2**	**43**	**48**	**4**	**46**	**3**	**2**	**1**	**17**	**3**		**4**	**9**		**1**
SUBSTITUTE						**1**		**2**		**4**	**3**	**4**	**2**	**4**	**3**	**6**	**2**	**10**		**11**	**1**			**1**	**6**	**1**	**6**	**2**	**2**	**1**	**2**	**1**	
GOALS SCORED					**4**	**4**		**1**	**11**	**9**	**5**	**10**	**1**	**37**	**4**			**1**		**24**	**7**	**1**	**5**		**2**	**1**	**2**			**2**	**3**		

GM VAUXHALL CONFERENCE

SEASON 1992-1993

Date	Venue	Opponents	Result	Atten-dance	Batty, L.	Brown, K.	Finch, J.	Nugent, R.	Baron, T.	Clement, A.	Brown, D.	Biggins, M.	Senior, T.	Puckett, D.	Fleming, M.	Steele, S.	Joyce, A.	Fielder, C.	Buzaglo, T.	Roffe, G.	Carroll, R.	Brodrick, D.	Murphy, A.	Milton, S.	Pape, A.	Wye, L.	Wye, S.	Horne, B.	Alexander, T.	Rowe, E.	Honey, D.	Coleman, D.	Bushay, A.	Peters, R.	Greene, Dave	Buzaglo, R.	Kelly, P.
22 Aug	(H)	Stafford Rangers	L 0-3	2,044	1	2	3	4	5	6	7	8	9	10	11	12																					
25 Aug	(A)	Kettering	W 1-0	2,127	1	2		4	5	6	7	8	9	10	11[1]		3																				
29 Aug	(A)	Stalybridge Celtic	L 0-3	968	1	2		4	5		7	8	9	10	11	12	3	6	14																		
5 Sep	(H)	Runcorn	W 4-0	1,890	1	2		4	5		7	8[1]		9[1]		11	3	6	10[2]																		
12 Sep	(A)	Kidderminster	W 3-1	1,759	1	2		4	5[1]		7	8[1]		9	12	11[1]	3	6	10																		
15 Sep	(A)	Bath	L 0-2	801	1	2		4	5		7	8	12	9		11	3	6	10																		
19 Sep	(H)	Witton	L 1-2	2,041	1	2		4	5		7	8	12	9[1]		11	3	6		10	14																
26 Sep	(A)	Telford	D 3-3	1,463	1	2		4[1]			7	8[1]	9	10[1]	3			6			11	5															
3 Oct	(H)	Altrincham	L 0-2	2,060	1	2		4			7	8	9	10		12	3	6			11	5															
6 Oct	(A)	Dagenham & Redbridge	L 1-5	1,648	1	2		4			7	8	14	9	3[1]	12		6	10			5	11														
17 Oct	(H)	Northwich Victoria	W 1-0	1,992	1	2		4	5		12	8	9	10[1]	6	11		3					7	14													
31 Oct	(H)	Bromsgrove	L 0-2	1,832		2		4	5			8		10	9	11		6						14	1	3	7										
7 Nov	(A)	Yeovil o.g.	L 1-4	2,911		2		4	5		7	8		10				3		9	12					11	6	1									
21 Nov	(H)	Gateshead	L 1-4	1,722	1			4	5	2		8	9[1]	10		11		7			12					3	6										
24 Nov	(A)	Merthyr Tydfil	W 5-1	380	1			4		2		8	9[2]		7			11[1]						10[2]		3	6		5								
28 Nov	(A)	Boston	W 2-1	1,135	1			4		2	12	8[1]	9[1]		7			11						10		3	6		5								
1 Dec	(H)	Dagenham & Redbridge	D 1-1	1,734	1			4		2		8	9		7			11			14[1]			10		3	6		5								
8 Dec	(A)	Welling o.g.	D 1-1	1,077	1	4				2	12	8			7			11	14		9			10		3	6		5								
12 Dec	(A)	Runcorn	W 3-2	953	1	4				2[1]	7	8		12[1]	3[1]			11	10								6		5	9							
19 Dec	(H)	Boston	W 3-0	1,652		11		4		2	14	8	9[2]	10[1]	7				12							3	6		5		1						
26 Dec	(H)	Wycombe	L 0-3	4,911	1	11		4		2	14	8	9	10	7				12							3	6		5								
28 Dec	(A)	Farnborough	W 3-0	2,287	1	11		4		2	7	8	9[1]	10[2]	3												6		5								
2 Jan	(A)	Slough	W 1-0	2,480	1	11		4		2		8[1]	9	10	7											3	6		5								
16 Jan	(H)	Welling	W 1-0	1,647	1	5				2		8	9	10	7[1]	11			12							3	6		4								
23 Jan	(A)	Gateshead	D 1-1	626	1	4				2	14	8	9[1]	10	7	11			12							3	6		5								
30 Jan	(H)	Yeovil	D 0-0	2,427	1	4				2	14		9	10	7	11		8	12							3	6		5								
6 Feb	(A)	Northwich Victoria	L 0-1	984	1	5					8		9	10	7	11		2	12		14					3	6		4								
13 Feb	(A)	Witton	W 2-1	930	1	6		5			7		9	12		11[1]			10		2					3	8[1]		4								
20 Feb	(H)	Macclesfield	W 4-0	1,868	1	8		5			7[1]		9[1]	12		11[1]			10		2[1]					3	6		4								
27 Feb	(H)	Merthyr Tydfil	L 0-2	2,049	1	8					7		9	10		11					2			14		3	6		4			5					
6 Mar	(A)	Altrincham	L 0-1	839	1	8		5			7		9	12	6	11		14			2								4			3	10				
9 Mar	(H)	Slough	L 1-2	1,948	1	8		5			7		9		6	12		2			11								4			3[1]	10				
13 Mar	(A)	Stafford Rangers	D 0-0	1,062	1	11		5			7	8		12	6			2			9								4			3	10				
20 Mar	(H)	Kettering	W 3-2	1,586	1	4		5		14	7			9[1]	6	12		2			8											3	10[1]			11[1]	
23 Mar	(H)	Bath	L 0-1	1,290	1	11		5		2	7			9	3	12		6											4			8	10			14	
27 Mar	(A)	Macclesfield	D 1-1	879	1	5				2	7		9			11[1]		12			8								4				10	3			6
30 Mar	(H)	Telford	W 3-2	1,317	1	5				6	7		9[1]	12		11[1]		2											4				10[1]	3	14	8	
3 Apr	(H)	Kidderminster	L 1-5	1,537	1	5				6	7[1]		9			11		2											4				10	3	12	8	
6 Apr	(A)	Wycombe	D 0-0	5,000	1	5		4		6	7					11		3											2				10	8	9		
12 Apr	(H)	Farnborough o.g.	W 4-1	2,471	1	5		4[1]		6[1]	7			12	2[1]	11		3															10	8	9		
24 Apr	(H)	Stalybridge Celtic	W 2-1	1,713	1	4		5		6	7		14[1]	12	2	11		3															10	8	9[1]		
1 May	(A)	Bromsgrove	L 0-1	1,808	1	4		5		6	7		14	12	2	11		3															10	8	9		
ISTHMIAN CHARITY SHIELD																																					
31 Aug	A	(Sutton) Grays	W 5-1	478	1	2		4[1]	5		7	8	12	9[2]	14	11	3	6	10[2]																		
THE DRINKWISE CUP																																					
8 Sep	1st R !st L (H)	Welling	L 1-2	1,363	1	2		4	5		7	8	12	9[1]		11	3	6	10																		
22 Sep	1st R 2nd L (A)	Welling	D 2-2	670	1	2		4	5[1]		7	8	9[1]	10			3	6			11	14															
F.A. CUP																																					
14 Nov	1st R (H)	Nuneaton B o.g.	W 3-2	3,280	1			4	5	2		8[1]	9	10	12	11		7			14[1]					3	6										
5 Dec	2nd R (A)	Brighton	D 1-1	9,208	1			4		2		8	9	10	7			11			12					3	6[1]		5								
16 Dec	Rep (H)	Brighton	L 1-2	5,870	1	4					7	8	9[1]	10	2			11	12							3	6		5								
F.A.TROPHY																																					
9 Jan	1st R (A)	Sutton	L 0-3	1,884	1	11		4		2	7	8	9	10	3				12		14						6		5								
SURREY SENIOR CUP																																					
5 Jan	1st R (A)	Dorking	D 2-2	656	1	11		4			7	12	9	10	2				14[1]		8[1]					3	6		5								
12 Jan	Rep (H)	Dorking	L 0-2	932	1	11		4			14	8	9	10	7	6			12		2					3			5								
APPEARANCES					**48**	**45**	**1**	**40**	**15**	**26**	**35**	**34**	**33**	**34**	**33**	**26**	**10**	**35**	**9**	**2**	**14**	**3**	**2**	**4**	**1**	**22**	**24**	**1**	**29**	**1**	**1**	**6**	**12**	**7**	**4**	**3**	**1**
SUBSTITUTE										**1**	**8**	**1**	**7**	**9**	**3**	**7**		**2**	**12**		**8**	**1**		**3**											**2**	**1**	
GOALS SCORED								**3**	**2**	**2**	**2**	**6**	**13**	**12**	**5**	**5**		**1**	**5**		**4**			**2**			**2**					**1**	**2**		**1**	**1**	

SEASON 1993-94

GM VAUXHALL CONFERENCE

Date	Venue	Opponents	Result		Atten-dance	Batty, L.	Clement, A.	Agboola, R.	Brown, K.	Tucker, M,	Berry, G.	Brown, Der	Biggins, M.	Morah, O.	Puckett, D.	Walker, C.	Brown, Del	Steele, S.	Fielder, C.	Greene, Den.	Dennis, L.	Rattray, K.	Swift, K.	Haylock, P.	Heritage, P.	Craddock, J.	Gray, A.	Wye, S.	Wye, L.	Fleming, D.	Lakin, B.	Hislop, C.	Bennett, G.	Read, T.	Hay, D.	Hutchinson, G.
21 Aug	(A)	Northwich Victoria	D	0-0	1,041	1	2	3	4	5	6	7	8	9	10	11	14																			
24 Aug	(H)	Welling	L	0-2	1,833	1	2	3	4	5	6	7	8		10	11	9	14																		
28 Aug	(H)	Runcorn	D	1-1	1,520	1	2		4	5	6	7[1]	12		10	11		14	3	8	9															
30 Aug	(A)	Dover	L	0-5	2,220	1	2		4	5	6	7	12		10	11		14	3	8	9															
4 Sep	(A)	Stafford Rangers	L	0-3	1,071	1	6	3	4	5		7	8			9	12	11	2		10															
11 Sep	(H)	Macclesfield	W	3-0	1,566	1	2		4		5	7	12			11[2]		8	3		9[1]	6	10	14												
18 Sep	(A)	Bromsgrove Rovers	D	0-0	1,097	1	2		4		5	7	12		10	11		8	3	14		6			9											
25 Sep	(H)	Halifax	L	2-6	1,848	1	2		4		5	7	6		14[1]	11[1]		8	3			12	10		9											
5 Oct	(H)	Merthyr Tydfil	W	2-1	1,266	1	2	3	4		5	7	8		12	11[1]						10[1]			9	6										
9 Oct	(A)	Southport	L	1-2	1,526	1	2	10	4		5	7	8		12	11			3							6	9[1]									
12 Oct	(H)	Dover	W	3-0	1,832	1	2[1]		5		6	7	8[1]			11[1]		3	12			10				4	9									
16 Oct	(H)	Witton	W	3-1	1,615	1	2		5		6	7	8		14	11[1]		3	12			10				4[1]	9[1]									
23 Oct	(A)	Halifax	W	3-2	1,201	1	2[1]	3	6	4[1]	5	7			8[1]	11						10					9									
30 Oct	(H)	Telford	D	0-0	1,876	1	2		5		6	7	12		8	11		3				10				4	9									
20 Nov	(A)	Stalybridge Celtic	D	2-2	524	1	2		5			7				11[1]		3	8		10					4[1]	9	6								
27 Nov	(H)	Kidderminster	W	1-0	1,767	1	2		5		14	7	8			11[1]		3	10		12					4	9	6								
11 Dec	(H)	Bath o.g.	W	4-1	1,463	1			4	2	5	7				11		8			9	10[2]						6[1]	3							
18 Dec	(A)	Gateshead	D	1-1	579	1			5	2	4	7			10	11		9[1]				8						6	3							
27 Dec	(H)	Slough	W	2-1	2,913	1			5	2	4	7				11		9			10[1]	8[1]						6	3							
1 Jan	(A)	Welling	D	2-2	1,762	1			5	2	4	7[1]				11		9[1]			10	8						6	3							
3 Jan	(H)	Kettering	D	0-0	3,130	1			5	2	4	7				11		9			10	8						6	3							
8 Jan	(A)	Altrincham	W	2-0	632	1			5	2	4	7			14[1]	11[1]		9			10	8						6	3							
15 Jan	(A)	Macclesfield	D	1-1	1,053	1	3		5	2	4	7				11		9			10[1]	8						6		12						
29 Jan	(H)	Southport	W	1-0	2,571	1			5	2	4	7				11[1]		9	6		10	8							3							
5 Feb	(A)	Telford	L	0-2	1,222	1			5	2	4	7				11		9	6		10	8							3	12						
19 Feb	(A)	Kettering	L	0-3	2,054	1	6		5	2	4		12			11		9			10	8							3		7	14				
26 Feb	(H)	Stalybridge Celtic	W	3-0	1,727	1	6		5	2	4	7				11[1]		9			10[2]	8							3		12	14				
8 Mar	(A)	Dagenham & Redbridge	W	4-3	894	1	6			2	4	7[1]			9	11[2]			5		10[1]								3		8					
12 Mar	(H)	Altrincham	D	1-1	1,816	1	6		5	2	4	7			14	11		9	12		10								3		8[1]					
15 Mar	(H)	Bromsgrove Rovers	D	0-0	1,192	1	6		5	2	4	8			12	11		9	7										3				10			
19 Mar	(A)	Kidderminster	L	1-3	2,705	1	6		5	2	4	7			9	11													3		8		10[1]			
22 Mar	(A)	Merthyr Tydfil	W	3-2	490	1			5	2	4	7				11[2]		9	6										3[1]		8		10			
2 Apr	(H)	Gateshead	W	1-0	1,669		2[1]		5		4	7			10	11		9	6			8	14						3		12			1		
4 Apr	(A)	Slough	D	0-0	1,433	1	2		5		4	7			10			9	6			8	14						3		12				11	
9 Apr	(A)	Runcorn	L	1-2	531	1	2		5		4	7			14	11		12	6			8							3		9				10[1]	
12 Apr	(A)	Bath	W	1-0	691	1			5	2	4	7				11		9	6										3		8				10[1]	
19 Apr	(H)	Dagenham & Redbridge	L	1-8	1,127	1	2		5	6	4	7			9			11	12			8							3		14				10[1]	
30 Apr	(A)	Witton	D	0-0	454	1	6		5	2	4	7			11			9	8			12							3		14				10	
2 May	(A)	Yeovil o.g.	W	1-0	2,208	1	6		5	2	4	7			11		14	9	8			12							3						10	
5 May	(H)	Yeovil	L	1-2	1,265		6		5		4	7			11	12		9	2			8							3[1]					1	10	
6 May	(H)	Northwich Victoria	W	2-1	692		6		5	2	4	7			12	11[1]			8			9							3					1	10[1]	
7 May	(H)	Stafford Rangers	W	4-0	1,428		6		5[1]	2	4	7			11[2]		10	9	8										3		12[1]			1		14
THE DRINKWISE CUP																																				
2 Nov	2nd R (A)	Welling	L	0-1	681	1	2		5		6	7	12		8	11		3				10				4	9									
F.A. CUP																																				
13 Nov	1st R (H)	Weston-Super-Mare	D	2-2	2,766	1	2		5		4	7	8			11		3	9		10[1]							6[1]								
23 Nov	Rep (A)	Weston-Super-Mare	W	1-0	2,623	1	2[1]		5		4	7	8			11		3	9		10							6								
4 Dec	2nd R (A)	Kidderminster	L	0-1	4,411	1	2		5		4	7	8			11		3	10		12						9	6								
F.A. TROPHY																																				
22 Jan	1st R (A)	Bashley	W	4-2	1,102	1	3	8	5	2	4	7				11[1]		9			10[2]							6[1]		14						
12 Feb	2nd R (A)	Dagenham & Redbridge	W	2-1	1,769	1	6		5	2	4					11[1]		9	12		10	8[1]							3		7					
5 Mar	3rd R (H)	Bromsgrove Rovers	W	3-2	2,342	1	6		5[1]	2	4	8				11		9			10[1]								3		7[1]	12				
26 Mar	4th R (H)	Billingham Syn	D	1-1	2,767	1			5	2	4	7				11[1]		9	6			8							3		12	14	10			
30 Mar	Rep (A)	Billingham Syn	W	2-1	1,176	1	2		5[2]		4	7			10	11		9	6			8							3							
16 Apr	S-F (H)	1st Leg Enfield (o.g)	D	1-1	3,841	1			5	6	4	7				11		9	2			14							3		8				10	
23 Apr	S-F (A)	2nd Leg Enfield AET	D	0-0	3,319	1	6		5	2	4	7			12	11		9	8										3						10	
26 Apr	Rep	(Wycombe) Enfield	W	3-0	2,674	1	6		5	2	4	7			12	11		9[1]	8			14							3						10[2]	
21 May	F	(Wembley) Runcorn	W	2-1	15,818	1	6		5	2	4	7[1]			12	11		9	8			14							3						10[1]	
SURREY SENIOR CUP																																				
14 Dec	1st R (H)	Dorking	W	3-1	622	1			5	2	4	7	14			11[2]		9[1]			10	8					12	6	3							
19 Jan	2nd R (H)	Walton & Hersham	W	3-0	1,022	1	3		5	2	4	7	8		11			9[1]	12		10[2]		14					6								
1 Mar	S-F (A)	Molesey	W	3-0	925	1	6		5	2	4	7	12			11[2]		9	8		10[1]		14						3							
10 May	F	(Kingston) Sutton	W	3-1	1,959	1	6		5	2[1]	4	7			11		14	9[1]	8			12							3						10[1]	
Appearances						55	46	7	58	40	56	57	13	1	21	51	2	48	34	2	25	29	2		3	8	9	15	36		10		4	4	13	
Substitute											1		9		12	1	4	4	6	1	2	7	4	1			1			3	7	4				1
Goals Scored							4		4	2		4	1		5	23		6			13	5				2	2	3	2		3		1		8	

SEASON 1994-1995

GM VAUXHALL CONFERENCE

Date	Venue	Opponents	Result	Atten-dance	Batty, L.	Tucker, M.	Wye, L.	Berry, G.	Brown, K.	Tierling, L.	Brown, D.	Fielder, C.	Steele, S.	Hay, D.	Walker, C.	Rattray, K.	Dennis, L.	Timothy, D.	Ellis, A.	Greene David,	Read, T.	Wye, S.	Ravenscroft, C.	Girdler, S.	James, C.	Alexander, T.	Benton, J.	Parminter, S.	Payne, G.	Crumplin, J.	Brooks, S.	Newbery, R.	de Garis, P.
20 Aug	(H)	Halifax	L 1-3	1,760	1	2	3	4	5	6	7	8	9[1]	10	11	12	14																
23 Aug	(A)	Welling o.g.	W 2-1	842	1	2	3	4	5	12	7	6	9	10[1]	11	8																	
27 Aug	(A)	Altrincham	W 2-1	925	1	2	3		5	6	7	4	9[1]	10[1]	11	8																	
29 Aug	(H)	Merthyr Tydfil	W 4-1	1,640	1	2[1]	3		5	6	7	4	9	10[3]	11	8	14	12															
3 Sep	(H)	Telford	W 2-1	1,650	1	2	3		5	6	7	4	9	10	11	8[2]																	
5 Sep	(A)	Stevenage	W 1-0	2,037	1	2	3		5	6	7	4	9	10	11[1]	8																	
10 Sep	(H)	Stafford	D 2-2	1,938	1	2	3		5	6	7	4	9	10[2]	11	8	12																
13 Sep	(H)	Yeovil	D 2-2	1,550	1	2	3[1]	14	5	6	7	4	9	10[1]	11	8	12																
17 Sep	(A)	Runcorn	L 0-1	368	1	2	3	4	5	6	7	8	9	10	11		12																
24 Sep	(H)	Southport	W 3-0	1,966	1	2	3	14	5	6	7	4[1]	9[2]	10	11		12		8														
27 Sep	(H)	Bath	D 2-2	1,591	1	2	3	4	5	6	7		9	10[1]	11	14	12[1]		8		1S												
1 Oct	(A)	Gateshead	L 0-2	537		2	3		5	6	7	4	9	10	11	14	12		8		1												
8 Oct	(H)	Kettering	W 3-1	2,277	1	2	3		5	6		4	9	10[2]			11[1]		8			7											
11 Oct	(A)	Yeovil	W 2-1	1,601	1	2	3		5	6		4	9	10		7[1]	11[1]		8														
15 Oct	(H)	Northwich Victoria	D 1-1	2,130	1	2	3		5	6	14	4	9		11[1]	8	10					7											
22 Oct	(H)	Runcorn	W 2-0	1,877	1	2	3		5	6		4	9		11		10[2]		8			7											
29 Oct	(A)	Stafford	W 3-2	766	1	2	3		5	6		4	9		11[1]		10[2]		8			7											
5 Nov	(H)	Kidderminster	D 0-0	2,368	1	2	3		5	6	12	4	9		11		10		8			7											
19 Nov	(A)	Kettering	W 1-0	2,330	1	2	3		5		12	4	9		11[1]	6	10		8			7											
26 Nov	(A)	Stalybridge Celtic	L 1-2	621	1	2			5	6	7	4	9		11	12	10[1]		8			3											
10 Dec	(A)	Macclesfield	L 0-2	2,186	1	2	3		5			4	12		11	9	10		8			7	14			6							
17 Dec	(H)	Bromsgrove	W 4-0	1,517	1	2	3		5			4	9		11[2]	8				10[2]		7	12			6							
26 Dec	(H)	Dagenham & Redbridge	L 3-5	2,406	1	2	3			14		4	9		11[2]	8			7[1]	10		6				5							
31 Dec	(A)	Merthyr Tydfil o.g.	D 1-1	664	1	2	3					4	9		11	8				10	1S	7				5	6						
2 Jan	(A)	Dagenham & Redbridge	W 2-0	1,392	1	2	3		5			4	9[1]							10[1]		7		12		6	8	11					
14 Jan	(A)	Bromsgrove	D 5-5	1,333		2[1]			5			4	9[1]		11[2]	6		3	8		1	7							10[1]				
4 Feb	(A)	Halifax	L 0-4	1,038	1	2	3		5	6		4	9		11	12			8			7				14			10				
11 Mar	(H)	Stevenage	W 3-0	2,024	1	2	3		5			4	9		11[1]	6[1]			8			7							10[1]	12	14		
14 Mar	(H)	Dover	D 0-0	1,320	1	2	3		5			4	9		11	6						7								8		10	
18 Mar	(A)	Kidderminster	W 3-1	1,616	1	2	3		5			4	9		11[1]				8			7[1]							10[1]	6		14	
21 Mar	(A)	Telford	D 0-0	608	1	2	3					4	9		11	12			8			7				5			10	6			
1 Apr	(A)	Northwich Victoria	D 2-2	829	1	2	3					4[1]	14	9	11	8			12			7				5			10[1]	6			
4 Apr	(H)	Farnborough	W 3-2	1,994	1	2				3		4	9	10	11[2]				8[1]			7				5			14	6			
17 Apr	(H)	Gateshead	D 1-1	1,585	1	2	3		5	14		4	9	10[1]	11				8			7								6			
22 Apr	(A)	Farnborough	W 2-0	1,749	1	2	3		5	9		4		10[1]	11[1]	12			8			7								6		14	
25 Apr	(H)	Macclesfield	W 1-0	2,325	1	2	3		5			4	9	10	11[1]	12			8			7								6			
27 Apr	(H)	Welling	D 1-1	1,125		2	3		5			4	9	10[1]	11	8					1S	7								6			1
29 Apr	(H)	Stalybridge Celtic	W 4-1	1,555		2	3		5			4[1]	9	10	11[2]	12			8		1	7								6[1]		14	
1 May	(A)	Bath	L 0-2	651	1	2	3		5			4	9	10	11	12			8			7								6		14	
3 May	(H)	Altrincham	W 4-0	1,614	1	2	3		5	12		4		10[1]	11[1]	6[1]			8			7										9[1]	
4 May	(A)	Dover	W 3-2	990	1	2	3		5	14		4		10[2]	11	6			8[1]			7				12						9	
6 May	(A)	Southport	L 0-2	1,160	1	2			5	3		4	9	10	11				8			7		6								12	
CHAMPIONSHIP SHIELD																																	
19 Sep	(A)	Kidderminster AET	W 2-1	1,007	1	2	3	4	5	6	12	8	9	10[2]	11				7	14													
BOB LORD TROPHY																																	
1 Nov	2nd R (H)	Farnborough	D 0-0	1,375	1	2	3		5	6	12	4	9		11		10		8			7											
29 Nov	Rep (A)	Farnborough	W 1-0	935	1			2	5	6		4	9			8[1]	10	3				7	11	12	14								
20 Dec	3rd R (A)	Kettering	L 1-2	964	1	2	3		5			4	9		11	8[1]						7			10	6							
F.A. CUP																																	
12 Nov	1st R (A)	Barnet	D 4-4	3,114	1	2	3		5	6	12	4[1]	9[1]		11[1]	14	10[1]		8			7											
22 Nov	Rep (H)	Barnet	W 1-0	4,859	1	2[1]	3		5	6		4	9		11	14	10		8			7											
4 Dec	2nd R (A)	Marlow	L 1-2	2,845	1	2[1]		3	5	6	14	4	9		11	12	10		8			7											
SURREY SENIOR CUP																																	
13 Dec	1st R (H)	Met. Police	W 3-0	386	1	2	3		5			4			11	10[1]			8	9[2]		7	6	12	14								
7 Feb	2nd R (A)	Chertsey	L 1-6	1,161	1	2			5	3		4	9		11	10			14			7[1]			12	6	8						
F.A. TROPHY																																	
24 Jan	1st R (H)	Chesham	W 3-0	1,488	1	2	3		5	6		4	9[1]		11[1]				8[1]			7							10				
14 Feb	2nd R (H)	Cheltenham	W 3-1	1,128	1	2			5	3[1]		4	9[1]		11[1]	8			6			7		14					10				
4 Mar	3rd R (A)	Stevenage	W 3-0	2,631	1	2	3		5			4	9[1]		11[1]	6			8			7							10[1]				
25 Mar	4th R (A)	Macclesfield	W 1-0	3,019	1	2	3		5			4	9		11[1]	8						7							10	6			
8 Apr	S-F 1st L (A)	Rushden & D	L 0-1	4,375	1	2			5	3		4	9	10	11	14			8			7				12				6			
15 Apr	S-F 2nd L (H)	Rushden & D	W 2-0	4,643	1	2	3		5			4	9	10	11[1]	7[1]			8											6			
14 May	F	(Wembley) Kidderminster AET	W 2-1	17,815	1	2	3		5			4[1]	9[1]	10	11	12			8			7								6		14	
APPEARANCES					**54**	**57**	**49**	**7**	**53**	**32**	**13**	**57**	**52**	**29**	**54**	**29**	**14**	**2**	**38**	**5**	**3**	**43**	**2**	**1**	**1**	**10**	**3**	**1**	**10**	**15**		**3**	**1**
SUBSTITUTE								**2**		**5**	**7**		**2**			**15**	**8**	**1**	**2**	**1**	**3**		**2**	**4**	**3**	**3**			**1**	**1**	**1**	**6**	
GOALS SCORED						**4**	**1**			**1**		**5**	**11**	**19**	**25**	**9**	**9**		**4**	**5**		**2**							**5**	**1**		**1**	

INDEX OF EXHIBITS AND PHOTOGRAPHS

This index refers only to **Exhibits** and **Photographs** found in the book, in page numerical order for easy reference. Every exhibit, cartoon, programme etc, is indicated with an asterisk*. Over 155 photographs and captions are included.

Page

Page

Page